More Readings From One Man's Wilderness

THE JOURNALS OF RICHARD L. PROENNEKE

Edited by John Branson

Lake Clark National Park and Preserve

SKYHORSE PUBLISHING

Skyhorse Publishing books may be purchased in bulk at special discounts for sales promotion, corporate gifts, fund-raising, or educational purposes. Special editions can also be created to specifications. For details, contact the Special Sales Department, Skyhorse Publishing, 307 West 36th Street, 11th Floor, New York, NY 10018 or info@skyhorsepublishing.com.

Skyhorse® and Skyhorse Publishing® are registered trademarks of Skyhorse Publishing, Inc.®, a Delaware corporation.

Visit our website at www.skyhorsepublishing.com.

10 9 8 7 6 5 4 3 2

Library of Congress Cataloging-in-Publication Data is available on file.

ISBN: 978-1-61608-554-4

Printed in the United States of America

CONTENTS

Acknowledgement

I would like to thank Raymond Proenneke and his late brother, Richard "Dick" Proenneke for donating the Proenneke journals and slides to Lake Clark National Park and Preserve. Thanks also to Raymond for sharing his knowledge and insights into his brother's life and times.

Many thanks to volunteers in the park, Jeanette and Jerry Mills, for transcribing and proofreading the voluminous hand-written Proenneke journals; and for proof reading my manuscript, many more thanks. Katie Myers, collections manager, and Katie Krasinski, archeologist, did a great deal of photocopying and organizing the Proenneke journals at the Lake Clark-Katmai Studies Center in Anchorage. Molly Casperson, archeologist, scanned the photographs and proofread the print-ready manuscript.

Biological science technician Buck Mangipane and archeologist Dr. Barbara Bundy are due many thanks for the excellent maps of Proenneke's world they produced for the book. Other colleagues who are due mention for assisting me with the manuscript are, Dan Young, his wife Amy Sayre, Jennifer Shaw, Chandelle Alsworth, Michelle Ravenmoon, and Angela Olson. Ranger Leon Alsworth has helped me recall details about Proenneke's life at Twin Lakes. Editor Thetus Smith and historian Frank Norris at the National Park Service Alaska Support Office in Anchorage also must be thanked for their suggestions on editing the manuscript and on content.

Several friends and neighbors have helped me on this project. For freely sharing their recollections of Richard, thank you very much Margaret Alsworth "Sis" Clum, Glen Alsworth, Sr., and Laddy and Glenda Elliott. Thanks also to Kimberley McKennett and Danielle Ryman for their help with early versions of the manuscript. Thanks also to Linda Leask, who was a friend of both Richard Proenneke and Helen White; she talked with me about Helen White and proofread the manuscript. Nan Elliott shared her knowledge of Alaska Task Force members and Ed Fortier with me. I am indebted to Denise Martin for her excellent design and layout of the book, and for her patience with revisions of the text.

Finally, I want to thank my supervisors for their steadfast support as I labored on the Proenneke manuscript: former Park Superintendent, Deb Liggett, Park Superintendent Joel Hard, Chief Ranger Lee Fink, and Chief of Cultural Resources and my immediate supervisor, Dr. Jeanne Schaaf.

Preface

Apparently Richard Proenneke's journalizing began in the late 1950s or early 1960s while he was spending a month at a remote cabin on Malina Bay on Afognak Island. From his very first visit to Twin Lakes in 1962, Proenneke kept a journal. Over the Twin Lakes years Proenneke wrote millions of words. In 2000 Proenneke and his brother, Raymond, donated all his journals to Lake Clark National Park and Preserve.

The publication of Proenneke's 1968-1969 journals in 1973 as *One Man's Wilderness*, edited by Sam Keith, was largely responsible for making Proenneke a public figure and putting Twin Lakes on the map as a destination. Proenneke both enjoyed his emerging fame and was dismayed by it. He liked the peace and quiet of Twin Lakes before 1973, but he also enjoyed the public recognition that he was living a rather amazingly inspirational life in the wilds of Alaska. I believe that public acclaim validated in his own mind Proenneke's decision to carve out a productive and positive life at Twin Lakes.

Nevertheless, Proenneke was not completely satisfied with Sam Keith's paraphrase of his journals. Proenneke told historian Ted Karamanski in 1990: "I think Sam probably… wanted to be an author so I said you just go ahead, I don't care. He [Keith] was editor, but where does author come into it, but the way he wrote it, it's pretty much,…he tried to make it sound like it was mine, my thinking…He tried to put words in my mouth." Nevertheless the book was well written and thousands of people have been inspired by it. Overall I think Proenneke was more pleased than not with Keith's version, at the very least it shone the spotlight on what Proenneke felt was a life worth noting.

Soon after the creation of Lake Clark National Park and Preserve in 1980, Proenneke allowed the NPS to copy several years of his journals. In 2000 Proenneke and his brother Raymond were living in retirement in California and they donated nearly 90 lbs. of journals to the NPS. When Proenneke left Twin Lakes for the last time in 2000, he walked away from most everything he owned at the cabin. He left a few items such as his rifle and revolver, a hunting knife, and some clothes to a few close friends, everything else he left to the NPS. As for his cabin, he also left it to the park and I am quite sure he would have done so even if he had title to the land on which it sat. The Proenneke Collection contains journals, letters, calendars, and tools that are part of the park collections at the Lake Clark-Katmai National Park and Preserve Cultural Studies Center in Anchorage.

In 2001 I was asked by my supervisor, Dr. Jeanne Schaaf, to edit the Proenneke journals for publication. Her choice was driven by two factors, my previous historical editing for the NPS and my long time friendship with Proenneke. I think I've probably spent as much time with Proenneke in the field on long hikes and working together at Lake Clark as anyone alive. I first met Proenneke in June 1976 when Alaska Governor Jay S. Hammond asked him to come to his Lake Clark homestead where I was caretaker to get me and Ralph Nabinger started building a log steam bath.

Proenneke told me in the mid-1990s that I had been on the longest hike he had ever made, from his cabin to the Gill's Camp in the Bonanza Hills, some 35 miles. In addition, we hiked to Lake Clark and were together on his last long trek searching for the legendary Chickalusion Pass east of upper Twin Lakes in 1994. We also worked together cutting firewood and logs, clearing land, and harvesting potatoes at Lake Clark.

I am honored to have the opportunity to edit the Proenneke Journals and appreciate the confidence my supervisors have in me. I wanted my edition to be true to Proenneke's style but enhanced with explanatory notes, maps, and a biographical sketch of his life. In addition, I wanted to document the creation of a four million acre wilderness national park through Proenneke's eyes. During the 1970s the great Alaska lands debate flared across the state and nation and few had such a front row seat or had potentially as much to lose as did Richard Proenneke.

In my conversations with Proenneke during the 1970s I was heartened that he always expressed strong support to preserve the Twin Lakes-Lake Clark country. Although I was not then working for the National Park Service I was raised to believe that national parks were very good for our nation and that we ought to have more of them, especially in unspoiled places like Alaska. Having little prior experience with the NPS, Proenneke was initially skeptical that the Service might not have been the best way to preserve the area because he feared national park status would bring far too many visitors who might overwhelm the resources. Gradually he came to recognize that the NPS was the proper institution to preserve and protect America's special places. While Proenneke second guessed and groused in his journals about some NPS management decisions, I never heard him condemn NPS goals of resource protection and wilderness preservation.

I have relied on the transcript made by volunteer in the park Jeanette Mills who has read Proenneke's handwritten journals and typed them to the tune of more than 1,600,000 words. Her husband, and fellow volunteer, Jerry Mills, has been the proof reader of her transcription. This effort has been Herculean in scope and a labor of love for the Mills, who were exceedingly fond of Proenneke and what he stood for. Without their accomplishments in this endeavor I would not now be editing this volume.

I have condensed the voluminous journals to about 250,000 words, covering the tumultuous years 1974 through 1980. My intent is to present a broad array of Proenneke's daily activities. Readers will find Proenneke during his adventuring days on the trail and battling strong winds in his canoe, they will see him on more prosaic days of cutting wood, mending his clothes, cooking, writing, feeding his "camp robbers," and contending with an apparent limitless number of porcupines bent on chewing his cabin to dust. His keen observations of brown-grizzly bears, great horned owls, moose, sheep, caribou, wolverines, lynx, and red foxes demonstrates just how knowledgeable Proenneke was of wildlife behavior.

Additionally, I wanted to document Proenneke's interaction with various NPS personnel as they planned and created the new Lake Clark National Monument in 1978-1979 and the national park and preserve in 1980. Starting in 1974, Proenneke shot thousands of feet of wildlife movies and slides for the NPS. Lastly, I wanted to make selections demonstrating how very close Proenneke was tied to the small community of Port Alsworth on Lake Clark, and of his particularly close relationship to the pioneering Alsworth family. Proenneke might have been nearly emotionally self-sufficient but he was tethered to the Alsworths for provisions, mail service, and friendship. In 1975 and 1976 he had a J-3 Piper Cub that he owned jointly with his brother Raymond at Twin Lakes which they used to visit their friends and to explore the proposed park area. All this and much more are presented in this volume.

It is hoped that this book will inspire more interest in the life of Richard Proenneke because he was truly a remarkable man who represented values of wilderness preservation and resource protection. Subsequent volumes covering the late 1960s through the 1980s are planned to round out Proenneke's most productive and unique years at Twin Lakes.

Aerial view of the Proenneke hometown of Primrose, Iowa in 1975 • *Photo courtesy of Raymond Proenneke*

Introduction

In the late winter of 1974 Richard Proenneke wrote, "During the winter of 1973 & 74 I received many nice letters concerning my book *One Man's Wilderness* and many times I felt guilty about receiving them in flat lander country. If Twin Lakes country was so nice, what was I doing in Iowa [?]" During 1974-1975 Proenneke would spend the entire year at his cabin.

Proenneke faced new challenges and new opportunities in 1974 because he had signed a contract to do wildlife photography for the National Park Service. Previously he had taken movies of his cabin construction and wildlife with the intention of showing his films to paying audiences during winter visits to Iowa. But now he was to be paid to do something he loved. Henceforth, Proenneke would devote much more time and energy to what had heretofore been a sideline for him; now he would devote his great powers of concentration and stick-to-itiveness to filming the neighboring wildlife.

The year 1975 proved to be a very interesting yet tragic year for Proenneke and the NPS, whose profile in the Lake Clark region was steadily growing. During the course of the year Proenneke got to know Keith Trexler, an NPS planner involved in determining whether the Lake Clark area, including Twin Lakes, was worthy of national park designation, and would be included in proposed additions to the national park system.

Proenneke had a good deal of company and there were the usual number of sport and meat hunters flying around. His brother, Raymond, flew a J-3 Piper Cub, the "Arctic Tern," that he had rebuilt and that they owned jointly, from California to Twin Lakes in late summer. The brothers flew all over the Twin Lakes country, enjoying their mobility.

Sadly, on September 12th Keith Trexler and six NPS Alaska Office employees were killed when their chartered float plane crashed near the Kijik River. Proenneke blamed himself for their deaths because the victims had been rewarded with an end of season trip to see "One Man's Wilderness." Ironically, they never met Proenneke, because when Trexler and his charges landed at Twin Lakes the Proenneke brothers were at Port Alsworth.

In the spring of 1976 Proenneke flew the "Arctic Tern" back to Twin Lakes from Iowa. This was to be his most mobile year, because he had the float plane all season, yet he almost died for that mobility. On the way "outside" to Iowa in early October, Proenneke crashed his plane between Sheep Mountain Lodge and Glennallen and was seriously injured. After spending time in the hospital in Anchorage he spent the fall of 1976 and winter of 1977 rehabilitating himself at his brother's home in Lynwood, California. He returned to Twin Lakes in June 1977 and resumed his vigorous life of hiking and canoeing, gradually regaining his strength.

Two film crews paid visits to Proenneke in 1977. One from the NPS later resulted in nationwide exposure on PBS when the video "One Man's Alaska" aired. ABC News also sent a crew to interview Proenneke and a segment about him aired in the fall on the Harry Reasoner-Barbara Walters program.

Proenneke wintered over at Twin Lakes during 1977-1978 and fully enjoyed himself with his usual activities of hiking, wildlife photography, wood cutting, and visits from the Alsworths and other friends.

In late winter 1978 a Nova/WGBH film crew came in for an interview with

Proenneke. The result was *Alaska, The Closing Frontier*, which aired nationwide on PBS in June. Like it or not, Proenneke now became an unofficial national spokesman for the preservation movement. Proenneke confided to his journal his worries about alienating some of his old Alaska friends who might not be pleased by the expansion of parks in Alaska. Late in 1978, frustrated by Congress's failure to pass Alaska lands legislation, President Jimmy Carter invoked the Antiquities Act, creating a number of new national monuments, including Lake Clark National Monument.

In the year 1979 Proenneke met the first NPS law enforcement rangers assigned to the new national monument. Proenneke was hopeful that his "neighbors," the local wildlife would now be spared from ending up on the wall or in the freezer of some of the hunters who formerly hunted at Twin Lakes. Overall, Proenneke had another typically busy and satisfying year with little impact on his daily existence from the more frequent NPS presence at Twin Lakes.

Proenneke probably was near the peak of his journalistic output around 1980. He had a great need to document his life in words, and write he did. More visitors than ever came to see "One Man's Wilderness" and the new Lake Clark National Monument. Proenneke could see his little slice of paradise was still intact and there were fewer hunters killing his wild "neighbors," but it was never going to be as quiet as it was in the late 1960s and early 1970s. On December 2, 1980, President Jimmy Carter signed the Alaska National Interest Lands Conservation Act, creating millions of acres of new wildlife refuges and national parks, including one of the most ecologically diverse, the four-million acre Lake Clark National Park and Preserve. Not having a radio for news, Proenneke was unaware of the momentous bill the president had signed into law back in Washington, D.C. It was just another productive day in Proenneke's Twin Lakes country, far from the tumultuous outside world.

Laura Bonn Proenneke and William C. Proenneke circa 1944 • *Photo courtesy of Raymond Proenneke*

Editorial Principles

Richard Proenneke told me he wanted any subsequent book of his journals to be in his own words not paraphrased. I have tried to honor his request but have standardized punctuation, spelling, and capitalization where Proenneke tended to be inconsistent. Proenneke was fond of abbreviations but I have only retained a few unambiguous ones such as "mt." for mountain and "Anch." for Anchorage. I have used notes to enhance the journals for readers by explaining people, locations, and events Proenneke mentions. In the notes I have referred to Proenneke as RLP, for Richard Louis Proenneke. I have also referred to the four cardinal points, North, South, East, and West as N, S, E, and W.

I have edited the Proenneke journals with some diffidence, for I did not want to step on his original intent but merely spruce up his text to make it more reader friendly and understandable in a few instances. However, I have edited minor content where feasible and appropriate. Although I have not paraphrased anything I have omitted a few unclear words with ellipsis and any words used to replace ambiguities appear in brackets. All the editor's clarifying words are in brackets and those in parentheses are Proenneke's. I have tried to identify all the people Proenneke encountered but occasionally I have not identified those who made very transitory visits.

A word about Proenneke's place names is in order. Proenneke named many locations around Twin Lakes; all to my knowledge are unofficial names but many are in common use by National Park Service staff, air taxi operators, and park visitors. Many people would like to see some feature of Twin Lakes country named for Proenneke. The official process of naming unnamed places in an officially designated wilderness area, such as upper Twin Lakes, is difficult, but it might be possible to name a "Proenneke Wilderness Area" similar to the Bob Marshall Wilderness in Montana, without naming individual features.

Proenneke often used abbreviations, for example in his daily summary of the weather Proenneke used "Breeze Up" to indicate a wind coming up the lake from the southwest or "Breeze Down" or "Breeze Dn" to indicate an east wind moving down the lake. Proenneke often wrote Crag Mt. and then he would write Crag "mt." or he would write Emerson Creek and then Emerson "creek." I have retained his upper case letter for Mt. or for example, Emerson Creek, but not for peaks, points, benches, or basins. When a Proenneke place name, such as Big Valley, has developed widespread use, I have retained upper case. Even if Proenneke lived at Twin Lakes more than 30 years it was still a mere blink of an eye when compared with the 1000 year tenure of the Dena'ina Athapaskans of Nondalton and Lime Village. The Dena'ina called Twin Lakes, Niłqidlen Vena, which means "lakes that flow into one another." The Dena'ina also had a name for Emerson Creek, Ts'izdlen, which means "flows straight." Readers will find that the journal notes provide Dena'ina place names for all locations where they are known.

Richard Louis Proenneke
1916-2003

Richard Louis Proenneke was born on May 4, 1916 in Primrose, Iowa to Laura Bonn Proenneke (1884-1966) and William C. Proenneke (1880-1972). He was the fourth of six children and was raised in a small farming community in the southeastern corner of Iowa about 30 miles from Keokuk.

The first Proenneke family immigrated to United States from Germany in the nineteenth century. William Proenneke was a house painter, well driller, and carpenter. He had a horse powered well boring machine that bored 19-inch diameter holes up to 100 feet deep. Proenneke bored wells in Iowa and Missouri in the teens and 1920s. Not much is known about Laura Bonn Proenneke's background but it is probable that her ancestors immigrated to the United States from Germany before the Civil War. Laura Proenneke was a homemaker and gardener.

Richard Proenneke attended elementary school in Primrose in the 1920s. His father purchased a Model T Ford for him to drive to high school in Donnellson in the early 1930s. Proenneke was not happy in high school, and showing an early independent streak, he dropped out after a couple of years. He was very interested in motorcycles and had a Harley Davidson as a teenager. Proenneke worked on nearby farms driving tractors and doing all manner of mechanical and building chores one had to do to maintain Iowa family farms during the Great Depression.

In 1939 Proenneke combined his love of motorcycles and independent spirit undertaking a long "working" trip with a friend, Roland Schrepfer, through the west in search of adventure. They drove their motorcycle south to Oklahoma to harvest wheat and then northwest to Hood River, Oregon to pick apples and then down the Pacific coast to visit the World's Fair in San Francisco. The boys returned home by way of Los Angeles and Albuquerque. Proenneke began the trip with $30 and returned to Primrose with $10, demonstrating early in life both frugality and resourcefulness.

While in Oregon they visited the Frank Wilkinson ranch at Heppner in the foothills of the Blue Mountains, a place where Proenneke would soon work setting up remote camps for herders grazing sheep and cattle. In the spring of 1940, Proenneke returned to the Wilkinson ranch and worked there until the day after the attack on Pearl Harbor. On December 8th 1941, he joined the U.S. Navy. He became a carpenter's mate and was soon stationed at Pearl Harbor where he worked for nearly two years. While he was in San Francisco to join a new ship, he climbed a nearby mountain and soon developed rheumatic fever. Proenneke was sent to Norco Naval Hospital near Corona, California for six months and WWII ended before he left the hospital. He received a medical discharge from the Navy in 1945. Regarding any lingering effects of the rheumatic fever Proenneke said: "After the doctor gave me instructions on what I could do and what I couldn't do. Don't sleep on the cold ground and don't get wet, don't get cold and don't get tired, this and that. Boy, you can't do that on a ranch, you know...but I never had any trouble." [Karamanski, 1990]

Proenneke returned to the Wilkinson ranch in Heppner, Oregon and worked until 1949 when he took a heavy equipment operator course in Portland, Oregon. Later in 1949, he flew to Alaska to visit a friend, Jack Ferguson, who worked for the Alaska Railroad. The winter of 1949-1950 Proenneke took a course in diesel mechanics in Portland and ended up grading papers. People who saw Proenneke working wood or metals or repairing everything from bulldozers to clocks considered him a mechanical genius.

In the spring of 1950 Proenneke returned to Alaska and went to Kodiak with Ferguson to study the feasibility of cattle ranching. The venture never came to be and Proenneke used his training to work seven or eight years at the Kodiak Naval Station as a diesel mechanic. He also fished commercially for salmon at Chignik and worked for the U.S Fish and Wildlife Service at King Salmon in 1952. Beginning about 1961 Proenneke worked for a defense contractor as a powerhouse operator and mechanic at a satellite tracking station at Cape Chiniak on Kodiak Island. During the years 1965-1966 he worked for another contractor as heavy equipment operator and mechanic. During the 1964 Alaska earthquake, a 32 foot fishing boat was carried two miles inland by the tsunami at a bay on the south end of Kodiak Island. Proenneke and another man spent three days winching the boat the two miles back to the bay where they were paid $800 apiece for their labors. Later at Twin Lakes Proenneke would become adept at salvaging submerged aircraft, the bigger the challenge the better he liked it.

Proenneke met Gale "Spike" Carrithers and his wife, Hope, while he was working for the defense contractor on Cape Chiniak. The Carrithers were building a cabin on a recreational site at Twin Lakes on BLM land. They invited Proenneke to Twin Lakes for a visit and he made his first trip there in 1962. After Spike had a stroke Hope Carrithers asked Proenneke to accompany them to Twin Lakes and since he was now working for himself he had more discretionary time. Soon Proenneke got the bug to build a cabin at Twin Lakes. While he was looking for a good spot and learning the country the

Richard Proenneke's family home in 1944 • *Photo courtesy of Raymond Proenneke*

Richard (left) and Raymond (right) Proenneke in 1927. Richard holds a model airplane similar to Charles Lindburgh's *Spirit of St. Louis*

The Proenneke children in 1929. Left to right: Richard, Lorene, Helen, Raymond, Florence, and Robert

William C. Proenneke with his well boring machine circa 1920

Photos courtesy of Raymond Proenneke

Carrithers let him use their cabin. During the years 1964-1967, Proenneke stayed at the Carrithers' cabin part time as the wilderness bug captivated him. "...I had looked around and found a location for a cabin and another friend...Herb Wright, he had picked a spot and told me to stake it and lease it. And right where the cabin sits he ...made a big blaze and carved [a] cabin on it. And so poor old Herb...got cancer and died and never got back to Twin Lakes..." [Karaminski 1990]

The summer of 1967 Proenneke cut his logs and let them season over the winter. In the spring of 1968 he began building his cabin and completed it that fall. For many years Proenneke had been an inveterate letter writer and diarist, so naturally he chronicled his life at Twin Lakes. He had met Sam Keith on Kodiak Island in the 1950s. Later, Proenneke shared his journals from 1968-1969 with Keith. Keith thought Proenneke's cabin story would have broad appeal. Proenneke agreed to allow Keith to edit his journals and they approached Alaska Northwest Publishing Company in Anchorage about bringing out a book. Both Executive Editor Ed Fortier and *Alaska Magazine* outdoor editor, Jim Rearden encouraged publisher Bob Henning to publish the book. In 1973, *One Man's Wilderness* was published and over time has become an Alaska classic. Neither Proenneke nor Keith were particularly happy with the modest 5 percent royalty checks they received from the publisher. According to Raymond Proenneke, his brother never signed a contract with Henning for *One Man's Wilderness* because he felt the royalties insufficient, but Keith did sign.

In addition, Proenneke wished that Keith had not paraphrased his journals in the book but rather had simply used his unvarnished words. Proenneke said he hoped any future editions of his journals would remain true to his words.

With the publication of *One Man's Wilderness* in 1973, Proenneke's extraordinary life became public knowledge. He acquired a following of people who found him inspiring during a time of growing national environmental awareness. Seven years later, Lake Clark National Park and Preserve was created with the passage of the Alaska National Interest Lands Conservation Act. Twin Lakes was part of the new park, resulting in even more general public awareness of what Proenneke stood for. The National Park Service mission to "preserve and protect" the resources and to provide for the enjoyment of those resources by the public were largely the same values Proenneke embodied; although he was concerned too many visitors might be harmful to wildlife. Many current and former National Park Service employees in Alaska were inspired to move north after reading *One Man's Wilderness*. The book was available between 1973 and 1986 when it went out of print. About 1991 the book was printed in Japanese and has since sold 5,000 to 10,000 copies in Japan. In 1999 Alaska Northwest Books, an imprint of Graphic Arts Center Publishing Company in Portland, Oregon reprinted the book and it has sold at a brisk rate. In 1999, *One Man's Wilderness* won the National Outdoor Book Award in the category for biography and memoir.

Proenneke's idyllic existence nearly came to an abrupt end on October 6, 1976 when he crashed his Piper J-3 Cub, the "Arctic Tern," near Copper Center, Alaska as he was flying back to Iowa for the winter. His plane was wrecked and Proenneke suffered a compression fracture of the lumbar region of the spinal column. He was able to crawl to the highway and was picked up by a motorist. He was in an Anchorage hospital the next day. Proenneke spent the winter in southern California rehabilitating himself at his brother Raymond's home. A consensus of opinion by Proenneke and other pilots around Lake Clark was that the crash was caused by carburetor icing. Proenneke told me in the mid-1990s that he attributed much of his physical decline to the trauma his back suffered during the crash.

In 1977 the National Park Service produced a 30 minute video entitled "One Man's Alaska." It was based on Proenneke's cabin construction footage and wildlife footage that he shot for the NPS under contract starting in 1974. Also ABC News ran an interview with Proenneke on the Harry Reasoner-Barbara Walter's program in the fall of 1977. In 1978 the Nova/PBS program, "Alaska, The Closing Frontier," brought Proenneke in a very public way into the great Alaska lands debate that raged throughout Alaska and the nation during the 1970s. Proenneke came out as a strong advocate for preservation of Twin Lakes region. He was the featured Alaskan in the program and his message was one of wilderness preservation as he quoted Thoreau's belief that the preservation of humankind is in the wilderness. By 1980, Proenneke was a hero to many preservationists and a public, if reluctant, advocate for the new national parks.

In 2003 videographer Bob Swerer of Fort Collins, Colorado produced a video entitled "Alone in the Wilderness" that uses Proenneke's original 1967-1968 film to present a thorough documentation of the construction of the cabin. The video is a fine visual companion to the book and seems to inspire and educate at the same time about Proenneke and the ideals for which he stood. "Alone in the Wilderness" has been repeatedly aired all over the nation by PBS stations to wide public acclaim. It offers the uplifting balm of a life well led, during these unsettled times in our nation's history. The wide spread appeal of the video has stimulated sales of *One Man's Wilderness* to the tune of some 85,000 copies during the past 18 months.

By the 1980s some were beginning to see parallels with Henry David Thoreau in Proenneke's singular existence at Twin Lakes. The more one examines Proenneke's life at Twin Lakes the more one sees Thoreau's philosophy put into practice. Thoreau preached material simplicity and a life in balance with nature in *Walden*. Thoreau wrote about the costs of building his cabin at Walden Pond and Proenneke wrote about the costs of his cabin construction at Twin Lakes. Thoreau lived in his cabin two years; Proenneke lived at his cabin the better part of 30 years. Thoreau has inspired millions about the value of wilderness to human survival, of low consumption and self reliance. Proenneke inspires by example, leading a full life, both of action and of the intellect. He had more constructive energy and could concentrate more than anyone I have ever met, whether cooking, hiking, wood cutting, cleaning up after litter bugs, or writing his journals and attending to his large correspondence. Proenneke's life at Twin Lakes runs back through some 150 years of American history to Thoreau at Walden Pond. Both men achieved great balance in their daily existence, tending both the mind and the muscles.

Proenneke had read *Walden* and greatly admired Thoreau. He shared Thoreau's ideas of self-sufficiency, thrift, and a reverence for the natural world. Proenneke also had read Aldo Leopold's *A Sand County Almanac* and was very much in tune with the concept

Richard Proenneke driving a tractor in Iowa circa 1936

Richard Proenneke in the Navy in
Hawaii circa 1943

Richard Proenneke on a Harley Davidson
motorcycle in Iowa in the mid-1930s

Richard Proenneke near Heppner, Oregon circa 1940

Laura Proenneke with sons Richard
(right) and Raymond (left) circa
1944

Photos courtesy of Raymond Proenneke

of land ethics articulated in the book.

Proenneke was not a philosopher like Thoreau, but he was concerned about how the individual could find contentment and purpose and fit into society and nature. He was a very practical man of action rather than a man of lofty ideas; supremely independent, he was a tireless chronicler and letter writer. Over the years he wrote thousands of letters, annotated calendars and kept voluminous journals documenting his Twin Lakes existence. What Proenneke lacked in eloquence was more than made up in homey and humorous observations about life. He had a sign in his cabin that read, "Is it proper that the wilderness and its creatures should suffer because we came?"

Proenneke was following the calling of his own dreams to Twin Lakes in 1968. He heard a different call than most of his contemporaries, as neither money nor material possessions held much interest for him. Proenneke put into practice much of what Thoreau preached and he did it with a hardiness and a kindliness to all those who had the pleasure of his company. He was true to his own ideals and was a heroic, inspiring figure to his friends and those who have been fired by his life through reading *One Man's Wilderness* or viewing "Alone in the Wilderness."

As the 1970s moved along, the story of Proenneke's life became known to a national audience through his book and television appearances. He shined the clear light of day on the natural untrammeled majesty of the Twin Lakes country and by extension all the wild lands in Alaska. Proenneke's ideals helped inform America about the legitimacy and worthiness of national park status for the area. In his own unique way he helped pave the way for the passage of ANILCA through educating the public about the lands being proposed for preservation. Proenneke corresponded with and hosted conservationist Mardy Murie and NPS planner John Kauffmann, and he avidly read and corresponded with nature writer Sigurd Olson. He also corresponded with a few congressmen and other political figures, but since he periodically burned most of his correspondence in order to save room the letters have not apparently survived.

During the 1980s Proenneke's fame spread, and as a result of his book and creation of Lake Clark National Park and Preserve he received fewer sport hunters and more back packers and river floaters as visitors. He became a volunteer in the park helping NPS personnel monitor weather, collect botanical specimens, assist with aerial wildlife counts, and communicated between visitors and rangers about float plane pick ups.

Proenneke continued to produce his journals during the 1980s but as the 1990s evolved he wrote less in journals and more on his wall calendars. His health gradually declined. Once in the early 1990s he slid down a mountain during the winter and broke some ribs. He also endured prostate problems, and apparently suffered small strokes. On our last overnight camping trip in 1994 he said he wanted to hike like he used to but his old heart just would not allow him to do it. Nevertheless he acquitted himself very well for a man of 78 years of age, climbing more than 3,000 feet.

Proenneke ceased spending entire winters at Twin Lakes by the mid-1990s. Frequently, he would housesit in Port Alsworth for part of the winter, and then visit his brother in California and his sister in Iowa before returning to his beloved Twin Lakes

Richard Proenneke in Portland, Oregon in 1949 • *Photo courtesy of Raymond Proenneke*

Richard Proenneke in Kodiak, Alaska circa 1950 • *Photo courtesy of Raymond Proenneke*

in the early spring. By the late 1990s, Proenneke gradually lost the urge to live at Twin Lakes as concerns for his failing health came to dominate his life. In 1998 he moved permanently to his brother Raymond's home in Hemet, California. The summer of 2000 Proenneke made his final trip to Alaska, spending two weeks at Port Alsworth with park ranger Leon Alsworth and his family. He made two brief visits to his Twin Lakes cabin, the last one for a filmed interview, before leaving Alaska for the last time. Proenneke's health continued to decline and by 2002 Raymond Proenneke felt it necessary to move Richard to a nearby nursing home. Richard Louis Proenneke passed away on Easter morning in 2003 in Hemet.

Proenneke's legacy is the example of his extraordinarily productive life, his advocacy of wilderness, his voluminous writings, his photographs, and his cabin. In 1998 NPS historical architect Timothy Johnson summarized the Proenneke legacy very succinctly: "The Richard Proenneke site within Lake Clark National Park is an excellent example of the wilderness tradition of bush country in Alaska...the Proenneke site is a prime illustration of a broad wilderness movement. Proenneke built his cabin utilizing, almost wholly, materials from the area and his own ingenuity. He has lived in a virtual symbiosis with the land, consuming only that which he requires to fulfill his humble needs. Following the notoriety of the book..., *One Man's Wilderness,* he has been sought after by hundreds of visitors and wilderness enthusiasts. Proenneke's understanding and insight into the daily workings of nature and his friendly way with guests has made him a very popular icon in the Lake Clark area. While others promote the salvation and preservation of our country's wilderness areas, Dick Proenneke has chosen to live his life in such an area. And in so doing, he has played an early and important role in the wilderness movement of this country." [Johnson, 1998]

A few final thoughts about Richard Proenneke, the man, are in order to finish this imperfect sketch. What sort of basic human qualities did Proenneke possess? He was humble and self-effacing in spite of his extraordinary physical and mental abilities. He had an orderly and methodical mind with great powers of concentration on the task at hand. He was very perceptive of other people's sentiments and acutely aware of his physical surroundings. Physically he was not a big man, standing five foot seven and weighing 150 pounds in his prime, he was very strong and endowed with tremendous stamina; he seemed almost tireless while hiking or canoeing. Proenneke was frugal and as self-reliant as his circumstances would permit. He was an independent thinker with a curious and inquiring mind, who kept his own counsel, and had a healthy streak of skepticism about life. In spite of living without radio or television he was able to stay reasonably well informed of the great events of the day by reading magazines and newspaper clippings sent by friends and family.

Proenneke had a copy of the nineteenth century classic, *Woodcraft and Camping,* by Nessmuk. In the book, Nessmuk described a Michigan woodsman very much like Richard Proenneke, "Not a misanthrophe, or taciturn, but friendly and talkative rather; liking best to live alone, but fond of tramping across the woods to gossip with neighbors...." Proenneke was no gossip but he liked to talk with his friends and neighbors. Proenneke had a healthy ego and was competitive by nature yet he was never arrogant or

Spike and Hope Carrithers at their cabin on Twin Lakes in 1965. To the right, Proenneke stands on a ladder. • *Photo courtesy of Raymond Proenneke*

Sam Keith at Emerson Creek in 1970 • *Photo courtesy of Raymond Proenneke*

condescending to those of us less endowed with his quick mechanical genius. He was pragmatic and able to improvise solutions to problems in a flash with few basic tools. If he did not have the tools he needed then he would make whatever it took to complete the job. Once at Turquoise Lake, he tore his pants and needed to mend them, but was without needle and thread. Proenneke quickly found an empty five gallon tin gas can and crafted a needle. Next he found some tangled monofilament fishing line and soon had sewn up his torn pants.

Finally, Proenneke had an understated sense of humor and was quick to chuckle. He had an active curious mind. His favorite exclamations were "Ho Boy!" or "Boy oh Boy!" Although a life-long bachelor, Proenneke liked women, and had many female friends. I never heard him swear, or brag nor did I ever know him to drink or smoke, yet he was no prude. He had a great many friends and his life inspired those friends and continues to inspire those who are newly acquainted with him.

Richard Proenneke on Kodiak Island in 1960 • *Photo courtesy of Raymond Proenneke*

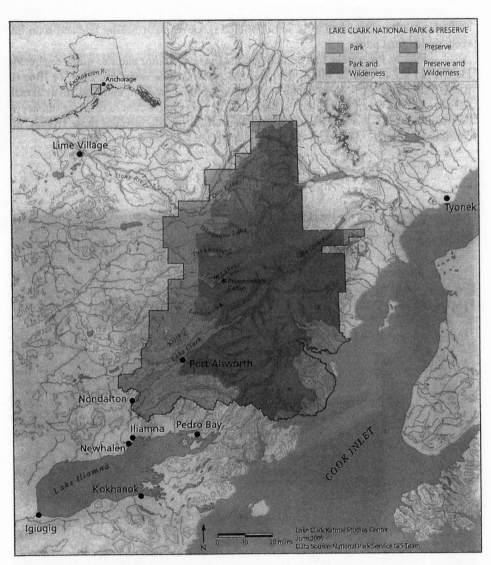

Lake Clark National Park and Preserverve, and environs • *Photo courtesy of NPS*

CHAPTER ONE – 1974

LAKE CLARK CONNECTIONS—A LIFE AT TWIN LAKES

[RLP drove back to Anchorage in late March from Iowa and met Babe Alsworth. They drove to Edmonston, Alberta with Fred and Charlie Roehl and picked up a new Taylorcraft. Babe and RLP then flew back to Anchorage arriving about mid-April.]

March 27

During the winter of 1973 & 74 I received many nice letters concerning my book *One Man's Wilderness* and many times I felt guilty about receiving them in flat lander country. If Twin Lakes country was so nice, what was I doing in Iowa.[1]

Babe[2] phoned Merrill Tower to clear him with no receiver and we headed on the last leg of our long journey. Ft. Nelson, B.C. to Anch. is a good hop for one day. Babe flew on home next day and I stayed to take care of last minute business. A few showings of my film and one of them for the National Park Service. They were very much interested and asked if I would shoot some film of Twin Lakes country for them. I would if we could agree on a deal. An easy outfit to deal with and it was soon settled. I purchased a new Bolex tripod for the project and Will Troyer[3] loaned (wouldn't sell) me his good Miller fluid head. Another show for the Anch. Prospectors Club[4] and I have never had a better audience.

Babe came to town and we flew to Port Alsworth[5] Apr. 17. The usual small jobs to do at his homestead. The far side of the greenhouse roof to recover. Several axe and splitting maul handles to put in. A trip to the mission[6] for a few small chores. He left me there to fly away with fare paying passengers. The girls[7] and I took Sig & Leon[8] on a picnic

---

[1] RLP flew the Alcan Highway with Babe Alsworth after meeting him in Edmonton, Alberta about April 15, 1974.

[2] Leon Reid "Babe" Alsworth, Sr. (1910-2004), born in Minnesota, pioneering bush pilot who began flying in Alaska in 1939, homesteaded on Lake Clark in 1942; the village of Port Alsworth was named after him in 1950, variant Tanalian Point.

[3] Will Troyer, NPS wildlife biologist and pilot.

[4] Anchorage Prospectors Club was a social organization that met in a downtown church and had monthly speakers present movies and slide shows documenting travel throughout Alaska.

[5] Port Alsworth, a small community on Lake Clark that grew up around Babe and Mary Alsworth's home. Tanalian Point is the name of the area before 1950 and dates from 1909. Port Alsworth is about 35 miles south of Twin Lakes.

[6] Arctic Missions, (now InterAct Ministries) evangelical Christian missionaries headquartered in Boring, Oregon, with missions in Canada and Alaska.

[7] Florence Hicks and Doris Hagedorn were missionaries from Arctic Missions in Nondalton.

[8] Sig Alsworth (1965-1982) and Leon Alsworth III who was born in 1964 were the children of Leon "Lonnie" Alsworth, Jr. (1945-1969) and Martha Bedell Alsworth (1948-1996).

on the creek. "B"[9] came for me in his Tri-Pacer. A nice quiet easy riding rig.

Babe was in no hurry for me to leave even though I had mentioned I was ready to go. Florence (the mission girl) came to my rescue. Babe and I made a second trip to Nondalton[10] and would go on to Iliamna.[11] At the mission I had a couple new faucets to replace some leakers and Babe came after visiting a friend. Florence says "Babe you are in a big hurry. I know Dick is in a big hurry to get to Twin Lakes. I'll pop some corn if you will stay." We stayed for popcorn and then on to Iliamna to deliver a fresh frozen salmon. Babe said when we returned to his place "Now Dick I don't want you to go until you are ready but if you want to go now, we can try it this afternoon." At three o'clock lunch and we loaded the new "T craft"[Taylorcraft].[12] He would have preferred the big tires on the old one but we would give it a try. Off and flying and she climbed good as we headed for the Kijik [River].[13] I was interested in snow cover and ice conditions. I could see no caribou trails on the snow patches near Pear Lake.[14] Where were the caribou? Over the mt. and a view of the lakes. Ruffled with remnants of old snow drifts. Not the best for smooth landings. It would be better below Carrithers' point,[15] I was sure of that. We carried two rocks in case we needed a second choice. Smooth from Hope Creek[16] to the point as we came close I let one go, down down and it hit and skipped. Good enough I let the last one go on the turn for a landing. The ice was hard and smooth, just like concrete. No water along the edge which is a good sign. We stopped 50 yds. out and packed my gear to the cabin. We had to wade soft snow to reach the door. The door was locked and I wondered how it would look inside. Not as I had left it but good enough. My kerosene lantern sitting on the counter. A bag of jelly beans on the window ledge above. The stove pipe for above the roof leaning against the stove. I had oiled my stove when I left but now it had rusted along one edge. That was no problem. Mahlon Troyer and his partner Ray Massey[17] had used it and I was glad I had seen him at Babe's as they passed on their way to Wide Bay.[18] He told me they had used it and seemed peaved when I said I had heard that they did.

Babe allowed it looked pretty good and after visiting a few minutes he decided to head for home. He says "you know this will be my first chance to fly this airplane without a load." He was anxious to see how it would clear the mts. on a straight course to Port

[9] Wayne "Bee" Alsworth, son of Babe and Mary Alsworth, is a pilot and aircraft mechanic.

[10] Nondalton, a Dena'ina village on Sixmile Lake, about 22 miles west of Port Alsworth; Nundaltin is a Dena'ina word for "lake extends below."

[11] Iliamna, hub village for the Iliamna – Lake Clark country, about 35 miles SW of Port Alsworth. Iliamna dates from about 1920, variant Seversens or Seversen's Roadhouse; Nilavena is a Dena'ina word for "islands lake," Iliamna Lake.

[12] Taylorcraft or "T craft," small single engine aircraft favored by Babe Alsworth. "T crafts" were manufactured by Taylorcraft Aircraft Company in Alliance, Ohio.

[13] Kijik River is a glacial river that heads east of Twin Lakes and flows 18 miles to Lake Clark; Ch'ak'daltnu is the Dena'ina word for "animals walk out stream."

[14] Pear Lake, a small lake about 8 miles south of lower Twin Lakes.

[15] RLP's Carrithers' point, location about 300 yards NE of the Proenneke site on upper Twin Lakes, named for Gale "Spike" (1898?-1985?) and Hope Carrithers (1908?-) who first brought RLP to Twin Lakes in 1962 from Kodiak Island.

[16] RLP's Hope Creek, glacial creek that enters upper Twin Lakes about 125 yards south of the Proenneke site.

[17] Mahlon Troyer lived for a time at Port Alsworth on land provided him by Babe Alsworth. After his son drowned in Hardenburg Bay the family moved to the Kenai Peninsula, later Troyer died in a plane crash. Nothing is known of Ray Massey.

[18] Wide Bay, a bay on the Pacific side of the Alaska Peninsula about 20 miles SW of Lower Ugashik Lake.

Alsworth. He took off and climbed fast. I stood and watched him out of sight. Silence closed in around me and it was a good feeling. This was the way I preferred it. Now I was geared to my own planning. I knew what I was going to do.

April 30

Clear, calm & 20° when I looked out. I had slept like a log but was awake long before sun up. I hadn't seen or heard my birds and wondered when they would find me. The only bird I had heard yesterday was a raven. I was up before the sun and had my spuds, bacon, & egg plus a bowl of oatmeal. Today would be a day to get further organized and keep track of the bears. Babe was coming so I had better stay close.

I spotted the four bears where I had last seen them last night. The cubs were stirring but the mother lay still.

It was 10:15 when I heard Babe and soon he was on the ice out front. Three dozen eggs yesterday and four today. I told him seven dozen is too many but he says "eat lots of eggs." About 60 lbs. of spuds, my sugar, beans and seasonings I had bought in Anch., 25 lbs. of oatmeal. Now I was really stocked. About all I could use in the food line was vinegar and I have a fair supply of that.

How did the "T craft" take the mts.? "Fine, I think it shortens the trip about five minutes by going straight across" he said.

He would be heading back and we decided on May 15th for the next trip. Put a little circle of spruce boughs on the ice and leave it till the ice goes bad he said.

May 4 – Clear, Calm & 25°.

A beautiful clear morning and I hadn't expected it. I figured that it would be overcast and I would stay home and celebrate my birthday.[19] I did sleep in till 4:45.

My bears had stayed put during the night and it would be nearly nine before the old girl gave the order to grub roots.

Again the call of swan and I looked without success. The next call I spotted a wedge very high. I should have put the camera outside for again I heard them and louder. Here they came much lower and snow white against the deep blue sky. I rushed for the camera but was too late. Once they are going away they don't show white any longer.

Today I would go up country again. I would try for some ptarmigan pictures. Only two days since I was there and I was surprised that the lake ice had deteriorated so much. Sand & dirt blows on the ice from the river flat in winter and this hastens the melting in spring. Ptarmigan right away and a wild pair. Run along ahead and into the

---

[19] RLP was born May 4, 1917 in Primrose, Iowa.

brush. Then one rooster in the top of a small spruce. Another one and this one very cooperative. I soon learned why. The hen was under a spruce nearby. When she flew so did he.

It was 2:15 when I reached the lake shore and headed down. The sun very bright on the snow white lake ice. One hr. and five minutes walking in a straight line to reach Carrithers' point. I sat down on the beach to check on my bears and was surprised to see the sheep bedded near where the bears had spent the night. Then I picked up the bears no more than 200 yds. from the sheep and working on a big slide. I came on down and took care of my camera gear. Put my biscuits in the sun to rise. This had been a pretty good birthday. While I worked about the cabin I heard the cubs squalling and rushed out to check. I saw no reason for the crying. Two with the mother and the third working a hundred yds. up country. The three headed that way and that was the last I saw of any. I started a letter and when I went to check – no bears. Perhaps they were there but in a swag. I hope they stay a few more days at least. The sheep had a good spot above so they hadn't climbed. No birds yet. I left a little meat scrap on the table out side. The first camp robber to get near would have it in a flash. It has been laying there for two days.

May 7 – Clear, Calm & 30°.

First thing after breakfast I searched for the cow moose and spotted a black bear just above the cottonwoods. Some difference between the black & brown bear. The brownie would be up on the mt. digging roots. Evidently the black bear was after the first shoots of green stuff. Brush is budding on the south slope and leaves will soon show.

I found my moose on the big slide – bedded down just her head and neck sticking out from behind a spruce. I would try for her so made preparations. I figured she would see me cross so I headed for Falls Creek[20] and then angled up when the spruce hid me. I traveled close to shore and the bank and timber covered me on that stretch.

Something dark out on the ice and crossing from the base of Crag Mt.[21] to the big slide country which was my destination. I was surprised to learn it was a porcupine. The first I had ever seen on the lake ice. I would meet him at the beach and get some pictures. It so happened that the bank was low right there and the cow moose was above. I had to let him go or risk being seen.

May 9 – Partly Cloudy, Calm & 36°.

Today was due to be the day of days. I slept in a bit and was up at 5 o'clock. Hotcakes out of the way and washing dishes when three camp robbers came. My birds! – I knew it was

---

[20] RLP's Falls Creek, a small creek on upper Twin Lakes across from the Proenneke Site.

[21] RLP's Crag Mountain, a 5, 328 ft. peak immediately east of the Proenneke Site.

them. A scrap of hotcake and one came to my hand. Little tender bill and I knew it was. I noticed that his beak doesn't quite close and that's the way it was when I left him last fall. Strong enough to tear chunks out of a hotcake now. The second one wouldn't come to my hand but would come close if I dropped it on the ground. The third was shy and stayed in the spruce. It is good to have them back again.

A few minutes later and I was outside brushing my teeth. Caribou, seven head of them passed from the point going down. Some with antlers and one with only one side. They trudged slowly down the lake heads low as if packing a heavy load. Then I spotted more along the far shore and a half mile below Jerre's cabin.[22] About 20 there. Down by the gravel bank a long string of them on the ice. Caribou in the brush at the lower end of the lake. Who was the Cheechako who predicted very few caribou would come to the lakes this spring?

I crossed to the high bank on the up country side of Beech Creek.[23] From there maybe I could see them go and perhaps get ahead of them. As if there never was a caribou and they had to be there. No doubt they traveled the beach below the bank and my line of vision. A beautiful shot up the lake from there and I ended a roll of film.

At the cabin and I heard a parky squirrel. There he was at the rock pile on the beach. I had left him there last fall. I took him a chunk of hotcake and I had no more than reached the cabin when he was sitting straight as a picket the hotcake bit in both hands. He is the guy that ate a batch of my cabbage last fall. The birds came for a hand out. It was just like old times.

May 11 – Partly Cloudy, Breeze dn. & 30°.

I was up at 4:30 to greet the new day. My birds were here before that by quite a bit. I heard them bumping the spruce buck horns on the end of the ridge log. The second bird came to my hand as if it had been a regular thing.

After breakfast a check of the hump and Crag Mt. No sign of life there. I walked out on the ice to check the moose pasture. One caribou cow over above the cottonwoods and while I watched a second and third cow appeared. Then two out on the lake ice from behind Carrithers' point. They seemed afraid of something on the beach and later I determined it was Terry Shurtleff's[24] pile of gas cans under the spruce on the beach. The two trotted across the lake and more followed. There was seven in all. I took glasses and scope and went up to the point. More caribou cows – a good bunch of them and they were also crossing the lake. 24 was my count and all cows – most with antlers. They stopped out in the middle and milled around before finally deciding to go up country. They headed

---

[22] Jerre's cabin was across the lake from the Proenneke cabin and was built by Homer resident Jerre Wills. Wills was a commercial fisherman and trapper.

[23] RLP's Beech Creek, a small creek on the south side of lower Twin Lakes, named for a crashed Beech aircraft. In *One Man's Wilderness* the creek was referred to as Bonanza Creek.

[24] Terry Shurtleff, a pilot and sport hunter who left a fuel cache on Twin Lakes.

for the mouth of Glacier Creek. And there above (up country) Glacier Creek[25] mouth was a cow moose and once I thought I got a glimpse of a dark yearling calf but I couldn't be sure. She was on the move and stopped often to stick her big nose high testing the wind.

May 12 – Snowing, Breeze dn. & 35°.

Visibility was low and the ground was white when I looked out at five. A strong breeze down the lake. I was glad to see it. The chore I had to do today would be much easier because of it.

Fried spuds for breakfast along with the usual bacon, egg, and oatmeal. My hot water, vinegar, and honey which I find the best drink of all.

Chores out of the way I made ready to write letters. Add to what I had and write more. The snow stopped but the wind continued down the lake. First get a fresh kettle of beans to simmering. Make the fire do double duty today. My two birds came for a hand out and were gone for the day. I didn't see mr. parky squirrel until afternoon. He sat up straight on top of the rock pile and munched a sourdough biscuit and then retired below. I must cut down on his ration or he will forget what work is. Not so with the camp robber. He is on the go from daylight till dark and anything he can pick up for free is just a bonus.

I wrote till late afternoon and then took time out to get cleaned up and do laundry. Supper over and my journal out of the way I went at it again. Some letters had gone [un]answered too long. Blue spots down country but a few small flakes of snow still come with the good breeze from up country. Temp. 37°.

May 13 – Partly Cloudy, Calm & 35°.

Babe had said, with spruce boughs, make a circle on the ice and leave it there as long as the ice is good. I had better get that chore out of the way. I didn't like to cut a small spruce for boughs. I would trim up the blow down tree behind Spike's cabin. With glasses & scope and my trusty axe I went up to the point. Another good look across the lake but no success on moose. I got my boughs plus a couple lengths of green fire wood for Spike's stove. I stuffed a burlap sack with tips of branches and went out on the ice. I suspected those rams on the mt. would take a dim view of this operation.

I would not only make a circle but lay out a runway too. Forty five feet wide and several hundred feet long. The markers along the side fifty feet apart. A circle twenty feet in diameter on the Port Alsworth end.

A large body of open water at the upper end of the lower lake.[26] The upper lake

---

[25] RLP's Glacier Creek is a small creek that enters upper Twin Lakes on the north side of the lake.

[26] Lower Twin Lakes, is about 6 miles long and forms the western part of the Twin Lakes. The Proenneke Site is about 5 miles east of lower Twin Lakes. Niłqidlen Vena is the Dena'ina word for "lakes that flow into one another."

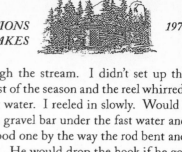

rising very slowly and so more water is going through the stream. I didn't set up the camera I would see if I could catch a fish first. First cast of the season and the reel whirred. The super duper [lure] plunked in out beyond the fast water. I reeled in slowly. Would I get a strike first cast. The lure came to the end of the gravel bar under the fast water and stopped. I pulled and it moved. I had a fish on. A good one by the way the rod bent and the reel turned. Probably a laker with a boney mouth. He would drop the hook if he got an inch of slack. I played him awhile and worked him in and I knew before it got close it was no lake trout. The color was wrong. A big Dolly [Varden] or arctic char. Hooked good both top and bottom so he wouldn't get away. A stone on the rod and I went for my camera gear. Sunshine every where but here and I waited for the cloud to move but clouds don't move. They just build up on one side and dissipate on the other. I scooped out a couple holes near the ice along shore. I wanted some pictures there. I moved him over and he was patient while I removed the hooks. A shot or two and I decided to move him to the other pool which looked much nicer. I would get some close ups there. After that I would slide him over the dam and under the ice with the camera running. No struggle while I moved him. A real nice fish, a good nineteen inches long. He lay in that nice pool along the ice. A pretty picture in the making. I moved back to the camera and before I realized it he was gone. Just swam and swam right over the dam. There was a spruce nearby. I should have cut a few boughs to fence the pool. I didn't mind him getting away but would liked to have a movie of it. I tried and tried and got one strike but no fish. An arctic tern, the first of the season, was working nearby.

I glassed the country and could count 16 sheep on Falls Mt.[27] and two on Black Mt.[28] No lambs or any lone ewes up in the rocks.

May 14 – Partly Cloudy, Calm & 36°.

Frank Bell[29] said years ago, "I feel better at Twin Lakes than any place I have ever been." I believe that is true. I sleep like a log. I wonder how Frank feels in Pekin, Illinois.

My early morning check. No lambs that I could see. Rams not four but six on Crag Mt. and close to the ridge leading up. Just in the edge of the rough stuff. The two half curls were there and the four, all good ones. It was six o'clock when I headed for the point with the scope to check for moose across. While I glassed the far side I heard the clack of horns on Crag Mt. Was those big guys bumping head at this time of year? I put the scope on them. Soon I saw two standing shoulder [to shoulder] and reaching with that inboard front foot. One turned and trotted back a few paces – turned again and stood head on. The other wasn't interested. Many false starts but pretty soon two did come together and it was four or five seconds before the sound of heads bumping reached me.

---

[27] RLP's Falls Mountain, a 4,790 ft. peak on north side of upper Twin lakes across from the Proenneke Site.

[28] RLP's Black Mountain, a 5,363 ft. peak on the north side of lower Twin Lakes.

[29] Frank Bell (1901-1992), a Kenai Peninsula based trapper who built 3 cabins in the Twin Lakes area in the 1960's and later sold them to Jerre Wills.

Too early for pictures. The sun was still behind Crag Mt. I headed for the edge of the timber on the creek trail and parked myself by a spruce. All four would get in the act at times. Two bump and bounce back and another would be on his way in to give that down hill guy a second blow. Once I heard four in rapid succession. If only I could get pictures. I could climb on the lake side of the mt. but the sun would be in my face – no good. It would be a real tough chore to get by them below without moving them. Keeping under the bank going up Hope Creek would be murder.

First thing this morning when I went to the woodshed for kindling[,] I was startled (when I entered) by a porkypine standing on my fish cleaning table and chewing on the end logs of my woodshed. Now! there was a porkypine[30] for pictures on the lake ice. I would take him out and turn him loose headed across. So – I urged him to enter a gas can box. I covered it with a board and set my chopping block on top.

At the cabin the tree squirrel perched on the stone house of the ground squirrel. The ground squirrel at the base of it. Finally both of them on the gravel within two feet of each other. The tree squirrel scampered away. The ground squirrel learns fast. He recognized me and didn't hide in the rocks when I went to the beach with a chunk of biscuit. I squatted down and held it out. Cautiously he came and took it from my fingers. Sat there and started to fill his cheeks and then ran to his house in the rocks.

The biscuits in the pan and film changed. 14 rolls ready to send in now. Now for the porkypine. I lugged my gear and the box of porky out on the ice and turned him loose towards the far side. A porcupine can lope and he did a few steps but only a few. A fast walk is his normal top speed. I found this project was not so easy. All I could get was departing shots. If I circled right or left so did the porky. His stern always towards me. He must steer by radar for he was always going directly away even though his back was turned. If I got too close he stopped and then no sound and he might turn towards me to whirl again when I moved. It's a long way across the lake as a porkypine paces it. When we got well over I circled very wide and waited on the beach. As soon as he heard the camera he turned and headed back. Back on the ice and him straightened out. A narrow strip of water between the ice and the beach. He wanted on the beach but didn't like the water. He turned this way and that. I encouraged him a bit and he finally slid over the edge and headed for the rocks. A good ending for the 75 ft. of film I wasted on the little porkypine.

May 16 – Overcast, Breeze up & 30°.

I came up along the edge and found a place to get off of the ice near Jerre's cabin. Snow hides the sins of winter. Now with it gone cans and trash lay every where. Nine carcasses of foxes lay in a heap. Fur buyers are not particular these days. These skeletons still had the feet attached. Nine foxes and one small wolf. I should waste some film on that

---

[30] "Porkypine," RLP's quaint spelling of his habitual nemesis, the porcupine, has been retained.

display and then a shot of my little decoration (in the cabin) which reads "Is it proper that the Wilderness and its creatures should suffer because we came?" With the weather thickening down country I headed for home. The ice 35" as of today but some places it is soft which gives one an uneasy feeling now and then.

May 20 – High Thin Overcast, Calm & 36°.

I traveled the beach on up and found that there was a perfect place to leave the ice at the old Watts Waddell sheep camp.[31] Many tracks of caribou but nothing fresh. I headed for the big slide and a view of the flats. I expected to see caribou across the flats on the meadows by the old beaver ponds. If I was lucky I would see a bear digging Eskimo potato in the dry water courses. I saw nothing except a few ptarmigan in the willow brush. On my way to the slide I had made a good find. A backpacker's cup. 5" across the top, 3" across the bottom and 1 ½" deep. A handle of wire and the type that hooks over a belt. One of Pollard's[32] hunters had probably lost it as it wasn't more than 400 yds. from the campsite. A good sturdy cup and stamped in the metal "Made in Japan." I came off of the slide and headed up the river. A chance of seeing a moose feeding on the slope. I turned in to visit the beaver pond. It doesn't appear that beavers used it last winter. Some years they do and others not. A pair of Barrow's goldeneye ducks were there and it was the same last time in spring (a year ago). Probably the same pair. On up and I hit a bear track that made me think of my big pistol hanging on the bunk post.

The front track a strong seven inches wide. A pretty impressive track for Twin Lakes country. Maybe a day or two old. I would bet it is the same big bear that got the moose calf last spring. A little farther on and little bear tracks, lots of them and then the remains of an old caribou carcass. Probably a hunter had killed it last fall. Again I climbed the mt. slope for a good view of the flat. I wanted to see that good bear. I glassed the flats and far slope for an hr. and didn't see anything move. More places he could be and not be seen than the other way around. Let him move very far on the flats and I would pick him up.

May 21 – Clear, Calm & 26°.

Another fine morning and I was up in good time for today I was going on a long journey. I would go at least as far as Trail Butte[33] (on the Nondalton-Telaquana trail).[34] A good hike from here as it is a good two hrs. hike below the lower lake.

---

[31] "Watts Waddell sheep camp," RLP refers to Hugh Watson and Guy Waddell (1890-1960), a big game guide. The camp was at the N end of upper Twin Lakes and was used by Waddell in the late 1940s and 1950s. Waddell was an old time guide and Watson frequently worked with him as an assistant, both men lived in Homer.

[32] George Pollard, a second generation Alaskan from Kasilof and big game guide who hunted sheep at Twin Lakes.

[33] RLP's Trail Butte, a 2,275 ft. promontory south of the Chilikadrotna River along the Telaquana Trail.

[34] Telaquana Trail, a 50-mile long Dena'ina trail that connected villages at Kijik on Lake Clark with those at Telaquana Lake.

On my morning check I spotted a 2nd new lamb. Born at nearly the same spot as the first one.

The lake was in good shape with the temp. 24° during the night. I would travel the ice of this lake but not the lower. A pair of Barrow goldeneyes right where the upper lake dumps into the stream. A gentle pair and I got as close as I wanted.

I headed for the [Trail] butte and felt sure when I crossed the old trail. A low saddle and leading to the river crossing was a natural gentle slope. I could just see those dog sleds sail on down grade to the river. I climbed to the summit of the butte. I had been there before but didn't stay overnight. No water on top but a few snow banks on the lee side. I pulled off my shoes and socks and buried my tired feet in the snow for a few seconds. Cold for just a little while will make your feet good for many more miles.

I dug out my film and rations. I had brought along five hundred feet of film, which is a load. Also my big pistol, mummy bag, combat rations & smoked fish. With my heavy tripod, Miller head and Bolex I was probably packing a good 40 lbs.

The sun was still high. 5 pm when I arrived [at Trail Butte]. Warm and a good breeze coming up the Chilikadrotna.[35] It was nice up there. I ate and glassed the country full circle. I could see a couple more single cows a long way off. I guessed they had calves. Across the river a little bunch of caribou and towards the Kijik [River] another bunch. Possibly one calf with them When the sun got low I could see more. A long way off but a change in color told me it was game moving about feeding. One lone cow on a high flat plateau towards the mt. High up and no chance to get close to her. I turned in at 8:30 and lay watching the sun light leave the flats and then the mts. It calmed and now the mosquitoes came. No more than a half dozen but they didn't sleep and it didn't get cold enough although in the morning there would be frost at the base of the butte. I slept a little bit – three hrs. perhaps and was awake when the sun cleared the mts. on the far side of Turquoise Lake.[36] I was ready to go at five. Ptarmigan roosters had cackled all night and now I could hear old squaw ducks on the river and so started

May 26 – Partly Cloudy & possibly 32°.

Two pairs of swan added to the sound. Two caribou crossed a good distance ahead of me as I passed the gravel buttes. Farther on I spooked a bull the first bull I have seen this spring. Past the gravel knoll and the spruce knoll – I traveled the shoreline of the lakes. From there only a mile to Arlen's cabin.[37] The bay...is very shallow there and near shore I could see water pushing up and creating quite a disturbance. A spring under the lake floor. Later as the day warmed I saw several. I was at the cabin by 7:45 and set about to

---

[35] Chilikadrotna River, flows 55 miles W draining Twin Lakes. It is the largest tributary of the Mulchatna River and is in the Nushagak drainage; Dena'ina word is thought to mean "tongue river."

[36] Turquoise Lake, a large glacial lake about 12 miles north of Twin Lakes and the source of the Mulchatna River; Vandaztun Vena is the Dena'ina word for "caribou hair lake."

[37] Arlen Colclature or Koklatcher, nothing is known of this individual except that he built a small plywood hunting cabin on the SW end of lower Twin Lakes in the 1960's. RLP called the bay Lake Trout Bay.

clean it up and cook myself a big feed of oatmeal. I had left a sack of it 2 yrs. ago and no one had used any. A can of beans with wiener chunks was also my breakfast. This squared away I lay down and slept a half hr. or so. I still had a long way to go. At least four hrs. steady going.

May 26 –Clear, Calm & 30°.

We did it again – a perfect morning. It would have to be Sunday but I could fix that I would take Monday off if it was cloudy.

Six head of sheep on Allen Mt.[38] was all I could see on the far side. Down country below Beech Creek I could see three caribou that I took to be bulls. I wanted to take a tour up into the big basin behind Crag Mt. See if the rams were there and if any of those caribou cows had calves up there.

I was away early headed up over the hump and along that miserable slope of Crag Mt. Steep, loose rocks in the brush, rock slides, deep washes, you name it that slope has it.

This morning from in front of my cabin the morning sun just lacked half of its diameter of clearing Crag mt. peak. Now, from here on the sun will be in the clear from sunrise to sunset. I traveled in the shade of the mt. for a time but finally the sun got around and it was in my eyes. I saw the caribou cow and her calf but failed to recognize her until she became alarmed and headed down country. At the entrance to the basin I saw a snow white ptarmigan which is a rare sight at this date. Over the hump guarding the basin and nothing in sight. The very long slope up to the saddle still deep in snow. I would circle left up under the peak to the high ridge over looking the river up country from the lake. I saw no cows and calves but did see tracks of both. The rams had been there no more than a few days ago. I ran into snow a half mile from the top. Deep washes are usually good. The snow is packed and good going. It is shallow snow 3 ft. or less that suffers from the sun. The snow will soften all the way down. I ran into trouble no more than a few hundred yds. from the top. Soft snow and I had a battle getting to the dry rocky slope along side. On top at last and a beautiful sight it was. Clear as a bell. Calm and the sun really warm. To the south Iliamna Volcano[39] was putting out a huge cloud that rose and flattened then trailed to eastward. I have seen the volcano from the high ridges many times but never with such a display of activity. To the east and the high mts. I tried to map a trail to Lake Clark Pass.[40] Some one told me "I think you would have some ridges to cross." I had thought one could climb onto the glacier and travel across it and down the far side.

The sun was very bright and warm. I pulled off my boots and socks – laid back on a grassy sheep bed and took a nap.

[38] RLP's Allen Mountain, a 6,340 ft. peak on the north side of upper Twin Lakes named by RLP for his Kodiak friend Roy Allen who hunted sheep near there in 1965.

[39] Mt. Iliamna, a 10,016 ft. volcanic peak about 45 miles SE of Twin Lakes.

[40] Lake Clark Pass provides a 50 mile long pass through the Chigmit Mountains, a section of mountains extending about 140 miles between the Aleutian and Alaska Ranges. The pass connects Cook Inlet with the Bristol Bay. The Dena'ina word for Lake Clark is Qizhjeh Vena, "many people gather lake."

The sun moved around – it clouded – a breeze came cool over the ridge. I could see caribou cows with calves up in the head of Lofstedt Creek.[41] Those cows are wise. They leave the river bottoms where the predators are and climb up into the snow country where there is a few bare knolls with feed.

I surveyed the possibility of climbing Crag peak. I was only a few hundred feet below. Rough going and I would want both hands free. The Japanese pack frame for the tripod.

I thought of the lake ice and Babe as I neared the hump. Just supposin' I came to my cabin and found that new "T craft" submerged wings to the ice on the lake. Babe perched on top of the wing waiting for me to come home. I was glad to see it wasn't true. A fire going, water on to heat, biscuits rising. A sandwich made and I heard a plane. The first to come near since I came. Sure enough the red & black "T craft." I went out on the beach and waved "Yankee go home." He circled and came by lower. Ok! he called down. I motioned go home go home. Again he went up past Carrithers' point and throttled back. He was coming in to land. I really got frantic and gave him the old wave off. He opened the throttle twenty feet above the ice and flew the length of it. Couldn't he see my cross at the end of the runway. The field is closed, go home. He climbed down country and came back. I suspected he would drop my mail. I went out on the flat. His door came open and down came a yellow mail sack. It landed back in the timber and I took a bearing and hurried to get it. I was waving it as he came back by on his way home.

Mail, lots of mail but it would have to wait until I got caught up with my chores. I read a few letters while my biscuits baked. I saw strange names on some and opened one. An Air Force boy in Texas. He had read my book ten times and wants to come to Twin Lakes. Build a cabin maybe two or three miles from mine. Any information I could give would be appreciated.

May 30 – Clear, Calm & 40°.

I got off to a bad start this morning first thing. The first spoon full of my good oatmeal tasted like Fels naphtha soap... I stirred it vigorously and I had soap suds. I won't mention any names but somebody put soap powder instead of dry milk in my oatmeal. Then, on the way to the woodshed there was one of my rabbits off to the side fifteen feet picking my new fireweed. Me, I go up to Spike's[42] for greens to let mine multiply and this character picks them one by one. Cuts them at the ground and then chop chop from the big end towards the top.

With all this tropical weather my roof is getting dry as tinder. It would really burn if a hot spark dropped into it. I packed six buckets of water and slung it on with a long handled stew pan and then two buckets more for good measure.

[41] RLP's Lofstedt Creek, a small creek into upper Twin Lakes and named for Kenai based pilot and guide Vernon "Bud" Loftstedt who had a cabin built there in the early 60s.
[42] Gale "Spike" Carrithers' cabin was about 300 yards NE of the Proenneke Site.

I headed for the woodshed and here came a parky squirrel. Was it Freddy. I came back for some biscuit and he met me at the corner of the cabin. He took it and headed for his stone house but was soon back cheeks bulging. I gave him more and he sat right there at my hand before he headed for his house. Later I saw him heading for the point and off on another tour. I hadn't seen the little guy for days and figured he had met with foul play.

Today I would stick around. Some repairing to do on my camera carrying bag. Cut some wood. This all the time burning and no cutting is not good. The temp. climbed to nearly 70° in the warm part of the day. Babe's airstrip has now turned blue. The sign that it is ready to breakup. Along the edge of the ice it measures about seven or eight inches and so loose I can paddle through it in the canoe.

Write letters, that was another job. A good wide strip of open water for floats now but I doubt that Babe will come till June 15th if then. If he puts the floats on the old "T craft" he may make it by then.

My oleo margarine and eggs went into my cooler box today and I notice the sourdough that I took out is starting to work. That little shot in the arm did it.

Near supper time and I paddled up to the point for fireweed green. I am real happy with the foam rubber construction workers kneeling pads (knee protectors). Very comfortable and the cold doesn't come through.

June 9 – Clear, Calm & 34°.

Sunday morning and a beautiful day coming up. It was due to be the start of the airplane season. I would liked to have gone up country but I half expected Babe. I figured that he didn't have floats on the new "T craft" yet but would the old one. So – I wouldn't go far. My early morning check made it easier. I was very much surprised to see another blond bear on Allen Mt. Straight across and up under the lower out crops. Lots of morning sun I would just go over and see what I could come up with. I paddled straight across to the bare knoll but on the way I noticed the bear wasn't feeding much and walking a lot. Moving down country so I paddled down to Falls Creek. When I beached I knew he would beat me to the canyon so I set up on the beach for a couple long shots. He stayed low and I figured he would cross between the waterfalls and sure enough in ten minutes he showed up on the down country side of the falls but in the canyon. I knew where he would climb out as I have climbed out there too. I picked the spot to start the camera. A nice green patch at the base of a rock face. Twenty five feet to go and the bear dropped in his tracks. Time to take five in the warm sun. I waited, no sign of life. It was dead calm on the lake but I knew if I headed up the trail I would soon feel a light breeze at my back. The air would be moving up the canyon like smoke up a chimney. Never climb below a bear in calm air. But what did I have to lose? The bear was on the move anyway. I would climb and see how close I could get. At rest rock I was in the clear but to low to see the bear

laying down. I set up and waited thinking my scent would reach him and he would move on out. No bear and I climbed again to a good view. I left the camera set up and moved across the mt. I had a fair view of where he had been but there was a low ridge along that climbing ledge. I was most sure my bear had moved out. Probably dropped back to the creek and went up the canyon and over the big pasture to Emerson Creek.[43]

Another plane and this time an orange one up the far side. It circled and landed at the point. With the glasses I recognized it as Howard Bowman's[44] souped up Stinson Voyager Stationwagon. He hesitated and headed down for my beach. I had better head for home. As I paddled across I saw he and his wife[45] over at the mouth of Hope Creek. They met me as I beached. Said he was up at Babe's and asked him where my cabin was located. "Halfway up on the right side and say take his mail along." So they brought my mail. They had to get back so couldn't stay for supper. Did Babe have the floats on the new one yet? No, but this week they would put them on. Will it be legal on floats. (Howard works for F.A.A.). Well, I think nearly so. He had the blue prints for installation. He has the old one on floats but not in the water yet. Teen camp[46] in progress at Babe's now. He had given them some land and the shop building. Where would Bee work on airplanes? Under a tree I guess. Bee is busy sawing 2x4's for his house now.

Well they had to go. We took a little tour of my layout. Howard was very much interested in my fireplace. They took my outgoing mail and flew away.

June 17 – Partly Cloudy, Calm & 35°.

A plane coming up and it was that [Alaska] Fish & Game Goose again. On by and up the lake. Soon it was back and on down and then here it came again and letting down for a landing. I packed the canoe back from the beach and turned it end on. I knew what the blast of those two engines will do to a broad side canoe. He tried the beach once. It was soft. He turned out and came in again. Hanging by one wheel and he shut her down. The man on the right slid the window open and asked if this was Lofstedt's cabin. They had a load of gas in 50 gal. drums to unload there. I told them where to find it and thought it strange when they acted as if they didn't know there was a cabin up there. The pilot thought it was here but close to it was a 900 ft. airstrip. Whose camp was this and I told them and asked if they had seen the book *One Man's Wilderness*. Never heard of it but the copilot took my name and said he would get one.

The reason for the gas cache – going to count the caribou. A helicopter would be here as well as that Super Cub. They had left a load of gas at Gatano's beach.[47] Couldn't

---

[43] RLP's Emerson Creek, a large creek that enters upper Twin Lakes from the north near the connecting stream; named for sheep hunter Bob Emerson (1920-2001). The Dena'ina name is Ts'izsdlen, "flows straight."

[44] Howard Bowman (1929-2003), long time Lake Clark resident starting in 1936, who worked for the FAA at Iliamna in 1974.

[45] Letitia "Tish" Bowman, wife of Howard Bowman and an artist.

[46] Tanalian Bible Camp (TBC) was located at Port Alsworth, on a donated part of Babe Alsworth's homestead, first year of operations were 1974.

[47] Ralph Gatano (1903-?), a hunting guide and pilot from the Kenai, who had a hunting cabin at a natural landing strip on the south side of lower Twin Lakes.

get in at the lower end – too shallow. The pilot said he had guided here back in 1960. Took a worlds record caribou out of here. He knew Fred Cowgill,[48] Watts Waddell, all of them. Another plane and it was the Super Cub. It cruised on by and then came back and landed. The Goose and the Cub set like ducks off shore while they held a meeting. They headed up country but the Goose didn't go so good – he hadn't raised his landing gear. So there would be much flying going on around here. I would have to talk to those boys and maybe they would report the location of the big herd of caribou if they see it.

Something else I would like to find is nesting swan. On my trip to Trail Tutte I saw two pair but they were flying and went down the river. And too maybe they will see that big mineral lick Lyman Nichols[49] told me about.

Doing dishes and the Cub went down again. Those boys were really flying today. It had sprinkled a good shower but had faired up again. I was writing when here came the Cub back. They came low and swung back by the point for a landing. A tall blond slim guy in the back seat and a heavy man in front. The reason for all the flying – looking for the big herd. They had it spotted over by Telaquana[50] Lake a week ago and later sent the helicopter out for a count and they couldn't find the herd. The helicopter is coming again tomorrow and they had to find the herd. They found it south of Snipe Lake[51] and moving farther away. It had passed below the lower lake maybe three days ago. Out of my range now and I'm sorry that I missed it. They came to the cabin and we chewed the fat till 9:30. The pilot had been around a good bit and had many experiences with bears. He had first hand information on a few of the maulings I had heard about. It started to rain and it was time they were going. They had burned a barrel of gas today.

June 19 – Overcast, Calm, Raining & 42°.

After writing last evening I was curious as to what the caribou counters had seen during the day. I would just take a paddle up there and find out. Better still I would put the little gas kicker on and make it in 25 min. It was raining lightly as I shoved off from my beach. The little kicker[52] sang a merry tune as I went gliding over the smooth water. Halfway and here came the Super Cub down and climbing. No indication that he saw me and went on down the lake. On the beach at the upper end that good looking Jet Ranger with a KAS[53] on the side. Kenai Air Service. That was Lofstedt's rig. Bob the caribou biologist was there and finishing supper. He offered me fried chicken and corn on the cob. They had more than before they started he said. Two others there. Don, another biologist and

[48] Fred Cowgill (1900?-1965), a Homer based guide who built a hunting cabin about 250 yards south of the Proenneke Site in the early 1960s. RLP's Cowgill Benches are a series of terraces running SE of the Cowgill cabin near Hope Creek.

[49] Lyman Nichols, a sheep hunter and pilot, perhaps from the Kenai.

[50] Telaquana Lake, a large lake about 25 miles north of Twin Lakes in the Kuskokwim watershed; Dilah Vena is the Dena'ina word for "salmon swim in lake."

[51] Snipe Lake, a large non-glacial lake about 6 miles west of Twin Lakes; K'adała Vena is the Dena'ina word for "birds fly out lake."

[52] The term "kicker" is an Alaska regional variant for a small outboard boat engine.

[53] Kenai Air Service (KAS) was owned by Vernon "Bud" Loftstedt and flew both fixed wing aircraft and helicopters.

Bud, Bud Lofstedt's son [Vernon Jr.] who was the pilot of the chopper. Mustache, long hair and beard. I wouldn't have recognized him as the kid who was acting as assist. guide for his dad back in the sixties. "Boy, if you saw what we saw today," Bob said. He would say that to a ground bound poor boy. Bears, wolves and many caribou. A sow with twins just over the ridge from Arlen's cabin. A big boar and sow. Two bears and three wolves in an argument over a kill and the herd – a mile farther away and still going. Maybe 5000 in the herd.[54] Sure wished he could take me along but it was against regulations (which I was certain of and rightly so). The bear-wolf hassle they had ended with the chopper with everybody running for the hills. The location up the valley from Pear Lake towards the Kijik and he doubted if I could see them if they came back as it was in brush country.

No money would be made counting caribou today. Of what value is counting 5,000 or 10,000 caribou and spending many thousands of dollars doing it. The only answer – man has to satisfy himself that he knows what he doesn't know. Like Henry David[55] said "All he really knows is that the wind blows."

June 20 – Overcast, Calm & 40°.

I had taken the shovel along to rebury a can dump which the bears had opened and scattered cans about. The camp that Hank Rust's[56] hunters had used on the beach towards a gravel bank. What I needed was a can smasher. A half bushel of beer cans take a big hole. A 75 lb. rock on a beach solved that problem. All the cans in and I lifted the rock as high as my head and brought it down with force. A half dozen blows and there was room for much gravel on top. The weather was really looking good over the upper lake. Clouds along the mts. and the lake very blue. I beached at the end of the gravel banks and hiked to the top of the high bank along Beech Creek. A good view of some moose country and also a good shot up the lake. Not enough breeze and the insects a pest. The white socks are beginning to work now. I headed up and put in at Low Pass[57] beach to check on the sandpiper nest. No bird there but the sun was warm. It is hard to realize that those four large eggs belong to that little sandpiper.

June 21 – Overcast, Calm & 41°.

Clouds were low again and there was some question in my mind if it was the wise thing to do. I had planned to celebrate the longest day and the shortest night by taking an over night trip to the low country.

I was up at four and by five it was fairing up. I shoved off at six after leaving a note

---

[54] The Mulchatna caribou herd spends part of the year in the Twin Lakes area.

[55] Henry David Thoreau (1817-1862), an American philosopher, father of modern environmental movement, whose book, *Walden* inspired RLP to move to Twin Lakes.

[56] Hank Rust (1920-2005), an Anchorage based bush pilot-guide who owned a lodge on Lake Clark and Rust's Flying Service.

[57] RLP's Low Pass, a pass through the mountains connecting upper Twin Lakes with the Kijik River Valley.

on the table that I would be gone for a day or two. By the time I reached Emerson Creek it was a picture taking day. I ran the stream[58] into the lower lake and water even more blue than the upper lake. Down the middle and around Gatano's point. 10 o'clock when I beached at Arlen's cabin. My gear squared away I took a break of two hrs. before heading on down to Trail Butte. Instead of traveling the flats with its countless ridges and holes I climbed to the caribou trails along the lower slope of the Volcanic Mts.[59] Trails well worn by recent traffic of many caribou. It must have been done by the great number of caribou that Jerre Wills wrote about.

Past the end of the mts. and onto the gravel buttes and I came onto the trails north to south made by the recent passage of the big herd. Many trails well worn but still the thousands of hooves didn't cut through the moss to the bare ground.

I heard a plane and thought, Babe would pick today to come. Two Super Cubs one on floats, the other on wheels came from the bend of the Kijik and headed up the lake. Now and again I stopped to glass the country but saw no caribou. Finally up Trail Butte with its 360° view. I had brought the scope along today. I wanted to look in the direction the big herd had gone. Since the boys left I had been thinking I should have taken off the next morning. Maybe I couldn't have found them in a day but I could have in a day and a half. The sun was on those hills and ridges but no sign of caribou. It was just too far to go not knowing exactly where they were. Not a caribou in that direction. I swung the scope towards the Chilikadrotna and right away I saw something that made my heart beat faster. A mile and a half away a good bunch of caribou on one of two ice covered areas on the whole low country flats. Springs had fed water during the cold of winter. Ice had built up a few feet thick. Now two pond like areas white with ice. The caribou bunched close and I could see many antlers of bulls. Right away I dropped down from my look out and headed that way. As I broke over a low rise I found that the caribou had left the ice and were feeding in a big spread toward the river. I moved in and set up on a small brushy knoll at the lower end of the ice patch. Insects were working on the bunch and there was much fighting and running about. When they turned my way I knew they were coming back. Here they came head on up a strip of ice and passed not over fifty yards away under the brow of the little knoll. This was a perfect set up. Some bedding down and others standing heads low to the ice. Sooner than I expected they fed out the other way towards Trail Butte. Now was my chance to climb a large knoll between the two ice patches. I made it and was set up on the sunny side not even a good hundred yards from their resting spot in case they came back. Not gone long and they turned back again and right to the bed ground. I was really doing good. They could hear the camera but caribou get used to it and ignore it. One or two watched me and would have left if the others hadn't ignored it. Finally they to went back to fighting insects. I was doing some real business now. The sun was in and out and I waited for the sun. Finally it was time to feed again and they started to leave the ice and headed around the large knoll and down country. This was fine as they would soon be out of sight and I could head for camp. Nearly 200 ft. of film exposed and never a better opportunity on caribou bulls. I loaded up and dropped down

---

[58] "Stream," also known as the "connecting stream" refers to the 1/3-mile long river that connects upper and lower Twin Lakes.

[59] RLP's Volcanic Mountains, are mountains that lie to the south of lower Twin Lakes.

over the point of the knoll. In the brush near the base and I came onto sign of old dens and then the den itself. Wolf tracks at the entrance and made since the last rain. The den itself had a fresh used look and I got close to see into the tunnel. Big tracks in the soft dirt. I had stumbled onto a wolf den. No sign of pups. An old caribou bone laying close. I didn't stay long and hoped I hadn't caused any damage a little time wouldn't heal. Out across the ice and up country – I had five miles to go and it would be near sundown before I reached Arlen's cabin. I had gone about a quarter mile and thinking of my find. Those tracks in the tunnel – were they going in or out? The wolf would have to slide in on its belly and I could easily tell. I parked my gear and hurried back. Two rows of tracks close together left and right going down and back and then up grade out of sight. No chance of tracks being made on top of them coming out. That wolf had to be in the den. I listened close to the opening but could hear no sound from within. If there had been pups I felt sure I could hear them. I hurried away and watched for good blinds along the way where I could watch the den from.

I had gone only a short distance when there on my right and about a hundred yards stood two young bull moose. Twins with little spike antlers. Really nice looking yearlings of the same size. No film in the camera. I had used it all on the caribou. They stood and looked until I moved to go and then hurried towards a patch of timber. Farther on I walked up onto a ptarmigan hen in full summer plumage and she would have made a good subject. A mile and a half and I saw a caribou cow coming down from the gravel buttes. The sun was getting low and she was a pretty sight in the big wide open. She had seen me from a distance and was coming thinking I was another caribou. I stopped behind a thick dead spruce. She trotted and stopped to look and trotted again. She had lost me. She had the right idea. She knew where I should be and when she got close began to smell the ground. No luck and she searched farther until she got down wind. She stood and looked for a minute and then got alarmed and took off at a fast trot. I headed for my trail along the slope of the mt. I looked back often to see if that knoll with the two ice patches was visible. From on the mt. trail using the scope I could check the den from a great distance. The sun had nearly set when I reached the cabin. I reloaded the camera and climbed the slope behind the cabin to watch the sunset on that longest day. It was a beautiful ending for a good day. The sky partly cloudy and it was warm with a light breeze coming up country. Near eleven o'clock when I turned in.

June 22 – Overcast, Warm & Calm.

I was surprised to find a yellow mail pouch on my table and my outgoing mail still there. About that time I heard foot steps and here came a young guy wearing a red shirt. Jim Shake[60] was his name he said. He had bought Spike's cabin. Babe had flown him in. Two loads and another to come yet today if the weather wasn't too bad.

[60] Jim Shake, a young visitor from Washington State who apparently briefly owned Spike and Hope's cabins. He left RLP a big kettle and a splitting maul.

I was glad to meet the guy and anxious to learn what his impression of the wilderness was after spending his first night alone there. It wasn't long until he said he had set in the cabin and was bored with that. He didn't know what he wanted to do. He had made out a list of places he wanted to see and things he wanted to do in Alaska. He would stay here a week and then travel to [Mount] McKinley [National] Park. Then go down the Inside Passage and then come back and hunt a bit. Fly the meat to Anch. – buy a freezer and put it in the back of his pickup. Load in the meat and drive home. He soon gave up that idea and would just look and take pictures. He liked pictures but would rather cut them out of magazines and mount them in loose leaf folders than take them. We spent the afternoon visiting, talking of his country and the orchard business. They had sold out and now he was taking a vacation before going back to work for big farmers raising sugar beets and corn.

June 23 – Overcast, Calm & 46°.

I was up at 4:30 to get my writing caught up and it took longer than I expected. I hadn't built my breakfast fire when I heard a quiet airplane coming and knew it was the old T craft. He landed up at the point and I got busy closing my outgoing letters. Soon he taxied down and tailed it into the beach. He had brought me 50 lbs. of flour, many onions, a gal. of vinegar, and many smoked salmon plus a gallon can of peanut butter. He was a happy guy and filled me in on all the news about the Lake Clark country. Bee was about ready to put the roof on his house. Glen getting married.[61] Floyd Denison[62] complaining because he can't buy food stamps with a check. That rascal is getting so fat living on food stamps he can't bend over. Mary[63] would like to go to Hawaii next winter for a little vacation but he doesn't care to go. He hasn't seen all of Alaska yet. Lots of moose he said. He sees lots of cows with twin calves.

Jim came down and they discussed this going out business. Jim said the 28th but then changed it to the 27th in case the weather might foul up. Here Babe had flown in three loads of his gear and grub $83.00 worth and he isn't staying a week and only plans to take out what he can haul in one load. I think that one night alone here on the point got to him. He says there is so much he wants to see that he must get moving but it goes deeper than that. Well, Babe would come in the 27th then and he fired up the little old bird and flew away. It fits Twin Lakes better than any plane that ever came. I told him it surely was quiet – no fuss, no muss and he said, "Yes, and it is getting quieter all the time." Only 600 hrs. on that engine and he thinks it is getting tired.

---

[61] Glen Alsworth, the youngest son of Babe and Mary Alsworth, pilot and college student at Lazy Mountain Bible College in Palmer. Alsworth married Patricia Elliott on July 14, 1974.

[62] Floyd Denison (1907-1986), resident of Lake Clark since the early 1930s, he lived about two miles south of the Alsworth homestead.

[63] Mary Alsworth (1923-1996), born at Pilot Point, and married Babe Alsworth in 1941, post mistress, weather reporter, ran lodge for many years at Port Alsworth.

June 26 – Clear, Calm & 38°.

Now as I headed up the lake I saw it at my beach. Who could that be and maybe they were tired of waiting and would fly away before I got there. As I got closer I could make out strange uniforms moving through the trees. Maybe it was BLM[64] in for a check up on the legality of my cabin. I had an answer ready. I am working for a branch of your outfit – the National Park Service and for Fish & Game too. When I got close I saw a slim guy with a crumpled cowboy hat and he came down to the beach. Bob Acheson formerly of Kodiak and now Ellensburg, Wash.[65] I was surprised and glad to see the guy. I had heard so much of that fine cattle ranch of his. The other man Bob Barnett, a shrimp boat owner from Homer and pilot of the [Cessna] 180.[66] Barnett has a cabin on Lake Clark above Babe's bay[67] ten miles or more.

From the looks of things they intended to stay the night at least. Sleeping bags, a box of grub and something else, a chicken halibut and some herring, salmon eggs and a bag of frozen shrimp all caught on the last trip out with the boat. They had intended to stay in Hope's cabin but I asked them to stay here. Get the Army cot from Spike's cabin and we would be in good shape. A good visit. Talk over old times on Kodiak of those still there and those gone. Bob Acheson had a freighting business out of Flat, Alaska (about 200 miles west of here) years ago and from there to Kodiak and the Donnley and Acheson store there.

I went to the point for greens even though they had lettuce and celery along. Feed them a good salad. We invited Jim down...We had shrimp with melted butter, mashed spuds and fireweed salad which was a big hit. I was lucky and got a good scold on my dressing. The dishes done and more chewing the fat. Bob's son and wife were doing a fine job running the ranch and Bob was free to visit the north country again. He would buy one and maybe both of Spike's cabins. It depended on Jim's deal with Spike. It was a pleasant evening with the insects a bit on the active side. We turned in, Acheson on the lower bunk and Barnett on the cot. Not a sound but Hope Creek during the night. In the morning sourdough hotcakes. Bob Acheson told of one woman after reading my book – promptly cooked a kettle of beans and got some sourdough going.

June 27 – Clear, Calm & 38°.

Babe and Acheson really hit it off except I sorta shuddered at all the cuss words Bob was using. They both knew a lot of the old timers, pilots, prospectors and fishermen. Bob said

---

[64] Bureau of Land Management (BLM), part of the Department of Interior was the Federal land managing agency that oversaw the Twin Lakes area before late 1978 when the National Park Service assumed management.

[65] Bob Acheson (1908-1993) born at the mining camp of Ester to an Alaska pioneering family, Kodiak businessman, who was acquainted with RLP on Kodiak Island.

[66] Bob Barnett (1915-) Anchorage pioneer and businessman who owned a cabin near Portage Creek on Lake Clark.

[67] RLP's Babe's bay, is Hardenburg Bay on Lake Clark at Port Alsworth, named for prospector H. von Hardenburg, circa 1906. The Barnett cabin was located near Portage Creek approximately 14 miles NE of Hardenburg Bay.

he would like to visit with Babe again and refresh his memory of the good old days.

Babe wondered if he could get his load off of the water as it was glassy smooth. Clouds were showing down country and he had said Lake Clark had ground fog this morning. He ran and ran and finally eased that one float out of the water. He had it made and was soon climbing along the Volcanic Mts.

We came down and they got underway. A last look around to see that nothing stayed behind. An invitation to Ellensburg and the ranch. If you get as close as Seattle I'll come get you Bob Acheson had said. And an invitation to Homer and a cruise on the shrimper too.

Babe had brought me a few oranges and bananas along with my mail. Another 50 rolls of film from the Park Service. I doubt if they have received a report or viewed that which I sent in. We had cut out a section of moss and buried the halibut, herring and eggs. The ground still frozen solid under that best of insulation. I would give a good portion of it to Babe as I couldn't make use of it all. Soon he was back and I dug it out. White with frost under the moss. Jim had said he had lots of time he would close up the cabin but I noticed the stove pipe still up and the windows not covered.

This time they got everything in and he said all that I found of his in the cabin I could have. He thanked me for the good tour and told me his latest plan – get a good camera and photograph ducks. They made a run down the lake but couldn't get off. Back the other way – there was some ripples above the point from a very light breeze. Off and flying. Once more I was king of Twin Lakes. I had a feeling that Twin Lakes as it was is a thing of the past. People coming and thinking gee! this is great. What a wonderful place, not realizing what a handicap it puts on a guy who prefers to feel there is no one closer than Lake Clark.

July 28 – Partial H. Overcast, Calm & 44°.

Up before the sun this morning and it is rising very close to the string of the mts. along the south side of the lake. Last night's overcast down country backed off and this morning the partial thin overcast was up country. This looked like a going day coming up and it would have to be Sunday and letter writing day. Babe just might bring the little boys in but I couldn't depend on him to do it. Operate as if he didn't intend to come and let the writing wait for a rainy day. Today I would visit Farmer's[68] ram mt. to see if rams did come back to it. It would be a climbing deal. Go to the second canyon and up it to the highest part of the skyline. That would be a good test for those football shoes. I put in my leather arch support insoles and wore a light and heavy pair of socks. Laced them good and snug and would tighten them up again on the mt. Take the old Linhof tripod and Bolex head as this would be mostly scenic shots. I was ready by seven with a note on the table with my

---

[68] Marshall Farmer (1920-2001) guide-pilot from Anchorage who purchased the Cowgill cabin in 1959. RLP referred to the cabin as the "Cowgill" or "Farmer" cabin. RLP's Farmer landing, Farmer point, and Farmer trail are all located near the cabin. RLP'S Farmer's ram mt. was probably off upper Hope Creek.

outgoing mail "Be back by five" and I baited the trot line[69] as I passed. Across the creek and up the trail on the Cowgill benches. Those shoes felt good and very light. A new caribou track on the trail up the creek. At the second canyon I climbed to my look out before going on up the canyon. Something on the bench at the head of the creek. Blond & black – it could only be a bear. Too tall to be laying down and it didn't move. I watched for a few minutes and thought I saw a variation in color and size. It had to be a bear but a strange acting one. I dropped down and crossed the second canyon creek and headed up Hope Creek. Climbed well up the slope and went a half mile. I glassed again. A rock with a bright face catching the morning sun. I turned back and up around the point into the second canyon. Good going all the way up into the big basin and then it is loose rock on all sides and lots of it. I picked a spot with lots of coarse rock and snailed my way up the steep slope. The sun really bearing down and no air moving. Up to a big outcrop and the angle not so steep from there. Those shoes were doing a good job. Holding perfect where there was anything to get ahold of. I broke out on a ridge and beyond it a very big bowl leading up to the skyline. A big snow field against the upper slope. Two cows and two calves standing on the snow high up. Noses to the cool snow which is protection from the insects. I headed up the ridge which was good going. Any time you find black rock (black lichen covered) it is stabilized and good footing. Either the breeze up there gave me away or the cows saw me and became alarmed. When I saw them at the bottom of the snow field I thought I had found more. Again they moved and circled below to where I had come up onto the ridge. Cows smelling the ground and trotting around before they took off down over the edge towards Hope Creek. I climbed out on top following a sheep trail with tracks made since the last rain. Droppings were dry so it had been a few days since they were there.

Redoubt[70] and Iliamna really stood out and miles closer than I had seen them from the head of Camp Creek.[71] I could see a lot of Kijik River country and a good view of Lachbuna Lake.[72] No sheep did I see in any direction. I followed the ridge a quarter mile to my left (up country) to see over a hog back running down to the Kijik low country. Tracks in loose stuff far down and finally I spotted a bull caribou standing on a snow patch in a deep wash. Many hundreds of feet down and loose rock all the way. Only an average bull anyway. I back tracked and would follow the ridge to the peak if possible and it looked doubtful. Sheep had used the ridge and here and there a sheep trail past a high point of rock. I dropped a few hundred feet and would have to gain it back twice over to reach the peak. Beyond the peak was Farmer's sheep country. Outside of one steep pitch of loose stuff I had no trouble. Always a way no matter how rough it looked. I pulled up to the peak which is pretty much a pinnacle of fairly solid rock. Very small on top but a nice little hollow lined with a mat of very fine green grass. I suppose that over the hundreds of years that sheep have bedded there – they fertilized the area and packed grass seed there

---

[69] RLP's trot line refers to a set fishing line of baited hooks anchored from the land or a float, also known as a trout line.

[70] Mount Redoubt, a 10,197 ft. semi-active volcano about 40 miles east of Twin Lakes.

[71] RLP's Camp Creek is a small tributary of Emerson Creek.

[72] Lachbuna Lake, a large glacial lake that the Kijik River flows into about 12 miles SW of Twin Lakes; the Dena'ina word is L'alił Vena, 'deadfall collapses lake."

too. From that peak I think is the most beautiful view I have seen of Twin Lakes country. Looking up into the head of the Kijik River valley – big and open – glaciers at the head. Beyond that the mts. and glaciers to Lake Clark Pass and beyond to the base of Redoubt and that huge mt. in the background. Sometime on a nice day I must make the climb again with the Exakta. Be there by one P.M. for at that time the sun is 90° to the view (for a pola screen shot). From the peak I could see all of the Kijik from the head waters to the bend below Lachbuna and only a few miles from its mouth at Lake Clark. One fast river, that Kijik. White water all the way as far as I could see. Still I failed to see sheep. A few tracks and from the size they had to be ewes and lambs. Beyond my peak to the west – a very large and rugged mt. and rams on there would be pretty safe. I shot a roll of film from on top and stayed till 2:30 before heading down and I hated to think about all that loose rock going down. I picked the first low pass with fine stuff leading down to the big tailing piles in the basin and dropped over the edge. I made real good time plowing down the slope in the fine stuff and was soon on a gentle slope of stabilized loose rock. From there onto a steep snow field and those deep lugs on my shoes did a fine job of holding. Soon I was onto the grass and dropping fast. One hr. from the peak to Hope Creek and I could make it to my cabin in one hr. from there. A cold drink of water and half of my chocolate square before I headed on down.

Getting a good start and I saw a young bull caribou trotting down the creek bottom. He had seen me and was on the go. He left the creek and came out on my side. The breeze was down so he had my scent and still he didn't get alarmed. He might be good for a few feet of film and I put my rig together. He fed and came my way. I exposed some film and moved ahead. He came on and I the same. Down wind at a hundred feet and still he showed no sign of alarm. He came within fifty feet and it wasn't until insects gave him a bad time that he headed for the brush of the creek bottom. Never have I seen such behavior by a caribou. I had lost a half hr. but would still make it by five. Past first canyon and Pup Tent canyon and over the trail to the Cowgill benches. No plane at my beach. I sat down to look for Jerg's [Jürgen Kroener][73] rams. From the peak I had seen two of them in a tough to get to spot. Now I saw all four. Three he would never find and the fourth near the top and he could shoot him from the ridge. Down the trail and my trot line stretched out. It pulled heavy and I suspected two fish. Sure enough two lake trouts – one a big one.

I had work to do. Get the biscuits going, get cleaned up and washing done, dress the fish, cook the rhubarb, gather greens. The big lake trout measured 19 inches exactly – the other about 15".

Now at 9:10, everything done and time to turn in. I have a feeling it will seem like a very short night. Overcast took over after I arrived, a light breeze down the lake and 64°.

The shoes did a very good job on a much tougher than average hike. I feel that

---

[73] Jergen or [Jürgen] Kroener, a German backpacker who spent three months in the Twin Lakes country.

their life would be short but for a one hunt deal like an average sheep hunter – they would be fine. To me it was like having wings on my feet – like losing my ball and chain. I would like to race Jerg in his $60.00 German mt. shoes to the top of Allen Mt.

July 30 – Overcast, Calm & 52°.

A plane came up the lake following the shoreline. It turned at the upper end and went down. A red & yellow Goose – not Fish and Game. Again it came up past Carrithers' point and then turned and landed. I suspect it was the Park Service. I headed down, full paddle. About halfway when it took off and came to meet me. Landed along side and I paddled close. The pilot, a little guy with mutton chop whiskers. He looked a little familiar. He says, I guess you don't know me. Jack Johnson of Kodiak. (One of twins Jerry & Jack. Their dad had drowned off shore in a little boat while coming from elk hunting on Afognak Island.)

We tried to get enough of the canoe in the Goose so the stern would clear the water and he would taxi down, but it wouldn't work so we would tow it along side. There is a Park Service man at your place he said. On the way down I wondered what the verdict would be. Was I doing ok at this picture taking racket. Near my beach he shut her off till I got clear and then taxied in. The man was Keith Trexler[74] (project leader). I had seen him at Anch. in the office there. He greeted me with a big smile. Four other young guys of various descriptions were on the beach. Then came the sad news. Your films were the best bar none, of any taken for us. With others, we figure about 10% useable but with yours we can use 90% or even more. That sounded pretty good to me but I figured maybe my cheap rate of pay had something to do with it. He gave me a memo from the man who reviewed them and he listed the scenes (most important) and their quality for each of the 34 rolls. He wrote – the overall evaluation is that the film footage is of high professional quality. In sum, this footage represents some of the very best we have gathered during our entire film effort. I therefore recommend that Dick Proenneke be engaged for a continuance of filming at Lake Clark Twin Lakes region for the remainder of the summer and fall season. End of quote.

That was pretty good but I should have done better and would try to eliminate those few overexposed and underexposed takes. And as far the guy who wrote that stuff – flattery will get him no where. In front of the cabin lay a duffle bag full to bursting. A gallon can of appliance fuel set along side. A big cardboard tag on each. Could they leave it here for three Sierra Club hikers who were hiking from Lake Clark to Telaquana Lake. They were due to pass here about mid Sept. From the names on the tags it sounds like two

---

[74] Keith Trexler (1932-1975), NPS interpretive planner with the Alaska Task Force. Died in a plane crash with NPS employees Rhonda Barber, Carol Byler, Janice Cooper, Dawn Finney, Jane Matlock, and Mickect (Clara) Veara on September 12, 1975. The NPS employees had spent all summer typing the field notes of the Alaska Task Force members and were to be treated with a day out of the office to visit RLP at "One Man's Wilderness."

girls and a boy. Bea Van Horne, Candy Downing & Walter Ward.[75] Experienced hikers so they could manage. The boys had a case of "C" rations out of the goose and they had their lunch at noon their time, eleven mine, and when that was over they prepared to take off. They wanted to see Lake Clark and Lake Clark Pass yet and get back early.

July 31 – Partly Cloudy, Calm & 40°.

I was awake at four and saw the sky was nearly clear, the lake calm. Today would be the day to go to the lower end and over the high ridge towards Turquoise Lake. I rushed around getting breakfast and my gear laid out. I noticed that the dark cloud bank way down was going the other way. That full moon was doing its job well.

I was loaded and shoved off about 6:15. I would paddle the eight and a half miles with the little kicker along for the ride. It is a pleasure to paddle early in the morning with the lake calm and the temp. 40°.

I had spent two days on the beach waiting for the lake to calm enough that I could risk a crossing to Arlen's cabin. Everything that would stay behind was under the bottom up canoe. My load consisting of camera and tripod (Linhof & Bolex head) 500 ft. of film. A few rations and my heavy pistol in case I had the opportunity to get close to a grizzly. Actually it is the brownie but Jerg refers to them as grizzly and so does the Park Service. 9:30 when I left the canoe and headed directly for that high open ridge. It looks like a long way and nearly all up hill. Across the upper boarder of the gravel knolls and a broad open brush covered flat and then a strip of cottonwood and spruce at the base of the first pitch. The sun was bearing down and that was no good. A few clouds were forming and as I climbed they multiplied. Good climbing, solid footing with only a few narrow brushy draws to cross. A couple pretty little ponds and enough steams for good water in route. Two hrs. and I was standing on the ridge. To the right the ridge leads up to the peak and to the left it spreads out into a big table land – little or no brush and as green as a golf course. Straight ahead it goes down at a rapid rate. A deep canyon coming out of the mt. and making a sharp bend to the right and into a valley that runs perhaps five miles into the mts. On the far side of the deep canyon sheep trails coming to the point of the ridge separating the canyon from the valley. As I continued down over the far side more trails and finally I could see the bottom and the stream. The trails all converged on the point not far from the steam. Suddenly it struck me. I was looking at the mineral lick that Lyman Nichols had told me about a few years ago. You should spend some time there, he said. There is bound to be lots of game come there to eat dirt. At least sixteen trails I counted coming down from the top and in from each side. With my glasses I could see hollows (where over the years) sheep had made eating this formation for mineral that they need. No vegetation on the mineral point. It appears like a huge mud bank, blue in color.

---

[75] Beatrice Van Horne, Candice Downing, and Walter Ward were undergraduate students from the University of California, Santa Cruz in the Environmental Studies Program who studied the feasibility of national park status in the Lake Clark area. They were funded by a Sierra Club Foundation grant, a grant from their university, and received logistical and village liaison support from the NPS Alaska Task Force.

A perfect spot to camp below the lick near the stream. Small brush patches for a blind. The afternoon sun would be just right.

I detoured a few hundred yds. to the left where I could get down with grass nearly all the way. On the stream I saw chunks of this blue very crumbly rock. If Lyman would have a sample analyzed I would pack some out. He will be happy to learn that I found it. Down the stream a short ways and into the big valley that I had seen from high on the ridge up Camp Creek. I headed up the valley expecting to see many sheep up under the rock ledges on the right hand side. A good start up the valley and now those clouds were grey and heavy. Down the valley scattered clouds and sunshine. No sheep and I kept going expecting to find them. Grass from the valley floor up to the first rock ledges. Sheep sign but nothing real fresh. Along the trail an old rams horn. Very massive and full curl, badly broomed and a real tight curl. That old guy had gone his twelve winters and more. Many parky squirrels – families of them. The old one standing motionless while the young ones did the complaining. Finally some sheep. Four ewes and four lambs high up in the rocks. While I traveled two of each broke away and headed up country and I suspected that was where the big bunch was. Up the valley which finally roughens and eventually becomes loose rock and tailing piles of glaciers past. Far up I could see many large streams pouring out of the face of a tailing pile. Maybe two and one half miles I traveled before coming to a side canyon on the right. The big bunch could be in there. It involved some climbing to get to a view point and it started to sprinkle. In this canyon and high up at the head, [a] few ewes and lambs on a ledge that looked pretty impossible to get to by sheep or man. Now I had seen it all. The sheep must be on the other side of the mt. reached by going up Camp Creek. The rain increased and there wasn't an over hanging rock in sight. Two o'clock when I headed down and was soon dripping. I picked up the rams horn as I passed and carried it to the mineral lick. One hr. it had taken me to come that far. Now the climb to the ridge again and I had only a good start when a young bull caribou showed up on the skyline headed down to the lick area. It saw me and that ended that. Much running about and it finally took off. Twenty minutes for the climb out and I could see down on the Chilikadrotna country which was grey with rain. It was clearing up country. Now I had it made – down hill all the way to the spruce timber and brush which was due to be wet. The rain stopped and I sat glassing the many ponds below in hopes of seeing a moose feeding in the water. It was 6:30 when I reached the canoe. The sun still high and the rain past. I shouldered my gear and headed down the river. I would go about a mile below Frank's [Bell] cabin. Many wide open gravel bars and a chance to see a moose or caribou. And too I wanted to see if any king salmon lay along the cut banks in the eddies. I had just left the canoe when a blue and white [Cessna] 180 came from over the ridge and to the head of the river. He banked sharply to get a look at me and then on up a mile where he turned and landed coming back towards me. I stopped and waited. He turned into the beach well out of the bay for it is shallow with big rocks. I went on and climbed to the brass plate rock. The plane had let out three on the beach and took off for Lake Clark. Fishermen for the greyling hot spot. Well, I would make the first track on the river bank anyway. I went on down and saw a recently made caribou track and a

fair moose track. No kings along the banks. I went past the tumble down trappers cabin and stood looking at that nice Alaska Magazine. picture in real life. A little tree squirrel crossed just in front of me packing a mushroom nearly as big as he was. The light failing and I headed back. I loaded the canoe and headed for Arlen's cabin. The intruders wading around in the brush behind the beach. A radio was going full blast. I had gone halfway when here came the [Cessna] 180 back and this time let off more people. Five in all and some were children. Arlen's cabin, just as I had left it last time.

I fried some lake trout I had brought and warmed up some beans. Dishes done and I turned in. It had been a pretty good day. To find that lick was more important than seeing a band of sheep. The sky partly cloudy, calm and warm, 50° perhaps.

August 2 – Partly Cloudy, Calm & 40°.

The weather is holding fair and it was a beautiful sunrise. Hotcakes for breakfast and I was just finishing dishes when I heard a plane and it sounded like the easy running T- Craft. Sure enough – a pass overhead – a turn down country and he came in to the beach. I could see heads of two little boys over the bottom of the window. At last Leon & Sig had arrived at Twin Lakes. Babe turned her around and tied the tail to a tree. Out came the little guys with their sleeping bags. Babe unloaded their luggage and a big plastic garbage bag, four doz. eggs, and a slab of bacon. "Feed them lots of smoke fish," he said. I went about getting my outgoing mail ready while we visited and the boys had a look around. The birds came and the fun started. They liked those camp robbers and the camp robbers knew an easy touch and made the most of it. When would the squirrel come and could we climb a mt. today. Would we see some sheep. That was high on the list – they had never seen sheep.

Some sad news. My brother-in-law Melvin had died of a bad heart attack. Eligible to retire from the telephone company this month of Aug. but he hadn't planned to retire.

When are we going to climb a mt. came from the little guys. The lake was good we would paddle the lake. Oh good! I fitted each with a life jacket. Leon would paddle out and Sig back. We headed for Glacier Creek point. Check the game trail and look at the bear tree with tooth marks higher than I could reach. The morning was warm and they wore their parkas. Going up through the brush and picking berries here and there. Sig got behind and when he came in sight – no coat. Where had he left it. Oh! in the brush back there. Well, he would have to find it on the way back. The trail crossing the creek had been used. A moose plowing down the steep trail in loose dirt had all but erased a bear track. A good little patch of berries picked and devoured and we headed down. Sig did pretty good but stopped short in the search for his coat. He scouted around through the brush and finally, oh, here it is.

We launched and headed across for first point and the cave high up the grassy

slope in the big rock. Sig the best paddler of the two. More serious and not so much playing around. The climb started and only a hundred feet up when there was an awful racket. I looked down to see them tumbling down the mt. Leon just missing a protruding rock. Such squalling I have never heard by both of them. And then I noticed bees swarming in the moss just below me. Yellow jackets and both had been stung a few times about the face and neck. The climb was off – they didn't want to go farther but I talked them into it. What's a couple stings anyway? Only welts formed and after a little delay to lick their wounds they made a big detour and we climbed keeping a sharp look out for yellow jackets. The cave I had only been to it once and wondered what had used it since. Ptarmigan had roosted there before. This time it had been the porcupine. We explored the big hole in the rock and enjoyed the view. Glassed the mts. for sheep but saw none. On the way down we circled the bees nest and cautiously came up from below. Yellow jackets covered a rock in the moss, crawling about. When they began to stir it was get out of here and down to the beach.

I had cooked a fresh kettle of beans early. It was noon Port Alsworth time. When do we eat. No eating till 12 Twin Lakes time but they had to taste those beans. I was busy on the beach and could hear that lid carefully being replaced every few minutes. Much tasting going on in the cabin.

In the afternoon we would pick blueberries to have some topping for hotcakes. Eager little guys when it comes to picking berries. Leon could keep up with me and not as many green ones. Sig slower and had to eat them from his pail. No eating from the bucket according to Leon. From the brush not too bad but not out of the bucket. A big pile of fresh bear dropping on the creek trail so someone else was picking too. All afternoon we scouted and picked towards the lake. A great thirst for water and they thought we would never get there. Leon spilled his in the moss and had to pick them up. Bet he could get them all but decided he could pick new ones faster when the clean up got slow. Nearly two gallons total when we worked our way out of blueberry country. A big sorting session on the beach and the green ones tossed in to the lake where a few good rises appeared. A little four incher came in close to shore. Much interest in fish by those boys.

Time for supper and it would be spuds, lake trout and beans, blueberries for dessert. Just getting things going when here came Jerg [Jürgen Kroener] paddling down along the beach. We would have a full crew for supper.

Jerg had gone way back the day I saw him last and stayed over night. 14 hrs. and fording streams. Climbing with a good load and the marmot he hoped to find didn't show. Last night he had a time at his tent. During the night he heard and felt something try to get under his sleeping bag. He found it to be a porcupine and it wouldn't go away until he threw something over it. He had shot pictures of the full moon over the mt. and thinks he might have some nice shots. We had supper and there were no leftovers. As usual Jerg refused no second helpings or to clean up anything left over. I am even now more thin than on the Yukon trip, he said.

Sig dried dishes and Leon casting in the lake for trout. The trot line was baited

and out. Jerg gave me a letter to mail to his mother, next plane. It was 9:30 when he boarded his little craft and with a "see you" paddled up the lake.

The boys tucked in head to foot in the lower bunk. We called it a day.

It was clearing up country, calm & 46°. The full moon was holding fair weather.

August 5 – Clear, Calm & 40°.

Sig didn't want to paddle across even though it was his turn. "I always have to paddle coming back when I am tired." Ok, Leon would paddle. We beached at the mouth of Falls Creek and left the canoe bottom up on the beach. Sig was guide going up the trail. A drink at the game trail crossing and that would be the last till we got on top the big rock face and into the canyon. A few wild currants and blueberries along the trail and that Leon has an eye for berries. The high waterfall is only a good shower bath now and if it was only warm they would like that. The smooth rock crossing on the rock face over it or around the bottom? Go over it cause it was shorter. No, they wasn't scared – so with Sig in the lead and me telling him where to place his feet we inched up across it. Leon got stuck with the wrong foot first and I retrieved him to the grass on the top end. On up and into the canyon for more drinks and the final climb to skyline. Leon and I had to wait at the forks of the canyon while Sig stopped to get first chance at the packet of toilet paper. On up the trail and Leon comes up with a little blue flower. He had never seen one like it. A forget-me-not – our State flower. He wanted a whole plant to take to grandma. On the way back we would dig one. On the skyline and over to Emerson Creek side of the big pasture. We could see a few sheep high up on the skyline or near it on Ram Mt.[76] across the creek. How long would it take to climb up there? Too long! I set up the scope and we counted five head. Now, we would make that long climb to look out peak. I was packing the gear in my camera pack bag and said, "You guys start up, I will catch up with you." "Are you sure you can?," came from Leon. "I think so." He didn't go but hung around till I was ready and then he took off straight for the peak. No zig zagging to make the climb easier. He would soon wear down. He was gaining fast but halfway and the steep half to go would slow him to a crawl. Sig was slower and lagged a bit. I climbed steady and would show that little 10 year old.

Down that steep grassy point of Allen Mt. they slid on their back sides and hollered and laughed and up ended a few times. By now I was beginning to wonder who would wear who out on a long haul. A stop on the rock face for a few minutes to enjoy the scenery and then down the tough stretch. Down and around the rock this time and no fun. A stop at rest rock and a second drink at the crossing. On the lake and to the canoe. The lake a little rough with quite a few white caps. Leon on the paddle and Sig to keep her level we headed out. I would rather risk a crossing in rough water with those two than with a 200 pounder on the front seat. No problem and they laughed when a seventh wave

[76] RLP's Ram Mt. was near the head of Emerson Creek.

splashed them a bit. We made it in good shape and after a sourdough sandwich they were off to Hope Creek fishing while I got the biscuits in the pan.

Soon Leon was back "Sig lost another hook" and he showed that he was proud of his record of catching all the fish and losing no lures.

"Hey! here comes that German fella" and sure enough – Jerg came paddling up along the beach. He had made a tour of the lake today. Hiked the connecting stream and fished in the lower lake. Caught two fish, "did we need a fish?" Oh no we can catch one but I knew he would like to stay for supper. "Why don't you stay for supper and we will have the fish," I said. "That is fine, you fix them better than I" he said. He had a big laker (19½) and a dolly about 17 inches. I dressed them out while he went with the boys to try for another to take to his camp. Mashed spuds, green beans, biscuits and trout would be our supper. Only three biscuits for four so I would have a cold sourdough hotcake. Leon always one to share insisted I have the biscuit and he the hotcake even though he had said many times he sure liked those biscuits. Supper over and as usual everything cleaned up by the chief cleaner upper – Jerg. He told me later that he had been short of money on this trip and had skimped on food. He was getting thin and weak and those 14 hr. days on the mt. were beginning to tell.

August 8 – Overcast, Calm & 44°.

Late in the afternoon a plane came down the far side for the decent going up. It was the red & black Beaver that brings the guide Pollard from Kenai.[77] He had used Jerg's camp nearly the whole sheep season last year. Where would he set up camp this time?

August 21 – Clear, Calm & 33°.

A Super Cub with big tires came low and slow up the river. He turned a short distance up and came back and circled many times, making low landing passes at a bench across the river. Nearly but not quite and he made a couple at a river bar below and chickened out. A guide I figured and he had something spotted close by. Would he follow the no hunting the day you fly regulation. Kill it, chop the horns off and get out of here would be my guess. Finally he made a low pass over me and on down the river [Kijik] and Lachbuna Lake.

August 25 – Light Rain, Calm & 42°.

We sat on the beach and he Jergen [Kroener] told me of his travels. He had spent two

---

[77] Kenai, a large community on the Kenai Peninsula S of Anchorage and about 75 miles SE of Twin Lakes.

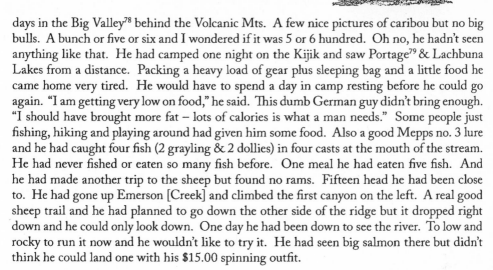
days in the Big Valley[78] behind the Volcanic Mts. A few nice pictures of caribou but no big bulls. A bunch or five or six and I wondered if it was 5 or 6 hundred. Oh no, he hadn't seen anything like that. He had camped one night on the Kijik and saw Portage[79] & Lachbuna Lakes from a distance. Packing a heavy load of gear plus sleeping bag and a little food he came home very tired. He would have to spend a day in camp resting before he could go again. "I am getting very low on food," he said. This dumb German guy didn't bring enough. "I should have brought more fat – lots of calories is what a man needs." Some people just fishing, hiking and playing around had given him some food. Also a good Mepps no. 3 lure and he had caught four fish (2 grayling & 2 dollies) in four casts at the mouth of the stream. He had never fished or eaten so many fish before. One meal he had eaten five fish. And he had made another trip to the sheep but found no rams. Fifteen head he had been close to. He had gone up Emerson [Creek] and climbed the first canyon on the left. A real good sheep trail and he had planned to go down the other side of the ridge but it dropped right down and he could only look down. One day he had been down to see the river. To low and rocky to run it now and he wouldn't like to try it. He had seen big salmon there but didn't think he could land one with his $15.00 spinning outfit.

I said, "Jerg, I guess I'll have to find you a caribou," and set up the scope. Right away I picked up that young bull or cow below Low Pass Creek.[80] I dressed out the lake trout and we took the fins to bait the trot line at Carrithers' point. With the scope two sheep up country from his old camp at the head of the lake. I would guess them rams but not legal. He would like to make another trip up country again.

All the while I had been figuring a way to help the poor guy on grub. He needed flour, sugar, salt, rolled oats, potatoes, anything at all. He had no money to spend and that wasn't important. In Spike's cabin I found about 4 lbs. of flour and a couple part packages of bisquick, some sugar and a box of potato buds, a small jar of honey and a little peanut butter. A part of a can of Crisco and in Hope's cabin a little rolled oats with raisins left by the Holts. He insisted on stopping with that. If he ran out he would come again. Anything he had leftover he would give to me plus some of his gear he didn't want to take back. He stowed the box full in his little boat and asked what he could give me in return. "Just send me a sample of your good pictures," I said. He would sure like to do that, but I would have to wait for he must make some money before he could get them processed.

One lake trout didn't seem like much for supper so I suggested we try Hope creek. I took my fly rod with Mepps spinner and he his spinning gear. Grayling were working. I saw four roll on the surface. One was due to get hooked shortly. He had a foul up with his reel and I hooked one. Good enough and we made ready for supper. "It is sure nice to sit down to a meal in a warm cabin" he said as I filled his GI tray with half a pan of trout. I had made a big salad from lettuce, cabbage, carrots, onion & cheese. A good big helping of beans and the old favorites – sourdoughs. We cleaned up two pans of fish plus everything else with blueberries for dessert.

---

[78] RLP's Big Valley is a 13-mile long valley that runs east from Snipe Lake toward the Kijik River; the Dena'ina name for the creek that runs through the valley is K'dalghektnu which means "where the caribou tear the velvet off his horns on the brush."

[79] Portage Lake, a small glacial lake about 12 miles south of Twin Lakes.

[80] RLP's Low Pass Creek, is a small stream that drains north from Low Pass basin to upper Twin Lakes.

August 29 – Partly Cloudy, Blowing dn. & 54°.

I just might butcher today. Cool with a good breeze. No flies or other insects. I loaded the old musket[81] and tucked a couple pieces of plastic under the lashing of the GI packboard. My Knapp saw and Denver hunting knife would go too. As I crossed the creek the cows [caribou] were working down country with the wind behind them. I would take the short cut and climb to the spruce clump on the lower bench close to Cowgill Creek.[82] I would wait there for them to come in range. I ran into a very good patch of blueberries (not too soft) at the base of the bench and marked the location in my head. I made the spruce cover in plenty time and got set. The pack boards and butchering tools standing by ready to go to work. On they came feeding a few bites here and there. The fall colors starting to show good and what beautiful footage I could get if the sun was out. A hundred yds. more or less and all five of them. Two small cows and I took them to be yearlings at the least and probably two year old. One cow with a grey cape and flank stripe. Ninety yards and closing. Make it seventy five and there would be no hole showing in the fleshed out hide. Through the neck at the base of the skull – the cut off spot. Head on shots, broadside, anything I wanted and I held my fire for that close up high in the neck shot. One made a pass at another – it whirled and trotted away. Then they spooked a bit from some imaginary object below and they trotted back and up. I had fouled up by waiting for the perfect shot. Should have taken one high forward in the ribs.

September 1 – Fog, Light Rain, Calm & 50°.

"This time I am bringing you some thing," he [Jürgen Kroener] said as he patted the kayak deck behind him. Carry-boo! "Did you get one" – "oh no – the four hunters got one near my camp." They had boned it out and left quite a bit. They had given him some food too. Now he was in good shape for the last two weeks.

I chunked mine and put it on to boil, well seasoned with everything on the shelf. Was there any left at the kill, "Oh, the bones." "Any neck or ribs?" Yes, the ribs but he didn't know about the neck. I would go back with him and see what we could scavenge.

Over under the tree lay the rib cage. Lots of good short ribs there. Why hadn't he taken some ribs. Oh, he didn't have a saw and his cooking pot was small. He hadn't thought of his hatchet. This was his first carry-boo. The backstrap and tenderloin long gone. I sawed down each side of the backbone and had two sides of ribs in short order. A few good pieces of fat laying about. He was cutting what he had taken in small chunks – frying and eating it. I was running low on bacon grease, I would render some and try it in cooking. He wanted no more. I will come up and eat some of your good cooking he said as I lashed everything on the packboard.

[81] RLP refers to his Springfield 30.06 rifle.

[82] RLP's Cowgill Creek is a small creek draining off Cowgill Mountain into upper Twin Lakes near the Proenneke Site.

September 2 – Fog, Calm & 48°.

I was up at 5:15 to build my spud frying fire. A nice little steak of caribou in a hot salted skillet instead of bacon. How would I keep the meat from souring after all the wet. I would try hanging it by the stove to dry. Dice the fat and render it out in my big skillet. Give the meat another dose of curing salt and let it drip again. The fat rendered until it was only slightly brown. The grease poured off and the cracklings drained and let cool. Add some salt, pepper & garlic salt and put them in containers to eat dry. Jerg could go many miles farther if he packed a bag of those to chew on. Fat, that's what he needed, this was fat.

I had salvaged the tongue too. Cooked it in yesterdays broth while the fat rendered. It done and a batch of short ribs went in and bubbled as I caught up on my writing. Now it was plain to see why I hadn't shot a caribou. I will be fortunate if I can save what meat I have.

The ribs were done to perfection. The bones came free easily. As I ate a good helping I thought of Seth Wright (Jerre's friend). He and Jerre had come over for supper and I had caribou short ribs. Seth was doing pretty good and finally said "This is the best meat I have ever eaten." I think Twin Lakes country had given him a good appetite.

It seems that Twin Lakes had its quota of sunshine for the day. Clouds were building fast. At my "diggings" I found only some strange boot tracks. I wonder what he thought of the neck and two sides of caribou hanging from the perlin log. I had given them two coats of sugar cure and they were nearly dry. One more should do it and I packed them out to my work bench for the application. Get a bucket of water, saw up a length of wood and it was time for beans, spare ribs, salad and sourdoughs, cold porridge and blueberries for dessert. The sky overcast again, a light breeze up and 58°.

September 4 – Clear, Calm & 40°.

I was up at 5:15 for this was another rare day. Must take advantage of the good light of clear days. Today I would go up Emerson Creek and check on those sheep. Climb out by the waterfall and go over the skyline. That old moon (past full) was very white in the still dark sky of early morning as I got breakfast. More meat to cook and I cut off some neck meat. No sign of it starting to spoil. A half hr. later getting started but not half as far to paddle so I was at the mouth of Falls Creek in good time. Two spruce grouse flushed as I climbed the trail and I found young moose tracks the last traffic over the game trail creek crossing. Higher in the timber a good bush of very ripe rose hips which are a good source of vitamin "C." Still higher many high bush cranberries. Over the big rock face and up the canyon I was soon looking down on Emerson Creek. There would be no climbing to

look out peak today for I intended to go down and up the creek. High up on the far side I could see a string of nine sheep like a string of white beads traveling a sheep trail heading for the ridge. At another place two and still another two more. That made thirteen of the sixteen I had seen the day before. It would be slim picking up the creek today. I didn't need a lot of sheep and I could see one laying on a high grass covered outcrop of rock a couple miles up and on the right hand side. Too far to tell for sure but I would gamble that it was a ram. I would make a try for that guy so dropped down over the side and headed for the mouth of a creek coming out of the big pocket behind Allen peak. Crossing the creek I would have to climb again and then follow a sheep trail across a big rock slide to the sheeps location. It was clouding up fast and I couldn't expect much help from the sun. I crossed the creek, made the climb and followed the trail. Getting close and I didn't want to spook that guy. Slowly I worked across the top of the outcrops. He wasn't where I thought he should be and I moved down to look over the edge to see if he was feeding below. No sheep and I knew he hadn't gone far. Another bunch of outcrops farther up and I suspected that was where he had been. Suddenly there was a sheep a quarter mile farther and at first I thought it was a big ewe. It turned its head – a half curl ram. Not what I had expected but I would try for him anyway. He fed behind a rise and I moved his way. Ridges & hollows would let me get very close and I made the last ridge and eased up for a look. There he was about a hundred feet away. No sun but the breeze favorable. I had shot out the last fifteen feet of film a mile back so as to have a full roll. I backed up and planted the tripod. I was ready when he first saw me. He stood and looked for a minute or two and then back to feeding and slowly moving my way. More looking and he didn't seem to mind me winding the camera. Closer and closer, fifty feet, forty, thirty. Enough light for my 75 mm 3X lens. A full frame filler. I could even use the normal lens. I was running out of film and he had shown no sign of leaving. Just a few feet left and I whistled quietly to see what he would do. He came a few steps closer and then more. At about twenty two feet he turned and walked away. That was something that I had never experienced before. What that little guy lacked in horn he made up for with cooperation. That was pretty good and I would like to see that 100 feet of film on the screen. Back over the rise he joined four head of ewes and lambs and the five of them traveled a trail around the mt. Later there was that young guy bedded down high on a rock over looking Emerson Creek country.

Yesterday I returned to find a note on the door. It read "Dropped in to pay you a short visit but don't blame you for not sticking around on such a nice day. Everyone is extremely happy with the footage you shot – the best any of us has seen. May drop by again in a couple weeks." Signed Bob Waldrop.[83] He is with the Park Service and if he had only looked inside the cabin. A package on the table addressed to the Park Service and in it 1600 ft. of exposed film waiting for Babe to fly it out.

---

[83] Bob Waldrop, a seasonal NPS park planner from Anchorage.

September 7 – Partly Cloudy, Breeze & 46°.

It was Bee and he had just flipped the prop. on the old bird in preparation for leaving. He saw me and shut her off. "I nearly missed you," he said. Terry[84] had told me "Bee is the worse. He will come but if you are not there to meet him, he will set your stuff out and fly away. Maybe you have a list to go or want to tell him or ask him something – you had better be there when he lands." I hurried to get my outgoing mail ready. Was he in a hurry? "Oh, not much I guess I was going to pick up some guys at Turquoise but it is pretty windy – they can wait." Terry and Vic are coming to Lake Clark by helicopter today and the chopper would then take him [Bee] up a side canyon in Lake Clark Pass to salvage an engine from a plane that had landed against a steep slope. He had found it – radio was still in it too. His dad had just got home with the second new "T craft" and he may get more. The price is going up a thousand soon. This one same color as the last one (red & black). This one for Bee. Took him five and one half days from the factory and was weathered in a day and a half at Ft. Nelson, [B.C.].

Bee had brought three boxes of pilot bread, a little pack outfit camp stove and a pressure cooker. Gear for the hikers headed this way, he said. "Where are they now," I asked. On the Kijik River. "Chuck Hornberger[85] took them across yesterday." Till now they had been touring Lake Clark and Lake Clark Pass.

My mail was ready and he loaded up and took off. He had brought some things I ordered. 50 lbs. of flour, 24 lbs. of rice, 25 lbs. of oatmeal, 7 lbs. of peanut butter, 2 lbs. of popcorn. About 3 qts. of bacon grease, some celery & cabbage and a good bundle of mail. I declared it a Twin Lakes holiday. Mary had also sent a piece of rhubarb pie. Little Sig and Leon are going to school at Soldotna this year.[86] The mission girls are outside and the school burned at Nondalton.

My mail read and lunch over I could still pick so I climbed the hump again. Nice picking as the wind was calm along that slope. I picked a gallon and there is still gallons more in the same patch. Leaves pick easy now so I had to run this gallon over burlap to take the leaves out. Sunday coming up and company (the hikers) soon so I raked my beach and neatened up my diggings.

September 8 – Partly Cloudy, Calm & 45°.

Through the stream and I didn't see his boat on the beach. I had taken some boiled caribou meat for him. A good start towards his [Jürgen] camp and I saw him traveling the

[84] Terry Gill (1909-1985), cannery man and miner in the Bonanza Hills beginning in 1958. Gill and his wife Victoria (1908-2004) had a cabin at the confluence of Bonanza and Little Bonanza Creeks. The site had previously been used by O.B. Millett and Jack Kinney of Iliamna in the early 20th century.

[85] Chuck Hornberger, a long-time resident of SW Alaska and lodge owner on Lake Clark; the property was purchased from trapper Frank Bell in 1969.

[86] Leon and Sig Alsworth attended Cook Inlet Academy in Soldotna, a village 8 miles SE of Kenai.

beach from Beech Creek. Packing his big lens on the tripod and a pack on his back. His boat was laying well back against the bank. "Just getting in," I asked. "I only yesterday got home from my long hike but today was such a nice day I just had to go a little ways. I saw you coming and I headed back." "Did you get to Turquoise Lake." His eyes got big and he said. "Much farther than that. I was four days away from my camp. I looked down on Telaquana Lake." He had crossed the first ridge and camped near the stream going up into sheep country. There he caught a big rainbow trout. Next he saw four good bull caribou but in bad light. Then six cows and calves. He had forded the river coming out of Turquoise Lake and met some hunters who gave him food and he ate scrambled eggs with them. He heard of hunters killing 20 caribou out of a bunch of forty and the meat was spoiling from the rain. He had gone on over the ridge looking down on Telaquana. Blueberries just blue everywhere and there he saw a black grizzly and got to within 250 feet of him and never did get found out. That bear was just very busy picking berries. He had seen the bear as a black speck – so far away and it took one hr. to walk to him. From there he headed home. "I was very tired," he said. "The pack very heavy, I have run out of oats and I count on it during a long hike." "Come up and I will give you some" I said. The wind was down on the lower lake and it took him two hrs. to paddle home.

We sampled my caribou meat and he said I will make you a bannock right now. A little fire going and he started with flour then baking powder and salt. A little shortening and then lake water and he worked it with his fingers. "This is how I get my fingers clean" he said and I took his word for it as he hadn't washed his hands. Some grease in his little frying pan which had fried fish and not washed. The mixing pan over the top for a cover. "Too fast" he said, the fire too hot. Pretty quick he knocked the cover off and the bannock was brown on top & black on the bottom. He tipped it over with "this one is mine." The next one turned out better. A light crust top and bottom and pretty doughy in the center. "How did I like it" – "ok, not too bad." With lots of blueberries it would be pretty good. "Yes, they would help" he said. Only seven days left and he would like to make another over night trip for rams if he only knew where to look. "Go 14 hrs. and see nothing," he said. He might come up country one more time and at any rate he would come by my place before time to go. Many things that he didn't want to take back with him that I could have. He wished he could stay till freeze up but he had to go. "I must be out of Alaska by Oct. 1st or your government won't like it," he said.

The sun was getting low when I pushed out and headed for the stream. I lined her through and headed up the flat lake. Fifteen till seven as I entered the upper lake and one hr. later I was on my beach. The sun had set and the cool of evening was taking over. It would frost tonight. Supper over and dishes done by nine. Through writing by ten. A light surf on my beach from an up lake breeze. Clear as a bell and 38°.

September 11 – Raining, Blowing dn. & 46°.

Before daylight I heard rain on the roof and the wind in the spruce – this was a good one.

I slept in till six and it was still half dark getting breakfast started. I had expected Jerg to pass today but not with the lake roaring as it was. He would probably hole up in Lofstedt's or Frank Bell's old cabin – that is if he had food enough to tide him over a day. For me it would be a letter writing day. Dishes done and I just got my writing gear laid out when I happened to look out the window. There humped up on the beach was the largest beaver I have ever seen. It was Jerg humped over (in his rain parka) closing up the cockpit of his kayak. I rushed out to greet him. How was the lake? "Pretty rough I tell you." Where had he spent the night? "In my old camp under a tree." Have you had breakfast? "A little oats, I didn't build a fire." By now we were inside and me stoking the fire. I started him out with my leftover porridge with lots of dry milk and sugar. A cup of hot vinegar and honey. Then I cut up some boiled caribou and fried it, mixing in a egg when it was hot. Then two or three cups of coffee and I popped a big bowl of popcorn. What had he seen on his last big tour. He had gone up the left fork of the river at the rock pile and then up the next left headed for the divide where he had been before. Past the first canyon on the left and climbing when he learned it was raining and snowing up high so he turned back.

We [RLP and Jerg] had shook hands in case we didn't meet again before he left. "Maybe I see you at Twin Lakes again or some other place," he said. He headed down… The last I saw of him he was trudging the beach along the lower end. It would be dark before he got to camp after all. What a wind up for the last big tour at Twin Lakes. Next year he wants to bring his mother to Canada for a sightseeing tour and then if he has time & money left-go into the wilderness of B.C. for a time. He will have to play it by ear from the time he reaches Whitehorse. He must get a job and where ? Only a few hundred dollars to see him making money again. I wouldn't like to play it that close in this day and age. But I can remember starting on a six months trip with $30.00 and getting back back with $20.00 (1939).

September 12 – Raining, Calm & 44°.

Some improvement over yesterday morning – no wind on the lake. Raining gently and it looked as if it could rain forever. Jerg and his appetite had upset my schedule. I would have to make hotcakes again and start a fresh batch of biscuits. The griddle off of the fire and I put the caribou pot of short ribs on. Get another batch of beans cooking and write letters. I felt quite sure there would be no German visitors today. His boat still lay bottom up along the gravel bank. He would be sleeping in this morning. My birds came and I have self feeders for them now. Three short "C" rations cans filled with caribou grease. Scatter them out front and let them work at it but don't forget or you will find them empty.

I wrote and wrote and tended the fire. A trip or two to the woodshed for fuel and I saw one of my rabbits. If only I could catch one in good light for pictures. The weather would fair up a bit and then rain some more. I checked the hump, benches, down country and across the lake during the intermissions but saw no game. The colors appear much brighter and a clear day would see some film exposed.

Lunch time, a sandwich, a sample of the beans and a spare rib or two, then back to my writing. Along towards five it began to clear down country. I happened to go outside and it was fortunate that I did. Crag Mt. and the country from here up was in light rain. The brightest rainbow I believe that I have ever seen and a second rainbow above it but faint. I had meat frying and biscuits baking but they would have to carry on unattended. I grabbed the 35 mm and launched the canoe. I backed off shore for a couple shots before the rain came and it rained hard after I reached the cabin. The meat was smelling of too much fire and I found it stuck fast to the cast iron skillet. The sun dropped behind the lower slope of Falls Mt. and the excitement was over. By about Sept. 15th the sun will set in the notch formed by the Volcanic Mts. and Falls Mt. Then in six more days it will have reached the halfway point between the longest day and the shortest.

On the beach brushing my teeth after supper and there was a rooster grouse towards the point picking gravel and just now as I write one flew across my front yard. The family from across the creek must have moved near.

September 14 – Overcast, Calm & 38°.

I came onto the benches to find white caps on the lake. I had told Jerg I would come down before he flew away. I could go alright but had better take the kicker to get back. Lunch over and my film taken care of I made ready to head down. Take the little kicker along for the ride. I headed for Jerre's cabin to get out of line with the wind and the stream and headed down. Two airplanes (one was Ketchum's[87] for sure) came to Low Pass beach and I could see another lean-to there. On down and through the stream. I could see a stack of gear covered with a green tarp near Jerg's tent. He crawled out as I came near. That was his disassembled kayak under the tarp. The skin folded and in a bag. The frame in another and the two weighed more than fifty lbs. He had a plastic bag of odds and ends for me. A first aid kit, shoe grease, fish lines, lures, plastic bags, bug dope and did I want his little tent. He had used it two trips and would get a new one next time. Get a bigger, higher, one that he could move around in. This one was for use with the kayak on a river trip. I liked the little orange nylon tent. It only weighs, 2 ½ lbs. Could use it packing out for a day or two and maybe this fall yet, but I didn't want it for nothing when he was so hard up for cash. He insisted I have it for I had given him food. Finally I told him I would pay half of Babe's trip in for he would bring me grub and mail and I would pay him five dollars extra on Jerg's half of the trip. We agreed on that. It would help him by cutting down his load back to Whitehorse [Yukon Territory]. The two [Cessna] 185's took off down the lake and soon one came back with another [Cessna] 180 and landed. Noise pollution galore today. It was calm on the upper end of the lower lake and sprinkling lightly as we stood on the beach and discussed his future plans. By this time next week he might be working again. 4:30 and time I was heading back with my sack of loot. There would be more. His leftover food, tent and green tarp. I would pick it up next time down. We shook hands

[87] Ketchum Air Service, a bush flying service based on Lake Hood in Anchorage owned by "Ketch" and Marguerite Ketchum.

and he said, "Maybe I will see you at Twin Lakes or someplace again." I paddled towards the stream and left him with his cold camp. Three months and never a warming fire. Just a little blaze to cook with. I would be in the woods and I would have the warm glow of a good fire when ever I wanted it. I hope Babe makes it in to get him out tomorrow.

I lined her through the stream and found the upper lake nearly calm with only a trace of a breeze. One airplane had flown away leaving one at the beach. Five o'clock when I headed up and at halfway I met a light breeze which picked up at the three quarter mark. Quartering to Farmer's landing I got out of it and got going, 1 hr. and 20 min. for the run. A fire going and the spare ribs on to warm up. The biscuits to bake and beans to warm. A big leaf of cabbage for greens. A fresh bucket of water and my loot stored away. It was nine o'clock before I got my writing done. Till now I had used my candle lantern but this Sept. 14th saw the little single mantle Coleman go into service. Now it would be six months before it would be retired for the summer again.

September 16 – Partly Cloudy, Blowing dn. & 44°.

The lake rough but I wanted to get the stuff that Jerg left. I could take the pack board and be back by six. A pretty good hike. I had told Jerg I could go to the lower end of the lake in a hour and fifteen minutes. He allowed I would have to travel some to do it. A square of chocolate for the return trip. A sourdough sandwich before I started and I was crossing Hope Creek at 2 o'clock. I cut across the mouth of Low Pass Creek and traveled blueberry hill to the gravel bank and was there in one hr. An hr. ten at the bend of the beach and I went straight to Beech Creek and down the beach a few hundred yds. to Jerg's campsite. All the stuff under a small spruce where he said it would be. I left his cooking gear, empty cans, a little vinegar and his worn out rubber boots. I would pick that garbage up with the canoe. The tent and his left over food plus his plastic tarp I lashed on the Japanese pack frame. 4 o'clock when I headed back. It was clearing and a pretty sight up country. A head wind too and cooler than running with it. 5:45 when I reached the cabin. Still a fire in the stove from a good cottonwood log. Everything on to warm and I unloaded the pack board. Grub, there was very little, rice, about three good hand fulls. About that much flour. A few tea bags. Some black pepper and bullion cubes a few. A little chunk of caribou fat and a hand full of macaroni. Baking powder two full cans and more than a box of matches. I soon had everything out of sight. A clear sunset and one more sunset will see the sun in the notch formed by the Volcanic mts. and the lower slope of Falls Mt. Another month and the sun will be looking scarce but snow will brighten the day for filming. Supper over and my writing done by nine. I am surprised that no stars are out (overcast) calm and 45°.

This evening I heard that mysterious thunder again and this time far ahead a vapor trail of a very fast flying jet fighter. A pilot hurrying home to roost.

Today with my mail a letter from the hikers[88] thanking me for keeping their

---

[88] Hikers, refers to Van Horne, Downing, and Ward.

supplies. Leaving Kijik the 10th Sept. and expect to be at my place Sept. 20. "Traveling slow for there is much to see," they said. A week at Twin Lakes to explore and then on to Telaquana Lake where they will be picked up Oct. 5th. I wonder how many lbs. of grub they will have left after a week here. I figure they will have to get rid of about a hundred pounds in order to pack the remainder. Good that I didn't take Babe's advice. He had said weeks ago. "They will never make it to Twin Lakes, you just as well use that grub." Not here yet but I'm thinking they will make it.

September 20 – Raining, Blowing dn. & 50°.

In Spike's cabin I had found some of the same material (tin pants which Hope had washed the character out of). A tan seat on grey pants. From the rear I would look like an elk with his buff colored rump. I spread the pants out flat on the table and the material covering the affected area – out lined one side and then folded it to get both alike. Pinned it in place. Stuck my narrow stew [?] pan inside the leg (bottom up) to keep from stitching the back side to the front side and nailed that seat patch on with grey (waxed) button and carpet thread. Looked pretty neat when done and good for many many miles and hrs. of sitting on abrasive rocks. Good to wear under my tin pants when the cold winds come. Another pair of pants got some stitching and a patch or two before it was time to bake the biscuits and heat up the caribou. One more batch and my caribou will be gone. Comes cold and freezing, caribou had better be scarce around here.

The rain stopped late in the afternoon and it was high overcast and low scattered. The wind all but died and I would take a paddle up the lake to check on the five rams still on Bell Mt.[89] On a close check I could still see white caps coming down so I cancelled out. Brushing my teeth at the beach and I heard two more shots at least as far down as Beech Creek and probably farther. Someone would be working late tonight as it was pretty dark. Now at 8 o'clock, raining down country, calm & 50°.

September 21 – Raining, Calm &44°.

I paddled across, rounding that last point before Emerson Creek when I saw three people coming up the beach, just leaving the creek flat. I suspected they were hunters and I would stay close to shore and see who it was. Trudging slowly my way and finally I could see they had packs and good sized ones. Could it be the hikers on the wrong side of the lake. Then I could see only one rifle and one wore red leggings. Closer and I could see two wore little Swiss felt hats with the brims turned down. It was the hikers. "Going some where," I greeted them. The boy said, "Are you Dick Proenneke?" Right. And then he introduced himself, Bea & Candy. He had a full beard and longish hair. Bea looked some what like

---

[89] RLP's Bell Mountain is a peak approximately 5,000 ft. high north of upper Twin Lakes.

an Indian girl. A good tan and hair in braids. Candy a blond with long hair. Both big enough to carry a load but I wouldn't expect them to pack such a mountain of gear. "How come you are on the wrong side of the lake," I asked. Floyd Denison on Lake Clark had on their map located me on the side they were on. How far had they come since yesterday morning. Last night they had camped in the cottonwoods on Emerson and the night before at the head of the Chilikadrotna River. There they had cleaned up a dirty campsite and asked some hunters to haul the garbage out and got snickered at.

I told them to dump their packs in the canoe and I would haul them to my place. I was surprised at the size and weight of those three packs. Three of them made a canoe load bulkwise. They could hike on up to Jerre's cabin and I would come for them. I headed for my beach with a following breeze. At my beach I set their packs under the over hang of the roof, built up the fire a bit for hot water and with an extra paddle aboard I headed for Jerre's point. Walter was bow paddler and the two girls the load. We came across in fifteen minutes. That was the easiest mile they had made in ten days and since they left the shore of Lake Clark. All preferred tea and popped some corn and made sourdough sandwiches.

I had prepared the cabins for tourists – just as well make use of them. I asked them how they would go for living in a cabin instead of the little tent. They would like that so I tried Bea's pack for size and weight and we headed up the timber trail. The load on that good pack frame was not to bad but on the mt., it would be too much. I left them to get squared away and came down to do some jobs I had been wanting to do. Cut my weak canoe paddle – shorten it six inches and make a new glued splice. The other splice had done well and I wondered how come it didn't give way by this time. I had wrapped the splice with nylon tape and when I cut and peeled it off the paddle fell apart. A new splice cut and glued and wrapped tightly with nylon cord to hold it until it dries. The kids came down to break into that heavy duffle bag of food & fuel.

Dry beans, split peas, lentils, cheese, a big chunk of it. Many big bags of mixed nuts. Loaves of heavy bread that they had baked in Anch. It was green with mold. Cooking oil and stove fuel. I told them I would camp right here until I got the load used up to an easy pack and then go. They had figured six days to Telaquana.

The kids all three from Calif. and in college. This was part of their college work. The gear for the trip they had to furnish but the supplies they had received a grant to pay for. It had been good so far. They had been flown up to the glacier in Lake Clark Pass and then ran the river back to Lake Clark in their three Klepper Aerous kayaks. They had visited in Nondalton talking to the old people learning how it was in the old days. One Native woman said she had been over the trail to Telaquana many times and it took five days if you walked all the time. At thirteen she had packed her baby (on her back) over the trail. They had searched out the old village of Kijik[90] at the mouth of the Kijik River. Part of the Russian Orthodox church (three walls) still stands. Here and there depressions where the huts had been. A squatter living there now had torn out the grave markers in

---

[90] Historic Kijik village is the abandoned 19th century Dena'ina village on Lake Clark and now part of the Kijik National Historical Landmark, perhaps the largest Athapaskan site in Alaska. The Dena'ina word for the village is Qizhjeh, "many people gather."

the cemetery and built a cabin there. The Natives very unhappy about that. Walter with all his other gear packs a book that must weigh six pounds or more. In this book the vegetation of Alaska and they must study and make a report of what grows here back in Anch. There will be much library study to complete their report. I think they hate to see Oct. 5 and time to fly back to civilization.

September 22 – Raining, Calm & 50°.

Raining gently – again the weather thickened, warmed and rained instead of cooler weather which I felt sure would come. I had invited the kids down for sourdough hotcakes this morning. They had no time piece as their only watch had been dunked in a river crossing. Breakfast well started I went up the beach and gave them a growl. This morning I had used three cups of flour instead of two (for Leon, Sig & I) and had none to many hotcakes. Only Bea went for a helping of porridge. Raining a steady rain and they stayed awhile. On their maps they traced their route till now. One narrow escape crossing a fork of the river in Lake Clark Pass. Candy had been swept down stream and lodged on a gravel bar along the far shore. Walter went too and couldn't get out of his pack and as luck would have it he drifted into shallow water. So cold he was helpless. Two on one side and one on the other. They threw Candy the end of a rope and after her tying it around herself she started across. Again she lost her footing but they dragged her ashore. For three days they tried to cross it and finally gave up. On the map of Twin Lakes they wanted to fill in all of my names for the streams and mts.

September 28 – Fog, Light Snow & 30°.

Down in the brush along the creek and looking for a good place to climb out I ran onto the one and only hornets nest I have seen here. A typical paper type, cone shaped with a round top. Built around the main branch of a large willow. A real substantial set up. Hornets to be seen through the small round hole low on southern exposure. It was good for a few feet of film before I climbed out and traveled on.

It was three o'clock when I reached the cabin. Many nice early snow scenic shots with beautiful cloud effects along the way down. A note on my open writing tablet. A Randy Jones[91] of the Park Service and he wrote that if the three hikers stopped here to tell them they could stay here on the lakes and would be picked up here Oct.5th. Perhaps they would pass Twin Lakes, he wrote and not to worry about it if I didn't see them. He also had a message from Bob Belous[92] who reviews my film footage. "Doing great- some of the best film we have." And on the next page another note. "Read your book and finally made it here. Sorry we missed you but we saw 'One Man's Alaska.' Ted Foss…& Charles Tulin…Anch."

---

[91] Randy Jones was an NPS Resource Planning Advisor for the Alaska Task Force.

[92] Robert Belous (1935-2001) was an NPS park planner, photographer, and subsistence expert with the Alaska Task Force.

I put in at the hikers campsite. One thing about them, you find nothing but their tracks after they leave. Even the stones from around the fire were gone. I made up my pack and cached the canoe bottom up in the stunted spruce. A good shelter for the gear I was leaving. I didn't pack much food for I expected to be back by noon tomorrow. Just as I was ready to start the old folks came by. Well into their sixties but very active and I had heard that they take a long hike every day. The lady allowed I would get caught out in the dark and I agreed but that would be no problem. Yesterday from the big rock with the brass plate the hikers and I had looked at the country they would travel. I knew where they would climb out of the timber and where they intended to hit the skyline. I took off packing my sleeping bag and grub on the light Jap. pack frame and my camera film and accessories in the front pouch of my ammo pack pockets. Skirt the beaver ponds on the right I had told them and now I found another new pond had been added since I was there last. Near sun down and a beaver was using the pond as a swimming hole. On across the brushy flat to the timber and a moose traveled game trail heading down country. To the big timber filled notch in the lower bench and a big patch of now spent cow parsnip. Across one clear running small creek and then a 2nd before pulling up a steep draw and then out onto the open point of the first bench. The near full moon was now clearing the right shoulder of Black Mt. A beautiful sight against the very blue sky. It was cool and would no doubt frost tonight. At the base of the 2nd bench and a good sized lake. My turning point when headed for the Bonanza Hills.[93] This time I climbed on towards the skyline. Enough light from the moon that I cast a shadow but still it was a problem to tell exactly where I was on the mt. I didn't want to get too close to the hikers camp in the dark. Walter was packing a Winchester model 70, .300 Magnum for bear protection. Early in their hike they had abandoned eight smoked fish because they thought it might attract the bears. I didn't care to be shot or shot at with a .300 Mag. so I planned to stay a little down country from their camp. A cool breeze was coming over the ridge so at the last bench I found where a bear had dug for a ground squirrel. A nice little notch into the hillside. I pulled some dry grass to cover the dirt and spread Jerg's plastic tarp. Next my chunk of sheep skin and then the mummy bag. I folded the other half of the tarp over the top and put my camera and other gear under the edge of it for it would frost heavy with such a clear night. I turned in and noticed that it was about nine o'clock. It was cool sleeping. The sheep skin wasn't long enough. Frost formed at the opening of the bag. I watched the moon travel across the sky and twice I heard geese going by. Finally I got the place warmed up and went to sleep.

September 29 – Clear, Calm & Cold.

Four o'clock and finally 5:30. I could see to travel so got up. My L.L. Bean shoe pacs stiff as a board and I had to pull hard to get them on. I jogged back and fourth along the gravel bench above to get warmed up before packing my gear. I looked along the edge of

---

[93] Bonanza Hills are a group of low mountains between the upper Chilikadrotna and Mulchatna Rivers about 20 miles west of the Twin Lakes.

the ridge for the hikers camp and failed to find it. I felt sure that it would be up country from me. I headed for the turned over Cessna 170. Their route would take them near it. I found solid snow cover on the crest of the ridge and came over a rise to see the airplane just a little on my right. Tracks in the snow there but only two people. Two sets of tracks coming in from the direction of the lower lake and two leaving towards Turquoise Lake. Certainly they hadn't passed already this morning. They must be camped on the creek coming down from the lick. Snow cover was only partial and I soon lost their tracks. Why only two people. I suspect it could be hunters who passed. A couple miles more put me on the slope looking down on the creek. A nice little stream crooked and lined with willows and grassy parks. I glassed the country up and down. No sign of the hikers or their tent. Now I was thinking I should have back tracked at the airplane to see where the tracks came from so I went back. The airplane a total wreck. Both wings damaged and part of the tail. One landing strut torn out, the engine and instruments gone. One seat missing and the other a wreck. I back tracked there and found they had only walked out and back taking pictures. No one had come from the lower lake. I made a big circle on solid snow and learned the two sets of tracks had come from and left towards Turquoise. The hikers must be still towards Twin Lakes country so I trudged back across the rolling hill country of the ridge. I had seen caribou tracks in the snow and now ahead of me a good looking bull. A long ways ahead but on my route. I came carefully over the last rise to find antlers facing me. I hurried to set the tripod for he was heading my way. A pretty sight in the view finder as he broke over the rise. He spooked and floated about in that graceful trot that means – if it's a race you want I am the guy who will race with you. He circled about and out of sight. I went on and down from snow cover. I was looking down on the lower lake again. By now the kids should be on the move but no sign of them. Now I suspected I had camped above them and they were out of sight lower on the ridge and heading for Turquoise so I circled down that way and again on solid snow cover on the crest of the ridge. I hit three sets of tracks going in the right direction. Tracks made in wet snow of yesterday. Now I was on the trail. On bare spots I would lose the trail but pick it up on the snow farther on. It passed below the plane and I now got the picture. They had passed it before they saw it and came back to take pictures. Only two. Candy had stayed with the packs. I followed on and was heading near to where I had stood when glassing the creek. Circling down the slope I saw them in a little hollow of the bank on a nice grassy park in the willows. No snow down there. Now was a chance to get some footage of them packing. It had gone so well yesterday they came all the way to the creek and arrived just as the moon was clearing the mts. The same time I was leaving the timber near the lower lake. Only four miles to go today so they had slept in and just now ready to start down the creek. As Bea was leader of the three I gave her the note. She read it and tried to figure why the Park Service wanted to stop them short of their goal. They (all three) agreed that they wanted to go on to Telaquana and be picked up there Oct. 5th so when and if the plane came here I would tell the pilot he would find them there. It was now 10 o'clock and the first order of business was crossing the creek. Rocks icy and not safe with a heavy pack. Better to find a gravel bottom and wade. So, off comes hiking boots and socks and on goes shoe pacs over bare feet. Wade across and change back again. Bea threw hers

across to me (even hers much larger than mine). A few seconds of cold water is good for the tired feet and mine felt fresh after several miles already today. Now they would go – pay no attention to me. I would shoot from all angles as I came to them. Down the creek and across the lower end of a ridge and a view of the Mulchatna[94] River which they would have to ford. Only about a mile to go and they stopped for lunch. Out came the peanuts, pilot bread, cheese, peanut butter, blueberry jam (they had made here), sardines. I said, "no wonder you don't go far in a day. Get a late start and spend the rest of the day eating." "Oh, but you must eat good to keep your strength up." I guessed that was true as they are strong under a heavy pack. They had lots of food – why didn't I stay overnight and go back tomorrow. That I would like to do but I still had enough time left to make it back and I didn't want to cross the river twice for no good reason. They would spend a day on Turquoise and then two days to Telaquana and a day to spare before the plane came. It was twenty till two, how long would it take me to reach the lower lake. On their map it was about seven miles. Bea said I might make it by five o'clock. I would stay low on the ridge, no snow and very little climbing. Just below us the creek we had crossed farther up and a stepping stone crossing. It was wide with many boulders. I stayed to get them shouldering their packs and winding down onto the big flat along the river. From the bottom they waved and trudged on towards a possible fording place. I crossed the creek and headed back along or very near the old Native trail from Lake Clark to Telaquana Lake.[95] It was clear and calm, the ridge climbing on my left and the big flat country below on my right. Nearing my lower lake to Bonanza Hills trail I would climb a bit to shorten the route and drop down again not far from the lake I had passed in the moonlight the evening before. A big country and there must be caribou somewhere so I stopped a few minutes to glass the country. A good sized lake in the distance and a camp of some kind on the far side. On my side and maybe three miles from me four caribou there with white capes and I would bet they were bulls. I was tempted to head that way but if I did I would be another night on the trail and I didn't relish that being prepared as I was. I should have taken some caribou hide for a ground cloth under my sleeping bag. I traveled on, entering the timber at the same place I had left it. My load was getting heavy by the time I threaded my way among the gravel knolls to the beach and the canoe. Ten past five my watch said. The tent campers were out on the beach in front of their camp taking many combinations of pictures of themselves with a caribou rack. I would have stopped by but had a good ways to go and a cool and strong breeze was blowing up the lake. I used the kicker and in less than one hr. I was lining through the stream. The upper lake more calm and I made it in twenty minutes. My gear packed in and a fire going. The caribou and bean pot on. Water heating for a bath and laundry. It was eight o'clock when I turned out the lantern. I just knew I would sleep good tonight. That four inches of foam rubber under me never felt so good.

---

[94] Mulchatna River is a 175-mile long river that drains Turquoise Lake and is the major tributary of the Nushagak River, known for its great fishing, beaver trapping, and hunting. The Dena'ina word for the upper river is Vandaztuntnu, "caribou hair stream."

[95] Variant of the Telaquana Trail, a Dena'ina trail that ran from the Kijik villages on the north side of Lake Clark 50 miles north to the villages on Telaquana Lake in the Kuskokwim drainage.

October 1 – Snowing, Blowing up & 23°.

This evening the surf is still heavy on the beach but the wind is nothing compared to this afternoon. I had told the hikers that I expected the fair weather to hold until after the full moon. That would put them at their destination. I did forget to warn them that once it is October winter can come over night. Snow can be sixteen inches deep and below zero by the 15th. At sunset it was only partly cloudy but now at 7:40 there is snow in the air, temp. 24°.

October 4 – Snowing, Blowing dn. & 34°.

As it grew lighter I could see the ground was white. That is one advantage of sleeping in the upper bunk. It was snowing, the lake still roaring. I was glad I came across instead of going to Jerre's cabin. From there I would have had to walk to the lower end and ford the stream.

Always at this time of year a wind down the lake is warm and brings melting snow.

My blueberries still frozen for I had insulated them with some sheep skin but they would thaw shortly. Today would be a blueberry syrup making day. I went up to Spike's cabin and got the big water bucket to cook them in. Stopped at Hope's cabin[96] for some bottles from the big glass box. On my stove I dumped in half the total and got them melted and lots of juice and then I emptied the storage can. The big bucket was two thirds full. What to use in thickening the juice after it came to a boil? The girls (hikers) had used flour and water in making the blueberry jam they packed away from here. I had some corn starch and would give it a try. No instructions for my operation so I mixed a generous amount with my sugar and mixed it good. Stirred in three fourths of it and cooled a sample. Not thick enough so I added a second generous helping. That would have to do. Probably I would be digging the syrup out with a knife. First before adding the sugar and corn starch I separated the pulp from the juice. Ran it through the wire strainer and then squeezed the pulp dry in a section of game bag. Half of the batch filled my large stainless mixing bowl (1 ga. 2 pts.) with juice. In went the sugar and starch and I stirred it until the sugar was dissolved. Cooked it a bit and funneled it into my bottles. Two batches and by that time my kitchen had taken on a blue look. To the last batch I added some maple flavoring. Five big bottles (one of them a big syrup can) and a stubby. Enough syrup to last all winter and then some. I had intended to use honey but at $50.00 per 5 gal. can this is better and I am thankful for the cold weather to pick the berries.

---

[96] Hope Carrithers' cabin about 200 yards east of the Proenneke cabin built by Spike Carrithers and RLP in the early 1970s as a guest cabin.

October 6 – Rain, Calm & 40°.

The sleeves of my black navy sweater were shot beyond repair. Cut them out and make a vest of it. I have more clothes with short or no sleeves. Lots of freedom when swinging an axe, sawing or paddling but it makes for colder hands hiking and packing the camera. My wool halibut jacket to mend, short sleeves, that one.

I stoked up the fire and popped a big bowl of popcorn to see my mending finished. By then it was getting dark and time to get supper. Still snowing and melting most places and in the morning I expect the snow to be near lake level.

Four journals and a half reread and some of the mistakes corrected. About eight notebooks filled in five months. I am well ahead of my usual one per month. The days ahead will see a slow down unless the weather cooperates. 2600 ft. of film to see me through Oct. but I have written Trexler telling him that I plan to be here at freeze up and if he wants to see it maybe I had better have 10 more rolls. So far I have averaged about 17 rolls per mo. and I wonder how many miles. I could read my journals and make a close guess.

Tonight a light surf on my beach, snowing (the ground getting white) and 36°. A good snow cover will expose the moose.

October 16 – Overcast, Calm & 25°.

This morning as I entered the woodshed for my fire starting kindling the place fairly exploded. The squirrel had been in a big cardboard box and I startled him as much as he did me getting out of there. He was plenty scared and angry too. Such language as that guy did spit out from a spruce behind the shed. What was he doing in that box anyway? The flaps folded and tucked leaving only a small opening in the center. I took it down and opened it. So that was it – after the kids had left I found two loaves of their heavy bread on the stump at Spike's cabin. I brought one down for bird and squirrel feed. The stuff saws just like wood and tastes only slightly different. I had put it in the box and forgotten about it. The squirrel has eaten about half of it. No wonder he leaves the smoke fish skins on the stump untouched.

October 18 – Snowing, Breeze up & 15°.

It was foggy and snowing – the lake steaming – it was a wintery looking morning. Hotcakes for breakfast and they really taste good with such weather conditions.

Only one helping of beans left so I put them in a bowl and got another batch going. I noticed that the last half gallon of my fresh blueberries were taking on a slightly moldy flavor so I cooked them a bit and added sugar. A few small repair jobs to do while

the kettle boiled. One shoulder strap on my camera gear pack sack was getting weak with age. Walter Ward had told me that he has one and knows where he can get one and will send me one. I hope he has a good memory. Snowing still and I dug out a stack of *"Grit"* newspapers that Babe had brought quite some time ago. I was the one who got Babe & Mary started with a gift subscription several years ago.

The temp. dropped slowly. By noon it was down to ten and I was due to get in more wood. The breeze was cold on the beach but in the woods, a perfect day for the job. I limbed and bucked two down trees for packing. I had heard and seen swan today. Like grey ghosts they were against the snowy sky. The swan really a beautiful bird in flight. Very long narrow wings and a neck to match. I had made seven trips over the timber trail. Each trip requiring the time to bake a pan of biscuits. I had been to the cabin and saw that my rising biscuits were starting to settle so I stoked the fire and put them to baking. Next time in I checked. Time for a cup of tea before they were ready to pop out of the pan. (Sig and Leon's term.) One last trip and I didn't take the pack board. I had a long pole to pack this trip. At the lot line between me and Hope I heard swan and looking up I saw three and they turned towards the lake. Getting dark but I could see they were gliding on arched wings. Out they went and circled back losing altitude fast. They intended to land near the beach. Talking as they came down behind the trees. I went down the path to Hope's cabin and very slowly made my way to the beach. Not down country so they had to be up and not very far. Through a spruce I saw one on the water close to the beach and two on the beach. A dark grey this years bird and an adult. I went back over the path and to Spike's cabin where I moved directly down country along the standing brush. They had drifted up and I saw the first one directly out and not a hundred feet away. Then the other two moved into view talking contentedly. The grey one noticeably smaller. The adults with very long buff colored necks and snow white bodies and wings. They moved out as if alarmed a bit but then drifted back in a bit farther up. I moved back and up the trail without disturbing them. Sometime back I had seen a large flock led by a dark grey swan – so – a young one was getting a chance to test his leadership.

Pretty dark when I got back to the cabin. Part of living just has to be coming back to a snug warm cabin after an afternoon in the cold. The thermometer said 7°, still snowing and that same cold breeze up the lake. Those fresh cooked beans tasted extra good and I fried some lunch meat that came down from Farmer's sheep trail on the mt., my usual green stuff, compliments of Babe. Again last trip he brought 5 doz. eggs. I wanted to pay but he said no, you built the chicken house.

October 25 – Partly Cloudy, Breeze dn. & 38°.

Along the trail in the timber a seven foot section of log (about ten inches through on the big end), leaning against a tree. Fred Cowgill had placed it there more than twelve years ago. I thumped it with my walking stick. Solid, I would come back to Farmer's landing with the canoe. Bring saw and pack board and pack it out.

Past two when I reached the cabin and just in time. The world turned grey and it rained on all sides. Only an Oct. shower and had nearly stopped by the time I had finished my sandwich. The log, (cut in half) made a fair load coming down grade to the lake. Along the trail I saw several eight to 10 inch dead spruce. Tall and straight real good wood. Bucked in lengths and packed to the lake shore before deep snow comes I could haul them in with the sled.

October 28 – Partly Cloudy, Calm & 23°.

I had the camera and scope along. I wanted to go down the Chilikadrotna as far as trap rock (a big erratic on top of a gravel knoll. Two steel traps have lain on it all these years since I was first there.) for from the rock you have a clear view of the low country. I had never been there this late in the season. But first I would check on the Oregonians camp. The nice old couple who took long hikes every day and their talkative son who took still longer hikes. They came from a beautiful state and the coast country with much wilderness. Around the last point and down along the beach. Their tent was gone and had been for weeks but there set the egg shaped sheet metal heater with a few lengths of stove pipe beside it. I came into the beach and went to investigate. Three gas can boxes of odds and ends that they didn't want to take back or didn't have room for. Spruce branches, firewood and big rocks lay everywhere. They had packed much gravel from the beach to anchor the wall of the GI pyramid tent. My nice little clump of spruce on the beach where I had camped two days waiting to cross to Arlen's cabin was a mess. The man had a chainsaw and just sawed the heart out of it. Cut a hole through six feet wide and put a pole across seven feet up. A meat pole for his caribou. The branches lay where they fell. Nylon cord in bits and pieces tied to everything. A knife had been used to hasten the chore of getting away. They may have taken long hikes for exercise but not to go to the bathroom. Toilet paper scattered from the tent back fifty yds. They had been there a long time and that heater required considerable wood to heat the big tent. Many spruce had been cut and not dead spruce. A few boughs tossed over the fresh stumps to hide them and the rest where they fell. Not particular about cutting close to the ground or using the tops. It had taken me three hrs. to paddle down and I had arrived at 12 noon. I had two fires going on the beach and worked nearly two hours before I called it good enough. I would go no farther today. I thought of taking the stove and pipe down to Frank Bell's old cabin[97] but it is in such bad shape the stove would soon rust out. I would haul it back and put it in O'Connel's cabin.[98] No stove for heat there. Some stew pans and other kitchen gear I would put in Spike or Hope's cabin. A thin foam rubber mattress could go there too. I loaded up and headed for Arlen's cabin. A big party had been there. The first thing I noticed when I walked up the path was that the roof covering had blown off again. Two courses of paper on the up country side and one on the other. Under the table 10 lbs. of

[97] Frank Bell's cabin on the upper Chilikadrotna River was used as a line cabin for trapping in the 1960s and early 70s.

[98] O'Connel's cabin, a variant of the Lewis Vanderpool cabin on the south side of the lower Emerson Creek. A hunting camp built by Lewis "Buster" Vanderpool in early 1960s.

potatoes that had frozen and now running black juice out onto the floor. Moldy bread and cheese on the table. The place left as if they had just gone down to the lake and would be right back. Evidence of a squirrel being in and I searched for a hole. Out back at the left corner the claw marks of a bear four feet above the ground. The building covered with _" insulating board with a tar surface on each side. Mr. bear had gone right through that but there was a lot of junk inside and I doubt that he had gone in. The paper blown off still in fair shape and I rolled it up and put it inside. I took an old gas can box apart and plugged the hole so the squirrels couldn't get in. Picked up some litter about the place and decided it was time I was paddling. I set the scope up on the beach for a quick look for sheep or caribou over on the high ridge towards the lick but saw none. I headed up on a dead calm lake and the sun getting low. My route would take me past the four empty jet fuel drums and I had brought two five gallon cans along plus a one gallon with the end out to pour with. Each drum had more than two gallons remaining and I ended up with 10 gallons of "Jet fuel B." Now if I had 10 gallons of stove oil to mix with it I would have lantern fuel from here on. By now I had a pretty sizable load and headed on up. A disturbance in the water ahead and as I got near a big fish rolled twice. A big red I do believe and the first one I saw roll this fall. This was the poorest year ever for reds at Twin Lakes. I paddled and followed rising bubbles. The water shallow and I saw two big fish and felt sure they were red salmon. Halfway up the lake and I heard a Super Cub and saw one on wheels coming from the low country and Turquoise. He came on up and gave me a high fly by and I knew what he was thinking. That guy has got a moose in that canoe. That big egg shaped stove laying on its side would look like a moose hide rolled up. He went on up the upper lake and in due time I heard him coming back along Falls Mt. A tour of the big timber patch at Emerson Creek and then here he came head on. This time he was going to see. He came plenty close enough and then headed on down and back Turquoise way. The sun had set and the light was leaving the peaks before I got to the stream. That big moon came out from behind Crag Mt. I lined her through and then stopped at the mouth of Emerson to deliver the stove. I hope the boys will make good use of it. Quarter till six when I left the beach and the moon climbing the slope of Cowgill Mt. The evening star was bright over Low Pass. This was a nice evening to paddle. I could see the snow on Hope Creek flat and used that as a guide to my beach. I was only a couple hundred yds. out when I caught sight of my cabin. Everything squared away and supper over by nine o'clock – my writing done by ten. Clear and calm (a beautiful night) and 22°.

October 31 – Overcast, Lt. Breeze up & 25°.

Last night when I turned in the full moon was out in force – very white as it is in the dead of winter. I expected it to be about 10° this morning and was surprised to see it 25°.

Dishes done and the up lake breeze had calmed and now it was down the lake. Later, a spot of sun down country and soon the overcast was clearing out. This would be the day to climb to the bear den above the cottonwoods. I didn't like to but I would wear

my Canadian pacs. Not cold enough for the felt liners but they gave me more room than the snug fitting L.L. Beans. I had been having a little trouble with the little toe of my left foot. It was sore and side pressure when traveling along a mt. slope made it rather painful. I had soaked it in hot water – doctored it with salve and sometimes I thought it was better only to have it flare up again. Let it hurt I would climb anyway This would be a climbing day so I loaded my gear on the Japanese pack frame. Good to have both hands free and a good walking staff. The breeze was just right as I paddled across. I would climb to the left of the big rock face and then travel into the wind along the slope to the canyon and the den on the far side.

November 1 – Snowing, Calm & 30°.

Pretty dark when I looked out – only a trace of snow came during the night but it was snowing lightly. It was good that I had climbed the mt. yesterday. It would have been a chore today.

After my spuds, bacon & egg, I lugged in the full five gallon can of honey – that had stood under an outside table since Babe brought it. Sugared and solid, it would take some doing to get it warm to the top. First I blocked it up clear of the stove top but soon decided that would be very slow so I went to Spike' cabin for Jim Shake's big dish pan. The can in and filled with water. Something like a bean cooking day – tend the fire and do odd jobs about the cabin. This would be a spoon sanding and finishing day. It takes a heap of sanding to get a good smooth finish and so I sanded first one and then another a few times around. The snow fall increased and began to pile up. Solid grey as if it could snow forever. By noon I had the spoons ready for the super satin Flecto. Lunch past and the spoons drying near the stove. I made an improvement on the Jap. pack frame for packing my 400 mm lens. A 4 ½" dia. can 4" deep mounted to the right of center. Just big enough to set the lens in (big end down). A strap at the top to hold it secure. Mounted separately from the camera and tripod I can use them without disturbing the lens.

By now the can was warm halfway to the top. Full to the top and soft to the touch. I would poke a clean stick down through and strike oil. It was a good idea but I hadn't anticipated pressure from below. Up and down a couple times with the stick – it was loosening up. Then clear honey appeared and I had no room for the excess. Over the top and down the side into the water. The top had been damaged in shipping and the cap refused to screw on. I was pretty busy salvaging honey as it came out. A finger licking good time and thankful that the pressure was soon equalized. All of my empty jars full and the can went outside to cool again.

November 8 – Overcast, Breeze dn. & 34°.

Slowly it circled down and past my cabin then a turn over the lake and me, then over the

cabin again. Soon it concentrated on me and I paddled on to the spit. A low pass up the beach and down the lake. Another pass and this time a couple scraps of paper drifted down as it started its pass. I wasn't surprised when the door pushed open and a box tumbled down 50 yds. in from shore. A hundred yds. from me and I hurried to pick it up to show them I had found it. A pass going down and the turbo twin otter flew on down the lower lake. The box, about 14 inches square and taped nearly solid with nylon tape. I knew it was film from the Park Service.

Now we would have colder weather again.

My gear packed in and the fire revived, I opened the big box. In the center with wadded newspaper packed tightly around it a second box. A box of 20 rolls of film and on top a letter from Keith Trexler. It read "your letter of 1 October arrived here just last week. Yes, we definitely would like winter footage! It's the one subject we're really lacking. Any wildlife action would be highly desirable. I also remember your ice shots as being really great. All your footage is great – no specific ideas for making them better. We're sending 20 rolls of film via an air drop by OAS I'm sending a copy of this letter to Babe and one with the film. Good luck! Keith."

So – now I have a good supply of film to work with. A total of a bit over 3000 ft. That should last a good long time in winter unless I ask Babe to do some flying in caribou country and perhaps over the proposed park area. After freeze up the moose should move back up the lake. If the snow gets deep the sheep will be on the face of the mt. All kinds of possibilities.

November 14 –Overcast, Calm & 26°.

Today I would do a chore I had been thinking on since last May. At that time I had received a big brown envelope from the Montrose, Iowa, Elementary School. One letter each from the 4th grade teacher and all of her 26 students. At that time I had a bundle of letters to answer. Her sending me 26 letters of questions seemed as if she was trying to get even for something I did or didn't do. She was sorry that she hadn't sent them earlier and I was sorry she had sent them. (period)

Those little people had really worked at writing. Some did a better job of writing than I and others had erased half a page and started over. Many had a half dozen questions and others none. It would hardly be fair to answer only those with questions but to answer 26, yee gods. Finally I decided on one letter to the teacher and class. Give them a run down on this years activities and then on each students sheet of paper answer their individual questions and a little note for those who had no questions. The main letter to the teacher and class amounted to 10 pages (both sides) and then the stack of 26.

The wind picked up and the snow increased. This could be a real Nov. snowstorm. I wrote and wrote and watched the weather. The light began to fail and I lit the candle lantern. It was time for supper when I scribbled the last note to one who wanted to know

what Alaska was like and how I kept warm at night. All through the pile, questions as only 4th graders can ask them. All liked the building of the cabin best but liked the birds and animals too.

So – I will put a new address on that brown package and send it back. The kids, most of them will be 5th graders I hope. A few may have moved or changed school. I'm trusting that the darling teacher will see that each gets his or her letter one way or another for I feel that those little guys put a lot of effort into the writing of them and must think I have forgotten just how much effort it was.

November 28 – Overcast, Breeze dn. & 36°.

The weather was clearing – patches of blue over head. It was like a day in May. Now, just suppose that Babe should try it on a Thanksgiving day. I wouldn't know if the ice was good for the "T craft." I would check that good ice off Carrithers' point. With my ice measuring stick and chisel I went over the snowshoe trail to the point. The ice clear of snow or frost and very slippery. I walked off shore and heard no complaint so I kept going. Out 50 yds. I cut a small hole. Real close to 3 inches of good solid ice. Good enough and I worked back this way a hundred yds. from the beach...About 2 ½ inches of ice out from my beach. If he came I would direct him up to the point.

The ice seemed good enough for travel, I would celebrate by traveling the ice on Thanksgiving day. From the woodshed my homemade ice creepers came out of hiding. Oil drum metal soles with short sheet metal screws going through from the top side. I had just put new bindings on a short time ago. I lashed them on and with binoculars hanging from my neck I headed for Jerre's point. Perfect traction with those extra sharp creepers but nothing under the heels, so I couldn't really stretch out and go. Three fourths of the way over and the ice began to crack. Far enough and I glassed for sheep. None, or any trails in the snow filled washes. I swung back a quarter and headed down country pushed by that nice breeze and how easy it slides over that slick ice. I was glad that I was rough shod and afoot instead of paddling. Down a half and I turned back. It would be time to start my special dinner which would amount to an early supper.

From the cache I had taken down some mixed nuts and some of Mike's fudge. I boiled some spuds, and some cabbage, carrots, and rutabagas. Opened a can of Alberta peaches and a small can of ham (Plumrose). I would have sourdough biscuits and honey. Feed my birds extra good. That young one is a character. If he is here alone he takes all the time in the world to eat his cold hotcake. Sit on my hand and take little nibbles, set and look around and then nibble some more. Dinner can be getting cold or hotcakes burning, he couldn't care less.

It was a pretty good Twin Lakes meal and all done in daylight. The full moon was just getting a good start when I emptied the dish water. I would just tie on my creepers and take a walk to settle my dinner. Against that warm breeze I headed for 1st point. The

moon hazy at best and now and again behind a cloud. To 1st point and not a crack from the ice. How long would it take to walk back. Twenty five minutes is good time paddling. The breeze maybe seven miles per hr. so it helped a bit. Twenty five minutes exactly so it's a toss up, walk or paddle, same difference. 6:30 when I came in the cabin and so ended my activities on Thanksgiving day 1974.

Now at 7:30, that hazy full moon, holding the weather fair, that warm breeze down and 37°.

November 29 – Overcast, Calm & 23°.

Hotcakes for breakfast and today I would take a tour up [to] the Lofstedt's cabin to pick up my groceries. The Matthews[99] would make a list and the price of things they were leaving and I would send them a check. A trace of snow last night or early morning so the ice would be better for travel. I would push my sled which would make walking easier and safer in case of thin ice. Also I could take my ice chisel and snowshoes along.

I was on my way at 10:38 and found the traveling good. Well up the right hand side and I spotted the Super Cub on the strip. I thought it had gone the same day the chopper left but there it was. Had they left it for some strange reason. It was 11:50 when I came to the head of Lofstedt's bay.[100] I appreciated my snowshoes for the short trip to the cabin. Mike's snowshoes still leaning against a spruce and the chainsaw still there. Smoke coming from the cabin chimney. Someone rattling around inside. As I got out of my snowshoes the door opened and there was Mike and his wife and the Cub pilot. (John) "Still here," Mike said, "and getting pretty low on grub. I guess you saw that dressed…porcupine hanging from the eave log." I had but didn't look close. I had noticed the beaver type teeth and figured it for a beaver. "We are eating rabbit now but that porky is next and we just finished most of the lynx cat," he said. "How was the lynx?" I had heard they were good eating. "It was real good, tastes something like pork but no fat." Well, what was the story about still being here. "Can't get out. The [Cessna] 180 came and the snow so sticky he couldn't get off with more than one and the Cub pilots wife had gone back in it. They could have gone on the copter but wasn't expecting to go that day and not ready and he was on flight plan and couldn't wait. Now it is clear every night and socked in every day and the weather between here and there not flyable according to reports."

"A plane down on a trip from Kenai to Port Alsworth. A Bill Johnson[101] in an all white Aeronca Chief. (He is building real close to Babe's between the beach and the runway.) He has been missing for a few days now but the weather so bad they have been unable to fly search missions. The weather has been mild and if unhurt he could be doing pretty good."

---

[99] Mr. and Mrs. Mike Mathews were possibly from the Kenai.

[100] RLP's Lofstedt's Bay, a small cove at the head of upper Twin Lakes near the Lofstedt cabin.

[101] Bill Johnson (1940-1989), a pilot, and carpenter who resided with his family at Port Alsworth. He died when his plane went down in Cook Inlet in 1989.

When it is flyable the Cub pilot will take Mike and his wife over in the Cub (legal for three) and come back for the gear. "Your letters are on the way," Mike said. "They are in the Cub over on the strip ready to take off." As for grub, instead of a lot left over we may have some and we may be down to beg some from you. They did have a large box of chili powder, a large jar of seasoning salt and a full can of black pepper. Out of sugar so we can't make any fudge today and out of flour. The menu for today macaroni and rabbit all cooked in one pot. Burning aviation gas in the gas lantern and doing pretty good.

We watched the weather and it went from a quarter mile to a 500 ft. ceiling but to late to start. When I had a reading of -10° they had a -25° over at the airstrip. That explains the bitter cold I have experienced above the upper lake a time or two. It can get very cold there and a big change no more than a mile down.

We ate on that poor rabbit and had tea to drink. Listened to the news and learned the search planes were still grounded. If the weather was no good tomorrow they would walk down and if it was flyable they would give me a flyby. I paid them for the groceries plus the 4 lbs. of beans they had given me and prepared to head down. They would go with me a stretch to see how the ice was. About five inches at the head of the bay where it had been iced over early. Out farther 3 ½ was about it. Past the first point coming down and the mouth of the bay they headed across to visit Frank Bell's cabin.[102] I followed my sled track under an entirely flyable overcast. That full moon of the 29th would be out tonight. Getting dark and still a few coals in my stove when I arrived. Supper over and that moon so bright I just had to take a little tour down the lake. The ice just starting to complain when I left. Better than a mile down I ran into a sharp breeze and fog coming up. Clouds coming over the mt. from the south to hide the moon. I turned back and soon the ice began to really act up. It is a frightening experience to have a crack come ripping by and see the ice turn wet along the crack and the ice cracking with every step until you get clear of the area. Up and down and across she ripped & tore. I felt more comfortable when I reached my beach. It kept up the disturbance for perhaps a half hr. and then stopped as suddenly as it began. I guess we shall blame it on the moon for now at 7:30 clouds have all but made it solid overcast and the lake ice is quiet. It is calm and 16°.

November 30 – Partly Cloudy, Calm & 26°.

Camera gear, ice chisel, snowshoes, spotting scope, binoculars and my lunch smoke fish and a square of Bakers semi-sweet chocolate.

I had gone nearly a mile when I heard another plane and here came Glen's yellow and blue Stinson on skis. Right down on the ice as he went by. I turned back and headed for the point. He turned and came back skis on the ice but with enough speed to fly. I waved him off and directed him towards the point. Behind the sled I jogged up the lake and directed him on the heavier ice and to stop at Carrithers' point. The ice creaked as

---

[102] Frank Bell's cabin was on the north side of upper Twin Lakes near the head of the lake.

he neared the beach. One ski against the shore ice. "How deep is the water under that outboard ski," he asked. "Oh, not deep," and I chiseled a hole. About six inches, safe enough. He had his wife Pat[103] along. He fished out two sacks. One a yellow mail sack in case they had to air drop my mail. The other a freshly dressed chicken and a cookie can containing a fruitcake like bread with a big square of pumpkin pie in the bottom. We headed down along shore with the sled. Had they found that man Bill Johnson. Glen grinned and said, "Yes, we and he spent the night in the pass." One on one side of the big glacier and one on the other. Johnson had iced up – full power and 65 mph was the best he could do. He made a wrong turn and first thing he knew he bounced off the glacier once and a second time. He lost his ice and was flying again. He landed below (Lake Clark side) the glacier in the pass. Glen got trapped before he reached the glacier and set her down on chest deep snow. There they spent the night. He, his wife and another girl. It was raining and warm so they didn't suffer. Next morning they had visibility and got off and to Lake Clark. How was this Johnson as a pilot, I asked. Oh, he's a good pilot but doesn't use enough common sense. Doesn't know when enough is too much.

I stoked the fire and popped some corn. They had come down from school (mile 95) and had to go back tomorrow. How was everything at Port Alsworth, was Babe & Mary still planning on Hawaii for Xmas. As far as he knew they were. Dad was busy taking care of his three pigs.

December 9 – Clear, Calm & 0°.

This was one of those mornings – clear, calm and zero. It was 9:30 when the sun lighted Spike's peak and 9:50 when the Volcanic Mts. caught the first rays.

Today would be that day to go way down. Pack snowshoes and camera gear and see how the lower end lives. Smoke fish and chocolate in my jacket pocket, a little gas burner in each mitten (not necessary unless I have occasion to use my camera) and I was on my way. The lake ice like walking on concrete. One hr. to the stream and I didn't use my snowshoes for the short stretch of snow there. The bow wave of trout feeding in the smooth quiet running stream. Onto the lower lake and I have never seen it so bad when frozen. Rutted and gutted all the way. Not only the snow but the ice too. As if the wind had blown very hard when it was freezing up. I watched for a wolverine, wolf or fox to be traveling across or along shore. Lake Trout bay was better but only a little until I got near Colclatures cabin. 2 hrs. and 30 min. it had taken from my beach. On the ice out front I set up the scope for a check of Black Mt. and the ridge towards Turquoise. Both looked in good shape for sheep feed but going on down the ridge towards Bonanza Hills the snow cover became solid and the Hills themselves looked to be tough going for the rugged caribou. I couldn't see sheep and I looked close. Where would they be – perhaps behind the ridge and up the canyon past the mineral lick. The sound of a light plane up country and I saw a good looking late

[103] Patricia Elliott Alsworth, was graduated from Victory High School in Palmer and attended Lazy Mountain Bible College with her future husband Glen Alsworth in 1972-1974.

model Cessna with tricycle gear on skis. Flying with it a red and white Super Cub. Headed towards Whitefish Lake[104] and I suspect they would find caribou there. On my snowshoes for two times around Arlen's cabin to check for damage by varmints. It was still as I had left it after last patching. I scooped up my gear on the lake and headed on to a high knoll below the lake and from there over to the Chilikadrotna and the survey rock for a closer look at the mt. and the ridge. The sun had already set on the thick timber country at the foot of the ridge. Another plane and this one flying low over the timber looking for moose and if he saw one he would be sure to circle for a second look but soon he came back up, a blue and yellow Piper flying low and slow. I was sure he would see me traveling on the solid white but he showed no indication that he did. In about ten minutes on his present course, he would pass my cabin – for me it would take a good three hrs.

My first time at the head of the river this late in the season and I was surprised how low the water level was. Still open and a hundred yds. out into the lake. From high ground I checked again and good. No sign of sheep or caribou. Moose of course would be in the timber brush patches and I didn't have the extra hr. needed to go there. Twenty five till two when I packed up for the return journey and I found the left side coming up worse than the left going down. The snow wind packed, drifted and frozen. Much to rough for a landing on skis. In one area ice chunks five or six inches thick standing at all angles and frozen fast. What was the condition to bring that about? As if one heavy flow of ice had traveled down the open lake and collided with ice covering the lower end.

A cool breeze at my back as I trudged the five miles, dodging this way and that to avoid slick ice and patches of breakable crust. Well up and looking up Emerson valley. The sun light was leaving the peaks but the one at the head of the valley was lighted to its very base. I was tempted to set up the camera for a time lapse of the shadow climbing but decided I had better keep moving. It was good that I did for the light on the mt. just turned pale and went out as the light left its neighbors. Evidently it is line of sight from the base of the mt. to the horizon and the setting sun. 3:15 was the time of sun set. One hr. fifty five minutes to travel the length of the lower lake and five minutes along the stream. Three thirty when I stepped out onto that perfect walking surface of the upper lake. My shoulders getting a bit weary from the pack. My legs beginning to feel the effect too. I would make it in one hr. regardless of the miles traveled and I lengthened my stride. 20 min. to Low Pass another twenty saw me opposite Gold Mt.[105] and fifteen more to my beach. 55 minutes equal to a hurry up trip paddling the canoe.

I had put in two sticks of wood and loaded the stove with sawdust and chips before I left. Still portions of the two left and good coals for a new start. 2° the thermometer read. It had been a perfect day for the trip. No game, all I saw was fox tracks. Game, I have more across the lake than anywhere I know of. Now I will be content to concentrate on the upper lake area.

Now at seven, clear, calm and a very surprising 13°.

[104] Whitefish Lake, a large non-glacial lake about 30 miles NW of the Twin Lakes in the Kuskokwim watershed; Łih Vena is the Dena'ina word for "whitefish lake."

[105] RLP's Gold Mountain lies on the south side of upper Twin Lakes just east of Low Pass.

December 11 – Partly Cloudy, Lt. Breeze dn. & 28°.

No airplanes at Lofstedt's, no sign of life up country so I headed back over the trail a quarter before dropping lower and into the heavy timber. There, and I passed it once before – a sawed stump and just one – very old maybe 30 or 50 years. What was the history on that cutting. Who cut it and what was the occasion. A long way from the beach and in heavy timber. What was the game situation at that time? No sign of moose so I angled down and traveled the lake ice to the sled. Something strange in the clear ice along shore. Countless strings of air bubbles frozen in the ice from top to bottom. As if air bubbles (some large, some small) were streaming up from the bottom. As the ice went down it surrounded them leaving long strings of pearls from the surface down. No where else have I seen this.

December 19 – Partly Cloudy, Calm & 0°.

The visibility improved rapidly and I rushed around for fear Babe with his daylight savings time might come and catch me eating hotcakes. I got my outgoing mail ready and wrote an extra letter. One to Dick Weiser on Kodiak.[106] I had never written to him since he and Randy finished their cabin, hunted one day and flew away. I wanted him to know that his cabin is still dry and snug, waiting for him to come use it. Dick always took pride in his ability as a hiker. He believed he could equal Herb Wright[107] and Herb was a champion. In my letter I told him Twin Lakes is still waiting to see the man who can out walk Herb Wright and me.

December 21 – Partly Cloudy, Calm & -18°.

It was all cut and dried. If the shortest of the short days was a bad one, (non flyable) I would (in respect for the bears system of spending the winter) hibernate – sleep the clock around and fast for 24 hrs. If it was cold I would keep enough fire to prevent freezing of my perishables.

When I woke up the sky appeared clear so my plan was off. The temp. had dropped steadily and the moon and stars were bright at 10:30. I watched for the sun to light Spike's peak but no sign of it. Then a high thin overcast began to appear and finally a mirage appeared along the mts. of the lower lake. The trees and landscape distorted.

[106] Erhardt "Dick" Weiser was a Kodiak friend of RLP who began to build a cabin about 100 yards east of Spikes cabin in the early 1970's but never finished it.

[107] Herb Wright was a friend of RLP who in 1960 made the first attempt to claim the land on which RLP ultimately built his cabin in 1968. Wright never built his cabin because he became terminally ill. Wright's sheep hunting camp was located off lower Twin Lakes near the Vanderpool cabin.

Warm air was moving in. The last time I had seen this happen I was at the lower end of the lower lake. The Bonanza Hills were so distorted that they looked unnatural. Now my thermometer began to rise even though it was dead calm. I put water on to heat for a bath and laundry. Start the down grade clean. The temp. came up to -10° and finally 0°.

I had wanted to visit Beech Creek and on down that side a ways – today would be a good day. By now it was overcast and too dark for filming. Binoculars, walking staff and snowshoes would go. The temp. still climbing as I left my beach. Opposite Low Pass I picked up a side wind coming down from the pass. I was headed for Emerson but made a sharp bend for the bend of the beach down country from the gravel banks. I intended to come back by way of Emerson Creek. It was snowshoes from the time I hit the beach and I would be on them for a few hrs. I traveled the high bank along Beech Creek timber for a good view of moose feeding area. Not a track. On up towards the gorge I crossed and headed down country for Dry Creek[108] (next creek down and always dry). The snow wind packed in places and easy going. Other areas soft and slow. Ptarmigan tracks near the willow brush. Past Dry Creek I saw old moose tracks. Nearly snowed under and made during and soon after the heavy snows. I would angle towards the lake and my high lookout knoll, cross the lake and tour Emerson Creek timber to my snowshoe trail there. Moose tracks! – two of them and the freshest I had seen for some time. A cow and calf had left the Dry Creek brush and headed down country. Along their feeding trail willow leaves on the snow were dusted with new snow – droppings frozen hard and beds icy. A few days old but tracks have way of freshening up fast if you find the moose. I would follow a while and see where they went. Typical of a feeding moose, they wandered around but the trend was down. Sunlight hit the mts. up and down and the high ridge towards Turquoise [Lake] got the treatment, a pretty sight. The light yellow from a very low sun. It was getting late and I had a long ways to go. Till now I hadn't noticed any great amount of wind coming down. I went nearly to the pass that leads to the inside passage of the Volcanic Mts. before I turned off and headed for the lower lake. No more moose tracks but the trail of what appeared to be a land otter in the soft snow. Just a smooth trench where he had slid along. I had glassed the country from the slope of the mt. so didn't climb my look out knoll though I passed at the base of it.

Now I knew what I was up against. The wind was strong down the lake. Enough drifted snow to make it tough walking and packing snowshoes which have considerable wind resistance. More than a mile to the stream and then snowshoes to the upper lake. A nice flock of ptarmigan flew from along the stream. The upper lake was not a purty sight. Snow was blowing and so much of it that it appeared very much like vapor during a cold day before freeze up. Three miles of that to face without a break wasn't to my liking. When I hit the upper lake I didn't remove my snowshoes but headed for the cottonwoods near O'Connel's cabin. Crossed the creek flat and into the woods again. I had thought of this when I made the snowshoe trail to Emerson. I angled up the slope until I hit it. What a pleasure to travel a well packed trail – the wind in the trees over head and me cozy warm. It was getting quite dark and would be too dark to follow the trail by the time I reached

---

[108] RLP's Dry Creek is on the south side of lower Twin Lakes just west of Beech Creek.

Falls Creek. If I didn't miss the junction I would drop down to Jerre's cabin. Something nice about snowshoeing a broken trail in the heavy timber with darkness closing down on you. A spruce grouse flushed from a tree along the trail and further a second one. I would have expected them to sit tight in the near darkness. The trail very dim by the time I walked out onto the lake ice. I could still see Hope Creek gorge and headed for it. The wind not quite so strong and no snow blowing. 5:15 when I reached the cabin, temp. 26° and coals in the stove. It had been a good day. I feel sure there is a cow and calf moose feeding an area between where I left their tracks and the big opening by the Pyramid Mt.[109]

Supper over and dishes done. My journal up to date. The wind is still strong in the spruce – the moon visible and the temp. 26°.

By now I suspect Babe and Mary are somewhere over the blue Pacific or among the palm trees on the island of Oahu.

By this date we have gained three minutes in the evening sunsets and still have three to lose on sunrises – so – this is the shortest day of 1974.

December 22 –Partly Cloudy, Calm & 27°.

I discovered that I had a problem. Water was leaking in on the eave log and running down the inside. It appeared that either there was condensation between or a leak in the polyethylene and water is running down between it and the tar paper...I had tarred a patch of roofing paper...The paper warmed and neatly folded to make a good thick patch...my patch had hooked in the hole and torn it bigger. I soon had one cured only to have it start...to the left. This was a leaker for sure and a tough one to get at...A tarred patch was out of the question. How about some okum with tar. It went in solid and the hole in the dike was plugged. I watched for more but none dared to appear. Some jet fuel B to clean the tar from whatever needed cleaning. Soap and water to finish the job and I was soon ready for Christmas company. It would have been a sad state of affairs to have water running down the wall of this most famous of the famous cabins in Alaska.

December 23 – Overcast, Calm & 14°.

After breakfast I went for my days water supply. Coming up the path with my two buckets when I really got a jolt. About an eight foot section of the side of the cabin looked like a waterfall after freeze up. I had stopped the leaks on the inside and now it had run down on the outside. What a mess and something would have to be done. It was caused by heat from the stove warming the roof on both sides of the ridge. Water had come to the eave over hang but could go no farther because of ice build up the thickness of the moss.

---

[109] RLP's Pyramid Mountain is on south side of lower Twin Lakes near the Gatano cabin.

I fueled and fired up the little Coleman single burner stove. Made a bail to hang it by, drove some nails and bent hooks to hang it under the eave along the offending section. Soon I could feel the moss above the roof covering getting soft but very little water came to the edge. On a length of Jerre's no. 9 wire I bent a tight loop to prevent gouging the polyethylene and ran it up between it and the moss. I could get to the eave log but there it hesitated. A little prodding and poking and it broke through and out came the water in a steady stream. Soon it had stopped dripping at the wall. At three places I warmed the over hang but nearly all of the water had leaked out of the first opening. While the little Coleman did its work I chipped the ice from the logs and ran some hot water down to get what was left. The ram rod stays in place so next time if ever all I have to do is hang the stove or gas lantern under the eave to get that warm water started through.

December 24 – Overcast, Calm & 20°.

I did a bit of reading of magazines collected during the summer and went through half of my Dec. journal. Pretty tame reading now and I wonder how it will be in a dozen years from now. It would be interesting to reread from April 29 and estimate the miles I have covered since that date. 1,500 would be a real conservative estimate in my mind and I wonder how close I am.

Recently I have been thinking of a good hike on snowshoes and only one thing holds me back and that is perishables freezing in my cabin while I am away. Pack my Eddie Bauer sleeping bag, a tarp, axe and some grub and head for Port Alsworth. I could make it in two days easy enough. Go through Low Pass and down the Kijik to Lachbuna Lake and from the lower end take a sharp left and through a pass to the head of Portage Creek. Down the creek to the lake and travel the lake to Tanalian point[110] and Babe's bay [Hardenburg Bay]. It would be a good exercise and to return over a broken trail would be a breeze. It would be done after mid Feb. when the days are longer and less chance of things freezing here.

December 25 – Partly Cloudy, Calm & 2°.

And a Merry Christmas to you too. The sky appeared clear in the early morning light but it wasn't long before a high thin overcast made itself known. The temp. dropped to 0° as sunrise came near. Spike's peak caught the first rays at 9:45 my time, but it didn't last. The light turned pale and died. A low overcast began to form.

After getting my water supply and putting a tub full on the stove for a bath and to wash my bed tarp, I buckled on my snowshoes and laid out a neat little airstrip on the

---

[110] Tanalian Point was the original name of the location now called Port Alsworth (1950); it was also known as Walker's Camp and Tanalian, originally it was a small Euroamerican–Dena'ina hamlet dating from about 1909. The Dena'ina word Tanilen Vetnu, means "flows into water stream."

solid white to make depth perception easier. Six round trips 220 yds. long. That would test the skill of whoever came.

My Christmas dinner bird had come in to hang by the stove pipe again. To cook it all at one time I would need a bigger kettle – so I went up to the point for a good big aluminum kettle that Jim Shake had left. The bird thawed and limber I proceeded to dismember it. Two legs, two wings, neck, breast and back. As I worked forward I ran into a packet of chicken feed and it was fortunate that I found it. The kettle scoured and rinsed standing by. First I would brown the pieces a bit in bacon grease using my big cast iron skillet. First I salted & peppered and rubbed them with flour. The grease hot, I arranged them in the skillet and put the lid on. By now my bed tarp was taking advantage of the cooking fire. Out of the frying pan into the kettle of hot water, seasoned with various spices and fresh onion. The operation was going according to plan when I discovered that my dish rag was missing. Perhaps I had thrown it out with the last water but I failed to find it. It couldn't have gone far and I was beginning to think it was boiling with the chicken when I discovered it under foot.

Dinner would be served about three thirty if the chicken was tender and being small it probably would be. I saved the drippings from the frying for gravy. I had some raspberry jello setting up in my 0° cooler on the table outside. The chicken well along I added some egg noodles and later some dumplings. A chunk of carrot would be my green stuff. Dinner was served at 3:15 – the chicken done enough but required a little more salt. Mashed potatoes and brown gravy, noodles & dumplings. Sourdough biscuits and honey. Jello and hot chocolate later. I did away with a drumstick, thigh and two wings. A couple helpings of noodles and three dumplings. By the time I had finished I was uncomfortable. My birds knew it was Christmas and came for many helpings of hotcake. The young one is beginning to fit in now and the old ones accepting him.

Dishes done by a quarter past four. I would take a walk to settle my dinner. On with my tin pants, jacket and big wool shawl. I would go down the lake a stretch. The temp. 6° and clearing – the moon would be out soon. Dead calm, a good evening for a walk and I kept going. At the beach of Emerson Creek flat I turned back. The moon big and hazy. No problem to follow my trail. I was back by six and feeling much better. Fingers too stiff to write without a good warming. Now at 7:15, a light breeze up the lake, snowing lightly. The moon not as bright and the temp. up 4° to a +10°. Christmas of 1974 nearly past. Will it be an easy trail to the next one?

December 26 – Partly Cloudy, Breeze up & -2°.

The sun light had struck the peaks and started down the ridges but it was weak and soon faded. The wind picked up and the temp. started down. By noon it was a -10° with a chill factor maybe 40 below. No day for joy walking on the lake. I had more (only a few) letters to write and I would be caught up. Then there was the roll of maps covering the proposed Lake Clark National Park to study and wonder what some other areas of the park must

be like. It would be great sport with a little float plane to tour it and stop at all the good sized lakes for a day or two.

More studying of my flying material and correcting of my December journal. Before I realized it possible it was getting dark. A few items to get down from the cache and a couple lengths of wood to saw and split – keep a small deposit going into my wood bank. This wasn't a day heavy on the use of water and I would have plenty to carry me over but just to keep in practice I opened the water hole for one bucket. Down on the lake I could hear very sharp reports of the ice expanding in the cold.

Christmas leftovers for supper, chicken and noodles along with the fresh beans I had cooked and didn't sample yesterday.

A blast of fog as I opened the door to go empty my dish water and I knew it was getting colder still. The moon only two days till full boldly boring its way through the thin overcast. Light snow pelted me in the face. A thermometer check had it at a -15°. Cold weather is to be expected for winter is officially here.

December 27 – Clear, Calm & -36°.

Today I would go down country. I wanted to get the low sun traveling the ridge to the south. I dressed warm and tucked a little stove in each Air Force mitten and then I heard a plane. Who would be flying -36° weather. It came over the Volcanic Mts. and up the lake. A [Cessna] 180 by the sound of it. Closer and I could see red & white and blue – Voight![111] and he circled twice before touching down. His son David with him. He slid in close and shut her off. Merry Christmas was his greeting. "I'm sorry to be late but I couldn't get this silly thing started yesterday." Lots of cargo. Frozen stuff, fresh stuff, dry stuff, packages, and mail, lots of it. We lugged the stuff to the cabin. Would they eat some popcorn. "Oh don't bother," but it was no bother and I stoked the fire to super hot. I sorted mail and popped corn. "Now don't pop more this will do us." But I kept popping and the big mixing bowl didn't seem to fill. How was everything at the ranch. "Oh fine. Babe and Mary got away on schedule. Babe was so anxious to get going that he hardly had time to give me instructions on caring for the goats, chickens, & pigs (3). Mary was the same – like two little kids going on a picnic. They climbed in the 180 and were gone. Polar Airways is making money now, boy. Got another [Aero] Commander and fly two twin Pipers plus a Cessna 206. That run to Valdez is really paying off."

We had put the motor cover on the [Cessna] 180. A flashy red custom made job that can be put on while wearing mittens. Loops of heavy cord and big wooden toggles to complete the job. No caribou in sight but he (Voight) had bagged a tough old bull moose who had been in many battles – ribs that had been broken and healed. Old wounds in a hind quarter and he wasn't fat. Bee had got one too out of a bunch of seven.

---

[111] Voight Clum, aircraft mechanic and Alsworth son- in-law is married to Margaret "Sis" Alsworth, lives in Anchorage; David Clum was his 8-year old son.

CHAPTER TWO – 1975

FLIGHT AND TRAGEDY

January 7 – Clear, Calm & -35°.

After supper and doing dishes when I heard a rattling on the gas can cabinet. With the flashlight I checked and there sat another red backed mouse but he wasn't welded to the can. I don't like those little guys to suffer while trying to get something to eat. I took it down. Tomorrow I will pour hot water over one of the little cans of caribou grease. Take it out in cake form and put it where they can work on it.

The days of the bright moon are past and the next one about the 25th of January No doubt there will be a warming trend before then. Let it stay at least -20 below and there will be no build up of new snow on the mt.

Now at 7:40, clear, calm and -35°.

January 8 – Clear, Calm & -35°.

Another beautiful morning. This makes six days in succession without a trace of a cloud in the sky. This is ideal winter weather. How long can it last. Yesterday evening as I crossed the lake, snow was curling from the ridge down country from Spike's peak.[1] Blowing a fair breeze up there but on the lake dead calm.

Breakfast over and my hungry birds fed I made ready to go get my cable release and to check on my little band of rams. For some time now I have been expecting to see ravens and magpies concentrating in some area low on the mt. That would be the sign that mr. wolverine had run a sheep down and into deep snow for a kill. What is the wolverine feeding on at this time – I fail to see more than a track now and again.

I have made that run up the mt. through the cottonwoods so often that I have a perfect trail. Frozen hard and I wondered if I could travel it without snowshoes so I left them off but after breaking through just a few places I put them on. The trail must be very good before it is less tiring to travel without snowshoes than with them.

[1] RLP's Spike's peak, a 6,163 ft. mountain on north side of upper Twin Lakes.

I was still a hundred yards from were I had parked my gear when I climbed into sun light. The sun just peeking over Cowgill Mt. Would I find the cable release where I was sure it would be? It was laying in the trail lightly dusted with frost. A good two miles each way and half of it on the mt. just for a little piece of equipment weighing no more than one ounce, but in two hrs. time I could have it back doing its job and to order a new one and get it here would take two months or more. I could count four ewes where the rams were yesterday and no sign of the rams. Evidently I had gone too far yesterday and they didn't approve. The sun was bright and warm and I hated to go down into the cold shadow again. In case I climbed high again I could use a better route so scouted one out and climbed a couple hundred yards to clear brush line and a more gentle slope. Ptarmigan tracks everywhere and yesterday I had seen a nice little flock on the mt.

I had thought of going down country if I got back from my search in time so headed down. Again it seemed cold on the lake and I was surprised to find it a tropical -25° when I reached the cabin. It was late for a trip to Emerson Creek but a perfect opportunity to cut some wood, not that I am in need of wood for I have hardly made a dent in the wood bank.

Lunch over and my tools inside to warm while I got a few items down from the cache. Some white flour as well as fine graham flour which I mix two to one for hotcakes (2 white, one graham). A smoke fish came down to warm and be cut into packing chunks to go with my Baker's semi-sweet chocolate. Also a sample of Borden's whipped potatoes and a bag of peanuts (both Xmas gifts).

I headed for the woods across the creek and just past the bend in the beach towards Farmer's property I ran onto a nice bunch of small (6 to 8 inch) dead spruce and soon had a bunch of good poles leaning against the green spruce. Today, instead of making forty dozen trips packing, I would try the sled. I doubted that it would pull easy in the cold and very dry snow but would give it a try. Coming for it and packing a pole I broke trail on the ice. The snow no more than four inches at the most. It dragged heavy empty, what would it be loaded. At the other end I flopped it over and checked the runners. A coating of rough ice and frost on the bottom. With a sharpened stick I cleaned them as best I could and brought back a load. It didn't pull easy and I wouldn't care to drag a load to the lower end. Before going back I took the tea kettle out and ran hot water over them. That did it – no comparison. The second and last load was heavier than the first but pulled no harder. A few poles sawed to round out the pile and I called it a day. The sun had left the peaks and darkness was settling on the wilderness. My feet were starting to get cool and I would be sure to find my pacs iced inside when I removed them.

I found the whipped potatoes good. The package said 4-cup servings but it was no more than ample for one serving after my activities for the day. Now at 7:25, clear, calm and a -31°.

Last evening after writing I thought why wait till tomorrow to get the caribou grease for the red backed mice. I was sorry that one had died in such a tragic manner before I thought of it. I climbed to the cache and came back with a little ration can (2"

deep 3" dia) and poured hot water over the bottom up can. Soon it slid out and I parked it at the corner of the cabin in behind a table leg. Today I noticed that the edge had been nibbled on. Enough there to last those little guys all winter. In this cold it is so hard the camp robbers don't bother. If Milo the weasel comes by it is apt to disappear so I should run a wire through it and anchor it to the table leg.

January 9 – Clear, Calm & -31°.

Today I would follow my trail in past O'Connel's [Vanderpool] cabin and then split off and go farther down country before circling towards Black Mt. and the Emerson benches above the high waterfall. I wanted to learn if the moose had gone farther down or were hanging in the heavy timber below the high timbered benches of the bottom land. Up the first bench and on to the second and much higher. It, I would follow along its edge with a view below. Not much sign of anything but a few rabbits and then moose tracks going down and I made it a cow and calf. I crossed it and continued on towards the high open benches. Near the first steep pitch moose tracks again and not too old and again a pair, large and small. They had spent some time there and I half expected to see them but failed and was soon climbing a scrub poplar point to the benches. The sun was on that country when I left the lake and with glasses I could see many tracks. Very low down for sheep – farther below the high falls than I had seen tracks before. Now I would see who made them. Moose tracks on the high bench too but also the tracks of a wolverine and the further I went the more plentiful until it was just a mess of tracks. I was soon to learn what mr. wolverine is living on these days. He makes the most tracks where the meat is. Now I saw wolf tracks too and I learned the worst. I half expected to find a little red on the snow and a lot of moose hair. Tracks a plenty and on both sides of Emerson [Creek] just above the falls. I eased up to the edge of the high bank over looking the brushy bottom above the falls. There directly below me at the base of the high bank, blood on the snow. There had been a kill alright but what – I couldn't tell without going down. Off came the snowshoes and I slithered down the steep bank. Sheep hair, lots of it. The contents of the stomach and that was all except for some very large wolf droppings here and there. I searched for bones – the lower jaw bones with teeth they always leave but no sign of them. No horns so evidently it was a young sheep. How did this killing come about. I could see tracks of animals running on the far side of the creek. I crossed and climbed. Tracks of two wolves coming down and also the ever present wolverine tracks. No tracks of sheep, so I went back to the kill site and looked around. There, 20 ft. up was where they downed it and from there tracks angling up the high bank. A sheep running coming down followed both on the lower and upper sides by wolf tracks. Bunches of hair on the snow and here a hundred feet from the kill site the marks of an animal sliding along the slope so a wolf had grabbed it here. I climbed out and followed along the high bank. I came to where the sheep had angled down over the side from the top. Wolf tracks there too. A bold trail of tracks from Camp Creek canyon and from the far side I could see many tracks on the far

bank of the canyon. I put on the snowshoes and headed that way. The sun had dropped behind the mts. and a nice breeze was coming down Camp Creek. Now I could see where the sheep had come down the long slope from the point of Black Mt. Tracks four in a bunch eight feet apart. I followed the bold trail towards Camp Creek. Wolf tracks coming my way and running. A trail bold enough to have been made by a moose calf. It is surprising the crust that a big wolf will break. He makes the trail of a heavy animal. At the edge of Camp Creek canyon I found the tracks to be wolverine and I expected another kill site but couldn't see one. I climbed on towards the base of the steep pitch and rough stuff of Black Mt. I came to where sheep had been feeding. If surprised here I suspected they would drop over the edge and on the face of the canyon. Wolf tracks and sheep tracks – I climbed to the top and saw sheep trails towards the steep pitch of Black Mt. I circled to the canyon and down over the side as far as I dared. Three white tailed ptarmigan flushed and sat in the snow. Considerably smaller than the big willow tarmigan. I couldn't see sign of a kill in the canyon so climbed out and circled down country as if going around the point of Black Mt. I wanted to see where the unlucky sheep had come from. Down from the point of the mt. and a bit to low to see the start of it. I came to the tracks of the sheep bounding down. Wolf tracks following so it appeared the wolf had cut this one off from the safety of the mt. – it panicked and headed for the crossing to Falls Mt. at the high falls. I followed the tracks down. Sheep and wolf tracks a few yds. apart. The tracks of the running wolves from Camp Creek were converging with those going down the mt. so I suspect there was some team work there. Where had the wolves gone after the sheep was cleaned up or had the wolverine taken it away from them. He had made more than his share of tracks about the place. All of them long gone and only one lone magpie in a little spruce clump over the point. Hardly enough left for even the little guy who will lead you to a kill.

I circled down country a bit and hit a trail of wolf tracks leaving, single file and I followed for a short distance. Headed towards the lower end or somewhere to lay up and sleep it off and then kill again. I wouldn't be surprised to learn that the moose calf was their next meal.

January 13 – Partial Overcast, Calm & -33°.

That man John Davis[2] asked Babe what he was going to do with two more "T crafts." "Oh, one of my brothers died and left me just enough money for two. The money isn't worth anything so I just brought them."

Everything in a sack and they headed out. "It's warm up high, see those clouds," Babe said. "We went up to 8000 ft. and it was zero there." Here it was -30°. "I'll be back sooner next time," Babe said as he pulled the cover from the engine and told John to fly. "Boy, Dick, this is a good airplane on floats now with that long flat prop. Got her stripped down too. All the electrical gear out – starter, generator, battery, radio, 60 lbs. of junk

[2] John Davis, a Soldotna radio station owner who had a summer cabin at Port Alsworth starting in 1974.

and it really makes a difference and is a safer airplane too. Less chance of trouble and a fire." They took off for home and me to open some of my mail and packages. Nuts, lots of nuts, peanuts in the shell, English walnut meats, hickory nut meats, instant spuds, granola breakfast food (good stuff), peanut brittle by the old master, Hazel Schrepfer.[3] A package of seven Arizona Highways magazines from Rose Nadeau[4] in Maine. (Her gift of the book *Walden* was my start on this wilderness adventure).

Today too a check for $2000.00 from the Park Service for doing what I would have been doing if they hadn't furnished all the free film. I only hope that I get some real nice footage with the last twenty rolls. Patience is the watch word. The sun is climbing higher everyday…Babe said there are bunches of moose down along Lake Clark. Bunches would be nice but I would be happy with just one bunch feeding on the river flat up country and me up on the big slide. The lengthening days give promise of good things to come.

February 3 – Clear, Calm & -15°.

I stayed up past ten o'clock last night and then didn't get it all read (my mail). Tomorrow would be a Twin Lakes holiday (return of the sun). I would finish it then.

During the night I heard a rattling around out front. I had put the caribou grease back in the can and turned it bottom up as the birds were working on it. Now, I heard the can rattling. That would be Milo the weasel. I hadn't seen him since last fall. I got up and flashlight in hand eased over to the door. I pushed the top open a crack and turned on the light. It was Milo sure enough and he stopped to look into the bright light and then back to the battle. The cake of grease was a snug fit and he couldn't get it out so he would take can and all. Only one sticker and that was the wire loop through the cake. He would take the edge of the can in his teeth and pull & yank – run around a table leg one way and then the other. Finally it came out of the can and he settled down to feed. I watched a few minutes and then brought it inside – save some for another day.

That big meal. I had thawed some chicken thighs. Had the can of peaches thawing. Got the box of chicken flavored stove top stuffing mix (compliments of sister Florence[5] a year or two ago). An envelope of whipped instant potatoes. I soon had the chicken frying, the stuffing made and the spuds ready. A few minutes for some chicken gravy and dinner was served about 7 PM. A real good feed 2 chicken thighs, 4 servings of stuffing, 2 of mashed potatoes and all of the gravy, plus raw carrot and a chunk of cheese. A few big halves of cling peaches with my cold porridge. I just plain forgot my old stand by, beans. That was a good meal in honor of a most happy occasion.

Supper dishes done and wood in for the night. My writing done by 9:15. Temp. -22°, clear & calm.

[3] Hazel Schrepfer was a hometown friend of RLP from Primrose, Iowa.

[4] Rose Nadeau (1922-) a friend of Sam Keith and later RLP from Fort Kent, Maine who introduced RLP to Thoreau's *Walden*.

[5] Florence Proenneke (1918-2003), sister of RLP, during WWII she worked for Schaeffer Pen Company, homemaker, who lived on the family place in Primrose, Iowa.

February 4 – Clear, Calm & -13°.

I climbed into sunlight and for no particular reason I climbed higher than I normally do in summer. Finally, high enough and I head across the slide for a view farther up the flat. On the crest and I heard ptarmigan. Looking up the slope and I could hardly believe my eyes. Not two hundred feet above was about a hundred birds strung out across the slide for a distance of a couple hundred feet. Singles, doubles, small groups and some good concentration of a dozen or more. They were enjoying the bright sun. Why they didn't fly I'll never know. Just one of those things that happen but not often. I got out of my pack frame and unbuckled the tripod. Got the camera out of my belly pack and I was soon in business with a full 100 ft. of film. Still they stayed. Some preening their feathers but most just soaking up the sun. I moved a few steps closer and some started to leave on foot heading up country. I still had lots of birds and was making the most of it. I moved still closer and they started to leave. A pretty sight, birds trailing across the slope. The camera ran dry as they went over a rise. Just what I was wanting before they start to change to summer plumage.

This last mail call brought a letter from [Keith] Trexler. He wrote that Bob Belous and John Kauffmann[6] are in Wash. D.C. now editing the film in preparation for the movie. Please send along any more exposed footage as you have the opportunity and we will forward it to them. So – the wheels are turning on the way to the finished product. Now at eight clear, calm and -2°.

February 11 – Clear, Calm & -35°.

I missed my first fire check and then didn't wake up till daylight. The windows had that extra frost and that deathly white cast and I figured it was colder than thirty below. Hotcakes for breakfast and my birds came with frost around their eyes. Sun on Spike's peak at 8:15 and then it had crept down a bit. I watched the temp. and saw it a -36° after the sun was well on its way. Too cold for camera work I would stay home today. A few small odd jobs and I wondered how cold it was up on the hump. I had been to Hope's cabin for a container of salt and saw direct sun light lower than the spruce knoll. I would take my heat gauge and make the climb. I had no more than left the creek bottom when it read 20 below. At first rock a -10° and on the knoll a -3°. The sun had climbed leaving the knoll in the shadow so I climbed an extra hundred feet and into the sun lit area. In the sun a +5°. It was -33 when I left the cabin. I stayed until the sun quit me and headed down. Again, it was colder than 30 below near the lake.

February 12 – Clear, Calm & -45°.

Cabin logs popped during the night – a sure sign that it was pretty cold. This morning

---

[6] John Kauffmann, NPS park planner, writer, active in the Alaska Task Force planning for Gates of the Arctic National Park and Lake Clark National Park and Preserve.

the atmosphere loaded with frost and the landscape appeared a little out of focus. Clouds began to form up country and down (ice fog). I tried to catch the thermometer reading a -50°, but a -48° was the best I could do. I took it down on the lake but it refused to go lower. My birds came loaded with frost, grabbed a bite and took to the timber. I had planned to stay close today but after getting my water supply I decided to hike down the lake trail aways. The packed snow frozen hard.

The sun was on the mts. across and with my bare eyes I saw a dark spot on Falls Mt. and imagined I saw a trail leading up to it from below. I stopped and watched to see if it would move. A rock and an imaginary trail. My gaze swung to Allen Mt. and at the head of a slide and where the outcrops start there was what appeared to be a very small slide. A few trails to it and I wondered if a sheep or two had come down to feed. Then I saw ravens fly and then two dark objects and they had to be larger than a wolverine. Wolves! and I hurried back for the scope. Sure enough blood on the snow and two big wolves feeding. Ravens and a few magpies sitting on the side lines waiting their turn. Trails down the mt. and converging at the kill site. Some team work there. Probably started it on top and one to either side as it bounded down the mt. Some good rough stuff well to each side but nothing it could reach. Down into the deep snow and the end of the trail.

When I reached the bare knoll I could only see one though I hadn't seen the second one leave. First a shot of the mt. with the normal lens and then the 152 on target. The wolf had left the kill site and climbed a few yds. There he stood or moved about with the ravens hovering around. Now and again he made a half hearted rush at them only to return as if guarding some meat. I ran out of film. Boy, this would be something – changing film at colder than 40 below bare handed but it had to be. Again there was a spruce with a very promising bough for a table. Lay my pack frame on top. The garbage bag dark room crackled as if it would shatter when I unrolled it. Hands out of the big mittens and I went at it. I got the film out of the camera and in the can first heat. Back into the mittens for a minute and I started to reload. This would have to be a no hitch deal for I couldn't stand to fight long. Everything clicked just right and I soon slapped the cover on. My fingers stinging from a thousand needles.

Now I saw the second wolf. Darker on the back than the first. Both grey wolves and pretty big. I got them climbing. They were leaving the site and angling up to a big hump of a rock.

I noticed that my light was failing and at first I thought it was the meter. Clouds were moving in and killing the bright sun. Up country it closed in, down an overcast formed. Clouds crossing the lake at a rapid rate and coming from the south. I would break a trail towards the mt. Take only the tripod and camera. I climbed and that warmed me some. My feet had become cold from kneeling in the snow. Tight snowshoe bindings cause cold feet too. When I reached the upper limit of spruce and a good view I saw that one wolf had been back down and was now standing, headed up. Something that looked very much like a good chunk of meat (pinkish cast) lay in the snow in front of him. To my

great surprise he picked it up and continued up the trail to the big rock. There he was on the skyline a minute or two and then moved over the rock out of sight. The ravens were gathered round and I knew he was there. The light went bad and the sun getting lower. The wolf showed a time or two but not enough for a good shot. I could no longer use the 400 because of no light so I packed and headed down the mt. Before I crossed the lake I could see the weather was fairing up though it was still no good for my business. On this side I set up the scope and there was one wolf back down near the kill site and feeding on a chunk of meat. A few minutes later I couldn't spot him and went part way across but with no success in locating him. Bedded down on the rocks he would be hard to pick up.

February 22 – Overcast, Lt. Breeze up & 10°.

While getting my water and opening my roof drain I had a tub of water heating to wash my towels and canvas bunk spread. Have things looking sharp when Babe comes tomorrow (weather permitting). I still haven't put up the fancy sign board that he brought last trip. It is made from a board about eight inches wide and three feet long. The barked edges still intact. On it in black recessed letters "Set your affections on things above, and not on things on earth." A real nice job – finished with clear varnish and the letters black. Doesn't fit or belong in my cabin. I think we had better set our affection on a few things on the earth before we get it so loused up we can't survive on it. He could make a pretty good showing by cleaning up that junky looking place of his.

February 26 – Overcast, Breeze dn. & 30°.

Suddenly the sound of a plane and coming low up the far side of the lake was the little red bird. Very low, not more than 20 or 25 feet above the ice. He [Babe Alsworth] climbed a bit to clear the spruce at Hope Creek, turned and came out over the lake and down. Evidently he saw me headed back for he came over and passed before turning into the wind as if to land. It was badly drifted and that nasty pressure ridge was directly in front of his touch down point. I think he was checking to see if I would wave him off which I certainly did. He cut across and landed on my strip. He made a couple trips packing stuff in and then headed out to meet me. Wearing his red sweater and cow barn rubber boots, picking his way as I had done.

How has your weather been I greeted him. "Not good" he replied. Pass has been closed for a couple weeks. Weather is bad at Iliamna today and it was touch and go... coming this way until he was away from Lake Clark. It had been cold, about 30 below night after night. He says "I think Hawaii would be better than this..." He brought my list of stuff (lots of green stuff), 25 lbs. of beans, 4 dozen eggs, smoke fish and a few other things. Several packages and my letter mail. Not so many this time and I felt relieved,

thinking of all the answering. A short letter and bill from Mary [Alsworth] for past grub flown in which Babe had refused pay for and trips too. I was glad to see it though it totaled up to better than $192.00 dollars. At the end she wrote, "We are dreaming and planning on a move to Hawaii." And instead of her usual "love and prayers, Mary" she ended with Aloha, - that was a switch. Also that BLM had refused her my five acres.[7]

February 28 – Partly Cloudy, Breeze dn. & 27°.

Last night at 1:30 I awoke from a sound sleep with a pain in my abdomen – not too bad but it shouldn't be. I stayed quiet for a few minutes wondering what could have brought this revolting situation to my cabin. I finally got up and it got worse and rapidly. The word appendicitis entered my mind. If that was true I was in deep trouble. I walked the floor and sat at the table looking out at the moon lit night. I wasn't easing up and if anything was getting worse. I could take aspirin for the pain but then I wouldn't know where I was, getting better or worse. I tried to think of anything I might have eaten that could have poisoned me. On my hike I had eaten a couple pieces of smoke fish. One dusted white on one end but they had come out of a paper flour sack. If I was poisoned perhaps some vinegar would help. No thinning it. I took it straight. Time wore on and I wasn't improving. It came 3:30 and I thought of my old boyhood remedy for stomach ache. A raw potato. I peeled a medium sized one and ate it slow chewing it well. In about ten minutes I began to feel better and went to sit on the edge of my bunk. Still too much pain and I waited a few minutes longer. It gradually eased up and when I crawled in at 4 o'clock I felt pretty good. It wasn't long until it was gone and I went to sleep and slept sound until seven. I got up and felt pretty good except for a few butterflies still bouncing about inside. My hotcake batter was ready for mixing. I was soon in business.

The sun was slow in coming to the mts. across and a fair breeze down. I got my water and chopped away an ice buildup below my counter window. I looked for sheep and spotted three head on the edge of the big pasture on Falls Mt. I would stay close today and see what developed. I studied some of my new books and magazines that came on the last plane. I sawed and split some wood to see how it would go. I had felt better but I wasn't suffering.

About eleven when the sun just passed below the notch to the left of Cowgill peak. So near that sun light was on the trees just a short distance away. From there it followed up the ridge and just barely below it to the peak. A more abrupt rise there and it wouldn't clear at 12 noon. I put on the snowshoes and went up towards the point and off shore. Line up the cabin and the peak with the sun above. So close that I didn't change my watch.

I didn't want to eat much so I fixed a small hotcake sandwich with no onion and I

[7] Mary Alsworth filed on a 15 acre Native Allotment over the Proenneke cabin in order to ensure RLP would not be denied use. However, the Bureau of Land Management denied her claim because there was no proof of prior occupancy or use by Mrs. Alsworth.

peeled another small potato. I was feeling a little sore in the mid section but figured it to be expected after the way I felt last night.

The sun was out bright and warm – a good afternoon to take a tour of the point. Take the camera along and maybe see a grouse or ptarmigan. This morning early I had stepped out the door and nearly on a spruce grouse picking gravel. It showed no sign of alarm and finally ran back past me and around the corner of the cabin.

I headed for the cabin log timber. Snow drifts such as I have never seen at Twin Lakes. My old trail buried without a trace. On up the creek trail and into the clear. That was the end of the rabbit tracks. I would see no more until I came back past Spike's cabin. No point in climbing the hump so I cut down through the timber. Snow, just an awful lot of snow. Close to the lake shore and much drifting. Ridges and valleys caused by singles or clusters of spruce. Heading back towards the Weiser cabin when two ptarmigan flew but I couldn't see where they lit and failed to find tracks. At Hope's cabin water dripping from the eave on the sunny side. The first melting by sun alone.

An overcast was forming high and thin. The breeze had picked up during the day. I looked for rabbits as the light began to fail but saw none. That pile of wood ashes behind the woodshed is a drawing card. Yesterday evening while I watched one came to get his daily ration of ashes.

For supper a few beans, a can of V8 juice left from Christmas, my cold porridge and sourdough biscuit. I wouldn't use the Coleman lantern burning 80-87 av[iation] gas. It does give off offensive fumes not noticeable after the first time. Go to bed early and get a good night's rest. Hope it doesn't happen again and be thankful it didn't happen at 40 below. Trouble of a very serious nature could be the result.

March 1 – Partly Cloudy, Calm & 4°.

A good night's sleep (8 to 6:30) – no pain. I felt physically fit but went a little easy on the breakfast. I had no more than finished when a blue Aeronca Sedan flew up the far side and came back low before landing between the mouth of Falls Creek and Jerrie's point. In a few minutes a Cessna (red & white) 170 joined it. And here came a brown Interstate 150 (on the lines of a Cub P.A. 11 but bigger) and finally another Cessna (red, white & black). The spring caribou hunting season was about to start. A big pow wow and a couple cases of gas unloaded. I went about my chores and would cut a hole off shore to check the thickness of the ice this first day of March. I found it to be 33 inches which is about a foot short of other years. That heavy snow cover during the Feb. cold insulated it.

Airplanes were flying back, climbing to clear the high stuff. Down the lake I could hear more and saw a couple in the air. Two started to taxi across the lake towards my place and soon a third one snailed across. The light flashing from the wings as it crippled over the rough going. I suspected they were loaded heavy and decided it was too rough to risk a take off. Coming to my place to use the strip. When I came around the point there was

five airplanes parked out front. A red one had joined the four. They said it was to rough over there and one guy in landing had nearly hit the pressure ridge. Had they done any good? Every plane was loaded with caribou but I suspected not all of each caribou killed. I wished that I had all of the rib cages they had left on the snow. Thousands of caribou on the far side of Turquoise Lake and a couple hundred this side of it and a couple miles this side down on the flat, off of the point of the ridge. Still a long way on foot from here. Had they seen moose. Yes, five head just down below Emerson Creek. That was good news. One old boy ask me if I built the cabin. That was the nicest piece of workmanship on a log cabin that he had ever seen. Someone wanted to know if there was a story about it and me in Alaska. Another guy had the book. Someone had left me a newspaper and a note they said.

The sun was getting low and they had better be flying to make it to Anch. before dark. Three used the strip and two headed right on out past Carrithers' point. Some didn't come back but two circled and climbed before heading for the peaks.

On my outside table a fresh paper and Time magazine. Stu Silvers[8] and Ginger had left it and five gallons of gas that he didn't want to haul back. A note from his buddy Jim Okonek. "Hate to say so but we each got a caribou," he wrote. Had I been here I would have told him "Don't feel badly about it. I shot two moose and 150 tarmigan today." And a business card Bob, Gayle & Robert Curtis,[9] Tikchik Narrows Lodge, Alaska's top fishing. Bob Curtis is the famous fishing guide who flies a Helio Courier. On the back he wrote, "stopped to say hello. We are your nearest neighbor west 170 miles. Will stop again."

A lot of business this first day of March. I had the fire going and water heating for a bath. Got a chunk of steak down from the cache. This had been a good day. Now at eight, it is partly cloudy down country, calm and the temp. 6°. Feeling in top shape after 14 miles.

March 2 – Clear, Calm & -2°.

I was up at 6:30 to greet the new day and this morning, I was on full feed. Spuds, bacon from a fresh slab. One egg and the chicken house is paid for.[10] Eggs $2.00 per doz. and my every morning porridge, (rolled oats, rice & raisins).

The sun caught Spike's peak at about 7:30. The days are building very fast and before long I will be having sunshine at 8 o'clock.

Today I would go down and shoot the five moose. I had it all figured just about where they would be. Chores done and I was away in good time. Sunlight wouldn't catch me until I was near the far side. I would go by way of Jerre's point for the snow cover is

---

[8] Stu Silvers, a hunter from Anchorage who cached aviation gas at Twin Lakes.

[9] Bob and Gayle Curtis, owned the Tikchik Narrows Lodge approximately 150 miles west of Twin Lakes.

[10] RLP had previously built a log chicken coop with a shed roof for Babe Alsworth and was apparently compensated with groceries and flying support from Alsworth for the labor.

smoother from there if you hug the shoreline. Going across I followed the many airplane ski tracks which made for better going. The very sharp report of a high powered rifle when I was about half way. It was the ice of course but such a loud and sharp report I have never heard. Getting over there and I saw something where the airplanes had been parked. A red cast to it and I figured someone had left part of his caribou. I went over and there it was untouched by birds or beast – just what I have always wanted - a rib cage of caribou. Meat had been cut from it – back strap was gone but a bit of neck bone was there. Lots of good short ribs boiled to perfection is my kind of caribou. A big chunk of plastic nearby. I put them both in Jerre's little cabin so the sun wouldn't hit it before I came back.

I picked up the rib cage and headed across. The sun just dropping behind the hills when I reached the cabin at 5:30. The ribs hung in the woodshed and a fire started. Another card near the door. Dept. of Public Safety, Fish and Wildlife Protection. On the back, "Dick 3-2-75, 2 PM, Stopped by checking on caribou hunters. May see you in a couple of weeks," signed Steve. Couldn't make much out of it. That man was a dollar short and a day late. Yesterday he could have had a field day checking caribou hunters.

The temp. was going right on down. Now at 8:30, it is clear, calm and 4°. It may go well below tonight. The low for March of 69 was a -28°.

March 12 – Partly Cloudy, Calm & 24°.

I went down to the mouth of Falls Creek and broke trail to just below rest rock and then found a good crossing for snowshoes and climbed on up on the lower side. At first gravel I poked my snowshoes into the deep snow and climbed on up, thankful for my Bean packs with the rough soles for climbing. Up and clear of the snow I moved away from the edge and parked myself on a bed of creeping juniper. A good bed and I laid back. The sun was warm and I nearly dozed off. Soon clouds hid the sun and it was time to move. Back down through the spruce and both going and coming I saw a rabbit or two. The wind was strong and cold as I crossed. The cabin warm I dug out the book *A Sand County Almanac* by Aldo Leopold. A new book and I can't remember who sent it to me. Very much on the order of Henry David Thoreau's *Walden*.

This morning while I worked inside I heard a spruce grouse fly and wondered if one had come for gravel. A bit later I was going outside for something and nearly stepped on one outside the door. Only one and it stayed for five minutes or more. Later I saw it perched on a spruce bough low down in the spruce near the cache. Babe saw two in front one day when he came. "One of those would find his way into a cooking pot if I was here" he said. Like the Nondalton Natives he would have every bird and animal killed off near his camp. To me it is nice to have wild things about that trust you. My camp robber. Spruce grouse, rabbits, and the cow and calf moose.

March 14 – Clear, Calm & -5°.

When I looked out at six I saw that there had been company last night. One hind leg of caribou was about twenty feet from the pile and the pile looked much smaller.[11] Then I saw wolverine tracks at the clothesline and beyond. While I was getting breakfast I wondered how much damage had been done. If that character had gone to the bathroom on that pile of front and hind legs they would be no good for human consumption. There was no need to hurry so I did my chores and then went for a look see. Everything frozen into one chunk except that hind leg. It was pretty heavy and frozen hard. I could see his toenail marks on the crust made during the scuffle. The pile had been covered with chunks of skin, hair side up. Everyone of those were missing and many wolverine tracks going and coming from the timber. I put on my snowshoes and followed. About fifty feet in from the edge of the brush a big hole in the snow and in it a chunk of skin. Close to the hole a second hole and I could see a tuft of hair at the bottom to one side. With the shovel I prospected. The skin was in the first hole and showing in the second. One had [been] put in and covered and a second one on top. Off a stretch another hole and skin. Another set of tracks leading into the woods. Here and there drag marks with the tracks. Near the trail leading to Spike's cabin and out from my woodshed a couple hundred feet another hole and skin. That guy had been busy while I slept. I packed them all back – covered the pile with them again and covered the works with plastic and loaded it with snow. The second pile (rib cages and necks) covered with the green plastic tarp hadn't been touched. I hoped John[12] would come for his meat today, a perfect flying day.

At my place I discovered that the [Aeronca] Champ didn't take all of the pile of legs and hides. He covered the rest with the plastic. Nothing to keep Mr. Skunk Bear [wolverine] out. At dark I took my old wool pants (much in need of washing) and an old shirt out and draped them over the stack of meat. Will that bluff him, I wonder? When I unpacked I took the smoke fish skins and the hammer to the stump where I have a stack of tails and skins four inches thick for the squirrel. I was very much surprised to find he had climbed and pulled the long nail holding the skins to the stump and packed it away. That wolverine is something else. Perhaps I should leave my lighted cow barn lantern on guard at the meat cache tonight.

March 15 – Partly Cloudy, Calm & -8°.

Another couple chapters from the *Sand County Almanac*. Aldo Leopold and Henry David Thoreau would no doubt have been great friends if they had lived at the same period of time and within walking distance.

---

[11] RLP refers to a pile of caribou meat that was left on the ice under a tarp by meat hunters from the Kenai Peninsula for future pick-up.

[12] Perhaps this was John Davis, a Soldotna based hunter who had a cabin at Port Alsworth. Roger and Tom were other hunters who hunted with Davis but their last names are not known.

The snow showers over for the day by six and I had supper without the light again. About tomorrow evening the sun will set directly behind the Pyramid Mt. along the lower lake. Halfway between the shortest day and the longest.

Another good feed of caribou ribs and beans with a green salad plus sourdoughs, honey and cold porridge for supper. Overcast, calm and 17° now at eight. No plane came for the meat so I hung my stand alone wool pants on my walking staff.

March 20 – Clear, Calm & -33°.

I was a little bit surprised to see the -33° after the fog rolled in the open door. Winter isn't giving up without a battle.

My birds came for breakfast with much frost on their backs. It will soon be nesting time for them but surely not until April and after the mid part.

My chores done and I was preparing to wash my sleeping bag liner. Was it a plane I heard or the tea kettle vibrating as it sometimes does on the hot stove? I lifted it and the noise continued. I looked out and there went that tired looking little [Aeronca] Champion down the left side. That was Roger and he was out to molest the cows again. Another plane and this one taxiing down along the beach. The yellow & black "T craft." Tom crawled out and his passenger (a big man on the other side). Now the [Aeronca] Champ was back and Roger was out cranking it. He had landed in the very rough crust nearly a hundred yds from the end of the runway and of course the engine stopped. He had his wife with him. Now that they have their foot in the door, there is no hesitation – head for the cabin and coffee. Everybody cold except Tom who has plenty of padding and dressed for the trip. "How cold in Kenai" I asked. "18° and up high coming over a -10°. A low is due to move in over there tomorrow." They were laughing at the effort of Tom's passenger getting into that little airplane at Kenai. He tried it rear end first, feet first and a combination of both before he made it. He says, "you know I think a man could run just as hard as he could and couldn't make it into that thing the first try." John was planning to come tomorrow for his meat if he could find an airplane. The Cub had required a complete new landing gear which costs right at $500.00. His caribou meat will be higher than Japanese prime beef at $17.00 per pound.

Finally they got warmed up and Tom's man says, "Let's go shoot some caribou." That did it – they filed out and gassing up and the bathroom got about equal time. It was still -25° when they took off and headed down country. Frost was starting to form in the clear air and soon it was falling like rain. A pretty sight against the light of the bright sun.

The planes came back and landed from the point on down. What would they do when they discovered me not at home. Everybody out and headed for the cabin. Inside and the door closed. I glassed the mts. and spotted six head of ewes and lambs on Falls mt. About two thirds of the way up and down and to the left of the bear den. I climbed

on not intending to try for pictures as it was still frosty and the sun getting around to the west and behind them. I came to the end of my snowshoe trail and took off my snowshoes. I would climb a bit for a better look. Above brush line and in the clear. The airplanes still roosted alone. Now I have something going. Running a rest stop for non-fair chase pregnant cow killing airplane drivers. Enjoying my hospitality and killing my actors. I suspect the traffic will be heavy until the end of the month now. April will find that no hunting (shooting) the day you fly in effect and they would rather stay home than camp out over night. I climbed on and before I stopped I was looking across at the sheep on my elevation. With my glasses the view didn't look too bad and it might make a fair shot. Should I or shouldn't I. After climbing so high I would give it a go. The airplanes had started and taxied up to the point so they were loaded heavy with meat. Down along the beach and they used my strip for the final lift off. Down the lake and back up climbing slowly. So much frost I couldn't see the high peaks but they would before they got there. A couple runs of the sheep and I packed for heading down. It was slow going wearing the Canadian pacs which are big, loose and not a rough sole. It had been very cold up there with a sharp breeze out of the southwest.

Down the creek trail and across to find a couple small cans of juice, three candy bars and a cinnamon roll on my table. A down payment for next trip.

It was -4° instead of +4° as the sun neared the mts. this evening. It could get colder than -35° if the low doesn't interfere. After supper I prepared another kettle of beans and mixed my hotcake batter for morning. Now at nine, a half moon, clear, calm and -28°.

March 21 – Clear, Calm & -36°.

At timberline and bare gravel I left my snowshoes and wool lined pants. I would be warm enough climbing. I followed my route of yesterday until I came to a big rough looking rock face that looked as big as a mt. itself. Before I had always gone around it but this time I searched for a route up through and had solid climbing instead of loose fine stuff. On top of the rock face and only a short haul to the bear den. To get down to it I would have to go down over a snow cornice and this I didn't want to do. I could see from a hundred feet that it was plugged tight. I climbed on up the point to find real good traveling on the big pasture, the snow had been swept clear for the most part and what there was, was hard packed. I started up along the edge and the farther I went the more I wanted to climb to Falls peak where I had never been. An easy gradual climb. What loose rock there is was filled in with snow and frozen solid. I moved to the very edge a couple times to look for sheep and spotted nine head down a ridge. One a very small sheep and must have been a late lamb of last spring. How it survived the deep snow is a wonder. A good old mother ewe looked out for its welfare no doubt.

Below there had been a cold light breeze from the southeast but on the peak when I arrived it was calm. What a view. A good view of both lakes and nearly a full circle

of peaks. I could see Iliamna Volcano putting out a big cloud of steam. Below a perfect view of Emerson Creek flat and the timber. On a clear day and with snow on the ground one could easily spot a moose or caribou most anywhere in the timber if it moved. Two days ago from the lower end of the lake I could see coming down the steep bank above the high falls on Emerson Creek what appeared to be trails of a herd of caribou going down or coming up from the creek. No crossing there and I suspected I was looking at a few small deep washes. Now from the peak I could see they were trails and more than a half mile farther up they crossed the creek again going to or coming from Camp ridge. Old trails so no telling where the herd was now. I have no idea how cold it was on the peak but felt sure it was well below zero. My thumbs were getting cold in my big mittens. I had seen all there was to see today. Ice fog made distant viewing no good and now a sharp breeze had come. How long would it take to reach the mouth of Falls Creek and the lake. Coming down was faster and colder than climbing. No rushing but steady going. Down to the point of the mt. and on down through the big rock to timber line and it seemed warmer there than on top. I was on the lake shore in one hour and up my path in an hour and a half. The temp. a -14°. A sandwich and some fresh cooked cold beans. A warm fire going I searched for some suitable material to mend a shirt sleeve. I dug into the grey ammo box that Spike & Hope had left. There was Hope's sheep lined coat. Just what I needed for this frigid weather when traveling the lakes. I tried it on. A trifle snug across the shoulders and the sleeves none too long but not a bad fit. I could move the buttons a couple inches and give a little more freedom. A bit of mending to do on sleeve lining and cuffs, I was soon hard at it and proud of the results. Yesterday afternoon the temp. stood at -4° before sun down – today it was -14° at the same time of day and at eight instead of nine it was a -29°. It could hit -40° tonight if all goes well. The moon one day past half and if this weather holds until after the moon is full, it is going to be a good long spell of frigid temperatures Let it stay cold – perhaps it will discourage the Kenai flying wolves from working on the caribou.

March 23 – Clear, Calm & -29°.

Noon came and the temp. had climbed to the minus teens. I wanted to cross to the far side and then decided on a tour of lower Cowgill Creek and Carrithers' point. I would climb the hump in my wandering. I scouted out more good wood and saw quite a few rabbits before I crossed Hope Creek below the gorge and headed for the hump. A Piper Family Cruiser went up the lake and down my side. It circled and circled as if he wanted to see someone home before he landed, but while I watched he did and I headed down. Coming down Hope Creek flat when here came the new "T craft." Both were on the snow when I arrived. Two complete strangers from the Cruiser and Glen and Terry Gill in the "T craft." Glen jumped out and came rushing to shake hands, a big smile on his face. He hadn't been here since Thanksgiving. The two strangers from Anch. Looking for caribou and saw a smoke and thought they would stop to say hello. Some people get lonesome no more than two hrs. from the big city. Glen was rolling out the packages and

mail and commented we haven't started yet. Packages! I hadn't ordered a batch of stuff. Every body loaded up and we trudged to the cabin. The place was loaded. One stranger a big man and his head so high I had to take the lantern down from the ridge log to give him room. I started to get my outgoing mail ready and there was questions to answer – I was confused. I laid brother Jake's[13] outgoing letter aside for I wanted to add a note and after everyone was gone and I reading my mail, there it was. Everything squared away and the drivers ready to fly. Glen and Terry had seen quite a few caribou in the big valley beyond the Volcanic Mts. and told the strangers where. The driver a very cautious pilot and I figured he wouldn't hurt the caribou unless he had a nice smooth strip outlined with spruce boughs. He questioned me as to the condition of mine at the far end and how long it was. Glen and Terry were going by way of Terry's camp on Bonanza Creek to check on conditions of snow and cabin there. The Piper Cruiser a STOL[14] job with 150 hp engine and he got off in the length of the runway (250 paces). Glen was pushing it I know for he got off nose high and staggering but he didn't touch down. Better than the Cruiser but not as nice from my point of view. I had asked him about wrecking his Stinson. A high speed stall on take off he said. In a hurry and pulled her in a turn to hard. He lost her and hooked a wing in the brush.

A Twin Lakes holiday and after reading till near sundown I counted 35 letters. Again some from strangers and another boy wanting to come stay a few days. Eddie Yeakle from Penny. working hard and saving his money. He would like to come at Xmas time in '75 as well as '76. A letter from Keith Trexler of the Park Service. "The film editors Bob & John[15] have nothing but praise for your work," he wrote. "All are so pleased with your Twin Lakes footage that we are hoping to make a separate production of it. "All that is missing is midwinter coverage to make the four seasons." (They have all the midwinter I could possibly get.)

They also sent a package containing 15 more rolls of 16 mm and 10 – 36 exposure rolls of Kodachrome (6 and 4). If you come to town please give us a call as we'd like to chat about the Park Proposal and ideas we have for your possible future involvement with the National Park Service.

A little package from Walter Ward (the hiker). A tape of music and songs that fit Twin Lakes country. Also he wrote and sent an announcement that he and Candy (a hiker) are being married on a point over looking the Grand Canyon. A letter from Bea Van Horne (a hiker) saying in her report she is recommending that any installations built in the Park will be restricted to Lake Clark – leave the lakes country to the northwest as is for a sort of game reserve. She will send me a copy as soon as the report is published. A letter from brother Jake and a copy of a letter to him from Bob Henning[16] blocking our deal with Professional Photographic Services to pay us a royalty on prints sold of my

---

[13] Raymond Proenneke born in 1923, youngest Proenneke brother, worked for Douglas Aircraft in Long Beach, in the U.S. Army Air Corp during WWII, mechanical inspector in machine shops and in the aerospace industry, and aircraft instrument repair, and pilot. Raymond's nickname was "Jake," after an old man by that name that young Raymond had admired in Primrose, Iowa.

[14] STOL, an abbreviation that stands for "short take-off and landing."

[15] Probably Bob Belous and John Kauffmann of the NPS.

[16] Robert A. Henning (1915-1999) publisher of Alaska Northwest Publishing Company who published the book *One Man's Wilderness* in 1973.

blueberry slide which appeared in Alaska mag. Henning wants to do any dealing done on that slide.

The sun set behind the mts. and I began to get my diggins in order. Mark things so I know who to thank for what. Burn scrap paper and stow provisions in the cache. The thing is full to the door. A sack 25 lbs. of brown sugar. I wanted to make some hotcake syrup. Hot water on the stove and imitation maple flavoring. I mixed a batch and had it cooling in the snow while I got supper.

Partly cloudy this evening but that moon says it will be cold again. It was -15° at sun down and now at 9:30 it is clear, calm and -24°. This was quite a day and I doubt that I will sleep sound tonight because of it. One letter of sad news. My good friend Art Vance of Heppner, Oregon[17] died after a short illness. He was a ranch hand at the time I was and eventually worked up in the REA until he was boss of the Heppner area. A good man, that Art.

March 24 – Partly Cloudy, Calm & -24°.

Terry Gill had tried to convince me that I wouldn't find 40 inches of ice on the lake April 1st after having 33 March 1st. I felt pretty sure that I will. We shall see. Too cold to do any good with camera gear. (It seems colder at -24° than it did in Jan. & Feb. at that temp. More humidity, perhaps.) I worked at rounding out my wood pile and then packed three gallons of roof coating to Hope's cabin. It came in yesterday but won't go on the roof until July. I had just returned and finished shooting a roll of 35 mm that I had in the Exakta. I would load it with Park Service film and try for some winter shots even though it is spring. Just finished reloading when here came a Super Cub up the lake. He dipped a wing, circled and landed on the strip. A good looking Cub and in it two strangers. The pilot introduced himself as Dave Barnett[18] and John somebody was his flying partner. Barnett it sounded familiar. Then he said his dad and Bob Acheson were here last summer. Now I knew – his dad had said that he flew his son Dave and a friend in years ago to hunt sheep and all they saw was ewes and lambs. Last summer I had seen Dave's name carved on a cottonwood tree at the mouth of Emerson. They came in – I stoked the fire and gave them a choice tea or coffee. They had stayed on Lake Clark last night and planned to again tonight. Dave's dad has a cabin there, next to Howard Bowman's. Howard had wrecked his souped up Stinson that Bee had built up for him. Landed hot on a little lake close to his house. It was either ground loop her or go into the brush. Sliding broad side and hit a ridge of packed snow (snowmachine trail). Got the gear, one wing and the propeller. Better that he should have landed on Slop Bucket Lake[19] which was a little farther from home but larger. Haste makes waste besides a mark on his record for he works for F.A.A.

---

[17] Heppner, Oregon in Morrow County about 40 miles SW of Pendleton where RLP worked on the Frank Wilkinson ranch before and after WWII. REA refers to Rural Electric Association.

[18] David Barnett, Anchorage businessman, pilot, and long time summer resident on Lake Clark, son of Bob Barnett.

[19] Slop Bucket Lake, a small float plane base at Iliamna village named by old timer John "Jack" Hobson (1868-1949) for his outhouse that hung over the edge of the lake.

March 25 – Clear, Calm & -24°.

It was two-thirty when I came to my beach. The wind strong in the spruce tops and the temp. 25° above for a change. Still coals in the stove and I soon had water heating to get cleaned up and soak that weary foot. Time to read Bob Emerson's book *I Heard the Owl Call my Name*. A story of a young priest who was sent by the Bishop to patrol the Indian villages along a section of the Pacific coast of British Columbia. The young man had only about two years to live (the doctor had told the Bishop). He lived and worked with the Indians and they grew to treat him as one of their own. It was their belief that the owl will call your name when it is time to die. Finally the young priests health began to fail and one evening he heard the owl call his name. He was killed by a land slide that came down the mt. into the river where he and his Indian boy helper were traveling by boat. Of the book, Bob wrote "the writer really touched a nerve," and I agree.

Ready for supper and for dessert along with my porridge hot chocolate and one of Anna Marie's[20] good cookies – I must make them last.

The overcast heavy and fog around Bell Mt. peak and its neighbors up the line. The wind blowing snow on the lake and the temp. 20° now at 8:30.

March 26 – Overcast, Blowing dn. & 24°.

My foot still sore but better. Today I would take it easy. I had my mail to read again as it was just once over lightly the day it came. Study that letter to Raymond [Proenneke] from Henning. "A straight 10% across the board" he writes as if it is a big deal. "Good and fair payment" in his famous last words. I dug out a 1968 copy of his magazine. In his mast head column "what we want and what we pay and the price per year for the magazine." $5.00 for a one year subscription. $9.00 per year in 1975. What we want and what we pay is one and the same in both 1968 & 1975. A letter came concerning *Alaska Geographic*. It seems they are having trouble getting out four issues per year. There is a choice – pay $8.00 per year for the *Alaska Journal* or continue to pay $16.00 per year and wait for the *Geographic*. He doesn't say so but I'll bet he can't find material to keep the *Geographic* going. Economize and drop them both. I read my letters and a story in the *American Hunter* by Roy & Sam Allen. A story of a sheep hunt in the Brooks Range by them along with Bob Emerson and his son Joey. It is Roy that Allen Mt. is named for. He climbed it the hard way – straight up the face and remarked later that he knew how a cat that had to be rescued from the top of a telephone pole felt – scared to come down.

April 1 – Overcast, Blowing up & 6°.

Today was the day to check the ice and the chill factor made it about 30 below. First my water supply and restock the cabin from the cache. I dug out the 25 lb. box of small white

---

[20] Anna Marie Dobson was the wife of Garland Dobson, warden-pilot for the Alaska Department of Fish and Game, Protection Division, based in McGrath.

beans Babe had sold me. A square box about six inches deep. A good sturdy box for it hadn't leaked. I noticed something that I hadn't when he brought them. On the box "Alaska Packers"[21] (fish cannery outfit), Pilot Point, Alaska (out beyond King Salmon[22] and Naknek). I'll bet those beans are 20 years old. First cooking, we shall see. Refill my flour bin and rolled oats jar. Now I was ready to test the ice. Little double bit to get the first foot and then the ice chisel and shovel. The wind was really blowing and cold like midwinter. Earlier I had snapped a 35 mm of the sun low over my cabin roof. A round bright spot behind the grey and it looked like midwinter, sure enough. I was getting right down there and figuring on 40 inches of ice when the chisel broke through. Quickly I enlarged the hole to get my gauge stick through and hooked under the edge. A low blow and Terry will smile when I tell him. 37 inches and a weak 37 at that. Any kind of decent spring and the ice will go out early in June if not late May.

April 5 – Snowing, Breeze dn. & 30°.

All the while I had seven heaping handfuls of those little white beans trying to boil on the stove. I just knew they were very old by the looks of them. Hard as buckshot, they would take some cooking. Boil them in soda water and then drain and start over with all the ingredients added. It was seven AM when I started.

The snow stopped and for a time I could see the peaks down country and then it closed down from that end. I finished my letter writing with one to Will Troyer who transferred from the Fish & Wildlife Service to the National Park Service. He likes it so much I accuse him of being on vacation with pay. This winter he flew a game survey of Katmai [National] Monument[23] and this is what he saw in four days flying. Counted 1100 moose, 25 wolves, 4 wolverine, and several lynx & fox. Saw lots of wolf tracks in areas other than where they saw the wolves. Ptarmigan & rabbit tracks by the millions. What a place that would be to film wildlife. Four o'clock when I added the flour and water to thicken my bean soup and 4:30 I called them purty good. More than nine hrs. cooking time. Next batch I will soak for two days before I put them on to cook.

My wood pile looking as if it had been 50 below and I took a good turn with saw and splitter to round it out.

Beans for supper and pretty good. A real nice green salad. John had brought me lettuce and a very large cucumber which makes a salad (a few thin slices).

As I wrote I heard a couple flies buzzing about. The first of the spring season. Now at 7:30 fog hides all but the black rocks on the mts. down country. It is calm & 30°.

---

[21] Alaska Packers Association (APA) largest consortium of salmon canneries in Alaska. Mary Alsworth's father, Gust Griechen had been the long time watch man at APA's Diamond U cannery at Pilot Point.

[22] King Salmon, an air hub on the Alaska Peninsula first built as Naknek Air Base during WWII and located about 150 miles SW of Lake Clark.

[23] Katmai National Monument was a 2,923,000 acre unit about 90 miles SW of Lake Clark.

April 6 – Snowing, Calm & 26°.

Snowing a lazy snow and I would shovel again though it was no more than an inch and a half.

Chores [done] and my laundry drying around the stove, I got an early start on my letters. A sharp breeze came up the lake and snow began to move on the surface. At no time today would the temp. climb higher than 28°. Near noon the sun tried to break through and I could see past the lower end and then it began to close in again. I wrote on until I declared a break. I would do something else awhile. I studied a *Grit* newspaper a bit and looked around for more productive work. I thought of old Frank Bell "I'm going to clean this place up but I have more important things to do right now." I would do some spring house cleaning and unlike him I would do it right now. Scrub the face of my fireplace and the hearth in front. Sort, discard, burn and neatly stow the garbage on my book shelves. Tear up my dog bed right down to the poles and redo it. I was surprised at what I found. Many thicknesses of plastic on the poles and then a few of Babe's big paper egg maker feed sacks with my four inches of sponge on top. The paper sacks had worked to the end and touched the chinking between the logs. Frost had come through and the sacks absorbed the moisture halfway to the head end. Wet and soggy – what a mess. The sponge wet on the bottom side. I hung it near the stove and burned the sacks. Wiped the plastic near dry and let it air dry. I found something I had thought souvenir hunters had taken. My cast of a moose track which hung from a nail along side the bunk. It had fallen to the ground next to the wall. Wet and moldy I chucked it in the fire. A batch of old letters to sort and burn. Before I looked at the clock it was quarter past six and I started to put things together again. Biscuits had been rising and went on the stove along with the caribou pot and a helping of beans. I made another good salad and dinner was served.

The wind had drifted my path to the lake and a small amount elsewhere. It could wait till morning. The temp. had dropped to 25° and a solid cloud bank lay across the lower lake. Moving north to south but not advancing up or receding down. Now at 8 still a light breeze up, temp. 25°.

April 7 – Overcast, Calm & 20°.

Today, I would liked to have gone somewhere. The snow was good early but it would get wet and sticky later. It would be a grey day for pictures and I prefer sunshine. Moose would be my only possible game and finding them in the spruce not easy. I would cut wood. Cut and pack in the big dead tree I robbed the burl from. Leave no mutilated trees in the forest. On the sled, snowshoes, saw & axe and my long handled shovel to clear the snow for a low cut. On the way I learned that I should have marked my packed trail on the lake with a few snow stakes. Snow and drifting had wiped it out. Time and again I went over the edge and had to alter course. Near the far shore, over the edge and I was

knee deep. The tree a big one and disfigured with much pitch showing. It would make a hot fire. I was a little disappointed when the sawdust showed yellow and soft. It would be light and not the best but it would make some heat. Down she went half buried in the snow and one nice thing about deep snow is when bucking logs you can stand and saw down. The end of the blade running in the snow below and not reaching the ground. On the butt cut one stove wood length made a load and finally two and then three. A lot of packing to the sled and several trips to clean it up. The weather had faired up and the sun bearing down. The temp. had climbed to 38°. Snow sticking to my snowshoes which I didn't approve of. It would have been a nice day to go on a tour. I was packing at noon and watched the sun for a time check. My Baby Ben runs fast and one time I forgot to wind my watch. Set it by guess and now the sun had me only ten minutes slow. My wood packed, hauled and packed again before it reached the woodshed. I split the butt cut and found it better than I figured. Another cut on the second length made two blocks and tough splitters with Jim Shake's 6 pounder. Real good wood and much bark and heavy pitch came free to be raked in a pile and burned.

April 12 – Clear, Calm & -13°.

I could hardly believe my eyes. It was -10° at sunup but nearly one hour later I saw it a -13°. This just has to be unusual. Hotcakes, my birds fed and chores done I set about to bring my outgoing mail up to date in case the plane came. I had just finished when I heard a plane and congratulated myself on being so on the ball. A red and white Super Cub and it came in for a landing. Two guys I had never seen, from Anch. Tired flying and saw my place down here. The passenger was the owner of the good looking two year old Cub. The pilot knew the country and was the guide. Water running every where in Anch. they said. Lake Hood[24] had a few inches of water on the ice. The town really booming from the pipeline activity. They had seen a good bunch of caribou in the gravel knolls to the right of the lower end of the lower lake. Three or four moose not very far away. Boy, I was all ears for that bit of news. The snow good for travel I could make it down for the afternoon pictures and come back in the twilight if necessary. After about a half hr. they was ready to tour again and would go to Lake Clark and through the pass. They took off and I rushed around to get headed down. It would be eleven before I got away. I would be there by two thirty or three. Head back by five (maybe) and get home at nine or later. The pin in the map and I was off and trudging on snowshoes. Two miles down when I met a blue and white Cub then a yellow & white [Cessna] 180 and another Cub coming high along the mts. to the south. I recognized no one so kept going. I heard the [Cessna]180 snarling and saw it turning over my place. I could see the blue and white Cub parked and while I watched the other Cub came in. I had better turn back and figured they may all fly away about the time I got halfway. The [Cessna] 180 took off and flew down country.

---

[24] Lake Hood, the float plane base for Anchorage, Ketchum's, Rust's Flying Service, Sea Airmotive, and the Office of Aircraft Services were located there.

I arrived to find one Cub and pilot from Iliamna. Chuck Rodgers the game warden.[25] The other guys I had never seen. The pilot, a heavy man and a Native – the other pretty stout in his flying suit and behind a full beard.[26] The Native from Sleetmute and the other from Bethel and a school teacher there. The Native asked me about the cabin up on the point. He had been here about ten years ago and visited a couple there. Did I know them and where were they now…The warden had his book of licenses along and was prepared to sell me one on the spot. He offered to pay the cost of the license $12.00 (hunting & fishing) if I would carve his wife a wooden spoon. I said no, I would settle for a gallon of cookies and that's the way we left it.

The Native and the school teacher wanted to see the inside of my cabin so we came in. I stoked the fire and dragged out the tea & coffee. I popped a big bowl of popcorn and we had quite a visit. The boys to the west were interesting. The Native had flown a long time and had seen lots of game. He knew where the big beautiful wolves were – snow white and he hoped no one would clean them out. He had counted 58 caribou kills in a straight line on the other side of Telaquana Lake. A lot of butchering had gone on there. He saw several wolverine and wanted to trap but those guys will steal the wolverine and your traps, he said.

I ask the warden if they ever found the Air Force pilots they were looking for. They were found the next day after he and Dobson were here, he said. They had landed in bad weather at Chakachamna Lake[27] on the Anch. side of the mts. A hole opened and they was sure they could make it. The hole closed and they lost every thing. Rolled her up in a ball and were there a couple days before someone accidentally found them. Broken jaw or two and other broken bones. Searchers on the other side figured they were on this side and had heard the weather was bad. A real mess. Finally Chuck says I had better get back to work and prepared to go. The popcorn was about gone anyway. He flew away and we kept the conversation going. My flight plan has expired, the Native said, but I radioed my wife that we was landing at Twin Lakes. He would be back again, he liked this country. The school teacher knew Dick Winholt at Bethel. I had worked with Dick at Harry Felton's back in 1966. Winholt a very nervous sort of a guy and always going on the run. He and another character run a repair shop in Bethel. The teacher said, "one is as bad as the other. Always much shouting and throwing things. When I take my snowmachine there to be worked on I never know how I will be greeted – maybe good and perhaps they won't even speak to me." Winholt now owns and flies a Cessna 170 and if he is as wild in the air as he is on the ground he is one crazy bird.

Well we had better head back. Only a couple hrs. of gas so we can't mess around much on the way. I set up the scope to show the teacher some sheep and he counted nine above the big rock face. They shook hands and thanked me for the popcorn, coffee and good visit. I'll be back after break up the pilot said. They flew away and I was back where

---

[25] Charles "Chuck" Rodgers, warden-pilot for Alaska Department of Fish and Game, Protection Division, based in Iliamna.

[26] Nick "Nixe" Mellick, Jr.(1932-2003), pilot-guide, lodge owner, local historian, Native regional leader from Sleetmute, a small village on the Kuskokwin River 78 miles E of Aniak.

[27] Chakachamna Lake, a large glacial lake on the east side of the Alaska Range, near the eastern entrance to Merrill Pass; Ch'akaja Bena is the Dena'ina word for "lake where tail comes out."

I started. Had I gone on I would be just heading the eight miles up the lakes and packing some good footage perhaps. If Babe comes early enough tomorrow maybe I can have him drop me off at the lower end on his way home.

To fill out the less than slightly productive day I worked at bringing my wood pile up to par. A kettle of flint hard beans I had been soaking since yesterday morning. Boil them ten or fifteen minutes in soda water and drain. Drown them again and add all the fixens. The sun was getting near the slope of Falls Mt. In the low sun the thermometer read 27°. Clear and calm, it would get pretty cold again tonight. At 7:30, 15°.

April 13 – Overcast, Calm & 4°.

He brought me up to date on the news as I checked my mail for threatening letters and to see if anything need to be said for the outgoing flight. One package, quick service from sister Florence. I had requested she make me a film changing bag (portable dark room) for the Bolex. It was here already. "Three more "T crafts" coming to the area. – local boys who bought them from Reeve,[28] the dealer in Anch. Had the same luck coming up as I did," he said. "Got too cold and they parked them in North Dakota." Glen is going to fly for a man at Pilot Point this summer. Guaranteed 130 hrs. flying time per month. Babe says, "I don't know about that guy – he is one of those that goes up through the fog and comes back down on the other end. There is one old pilot out that way and if I was Glen I would ask him if he approves of that procedure and if he says no I would agree with him."

Terry and Vic haven't gone to the hills yet. Glen and Terry had flown over and saw lots of snow. I had written Terry that all the snow from here had blown into the Bonanza Hills. Today a letter from Terry saying he had gone again with Bill Johnson (who flew into the snow at the glacier in Lake Clark Pass). The landing very rough and they had sprung the gear. Four feet of snow in the creek bottom about the cabin. Lots of water this summer. Bee is busy salvaging airplanes wrecked by caribou hunters. Has a [Piper] PA 12 to rebuild. A Maule on Snipe Lake to put a new landing gear under. Howard Bowman had landed short and dinged up another Stinson. Wrecked airplanes every where and old Babe the master of them all, still flitting happily about on a special permit because of his eyes. May have to drop back to private ticket next physical he told me last spring.

First thing I knew he was dipping in my bean kettle again. "How long does a pot of beans last you," he asked. "Oh, about a week if I am not too hungry," I said. No hurry today he stayed and talked about this, that and the weather. I believe it is colder at home he said. Here it had jumped from 30 to 40° in minutes when a sudden blast came down the lake. It died and soon it was near 30° again.

[28] Reeve Airmotive, bush airline specializing in the Aleutian Islands owned a hangar and parts store on Merrill Field in Anchorage, the company that had a franchise to sell Taylorcraft airplanes, owned by Bob Reeve (1902-1980), pioneering Alaskan bush pilot.

I had everything sacked up and ready to fly when he decided it was time to head back. The weather was lowering over the hills down country when he took off. We had decided on the first Sunday in May as the next mail day for Twin Lakes. "Can I come on wheels then," he had asked. Maybe but it sure didn't look that it was possible now.

Read my mail. Twenty one letters. One forwarded to me by Alaska Northwest Pub. Co. A military Sp4 Clyton Kepley wrote I am planning to take a long journey into that particular area that Mr. Proenneke had built his fine cabin. I am trying to find out if it is possible to find some way to use his cabin for a length of time. Isn't that something. That boy got the book for Christmas.

April 18 – Partly Cloudy, Blowing up & 0°.

In a letter to the old master bear hunter Sid Olds,[29] I asked him to make a guess as to when the first bear would come out. I predicted April 22 for the first one. How wrong could I be – the mts. south slope looks as it did in February. I doubt that there will be bear feed on the mt. before May 10th unless there is a sudden change to warmer than normal weather. A chance to see if the time of year brings the bears out or if it is time of year and favorable weather conditions. But, after the bad winter of 1970 & 71 I saw a black bear crossing the river flat up country when it was still solid snow cover with deep drifts.

April 19 – Clear, Calm & -10°.

A Cub came by and circled the lower end of the lake and I thought it had landed but didn't see it again. Soon another Cub and over the ridge from Turquoise. I recognized it as Fish & Game and probably Garland Dobson from McGrath.[30] He crossed the river and then a left to fly up the lakes. He would probably land at my place if I was home.

The caribou resting and I made a wrong decision. I would change angle and get closer. I should have moved to a new location along the ridge and waited for them to feed again. Too many soft snow patches and I had to use snowshoes. The air dead still and the crust very noisy. They could hear me in the spruce and didn't approve. The far ones went first in a caribou trot and then my close four. How far would they go before they settled down. They might go miles and certainly a mile or two. I followed and saw diggings and tracks as if a hundred caribou had been there. Feed is not plentiful and the easy place to dig is close to the spruce trees. I circled down country of trap rock and could see the big flat country but nothing but lots of snow on it. I swung left towards the river, still on the track of traveling caribou. Near the river I had a good view down the river and saw my eight head about a half mile down and on the river bank. I had to cover a third that

---

[29] Sid Olds (1890?-1975?) Kodiak cattle rancher with whom RLP consulted in the late 1940s and early 1950s about the possibility of starting a cattle ranch.

[30] McGrath, a regional hub of the upper Kuskokwim River about 100 miles N of Twin Lakes.

distance and went that way. When I got to my blind I saw they had crossed and were trailing across a big snow field towards the Volcanic Mts. A parting shot and I headed up following the river which is open and with a few good safe snow bridges. The Fish and Game Cub hadn't returned. My pin marked my destination and if he looked in the cabin he would know. I cut across behind Frank Bell's cabin and headed for the head of the river. I was in the wide open when he came down my sled trail. He didn't miss me but little and I waved but no dipping of a wing that he saw me.

Now that eight mile journey home. I had made four or five down there plus the eight going down. This was going to be a good day. Twelve thirty and the crust still good but not quite as good as going. I was facing a cool breeze coming down. To the stream by 2:30 and I soaked my tired feet in ice water for a few seconds before heading up the upper lake. The snow on the upper lake decidedly softer and though the sled was not much load, sixteen miles can make it seem heavy. Looking back I could see snow that had been turned up by my wooden shoes for a mile.

I had been thinking – bet that Dobson brought more cookies. I had written and thanked them for my favorite brand (oatmeal). Sure enough Cub retractable ski tracks on my strip. Tracks leading to the cabin. No note on the outside but on the wash table inside the door a gallon can and a two lb. coffee can on top of it. Cookies – a gallon of oatmeal but with a different flavor. The two lb. can had some thick frosted cookies. No note or name. What if it was Chuck Rogers paying in advance for the spoon his wife wanted. The plane came and went back Turquoise way so I think it was McGrath and not Iliamna. Who to thank and know that I am right.

A fire going and water on to heat. Get my days water supply. Change the water on a fresh kettle of beans. Supper warming. This had been quite a day for 8 measly carry-boo. The sun fell behind Falls mt. soon after 6:30 but it would still be light at nine. Now at 8:20, clear, calm and 12°. It was 25° when I arrived at 3:50. I plan to sleep good tonight and may or may not go up the lake tomorrow. The moon past half and coming full. This fair weather could hold for a week.

April 20 – Clear, Calm & 11°.

Today the only place to be would have been above and up along the ridge towards Falls peak but then I couldn't have seen my bear and probably wouldn't have seen very much of him. Now I must climb soon and check out the den. See what kind of quarters he had. How deep and how much room and did he have a bed of grass as I had seen on Allen Mt. I think not for there was none close and I didn't see him carry material for a bed last Oct.

So, it was Oct. 10 when he turned in and April 20 when the came out. 192 days in hibernation. In the calendar year (365 days) he spent more time in hibernation than out. 19 days more.

I had left a kettle of beans (soaked two days) boiling when I left this morning so

got the fire going to finish the job. I got my film squared away and find that I have about 850 feet to go on Park Service film.

Clouds had started to form while I was on the mt. and now at 7:30 it is nearly solid overcast, calm and 29°.

After supper I rounded out my wood pile and checked the slopes for the bear although I feel sure he is on Emerson Creek. Would he have gone back to the den to spend the night if not disturbed – I wish that I knew.

April 21 – Snowing, Breeze up & 25°.

I had letters to write, did pretty well at it. One to Will Troyer telling of my bear observations for he is an expert on brown bears. Noon time came and went and I wrote on. The sky opened up somewhat but scattered flakes of snow still swirled in from the lake. It cleared to the extent that I would take the glasses and scope and go to Jerre's point for a good look at the mt. On the lake I changed my tune. Get away from the beach and the wind was strong and moving snow. I could make more money writing letters and sampling one of Anna Marie's [Dobson] cookies now and then. Cookies, I have a good supply of. Still a 4 lb. box up in the cache that Lucy & Lindy had brought in 73. Still fresh as store bought, I'll bet. Stale isn't part of Twin Lakes vocabulary.

The day was ending with still a good breeze. I would have given a lot to see the bear near the den today. I would like to know where he went. Emerson Creek is certain to be well snowed in.

Now at eight, a thin overcast overhead with a grey cloud bank down country. Enough moisture in the air that I can see nothing but the dim image of spruce timber at the base of the Volcanic Mts. Temp. 27°.

Another year I saw ground squirrels out on April 20th and robins about May 1st. Not one of the migratory birds have I seen but yesterday I did see a butterfly. Insects crawling on the snow the day before and it had been -10° that morning. Hardy natives of "One Man's Wilderness."

April 26 – Overcast, Calm & 25°.

I rigged up the casting rod with a new leader and my old trusty Super Duper No. 506 (only one in captivity). No camera gear this trip – just my glasses and the casting rod. I wore my tin pants over my Frisco Jeans and my L.L. Bean pacs. My GI shawl around my neck in case the wind blew and I stuck my buckskin mittens with wool liners in my jacket pocket. It seemed like an unnecessary precaution but I didn't kick about it. A sandwich and I headed down. Good going until I picked up a cold breeze coming down from Low Pass. Cold enough that packing a casting rod seemed out of place. Near the lower end it was

no longer steady and not too bad. I have never caught anything from the lower end of the upper lake where it dumps into the stream but I would give it a cast or two. In early spring or until melting started the ice is good right near the water but I stopped ten feet back anyway. I was getting my rig ready to cast when crunch and down I went. I was facing the water and got turned a quarter turn by the time I was up to my knees. I fell forward over the edge of the ice and tried to climb out. More ice broke and I wasn't doing so good. I got a foot on top of the ice behind and lifted myself so I could slide out on top. Just got to my feet when down I went a second time. Just a matter of repeating the performance and I was out again and this time to stay. I had been in deep enough to get water into the hip pockets of my tin pants. Wet, pacs full, I trudged to the bare gravel along the head of the stream. My glasses a ball of snow, gloves wet. I was a sad sack for sure. Off came the pacs and pants. Wring out everything wringable. Not too cold yet but I would be before long. Back in shape again and not feeling too bad – I tried a cast in the stream. Rattle-d-clatter, I had bent the handle on my reel and it was striking the reel bearing cap as it went around. I tried to spring it clear and did help it some. I would go on to the lower lake and give it a test. Now I began to get cold and my fingers turned dead as sticks. Feet getting colder by the minute. I dropped the rod on the beach and ran around trying to get warmed up a bit. No chance (I hope) of anyone seeing me or they would have hid behind a tree and wondered. At last I was ready to fish but after a half dozen casts I decided I had better run home and climb into my wheel chair. My big wool shawl and heavy mittens were worth quite a bit on the way up. As I past the dunking place I took a good look. I could faintly see where the edge of the heavy ice was and I was past it when I broke through. The big wind of the past couple days had blown snow over the edge. The water too cold to melt it and it just choked up a ten foot width and froze but not enough to carry my weight – for very long. How lucky I was that I didn't have the heavy Bolex hanging on my chest and the tripod and big lens on my back. About 30 lbs. combined, and I would have had one tough time getting out if I did. About my only chance would have been to break ice to the open water of the stream for there it was shallow.

I marched right up the lake, cold, very cold feet – colder than they had been any time during the winter. Again that wind out of Low Pass and dead calm farther up. I had left a full tea kettle of water on the stove and banked the fire to hold until I got back. Out of my wet duds and a hot bath. Into my cold weather wool lined Navy pants and felt lined pacs. I was warm again.

The big ladle had been sanded on the outside – now the bowl would get it after some very careful gouge work to eliminate extra sanding. I hadn't given up the fishing idea. I baited the trot line with bacon rine and old salmon eggs and lowered it in the water hole. Probably no fish but much safer than playing near the open water.

Supper over and writing done by eight. It is clearing down country. It is dead calm and 22°.

Now I have had my dunking of the spring season. I won't soon forget it & don't expect to be trapped again by rotten ice.

April 28 – Partly Cloudy, Calm & 23°.

I raised up in my bunk and looked at the new day. Same old stuff, a grey day and then I discovered that the window was steamed over. About 50% cloud cover and it looked like a fair day in the making. Six hotcakes and the dishes done. I was ready to go somewhere. I stuck the pin in the map on mother moose country (Beech Creek) and was on my way by 7:30. The crust was real good and I made short work of the first three miles. The sun would be wrong for Beech Creek. I would rather hit it from the down country side with the sun to my back. I would change my destination and go up Emerson and see what was on Camp Ridge.[31] Snowshoes required on the creek flat. Not a moose track crossing as I traveled to the climb out for the benches. Snow free for the first few hundred yds. and then scattered patches to the high bank above the high falls. As I walked to the edge a nice bunch of ptarmigan flew from just across the creek. They lit again in a little grove of poplar and soon started to search for food. The flock travels as one, on the snow. Birds running and all in the same direction. From one little brush patch to the next, on the go. I counted 45 but I suspect 50 would be closer. Many roosters with brown necks and speckled heads. They circled high on the slope and in the short time I had watched them, they had traveled three hundred yds.

I went on down and hit my snowshoe trail on the creek. Now would I go visit the moose or head up. It would be quite a journey to make the full circle. 11:30, the day was still young, I would cross near my dunking spot and head for Beech Creek gorge. Where would I find my moose, if I found them? I favored the down country side as I came to the end of the timber and the start of the brush. There was the calf bedded down along the creek bank and there was his mom resting along side a shaggy spruce. Slowly I moved their way and was quite close before they learned I was there. Both got up and looked my way but didn't move away. This time the calf was gentle from the start. I saw right away they had both lost weight since I had seen them on Dry Creek. The calf's hip bones protruding and back swayed. The cow too was looking rough. They had only moved a few hundred yds. from where I saw them from Jerre's point yesterday. I moved around them trying to find an opening for pictures. Wind ward or lee side, it didn't matter. They didn't want to leave. Finally the cow stepped into the clear and I was in business. She fed high and broke branches down. She peeled bark and the calf did too. The first time I had seen moose peeling bark here at Twin Lakes. I moved to a hundred feet and closer and they paid no attention. Now would be the bad time for wolves to find them. They are no longer strong and the snow deep and crust hard enough to carry the wolves. I shot 80 feet of film and called it good. Left them not ten feet from where I found them. I finished the roll on scenery as I came down the creek and headed for the lake.

---

[31] RLP's Camp Ridge, a ridge near Camp Creek on upper Emerson Creek on the way to the sheep lick.

April 29 – Partly Cloudy, Calm & 21°.

Just now I happened to look up and out the window. Something at the rock pile under the spruce. The left over rocks of my fire place are piled there and I have quite an assortment of skulls, horns, antlers and such garbage there. At first I took it for a porcupine and then I saw the cream colored stripe – a wolverine hardly more than fifty feet from my window. A very old bull caribou rack of antlers sets propped against the rock pile and buried deep in snow. He was trying to pull those old antlers out but what on earth for. They are old as the hills and bleached white. Just a small portion of skull connects them. He yanked them free and headed for the brush of the point. He lost them and came back to take them and go again. As quietly as I could I uncovered the camera and set it up at the counter window. There I was afraid I wouldn't have big enough field of fire if he circled behind and came to the beach on the other side. I took it outside and set up near the clothesline. Now I could get him full circle. I waited and watched my heart making more noise than I would like to admit. Now I could see him working in the brush but not good enough. My only chance was for him to come looking for something else and I figured the chance was good as those old antlers were very thin soup. I watched him and finally here he came headed for the rock pile again. I mashed the button and the racket stopped him. I stopped it and he came on turning up to his right and in full view. Again I started the camera. He stood looking head on then turned, back to the rock pile and behind the spruce. He gave it up and went back to the point. Again I waited the light failing by the minute. I could hear him chewing on the antlers and saw him move through the brush. He was headed for the clear of the point but I was afraid he would stay in the edge of the brush and head for Hope Creek. He came out on the bank and looked across the lake. Down the bank and out on the lake. Now I had him. The camera sound stopped him but as soon as it stopped he would go again traveling at that wolverine rocking horse gait. He stopped often to look back but finally got lined out and stopped only occasionally to look up wind. Headed for a point just down country from the mouth of Falls Creek. Twice he went to the bathroom while making the crossing. On the far side he traveled down country – stopping to investigate every snow free area under the spruce along shore. He headed inland and there his trouble began. Here he had to walk for with him it is as it happens with me. The crust gives way over some buried brush and he would go in up to his chin if not out of sight. Evidently he flushed a rabbit for he tried to run. Down he went and he bounced about and stood on his hind legs looking. Again he tried but gave it up. Last I saw of him he was swallowed up by the spruce timber. I can see where the wolverine might eat just about anything at this stage of the game. The only place he can make any headway is on the lakes, or open slopes where the crust will carry him and there is nothing to eat there. I wonder if he would eat Gravy Train dog food. I have part of a sack in the cache. I could put out some Kennel Ration but the camp robbers would get it first thing. And that's how the day ended. Now at 8:30, nearly solid overcast and a light breeze down. Temp. 33°.

April 30 – Partly Cloudy, Calm & 32°.

Last day of April month but all same as May 1st so I would check the ice. Already the ice is softer than midwinter or even April 1st. Over deep water I found it to be just an even 40 inches. April 1st was 37." March 1st was 33 inches. I had just finished when I heard a 150 Super Cub coming and it turned out to be two. A blue Cub flying low up the far side and an orange and grey one up the middle. He flapped a wing and I figured it was Chuck [Rodgers] the warden. Gone maybe ten minutes and they came back and landed out front. The snow nearly gone from the ice there. A new warden Leon something or other flying the blue one. "What are you guys looking for," I asked. "Bears and early bear hunters," Chuck replied. Bear season opens May 10 and closes May 25th. They hadn't seen a bear yet but saw tracks of what they figured was a sow with small cub over on the Kijik. Saw some tracks up the lake here they said. Leon said he saw tracks in the edge of the timber above the lake shore and Chuck saw tracks on my side and along shore on the lake. Many moose tracks above Lofstedt's cabin. The two I had seen, I figured. I asked them in and what would be their poison. Tea would be fine so I dug out a couple tea bags and didn't think to ask them if they wanted sugar and milk. It had been Chuck who left the cookies. His wife had asked him if he was going to Twin Lakes and he said he wasn't sure if he would get there that day. Well, just in case better take these along. Good thing I hadn't the chance to thank Anna Marie and Garland Dobson for more good cookies. "They just moved from McGrath to Talkeetna" Chuck said. Boy his eyes lit up when he saw the spoon. "Boy, my wife is going to be happy with this" he said. He insisted it was worth more than a gallon and a half of cookies. "Labor is cheap at Twin Lakes" I said. Maybe she can send me more cookies some time.

May 2 – Partly Cloudy, Calm & 27°.

I glassed up country and across with a glance at the den site now and then. I had left the beach at 8 o'clock and was at the rock at 9:30. At 9:50 I glanced over at the den site and there was my bear big and dark. Boy! that was a surprise and I made haste to get behind the camera. The bear stood and looked down and soon bedded down in front of the den. This was too good to be true. I used a little film and waited for some action. It came in 20 minutes when the bear squared around back end to the den and slowly slid back in and out of site. I waited – surely this wasn't all of the show for today. In maybe 15 minutes and with the glasses I could see activity just above the snow around the entrance. Much movement and I wasn't sure. I couldn't make it cubs as I couldn't see enough. Finally a little head and front legs appeared over the edge. Soon it climbed up on the edge. Dislodged some snow accidentally and watched it roll down the steep snow field. In and out and never still. Finally he was playing tag with someone below and I saw another head and arms. Then inside and all was quiet and I waited and listened to snow slides on the mts. across. The afternoon sun was working on Crag Mt. and the rest. It was 4:30 when

the old girls head appeared again and out she came with front feet and standing with rear feet in the hole. She stuck her nose in the air, turned this way and that as if thinking and wondering where she could find milk food for a couple hungry kids. I could see a cub trying to climb out past her but ma was plugging the hole. She moved up more and looked back down. Out one came and soon the other. Never a foot away from her and mostly along side or between her front feet. A couple times I saw her make a grab at one as if to set him straight. The sun had dropped behind the mt. and I had shot a hundred feet. I packed to go and left her laying in front of the den. The snow even softer coming down but at least it was all down hill. Now I have a broken trail to timber line. I crossed the lake on snowshoes as the crust was very soft. 7 o'clock and 35° when I arrived at my "diggins." A fire going and supper on.

May 4 – Clear, Calm & 30°.

The weather was getting no where fast and it looked as if he [Babe Alsworth] would be spending the night at Twin Lakes. The first time in all these years that he got trapped on this end. We prepared for the night. "Now don't cook a lot of stuff for me" he said. "All I want is one thing – beans." I put the kettle on and made a salad with my brown sugar, salt, pepper, garlic salt and vinegar dressing. He didn't care for any salad but once he got a taste of it, he was the one to clean up the bowl. "I like that vinegar dressing" he said. It was getting late, him being on daylight savings time. I started to clear the upper bunk which had a foam rubber mattress. "Oh don't do that, I'll just sleep on the floor" he said. "Nobody sleeps on the floor here in the cabin," I said and I soon had him comfortable with a GI mummy bag. He was asleep in five minutes. As usual with someone in the cabin for the first night I didn't sleep sound. Too much creaking of bunk poles and snoring on the top bunk. When I turned in it was snowing and 28°.

May 5 – Overcast, Calm & 24°.

My journal to bring up to date and my mail to read. A letter from Keith Trexler about the film. It appears definite that there will be a separate film on the Lake Clark proposal, featuring my footage, - featuring Dick Proenneke "doing his thing" and "using your words and your voice in the narration," he wrote. That scares me more than a sow with twins. I'll have to think about that. I'm thinking my journals for the past year would be very valuable in narrating the film and I am more than happy that I signed no contract with Bob Henning. Keith Trexler wrote that the film would be along the lines of my book. Henning would want a big rake off on that for sure:

May 8 – Clear, Calm & 23°.

The crust the best ever for crossing and I was soon at timberline. I had just left my snowshoes when I flushed a newcomer to Twin Lakes. A dumpy looking little snipe like bird with a long beak. It looked like pictures I have seen of the woodcock but surely there are none here. I could see 12 head of sheep on the slope just down country from me as I topped out on the big rock face. I could also see my bear in front of the den and one of the cubs above it. Climbing the slope I heard a rooster ptarmigan and saw him perched on an outcrop farther up. Close to me was a hen with a speckled head and I stood waiting for her to fly but she stayed put. I unpacked and got set-up just in time to see her fly up and join the rooster. I packed the set up and climbed. Cooperation this time and I was doing alright. This rooster still snow white except for his black tail feathers and blood red combs over his eyes. Closer and closer and using Park Service film as if it was going out of style. I had a rock roll under one foot and nearly spill me and it was fortunate that it happened, the birds flew and I had film for the bears. Still out when I got to my station and today I should have had the 16 mm. Action by the cubs like never before. The cubs reminded me of two little boys but I couldn't name them until suddenly it came to me – Leon & Sig. Leon the more aggressive one. Climbing the snow field above the den and ripping and tearing around. Carrying chunks of snow crust in his mouth to the den. There he would wrassle with little Sig who appears just a bit smaller. Then away he would go again. Little Sig stayed close to the den and his mom. She lay bedded down looking my way but unless I made a strong showing of myself I felt sure she wouldn't spot me. Quarter past nine and mid morning lunch. She laid back, rear feet in the den entrance and the cubs got their mid morning feeding. It lasted a good while – more than five minutes. She has quite a system to be able to supply milk from her fat alone for she hasn't eaten anything (except just a taste perhaps) since she came out. Now a nap for the cubs and she stayed put.

May 11 – Partly Cloudy, Calm & 36°.

He flew directly over me and I wondered if he saw that guy playing in the cold water. He circled down and came back again. This time he throttled back and I knew he saw me. Again down and in for a landing coming up. I headed for the cabin by way of the lake ice. He had stopped a couple hundred yds. out. Two men and they came packing a styrofoam chest and a hand bag. I couldn't imagine what this was about. It appeared that I had staying company. It was John Kaufmann of the Park Service and Charlie Allen[32] (the pilot who had picked up the hikers at Telaquana Lake just as the lake was icing over.) "Brought you some goodies," John said. A half gallon of icecream, two quarts of milk, oranges, bananas, grapefruit, cantaloupe & the Sunday paper. "This makes about three times we

---

[32] Charlie or Charley Allen, an Anchorage based bush pilot who flew NPS Alaska Task Force members to various proposed park lands.

tried to get here. Last time we ran out of ceiling in the pass." he said.

He came to talk about the production of the movie. They hope to make a separate production of my footage and would like to use my words and hopefully my voice in the narration. Did I have a journal of my time at Twin Lakes. I had just figured a day or two ago and came up with about 2000 pages 6"x 9". They didn't want to jeopardize my collection of writing so would want copies made by machine or typed. Now, that would be a time consuming job any way you do it, was my thoughts. I would be happy to let them use them as they are. I gave him brother Jake's address and no doubt he will be hearing from them soon.

And he brought more film. All of the 16 mm they had on hand (6 rolls) and six or more rolls of 35 mm which makes more than thirteen rolls of 36 exp. that I have on hand. And, they would send me more as soon as they get some in.

"We believe you have a problem with your big lens" he said. "The distant shots seem a bit out of focus." I had figured that this problem had been corrected with my present mounting. "They would be happy to take it in and have it checked but then I would miss it for use with the 35 mm. I would stop using it on the 16 mm. I figured it was vibration that caused the trouble and we mounted the thing and ran the camera. It did tremble. I wished that I had received this complaint earlier.

Everything pretty well squared away and they prepared to leave. John had said he saw a dall ewe with a new lamb over in the pass country and we could see four head of ewes on Falls Mt. Later I was to count 16 head, eleven of them near the lambing grounds.

They flew away and I came back to my icecream which was getting soft. A half gallon is a lot of icecream for one person. A big helping and there would be three more before supper time. The last one very soft icecream even though I kept it in my well frosted cooler box. A sandwich and back to the creek for more gouging of snow under running water. By the time I called it good I had about 75% of the water in the old channel.

May 17 – Partly Cloudy, Calm & 32°.

Along in the afternoon the wind had come strong up the lake. Clouds coming over the mt. across the big pasture. It was good that I hadn't climbed down country from my bears or I would have been to windward and a good chance of being detected. Film and camera gear taken care of. Supper over and writing when I heard a plane. I wasn't long in making it not a Super Cub so it would be Babe. I ran out to watch my bears. She heard it alright and was on her feet. He circled twice and dropped a rock. It bounced and by then I was out on the lake with the sled. He had brought spuds, a pineapple, 12 lbs. of raisins, some fresh pork, he had butchered Petunia, he said, packages and mail. He planned to go to Anch. tomorrow, so came this evening. I rushed around to get the film wrapped to go. My outgoing mail sealed. The wind came strong and he loaded a couple big rocks on my sled and parked it under the windward wing of the "T craft." It would have to blow very

hard to lift that load.

I had him ready to go but he said, "Oh, I'm in no great rush," so he sat and filled me in on all the goings on around Lake Clark and the world. Someone had drown in Iliamna Lake, broke through with a snow traveler. Been around the lake all of his life too. "If I was you, I would drag the canoe" Babe said. "Someday you may cross it and it won't carry you coming back." "Lake Clark could go out now with a good wind."

I had kept track of my bears. She had moved but not far.

Well, he would be heading back. I pulled the prop and told him, go easy and don't scare my bear. He took off towards Low Pass Creek and I came to the beach. She was moving again but not far. It started to sprinkle pushed by a strong up the lake breeze. When I brought the scope in she was bedded down, good for the night. Little danger of planes scaring her over the mt. now. The ice will keep them from landing.

Now at nine, row on row of wet looking clouds. A fair breeze up and 37°.

May 18 – Partly Cloudy, Breeze up & 34°.

Snow on the mts. this morning and my bears were up in the white stuff. She would sleep late this morning for sure. Who wants to get up and look for breakfast in the snow. That strong breeze up the lake had held during the night and it would be an ideal day to climb for footage. I was happy that Babe came last evening.

The old girl was nursing the cubs when I reached the far beach and it was near nine o'clock. In the mail I had received three packages which required opening. Such a batch of eating material, I don't understand it. All I need to do is say, "Babe bring me some raisins," and in comes 12 lbs. Spuds are free, green stuff is free if he grew it, eggs free because I built the chicken house. Yesterday he brought me some fresh pork. I am making out like a burglar.

At the beach I climbed the bare knoll and glassed the lower slope up and down – no bear. She probably would stay under cover for an hr. or more. I glassed till I was tired and took a nap – woke up and glassed some more. A dark blob in the brush and I watched it. It changed. I had located her not far from where I saw her last. Then I saw the cubs moving about. She was feeding again and climbing. She came to the edge of the brush and a snow patch. Here she let the cubs play while she stood nearby. Another roll used up and I changed. As I took the camera out of the film changing bag, I heard some[thing] fall inside and I turned it over and heard it fall again. Something loose in the machinery. I took the film out and searched its innards. A small nut blue in color was the foreign material but I couldn't find where it came from. Nothing in the film compartment took a nut like it. The camera still worked normal so I filed the nut in a safe place and re-threaded the camera. By now the bears in the clear, up the slope. I could climb again and do all right. Should I, or shouldn't I? The sun was getting around and sun and wind on the same side is not the best. I would let them go today and hope they didn't leave the mt.

I got onto the ice and came across. A sandwich, studied my mail and kept close watch. She was climbing as if she meant it and could go over the skyline.

My wood pile had been neglected the past few days and time I was building it back. I kept watch and she kept climbing. Up into the rough stuff and then she traveled along the slope headed up country. Directly above where she had spent the night last night and maybe 150 yds. above she rolled some rocks down the mt. in making a resting place against a rock face. It wasn't late in a bears working day but she bedded down as if she intended to stay put for the night. My wood pile in shape I went to Hope Creek to put my bridge log in position while the water was low. The creek had dropped steadily since the rain and warm weather came to an end. The lake level up maybe seven inches from winter low. Supper over, dishes and writing done by 8:40. The sky partly cloudy, a light breeze up and the temp. 32°.

May 19 – Clear, (Ground Fog), Calm & 23°.

I was climbing through the timber at eight when I saw my bear on the move. She was headed up country too. Crossed to the next hogs back up country and bedded down again. The breeze came and it was down the lake. A high thin overcast was forming to the southeast. The wind would be up the mt. so I moved down country a couple hundred yds. to make sure any scent didn't flow up the mt. and spook her. I was all set, if she came down to feed I would get some nice footage. I could barely see her back on a grassy bench high up. No sign of the cubs and after an hour I began to wonder if I was watching a bear. Her head raised, it was her sure enough. That made the waiting easier. 10:30 and she made a move – got up, took a little walk around and bedded down again. She is the lazy one. At last she decided to travel and headed down – came to my stand of three days ago and showed no sign that I had been there. Next I saw of her she had crossed the next canyon and heading up country. I climbed fast to get some footage of her and the cubs traveling. Out of sight over a rise. It was past noon. I could climb and follow or come down. No good following a bear unless you can see it nearly all of the time. Danger of passing above or below and then all is lost and I wanted her to stay as long as she wanted too. I came to the beach and then spotted her high up. I would have missed her on the mt. I came across and from here with the scope I saw them move out onto a big snow field. A quarter mile back the cubs came in contact with true climbing material for little boys. A few small willows poking up through a snow field. I wish I had been close. Standing on their hind feet worrying those spindly things. On their back pulling them down. Just like Leon & Sig would do. The old mother stayed close until they had their play out. Now, on the snow field she started to dig. Snow flew out behind at a rapid rate. Not one hole but four as if prospecting for deeper snow. Deeper and deeper she went. The cubs in one hole and she in the other. The cub came out the adjoining hole, so they had a tunnel. I was busy and didn't see them leave but I could see no tracks leaving so I suspected they were having a cool nap.

Later I searched for them and failed to spot them but below and close to the canyon near the big cottonwood grove a single bear. This one as light in color as she is dark. A real light blond bear. It appeared that it was heading down country. Ambling along but now and again he turned back and angled down. Perhaps he would loose all that he had gained before he headed down country again. Once he doubled back and ran as if he smelled something. He came low along the rock faces and went down to the base of them. He climbed and sat looking. He acted like a bear looking for caribou calves.

May 23 – Overcast, Lt. Breeze up & 32°.

I flung out the Super Duper [fishing lure]and retrieved it slowly. No fish first cast – not a healthy sign. I cast again and again. A cool breeze coming up the lower lake and my wet fingers cold. Rest them awhile and glass the country. Nothing to be seen but the sheep. Cast again and I hooked something heavy and it moved. It was a heavy fish but then the line went slack. I suspected that I had snagged one and lightly. It was encouraging anyway. More casting and I hooked another one. Keep a tight line for that laker has a very hard mouth. I led him in to shallow water. A nice big lake trout and very dark. Really a beauty. I worked it into a shallow pool behind the beach and then gouged out a pocket in the gravel along fast water. I wanted pictures of this fish. I put him in and first thing he tried to get over the dike. That would never do and I built it higher and lined the crest with large rocks to fence him in. The water cleared quickly and I got my pictures. If I could catch another I would turn him back but if I couldn't he would have to ride the sled up the lake. Many casts and nary a strike. I parked the rod and went to check the ice of the lower lake for travel. No problem to get on and nary a squeak over deep water. Back to my fishing but no luck. My captive climbed out of the pool out into the shallows behind the beach. I tapped him on the head with a stone and hung him on a fish stick for the trip to the sled.

My sheep had a big scatter. Eight lambs since May 12. A good sign that the winter was agreeable with them. Now if the number of lambs increased to a dozen or fifteen and the bunch moves up to my favorite lamb filming ground I will go over and climb even if I have to walk around the lower end to get there.

My fish measured 19 inches. A nice fish but not as filled out as I have seen them. Not much in the stomach when I dressed him out. Small white objects (part of the contents) and appeared to be a form of snail. Lake trout for supper the first of the season. I hung him to stiffen a bit and finished the rasp work on the spoon. Then came the heavy sanding and by supper time it was looking good.

The fire going and bacon grease hot I would chunk half of him – shake the pieces in my fresh sack of flour and seasonings - fry him brown. It was a good supper.

At 7:25 and just finishing my writing when the sun dropped behind the ridge. I was surprised to see it setting so near its turn back point. Spring has a lot of work to do

before it turns everything over to summer but no doubt it will meet the deadline. I have never seen it fail.

May 25 – Overcast, Blowing dn. & 42°.

The ice a very dark blue and looked unsafe but it was good yesterday and would no more than squeak a bit today. Babe had said, drag the canoe – some day you will cross and it won't carry you coming back.

It was 6:30 when I saw the sow and cubs and exactly where I saw her last night. The cubs playing on a snow patch. She walked onto it and layed down and with the scope I could see her mouthing those little guys. Which way would she go when she moved out. I had predicted she would cross the canyon to Falls Mt. They moved out of sight and didn't show again. I believe I could have still gotten onto the ice with sled and plank but I wasn't interested. The wind was roaring on the mt. and it was threatening rain. I took the glasses and scope and headed for the Farmer cabin for a better look into waterfall canyon. I couldn't see her from there so I moved on down along the crest of the high bank and sat close to a little spruce on the point. No bears but I wasn't seeing part of the area that I was interested in. I sat and watched awhile thinking they would show and presently there was two caribou cows just below me on the beach. Feeding slowly at the high water mark and headed up. Both with antlers. One brown and the other so white I almost took her for an albino. No pink eyes and her legs had some brown, so she was just a light cow and well bleached by winter. They moved on by and around the point. I gave up on the bears and headed back only to find the cows had me blocked out. They were feeding at the mouth of Hope Creek. What was there to eat besides sand. I could put all the vegetation in my shirt pocket and yet they stayed and fed. They moved on and the brown one out of sight on my beach. I doubted that she would pass the cabin and sure enough she soon came walking back. Again they settled down to feed at the creeks mouth. To give them time I would go still farther down along the timbered slope of the mt. for a good look into the canyon. At last I found her and not fifty feet from where I saw her playing with the cubs. She had bedded down for an extra rest period. Soon she moved and went down into the deep canyon to feed. The cubs played on the snow and took their spite out on a couple sturdy bushes. Cubs are like little boys. If there is something to climb, they will climb. Each cub his own tree and I could see that they were clear of the ground.

May 28 – Partly Cloudy, Calm & 35°.

Now, what to do. I was up and geared for an early start. I would go to the low country and check out the wolf den and also to see if and how many caribou calves there were. I wouldn't take the 16 mm or the 400 mm lens. I would take the spotting scope and axe instead. A sleeping bag too and a little grub. I might spend the night in Arlen's cabin.

I took the Exakta 105 and 180 mm lenses. It was quarter till seven when I walked out onto Hope Creek flat and it would be 3 PM before I reached the far end of the trail. The beach traveling to Low Pass not the best. Still many snow banks to cross and slush if you try to crowd the water line. I noticed the foxes have been active at the gravel banks and I suspect they will be denning there again. Along the lower lake I traveled the bank to keep out of the snow on the beach. On Black Mt. I could see a few sheep and before I got to the lower end I would count 25 ewes and eight lambs. The first caribou calf was near the notch of the Pyramid Mt. Two cows and one calf and it was good size. I saw a half dozen more caribou before I got to Arlen's cabin. It was 11:30 when I reached his cabin and stayed till twelve. The place a mess. Some one had dirtied some cooking gear and left them full of water. Another or two they left the contents of whatever it was in the cooking pot. The granite coffee pot was bulged from freezing. A big racket outside. A squirrel really having a fit. Much scolding and bouncing around on the roof and at the windows. The place looked as if he had been inside and it wasn't long till he was inside. I found the hole after his leaving. What was wrong with that guy. I tacked a piece of tar impregnated insulating board over the hole.

Three courses of roofing paper had blown off last fall. Useable, and I rolled it up and put it inside before freeze up. The cabin getting wet inside with every rain. I would have to mend the roof, but as Frank Bell said "I have more important things to do right now." I headed down the flat along the string of three lakes. No ducks and I was surprised. Soon I saw a lone caribou cow who acted a fool and stayed with me for a mile.

From some distance back I had seen caribou beyond it. Now I was up where I could look down on them. 24 head of cows and five small calves. None of the calves as much as a week old or not two weeks old for sure. It was raining again and dark. They were moving out of range and I didn't bother them. From on top I could see more cows. The calving area is very large and I suspect it is well covered with cows calving. Predators would have no trouble finding calves if they worked at it. A mile back on my trail and the sun came out for a few minutes and soon it was raining lightly and me getting damp. 5:30 when I reached the cabin again and first thing I checked to see if the squirrels had opened the hole. Sure enough, and during the afternoon I wondered if it has some young ones in the cabin. No squirrel scolding now and I didn't see it again.

I would spend the night there and come on up next day. My supper over I started to clean the place up. It was eight o'clock before I called it good for the day. Mosquitoes were active before I went to sleep and my best sleep didn't come till near midnight. It was overcast and dead calm, temp. above 40 at sunset.

May 29 – Overcast, Calm & + or -40

At four I was very sleepy but during the night I had decided to repair the roof before heading up the lake. I cooked a big batch of oatmeal that I had cached there. I added lots

of raisins that I had taken along, borrowed a big chunk of margarine to make it better and soon was ready to carpenter. A good supply of 1st quality battens and some good holding nails to put them on with. I would batten her down on each rafter and cross wise on the seams. Three times it has blown off and this time it wouldn't. By seven o'clock I had it done and would feel better about leaving it in a dry condition. I have occasion to stay there now and again, I like to find it dry when I do.

I loaded up and headed for the upper lake and home. Bumped into a cow first thing and watched for a calf but she had none. On up and I traveled the high ridge that parallels the lake. Coming down and nearing the beach. In the brush ahead I could see a yellow back and big hump. It was no caribou and if it wasn't an old cow moose it was one big brownie. I had better check this one out pretty good. Slowly I worked closer and still couldn't tell for sure. The breeze was good so no danger of getting found out. It raised its head and there was those huge ears. An old cow moose, bleached out and thin.

June 7 – Clear, Calm & 30°.

Another nice one and more new ice than yesterday morning. Where is the wind that was forecast by those fast moving clouds.

After hotcakes and a check on my sheep. Seven or eight missing and I am short four lambs. So a little bunch has split off. I saw one ewe rubbing against a rock to get that annual shearing job done.

I got busy on my outgoing mail as if today was the day. I added a couple to the stack before I called it good. This old business of waiting for a plane that may not come for two weeks is no good. Better to go about your business and forget it.

I climbed the hump to see how the ice was doing and was surprised to see it had advanced a quarter mile down. A fair breeze was working the edge with a light surf.

While I sat there on the hump I got to thinking about all those caribou down country. I was thinking of waiting until the plane had come and gone but that was no business. Why not pack up and go. I still had time with lots of daylight. I headed for the cabin and got everything in order. Take a little grub, sleeping bag and Hong Kong boots to ford the Chilly [Chilikadrotna] River. Take the Exakta and three lenses. It was four o'clock when I walked away. It would take nearly four hrs. to walk it.

As I traveled the beach next to Gold Mt. I could see the sheep in a very favorable spot and wished I was on the mt. On down along the lower lake and near where I had seen the cow moose and twins. Something high in a willow. A round yellow ball. That could only be a porkypine and I detoured to the side. Sure enough and picking the new growth of the willow. The leaves just now forming and that was food rich in vitamin C. Like a boy picking apples the porkie was up in the spindly branches – holding on with one hand and reaching way out to drag those branches in. I unpacked and set up nearby and porky was none the wiser. A pretty sight in the low sun and through the 400 mm. Just packed

and leaving when I saw a caribou cow with small calf up on the ridge so I went that way. She was moving up country and I let her go. It took just four hours to reach Arlen's cabin and it was nice to find it just as I left it. Later I climbed the slope to see the sunset. No clouds so it wouldn't make a picture. It was cool and the mosquitoes of mosquito creek were not active. I didn't build a fire in the heater so would sleep comfortable. It was a fine evening.

June 8 – Partly Cloudy, Breeze dn. & Ice in Mosquito Creek.

Good going and I would soon be in the picture business. How to do this. The wind was strong and blowing down. I thought of getting on the mt. behind them but the wind might give me away while I was getting there. I would stay below. The sun at 90°, a mt. with snow patches behind, blue sky and white clouds. The big open slope just lousy with cows and calves. Spruce timber between me and them. I was heading for one of my look out knolls and it is good that a caribou was in the way and I couldn't make it. I picked another spot and got busy. Later I moved to another knoll with good spruce cover. Cows and calves like you wouldn't believe. Not the big herd but more than a thousand. Soon they started to move left to right across in front of me. How does so many calves keep from losing their mothers. One little guy did. He would run one direction very fast. Stop, look and grunt and then turn and run the opposite direction and repeat the performance. Calves, various shades of brown and grey but just one real darkie. Slate color with black legs and head. I was using lots of film. I had brought two extra rolls and would come back up with two ready to go. Cows and calves were moving through the timber and passing on both sides of me. Some as close as fifty feet. The weather had been perfect. Lots of sunshine with a few scattered clouds but now the clouds were building and I had much shadow and waited for sun. I finally called it good and packed up. It was eleven o'clock and it would take one hr to reach Arlen's cabin. The wind very strong and I would be bucking it all the way home. I had my lunch at the cabin. Put everything in good order – left my GI sleeping bag and leaky boots. I would stop by with the canoe sometime. It was one o'clock when I left. Climbed an open ridge behind his cabin and headed up country. A straight shot and no beach gravel which makes slow going. I made it to the stream in two hrs. which is good time. I found the ice of the upper lake in better shape to go out than the lower. Much ice broken up and ice pushed up on the beaches. Just 3½ hrs. to make the trip from Arlen's cabin. Everything as I had left it. Note on the table, pin in the map. They couldn't have landed if they had come for my open water along the beach was now jammed with drift ice. First thing the fire going and water on. A good bath, the best way to end a long hike. Supper over and my birds came. It looks as if I will have seven on welfare. Those black ones here every time the regulars come.

June 15 – Overcast, Fog, Calm & 41°.

Nearly as socked in as yesterday morning. A very low ceiling with fog below. It didn't look at all favorable for Babe to come in. More ice had gone and it appeared certain that today would see the end of it. My birds came and all four young ones came to my hand. It is amazing how suddenly they lose fear and swarm all over me. The old ones very polite and wait their turn.

I went up to check my hatching hen after spuds and chores done. Still pointed down country and the few sprigs of blueberry brush around her leafing out. It would be interesting to know how often she leaves the nest if she does. Maybe she doesn't. If a bear can go 195 days without food surely the hen can go three weeks.

A package to wrap when I got back and the Park Service film lined up for quick wrapping. A couple more letters to write and by then the day was looking entirely flyable. A noon time check and I paddled up to the point to get the little kicker out of storage. I see my garden is coming up. Radishes and rows and rows of other vegetables. The strawberries look poorly but a couple dandelions that came with them are doing fine. It would be good to have a dandelion patch for greens. Vic Gill has a good patch on Bonanza Creek that furnishes them with greens all summer.

The little kicker, I hung it on the rack and plugged in the tank. Filled the carburetor and gave it three pulls of the starting cord. She started and ran like an Elgin. Good enough I brought it down and checked the lower end for grease. She stands in the corner under the roof over hang ready to save the day when the wind blows.

By now it was a beautiful warm day. The sun bright and the day calm. I sat on the beach and read a *Grit* newspaper while waiting for Babe to arrive.

I would take a little paddle down lake. If I had brought my casting rod I would go to the lower end. No problem there I could borrow the mystery hunters spinning rig from Vanderpool's cabin. I headed down. Maybe a half mile and here came a plane. I drifted and waited. A Super Cub and when it got close State Fish & Game, Chuck Rodgers. He dipped a wing as he passed, circled and landed. He hadn't been here since the ice was unsafe. He shut her off and climbed out on a float. After greetings he asked if I ever found lots of caribou. I had—well over towards Fishtrap Lake the hills are covered with them. Did he catch any bear hunting violators. "One" he said. A guy from New York who killed a bear last year came again using his brothers name. Much checking and they caught up with him. By that time he had killed another bear. A thousand dollar fine. His hunt $3,500. and two bear hides, a black and a brown and his fancy Weatherby .300 Magnum rifle with 18 power scope. The money he didn't mind losing but the rifle and bear hides—that hurt. We set and talked and drifted for now a very light breeze was coming up the lake.

I asked him if he had ever been over to check the mineral lick. No he hadn't and why don't we do that right now. You know where it is and I'm not sure. Fish & Game doesn't

make it a practice to haul passengers other than employees but this is an exception.

I headed for the first good beach and he taxied over to pick me up. We took off down country. Over Emerson Creek timber and on down and around the end of Black Mt. We saw no sheep until we made the bend. Four head first and then the big bunch. I counted fast and counted everything. 54 head was my count. A long ways from the lick. I wondered how often they went there for mineral. Over the ridge and down. Nothing at the lick and it showed no recent sign of use. We flew up the nice little valley of Beatrice Creek[33] where the ewes and lambs spend the summer and early fall. Nothing there so we came back down and over the ridge for a better count of the bunch. It was hard to count lambs as when spooked the little guys run close along side their mothers. I counted about 15 but I suspect there are 20 more....We saw about ten head in another bunch that we missed first pass. We came on up Emerson Creek. I looked sharp for the sow and cubs but failed to see them or any sheep and I was sure my bunch had gone there. Up at the forks a turn to the left and through a saddle of Ram Mt. Down Camp Creek and then we saw sheep on the point of Ram Mt. That was my bunch and he turned in close. 5 head of lambs I counted. That was about right for I had seen five on Falls Mt. On down Emerson and up the lake. A landing on a lightly rippled lake next to the canoe. That was a good tour taking 30 minutes. Me, my camera and walking stick it would have taken two good long days. We talked a minute and he had to go. Did I need anything. He didn't see Babe often but he saw Bee at least once a week. Four items- flour, sugar, bacon & popcorn. He wrote it down. And I added, "If you see Babe tell him I said the ice went out in June this year." He took off and I paddled up the wide open lake. Really a beautiful evening.

June 22, 1975

I headed on up on a glassy lake. A rain shower or two before I reached my beach. What would I find? Had anyone been to my cabin. Someone had, the locking lever had been turned and I never lock the door. A couple notes on the table plus a business card. Keith Trexler of the Park Service and a Mardy Murie.[34] "We're going ahead on the filming and will get in touch with you soon," wrote Keith. Mardy (who evidently works for the Park Service of Wyo.) wrote that she had "read the book three times, lives in a log cabin and thankful to see this one." Wish I had been here to greet them when they arrived.

June 24 – Overcast, Calm & 34°.

During the night I woke up to hear a nasal whining and quite loud. It could only be a porcupine. It went on and on and I finally got up to check. Two porkies by the stump

---

[33] RLP's Beatrice Creek, heads in mountains north of Twin Lakes and flows past the sheep lick emptying into the Mulchatna River. The Dena'ina name is Vich'andaghedlen which means "flows out from inside" and is a literal description of its course.

[34] Mardy Murie (1902-2003), was the first woman graduate of University of Alaska, conservationist and writer who lived in Moose, Wyoming, married to Olaus Murie.

near the clothesline. One rasping on my prize caribou rack and the other (a big one) talking to him. He was up on his hind feet and down shuffling around complaining about something. I finally spoke to them and the young one took off for the brush and I suspected he had been the one I had helped around the rear of the cabin with my walking stick. The big one I had to encourage to leave.

I was up early for I needed to check on my hatching hen. After so much time and effort I had to see this hatching through to the bitter end. I was cool at 34° and Twin Lakes very lucky to have prospects of a big blueberry crop. Had the night been clear it could very easily have been 20° this morning. My hotcakes and I made ready to go. A beaver left the beach as I drew near to my climbing trail. What would I find this morning? She was pointed up and sitting tight and right along her port side was a chick snuggled up close to her feathers. I feared the worst. Had that little guy who tried to climb out yesterday made it and got back that near to the warm covers. Certainly no little chick could live long exposed to this mornings cold damp air. I went close and watched for sign of life. I saw it open an eye and then turn its head. If only I could get him where it was warm. I could move her but then I might have chicks scattering as instinct directs them to do when she flushes. Better to leave things alone and watch from a distance. I angled up the slope nearly a hundred yards and sat motionless glassing the nest. After a while I saw activity under the edge of the depression formed by the nest. The chick, that little rascal was toddling around the mother one. First to the right and then back around and then I lost him. I stayed until I got cool. Fog and a breeze had come up the lake. I decided to go and went near on my way down. No sign of the little guy, he was under the covers.

I cleaned up and raked my beach which had been messed up by the blow. Now I would check further to see what happened to my moose. Coming back I had followed the game trail again and was surprised to find fresh bear droppings and a good sized track coming this way. I wiped the dust from the old .357 and put in five rounds. Take it along just for the ride. I crossed Hope Creek and worked up along the other side. Up the high bank and back through the timber. Again fresh moose droppings but only one place. No sign of moose crossing the creek going up country but a large track (not smoking) going down. The weather had faired a bit and I would go check the hen again (now 10 o'clock). Traveling the game trail I saw my small moose had gone down country again.

Climbing, I had always come across the slope above the nest about 20 feet. This time I was near and looking for the hen when I heard clucking ahead of me. There she was directly ahead and sitting in a small depression. Three chicks not under her but maybe a foot away. One with his head buried in the sand (under the moss). Another in plain sight and another facing away and motionless. So she had left the nest. I shot a couple frames of her and the chicks and then went down to the nest. Eight shells instead of nine (I had miscounted). The shells cut in two at the largest diameter and the small end reversed and seated in the big end on more than half of them. I had seen this before and wondered why it was done. Perhaps to make more room in the nest for chicks and shells as no shells were removed. I moved away and watched over a rise with the glasses. Perhaps it was thirty minutes before the hen started to show sign of moving. She turned her head looking in all

directions. She got up and started to feed on leaves and the chicks came alive. They spread out and traveled with her. Tripping and tumbling over moss and twigs but pulling leaves too. It was a pretty sight to see those little guys tugging and nearly up ending getting the leaves free. I watched them move over a rise and into near open and then slowly went towards them. I found her covering the covey and clucking softly. I wanted pictures of her and moved close. She stayed long enough and then raised up and walked calmly away leaving the little guys in a huddle. Perfect and I did good. She didn't go more than thirty feet and was feeding. I moved away and she promptly went back and covered them again. I climbed above, out of sight and out of the wind and watched below. Again it was twenty minutes or more before I saw them feed out. Same as before the little guys spread out and really working at making a living. She didn't go more than thirty feet before she stopped feeding. They all ran to her and crawled under the covers. I circled down past her and came up from below. As close as seven feet, as close as I could focus the 180 mm lens. She was half standing and spread like an umbrella to cover the eight of them. On the last frame she raised to go but I talked softly to her and backed away. As I packed to go she had them all under cover. No doubt this would be the last time I would see her and the chicks. No telling where her wandering will take them. I wished them luck and came down the mt. June 11 I had discovered the nest. 20 times I had climbed the mt. checking on her and it was worth every step of it. I only wish I could keep track of them until they fly.

June 25 –Fog, Calm & 37°.

The weather lifted slowly near noon and a fresh breeze came up the lake. This afternoon I would take a tour up Hope Creek. See if there had been a bear over the trail. An early lunch and I crossed the now respectably low Hope Creek. Up the far side and I flushed young birds from a dead spruce. So, it is that time already, young birds hatched and flying. It will be time to head south before we realize that summer is on its way out. Up the Cowgill benches and no bear tracks on the caribou trail up the creek. He could have traveled Crag Mt. slope but I suspect he went on up the lake. Only a good start and I saw a cow caribou on the other side. Two calves came running and I thought, here I have the first pair of twins in the caribou tribe. They looked like twins and came running as if wanting to be first on the bottle. The old cow refused to recognize one of them. I looked for a second cow and finally directly across from me in the brush was a second cow. Several hundred yds. from the other and I wondered if she was the mother to the imposter. One of the calves climbed the bank alone and onto the very green slope. It was looking for its mom and wasn't finding her. Finally it took the attitude of the freckled faced boy with out standing ears and big tooth missing in a wide grinning face. "Who, me worry!" and he layed down and curled up like a dog. My cow nearby worked lower towards the creek and then suddenly decided she had better go check on [junior]. She climbed right out and headed up country. As she came in sight over a rise the calf jumped up and came running, starved half to death.

June 27 – Partly Cloudy, Calm & 38°.

I had the canoe ready to launch when here came that big yellow Beaver. The same one that was here the day I went down country. He made a big circle and landed. Tourists began to climb out as it came to rest against the beach. Keith Trexler and a party of four besides the pilot. Ketchum Air Service painted on the side of the big bird. "Oh, we caught you at home this time" Keith said as he stood on the float. "Brought you some film, - didn't know you was out. Your letter came the day after we were here last time." I was glad to see that box of 16 mm. 35 rolls of the stuff plus more 35 mm, 10 rolls of that. It's a good thing that Jake is coming and Keith said they had talked to him and he intends to get started by July 4th.

The tourists, two men and two women. One young man along with companions intend to do some hiking over this way from Telaquana later on. One woman commented on how neat the place looked so picked up, as she put it. Open house and Keith and I had things to discuss. The possibility of another camera for Jake to use, a timer for my Bolex with a longer delay before running the camera. And did they want any footage with that pretty little yellow Cub in the scenery. Sure, airplanes are a way of life up here. Jake will be happy to see that Cub in the picture.

They had brought airline box lunches along and had a picnic in front of the cabin. Oh, that Mardy Murie wants to come back and when would be a good time. An elderly lady maybe 70 and she liked the book very much. She is touring farther north now but will be back to Anch. about July 4th. We set July 6 (Sun.) as the day she would come here.

I had checked my trot line soon after lunch and had a nice lake trout on. A 16 incher this time and I would have it for supper. I put the baited hooks in the bait can and a rock on top. Something tells me I have a winner in that trot line.

Fairing up and I went for greens. The cow and calf caribou's tracks in the sand on the point, headed up. Blue sky and the sun in and out – the lake glassy again. This was a fine evening.

Now at eight, partly cloudy, the sun just behind the edge of the big pasture. It is calm and 57°.

Keith had said, "We have scads of aerial shots but not much from the ground." The Exakta is going to get a work out on flowers and other vegetation. I found my cow moose again. A wise old girl she would lay quietly if she knew she was hidden from sight.

On the quiet water out front, a lone seagull. Fish scraps will be picked up promptly from now on. Two loons also decorated the calm water for a few minutes. A brown rabbit fed on willow leaves nearby as I cut up the lake trout. I have many friends and neighbors this early summer season.

June 28 – Clear, Calm & 44°.

It was getting late and the light was failing. My watch said 2:45 but it had stopped because I hadn't wound it. I waited for the cow to move into the brush or bed down so I could go. She finally was very obliging and layed down facing the other direction. I moved down country along the slope and down wind of her and ended up at Jerrie's cabin. Now, I could stay there tonight or battle the lake. I walked right on by and out on the point to have a look. It was rougher than a cob but not as rough as I have crossed it. I headed up the beach to the bare knoll where the canoe lay bottom up. There I sat out of the wind and watched those seventh waves roll by. Not one seventh wave but two big ones. Watching wasn't getting me anywhere. I loaded in a couple rocks for ballast. She would ride better or sink like a stone. I couldn't hope to make my beach and I doubted that I could make Farmer's cabin. Maybe one mile rock down the far side. If so I would beach her – tie her to a bush and walk. Into it and it was no worse than I remembered other crossings but the worst was to come. Halfway out the wind was strong and I was drifting at a good rate. Now and again a big one would break just as it hit the canoe and I would take a cup full or two. I kept at it – wouldn't make Farmer's cabin or even the bend of the beach below but I would beat one mile rock. I ended up a few hundred yds. below the bend of the beach and could have beached and walked. I would give it a good try at getting to my beach and so battled my way to the protection of Farmer's high bank. I had it made and was soon in quiet water near Hope Creek where I stopped to put out my fish trap (trot line). "Sure tasted good to be back home again." Better than staying at Jerre's and walking around the lake tomorrow for the clouds were moving fast and it could last several days. A fire going and beans on. A salad to make and half of the greyling to make ready. It took no time at all.

Now with the strong wind came rain. Now at 9:15 grey with rain and the wind strong, temp. 50°.

June 30 – Partly Cloudy, Blowing dn. & 51°.

Again I woke up to the tune of rasping on the front left corner. I hurried out and there was the young culprit at the scene of the crime. I took the shovel and fanned him good as he headed out back. I wonder if a porcupine has a memory – if so and a good one, it is awfully short. I hate to do him in but this old business of chewing up everything in sight has got to stop. The next offense is punishable in the form of deportation – box him up and haul him away to start life anew.

It was early and I wasn't about to crawl back into my dog bed. The sun was out and white caps were chasing those ahead of them down the lake. I built a fire and fried my spuds with onion, bacon and egg.

Today, a letter to a Jerry Knobton of Rindge, N.H. A boy of 21 who wants to live along with nature in the wilds of Alaska and the colder the better. My advice to him.

Work until you are 50 and then if you can afford it, do it. He wrote that people thinks him crazy to do such a fool thing. I told him I would have to agree with them.

July 2 – Partly Cloudy, Breeze dn. & 44°.

It took time for it to soak in, I was sleeping very sound. Rasping on the northwest corner and the time 11:30. I was prepared. The long handled shovel at the corner. A gas can with the top cut on three sides sat on the table. I slipped into my pants and pulled on my pacs. Quietly to the door and then I went into action. A porky does have a memory, all it needs is to be jogged a bit. He was nearly to the rear of the cabin and traveling in a lope (fast for a porky). The shovel blade was in front of him when he got to the brush. Then for a time it was like trying to keep popping corn in a skillet with no cover on it. He wanted in to the brush and I wanted him in the corner by the fireplace chimney. To go into fast action so soon after sleeping very sound winds a person in a hurry. A few times he nearly ran into my legs and then he began to slow down. He didn't want to go head first into the can but he did and I pushed the lid down and crimped the three edges. I had him where he couldn't get away. The lake was flat calm, a nice night for a little paddle. I would take him to the far side. It was an enjoyable trip over and back. On the far beach I opened the lid and waited. Soon he stuck his head out and looked around at this strange land. He walked out and into the brush. I felt pretty sure that he wouldn't give me more trouble for quite some time. It was July 2 when I beached at my place. 12:15 to be exact. Now, to get some sleep and it took a little time. Before I dozed off I heard a porkypine walking outside. A nibble or two at my cache ladder and then no more. I woke up early to the tune of rasping but it was on the moose antler by the rock pile. When I got up he was still there. That's alright, I have lots of antlers, but not many cabins.

Spuds for breakfast and it was a pretty summer morning. I glassed the country and saw nothing. The lake was getting noisy out in the long run. I would stay on the beach. I did some laundry and hung it to dry in the sun. I would go up Hope Creek and into the big basin behind Crag Mt. I might even climb to Crag Mt. peak if all systems were go when I got up into the big pocket. I have wanted to climb to Crag peak for a long time. Much higher than the peak above the hump and overlooking the lake. At least 600 feet higher and maybe more. A full load of gear and it was a heavy load. No tracks on the trail up the creek and still several snow filled washes. I looked for bear tracks for near the second canyon on the far side of the creek is prime bear country in summer. Much green stuff due to subirragation. I had taken my rubber socks along to use in fording the creek which I did above the second canyon. I draped each of them over a dead stub to wait for my return and headed up the steep knob that guards the entrance to the basin. I had seen no fresh caribou tracks so guessed they had moved to fresh pasture. I climbed on, headed for the peak and I had my doubts if I could make it. It is very rough the last third of the way. I figured I would run into something I wouldn't want to risk while traveling alone. Above the grass and into the fine stuff and then the rough stuff itself. I kept going,

stopping now and again to look for a route I could navigate. I was getting there but it was still a long way to the peak. Near the peak the going was better. Lots of loose rock but very coarse which is like climbing stairs. Maybe 20 feet of solid rock near the peak and I learned there is only two climbable approaches to the peak. The one I had taken and one leading up from the ridge coming from the lower peak. The peak very small and hardly big enough to set a camera tripod. The very peak a loose piece of rock about a foot long and eight inches wide and maybe an inch and a half thick. It is covered with green lichen. The peak is split and spreading and some time in the future there will be a mighty roar when many, many tons of rock fall hundreds of feet down the straight side facing the lake.

White caps on the lake but dead calm on top. A very beautiful view of the lakes and mt. peaks unlimited. Cloud cover prevented me from seeing Redoubt and Iliamna volcanoes. I stayed till three glassing and taking both movies and slides. I hated to start down and hoped that I remembered my climbing route. Coming down was better than I expected and I was below the rough stuff in thirty five minutes. It would take maybe an hour ten minutes to reach Hope Creek from the peak. On to the grass and I stopped on the knob to look a bit before heading to my fording place. Right away I saw a bear and a pretty big one. Not far from the creek and in the green stuff. The breeze down the creek. I was really in luck. My rubber socks could wait. To go that way would really mess things up. I can't imagine where the bear was when I went up that it didn't wind me. No more than a few hundred yards below where I forded the creek and no more than a hundred yds. from where I passed going up. I was set up in short order and using film. While the camera ran two cubs ran into the open. So, it was a mamma with twins and this years cubs at that. She is lighter in color than the sow on Allen Mt. but a big bear. I would travel high on the slope of Crag Mt. coming down in hopes that she would stay and I would visit them again soon. Twice I set up and used some film. Close enough and a pretty sight. The bears on a little green meadow and Hope Creek running lots of white water in the scene too. The cubs tried to climb a willow which is standard cub procedure. I had taken only two rolls of film and had used one on the mt. The sow fed into the heavy brush along the creek and failed to show again. I finished the last few feet on scenery, packed up and headed down. Again the lake noisy when I came over the hump. From the peak it appeared that there was smoke to the west southwest.

Past six when I reached the cabin. A fire going and water on for a bath and washing. Beans warming and a salad in the making. This was a very good day and the bears a gold mine if they will only stay awhile and I feel that they will if they don't climb the mt. to sleep and strike my trail coming down. They are close to the noisy creek with a high bank to work from. A good breeze up or down is good. I must see them again tomorrow.

Everything in order for the night except getting my canoe back from Cowgill beach on the far side of Hope Creek.

Nine ten and nearly clear. The sun advancing one third of one diameter towards the peak when it dropped behind the ridge. A strong breeze down and 51°. From the

peak too I saw just an awfully lot of snow and I feel sure that there will be a big hold over of 1974, 75 snow when snow comes and stays again in Oct.

July 3 – Overcast, Breeze dn. & 48°.

An airplane came and turned back at the lower end. It was eight o'clock my time and I wouldn't wait longer. I would go up Hope Creek and try for the bear. A full load of gear and I paddled to the far side of Hope Creek and the start of the Cowgill trail up Hope Creek. I had climbed the high bank and was to the second bench when here came another plane. An orange and white Cessna 185. That could be Charley Allen the charter pilot who flew John Kauffman in while the ice was still on. When he circled my place and started to set down I knew it was for me and headed back. I found his plane nosed in at the sandy beach at Hope Creek and him sitting by the rock pile on my beach. Three more people present and Keith Trexler was one of them. Also a fellow named Bill and young woman names Michelle, a lawyer (for the Park Service, I understood) from Washington, D.C. Keith was in the process of writing a note to leave when I came. We had a few things to discuss while the tourists inspected the lay out. Then I gave them the twenty dollar tour of my cabin and cache. Made Michelle a sourdough sandwich. She wants a gold nugget but I had none here. Charley Allen says, Oh! look under the bunk. I'm sure you have some. They must have stayed close to an hour and then it was time to fly. The wind was strong down and the air rough. Michelle wanted to see a bear too and I told them I had one up Hope Creek but I didn't want her disturbed. It would be very rough flying the canyon anyway. They flew away after Keith saying they would try to get Mardy Murie in Sunday. That old girl is an old time Alaskan. Wrote a book or two, traveled by dog sled. Her husband (now deceased) was with Fish & Wildlife Service [Olaus Murie].

She dug for a ground squirrel and really plowed the earth. The cubs were busy too after she had caught the squirrel or give up, they got into a fight and I could hear them above the roar of Hope Creek. Now I was to see something I had never seen before. A mother bear show her authority in a cub fight. One cub broke away and ran down the slope, the other started after him. The old mother followed and passing him, stopped and turned in front, looking at him. That ended that fight and soon everyone was back on the job. I noticed the wind had died and now I felt a puff of air from down the creek. I was quite sure the old mother wouldn't wind me from so far away possibly 400 yds. and across the creek. Both of us high up. In a very few minutes she exploded into action. She ran up the slope a few yds., turned and looked and then took off with the cubs trailing as fast as they would go. She would stop and look back now and then to see if everyone was coming and then race on. She angled up the long slope and for the big basin where I was yesterday. It would be a good three quarter mile to the canyon. No stopping to rest. Those little cubs ran all the way and out of sight over the ridge before the canyon. I had lost my bears.

July 4 – Fog, Calm & 44°.

I read from Bea Van Horne's book *Planet Steward* by Steven Levine, journal of a wildlife sanctuary. She wrote – "the author is very much a poet and it takes place in the desert but somehow it reminds me of you and Twin Lakes."

A long haired whiskery guy and his small family taking care of a very small sanctuary in Arizona and he reminds her of me? Maybe it would. He is on speaking terms with all the birds, animals and insects. Instead of canoeing the porcupines across a lake he hauls them to a foreign land in a burlap sack. Read and write and dig a few nik-naks out of the cache to celebrate the 4th. Towards five the weather was clabbering and I lost hope of seeing a plane today.

A new evening meal dish in a fashion. Instant mashed potatoes with a generous amount of pure calories (bacon grease) added seasoned with salt and pepper. To this add my bowl of famous Twin Lakes navy bean soup. As sensible as onion and honey in a hotcake sandwich. That purty good looking Washington, D.C. lawyer took hers without the onion. More Labrador tea. If it has ill effects a generous portion should make it noticeable. Dishes done and the weather is on the rise over the lower lake. The breeze continues steady and the temp. stands at 48°.

July 5 – Partly Cloudy, Calm & 46°.

[Bush pilot Bud Loftstedt stopped at RLP's to inform him that an elderly Hawaiian couple, staying at his cabin at the head of upper Twin Lakes, were missing and he sought Proenneke's help in locating them.]

They [the Loftstedts] took off...I would paddle up the lake close to the shore to see ...I was nearly opposite Frank's [Bell] cabin and came onto an oar adrift at the waters edge. I leaned it against a small spruce to keep it at that location ...I was looking for anything that may have drifted ashore...across the upper end I ran into three baby sea gulls...Down the far side [north side] to Bell Creek and on down...past the poplar point below Frank's cabin and...something out of ordinary on the beach. I soon made it a person in waist high waders—feet in the water and head towards the brush. It was the woman and I could see she had been dead for some time. I couldn't do her any good...I could see the... motor and green river boat... only a very short distance from the good gravel beach of Glacier Creek... A complete turn around with the line and two half hitches for a knot. The spinning rods laying nearby – one taken apart and the other assembled. I was doing pretty good at finding where Bud had failed completely. Where was the man. The knot looked to me that a man had tied it. I would go home and get a tarp to cover the body – bring some emergency gear and hope to find him with a spark of life remaining. At the first point below the creek I cut across. I had found her at about 5:15. Here by 6:15 and

I loaded my gear – Jerg's green plastic tarp, survival rations, honey, tea and the little one burner Coleman and a can of sterno. My axe, a blanket, sleeping bag and first aid kit. I hung on the little kicker and headed back to her. I covered her and loaded the tarp edge with rocks to keep the wind from blowing it off or the rising lake from carrying her away. Went on up along shore watching closely for sign of him in the brush near shore. Past Bell Creek and to the old sheep camp. He would make good tracks there if he traveled that far. No tracks – not a sign of a track. I motored back to the boat and followed the game trail up country. Soon I saw tracks on a muddy spot and soon a second time and this time the tread mark of two different boots that appeared to be made at the same time. They had traveled together as far as she lay I figured but I couldn't imagine him leaving her laying in such a position. I figured he had died, but where. Not between her and the boat I was quite sure. It was now ten o'clock and I wasn't making any progress. I paddled down the beach opposite to my place and came across. Just on the beach and here came a Civil Air Patrol Beaver. I signaled with my flashlight and he blinked his landing lights. A few circles and he came in for a perfect landing on the glassy water under poor light. Four guys. Lofstedt had reported and they came. Too dark to search – they came in and I built up a fire for coffee, tea or whatever. Popped some corn and waited for daylight. The night clear as a crystal, calm and I didn't think to check the temp.

July 6 – Clear, Calm & 40°.

Nothing new turned up. Not a track. The pilot and his man had searched the Bell Creek point. Nothing to do but go back to Anch. and they let me off at my canoe at Glacier Creek. They flew away I went across to where the oar stood against the spruce and worked down close to shore hoping to find the other one. A red airplane with red floats came up the lake and it looked like Babe's "T craft" but his had aluminum floats. I had heard a plane earlier and now it registered, I had left a note on the table. "Tragedy up the lake, one dead & one missing. Please let me know you are here." Babe had read it and came on up. I paddled out so he could see me and soon he passed headed for my beach. When I arrived, he had unloaded a stack of stuff and there was little David [Clum]. He had made it to Twin Lakes at last. Babe was interested to know what Raymond had to say. He thought that he would be here by now. He had butchered more hogs and got Chuck Hornberger across the lake to help for which he gave him half a hog. I got my outgoing mail ready and he headed for home. It was "Bee's" "T craft" on his old 1320 floats (from the little black bird).[35]

He was hardly more than gone when here came Bud Lofstedt and son[36] with a state trooper, Dave, (his first name). Many questions by the man with the pistol on the hip and he wrote notes like mad. My address date of birth etc. Now a new crew and no one familiar with the findings. As this was my stomping ground and knew the developments

[35] "little black bird" refers to a black and silver "T craft" owned by Babe Alsworth that had small floats.

[36] Bud Lofstedt's son's names were Vernon Jr. and Craig.

would I get them started. I would if they would take care of my partner, little David. We will take him along Bud said and soon they were flying to Glacier Creek and me with the canoe a second time. They would bail out Bud's boat and we would use it to haul the body to Frank's beach for loading into the new [Cessna] 180. By now a fair breeze was down and it was rough at the scene of the tragedy. The trooper had brought a body bag (strong rubber coated zipper full length) with strong canvas loops on each side. I towed the boat with the trooper up the splashy lake to the body. He had suggested we leave David at the airplane but David didn't get the message and skipped and hopped the boulders along shore like a dog following a boat. We went ashore on the rocks and got the canoe and boat up away from wave action. He said, "Maybe we should send David up the beach a little way." "Oh! let him stay, he is tough," I said, "unless you insist." He removed the rocks and pulled the tarp away. He took many pictures and examined the contents of her jacket pockets. A paper bag of fishing lures. That accounted for no tackle box. David was as interested as anyone and would make a good trooper.

Bud had the door removed from the [Cessna] 180 when we got there and the four of us easily transferred her to the airplane. He tried the Sea King kicker motor on his boat. It ran and good but evidently the man had been unable to start it for we had found it in gear, the choke on and the fuel line unhooked. Bud's son would take the boat over to his place. They flew with the body to his bay and David & I headed down a pretty lumpy lake with gas getting low but no matter, it would be easy paddling. We made it and no more than on the beach when here came Charlie Allen's orange and white [Cessna] 180 with the Park Service and Mardy Murie that old sourdough lady aboard. Me well past 24 hrs. without sleep and company aboard. Again Charlie beached over at the creek, his favorite sandy spot. They came trailing in packing a fresh batch of greens from his garden. A good man that Charlie Allen. Mardy and it is Mardy not Maudy, greeted me as if she had known me all her life. Not a spring chicken but very active and really enjoys the outdoors. I had hotcake batter ready to go (my breakfast which I hadn't had yet and it was past noon). They had brought lunches. Bob Belous was along and also Ted of the Park Service.[37] They ate mostly on the beach until I got a stack of hotcakes and then Charlie sat close and sampled one after another trying to make up his mind if he liked them. Mardy had a couple with peanut butter, honey and onion, try anything once she said. She liked the combination. Bob couldn't see the onion and Ted didn't dare. They stayed and visited a couple hrs. I guess, and then made ready to fly away. We saw them off and now rest and read my mail and stow the grub that Babe had flown in. David wanting to take a hike and go fishing. First things first and I opened some of my mail. I would be reading and suddenly wake up with a start. Getting by and here comes another Beaver with CAP colors.[38] Troops aboard, a ranger and two boys to search the area.

Now could I fill them in as to where everything had been found to date. They had a very crude map of the area drawn by someone who saw it once. I could go with them and point everything out if they would bring me back. My first ride in the copilot's seat

---

[37] Theodore R. Swem, (1917-) chairman of the NPS Alaska Planning Group that was charged to plan the new national parks in a Alaska during the 1970s.

[38] CAP – Civil Air Patrol.

of a Beaver. A big old bird and real comfortable. We flew up to Lofstedt's bay and down the far side. Here on the beach they made plans. The pilot suggested they camp here and use my canoe. I didn't agree to that. If the lake got rough I didn't want them on the lake with my canoe. We had too many dead and missing now. The ranger agreed that they should be camped on the same side as the search area or at Lofstedt's and use his boat to cross the upper end. The subject of bears again. Could a bear have gotten the man and would there be danger of bears. "Forget the silly bears. You will be very fortunate if you see one." Bears avoid people as much as they possibly can.

They had a radio to talk back to Anch. and four walkie talkies. They would leave one with me and call from the upper end to see how it came in. They took off and the pilot said I'll fly by to let you know I got off ok on my way back to Anch. Again David wanted to go fishing and I wanted to take a nap. I could sleep over by the creek and wait for the radio call. No call and I tried for an hr. but no answer. No fish and David said lets go to sleep so we paddled to my beach. We didn't get inside until here came a blue and white Super Cub with Dept. of Public Safety decal on the side. They flew up, down and landed. It was the trooper, Dave [Johnson][39] again and the pilot one from Anch. and just down from a tour up north. Dave said the second boot sole tread matched with those at Lofstedts. He had learned the man smoked Camels. They had stayed at the hotel advertised on the match book cover. They had phoned his son in Hawaii and learned he had a history of heart trouble and in his personal belongings they found pills for many different ailments. So – the man was not in the best of shape to cope with the upper lake on a windy day. Dave would be staying for a couple days with the ranger and his men. He asked me if I had had any sleep yet. No but I wasn't doing too bad. Again the subject of bears and what part they might have played in the mans disappearance. "No, the bears played no part in it," I was sure of that. A bear in the area and I would have seen its track somewhere. They flew up the lake and David [Clum] and I cleared the upper bunk for sleeping. The Cub went through Low Pass just before I called it a day. The next thing I remember was a commotion along side my bunk. David had rolled off of the upper bunk. No damage and I got him squared away again.

July 7 – Overcast, Calm & 52°.

Very early in the morning I woke up to hear a light rasping on the northwest corner and soon again. I got up and went out. There was a young porky on the stump by the clothesline. He started up a spruce as I went out the door but came down as I waited behind the corner with my porky trap and shovel. He went through the brush to the woodshed and there I trapped him in a corner and canned him for early morning delivery to the old country.

The Cessna had taken off and circled us a few times and my cabin as many, before landing and going to my beach. He could land along side of us had he wanted to see me.

---

[39] David Johnson, state trooper for Alaska Department of Public Safety based on the Kenai Peninsula.

We paddled up on our continuing trip around the lake and was past Low Pass Creek when the Cessna took off on down country. It was one thirty before we came to my beach helped along by healthy waves. We were hungry. David says I'll take my cold rolled oats mush now instead of for supper. I got him started and fixed him an open faced sourdough sandwich to his specifications. Two kinds of jelly and peanut butter. That one down he wanted another and got it. I was washing dishes and noticed he had quit and had half of his mush left. I asked him to finish so I could wash the dish. He was too full so I said oh, you can sit right there until you are hungry again and he did which took nearly two hours. We would not go hiking until the dish was washed and he could wash it. I went about reading a few letters I had missed yesterday and opening my packages. That lady Eveyln from Kansas sent me two gallons of peanuts salted in the shell for the spoon I had sent. A pair of chaps in a second package from sister Florence [Proenneke]. Pant leg type to which I would add belt loops. The material of these, hand made (by her), chaps like imitation leather with nap on the inside. Should be very satisfactory if not too warm.

David needed a ladder to get into that high upper bunk so I ripped a pole for side rails and rounds and was putting it together when he came out. He had gotten it all down but one spoon full and could he start washing the dish. When the bowl is empty and licked clean I said and he went back. He was just testing to see if I really meant what I said. He finished the job and we climbed the hump and over to the spruce knoll where he pitched half a wagon load of rocks down while I took ten.

This evening we would have a marshmallow and wiener roast for supper. Go over by the creek and build a fire. We took those two items plus potato chips, grapes, carrots and more. An enjoyable time was had by all. Rising biscuits to bake when we returned. Now at 10 partly cloudy. The up the lake breeze dieing and the temp. 53°.

No more airplanes came so the CAP ranger, his crew of two and the trooper evidently didn't find the man who is missing. I would like to join the search again but I hate to tour a rough lake with David aboard the canoe. Maybe tomorrow morning it will be near calm or better and we can take a run up to see what has developed.

The pilot of the Cessna, Jerry Yeiter of BLM.[40] The note "I stopped by to say hello. However you were gone. Hope to see you some other time."

July 8 – Partly Cloudy, Calm & 44°.

Today we would go up and help the trooper and the CAP crew search if they still hadn't found the man.

Today they planned to start where the cap & jacket were found and work straight towards Bell Creek which would lead them by Frank Bell's cabin on the upper side. Did they mind if David and I went along to help search. Come right along. David can stay in camp with the boy keeping in contact with the radio. David wanted to go and I allowed he

---

[40] Jerry Yeiter, trespass abatement officer for Bureau of Land Management investigating allegations of illegal log cutting around Lake Clark.

would be as good as a dog in the brush. We hit the good game trail at Frank's beach and followed it down country maybe 250 yds. then they took us straight up the slope a hundred yds. or more to the spot where the clothes had been found. Now we would spread out and head for the creek. I was high man on the slopes. David and a boy, Cook, was next down.

What was the one thing that caused the man and wife to die. The one thing more than any other. I think it was losing the oar. With it gone they drifted much to far away from camp before they came to the beach at Glacier Creek. He had not been able to manage the kicker. With both oars he could have made shore perhaps at Frank Bell's beach. They had both died trying to get back to Lofstedt's cabin.

The trooper Dave had said I don't think we need to look higher than we were at the clothes site. If he didn't object I would stay a little higher. We started and right away I was traveling along the lower side of some huge rocks half buried with moss and brush. David and Cook together below me. I said, David scatter out a bit you might be the one to find him. He came up slope a bit and almost immediately he said, "there he is." I advanced a few steps and sure enough there he lay just ahead of me. Laying on his back. Arms across his chest feet down the slope. Wearing chest high waders and a light Hawaiian print elbow length (sleeves) shirt. That second oar I had searched for was about fifteen feet above him. I had told the trooper that we had looked for it along shore down country yesterday and didn't find it and I suspected he had carried it to use as a walking staff. The trooper found his wrist watch minus the band maybe fifteen feet below where he lay. Both his and her watches had stopped not far apart in time.

One rear seat removed and we loaded the body in. A second trooper had come with him. He took the body and two troopers to Kenai. He brought the message that the Beaver would be due at 3:30. David and I would wait to see the CAP crew away and it was good that we did. 3:30 came and no plane. 4:30 and no plane. The boys were getting impatient and after it was more than three hrs. late we decided we had better go.

Here came the Beaver and we motored back to see the boys away from Twin Lakes. The same pilot that brought them. As we loaded gear in the plane we came to a full case of C rations. "Let's leave the rations with Dick" he said. We have lots of rations. Just what I was needing when Jake gets here with the Cub. The boys had given us five meals of rations and now we had twenty two. He asked David for his phone no. in Anch. He would call his folks when he got back and tell them that he had seen us and about David finding the missing man. The trooper had already given David his card. Trooper David Johnson was his name. David would cross out the Johnson and add Clum when he got home. Away at last and we motored down the ruffled lake. Maybe Twin Lakes would settle down to peace and quiet for awhile. What was the one thing that caused the man and wife to die. The one thing more than any other. I think it was losing the oar. With it gone they drifted much to far away from camp before they came to the beach at Glacier Creek. He had not been able to manage the kicker. With both oars he could have made

shore perhaps at Frank Bell's beach. They had both died trying to get back to Lofstedt's cabin.

July 9 – Clear, Calm & 42°.

This was one beautiful morning in early July and one would wonder how two people could die of exposure even though they were from the semi tropical Hawaiians. John Taplins was his name according to his hunting license, and he would have been 71 in August. She was sixty years old. On rereading my journals I learned that I was on Crag Mt. peak the day and probably at the same time that they were in trouble on the lake. A mt. between me and the lake prevented me from seeing that part of their course except the landing near Glacier Creek. Good that I didn't see them for I most certainly would have taken them for the two men who had passed here in the boat. Two men that could take care of themselves even with no motor and one oar. Now I am happy that no mystery of a missing man is connected with the lakes. I would have been looking for him along shore or any time I was inland from Glacier Creek to the upper end.

Spuds for breakfast and Trooper Johnson had given us a pound of Fiesta sliced bacon and some grapefruit juice.

A promising day for lake travel – we would cross and climb up and past the waterfall. Go over and look down on Emerson Creek and maybe climb to look out peak. A nice crossing with David really in great paddling form. He did a real good job and stayed with it all the way. I complimented him highly and I suspect it soaked in a bit. A picture of him at the waterfall and we climbed the big rock face. Him crossing bare rock that some grown men refuse to cross. Into waterfall canyon where the forget-me-nots grow along with many other wild flowers. Out onto the skyline and across to look down on Emerson [Creek]. Still some snow patches and on the first, caribou tracks. Tracks of three headed up. I watched closely and saw them on a snow patch before they saw us. We made a big detour for the wind was wrong. David wanted to take their picture. We got very close and as we slowly raised up to shoot – they spotted us and took off. I got them but David refused to shoot until they were nearly a hundred yds. away. Buck fever or what, I don't know.

Noon time and we ate lunch while looking down on the creek of a hundred waterfalls. Our caribou had circled onto the big pasture to climb the first snow filled wash and stand shivering the insects with noses to the snow. We climbed look out peak and flushed a young ram who raced down by us headed for the slope of Falls Mt. A skinny looking guy with his short coat.

From the peak I glassed up Emerson and spotted what appeared to be five more caribou on the snow. We stayed awhile covering the country with bare eyes and glasses. Me sitting down and I happen to swing my feet clear of the ground to face up Emerson my foot hit David's Instamatic Kodak and sent it bouncing down the steep slope. It flew

open and the film cassette flew out. Both over a ledge and I feared that the rocks below would be littered with the pieces for it was a few hundred feet straight down. Carefully I worked down to the edge and was surprised to see both the camera & the film on a ledge two feet down. Past that and it would have been goodbye camera. I collected them but we couldn't make it work. The film had loosened in the cassette and the film advance refused to operate properly. Lucky that he had only three exposures remaining on that roll.

Then came the frightening experience. I was glassing not paying attention to David. I looked over to see him on the steep side of the ridge with that shear drop only a dozen feet down the very steep slope. He was tugging on a rock that he wanted to dislodge and tumble down the mt. I really gave him the word for I had cautioned him before about rolling rocks down the mt. We headed back and flushed the three young bulls again. They went back to the snow of Emerson slope.

Several airplanes and now two headed up and climbing. The party of seven were leaving the campground near the stream. Here again David headed down the mt. on his own and at an unsafe place. It seems that the rough stuff is a challenge to him. Some stern words got him in line and he wore the stitching out of his hip pockets sliding down on the grass with hidden rocks. I was glad when we reached timber line. The lake still flat calm and the suns reflection very warm. I found my thermometer at 76° when we arrived. The warmest of the season.

We went up to water my garden and pull the fireweed. I have radishes that will soon be ready to use. We had hauled home the CAP empty ration cans so flattened the box full for burying. I did some washing and David played on the beach. Again this evening we would have a marshmallow and wiener roast over by the creek. A good selection of groceries in the styrofoam chest we trudged over. A couple cans of Squirt cooling in the creek. Few insects the lake nearly flat. The fast flowing Hope Creek. It was nice. And so ended this July 9th. The sky partly cloudy, a very light breeze down and the temp. 62°.

July 10 – Partly Cloudy, Calm & 50°.

A pretty morning and I was up early. Spuds for breakfast because of a surplus of cold hotcakes and my little guest suggested we should have something else due to the danger of eating eggs two mornings running. I allowed we would burn up the eggs on a hike today. If it was calm we would paddle to the upper end for some black sand (magnetite) which comes down with the river high water. A down the lake breeze came early so we would go up Hope Creek to look for iron pyrite on the Hope Creek glacier tailing pile. A good long hike and I suspected he would sleep good tonight. A few small chores done. The beans to finish cooking and we made ready to go. David was wearing his rubber boots which I figured were no good for the trip. He said that he had a blister on his heel from yesterday. I figured he was just telling the story so he wouldn't have to lace up his shoes. I asked him to bring this blister out for inspection and he did, the little rat. Sure enough, a small water blister. I drained it and covered it with a Band-Aid. Shoes on and strings

tied for all day. It was near eight when we paddled to Cowgill beach and secured the canoe (bottom up) to a spruce.

The lure of that valueless pyrite kept him going. It had been a few years since I saw Hope Creek glacier (the high one) close up. A snow bridge got us across the head of Hope Creek and we saw fresh caribou cow and calf tracks. I expected to see some on the snow near the glacier. It had been a warm trip but as we neared the upper end it cooled and there were no insects. A steep snow patch to climb and tailing pile rock humps to go over before we could see the glacier. I suspect we had climbed as high as yesterday. We found a few good specimens of the precious metal (in the eyes of little boys) and ate our lunch at about 12:30. It was ten past one when we headed down. It had taken four hrs. going up. If it took the same coming down, we would be home by five. David was in good shape and high spirits as we came down grade. We stopped to rest and glass bear country at the second canyon but saw nothing. A rubber sock crossing of first canyon and on down the trail. A hesitation to scoop up a couple handfuls of water at every spring and stream, boy that water is good. David was behind and some how got below the good trail. Brush choked deep washes but he continued on even though he knew I was on a good trail. He would be pooped for sure by the time he pulled out onto the Cowgill benches. He did it looking pretty good, that little eight year old. We crossed high up and watched the Cowgill willow thicket for awhile for we had seen a fresh moose track near Hope Creek. Down the mt. and the trail to the canoe. 3 _ hrs. to make the return trip. A couple peaches, sourdough sandwiches and corn chips would carry us over till supper time. David hadn't written for yesterday and he tried to convince me that he couldn't for he had made a mistake. He had been a day ahead on the calendar from the start so he would and should skip a day to get back in step. I got him squared away on that operation and he changed the dates of his previous entries. He wrote and did a good job of it judging from the number of words I was asked to spell.

July 12 – Overcast, Calm & 56°.

A very low overcast which reminded me of the dark days to come. Aug. can be like that. Spuds for breakfast, spuds with onion, salt, pepper and garlic salt and little David asked for the rubber scraper to get the last of the fried egg.

On my way to dump the dish water when I saw that darkie porkypine behind the woodshed. Here was a good chance to go out of the porkypine business. I hurried to get my porky can and shovel and called for David to come help can a porkypine. He had started up a tree but I broke his grip and he tumbled into the brush. A great thrashing around to get him stopped and David held the can while I crowded him in and mashed the ears over. We would go to the upper end for black sand and would turn him loose at the old sheep camp. David did the best job ever on the paddle. Paddled like an old timer and nearly the long three miles.

Again I saw the young seagulls and we paddled in close for a better look. Growing

like weeds and I wonder what help they get from their parents. From fresh hatched till they fly you see them on the open lake. A nice feed for a big lake trout when they are small. David up ended the can on the beach and our porky started a new life by crawling up the slope through the heavy brush.

It was raining and had been since we had left my beach. David was getting damp and fingers cold. We paddled across the end till we struck pay dirt. The slope of the beach black with magnetite. It wouldn't take long to fill his four ink bottles. But first we had to dry out and warm up. We beached and headed for Lofstedt's cabin. That school teacher Whitney[41] had left the cabin very neat and we would do the same. I cut a small dead spruce and the branches went for fire starter. The tree sawed up for a heating fire. Some water on for hot tea and bouillon broth. It rained a real get wet rain and on the metal roof it sounded like a down pour. A couple army cots for us to stretch out on and we passed out for a few minutes. More than an hour we stayed by the fire before the day brightened down country. We headed for the canoe in a light drizzle. Two pans of material and we had the bottles full and more. Fog was traveling at a good rate along the mt. sides and at a very low elevation. It was strange that we weren't getting a head wind at lake level. We beached at first point to eat part of our lunch and met green water soon after. Head for the bend of the beach above Carrithers' point and have dead calm nearly to the point. White capping and a little battle to reach my beach. We had stopped to look at the transplanted red radishes. The damp day was good medicine. Nearly all standing in good shape and I was happy for the extra three rows of radishes.

Build a fire and dry the black sand was the next thing on the program. Wet and packed in the bottles. David had to dig it out, soon it was steaming in the gold pan. Much stirring to get the lumps out and next the rebottling. All had to be labeled with the persons name who would get a sample. One for each his brother, sister and the Japanese prospector, Tak.[42] Saturday, take a bath and wash clothes day. Why couldn't he just wait until the day before he went home. Save a lot of extra work. I allowed we would make this time a practice run and the real thing the day before.

July 13 –Fog, Rain, Calm & 46°.

Sunday morning and with the weather as it was, a good morning to sleep in a half hr. longer. A little stitching to do on David's sweatshirt before I built the breakfast fire. I was surprised to see that little sleepy head come tumbling out without being called for hotcakes. It was a morning for small chores. Repair my water bucket, shuffle the contents of my cooler box to see what I had and what wasn't keeping too well. Answer a million questions that patience and observation would have taken care of. Small boys live in a very slow moving world.

---

[41] Clark Whitney, teacher and principal at Nondalton and Kenai Peninsula schools.

[42] Probably Tak Yamamoto an individual who apparently lived in Anchorage and did assessment work on the copper deposit at Kasna Creek on Kontrashibuna Lake.

We waited for favorable weather to go fishing at Emerson Creek. Finally we could see the far shore and then the lower end. A light breeze had come up the lake and died. As we shoved off it was breezing down. A pretty good trip down with the usual are we halfway yet and where is two thirds of the way. He did pretty good for the half but then he began to fizzle. He wasn't tired, he just couldn't see the end. It was, "I'm tired" and he quit. I wondered what he would do if I got tired too so I quit and we drifted and I looked for caribou below Low Pass Creek. It wasn't but a few minutes until he said, "We had better go, I have to go to the bathroom." Emerson was running a nice stream but not as much as I expected. Would we catch anything. The party camped there said they had caught only a couple fish. David hooked one first cast with his spinning rig, and I have never seen a boy so excited. I was afraid he would lose it in his hurry to get it flopping onto the coarse gravel. Then I hooked a nice grayling. He lost a Mepps and that 2 lb. test line he insists is the only thing is a mean one to tie a lure to. "Fish can't see it," he said. I allowed that the fish have better eyesight than I. He lost a second lure and wasn't very happy about losing his good Mepps. I hooked one and lost it only to hook another and lost it before the lure came in. Next cast, one on and off and another took it in shallow water. A seventeen inch grayling. Four good fish – the first one of his a dolly or arctic char 15 inches and his last one a greyling 17 ½ inches. Four good fish, enough for two days but he wanted to catch more and turn them back. I didn't approve of hooking grayling with barbed hooks and turning them back. I have seen nice ones die within a few minutes after being released. He agreed it would be better to come fishing again. Next time I will let him catch them all.

The down lake breeze had died and we would have a good trip home. A check on the campsite of the hikers and if it wasn't for the trail leading inland to their tents you would never know that they had been there. Some of those long haired folks wearing granny glasses have a feeling for the land. We went to visit Vanderpool's cabin and found it as I had seen it last.

Light rain was falling as we headed home. David in high spirits but he didn't care to paddle. Get him lined out and taking it easy and in a minute he would be playing in the water with his paddle. Ok! stow the paddle in the canoe and sit very still while I paddled. A canoe is like an airplane – trim it for straight and level and it is easy to keep it that way. Foolishness from the front seat and you are busy correcting all of the time. He sat and dozed, nearly tipping over in the seat at times. We eased up on a little bunch of white winged scoters past the halfway.

Fish cleaned and hung to stiffen. A sourdough sandwich. David had taken his camera out to get a picture of a sea gull feeding on fish scraps. He came back and asked me if it would hurt his camera to fall in the lake. Why do you ask, I questioned him. "Because I dropped mine in the water, but it wasn't in very long and it floated," he said. I shook a few drops from it and hung it over the stove. He would like to carve something with his new Western hunting knife. He liked my little model boat. I got him started and ended up doing the carving.

A good fish fry for supper and he was counting the days till he would be going. "I wish I could wait and go home on my birthday, then I could stay longer." "Now lets not get carried away with the program," I said.

Now at 8:30, cloud deck above the peaks down country. White caps running down and the temp. 52°.

July 18 – Overcast, Calm & 52°.

The afternoon passed quietly and before it seemed possible, it was time to have porkypine and beans, fresh baked biscuits and a green salad. The meat was good. One hind leg a good big portion for one meal. A porcupine would furnish a weeks supply of meat. I stepped outside to watch the sun drop behind the ridge leading up to Falls peak. More than halfway to the peak now. A couple weeks will see it about ready for that long slide to Emerson Creek.

The lake flat calm and fog patches lay along the slopes. A beautiful evening with the setting sun lighting the fog and green of the slopes still fresh from the afternoon shower. I slipped the canoe into the water and headed for Low Pass Creek. I didn't intend to be gone long but had no more than started when I knew I would see the connecting stream running bank to bank. A few nice trout were feeding on the surface along the way and especially out from the gravel banks. I beached at Emerson to watch for action there but it was quiet. I paddled on following the shore to Jerre's cabin and then cut across. It was clearing and the air turning cool. 10:20 when I came inside. The past three hrs. had been true wilderness living. Temp. was 46° when I called it a day.

July 22 – Partly Cloudy, Calm & 46°.

It was clearing as I paddled the dead calm lake but I noticed the clouds were moving down at a rate that could bring a good breeze. Just as I beached a light ripple covered my end of the lake. No luck on the creek mouth so I turned the canoe bottom up and headed up the flat. In the brush and out as I was wearing my L.L. Bean pacs. I came across a rounded rock. I have often wondered why Emerson Creek puts out so many perfectly symmetrical shaped stones. Round and egg shaped. Soon I came across another one.

An airplane and I stopped to get a good look at it. Yellow in color but not a J-3 Cub. A Cessna 180 on floats traveling up the far side. A good looking rig that I didn't recognize. I went as far as the lower falls which is running lots of water. The [Cessna] 180 hadn't come back and I suspected it was at my place. I headed down picking up my smooth stones as I came to them. Suddenly it hit me how they come to be so perfect. The waterfalls, many of them on the creek. The low falls and another just above it that can't be seen except from the air. The high waterfall. Pools at the bottom of each. The

stones worn smooth grinding and churning in the turbulent water. All the same as a giant tumbler. Comes a flood and a lot of water they are thrown over the edge of the pool and are scattered on the creek flat. Gold, if there is any could be found in those pools in bedrock.

Lunch time and I could see the sun. My Baby Ben still a half hr. slow. This afternoon I would make a scouting trip up Hope Creek. I just might see a bear up there. Only the Exakta went for the ride. I might see a good flower shot or two. I had just hit the caribou trail leading up the creek when I saw one fair track of a good big bear coming down. It wasn't there when little David and I traveled the trail. Farther another and smaller track, so there had been bears on the creek. At Pup Tent canyon I climbed to the high bench for a good look at the creek bottom and on up to bear heaven. No sign of bears. I went up 1st canyon to my crossing and found too much water. With some big stones in the right places I might make a crossing. Stones that were a heavy load and each was swept away by the fast water. Finally a big one held and I made it with only a slightly damp foot. I stayed high on the slope headed for 2nd canyon. I stopped to glass and saw a black spot up near the head of the creek. Very green there with many springs gushing water. The black spot, the shadow side of a rock, but while I watched it moved. Then another. The cubs! The old mother one and the cubs had come back to the creek. I picked her up. All three feeding and moving about in the wide open. If I had the Bolex I would be in business. I watched them awhile. Moving down a bit if anything. They climbed the high bank to the left (from me) and she flushed a squirrel. A big chase and some digging. A good patch of saxifrage nearby and I used a little film before heading down. The sun getting around and it must be five.

It was after six when I reached the cabin. A trip to the point for new radishes, nice size and very crisp. A fire going and I was soon ready for supper.

Freddy the squirrel came and I got a surprise. I expected the timid approach and gentle reach for the hotcake. Instead she came rushing and knocked it from my hand. A second time but I was ready and got out of the way. I tossed it on the ground. She grabbed it and ran to the spruce. That squirrel has a good capacity for such a little runt. Looking fatter by the minute.

August 6 – Partly Cloudy, Calm & 36°.

Again a young rabbit in the woodshed. Yesterday I saw two of a size feeding on green stuff there.

Supper time saw the last of my porkypine meat and I am sorry that I don't have a live one nearby. Deported five and ate two. Probably seven was the population on Carrithers' point.

The sun is on the big slide to Emerson Creek. This evening it slid in behind Falls Mt. above five diameters below the peak. Time is wasting at a rapid rate.

Now at eight o'clock, partly cloudy, a light breeze up and 55°.

August 7 – Partly Cloudy, Breeze dn. & 52°.

It had been a long time since I climbed to the bear den site but I knew the trail well enough. Right away I saw some good bushes of berries and some ready for picking. Up the long brushy slope leading into the canyon and I saw my tracks of last time down (Oct. '74). I was packing a full load of gear and it was a heavy load for the day and the grade. Much of it was just along for the ride. Out of the loose rock and onto the grassy slope and soon I could see the dirt and rocks below the den. I was too late, as I suspected. The overhead of the den had softened from the melting snow and rains and had fallen in except for about three feet covering the rear of the den. Many heavy rocks had come out with the dirt and I saw where she had started a few feet away and changed her mind. About eight feet back into the mt. was the length of it and close to four feet wide at the rear. Wide enough that she could turn around for I had seen her enter head first a few times but as a rule she backed in. The entrance was wide (about three feet) and it dropped sharply which might account for the very wet and dirty condition of her and the cubs when they came out. No chance for any melt water to drain away and some no doubt drained in. I looked at it from all angles but couldn't see a picture that anyone would recognize as a bear den. It was about thirty feet down and to the right from the den used two years ago and the den where I disturbed the bear (which left) the year before that. I wonder if it was the same bear all three times and will she come back with the twins this Oct. and dig still another den.

August 8 – Foggy, Calm & 44°.

Visibility was not good at five o'clock but I heard a powerful airplane engine snarling as it made the turn between the lakes. The hunting season air activity is about to start.

For me, today would be a stay at home day. I had beans to cook and laundry to do. If it faired up I hoped that Babe would come and make me free to travel again.

Hotcakes for breakfast and the day was clearing as I did my dishes. This was due to be a beautiful day. Just a little snow left on Gold Mt. and it will be gone before new snow comes and stays. Cooking great northern beans for a change and they cook in a fraction of the time that it takes Babe's Pilot Point small navy beans.[43]

I was hanging my washing on the line when a black and white [Cessna] 185 flew up the far side. In less than ten minutes another of the same colors. They didn't come back for perhaps three quarters of an hr. and then both together climbing for altitude to clear the high ridge at the head of Hope Creek. Probably they brought the guide [George] Pollard and some sheep hunters. I have never met that Pollard from Kasilof and I have never been to his camp. He does leave a clean camp when he goes.

---

[43] RLP refers to old beans that Babe Alsworth had obtained from the cannery store at his wife's hometown of Pilot Point.

August 10 – Partly Cloudy, Calm & 36°.

[Raymond "Jake" Proenneke flies to Twin Lakes in the "Arctic Tern" that he had rebuilt and co-owned with RLP.]

A small plane flew up the far side. Another sheep spotter. Getting towards Glacier Creek when I noticed it was a Cub and yellow. I could see the eyebrows over the cylinders so it was a J-3 [Cub]. It turned and came back down. Still I refused to get excited. I had about given up on seeing Jake fly in. It turned again and came in for a nice landing. As it passed slowing down I could see 7335H on the side and could see Jake in his easy chair rear seat. He had at last made it to the land of the future. That was the nicest thing that has happened at Twin Lakes for a long time. I told him that I had given up and expected that he had junked the remains and hitchhiked back to lower Calif. A late start was the reason. Couldn't get away from L.A. until Aug. 1st. Nearly impossible to get a float plane into the water there. A delay in Seattle. With the fork lift, picking the Cub out of the water for the night they had bent the spreader bars between the floats and had to get new ones air freighted out from New York State. Onward and upward and it got wetter as he went until it was just rain. A great experience for the first long float plane trip. We unloaded his gear and here came another Cub. An old blue and yellow [Piper] PA11 (after the Cub). A heavy set stranger climbed out and introduced himself in a very broken English and I didn't quite get it. As it turned out he was from Switzerland and had been over here for 12 yrs. at least. Hugo Dietrich of Anch.[44] A woman crawled out of the rear seat – his sister from Switzerland over here on a visit and going back soon. They had read the book and wanted to see Twin Lakes country. I invited them in and they were good company. Great hikers and wanted to climb a mt. yet today but visited so long they didn't get it done. Was there some place they could camp. I suggested the old campsite on the other side of Hope Creek. We walked over to see it and it suited perfectly. A nice up the lake breeze to keep the bugs away.

Jake had told Voight and Sis that he would check in with Babe and Mary in time for evening radio schedule so we had better fly over to Babe's. I got my out going mail in order and we took off. My first time away from the lakes area since I came in late April of '74. A good smooth flight over and I could see the Cub was going to be a great little rig for seeing the proposed park area. Past Fishtrap Lake and Lachbuna, down the last stretch of the Kijik and out over Lake Clark. Air traffic over the busy Lake Clark Pass route. Soon we came in for a landing in Babe's bay. His new T craft was resting at his tie down. Jake had written him on his progress up the coast and so there was no reason for him to come to Twin Lakes. Bee [Alsworth] was there on the beach to meet us. Mary came down to see the new Cub and invite us for supper. Bee's wife Betty[45] would give us a big red salmon to take back. Reds were running pretty good and jumping in the bay. Mary had some smoking in the smoke house. A crew from [the]

---

[44] Hugo Dietrick, aircraft mechanic specializing in avionics for Wien Airlines, taught aviation at University of Alaska Anchorage, mountaineer, and river rafter.

[45] Betty Roehl Alsworth, wife of Wayne "Bee" Alsworth.

University of Washington[46] (fisheries research) had just arrived and start work as they do most every year during red salmon run. They would be eating and sleeping there. Mary had no time to eat with us – had to milk the goats and run radio schedule. After supper I collected my mail and we went down to Bee's to see his new house and airplanes he was rebuilding. It was near sun down before we got started back. Again a very smooth flight and as we came in close we could see another airplane on my beach. A stranger, and who would that be? The pilot came walking over from the Swiss camp and who was it but Will Troyer (now with the Park Service). They had fixed him up with an airplane for his own personal use and he was busy flying. First at McKinley and then Katmai Monument from where he had taken off for the flight to Twin Lakes.[47] He had told the powers that be that there was a guy over there who had made a good bear study and he wanted to ask him some questions. He had really come for some good sourdough hotcakes. He had brought a small game hen along from his freezer to pay for his meals. He would spend the night with us and go back this morning. Sis had sent a big strawberry pie with Jake and with it a can of pressurized whip cream. Will made a big fuss over such luxury. Jake gave the pie a blast and part of the gravel floor. It was late before we turned in. I had gone to Spike's cabin for a folding cot. We settled down for what was left of the night. The sky was clear, calm and about 50°. It had been quite a day.

August 11 – Clear, Calm & 35°.

We got busy getting squared away. Jake had some laundry to do. Here came the Swiss down the trail through the woodshed. They had got fouled up on the trail (creek trail) and not feeling very ambitious this morning they didn't climb the hump. They would rather visit, take pictures of my birds and squirrel who were making the most of a good thing. Did she like this country. "Oh, very much." Was it very much like Switzerland. "Yes, but no people and no big hotels on the mt. sides or homes everywhere. There you must stand in line to go hiking or climb the Matterhorn." After a bowl of blueberries they had to be flying. They wanted to go by Telaquana Lake and through Merrill Pass back to Anch. They headed for Hope Creek camp ground where they had their camp gear drying in the sun.

I had that big red salmon to butcher. Yesterday morning I had a small burbot on the trot line. That and our dolly would be our supper. Jake cleaned up the Cub and I got to my writing which was a day behind. There was the berry picker to finish after the Cub was washed and dried. We would have an early supper so the cabin would cool out for sleeping. I went to Spike's garden for radishes. Sourdough biscuits had been rising in the sun until clouds had moved in from the southeast. There had been a down lake wind since before noon. A big green salad of fireweed. Twin Lakes lettuce, onion, carrots, and radishes, beans and fish, sourdough biscuits and honey.

---

[46] Fisheries Research Institute (FRI) from the University of Washington, Seattle.

[47] Troyer's duties had him flying for Katmai National Monument, Mount McKinley National Park, and the proposed Lake Clark NPS unit conducting wildlife surveys.

The dishes done and still enough light to try that new blueberry picking machine. Two cans and two berry pickers went to the Cowgill benches. Light was failing but we had them both full (cans & pickers) in a short time.

To make the Cub secure we anchored that down lake wing to a very heavy stone. Small chance that the wind would change but better secure than to wish it had been. Nine fifteen when we came to the cabin. It is overcast, a good breeze down and 56°.

August 13 – Partly Cloudy, Blowing dn. & 52°.

Jake had his log book to bring up to date and figure the cost of his trip up the coast on floats. He found that it cost him just twice as much to get from the Long Beach airport to the harbor for take off. He had planned to take off from a flat bed trailer pulled by a pickup and it looked as if he had it made and then the airport manager got cold feet. $300.00 to haul it from the airport to the harbor. About $150.00 to cover cost of gas and oil coming up. I did tinkering jobs while I thought about that big chunk of red salmon that we wanted to bake. We could build a fire on the creek flat but it would take a lot of burning to get enough coals. Why not bake it in the stove. Season it good and wrap it in foil. Let the fire burn down to coals and then load him on the fire shovel and slide him in. Sort of a cremation of Sam McGee sort of operation. The entry was a huge success and I would bake it for 20 minutes. Jake went to the creek for a bucket of water so I added an extra five to bring it out when he returned. Steam was pouring from the seams in the foil when I got ready to remove a carcass. I lifted the end with the poker and slid the shovel under just as easy as that. Out it came and to the gravel outside where we opened the foil and loaded our plates. Came loose from the back bone in good shape, smelled fit to eat and it was, we thought. Half of it was enough for supper. The remainder we will have tomorrow. It was a big meal. Jake allowed a guy sure gets an appetite in this country. Just as the birds and squirrel will miss welfare when I leave, he will miss Twin Lakes when he leaves.

August 15 – Overcast, Calm & 46°.

Another one, but slightly improved as if the storm was on its way out. Good that it should be this way for awhile. We would have all of the film exposed before Sept. and the fall colors. Hotcakes for breakfast and brother Jake is eating better than I have known him to for years. Clean air, exercise, good water and no clock to punch is good for a body.

No game visible and I thought that there should be. The big sow and cubs could be anywhere and I hope she doesn't find that super patch of blueberries on the Cowgill Benches. I would do well to visit the place once each day to let her know that I have it staked out.

Jake had some washing to do. I did a few small jobs and decided to visit the

hump. See if the caribou were still there and pick a can or two of wet blueberries. Not good to pick them wet for they will mold if kept too long. We are using them at a good rate so no danger there.

Jake wrote cards and letters. I read *How to Fly Floats* and this morning I had read part of Mardy Murie's book *Two in the North*. It had come in the mail that Jake and I flew back from Babe's. Inside she had written "To Dick Proenneke who gave me one of the most precious memories of my return to the north in 1975... Mardy Murie, Moose, Wyoming." A real nice old sourdough lady, that Mardy.

August 17 – Overcast, Calm & 45°.

Jake wanted to take a shower and I could use one for I can't remember when I had the last one. Where to hang that portable job and have some degree of privacy. I knew of a good place – the meat tree out back. A rope over the big crooked limb. Fill it, hoist it and pull the cap off (unscrew). Jake would test it first while I did my writing. He came back with a good report. The best and only shower bath in Twin Lakes country.

Now at 8:10, overcast, calm with a light ripple down and 57°.

August 20 – Partly Cloudy, Calm & 39°.

Jake busy on the flying record for the Cub and himself. I asked him how he liked bush flying and he thought it was pretty good. Glen Alsworth would fly Hunter and Skip to Anchorage tomorrow. This afternoon they, guided by Leon & Sig, would hike up to Tanalian Falls[48] to fish for grayling. A good hrs. hike and would require much more effort than climbing the hump. They will sleep good tonight.

August 21 – Partly Cloudy, Calm & 34°.

Breakfast out of the way and we prepared to start filming. This was it. We would shoot Jake's arrival over and then follow it with footage of camp activity after his arrival. It ended with him putting Alaska flag decals on the rudder of the Cub. Clouds were building as they will on a summer afternoon. We had planned to visit Snipe Lake (Dark Lake) if there was a chance of sunshine. I rode the rear seat with the camera. We headed down and would try for a few scenes of the Chilikadrotna on our way to Snipe Lake. The air was not smooth and I felt sure my footage wouldn't be of much value, so I didn't waste too much. A camp at either end of Snipe Lake. Jake landed opposite the long gravel spit that separates Snipe Lake proper from a small lake where Frank Bell had built his third cabin. A small very rustic looking cabin. One that looks a part of the wilderness and as if it had many stories to tell. We hiked the few hundred yards from Snipe Lake to visit it. A real

---

[48] Tanalian Falls is a 44 ft. high waterwall on the Tanalian River 3 miles east of Port Alsworth.

mess inside. The roof leaks badly, squirrels had built a huge nest on the upper bunk. Jerre Wills (the new owner had told me) that I was welcome to use it if I got down that way. I never did and doubt that I will with intentions of sleeping there. The location does have its advantages. The cabin on a gentle south slope where the sun would reach it in winter and very large blueberries grow there. Clouds had hid the sun so we picked and ate blueberries until it came out again. It rained a summer shower of very large drops which reminded me of Bonanza Hills rain showers. Water can be squishing in your shoes in minutes. The sprinkles over, we headed back for the Cub and found more berries. Jake dug out a plastic bucket from the Cub and we picked until we figured it would take a gallon can to hold them. The sun was on the slopes toward Turquoise & Telaquana. We would fly that way and check on possibilities for pictures and on the big mineral lick of Beatrice Creek. Jake turned the Cub over to me and I herded it in that direction. Turquoise is just that in color at least. Not a long lake but wide. I had never been as far as Telaquana although I had seen it from the air so I flew farther than intended. Once over the lake I wanted to locate Dick Straty's cabin.[49] He had written me to feel free to use it if I ever got over that way. Upper end on the right side he had written. Jake spotted it as we made the turn at the upper end. A cold dark place in winter I'm thinking. I wonder when the winter sun drops below and when it peeks over the mts. again. Telaquana is a pretty lake with many small islands and it is a clear water lake. Straty had written that red salmon come to the lake and that he catches pike there.

August 22 – Clear, Calm & 35°.

We would rerun yesterdays flight. The fog had cleared out by the time we took off headed for Snipe Lake. The lower lake a beautiful sight in the early morning sun. A nice looking air shot of Snipe Lake and then we landed on the glassy water. A few ducks jumped as we came in and that was good. Ripples on the water and the ducks themselves indicated the surface which is difficult to judge from the air. We beached and climbed a knoll for some ground shots. Again, blueberries and even though we had a long way to go we had to pick a few. By now clouds were forming over the high mts. and would be in our area before we got to Turquoise Lake. On landing we saw a man packing his gear to the beach a few hundred yds. away. He came on down the beach and told us we would have to go – that we was invading his privacy. I had heard that story from the game warden. A writer had come to the lake last year. He wanted peace and solitude. This very same man and his party had come to hunt as they had years before. The man had ordered them to leave and had used words that could mean that he intended to do them harm if they didn't. Hank Rust their pilot had contacted the State Troopers and Fish and Game. They came in and straightened things out. Later the man apologized and everyone was happy.

I found Jake on the beach with a little fire going. He was preparing to make some add hot water stew and a cup of noodles. He had caught a grayling. The sun was getting

---

[49] Richard "Dick" Straty, fisheries and wildlife biologist who worked for U.S. Fish and Wildlife and National Marine Fisheries Service starting in the 1950s. He has had a cabin on Telaquana Lake since 1959.

low and we waited for sunset before heading back. Telaquana is a beautiful spot. We climbed over the high table land and passed below Turquoise then over the ridge to Lower Twin. It was getting dark as Jake said it would if we didn't get going. As we came up the far side of the upper lake we could see a plane at my beach. Who would that be. As we came down along the beach I could see that my door was open and two men walked to the beach. Two guys from Eagle River.[50] One had read my book many times and wanted to see the country. Were there any cabins they could use. I told them the cabins were private and not for public use. I could put them in Hope's cabin for the night as I hadn't closed it up. Save them pitching a tent in the dark. I had told them the camp ground across the creek. "Well, I will get our gear," one said and headed for my cabin. Those guys had moved in bag and baggage. Had seen our pin in the map and figured if we were walking back from Telaquana, we wouldn't be home tonight. I took them up the beach and got them squared away. Back home I built a fire while Jake cleaned his greyling. We had a sourdough sandwich, our cold porridge puddings with lots of blueberries and a cup of hot chocolate. Took care of our film exposed and fresh film for tomorrow. The sky had cleared the moon was full and the temp. 43° at eleven o'clock. It would frost tonight. In the morning I would have to get squared away with those Eagle River boys.

August 23 – Clear, Calm & 34°.

I didn't sleep very well thinking of the days events and especially the Eagle River boys moving into my cabin. What did they have in mind? If they intended to airplane hunt from here they had better make other plans.

We would fly again today, go up the Kijik River to the second forks and then back down to Portage Lake, Otter Lake[51] and Lachbuna Lake. Jake was busy getting the Cub ready for the day and I walked up the beach to talk to the hunters. "Ah! here comes the friendly Inn keeper," one greeted me. They still had their little cooking stove going. We chewed the fat a few minutes and one asked me if he could get gas at Port Alsworth. They wanted to look around a bit and might need some gas to get back. I asked them where they would be camping tonight. "Oh, down country some place." I said, that is good for I couldn't open the mans cabin to strangers except for one night or in an emergency. "Oh no, they didn't expect to hunt out of here – just stopped by to say hello." They would leave the cabin in good order when they moved out.

Jake and I took off down the lakes.

August 25 – Overcast, Calm & 43°.

I did turn in early and didn't hear Jake climb the ladder to the upper bunk. He had read

---

[50] Eagle River, a suburban town about 10 miles north of Anchorage.

[51] Otter Lake, a small lake in Lake Clark Pass; Huten Vena is the Dena'ina word for "trail ascends lake."

by lantern light until a fair breeze came up and surf was slapping the beach and the floats on the Cub. He pulled it higher and then started a rock breakwater that we had talked of doing on the windward side.

My legs and ankle were feeling better when I rolled out at five. I went to the woodshed for fire starter and spuds. Under a spruce at the rear corner two familiar looking objects. A cube of butter with the wrapping looking pretty ratty. A second chunk half eaten. Yesterday morning I had left the cover off of the cooler box to let that cold air settle in and also to air it out a bit. A short time later I noticed a butter carton laying unfolded on the moss nearby and there was that pesky squirrel climbing out of the box. The butter was missing and the squirrel wouldn't show up for welfare hotcakes during the day.

I salvaged the squirrel chewed chunks of butter and we would splurge by adding a good big chunk to our mornings porridge. If Freddy could afford butter we could too.

Lunch out of the way and Jake retired to the woodshed to saw and split. He had done some low tone complaining about my pet saw buck. Legs not spraddled enough and it tipped easily from his Cheechako sawing. I demonstrated that it was the sawyer and not the saw buck at fault but secretly I had thought of improving it for a long time. The sawing end was the offender so we sawed the legs off flush and augured new holes giving the legs wider stance. This lowered it six inches which was an improvement too. Much better he says and I must admit that it does stand solider under heavy bucking.

It had been quite some time since we picked blueberries and had only one gallon in the bank. We would break into that super patch on the down country side of Cowgill Creek. We took a gallon can, two halves and his picker which holds more than a qt. We had paddled and beached at Farmer's landing before I discovered that I hadn't brought my picker. I would pick the old reliable way and see how it compared with that ultra fancy Lumber Jack picker. The berries still there and ripe. Oh boy! such a mess of berries. We both agreed that in our recent touring of the lakes we had seen larger berries but not nearly so many in a small area. I pulled a Leon on him. I picked the good patch once over lightly. I had a half gallon by the time he did but he had more than a gallon by the time I put the cover on mine. I picked and ate while he filled his picker. I do believe a person could get sick on blueberries without sugar. I noticed it before and again this time. They didn't taste as good by the time we headed down.

August 27 – Partly Cloudy, Calm & 32°.

You guessed it – before I was ready the bear was out and chasing a parky squirrel. Such good action and we missed it. He ran the squirrel into its burrough and started to dig. In no time he had a good sized excavation and raking dirt as he backed up to make room for more digging. He acted like a tired dog. Raise his head with mouth open, half panting – was it worth the effort and then into the hole again. At one point it appeared that mr. parky had given him the slip. He backed out and looked around as if all was lost. Then back to digging again. I was watching with the scope and Jake had his eye to the

viewfinder and finger on the button. Because I could see the action better I told him when to mash the button. The bear backed out and turned crosswise. He was eating something – the squirrel. I could see him pulling it apart. I have seen many bears dig for squirrels but none to catch one. Another first for Twin Lakes. A small meal, that parky squirrel and the bear left the diggins and picked a few berries before heading for the brush patch and another snooze. Another wait of more than an hour and he was back in the berry picking business. He found some good patches and was really canning the blueberries. Only room for so many and what appeared to be about two gallons spilled out behind. Now and again he used the claws of a front foot to rake a bush in front of the picker head. We had left the cabin with 400 ft. of film and had used about three. Intending to call it good at three when here came the cow and calf running along the slope below the bear. He stopped and sat like a big dog to watch the crazy caribou.

September 2 –Raining, Lt. Breeze up & 40°

A good paddle and just beached when here came a Cessna 210 retractable up the far side and back cutting across to our side at mid lake. CAP in red under the left wing. Some one is overdue and the search is on. Next came a green and white turbo Beaver 44 "Tango" the number. Sea Airmotive,[52] the air service. Jake says "Is it the Park Service?" I said, "no I don't think so, they have never come in that rig." It turned up country and came down along the beach. We had better head for home and we took off fast paddle. It would be standard procedure if it took off and flew away by the time we reached the halfway. It didn't, and the reason – having a picnic on my beach. I'm glad I wasn't there – stand by and watch them eat a lot of fancy grub. It was Trexler and a plane load. Names too numerous to remember. He had brought 10 rolls of fresh 16 mm film and had a list of questions and answers to hash over. Tom Grey,[53] the pitcher snapper, wouldn't be in but Bob Belous would take his place for four days later when the colors are bright and the weather probably stinko. How long was Jake staying and when would I be going out. The Park Service would take me direct to Anch. if I wanted to go that route. I put the scope on a good ram in the rough stuff high on Bell Mt. A snow white sheep on bare rock and one guy couldn't see it. One or two had never seen dall sheep. Three sheep on the high bench up Glacier Creek.

Time was up they had to go. The pilot was up front behind the wheel and looking anxious. Keith had told me a V.I.P. party would be here the 9th Sept. A man so well off that he was paying his own way to Alaska and has his sights set on becoming Secretary of Interior. They would be in again Sept. 20 to make final decisions on my going out, etc.

The big green bird started with that turbine engine making no fuss no muss. She took off easily and climbed at a good rate. A fine airplane the pilot had said.

---

[52] Sea Airmotive, a Lake Hood based air taxi owned by brothers Ward and Al Gay.
[53] Tom Grey, an NPS photographer from the Harpers Ferry Center in West Virginia.

September 6 – Raining, Lt. Breeze up & 34°.

After lunch we just might film some blueberry picking or fishing in the Chilikadrotna River. Either way we would have to travel by canoe or plane. Our choice blueberry filming patch was down country from Gold Mt. We doubted that the weather would hold fair. Too much sun would cook up some clouds and showers. We would pick blueberries on the Cowgill benches. A good patch that hadn't been touched. Take the camera along and if we had light, film the operation. We went prepared to bring back more than three gallons and would come back with everything full. The light only fair but good enough. Jake recorded my blueberry harvest from start to finish. The sun refused to come out bright until we reached the cabin and then only for a few minutes. I rushed around to get a fire going. We had cut up the porkypine at noon. Jake ran the berries through the sorter and I browned the porkypine in bacon grease after shaking them in my fish seasoning sack. Water was heating in the Jim Shake kettle. In went some carrots, spuds and onion. The meat browned, I dumped the whole smear into the kettle and it was soon boiling merrily. A young tender porky, it wouldn't take long. While it boiled I baked the sourdoughs. The berries done and in storage, Jake went back to Hope Creek to give the fish a bad time. Catch one to take to Terry and Vic if we can see in that direction tomorrow. He came back at 5:45 – no fish but a nice grayling had come in close and looked at him. Letting him know that he was there and not a dumb one.

The porkypine tender and very good. Jake couldn't decide whether it tasted like Iowa rabbit or squirrel. An extra big portion of blueberries with our dessert. It was clearing and calming. It could freeze tonight. Now at 7:45, it is 39°.

September 7 – Partly Cloudy, Lt. Breeze up & 34°.

The little old Cub looked pretty good even though we were not certain it would get out of the small lake with two of us aboard. While we made ready three beavers came to investigate the intruders to their pond. I was elected to make the take off. We turned circles until the engine warmed enough to take full power. She got off easily and we soon cleared the ridge and over to the side of Ptarmigan Creek.[54] Up a valley between it and the Chili [Chilikadrotna] River and then follow the river to Twin Lakes. Visibility was not the best but no problem. Past Snipe Lake and we could see the lower lake dead ahead. Two planes at Arlen's cabin. A fair breeze up the lakes and a few white caps. On past my cabin and a turn to come back by Carrithers' point on landing. The landing not as nice as I would have liked but the master was on the monitor so we made it safely.

Sure tasted good to be back home again. Wet and showing some mileage. I rushed around to get a fire going. The porky kettle and some beans on to heat. My wet socks and pants rinsed out. Jake to doctor blisters on both heels.

[54] Ptarmigan Creek, the first major tributary of the Chilikadrotna River from the Bonanza Hills; Yuzheghnitnu is the Dena'ina word but its' meaning is unknown.

137

Stars and lots of them were showing at ten. It would freeze tonight for sure. A lot of writing to do and Jake turned in as I was near done. In less than five minutes he was snoring. Now at 10:30, it appears to be clear, calm and 34°.

September 12 – Partly Cloudy, Calm & 34°.

We recognized Ketchum's yellow and blue Beaver which came from Turquoise way and gave the Cub a circle. I wondered if it was the Park Service. As I traveled the beach I found where some one had boned out a caribou bull. They certainly took no bones and left a lot of good meat which was too far gone for human consumption. The entire rib cage with all that good boiling meat between the ribs. The head and neck in one chunk. Enough meat there to last me for a couple weeks. A nice hide folded on the beach but it too had been skinned too long. Jake picked me up and we flew up the lakes. We met Ketchum's Beaver along the upper end of the lower lake. On up and a [Cessna] 180 circling to land at my place. He touched down up from Carrithers' point and we followed him down to my beach. 95 "Tango" yellow & white. It was Dick Straty from Auke Bay near Juneau. He had written that he was coming to his cabin at Telaquana in Sept. and would stop by. He had read my book and wanted to meet me. He and I had worked for the Fish and Wildlife Service at King Salmon back about 1954. He had two passengers with him – boys from Juneau who were helping him move a plywood shed from in front of his new log cabin to a location behind it. He didn't want to cut any trees so they would have to cut it in two and move it half at a time. We came to the cabin to find a package on the table and a note. The package contained my journals that the Park Service had copied and the note from Keith Trexler of the Park Service. It read, " Dick & Ray, Word now is that no movie people will be in. We'll depend on Ray's footage of Dick for the Proenneke Special Super Spectacular. I will be here on Tues. (16 Sept.) with room enough to bring you out to Anch. if you'd like to come then. I have to come anyway, so no obligation. If you'd rather come out later either leave me a note or see me on the 16th. I'll arrange a flight whenever you say (at our cost). Sorry we missed you. We had 6 young ladies who really wanted to meet you. (signed) Keith...

The Proenneke film will not be scripted till spring. We will contact you by mail, please let me know where, and we can go where ever you are to do the work. Please call me in Anch. if you come in before the 16th. Many thanks, Keith."

Now, wasn't that something! Wait till spring – doesn't he know that spring is the rush season in the wilderness and as chief inspector of snow storms and rain storms, I must be here. Also on the table a copy of my book. He had said he was going to get one in here and looked for a copy here last trip. They had mailed one but I never received it. So much for the Park Service. Dick Straty and the boys came in. We compared notes on the two lakes. I told him Telaquana was like Kodiak. Alder thickets that a rabbit couldn't get through. How much sun light did he have in winter. He didn't know for he hadn't been

there in winter. Where was the good fishing there and where did he look for sheep. He doesn't see many sheep any more. Today Telaquana was as busy as Lake Hood. Airplanes a plenty.

September 13 – Clear, Lt. Breeze up & 28°.

Not much we could do about the situation. We wanted to fly and felt sure the fog would clear out. It did start to and then closed in tight as ever. Jake made the Cub ready to fly and I did odd chores about the cabin. We heard a plane on the water and close. Here came a beautiful red, white and blue Cessna 185 down along the beach. It was really a beautiful thing with the solid grey fog for a back ground. He nosed in to the beach and a little good looking guy climbed out. Ketchum in big letters on the tail. He introduced himself as Ketchum's son.[55] Had we seen the Ketchum Beaver.[56] We had met it yesterday as we came up the lake. Well, it didn't get back to Anchorage yesterday and the telephone had been ringing all night – relatives and friends inquiring about the people who didn't come home. He figured they landed on a lake and had starter trouble. He had three passengers aboard. Could they see the cabin. Sure, and we had open house. One asked if the cache was for storing provisions or just for show. "That cache is loaded," I told him. They were looking for a caribou as well as the Beaver. If we saw or heard of it would we please get in touch with Ketchum Air Service. By now the fog had cleared out from Carrithers' point on up and they took off up the lake, climbed and came down the far side on the trail of the blue and yellow Beaver.

Now we would fly towards the coast and lower mts. Climb and head north towards the entrance of Lake Clark Pass. A beautiful view of [Mount] Redoubt as we passed. On to Drift River[57] and a very large glacier feeding bergs into the pond at its toe. I ran out of film and spent some time changing while Jake circled out over the flat. Ready to roll and we entered the pass. Good filming until we reached the bend and headed for Lake Clark. Into the sun now and visibility was limited. Jake shaded his eyes with a hand to see and I tried for decent shots. From broadside to the rear it was perfect but out and forward it was very bad. Lake Clark Pass is noted for its heavy air traffic and in the pass is no place to be making radical changes in course just so a pitcher snapper can get a decent shot. I got what I could and let it go at that. I shouldn't have wasted the precious film. It's a long flight from Crescent Lake[58] to Port Alsworth by way of the Pass and our gas gauges were getting down to the add gas mark. Babe's bay would look pretty good and Babe did too as he came down to the beach shortly after we landed. A big grin on his face. "Are you boys having fun," he said. A new "T craft" parked in front of the gate and I asked him how the last trip was. "You know, I can't make it in less than seven days." "Weather

---

[55] Craig Ketchum.

[56] The Ketchum de Havilland Beaver that had brought Keith Trexler and six NPS seasonal employees to the Proenneke Site was missing.

[57] Drift River, a glacial river that heads in the Chigmit Mountains and drains into the Cook Inlet.

[58] Crescent Lake, a large lake in the Chigmit Mountains on the west side of Cook Inlet.

always ties me up somewhere. This last time it was Sheep Mt." (About 120 miles out of Anch.). We needed gas and he got us lined out on that. He would have to go pick up Mary at Nondalton. It would only take about 30 min. "You boys run the ranch and help yourselves to spuds, lettuce, cabbage, carrots and whatever else you want." He took off and we finished gassing and oiling the Cub. Dug some spuds and they were really nice. Soon we heard the "T craft" coming and it pulled in at the hanger. Mary came down through the garden. Looking real trim now after being on weight watchers. We would have to eat a dish of ice cream and set and visit awhile before heading back. I paid my grub bill and for gas and oil. We wanted to help them dig their spuds if they would say when. Sept. 20, weather permitting. The mission girls would be there to help too. Mary dragged out a brand new Canon 35 mm single lens reflex camera she had won by working puzzles. A really expensive camera with two lenses 50 mm and 135 mm telephoto.

It was getting late, we had better be flying if we could get off with all our loot. "Oh you can fly till nine o'clock," Babe said. Not at Twin Lakes on Twin Lakes time. It is pretty dark at 7:30. We loaded our produce and mail, shoved the little bird out from the beach and gave it a try. She got off easily, as if it had taken lessons from the little black bird "T craft." I put it in a steady climb, four and five hundred feet per minute at 65 miles per hr. We were at 3,500 ft. by the time we reached the bend of the Kijik below Lachbuna Lake. On across the rolling hills and around the end of the Volcanic Mts. A steady decent as we came up the lakes and made a landing from Carrithers' point on down.

The Cub taken care of and our grub and gear to the cabin. I started supper while Jake went to check his trot line. Nothing on. I had cut up two grayling. Dishes done and it was 10:15 before my writing was done. That moon coming full was pushing a cloud bank back. It was calm and 37°. This had been quite a day. We had seen a lot of the proposed Lake Clark National Park. All of it very beautiful and very forbidding.

September 16 – Overcast, Lt. Breeze dn. & 43°.

At daylight the weather appeared flyable and I hoped that Keith Trexler would come today. I would try to get more film (to Babe's by the 20th when we go to help harvest the potatoes). If Trexler got busy we just might be able to do some good between now and Oct. 1st.[59]

September 17 – Overcast, Blowing dn. & 48°.

At Babe's, Mary had said, how is the mossberries[60] and cranberries over your way? Very few of either at lake level but quite a few mossberries up Hope Creek. I knew that she

[59] RLP was unaware that the plane carrying Keith Trexler and the others had crashed near the Kijik River killing all aboard after leaving Twin Lakes on September 12, 1975.

[60] Mossberry, variant of the crowberry or blackberry, Empetrum nigrum L., a small evergreen shrub with a white or purple flower that produces a black sweet juicy berry.

likes them both. This afternoon I would go up to 1st canyon and pick her a couple gallons. The sun was nearly in the clear when I left. Jake had water on to take a shower. He is the cleanest brush rat at Twin Lakes and no doubt about it. The reds of the hump and the benches a sight to see even without the sun. I could see rain spilling over the wall at the head of Hope Creek as I traveled the trail. The berries not as large as those found at lower elevation but there was plenty of them. 30 min. for the first gallon. The same for the second. I filled the picker (3 to the gallon) I should have brought more cans. I lined my pack sack with my rain jacket and filled the back pocket. I would have more than three gallons before I headed down. Crossing the creek and I have done it there many times without mishap. This time a rock turned under my shoe pac. My walking stick slipped from a rock and down I went with a splash. One gallon of berries dumped out into the water. (Good that I had taped the cover on) My walking stick and Lumber Jack picker afloat and as luck would have it they didn't go down the chutes of fast water. The old picker I had in my right hand and it had suffered some damage. The 2 inch wide aluminum strip that keeps the berries in was torn loose at one end and bent out of shape. The base of my right thumb had a chunk of skin half as big as a dime flapping in the breeze. Blood would be running shortly. I had a sore knee and a damp right foot. Pant legs both wet to the knee. What a creek crossing that was. I collected my gear and across the high bench to Pup Tent canyon.[61] Blood marked the trail and it was good that I had a mile and a half to go. It would stop by the time I reached the cabin. The fair weather had fizzled. A grey day as I crossed Hope Creek and the short distance to first aid. My luck was not all bad. It started to rain a get wetter as I attempted to clean up the pocket full of berries. The water treatment not as successful on mossberries as blueberries. Jake was busy doing more improving on the breakwater. Hip boots and shovel bringing coarse rock up above water line to keep the surf from carrying away the fine stuff.

It rained a good rain as I cut up the two burbot. Not a lot of fish there so I would fry the heads too. Not a handsome looking face on that burbot but it has flavor out of this world.

Now at seven, blowing strong down. Very rough and ragged looking grey clouds down country. The temp. 46° after a high of 54° today. A Gulf storm can be like that at this time of year. 7:20 and raining a good one.

September 20 – Partly Cloudy, Blowing dn. & 42°.

I built our breakfast fire early in case we went to Babe's to pick spuds. There had been a good showing of blue and the full moon was bright in the western sky. Spuds and dishes done clouds were taking over and the clouds were moving too fast for a good thing.

It tried to rain and we debated whether to go and finally rushed around to get there before the operation was half completed. Mary would get better than three gallons of mossberries and a gallon and a half of blueberries. We had a good load of out going mail.

---

[61] RLP's Pup Tent canyon, a small canyon in the Hope Creek drainage.

I wrote a note to Keith Trexler and left it on the table. In case he came he would know where to find us. Little did I know what we would learn about him, his friends and the big Ketchum Beaver.

Again I was to be the pilot and this trip would be slightly bumpy. The weather improved as we neared Lake Clark – spot of sun light on the yellow fall colors formed by the birches among the spruce. Only a light breeze at Babe's. No sign of activity in the potato patch. We saw Mary first and she told us he was going to let them stay in the ground awhile longer. That they mature if dug after the tops have died and wilted awhile. So – I was right, I worried more about his potato harvest. He appeared and said, "I want to show you the engine from the Beaver." "What Beaver" I asked. "Ketchum's Beaver, haven't you heard? You asked about it last time you was here?" "What happened" "It crashed over on the Kijik and all were killed." The entire group, Trexler, the girls and the pilot were dead. That was a shock. Mary gave us the newspaper with the story. The women were all from the Park Service office and only one remained. A big loss for the Park Service. A couple of the girls were single and the others left families – too bad, to say the least. It had happened up the Kijik a few miles from Lake Clark. The river makes a sharp right bend. A very deep canyon leads straight on towards Fishtrap Lake. Mary showed us on her map where the crash site was. Search and rescue had dropped many flares during the night while the rescue crew removed the bodies. Babe took Jake and I up past his hanger where the broken engine layed on the grass. Cylinders of one side crammed with debris, the propeller bent back. He figured the pilot had stalled the big bird and it spun to earth. The story complete we would have to go eat a big dish or two of ice cream with chocolate topping plus nuts and banana and some of his white fudge on top of everything. Mary was preparing a big apple pie for baking. John's wife Esther and two and one half month old son Joel John[62] was there. John, Bee & Glen were moose hunting up the lake. Noon time and dinner with caribou barbequed ribs, a real treat. Floyd Denison came for his mail and later Chester Whitehead[63] came for a long visit after he inspected the Cub. The boys came back from moose hunting up near the Camel Humps.[64] The meat of a big bull moose in the boat. A rack of antlers that measured 70 inches. Glen had been the lucky one. Not the neatest job of butchering and the meat got a good scrubbing in the lake. Babe says we have too much meat. How about taking some caribou ribs back with you. From the smokehouse he took a full rib cage plus the neck. At the woodshed he and I bucked it up with a Swede saw[65] so we could get it in the Cub. Why not stay for supper, Mary had two turkeys roasting in the oven. We should be getting back, so prepared to take off. Again I was the pilot. We would fly up the Kijik to the Beaver crash site and then follow on up to our Twin Lakes Port Alsworth crossing – from there the route back to the lower lake.

[62] John Alsworth, the third oldest son of Babe and Mary Alsworth, a pilot and aircraft mechanic who was married to Esther Bower Alsworth. They had an infant son, Joel John.

[63] Chester C. Whitehead (1903-1985), a resident of Tanalian Point and Port Alsworth since the late 1930's, trapper, and Bristol Bay fisherman.

[64] Camel Humps, two low hills lying near the Lake Clark shoreline and about 6 miles east of Port Alsworth; the Dena'ina name is Nił hałgheldeki meaning "one packing together."

[65] Swede saw, a large bow saw between 36 and 48 inches used for cutting firewood in bush Alaska. Sawing birch firewood for the family cook stove was one of the pleasures of Babe Alsworth's life.

We flew through snow showers at near 5000 ft. but found the weather fair as we neared the Volcanic Mts.

September 21 – Partly Cloudy, Lt. Breeze dn. & 59°.

It was midnight before I called it a day. Stars were out and the full moon making itself known. Early in the morning from my bunk I could watch that big moon slant down across the big window. It looked like a beautiful day coming up. Hotcakes devoured and dishes done, clouds were taking over and it was due to be another day of little direct sun light. Jake had laundry to do and I had the caribou rib cage to take care of. I filled the Jim Shake kettle and sawed a couple chops from the backbone before sacking the remainder and hanging it high under the cache. Into the kettle with the ribs went plenty of my favorite seasonings plus potato, carrots, and onion. Soon I had it putting out a good aroma.

     I started supper and an early supper it would be. Boiled ribs and chops from a hot salted skillet. Which would be the favorite. For my part, it was a tossup. Jake allowed that if he had to choose one and stay with it, he would take the ribs because the meat came free from the bones. The camp robbers didn't agree. They would like steak every day for I spiked the vertebra sections to the stump. Much bracing of feet and tugging to get them free of meat. At present Anch. meat prices a caribou bull would be worth considerable. I see $1.49 stamped on the bottom of a can of corned beef that Jake brought.

September 23 – Partly Cloudy, Calm & 32°.

Nearly there and a plane came up the lake. Planes had been flying high and in two's headed towards Whitefish Lake country. This one low and a little rig coming up the far side. I could see red with aluminum floats. Babe, and what was his business at Twin Lakes. Only bad news could bring him over this way now with the Cub parked here. Over the gravel banks and headed our way, gave us a fly by, turned up country and came back down to land near us. He had a big elderly man with him. What did we know about the upside down plane. We had examined it close up with the canoe. The man with him climbed out on the float and Babe introduced him. Jack something or other and Babe butchered up my last name as he never fails to do. Jack was interested in salvaging the airplane. Working as a go between (insurance company and whoever would tackle the job of turning it over and floating it to a beach). Would we be interested in the job? We had no gear to do it with. Babe came into deal with an offer to furnish anything we would need in line of ropes, anchors, winch. He would fly them in. Jack wanted us to set a price to do the job (contract) or how much per hr. to work at it or would we help if they sent in a helicopter or a salvage expert. We hesitated to set a price, not knowing what was a fair deal for airplane salvage work. I wanted Babe to set a price. No! he wouldn't but he would

give us help in the line of equipment. I asked Jack what was fair. He wouldn't say for fear of doubling what we would bid at. Finally he asked if we would do it for a thousand dollars. No, we figured that was very cheap. To bring in men and equip. from Anch. would cost them plenty. Would we do it for $1,200 – not interested. We hacked away at it and Babe kept talking in our favor. We could do it and they couldn't do better than us at any price. Finally Jack asked if we would do it for two thousand. We would give it a real good try. He wrote down our names. He would pass the word and get a message back to Babe in a day or two. Babe says – well just as well give you guys this rope I brought along, no need to haul it back. He fished out a spool of synthetic line along with another odd chunk he had brought. Maybe we had talked when we should have been listening. It would be not so bad if the wind blows up the lake but if it blows down it could be a rough row to hoe. Five miles for the rough stuff to build could make a sloppy job and we would have to wait for calm weather. The plane hard aground. It would have to be raised a few inches to get it free of the boulders then floated to deep water and to a beach that has deep water close in. There we would attempt to turn it right side up. On its back position it with nose towards the beach. Place a heavy anchor out in deep water behind it. Tie the nose to the anchor line. A line from the outer ends of the wing struts to shore to hold it from swinging around. A long line over the top to the tail and a winch to pull with from the beach. Hopefully she will first stand nose straight down and then pulling the tail on down she will end up looking like a Cessna 185 Skywagon on floats.

September 24 – Foggy, Calm & 30°.

Fog was well established over the lake at day light. Frost on the roof so it had been clear to a good extent during the night.

     Spuds, eggs and caribou chops for breakfast. The good smoking had given them a very good flavor. By the time chores were done the fog was clearing out. I wanted to go to the far side below Jerre's for a few good straight poles to use in the plane salvage operation in case we got it. Last night I was awake a long time figuring an easier and quicker way to get that big bird on its feet again. It simplified so much that if we got the job for $2,000.00 we would make $1,995.00 or more profit. Today we agreed that we should have taken it for a good bit less, but does the insurance company give anyone a real good deal. Let it stand. If someone else does it, it will be interesting to see if they do it easier than we would or could have done if all went according to plans.

September 26 –Partly Cloudy, Calm & 36°.

We took off and down past the wreck and around the end of the mts. headed for the bend in the Kijik. Just past Pear Lake and suddenly there was Babe's "T craft" passing under us headed for Twin Lakes. We turned back and followed. He cut through past the Pyramid

Mt. and we did the same and shortened the route. He cut on around towards the end of the lower lake and the wreck, descending steadily as if to land. We circled down and came in after he had touched down. The water pretty smooth and I bounced but caught it and set her down again and better. It wasn't Babe but John [Alsworth] who climbed out and stood on the bow of the float. We stopped nearby. After greetings he said, "They want you to go ahead on this thing." That was the best news I had heard in a long time. He had a load of gear. Two life rafts, a winch and a bunch of rope. Where was a good beach to unload? Over behind the point at the entrance of the bay. Near the wreck it was a boulder beach. We taxied over and unloaded his gear. How soon did we intend to start work. I told him we would start right now. Well, he would stay and help us until near five then he had to go. He said they were digging spuds at home and I suspected that was his reason for staying. We attempted to inflate the two rafts and found them both leakers and one of them very bad. He stayed and Jake and I flew up for the canoe load of gear. My brain was working over time trying to list all the gear we would need. A fuel drum, 4 cases of empty gas cans, ropes, tools, planks, poles, nails, a batch of stuff. I was running around gathering and stacking it on the beach. We had a sandwich and loaded it aboard. I had a good load but would still make a stop at Farmers gas can dump for two cases of empties and also at Jerre's for rope, a huge chunk of styrofoam and a bunch of 6 gal. plastic Prestone cans for floatation purposes. I headed down the lake at a good clip. The lake still smooth but it would ripple before I came to the stream. Jake flew by me there on his way down. Into the lower lake and the breeze picked up. I wanted three empty drums from the beach below Gatano's cabin. I loaded the three but it was to top heavy and I left two. I found Jake and John patching the repairable raft. I had suggested the good one from Arlen's cabin. The little rubber boat owned by Erick the Dane years back when he got the ram. Tried to pack it all and couldn't so left it all and a bear found it and wrecked the cape which he prized higher than the meat which he said I could have if I helped him get his sheep out. I did help him and gave him all the meat he could use too.

I left the boys with their patching and hauled my load on down to the scene of the wreck. I came back for the remaining two drums and stopped at the raft repair shop. Still patching and I headed for Arlen's cabin. That raft larger and heavy. An Avon raft "safe as the Ark" said the tag in the bow. We blew it up and found no comparison between it and the swimming pool play toys.

The lake was rough, we wouldn't work on the wreck today. Get all the gear there and maybe the bridles made for our floatation gear. John took off for home and might be back tomorrow to see how we were doing. With two rafts and some gear aboard we headed down. The lake starting to calm and the sky clear. On the beach we got our gear sorted and back from water line, the bridles on the four drums, and four cases of cans plus the four 6 gal. cans. The sun was near down and we headed back for the point and the Cub. A swing to the right to get protection and less pounding. We cached the canoe and motor in the spruce clump on the point and took off for home. Some difference between three hours with the paddle and maybe six minutes with the Cub. The nicest landing I have made so far I think – takes practice. A fire going – beans and caribou on to hotten.

A good salad and sourdough year round favorite dessert. Jake busy reading our mail as I wrote – finishing at nine. This had been an interesting and a very challenging day. "Will she or won't she come unstuck from the bottom, only the man upstairs knows for sure." I think she will but I have been wrong many times.

Now, clear, calm and 45°. We want to get a daylight start in the morning. I doubt that I will oversleep.

September 27 – Clear, Calm & 45°.

By the time we started rigging the drums to the wing struts it was breezing up. Water sloshing through, between the float struts and tossing drums and raft about. Today we would wear life jackets and it was a good thing that we did. Jake would test his right away. A wave had pitched the raft with him riding the edge. He was in the water and neck deep. I had gotten my face washed a time or two while working the length of my arms under water. "This airplane salvage doesn't come easy," I told Jake. We worked on but should have quit. We sunk two drums the desired amount and made them secure. Jake on the bilge pump and me holding the raft to the drums. We had problems. Drums nearly full of water want to stand on end. It was a battle but we got them pumped and stable after a fashion. The lake was too rough. We went to the beach after putting out Babe's big anchor. Jake was shaking from cold. I suggested we walk to Arlens cabin, build a fire in the heater and get warmed up. We found the cabin looking more like someone lived there than I have ever found it. A start of a warming fire already laid in the stove. A window pane has been out and patched with cardboard and it was about gone. I took my tin snips along and cut up a gas can to make a tin blank to fill the opening. I dug a new hole for garbage and cans, chopped up a batch of down stuff for firewood. Jake was getting back to normal.

Babe's "T craft" had come and landed next to the Cub. Several airplanes circled us during the day as if the accident had just happened. I headed back to the job to see how the drums were doing. In close I saw one missing and went on down the beach to find it. Packing it back I saw a second one leave the plane. This would never do. I paddled out to save the remaining two. I pulled on the anchor line to see if the anchor was holding. A good steady and heavy pull made it climb over the round boulders of the bottom. I kept pulling expecting it to lodge in the rocks and hold but it never did.

A big 300 hp. Cessna circled a few times and landed in the rough water. Hank Rusts airplane from Lake Clark.[66] It must have been a hunter who yelled "Is everything all right – need any help?" I waved them on and they took off in a cloud of spray. Airplanes on wheels, airplane on floats circled and crisscrossed the area at low altitude. If I had some of that horsepower on the end of the anchor line we would have the [Cessna] 185 in deep water in no time.

[66] Bush pilot Hank Rust owned Chilitna Lodge on Lake Clark across the lake from Port Alsworth.

I set about to develop a new rigging for our drums. Use them separately and stand them on end, the position they like to take when nearly full of water. Rig a bridle with a loop in the center below. Jake came and we worked at rigging all four drums. An Aeronca Sedan landed and came to the beach towards Arlens cabin. Two guys hiked down to see how it was going and was there anything we needed. From Soldotna and going to the Bonanza Hills. John had told us yesterday that Terry and Vic had come out early. The helicopter came so they closed up shop and came to their cabin at Port Alsworth.

We did all that we could on the beach. The lake too rough to work.

September 28 – Overcast, Breeze dn. & 45°.

I awoke during the night and felt sure it must be time to get up if the wind had died. What a relief to find it 2:00 o'clock. I was very sleepy and slept till near five thirty and didn't roll out till six for I heard a good puff of wind in the spruce tops now and again. There would be no working in the lake today.

After spuds I had a kettle of caribou to boil. Jake had his jeans to wash (a little mishap while wrasseling his caribou with the plate to close to the edge of the table). The lake seemed not so rough but I knew that with a run of five miles from the stream the waves would be sloshing through the float struts on the [Cessna] 185. Jake suggested we make an underwater viewer. A rig that would allow us to see better what we were looking onto. A good idea but what to use. A one gallon Blazo can with both ends cut out. A transparent covering on one end. I had some clear mylar that would be satisfactory. Cut it to cover the end and tape it watertight.

September 29 – Partly Cloudy, Breeze dn. & 42°.

Dishes done and I had beans to cook. Have a supply cooked up in case we get busy on the lower lake. Then I had a letter that needed writing and I hardly knew how to go about it. A letter to John Kauffmann of the Park Service. For all they knew Keith Trexler and his party had visited us here at my cabin before flying on to die in the deep canyon. I must write and tell him the story as it unfolded on this end. We hadn't seen them but met the Beaver flying down country as we flew up. That we hadn't heard of the crash until Sept. 20th, eight days after it happened. Too shocked to think of writing or calling from Babe's when we did hear. I would send the note that Trexler had left on my table and the note I had left for him if he came and we were at Babe's digging spuds on the 20th. I hope that my letter will answer a few questions and ease a few minds. That chore done I had my GI sweater to mend. The same old story, sleeves giving out on the lower side from the elbows to cuffs. Many feet of synthetic yarn went into the repair.

September 30 – Partly Cloudy, Lt. Breeze dn. & 40°.

During the night the lake was talking and still whitecapping when I got up near six. It would be another of those waiting days with cold weather getting ever nearer.

  By the time dishes were done it was calming and we watched it closely. It doesn't calm often during the day but it was calming now. We decided to go down and be ready when and if it calmed at the lower end. Still whitecapping off Emerson Creek as we flew by and wind streaks on the lower lake. Should we land or come back. We would land and paddle to Arlen's cabin from the point at the entrance of Lake Trout Bay. There we gave the cabin a good house cleaning. Patched the squirrel holes and deposited his dried mushrooms under a shaggy spruce – covered them with plastic and tar paper. A real cache and I wonder if he approved. I found mushrooms on the shelf above the counter. A square plastic container had been nearly filled with them. Another cache in the gas can box storing canned goods and dry stuff. We got the diggins in order and decided to paddle over to the wreck. It was still rough enough but we took the raft out and opened the big rectangular compartments of the floats. Upside down now and mostly out of the water. Full to the top with personal gear, camping gear and moose meat. A hook on the end of the pole was a good tool. Hook into a game bag, twist it up tight and pull. The meat wasn't in bad shape but starting to head that way. We unlatched and opened the baggage comp. door and the cabin door (left). The right door was missing. More gear came out and even the battery for the airplane. The lake was calming in good shape. We started to hook on our floatation gear. Gas drums in pairs but they gave trouble. The strap around the wing struts out end would slip under a heavy strain. No good we wouldn't get much floatation there. Jake came up with the idea of hooking into the wing strut tie down ring. A retracting device that lays flush with the strut surface when not in use. He would use our clear vision viewer to see down the six or eight feet. Use a pole to push a little tab exposing the ring, hook it to hold it open and then with another pole feed a messenger [rope or cable] through. Our heavy line would follow. It worked and we made good progress. Two drums on each side. 4-6 gal. Prestone containers under the bow of the floats. Also a 2 can case of 5 gal. cans pushed under the floats and slid forward. Tied in place they looked pretty secure. The nose of the airplane came up. Now if we could get the wing up a few inches we could move it to deep water. Two more cases of cans on each side at the inboard end of the wing struts but still she stuck to the bottom. The wings leading edge heavily damaged and sand had drifted in. She was heavy. No more cans and Jake made a rush flight to my cabin for more. He was soon back with eleven. We stuffed them in the baggage comp. and main cabin. Tried to add more to the wing struts but our line wasn't strong enough. I got dark and we gave it up. Took the Cub and taxied to Arlens cabin. So dark we had to guess where it was and was lucky. Came to the beach no more than 50 yds. from the little stream entering the lake near the cabin. Some GI rations and we called it a day. No sleeping bags so each slept under a deflated air mattress. I was up a few times to check the fire and the weather. It was nearly clear and holding calm. I slept very little until it was about time to get up. So ended Sept. 1975. It would be a frosty night.

October 1 – Partly Cloudy, Lt. Breeze dn. & ? (Frosty)

A plane and here came the "T craft." Circled us and headed back down country. Babe checking on that easy deal. We thought he had gone back when here he came down the slope with a paper feed sack on his back. He had brought apples, nuts, and our mail. He knew the [insurance company] was wasting valuable time in the delay to give us the go ahead. He had landed on one of the lakes of the chain of lakes below the lower lake and close to the slope of the Volcanic Mts. Nice there – run right up to the willow brush and tie her down. We completed our chore and headed for the cabin. He and I ran into a real patch of very ripe blueberries – large ones and Babe just dropped to his knees and started raking them in. "Just like a big brown bear" he said. We picked and ate – it sprinkled and his paper sack was getting wet. We had better go. He allowed that was about the most berries in a small area that he had ever seen. We sat in Arlens cabin and watched the lake get rough to the point of being pretty wild. He would like to come back if only he could tell when it was calm here. We talked about Hawaii and I asked him if he and Mary were going back this winter. "Yes, Sis was already making preparations." Finally he said I had better go before it storms and we walked with him to the lake. The new "T craft" jumped out of the water against the strong breeze. He had left us a can of gas. Back at the cabin we waited and watched. Lake Trout Bay was rough but the day had turned from fog & rain to a bright partly cloudy windy day. I cut a few small dead trees and Jake sawed them up. A white Super Cub came from up country, circled the wreck and went on towards the Bonanza Hills. Terry and Vic had come out from the hills in time to help Babe dig his spuds. Spuds nearly to the ceiling in the bin he said. Five trailer loads they had put in. About ten in the crew. We decided to head for home. A rough water take off and I could shudder along with the "little ol Cub." We needed more of Jerre's good heavy wire and a couple steel hooks he had. I must write to Jerre and tell him I have borrowed and insist on making it right with him. Again we splashed into the air and came in at my beach. Sure tasted good to be back home again. While Jake tended the Cub I got a fire going to make it really home. The two drums under the spruce past the woodshed to get ready to go down early in the morning. We would lash one on each float and taxi on the step to the stream. Turn them loose and pick them up in the lower lake and taxi them on down.

     I had brought a chunk of that moose meat. I would slice some good steaks and trim the edges and see if I could smell sour meat. It had no offensive odor and I fried two each in the big skillet. Jake allowed it was real good meat. I wish we could save it all.

     The lake was calming and the sky clearing. Temp. 38°. This would be another short night. If only it would calm for two days or even 24 hrs. We just might get that big bird where we want it. Will tomorrow see it move from its resting place on the rocks.

October 2 – Clear, Calm & 26°.

I touched a match to the spruce tips of our breakfast fire at 3:50. The stars were still

bright and the lake flat calm. This was due to be a busy day. An all out effort to float the Skywagon and move it to the point across the lake. If it stayed calm we just might get the job done. Five hotcakes each for there probably wouldn't be lunch. We had the two fifty five gallon drums to move down. That would take time if we had to float them through the connecting stream. We lashed them to the float struts by the light of the little Coleman lantern. Jake used some warm water to remove the frost from the windshield. A good warm up as we taxied down the lake by way of Jerre's point to be close to shore in case the drums gave trouble as we ran on the step. I rode the rear seat and acted as observer – see if and when they decided to leave us. Jake climbed the Cub up on the step and the drums hardly got wet. He broke water and she flew like a bird – like her name sake, the "Arctic Tern."[67] Well, we were flying, no sense in landing to float the drums through the stream. No problem – we flew on down and landed at the salvage site.

It was a frosty morning there too. Ice in gas cans that had taken on water while submerged. We had the two drums to make bridles for. That took a little time but not too much. A heavy wire link would connect the drum bridle to the hook in the tie down ring. There would be no stretch in this lash up. We paddled out and measured the water depth to the tie down rings to get the proper length for the links. Ready to hook on and we flooded the drums right down to bare buoyancy. As luck would have it the hooks had a flat tang above the hook. In the tang three one inch holes. We had a small pole just the right size to slip into a 1 inch hole. I pushed the drums down and with the pole Jake hooked the tie downs. They looked good just barely showing above water. When we pumped them they would stay right there if the airplane didn't come up. An improvement over the nylon bridles and lines – too much stretch there. Both in place and we towed out the four in two pairs. Now we had three drums on each wing. We figured the six of them would lift nearly a ton. We pumped and one by one they went dry too soon. We hadn't seen a lot of change in the airplane except that the left wing raised from the bottom. The right wing and engine still down. We put the 4-6 gal. Prestone containers under the nose of the floats. 2 cases of five gal. cans behind the 6 gal. plastic containers. (One case on each side) Seven five gal. cans on the inboard end of the right wing strut. We pushed some singles (5 gal.) down and into the cabin. Now, we could see a radical change. The tail had raised considerably and the drums had lifted half out of the water. It was as if water was draining slowly and it took time to see a change. We had pulled on the anchor line and moved the plane only to get hung up on a boulder. More buoyancy and the chunk of styrofoam was pushed down and secured to a big flex line inside the engine compartment. Slowly she was raising as if water was draining. The lake had stayed calm but by now an overcast. Again we pulled and she pulled hard. I put the orchard growers prune hitch in the line (used in securing a load of apple boxes on a truck). This gave us a near two to one advantage in pulling power. She moved and came free in deeper water. We were ready to tow.

It was getting late – time we should be heading home. The lake was calming. We would let her float free anchored to the mud hook in the lake and to the spruce on

---

[67] RLP's "Arctic Tern" was the name he gave the Piper J3 Cub he jointly owned with his brother Raymond Proenneke.

the beach. We sorted out a few items we wouldn't need and loaded them in the Cub. In less than ten minutes we pulled into my beach. This had been a good day and I knew that I would sleep well tonight. Tomorrow morning we would bridle the bow of the floats (which were near the beach to the anchor offshore). Run the winch line up along the belly of the plane and hook onto the stinger of the tail. Remove buoyancy on the bow of the floats and the engine – start cranking in the winch line. If all goes as planned she will come up and over, stand on her nose and then the tail come down to its normal position. Then we must beach her. Slide her on poles under the floats. Bury dead men to tie the wings down against the strong lake winds. Do what we can to preserve the engine until the insurance co. can take over. They wanted to be notified as soon as possible after we beached her. More moose steak from a hot salted skillet, more good beans, carrot sticks, raw turnips and cheese (Velveeta).

Now as I finish my writing at 8:10, it is overcast, very near calm and 37°.

October 3 – Overcast, Breeze up & 33°.

It had been a raw cold day with a trace of moisture now and again. Snow showers over along the ridge towards Turquoise Lake. It was getting late. My hands very sore from being in the cold water and pulling on ropes. What would happen if we let her rest right there for the night. Would we find her with tail pointing high in the morning or would the line give way and she fall back with a mighty splash. We gambled she would stay. If we stayed much longer it would be too dark to fly home. We got our tools and other gear in order and under the stunted spruce in case of snow. Jake would fly and taxied up towards Arlen's cabin for smoother water. As we turned over the lower end and came back there was Cessna N70039 standing on it nose off the point. I won't soon forget that number.

We found hardly a white cap on the upper lake and soon came in to my beach. I got the fire going while Jake took care of the Cub. The caribou and beans on, a pan of biscuits baking. We would soon have a hot meal and forget the miserable cold wet job. It is alright just for the fun and challenge but for money alone it's a waste of time. After supper a session of hand doctoring. Grease them good and hold them over the hot stove. That helped but they would be very sore and stiff in the morning.

Now at nine, a breeze up, overcast with slight moisture and temp. 33°.

October 4 – Lt. Snow, Lt. Breeze up & 31°.

Again I lay awake until after twelve – that infernal airplane occupied my sleeping time as well as working hours. How would we find it this morning. Would it still be standing on its nose or flat on its back in the water.

It was Babe. He gave us a fly by, circled and landed. He tied his "T craft" over next to the Cub in quiet water and came trudging the beach. Stocking cap down over his ears. Wearing a parka and hip boots. "This is some country" he said. "It is nice down on Lake Clark – 40° last night." He had to fly a crooked path to get here. Come down the big valley behind the Volcanic Mts. and nearly ran out of landmarks at Pear Lake. He had carried a little round orange container. "Some apple pie for you boys in there" he said. He had also brought spuds, a head of cabbage and two doz. eggs. He was chief observer as the Cessna came over the center line and started down in the up right position. I was cranking the winch and Jake was the camera man. She came down not with a splash as we had figured but came as if she didn't want to. We would snub her tight to the spruce and let her rest till it calmed.

Now right side up we could empty it of all loose or removable gear. One pair of scrawny moose antlers, a rifle with barrel poking out through the side of its case, a bow and arrow case and two real nice pack frames. A sleeping bag or two, jackets and emergency life vests for the passengers. Much clear plastic and other items to numerous to mention.

Before emptying the plane Babe had suggested we take a break for apple pie. He wouldn't have any but did take a chunk of smoke fish. We sat in a hollow on the lee side of our spruce clump and visited. Babe in a happy mood and told us a story such as I have never heard him tell. "A little boy had been using many swear words and the minister was asked to talk to him. The minister said I hear that you have been using bad words and the little boy said, who told you. A little bird, said the minister. The little boy scowled and said and here I have been feeding the little sons of B-----." That was the best story of the day and we started getting gear in order for easy finding in case snow came. Swan continued to go by. Babe took off for home and we taxied to Arlen's beach. I wanted to hike over for more moose meat. Something good about the snow on the mts., chill in the air and water puddles iced over. I hiked on by the meat to check the beach. A Bethel aeronautical chart and a nice blue nylon tarp had washed ashore. The meat still in about the same condition as it was when we removed it from the floats on the airplane. I took three good chunks one of which was tenderloin or backstrap. We flew up the lake and passed a few swan winging their way up the lake past Carrithers' point. We were surprised that they didn't show alarm as we flew by not a great distance away. A big flock of ducks took wing as we landed behind the point and taxied slowly in the choppy water to my beach.

Now we could live a no pressure life. We had the airplane where it couldn't get into further trouble. When it calmed or the wind blew down we would put some buoyancy under the floats forward, bring them to the surface and pump them out.

I built a fire and popped some corn. Time out for a sourdough sandwich. More (and the last) of the caribou to put in the Jim Shake kettle. Some tenderloin to slice and trim. Beautiful red meat and aged just right. Boiled cabbage for Jake (mine raw) along with moose steak and beans. A good supper after a good day. I could sleep tonight

knowing we have it made (if we don't louse up).

Tonight at eight, the lake is noisy and there is snow in the air and on the ground. Temp. 30°.

What we need now is a few days of reasonably good weather to travel the lakes returning gear to my place and Jerre's and the good little rubber boat to Arlen's cabin.

October 5 – Overcast, Breeze up & 27°.

The kettle of caribou to cook and the cabin to restock from the cache. Rain jacket to mend and heavy socks to darn. Jake took a tour with his 35 mm. A good cover of snow but we needed sunshine to go with it. The breeze had been light early but as the day progressed it picked up to a good blow. The lake very rough and the Cub resting easy on its rack behind the high breakwater. A real safe tie down with the lake level low.

A sourdough sandwich and a sampling of caribou ribs with broth for lunch. This afternoon we would light off the fireplace for the second time since Jake came. He mentioned someone roasting steak cubes at a beach party so I diced a couple moose steaks. Smeared them with bacon grease and seasoning and prepared a couple roasting sticks. Real good, but I think roasting them through the open door of the stove would do better but lack the open fire effect.

A few bunches of swan passed and one large flock of grey geese. The weather down country looked very cold and wind blown. I sliced and trimmed more moose meat and wished that I had the remainder that lay on the beach near the head of the Chili River. If it is a bad day tomorrow I just might spend the day hiking down and back with the light load. See how N70039 is doing as I pass.

The sky was pink above a huge roll of grey clouds at sunset. The wind strong and cold. I put the thermometer in my potato box in the woodshed. When I went for it, 30° and I brought them in. It went into my cooler box for there is green stuff there. 36° when I went to check – good for a few days at least.

A good supper with boiled spuds and gravy. Moose steaks, tender and juicy. A big green salad and beans. Our old standby for dessert. Two gallons and a qt. of blueberries in the bank. The picking season is over. Now at 7:50, the surf is noisy on the beach, a few flakes of snow in the air, temp. 27°.

October 9 – Overcast, Calm & 25°.

Now we could pull her back with the winch. Lay a drum behind the float (left float first). Run the winch line over the drum and tie it to a line tied around the float forward of the rear cleat. The winch line tied to the belly band on the underside to get a good lift when pulling over the drum. She came back on the left. We switched to the right and got the

same results. Coming up the incline of the beach and compartments of the floats being made ready for pumping. All were full of water. Starting at the tails we worked forward. One side and then the other. The big cargo compartments would give us a real lift. We had pushed empty gas cans down into them and closed the doors. Now the deck dry above them we opened them and bailed them out. Only the bow sections remained and after one was empty Jake took off for Port Alsworth to report that she was riding normal and would come out of the water in the morning. After he took off down and around the mt. I finished the pumping and then unbuttoned the cowl to see what could be done with the engine. I pulled the top spark plug and rotated the engine with the propeller. One cylinder had water and ice in it. Squirted me in the face and bumped solid against the ice. I poured in a few ounces of JP-4 Jet fuel (like kerosene) in each cylinder and rotated the prop back and forth. Still she bumped up solid on one cylinder. All I could do for today the sun had set behind the Volcanic Mts. A nice flock of swan went by and there was small talk about that man working on the junker airplane below.

I went about picking up gear and getting things shipshape. Just finished when here came the Cub for a nice landing on a very smooth bay. Jake had reported and picked up a batch of provisions and green stuff. He had learned that the wheels for the Cub are in Anch. Babe would be going in tomorrow and would bring them back.

This evening we figured up the no. of days on this salvage job. Close to five days till now. Six should see it well done. Not bad considering the time of year and weather to contend with.

Getting dark when Jake landed out front. I had a fire going in no time. The beans and caribou kettles on. This had been a very satisfying day. We have it made for sure now. Tonight she rests with floats nearly half out of the water and the battered wings tied to spruce stakes driven deep into the gravel.

Tonight is a night for no nonsense sleeping. It is clear now at 9:45. It is calm and it is 22°.

October 7 – Clear, Calm & 20°.

It was 20° when I turned in and I figured 15° for this morning. Near sun rise we could see a very high scattered thin overcast and there was a very light breeze down.

Again last night I lost a lot of sleep. My hands throbbing they were so sore. I had doctored them but at midnight I got up and swallowed a couple aspirin. That took the sharp edge off. While I lay awake I thought of fast and easy ways to salvage big airplanes. Rubber tanks or Avon life rafts would be better than drums. Install long air hoses to the air inflating valves. Wear a scuba diving outfit and go down and attach them to the wreck deflated. Have an air compressor in a raft on the surface. Make the rounds of all the hoses and soon she would be afloat. In Alaska, insurance companies would be knocking at your door if you were equipped to do a fast efficient job.

Spuds for breakfast and again a good start. The frost would have to be sawed from the top of the Cub's wings with a rope. Heavy frost disturbs the smooth flow of air over the wing and rising the stalling speed. I could tell on take off that she didn't lift off as easily as usual.

It could be no other way the [Cessna 185] Skywagon was sitting hard on the gravel in shallow water. Today we would take care of the engine and move the plane high and dry. Tie the tail to a strong stunted spruce and drive stakes up in the beach gravel to anchor the wings.

All the gear on the beach plus the moose meat went into the canoe and it was a load for sure. That plus all the gear we had unloaded from the plane when we turned it over would make a real load and I am not surprised that the lady pilot sunk a float and rolled it over. Babe had told Jake yesterday that he talked to the pilot who saw it happen. She had tried to make a step turn at the upper end of the lake, had lost it and drifted the length of the lake bottom up.

Me back with the load and the engine free of ice. Now we could turn the prop full circle. I drained the oil and got considerable water. Jake pulled the lower spark plugs and we propped her over many times to blow the water from the cylinders. We salvaged the oil and mixed a gallon of JP-4 jet fuel with it to flush the cylinders and refill the crankcase. Jake hooked on a battery that John Alsworth had brought. One feeble effort and no more. We suspected it was dead. Now we would beach her, one side at a time we inched her back until she was on the beach. A Super Cub came and landed. Two guys and they asked us where the caribou were. "In the Bonanza Hills I suspected. No caribou here at this time of year." "Where were we working out of?" "Right here on the lakes." "How about this guy that built the cabin and wrote a book about the lake country." Jake pointed me out as the guy. "He doesn't look like the guy in the book." "He was a better looking guy." Anyway they knew the woman pilot who tipped over the Skywagon. One of them had flown for Ketchum last year. They took off for the Bonanza Hills. The sun was going behind the mts. and we rushed around to get picked up and fly home. Jake had salvaged about 12 gal. of gas from the wreck. Enough to bring down the price of Babe's $1.40 per gal. gas a bit.

About 50 lbs. of pretty ripe moose meat flew up the lakes with us. If I can't save any of it, the birds will have a happy time when we leave.

This morning I had seen a little rooster grouse strutting in the brush at the point. I wondered why and then a hen flew from a spruce nearby. Later she was picking gravel by the cabin. Very tame and she reminded me of my visitors of last winter when the snow lay deep and I had the only gravel in sight.

Again a good supper and it ended with apple pie. Mary had given Jake one yesterday evening. We had part of it last evening.

Tonight, clear, calm and 28°. Tomorrow we will return the borrowed gear and end up on my beach.

October 8 – Overcast, Lt. Breeze up & 26°.

No more than done when I heard a plane and saw Babe's "T craft" coming. I would bet he had some one along who wanted to see the airplane. It was Babe and he had a heavy good looking middle aged man with him. He introduced himself as insurance adjuster for Northern Insurance Adjustors. John C. Smith, his name. The manager himself. He asked about the plane and its condition. Was there any water in the floats now. There had been an expensive camera aboard, had we seen it. Not insured by the company. Ketchum would have to pay damages for the hunter gear out of his own pocket. The airplane – a helicopter was coming tomorrow. Pick it up and pack it to Anchorage. $750.00 per hr. for flying time to the lakes and back to Anch. Would we go down and assist them if need be and see that they got away in good shape. He would have the copter give us a fly by when it arrived. Where should he send our check. He seemed like a good man to deal with. He had said 16 planes insured by them had ended up like this one, this year. He had helped salvage many a float plane. They used a wet suit and inserted deflated inner tubes in the floats. Air lines to the surface to inflate them. An easy job to turn one over in deep water that way. A helicopter could turn one over easily too. Ketchum's Beaver had been insured by them too. He had been in to inspect the wreckage and they may carry it out and try to reconstruct the accident. There is hundreds of thousands of dollars involved in that case, he said. If they can prove Ketchum Air Service at fault he will really suffer a loss.

Right down to the bitter end of things and I still had that stinky moose meat to sample. If it was no good, into the woods it would go. The chunk that lay on the bottom had top priority. I found it lighter in color as I skinned the outer layer off. Not quite as red as that picked from the beach. It seemed perfectly good. A couple big chunks that must have come from hindquarters. Smelly on the outside but nice and red a quarter inch in. I was pretty reckless with a very sharp and thin butcher knife. Scraps were piling up at the end of the work bench. The birds were working hard but most pieces to heavy to pack. Jake had been busy beefing up the breakwater with rocks exposed out front by the recent storm. He came with the long handle no. 2 and packed shovels full out the timber trail. All the birds but one went with him and I had that one. The meat sacks soaking in the lake and later hung on the line to freeze tonight. The cleaned up meat in an onion sack hanging from the ridge log of the woodshed and it was time for supper. I had cooked a fresh pot of beans after we came up from the lower end. A couple good steaks, boiled cabbage for Jake (mine raw). Dishes and my writing done by nine. Still a very gentle breeze up the lake. Nearly clear and the temp. 26°.

Now after the chopper comes and packs the Skywagon away we have nothing to do but close up shop in a neat and orderly fashion. Fly out to Babe's and trade the floats for the wheels waiting there.

I hate to think of leaving.

October 9 – Clear, Calm & 16°.

A sandwich and I started cleaning up the little kicker for storage. Jake hollered helicopter! and here one came flap flapping down out of Glacier Creek. He gave us a fly by but it didn't look big enough to pack the Skywagon. KAS in red on the side. It was Bud Lofstedt's. He flew on down the left side and we rushed to get going. The rotors hadn't stopped turning by the time we passed to turn and come back into the wind for a landing. As we hit the beach two men were looking the Cessna over. I recognized Bud from a distance and closer he introduced a young guy named Buzz. They had wire rope bridles, chokers, shackles, swivels, everything it would take to hook onto that big bird. Two two by fours to tie to those butchered wings to act as spoilers which would prevent it from trying to fly.

How did they plan to make the hook up – they hadn't quite figured that out. Buzz would have to do it from the top of the Cessna and then climb in while Bud hovered very close. I volunteered to make the hook up which would have them both aboard. I would stay until the cable tightened to make sure there would be no snarls and then jump to the gravel below and eliminate unnecessary hovering close to the wreck. Bud said, from the ground you watch the plane. If it doesn't act stable and looks unsafe to carry give me the wave off and I will set it down again. They took off, moved in close to the wreck from the right wing tip. Closer and closer that monster came. It looked big as a house from close under. The big hook directly under the belly came within reach and I hooked the big swivel hook into it. Buzz was leaning out the door to keep Bud posted on operations below. Slow and easy he started to rise and stretch the cable. I, keeping it free of tangles. I was surprised that there was hardly any down wash of air from the big rotor bladed rig overhead. I was too close to the center where they were moving slow. The cable jerked tight and I went over the side. The Skywagon lifted a bit turned and settled. Bud was getting the feel of it. Now it lifted and he moved slowly up and out over shallow water. I had told him, whatever you do, don't drop it in the lake for I don't want to fish it out. He smiled at that. He would drop it sure enough if his big bird was in danger. He had dropped a light plane once and it glided down as if someone was at the controls. Didn't even turn over when it landed, he said.

He passed near Arlen's cabin drifting sideways with the wind. Farther down it was a pretty sight. The Skywagon flying along as if in a steep glide with the big copter just above it. The last we saw of them they were making the turn around the lower end of the Volcanic Mts. The beach looked bare with just the plastic covered mound of hunters gear remaining. Our work was done. We loaded up and flew home.

I had put beautifully raised biscuits on to bake just before we left. I couldn't leave them so set them aside and closed the stove draft. Now the center one had fallen flat. Never a bad batch of sourdoughs so back on the fire and they turned out to be entirely edible if not prize winners for looks. Two moose steaks each for supper. A real good meal to celebrate the flight of the Skywagon. Now as I write at 8:20, the wind is up and coming down the lake. Did Bud make it back to Kenai or did he cut her loose or set her down in

Lake Clark Pass. I would be most interested to know. I must drop him a line (later) and ask him how she went from here. A high solid overcast at dark and the temp. now at 8:25, 38°.

October 12 – Partly Cloudy, Breeze dn. & 38°.

Still the lake was rough out in the seven mile run and I wondered if this was the day we would leave Twin Lakes. Hotcakes for breakfast and our usual supply to carry us over until hotcakes again – we could go or stay. If we were going it was high time we made a start and I said as much. Jake agreed and another check of wind and weather made it the day to close up shop. Jake would take one load of gear and return for me and the remainder. Operation close up was set in motion. It wasn't long until Jake had a plane load and prepared for take off. The two good paddles had received each a coat of Flecto clear finish and had dried over the stove during the night. They and the canoe plus a few other items would go to Spike's cabin. I made that last paddle up to the point after Jake had disappeared down country.

I set about completing close up. Still numerous things to go into the cache and it would be full to the door when I finished. The chimney pipe came down and the top section given a good stamp of the heel for it wouldn't be serviceable for further use and also to discourage those who would move in. The good stove I gave a good coat of oil and I would be happy if the oil hadn't been burned off when I returned.

The sound of a plane – Jake coming back for that last load. I had the job nearly completed.

I would be pilot this trip and taxied down towards Farmers cabin so as to get airborne before reaching Carrithers' point. Jake wanted to shoot pictures as we passed my beach. The side window (top door half) swings up and latches under the wing. As if the picture wasn't to be. It dropped down and interfered with his filming. Fly away if we must but don't take a picture of me, the lonely cabin. Up past the point to gain altitude and then down the far side and a search for the moose which I failed to see. Past the connecting stream and down the lower lake. The mound of white at the entrance of Lake Trout Bay indicated the moose hunters possessions which we had stacked and covered hoping someone would come and fly them out. It was good to see the lower lake free of the wrecked Skywagon. I had suspected it would be robbed of engine and floats, the remainder to be an eyesore for years to come. On down around the end and I climbed for the 3800 ft. necessary to comfortably cross to the Kijik. Pear Lake passed under us. Soon Fishtrap lakes were on our right wing – then Lachbuna on our left. I detoured from the usual route to fly down the Kijik and past the crumpled wreckage of the yellow and blue Beaver. It would have been better that "One Man's Wilderness" had never been than to lose the lives of eight because of it. Later we would learn that the women had taken pictures of my cabin and of their picnic on the beach.

Out over Lake Clark and the journey was about over. The breeze was from the pass so I would fly down along shore and make my landing approach over the airstrip towards Babe's bay. As we taxied back to the beach Babe was busy getting the three wheel float plane dolly down to the waters edge. As we climbed out he said "I guess you want to take the floats off right away." To me it was as if he was jealous of my heaven and would eliminate any chance of me getting back to it anymore this year. From April 29th of 1974 to Oct. 12, 1975 I had been there. In many ways it was the best year and a half (nearly) I have ever spent there but in other ways it had been the worst. Too many people had died because I was there. Because I was there I am truly sorry. The End.

> *In many ways it was the best year and a half (nearly) I have ever spent there but in other ways it had been the worst. Too many people had died because I was there. Because I was there I am truly sorry. The End.*

[RLP had wintered in Iowa and returned to Anchorage in April 1976 flying a Piper J-3 Cub with an 85 horse power engine. Raymond Proenneke had purchased the Cub and had rebuilt it by the summer of 1975 and it was jointly owned by the brothers. RLP had first learned to fly in 1948 while working on the Wilkinson ranch near Heppner, Oregon but had done little flying since moving to Kodiak in 1950. The Proenneke brothers flew the plane back to Iowa in the fall of 1975.]

CHAPTER THREE – 1976

A CLOSE CALL

April 30 and 4 days of May

I was in Anch. John Kauffmann of the Park Service picked me up and took me to the Park Service offices. We talked over the results of my journal searching for the film. He was flying back to Harpers Ferry within the next few days. He still had that big batch of slides that I had shot. Still unidentified and I asked him to mail them to Port Alsworth.[1]

May 10 – Overcast, Calm & 30°.

I had better get at the chore of identifying all those slides I had exposed for the Park Service in '75. First I would get my Cub log books and my pilot's log book up to date. In figuring I learned that I had flown about 48 and one half hours. Spent about $146.00 for gas and about $7.00 for oil. Figuring my two nights in the Prince Charles Hotel in Lloydminster, Sask. it would amount to about the cost of driving my dependable 53.

I had biscuits rising while I wrote captions for the slides. I could recognize them all except for some flowers which I will have to search out in Helen White's flower book.[2]

A wind shift and a good breeze up the lake. I had put heavier tie down ropes on the Cub. I will be happy when it leaves the ice. Still plenty strong and I think the platform would support it on ice that I would consider unsafe for me. It must leave that platform to fly though.

It would have to leave the ice and it wouldn't do to beach it even if I could get off

---

[1] Proenneke and Kauffmann were conferring about a documentary film the NPS was preparing at the Harpers Ferry Center, Division of Reference Services in West Virginia on the former's life at Twin Lakes. The video entitled, "One Man's Alaska" was released in 1977, but is no longer available.

[2] Helen White (1905-1994) was a writer-editor and naturalist from Anchorage who worked for Alaska Northwest Publishing Company as an editor. She was a friend of RLP, and he sent his journals to her for reading. She wrote several Alaskan cookbooks, edited the *Milepost* travel guide, and in 1974 wrote the *Alaska-Yukon Wild Flowers Guide*.

of the ice to the beach. There I would be stuck till freeze up again. I would fly it to the upper end and park it on one of the two airstrips until I could fly to Babe's.

May 17 – Partly Cloudy, Calm & 30°.

The cloud build up in the southwest had dissipated. It looked like a fair day coming up. Dead calm and a very thin, partial overcast.

After breakfast, what to do, go up or down. Little hope of seeing game either way, I figured. Why not exercise the Cub. It had been a week since I had flown. Just a short flight – check the lake area. I went out and removed the wrappings from the engine and untied those super strong tie downs from the wings. I gave it a good preflight and rolled her away from the rack. An easy starting rig she fired right off and I warmed her good. I would taxi down below the Farmer cabin and come back by the point. She got off easily and climbed right out. I flew up the right side past the head of the lake nearly to the rock pile and the forks. I watched for moose or caribou on the flats but saw none. Back down the far side and I missed the bull moose that I saw yesterday. At 500 ft. and climbed a bit to check on ewes up in the rocks. None there and I dropped down to 400 ft. to fly the lower slope of Black Mt. looking for caribou. On down and over the knolls at the head of the Chili River. On down across the flat and I turned at the wolf den opposite Trail Butte. Back up the chain of lakes and I saw an arctic tern, the first of the season.

Past Arlen's cabin and duck lake which is now completely open. On up the lake along side the Volcanic Mts. I landed and taxied up to the rack. Just about 30 min. and I had seen all that I could have seen on foot in two good days but I didn't hear a robin sing or the croak of a rooster ptarmigan. I didn't see a snowshoe rabbit or even a parky squirrel. The man who walks is the man who knows the land.

Still some day left and I worked on captions for the Park Service slides. A problem with the flowers I had taken some that I don't find in Helen White's Alaska flower book, so I wrote a note "Have an authority on wild flowers check the flower slides."

May 20 – Partly Cloudy & 36°.

It was calm and the weather promised to improve. Before we pulled the wheels off we would fly to Nondalton and visit the mission girls. Doris had her mother at the mission for a short visit and then she would return home to Wycolt, Wash. I had told them one time that I would like to meet her. She is in failing health and this will no doubt be her last trip north. I flew and Babe rode the back seat. A nice smooth flight up. I really wanted to do a good job with the old master along but my landing wasn't the best. He allowed I was landing too fast for that uneven runway.

We found the girls at home and frail Mrs. Hagedorn was sitting in the rocking

chair by the window. She seemed cheerful enough but very thin and not very strong.

First thing – get out the corn popper and pop a dish pan full. Open some Pepsi and 7up. Sit around the table and hash over the winter and all the happenings.

Time to go. Babe had suggested we stop by and check Hornberger's on Chulitna Bay on the way back. "Ok, you drive," I said and he didn't argue. We saw a cow moose no more than a couple miles from Nondalton. I was glad that Babe was driving for Chuck's strip looked short and narrow with a high bank at the upper end. Chuck's [Cessna] 180 stood at one end so we should make it. Babe flies the Cub just as well as he did his little black bird. Sit her down right on the end and we didn't go far up grade.

Chuck has the nicest place I have seen in this country. The buildings and garden on a gentle south slope. A nice log house a small one and a cabin or two plus work shop and woodshed. Good protection from the wind and a beautiful view down the slope and across a lagoon. A nice big green house with green stuff, a jungle of it. Tomatoes already good size. A mouse had nipped a flat of cabbage plants the night before. Chuck and his wife were both school teachers but now he is mechanic and all round handy man.[3]

Couldn't stay long and we had to go or be late for dinner. Again Babe was driver and I think he enjoys flying the "Arctic Tern."

After dinner we put the Cub in the hanger but soon two planes came. One wanted to pick up a pair of floats he had there. A Super Cub, and the [Piper Cub] J-3 went outside. With all hands turning too it didn't take long to have that Cub ready to take to the water. The ice floes in the bay was shifting back and forth. As it happened it was wide open when he took off followed by the second Cub hauling his landing gear.

Him out of the way Glen and I backed the [Piper Cub] J-3 in again and proceeded to put the floats on. Everything fit and by supper time she sat ready and waiting to be towed out of the hanger and dumped in the bay. The weather was fairing up even more and Babe kept saying the forecast is for better weather and holding a few days. The next morning would see frost.

May 31 – Partly Cloudy, Calm & 25°.

At Low Pass Creek I climbed the bank where I had seen the cow moose and was surprised to find her not fifty yards from where I had seen her on Saturday. Not fifty yds. away and she stood and looked at me. I saw movements in the brush at her side. Did she have a calf? Finally I saw ones head and then another, twins. Not as red as some I have seen. I returned to the beach and went farther before climbing again for a better view. A good look at them and then another – triplets. Three of the little guys and won't that old girl have a chore raising all three of them. She moved slowly away with the little guys trailing

---

[3] Hornberger's place, Koksetna Lodge, was near the mouth of the Chilitna River about 13 miles SW of Port Alsworth on Lake Clark. Sara Hornberger, long time teacher and principal in various Bristol Bay villages and first local historian hired by Lake Clark National Park and Preserve in 1985.

along behind. The first set of triplets I have ever seen.

No activity at the fox den but the white feathers were missing. The Cub as I had left it. Remove the radio, check the floats, and do a few tinkering jobs before crossing that cold stream again. The shoes I left hanging in a little spruce tree.

A cow and big calf moose crossing Emerson Creek near the mouth, headed up country. Four o'clock when I finished lacing my hiking boots and headed up. No sign of the cow with triplets as I passed the creek. A young porkypine at Hope Creek. Eight head of sheep on Falls Mt. and I saw only one lamb. 5:20 when I came to my beach.

The evening warm and mosquitoes active. Supper over and everything squared away by 8:45. A high partial overcast. It is calm and 44°, the highest evening temp. to date. Tomorrow, June month. The green will come and the ice will go. The month that says there will be or there won't be blueberries.

June 4 – Fog, Calm & 40°.

A good looking [Cessna] 185 on floats coming up the middle headed for my cabin. He varied power as he passed to let me know he saw me. A circle and down the far side. Here he came back and at reduced power. A notch of flaps and the right hand door pushed open a bit. I was out by the breakwater when he passed and out came a package. It struck the tree by the clothesline and stopped in the low spot no more than fifteen feet in front of the cabin. That was an accurate air drop if there ever was one. I rushed to get it and took it to the beach for him to see as he went back by and on down the lake.

From the Park Service and in the center, well packed with crumpled newspapers, 6 rolls of film and a letter from Bob Belous. "Any wildlife footage that you might get would certainly be useful in our current film projects," he wrote. Sorry he wasn't able to get here to do some shooting of sequences with a winter background and may get over later for a few days gathering the kind of connective sequences needed for the films story line. John Kauffmann still in Washington.

June 12 – Clear, Calm & 38°.

To my beach and no one to greet me. A note on the table outside "Dick – came by to see you. I will be working on the lake this summer sometime in early July. The work we will be doing is concerned with the historical and archeological resources of the proposed Lake Clark National Park. Looking forward to seeing you." George S. Smith N.P.S.[4]

Today while I was high on the slope a Super Cub with big wheels flew up the far side and down my side. On down the lower lake and he landed at Gatanos airstrip. It set

---

[4] George S. Smith, NPS archeologist from Anchorage.

there a good while and I wonder if it is a guide interested in setting up camp there or at Coleclature's [?] cabin on Lake Trout bay. The Cub was there long enough for a man to hike that far. I hope that isn't the case. Enough hunters at the lower end each fall without a guide moving in but I suspect guides have used Arlen's cabin in the past.

June 16 – Overcast, Breeze dn. & 46°.

Everything going according to plan but the lake beginning to roar. Here came a good looking red, white & green Cessna 185 on floats. It circled, landed and came to my beach. Out climbed Chuck Hewitt[5] of the Park Service and then big Fred Eubanks[6] with the waxed mustache – the ends curled in a full circle. Then the pilot Chuck from Sea Airmotive. Had I seen a Widgeon? Yes I saw one yesterday at Lake Clark. It had circled twice and Babe said it would be landing at Glen Van Valin's.[7] They had just come from there. It was missing, didn't get back to Anch. last night. Two and the pilot aboard. Jerry Yeiter of BLM (the man in charge of clearing out illegal cabins) was one of them. I understood that it was coming to Twin Lakes from Lake Clark. The weather had been fair in this direction. A mystery where they could be.

They came in and visited awhile. Only Fred having a cup of chocolate. The others had coffee at Lake Clark. I ask them when the boys from Harpers Ferry[8] were coming. July 12th the day, and they needed a portable generator which would probably come in earlier. A generator to charge batteries for those fancy electric drive movie cameras and maybe for flood lights.

They stayed maybe a half hr. and here came my birds. The young one too and the pilot tempted it to come to his hand. Later today while I was using the scope on the beach a bird lit on my shoulder and stayed several seconds. It was that young one.

June 17 – Overcast, Calm & 40°.

I wanted to check on my caribou but should I canoe down or fly. Ruffled water moving up said flying was the way to go. I would take camera gear along just in case it turned out that I could use it. I taxied down on warm up and was nearly to Low Pass Creek before she was ready for full power. Off and down the lower lakes right side, watching the lower slope of Black Mt. At the lower end I cut in towards the ridge for I figured I might see caribou above the strip of timber. Light rain streaked the windshield but the Bonanza Hills in fair weather. I saw a cow moose with twin calves a couple miles below the lake.

---

[5] Charles "Chuck" Hewitt, an NPS seasonal employee who worked with Eubanks.

[6] Fred Eubanks, NPS planner with the Alaska Task Force.

[7] Glen Van Valin, former school teacher and pilot, and fishing lodge owner on Lake Clark.

[8] "boys from Harpers Ferry" refers to NPS video crew from the Harpers Ferry Center in West Virginia who came to document Proenneke's life at Twin Lakes.

Then a small bunch of caribou. I flew on to Ptarmigan Lake[9] at this end of the Island Mt.[10] No caribou where I had seen so many two days ago.[11] I turned left and headed up the Mulchatna River towards Turquoise Lake which is now nearly ice free. Now, I was seeing a few good bunches of cows and calves. A bunch or two of a hundred or more and smaller bunches but not nearly the amount I had seen on the mt. A rain shower extending up Turquoise ridge so I turned back and then across to trail butte and on up. No caribou on that side of the river. I came on up and found I had flown nearly three quarters of an hour. That tour would have taken two good days afoot and with the canoe. I was satisfied that there were no caribou within reach.

While the Cub engine was warm I would clean it. I didn't want Voight to see anything but a clean airplane from prop to tail end.

June 20 – Clear, Calm & 26°.

I wanted to check on my caribou herd. If I could catch them in an ideal setting I would squander more film. The weather was building as if it could rain again and I had better fly while flying was good. I would also take the airdrop package to Terry & Vic. It was 10:30 my time when I was ready to leave the beach. Although the lake was glassy smooth the air was turbulent at three hundred feet. From the air I took a good look at my beaching spot of yesterday. Not a big boulder anywhere near so I will remember that tie up spot when I fly to the lower end. On down by where I had turned back yesterday. Only a few minutes and it had taken me two hrs. Now, I would look for the herd. I wanted them near Snipe Lake. A good spot to land and some high ground to shoot from. Some blue water to improve the setting. No caribou and I flew on. Scattered timber now and I didn't expect to see them there. Down the Chili River and then across to the Ptarmigan Creek and the Bonanza Hills. Synneva Knob,[12] I was getting close. I saw Terry then Vic come out of the cabin door and wave. I flew on past and would drop the sack on the way back. Working alone I didn't want to fly below the hill behind the cabin. In the wind blast the big paper feed sack was hard to manage. As I passed I pushed it out and saw that it would land on the hill behind the cabin. I didn't see it hit the ground so I turned back and flew the area. I couldn't see it and figured that it went into the high brush. Terry hadn't started to climb and I wouldn't blame him if he left it up there until I came to visit again. Vic is trying to lose weight. Maybe she will climb and look for it.

I removed the window covers from Spike's and Hope's cabins. Bob had written that he didn't expect to use them this summer and to use them as if they were my own. I had written asking his plans for them and that I might use one or both for sleeping cabins when the Park Service boys from Harpers Ferry come.

---

[9] RLP's Ptarmigan Lake, a small lake in the eastern foothills of the Bonanza Hills and a source of Ptarmigan Creek.

[10] RLP's Island Mountain, a 3,090 ft. mountain near Ptarmigan Lake.

[11] RLP was looking for the Mulchatna caribou herd.

[12] Synneva Knob, a 2,615 ft. mountain in the Bonanza Hills; the name is of Norwegian origin but nothing particular is known of it, however, a nearby creek of that name appears on the USGS topographical map Lake Clark (C-5) Quadrangle 1:63

June 23 – Overcast, Calm & 40°.

A green and white Goose flew by and landed coming down along the beach. I hid the canoe for I knew what the 90 m.p.h. blast of a twin engine goose trying to turn on a soft beach could do. He came in a little to far and got stuck half way around. The left wing over the beach so I gave him a push and he went on around. He shut her down and tourists began to pour out. Fred Eubanks, Chuck Hewitt, and a couple more plus tall John Kauffmann. All of the Park Service. The pilot Tommy Belleau[13] who had been here before. He would have to go to Iliamna to gas up so blasted off into deep water and was gone. We came to the cabin and I stoked the fire for coffee.

Kauffmann had a gift for me from a friend of his in Maine. The man an outdoors man, legislator, farmer, master of many crafts and lore. One morning while John was there he was working on a wooden ladle, using a crooked knife. This is a now rare knife used in Canada for canoe building and a variety of crafts. John thought of me and was telling his friend about me and Twin Lakes. The man said "I have some crooked knife blades at home, bought long ago and I would like to have you give one to your friend." So, there it was all wrapped and in a box. No handle, you make your own. The handle is made with a hollow for the thumb near the extreme end and you use it with the sharp edge towards you as you would a draw knife or spoke shave (only with one hand). The mans name, William L. Vaughan, Elm Hill Farm, Hallowell, Maine. The blade very sharp and Sheffield speaks for the quality of the steel. I must write to the man and learn more about its use.

Now, how was the film coming? Well, Brain Jones (the producer) Hubbard Blair (the sound man) Tom Grey (the camera man), Carl Dean (big wheel) and I had a good session at Harpers Ferry.[14] We talked at length about your idea of the hikers coming to see you, finding the journals and reading from them. While we all recognize the idea was a good one, the Harpers Ferry veterans pointed out that it is an approach that has been done many times before and introduces complications and contrived situations that are far less likely to make a top notch film than to have the narrative come straight from "the man involved."

So – we would like to proceed with our original ideal of your providing whatever spoken commentary is desirable. Boy! right back where we left off at Harpers Ferry – the place I was really happy to see the last of. I find myself not looking forward to the coming of those guys and their sneaky listening device. If it's the same approach that they tried there, it's a lot of garbage. Like the TV interview in Anch. I find myself not wanting to see it or even hear it (the film).

"How long will this film run?" I asked. "28 minutes," was John's reply. "A four season film in 28 min, sounds pretty skimpy to me." Oh he didn't know maybe they would

---

[13] Tommy Belleau, an Anchorage-based pilot with the Office of Aircraft Services who flew NPS personnel to various proposed park lands.

[14] RLP's " boys from Harpers Ferry," Brian Jones, Tom Grey, Hubbard Blair, and Carl Dean were film makers from the NPS Interpretive Center in Harpers Ferry, West Virginia; their resulting film was entitled "One Man's Alaska."

make it 48 minutes. So – they are due here July 14. A portable generator coming in soon to be used by them.

Eubanks & Hewitt coming through from Lake Clark soon too. More coming in July. Good thing that July is dead gamewise or I would be loused up.

July 7 – Clear, Calm & 36°.

This was a truly beautiful morning after a night of some activity. I dreamed that I was notching logs and I woke up to hear rasping. Out of a sound sleep it took a little while for it to soak in. A porkypine was rasping on my cabin or the cache ladder. I pounded on the wall and hollered. Quiet for a few seconds and then the same old stuff. I finally got up and went out. No body at the cache ladder and I figured it a wise one and had taken to the brush. Back in my bunk no more than a minute when there it was again. As I eased out the door I spotted parts of a porkypine under the table on the left. Up on the rounds between the legs and gnawing on a log end at the corner. With my walking stick I poked out a hand full of quills getting him unlodged and headed for the brush. As it passed the rear of the cabin I tapped it severely on the head. Sorry to do that but we just can't have the cabin eaten up. An old one and I wouldn't cook it so I left it till morning.

July 9 – Clear, Calm & 42°.

A few tinkering jobs to do on the Cub to make it ready for inspection. My log books to bring up to date. I learned that I have flown about 100 hrs. solo since last Oct. and am now a 150 hr. pilot. The Cub has flown nearly 230 hrs. since last July. Everything layed out so I won't fly away and leave half of it. Voight had said it is important that you have your paperwork up to date.

July 11 – Raining, Calm & 46°.

The rain stopped, fog got better and worse. A broad band of the stuff cut the Volcanics in half. I wrote and watched. From here it looked pretty bleak on the far side of the mts. Finally it was go – fly down and see what was in my way from Pear Lake to Kijik Mt.[15] I loaded up and was away soon after ten.

Around the lower end at 3,800 ft to clear the high plateau. Fine weather to the Kijik. The sun was spotting the hills but I couldn't see Kijik Mt. To the Kijik and very dark down towards Lake Clark. A dark blue haze and so thick I could hardly make out

---

[15] Kijik Mt., a 3,351 foot peak overlooking the mouth of the Kijik River on Lake Clark. The mountain dominates the river delta and the Kijik National Historic Landmark, a sprawling Athapaskan site that represents a thousand years of Dena'ina occupancy on Lake Clark. The Dena'ina word is K'unust'in, "one that stands apart."

the far shoreline. As I let down it improved and I picked up Tom Island[16] and Babe's Bay. I cut across to check on Voight's cabin.[17] Still at a thousand feet and letting down. I saw that his garden had been tilled, a boat, two boats on the beach. Someone in the garden. Voight was there. The lake with only a ruffle and I circled back and landed off a point of land near his cabin. A good beach. David and Daniel there to meet me.[18] When had they come? Yesterday and spent the night in the cabin. We took the trail through the brush to the garden. There sat Voight and Floyd Denison (Babe's neighbor) visiting. Floyd and his new wife Helen had come up by boat to try for grayling at the creek there.

Voight had a good looking patch of ground tilled and if I would watch the crop he would put it all in strawberries.

Floyd had to go and look for fish elsewhere. Voight said his AD notebook[19] and rubber stamp was at Babe's. He wanted to plant some potatoes. I would fly to Babe's for 20 lbs. of spuds and a sack of chicken manure for his two anemic looking rhubarb plants. I suggested he fly the Cub up and see how it behaved. "Oh! I wouldn't do anything as dangerous as that," he said. "I haven't flown floats for three years." So – I took off. Glen Van Valin was at Babe's beach with his river boat and a big crew of kids and women. He had to inspect the Cub and visit awhile. Sis had come out and I told her what I wanted. By the time Glen left she had everything ready including the sack of fertilizer. A real good little house wife that Sis. Back to Voight's and we cut and planted the spuds. Gave the rhubarb a big shot in the arm, had lunch, which David & Daniel prepared. Now for the Cub. Voight dug into his big book for the A.D. notes on J-3's [Cub] and went through the log books to see that they had been complied with. Looked her over thoroughly and gave it his rubber stamp and signature. The Cub was legal for another year. Babe would ask me and I would say she is a legal airplane (which his isn't).

July 12 – Partly Cloudy, Calm & 48°.

I went up to get Spike's cabin in order. The posts to remove from under the perlin logs. The chimney top to put on. Wipe the Volcanic ash from counter and table. Level the floor and it was ready when I parked the work bench outside. How would John Brown's boys take this primitive living?

Now I had that bundle of 40 [Swede] saw blades waiting to be set and filed. In the bunch I found three broken ones. Just what I was needing for my short bow saw. Break them off at the right length. Stick the end in the stove and bury it in a can of ashes when it was red. No problem to drill a hole in the end after the temper was destroyed. I

---

[16] Tommy Island, an island in Lake Clark east of Port Alsworth named for fisherman-trapper Tommy Rasmuson who died near Kijik circa 1917.

[17] Voight's cabin was near the mouth of Tommy Creek about 4 miles E of Port Alsworth. It was built by Art Lee about 1935 and sold to retired school teacher Bill Park about 1940. Park willed it to Babe Alsworth. Alsworth gave it to his daughter Margaret "Sis" Clum. Ts'ananiłghldełi is the Dena'ina word for Tommy Creek, meaning "spawned out fish come out stream."

[18] David and Daniel Clum, 10-year old twin brothers, and sons of Voight and "Sis" Clum.

[19] AD notebook refers to air worthiness directives from aircraft manufactures and the FAA about various air plane parts that mechanics use to guide their maintenance.

sat on the beach and set the teeth on eight, filed them and then eight more. When I finish Babe will run out of lifetime before he runs short of sharp saw blades.

July 13 – Overcast, Calm & 46°.

A Goose white with orange wing and tail. That was my boys for sure and I headed out. He went on by, circled and landed off Carrithers' point. Slowly he taxied down my way and made very little fuss getting into position for unloading. I had only a good start up when the fans started turning and soon a cloud of spray as he blasted off headed down. Action on my beach and I could count three people. In close and a mountain of gear. Luggage and equip. cases. Warner Brothers or Metro-Goldwyn-Mayer couldn't have done better. It was Tom, Blair & Brian alright. Good to see them again and I wished they had just come to loaf a week or two. I tried to act friendly but at the first opportunity Brian told me John Kauffmann had let him read the last letter I had written to him. That the Harper Ferry decision was giving me a lot of trouble that many times I wished the book had never been and now it was in second place, that I felt "One Man's Wilderness" was in trouble as never before. Brian was sorry about that and understood how I felt. Enough of that garbage and we would move them up to Spike's cabin. A canoe load wouldn't clean the beach and it was two loads before I got all the gear and groceries moved up. This is sure going to beat living in a tent Tom said. So much gear that we cleaned the empty boxes out of Hope's cabin and one or more could sleep there.

July 15 – Partly Cloudy, Calm & 46°.

This morning at three a loud rasping on the lake hind corner of the cabin. Silently I opened the door with the stove poker in my hand. No sign of the culprit as I looked along side but just around the corner sitting on its haunches, a very large porkypine. My scent had reached it by now and slowly it turned to go but it didn't go far. A big female and too old for eating purposes I figured. I would skin her out for the birds and animals. Back to bed and up again at 4:45.

Brian the producer had a long list of activities. Cut wood was first on the list. Jake [Raymond Proenneke] and I had filmed the cutting, packing in and sawing of a big tree last Sept. (late) or early Oct. and I had filmed two cuttings this spring. He was more interested in sawing and splitting. Too dark in the woodshed so we moved the saw buck out in the green area in front where no wood had ever been sawed. Didn't look to authentic to me but I sawed and split while Tom filmed from all angles and from below. Blair got it all on tape while Brain made any suggestion of improvement that he thought necessary. The best thing about the whole deal was that I gained a few days supply of split wood. Now, they needed me starting out for a days filming. Pack up my gear and come out the cabin door. Gather up paddle and knee protectors before going to the beach

to launch, load on, paddle away. A few dry runs to get the bugs out and then the birds got into the act. I had to feed my birds before I left. Then Tom in the bow filming me paddling and finally Blair in the canoe for the sound of the canoe travel.

By now it was near twelve their time (eleven mine). Take a break and they would see me again in a little while. Brian mentioned the subject of statements and comments on tape for the afternoon session. I was afraid of that and thought what a way to go – no one was ever more relieved than I was at Harpers Ferry when John [Kauffmann] and I left after the last session of recording and now the same garbage had followed me to my land of no problems. "One Man's Wilderness" would never be the same.

[RLP flies his plane to the Hammond homestead on Lake Clark]

July 17 – Partly Cloudy, Calm & 42°.

A boat coming and it was the Governor's[20] and his guest. He greeted me with a big hand shake and thanked me for getting the boys off to a good start. He was well pleased with their work. He knew that his man John[21] was a good worker – all he needed was some one to show him how to do it. His guests Ed and Peg Wayburn[22] of San Francisco. The man a doctor, oldish like with long sideburns. A real friendly person and so was his wife Peggy who is doing a book about Jay.

Lunch time and they retired to the lodge to get some thing stirred up. Tuna fish salad on pilot bread, soup and sandwich cookies. A real nice get together and the weather clearing fast. Jay and the Wayburns got started on politics and it ended up by a lengthy speech by Jay. I couldn't get an edge in side ways to excuse myself. Peg was taping the conversation and the tape ran out. My chance and I said "Excuse me please, I must fly over the mts. to the land of no problems" as if Twin Lakes was still that way. Dr. Wayburn said he had read my book and had been pleased to meet me.

Jay says, "I'll run you around to your Cub in the boat." Oh no, I would go over the trail. He would do it anyway. He wanted to see that airplane. He had seen it fly by. All three of us went and the Governor and I got our pictures taken with the "Arctic Tern." The Wayburns wanted to walk the trail back. I would show them where it led out from the Cove. A fork in the trail so I went as far as cotton grass meadow. The good doctor says "You will soon be back where we started from." We stood and talked a minute and he quizzed me about my thoughts on the park proposal. I told him I wasn't sure it should become a park. "Oh, but it must," he said. If you knew of the plans to develop this country you would think it a subdivision of Anch. I suggested it be a wilderness area or refuge. "That would be good," he said. "The park has plans for improvements at the lower lake and we don't think that should be. Do no building closer than Lake Clark. Keep it a wilderness." I suggested eliminating the airplane and he agreed but added, "That would

[20] Governor Jay S. Hammond (1922-2005), governor of Alaska from 1974-1982 and Lake Clark homesteader starting in 1952.

[21] John Branson, former school teacher and caretaker at the Hammond homestead.

[22] Dr. Edgar Wayburn (1906-), medical doctor from San Francisco and president of the Sierra Club, and his wife, Peggy Wayburn (1918-2002), conservationist and author.

be like eliminating automobiles." He gave me his card and they both insisted I come to see them in San Francisco. Now it was 1:30 and I wasn't flying. My crew would suspect I was giving them the run around. Off and flying and I found my route clear if it was a little bumpy. At 4,000 I slipped by the Pyramid Mt. More than a little lumpy that short cut off but I saw a few caribou up near the peak. White capping and raining lightly as I came up the upper lake and I landed above Carrithers' point. On the water when I saw Tom & Brian with the canoe along the beach. Blair came trudging down the beach to help me take care of the Cub and pack my load to the cabin. I had bought 25 lbs. of Navy beans from Babe for $15.00. Hard as shot and 20 years old I suspected and on biting one I was convinced.

July 25 – Partly Cloudy, Calm & 42°.

Tom had shot right at 5000 feet of film in the past two weeks. I would have to work very hard to use that much in six months.

Brian left for a walk on the beach. Tom stayed awhile and then headed for the little cabin. Some packing to do in order to be near ready by morning. In early Aug. (Aug. 8) he goes on a filming assignment to Isle Royal [National Park], Michigan. He has really been around, that guy.

July 26 – Partly Cloudy, Lt. Breeze dn. & 40°.

I had thought the Otter a lot of airplane for two and their gear and I suspect it was but it seemed like a load by the time the canoe was empty. The boys went to the woodshed for the new Homelite alternator. It was the last to go in. "Well I guess we have everything but I suspect we forgot something," Tom said as they made ready to board the plane. "If you forgot something, it will be here when you come back," I said. They shook hands and Tom said "Well, we will see you on the cutting room floor" and I allowed that is where most of the footage would end up – on the cutting room floor.

July 27 – Partly Cloudy, Blowing dn. & 47°.

At Emerson Creek I could see a blue tent in the poplars. The yellow raft at the head of the connecting stream (on the left side). I looked for people but saw none about the stream or beaches. Then it struck me that they may be the Park Service party that was coming to study Twin Lakes area. An archeologist looking for sign of early inhabitants, other checking vegetation for maping. Babe had told me that Glen Van Valin had flown seven hours hauling them around searching for beetles.

July 30 – Overcast, Calm & 46°.

I would rake the beach if I had time but I didn't. I heard a plane and here came that pretty [Cessna] 170 on brand new floats. "Sure is a nice beach you have here," he [Governor Jay Hammond] said as we tailed the bird in to the beach. Everyone in hip boots for his wife[23] and daughter[24] are fisherman or women and fish commercially every season out at Naknek.[25] They had read the book and had to examine the cabin, woodshed, and cache. Those door hinges and that latch was the big attraction and on the inside the fireplace, it was beautiful. We talked a minute and Jay says, "How's your water?" I would go to the creek for some fresh. How about going along and try for a fish with my old bamboo Shakespeare. So we went all of us. That Jay is a fly rod man first class. That line curled way back and far forward with each cast. He got one on, a nice greyling. "All we catch at my place anymore is little ones," he said. This one about 15 inches. His wife interested in the flowers and other vegetation. Some she hadn't see on Lake Clark. His daughter interested in photography and packing a new Pentax. His daughter tried her hand at fishing but did no good. I tried and got nothing. Jay gave it another whirl and gave up. We came back and sampled my fresh kettle of beans cooked before I flew this morning. His daughter had never been in a canoe so we went for a little paddle, visited more and then they had to go. He set a little goal for each day and today's goal hadn't been gained. He says, "You know, I brought a batch of work along to do and you know I haven't touched it." He invited me down to use his steam bath, best thing in the world to take the kinks out he said. For the first lady of Alaska a special souvenir from Twin Lakes. The wooden ladle that I had kept as the best I had ever made. She was really pleased with it. Jay examined it and said, "I could never do that." They climbed aboard and taxied up to the point. A nice ripple coming up the lake. The [Cessna] 170 STOL with three aboard wasn't too impressive on take off and Jay had told me that he wasn't impressed with its take off, but, once in the air it climbed fast and was soon up along the high ridges of the mts. down country.

August 2 – Overcast, Calm & 46°.

As I came down the bank an arm raised from the beached boat. Some one was sitting in the bow. He stood up as I came near. Long hair, full beard, down jacket and soiled cap. "You must be Dick Proenneke," he said. He introduced himself as Harvey Shields.[26] His buddy Mike wasn't back from a little scouting trip to a nearby knoll. With the Park Service, they were archeologists looking for sign of prehistoric man in Twin Lakes country. Had they found anything? No, not yet but the weather had kept them from traveling on the

[23] Bella Hammond, wife of Governor Jay S. Hammond.

[24] Heidi Hammond, college student and daughter of the Hammonds.

[25] Naknek, a small Bristol Bay coastal community and salmon canning capitol of the world, home of the Hammonds, about 200 miles SW of Twin Lakes.

[26] Harvey Shields (1948-1993) NPS archeologist-anthropologist who along with George S. Smith conducted a survey to locate and describe archeological and historical sites in the proposed area of Lake Clark National Park and Preserve. Mike's full name is not known.

lake. They had found evidence at Telaquana and Turquoise where they had found a small spear or arrow point. Mike came, a young guy, long hair, full beard, soiled cap. Both young, Harvey from the University of Alaska and working on a grant. Mike was hired for the job I understood. They had planned to move to the upper lake in a few days. Their boat a Zodiak made in France. Inflatable and with an inflatable keel no less. A real good looking boat and would take any rough water that Twin Lakes could dish out. A new 6 hp. Evinrude kicker. $1,200.00 for the boat they said. $100.00 per foot. They wanted to go a bit farther down and invited me to go along. We went splashing to my high look out knoll. If I used it as a look out point no doubt prehistoric man did too. Look for rock that appeared to have been worked, chipped, shaped or whatever. Harvey and I climbed it and Mike traveled a long open ridge behind the beach. We found nothing and I hadn't expected to find anything. I had been there too many times and always looking for the unusual. Harvey dug a small hole in a likely spot with his shovel. Checking for anything out of the ordinary, chips of stone charcoal anything. That was how they made the find at Turquoise, digging in the blind. We went on to the next bare knoll and skunked again.

August 6 – Overcast, Blowing dn. & 52°.

Strong gusts in the spruce tops, the lake roaring wild and me very comfortable after a dead to the world sleep. I listened to it till six before I started a fire.

The Cub altimeter was climbing and it might equal the 400 foot rise of the last good blow from the gulf.

I had told Mary I would be back in one week and this was the day. It would be blowing on Lake Clark too and they would understand.

I had repairs to make. One of my hip boots, new in early May was giving out but what can you expect from Hong Kong for less than $13.00. The lining very thin and poor quality. It fails and the thin rubber tops fail. I had tried to find nylon tops but found none in Anch.

The anti-skid mats on the Cub floats coming unstuck (right hand float only) so I nailed them down with some "boat life" compound.

The lake got really wild. I don't think that I have seen it churning more at anytime since I came this year.

At least I have come up with a refillable ball point. My Schaeffer writes too heavy. My Parker doesn't write half of the time. Ball points go dry one after the other. I have bottles and bottles (plastic now) of Quink. Ed Fortier[27] had given me some (Bic's) ball points. Long like a lead pencil. Clear plastic with a small tube of ink in a large full length cylinder. Pull the guts out and cut the ink tube off close to the point. Put it back together minus the tube. Fill the big tube with ink using a fountain pen for a filler. Bottle ink

---

[27] Ed Fortier (1917-2001) was executive editor for *Alaska Magazine* and in 1972 was the driving force behind Alaska Northwest Publishing Company's decision to publish *One Man's Wilderness*.

won't feed through a ball point. Thin it, with what? Alcohol, from where? Hope's cabin. Bob Emerson had left some Everclear 100 grain. It got some, thinned the ink, it worked. One filling would write all day, maybe two. So – I wrote letters nearly all afternoon. Light rain at times, a patch of blue but always wind. Now at 7:45 a patch of blue, blowing down and 55°. Tomorrow to the sheep lick maybe.

August 9 – Overcast, Lt. Breeze dn. & 46°.

Glen [Alsworth] and old Harry Baker[28] of Anch. came to the beach to meet me. Harry was a long time resident of upper Lake Clark and still has a cabin there. Glen asked me if the Cub runs better since Voight annualized it. "Yes it did, the EGT [Exhaust Gas/ Gauge Temperature] worked going home and it hadn't coming in…it only runs better on paper and that is what FAA is interested in."

While I was unloading my incoming load, Babe came down. I was surprised when he said, "Are you sleeping good these nights?" I wondered what was coming next. "Real good," I said. "Well, if not you can count sheep," he said and that was the end of it.

At the house Mary says, "How are things at Twin Lakes?" "Been blowing for three days," I said. Making an excuse for being three days late. I closed my letters and she stamped them. The mail plane was on the field. I needed gas and was given the word to help myself. 25 gallons went into the tanks and I might have squeezed in 5 more. It was sprinkling so I put the caps on and called it good. Back to the house to pay and pick up my groceries. "Come into the living room with a plate and fork," Mary called. I washed my hands and kicked off my hip boots. Mary, Pat, and two more young woman eating cake. It was Mary's birthday and the cake a carrot cake came from Mrs. Woodward[29] across Babe's Bay. "I'm off of weight watchers for today," Mary said. This is a special occasion. The cake real good, very moist, my kind of cake. Mary finished hers and said, "I'm not bashful" and cut another one. I finished mine and waited for her to invite me to have more and she did.

August 19 – Raining, Breeze up & 44°.

Identical except for no fog patches – the ceiling too low. It had rained enough during the night that the eaves were dripping. No doubt there would be new snow on Spike's peak.

A few mending chores and I got with my study material and letter writing. Mary will have a pay day this trip. The weather began to fair up along towards noon. A big clear spot appeared over head and I went out to check on my prize bull caribou. I didn't see him and I would have been surprised if I had. When he got my scent he would move out.

---

[28] Harry Baker (1913-1997), Anchorage businessman and long time summer resident of Lake Clark.

[29] Clare Woodward (1896-1983) long time summer resident of Lake Clark, wife of Earl and mother of Allen Woodward.

Looking pretty good after lunch and I would just make the climb to make sure. Maybe I would see him farther up or across the canyon. Still raining over the lower lake and heavy grey clouds as far up as Low Pass Creek. I waited awhile on top but saw nothing so I moved over to the knoll. Finally, a moose at the cottonwoods across. In the wide open but not for long. No antlers, so a cow it was.

My blue spot turned to blue and grey and it started to sprinkle. I headed for the homestead. Who did I find in the woodshed but mr. porkypine chewing on a big card board box the Harpers' boys had left.[30] With a pole I headed him out the trail towards Hope Creek. With my glasses from the flat I glassed across on the slope of Cowgill Mt. There above the Farmer cabin was the big bull. Feeding and staying put pretty good. Let the weather fair up a bit and I would go over and see what I could do. Next I saw of him he was headed up country and traveling. Where would he go, not up into the high pocket I hoped. While I watched he stopped to feed on brush. A bug bit him and he began to dance around. He took off on the run headed down country. He circled back and down into the heavy brush and spruce timber. That was that for today.

I was getting low on blueberries and decided to see if I could scrounge a few. Try the big blueberry bank and work towards the lake. Wet in the brush and I wore my rain gear. Over that way I found a few here and there and on the bank fair picking in places. Towards the lake I found a few pretty good small patches and the berries mostly small too. I had taken my big green tin cup holding maybe a quart and a small peanut can. I would fill them both by the time I reached the lake and found the best berries near there.

August 20 – Foggy, Calm & 44°.

That two airplane party was a bunch of litter bugs. The remains of a campfire, burned cans, foil, candy wrappers, cigarette packs, a broken broom. Just what I always wanted to brush my floor. Only a half handle but I could extend it. I cleaned up the place and headed on down. At the head of the stream more litter. Another fire and a half burned sock and a good one, burned bug dope cans. I suspect if they came and found such a mess they wouldn't notice it.

The fourteen year old land mark is no more. Herb Wright's sheep camp. The dead tree with tent or lean to poles leaning into it. It was fourteen years ago that I saw it first. The tree cut and it and the poles used for the firewood.

I took the blazed trail to the turn off to the Vanderpool cabin. Someone had camped there and set up the heater that I had hauled up from the Oregonians camp two years ago this fall. A few cans of grub and some pilot bread left for the next hungry traveler. Next I would visit the camp in the cottonwoods this side of the creek. The Park Service ecology team had camped there and I knew it would be clean. Neat as a pin and a worn trail to two tent sites a hundred feet or more apart. I walked to the far one and

---

[30] "Harper's boys," the NPS film crew from the Harpers Ferry Center in West Virginia.

was surprised when something moved in the brush. A young cow moose and no more than fifty feet away. She didn't act alarmed and didn't attempt to leave. Had she become acquainted with the campers there. Then I saw a calf in the brush nearby. A good big calf and the color of slate. It too acted tame and went about it business, picking brush and fireweed. The cow laid back her ears and shook her head when I attempted to get in the clear for a better view. She started slowly my way and I knew what that meant and backed away. I stayed and watched them move into the open and then move slowly away. The calf half the distance from the cow to me and yet it ignored me. Why only a single calf. At the litter bugs camp part of a caribou skin in the shallow water along shore or was it part of a calf moose skin. I wished I had examined it when I fished it out and draped it over a drift tree, hair side down. So – the airplane yesterday had only stopped awhile and then took off to fly for sheep and camped somewhere else.

August 27 – Partly Cloudy, Blowing dn. & 46°.

Very early in the morning I was awake and heard a porkypine along side and I figured he was after glue on the cache ladder. As long as there was no heavy rasping I didn't mind. Then I heard him in front and he had better not start on that table leg. A light nibbling and I remembered my hip boots, tops turned down setting on the gravel by the table. I got up and with flashlight in hand I went out. There he was perched up under the table but not for long. Hurriedly he climbed down and headed out the path for the woodshed. Me walking right behind with my porkypine dispatcher. On through and in the clear past my standing wood supply and that's where I stopped him. The top of my boot had a ragged hole 4 inches long.

So this morning I had a skinning job and it was a nice tender meat on the table kind of porkypine. My boot to mend and I was happy that they cost no more than $12.50 or so. $35.00 boots would have tasted just as good.

August 28 – Partly Cloudy, Calm & 40°.

Off again and I landed on glassy water in Babe's bay. As I went to the house I saw activity up at the hanger. The old Stinson fuselage had been towed outside and I could see other odds and ends. I knocked and got a come in from Mary. "Where have you been? I was about to send out a search party." "The wind has been blowing at Twin Lakes," I said. Something new in the kitchen. A brand new propane gas stove. Boy, what a luxury after all these years of feeding a wood fire. I presented her with a nice wooden plaque that Babe had flown in the winter before last. A nice 10 inch wide board with bark edges, varnished and on it neatly carved "Direct your attention to things above and not on things on the earth." I was glad that Babe wasn't there. I told her I would like to present it to their church. I thought it was very nice and should be where people could see it. She thanked

me and put it in the Post Office. I mentioned the activity at the hanger. Yes, Babe was cleaning out two rooms and would put concrete floors in them. ... Hauling all of his tools home and going to put them in those rooms. So, it was as I suspected when his "T craft" wasn't getting the new 135 hp. engine put in, he started gathering up his tools and hauling them home. My mail taken care of I went up to the hanger. Ralph[31] the young carpenter was there and working like a beaver. He will have plenty to do as long as he stays at Babe's. For pay he might get the little black bird but it is a sorry looking rig now and he would be wise to have nothing to do with it.

The floors in the rooms to be used had many low spots and these were being filled with rocks picked up on the runway. Loaded on the two wheel flat bed trailer pulled very slowly by the Ford tractor steered by Sig or Leon. I helped them pick up a load before it was time for lunch. Glen was busy putting the new 135 h.p. engine in Babe's "T craft." In, and hooked up, all it needed was a new cowl and it would be ready to fly.

Lunch past and I started gathering up to fly back to the lakes. "Take anything you want from the garden," Babe said. He dug me some new red potatoes and pulled some carrots. I cut a head of cabbage & lettuce. Going out the gate I met a man I had heard a lot about but had never met. Earl Woodward[32] who lives (summers only) at the mouth of Babe's bay. More than 80 yrs. old now but still runs his own boat pushed by an outboard motor. He looked like he might have been a strong hiker in his day. He told me he had read my book and liked it. He had hunted sheep in Twin Lakes country years ago. At Turquoise and 7 hrs. back was a big basin and he had seen 15 good rams in there at one time. At Twin Lakes he had hunted up the lake and the river. At the rock pile you could glass and pick the ram you wanted to climb for. He had crossed that rock pile at night with a load of sheep on his back. The flashlight gave out and it was an awful stretch of going. He nearly got swept away crossing the river and then he told of spending a night on a high ridge in the rain and wind. He had talked to Fred Eubanks of the Park Service and was asked how he felt about the proposed park. Yes, he thought it was a good thing. Save some of the wilderness from being abused to the point where it wouldn't be wilderness anymore. He had read where in over 500 guides in Alaska only fifteen didn't use airplanes. But, we have to use the airplane he said, and I knew why. Too many not able to walk and pack or ride a horse, or have the time. He invited me over to his place[33] and he and his son Al[34] had talked of coming to Twin Lakes some day.

Babe had asked me if I was wintering here this time and I said I doubted that I would. Too much I could do outside and not enough reason to stay. Was he going to Hawaii again. "Well, we will have to stay here part of the winter, but I want to go as much as I can to see if I can find something to buy," he said. "This country is alright when you

---

[31] Ralph Nabinger, a young carpenter from Palmer who was a friend of the Alsworth's and who was hired by Governor Hammond to help build a log steambath.

[32] Earl Woodward (1897-1983), a retired railroad conductor from Nevada and long time summer resident of Lake Clark.

[33] The Woodward's place was originally built by Dr. Elmer Bly of Anchorage and was on Hardenburg Bay across from the Alsworth homestead.

[34] Allen Woodward, air traffic control evaluator and pilot with the Federal Aviation Administration, and a summer resident on Lake Clark since the early 1950's.

are young but when you get old, it is too cold in winter."

September 3 – Partly Cloudy, Calm & 25°.

Moose swimming across the lake, two of them. I had the motor laying in the bottom and camera gear all stowed forward. I headed for the mouth of Glacier Creek full paddle for that is where they were headed. Still in the shade of the mt. and they looked dark. I was gaining and they were loafing along. I was getting close when they hit the sunlight. It was a cow and young bull and I am sure it was the two that I saw yesterday. The cow in the lead and she turned her head to look at me. No problem and she continued on. I was abreast of them when she looked again. Now, the race was on. Moose are very strong swimmers and I doubt that a caribou is much faster if any. I wanted time to get my camera set up and it would be close. I paddled on and cut across in front of them. They turned down and would cross behind me. I made it to the beach and got the camera on the tripod. I ran down the beach to get close and this turned them back. They headed back across. A good run of them in sunlight and I hurried to get the kicker on. Back into the shadow by the time I got going. I caught them easily and as I passed they acted confused. Stopped dead in the water and I thought they would turn back again. I didn't want to do them harm so I moved away and let them decide where to go. They continued on towards first point. I got some footage hand held which is never the best. Getting close and the bull took the lead. He swam very hard, he was going to make the beach this time or else. His feet hit bottom and he lunged ashore. Water flew as he splashed out and raced down the beach as if he had been resting. The cow also showed no sign of weakness.

Some steep mt. side travel and a few dry washes to cross but I could go from the lake to the marmot colony in one and a half hours.

No sign of sheep and I would have to cross the big tailing pile to get to my friends house. Clouds were building and I was getting there none too soon. I could see sentries as soon as I came in sight of the colony. Two on guard and each laying on the big rock. No whistling and I wouldn't hear a chirp all the time I was there. Good camera subjects. Move slowly and you can get close enough. The one problem is that there is little action. The first one I came to retired to his house in the rocks so I went over the green ridge to where I had seen five. Still five and three smaller, so, I took it to be the father one, the mother one and three babies. A strange thing happened. One of the large ones moved away across the jumble of rock and came to the open level flat with no cover at all. Run a few steps and then stop, run and stop, all the way across to the base of a big tailing pile. I didn't expect one to do this with me so near. The sun was in and out and I waited and shot. One roll and then the second. As close as fifty feet and closer. They were easier to film than parky squirrels. I wished for the 400 mm and a few super close up shots and I could shoot some slides too.

The little pika's were busy and it is strange that you seldom hear them there. Perhaps they depend on the marmots to warn their neighbors. The pika's feeding on the

green ridge slope. Cutting grass and packing it back to the rock pile. I shot all the 16 mm I had taken (300 ft.) so packed for the trip down and this time I would travel the down country side of the creek to eliminate crossing the big tailing pile. The going not too bad. Going up I had flushed seven willow ptarmigan (one family) and down, five rock ptarmigan.

September 4 – Partly Cloudy, Breeze up & 34°.

I set up my equipment some distance away and suddenly I was in shadow. A big grey cloud had moved in covering the sun. Blue sky, miles of it, but the big hole was in dark shadow and would be for an hour and a half. The marmot soon learned that I was there and three were ready and waiting for pictures. One old one and the two young ones. At the upper ranch I could see five. I was set up and watching that cloud. I figured that after the heat of the day had passed the cloud would dissipate. As it was, it was building on the north and fading on the south. Not gaining much but the sun was moving slowly.

My actors had patience unlimited but even with them there is a limit to waiting. The old one decided to move just as the sun was about to cooperate. The young ones good subjects and I shot from different angles until I finally got too close. One sharp whistle and into the rocks they went. I headed for the high one but got no cooperation. Into the rocks and waiting wouldn't bring them out. I went back down to find my two star actors out and eager to get it over with. I learned something about the marmot. Sound as well as sight can cause alarm. A jet went by high above. One showed much interest and whistled the alarm.

September 20 – Snowing, Calm & 30°.

During the night I heard it raining gently and then no more. When I looked out at six I learned why – the silent one had taken over. It was snowing large flakes and many of them. Maybe close to one inch on the ground.

Hotcakes for breakfast and my birds slow in coming. What did they think of this first snow of the season. Eight o'clock and still coming right down. A light breeze up the lake. The snow building up and the temp. climbing a bit. It was starting to slide on the top side of the Cub. Chunks of the white stuff sagging and falling from the wing and fuselage.

It was one year ago today that Jake and I flew to Port Alsworth and learned of the Beaver crashing and eight losing their lives. On the way back we came onto the Ketchum Skywagon bottom up in the lower lake. A beautiful day weather wise, but give me the snow, peace and quiet of Twin Lakes instead.

A day for getting gear ready for storage. My…hiking boots to clean grease and

stuff with paper. My L.L. Bean pacs to clean and get ready to send in for new bottoms. I felt sorry for the Cub and when the snow over the engine cowl skylight and horizontal stabilizer refused to slide off I gave it assistance.

Still letters to write and others to bring up to date. If the weather holds foul I would get caught up. Early in the afternoon a fresh breeze came up the lake but the weather refused to lift more than a couple hundred feet. It continued its half rain half snow early fall weather.

As evening drew near and the day cooled a bit it was snow 100% that pelted the big window. The wing on the Cub started to turn white again. I thought, wouldn't this be something if this was the start of it all and just acted like winter until winter took its place.

I wrote till four thirty and then decided to have a light supper. I opened the big grey chest behind the stove and took inventory. I found a can of beets that had bulged and leaked. Two cans of ham, dried eggs, milk, vegetable, dried spuds. I could live a long time from that chest alone. The mess cleaned up, I selected a big can of peach halves and a can of white bread. That with my extra big helping of cold porridge pudding would be my supper (half of the peaches reserved).

The wind calmed a bit and soon the surf was gentle on the beach but the snow continued and now at six it appears that it could snow from now till spring. The willows have not yet dropped their leaves and load with snow easily. Every trail is blocked with willows bent to the ground. Temp. 32°. Does Babe have his spuds in the bin. I doubt that it would be snowing on Lake Clark but rain will make for muddy potatoes.

My camp robbers failed to come for supper and where would they roost. I have never seen one except on the go from tree to tree searching for food.

September 29 – Partly Cloudy, Breeze dn. & 34°.

I was up early to see it white capping down instead of a white frost. Today was the day and I would be away before noon. Time for a very neat and complete close up.

Breakfast out of the way and I went to work. My good wood cutting tools to oil and tuck away under the thick foam mattress of my bunk. It had appeared that the cache would have room to spare but it was filling fast and would be full to the door. Winter visitors had respected the privacy of the cache till now and I hoped they would one more time for it was loaded with valuable gear this time. The ladder would stand with my 16 footer out near the meat tree. The big spruce under which it stood would be complete protection from winter but a rabbit hunter looking for easy meat close in would find it.

At last the window covers went on and I closed the door. Again my note had been tacked on. It read "My cabin is closed for the winter, Thanks! if you leave it that way." It could be taken two ways. Thanks if you leave it closed or close it when you leave. Those

wanting to stay awhile would choose the later meaning.

I raked the beach one last time and with that, the operation got my stamp of approval.

A light load for the Cub. It would be a no strain trip. Away from the beach and I taxied towards Farmer's cabin. I turned circles in the bite of the beach past Hope Creek while waiting for the oil temp. to rise. Then down around the Farmer knoll for the take off run towards the point. A little turbulence out of Hope Creek flat as I passed and I was in the air as I passed that famous little cabin. A turn up lake around Carrithers' point and climbing at a good rate. A turn across and down. I was on my way [to Port Alsworth].

Babe asked me if I was in a hurry to switch to wheels. He had some machinery that he wanted to move into the back room of the hanger which now had a concrete floor. I was in no hurry and would like to fly up to visit the mission girls while still on floats. So – we moved machinery, visited and inspected the caved in cesspool that had been in that condition all summer waiting for the lake level to go down. Babe had insisted that it was lake level that we saw in the deep caved in hole. Not so, we found the lake level was 5 or 6 feet below. No need to wait longer as much as he would like to put off the disagreeable chore of digging a new one. It could start freezing any day. He would like to get Chuck Hornberger with his back hoe to do it, but I could see that he would rather have Chuck to volunteer to do it than be contracted to do it. While we poked and probed Chuck came for his mail. "I could sure save you a lot of hard work," he told Babe and Babe agreed that he sure could. And so the wheels started turning and Chuck would dig the hole. The man came with a mechanic to check the Otter. He had phoned a mech. in Montana and listed the symptoms. Sounds like an air leak in the oil suction line the mech. had said. Sure enough that is what they found. A nut on the suction hose not so much as finger tight. A few pulls of a wrench and the trouble was corrected. A happy pilot as he was prepared to spend $14,000.00 for a rebuilt engine. While Babe did his chores I worked at splitting slab wood. I would complete that job before I left Port Alsworth, Leon and Sig would help. Sig had volunteered to help on one other occasion and I gave him a spare pocket knife that I had. Now, it was no mystery when Leon offered to help. No more spare knives and I would learn later in Calif. that pocket knives don't come cheap these days.

September 30 – Clear, Calm & No Frost.

A fair morning [at Port Alsworth] with the [Hardenburg] bay calm. I would fly to Nondalton to see the mission girls. Mary had two big boxes to go. Clothes to be given to the Native kids of the village. A bulky load for the little Cub and we stuffed it in. A nice flight up country out of the bay and then down along the beach past Floyd Denison's and on down to see an Indian fish camp or two among the small coves and islands. I flew the length of the village and came down along shore. Doris and Florence with their Native neighbors Pete and Ruth[35] came to the beach to meet me. Pete is not a young man but

last winter he went marten trapping with his son[36] on the Mulchatna River.[37] Ruth has her own dog team, traps and tans skins which she makes into articles of clothing and foot gear. Very wise about nature and told me one time "I know everything" (in answer to a question).

The mission girls opened their little garage and wheeled out a new Honda motorized tricycle. They had traded the big tri-sport [ORV] for it and happy as kids with a new toy.

October 6 – Partly Cloudy, Calm & Cool.

[RLP makes ready to fly from Anchorage to Iowa in his Piper J-3 Cub.]

It was near ten o'clock when we untied the Cub and started the engine. While we stood and talked the engine slowed and I pulled carburetor heat. It ran rough for a few seconds and then smooth again. Carburetor ice, this was a good day for it. Tom and I[38] shook hands and he left. I got clearance to taxi to Wilbur's Flight Service[39] where I would gas up. All three tanks full and check for water. Oil full up and clean. I had changed it before leaving Twin Lakes. Clearance to take off on 06 and I was on my way at 10:40. At last I was on my way. The new David Clark head set did a nice job of cutting engine noise and I expected an enjoyable flight. Eagle River and Chugiak passed below. I talked to flight service at Palmer as I passed. Up the Matanuska River and I looked forward to getting out on top and away from that deep river valley with rugged mts. on each side.

Coming up the river I had used carburetor heat a few times as was customary with me when in rough country. Now I passed Sheep Mt. Lodge and its airstrip that appeared to be fair. A family lived below the highway and under me but I knew of no airstrip there. I pulled the heat on again and after several seconds I pushed it off. No indication of ice. Probably it was a couple minutes later when sudden silence took over. The engine had quit as if the switch had been turned off. Again I pulled the carb. heat on and flipped the switch to off and

> *It was near ten o'clock when we untied the Cub and started the engine. While we stood and talked the engine slowed and I pulled carburetor heat. It ran rough for a few seconds and then smooth again. Carburetor ice, this was a good day for it.*

[35] Pete (1905-2004) and Ruth Bobby Koktelash (1917-1988). Both Pete and Ruth were born at a Dena'ina village on the Stony River and moved to Old Nondalton early in the 20th century.

[36] George Koktelash Sr., son of Pete and Ruth Koktelash, and a resident of Nondalton, Bristol Bay fisherman.

[37] The Koktelash trapping cabin was near the confluence of the Mulchatna and Chilikadrotna Rivers at a place called Niłqidlen "where streams join."

[38] Tom Gregory (1914-2005), and his wife Marion were friends of RLP who hosted him when he came through Anchorage.

[39] Wilbur Flight Service was based on Merrill Field in Anchorage.

back to both mags again. Nothing, I tried the primer and got no response. I worked the throttle which would do no good unless it was ice on the throttle plate that was causing the stoppage. By now I was in deep trouble. The river fork lay down to my right but it would put me a long way from the highway and I doubted that a safe landing could be made there. To my left was up grade and I would be on the ground sooner with less time to pick a landing spot. Getting low, a landing was about to take place. I remember being perhaps two or three times the height of the spruce timber and descending at a good rate. Too fast I knew but I couldn't dive to gain speed and flatten my glide. I suspect that I pulled the stick back to slow as much as I dared if I wasn't already stalled out. Then, no more until suddenly I was standing forward of the right wing and facing the Cub. At first glance I took it to be totaled out. It had struck on the nose and landing gear. The gear folded tight against the fuselage. The under side of the nose cowl mashed and one blade of the propeller bent back. The wing tips had come forward and down to the ground. The left wings rear fitting had pulled loose from the fuselage. The tail undamaged and three or four feet in the air. Wrinkled fabric everywhere from the rear of the baggage compartment forward. A real sad looking Cub.

Gas was draining from the right wing tank. The side window was up and latched. It was holding the tank drain open. I dropped it down. My new David Clark headset lay stretched to the end of its cord as if it had pulled from my head when I crawled out. My sleeping bag was laying off to the side under the wing.

Now, how about me. My face felt numb and was dripping blood. The instrument panel had a deep imprint of my face in it. No wonder I was feeling not quite right about my head. My back hurt and when I moved to pick up the sleeping bag muscle spasms hit me hard. There was an urge to just unroll that bag, crawl in and rest awhile.

I could hear traffic on the highway and could see cars and trucks going by. I decided that I had better go while I was able. I headed for the road after one last look at the "Arctic Tern." This, I figured was the end of the last flight of the "Arctic Tern."

Going was slow and painful. Twice I rested during the 200 yds. to the highway. I came to the steep gravel grade and decided I couldn't climb it on foot so I crawled up to the shoulder. I was still on hands and knees when a camper came by, headed for Eureka and Glennallen. It passed and then slowed, stopped and backed up. A middle aged man and women got out and decided I was in trouble and had better get to a doctor. They loaded me in the seat with them and as we started to leave I looked and could see the yellow tail of the Cub over the brush. What a way to end the enjoyable year of 1976.

So I walked painfully to the highway on the lower slope of Sheep Mt. from the wrecked Cub. It would be nearly three weeks before I would walk again and then it would be slowly, on crutches. I had hitched a ride with a young couple in a camper on their way to Copper Center[40] and along the way he had phoned for an ambulance and the troopers, which we met father down the road. The trooper would salvage my gear from the Cub while we proceeded to the little five bed hosp. at Glennallen.

---

[40] Copper Center is a small village on the road system about 66 miles NE of Valdez.

I was admitted at 7:30 P.M. X-rays were taken and showed a fractured vertebra in my lower back. The young doctor ordered fifteen lbs. of traction on my hips and with a dripping bottle feeding my blood stream and a hypo in the arm I was ready for the night which would be a long one. Traction was very uncomfortable and I decided to do something about it. By reaching the limit on each side I could get a hold of the lines attached to the belt above my hips. I could lift the traction weights and ease the pain. This I did for much of the night.

[October 7 – Glennallen and Anchorage, Alaska]

Next morning (Oct. 7) I was due to be air lifted to the Providence Hospital in Anch. Morning finally came. My face was giving me some trouble. The lower jaw didn't meet the upper properly (slightly to one side). Six or a dozen stitches had been taken in my lips, chin, and nose. My forehead felt thick and heavy.

Another ambulance ride to Glennallen's airport at Gulkana fifteen or so miles away. A Cessna 206 was the ambulance plane. We took off, a nurse along as my attendant. Slightly turbulent but a much more comfortable ride than the highway would have been.

At the Providence end a young Irish doctor Dr. Nolan took charge. A look at the x-rays and he ordered two weeks on my back and then a cast would be put on. Friends began to come and I was quite a sorry looking sight. Voight and John would go get the Cub. Brother Raymond was notified and flew up to take charge of the crippled bird.

I had a little trouble with my mid section due to the injury and a tube to the trouble spot by way of my nose was in order.

In due time it was removed and I was making good progress. Doing so well that the cast idea was dropped and whirlpool therapy was started. I looked forward to those trips to the hot spring in the basement each day. Too warm (110 degrees) and to long unattended one day and I came out red as a beet and so weak I could hardly move.

I graduated to crutches and a back brace which I must wear any time I wasn't lying down. Sooner than I thought advisable Dr. Nolan wanted to get me out of the hosp. I asked for an extra day and he agreed. I would be flying to L.A. the day of discharge and I knew it wouldn't be easy.

The day of discharge arrived. Oct. 30 – and Tom Gregory and his wife Marion delivered me to Anch. Int. Airport. It wasn't an easy parting for me. Everyone had been too kind and helpful.

Western Airlines and a DC10 hauled me away and in less than an hour of five it would take for the trip. I was feeling pretty beat. I had to trip the latch on the back brace to relieve the discomfort to some extent. A landing at Seattle-Tacoma airport and then on to L.A. Raymond was on hand and I asked for a wheelchair. It had been a pretty demanding day for my pretty beat up condition.

Lynwood [California] weather was perfect for the work at hand. Even though it was a project to get out of bed in the morning I was determined to get on my feet and walk as much as possible each day. No more than a few hundred feet on crutches those first days. Then a block, two, three, and more. Finally I could carry the crutches and use then only to lean on while resting. Days, weeks, months went by. I was walking miles every day and the crutches had been parked long ago. In mid January I flew to the east coast on Park Service business concerning the film nearing completion and came down with encephalitis not a half day after completing the job. Severe headaches, vomiting and messed up memory were the symptoms and I ended up in the Georgetown University Hospital for a week. Another week and a check up before flying back to the west coast. It was a set back in my recovery but I worked at it and in due time I was walking strong again. It was very doubtful that I would be able to go to Twin Lakes in 1977 as much as I would like too. I could walk twelve miles easy enough but there is much more to it than walking. It was as if the muscles of my hips had been welded in a chunk and each one had to be torn loose and worked into shape again. I needed some work to do that. I volunteered to clean up the lawn and shrubbery for Raymond's landlord (a widow). Six hours of bending, twisting and lifting. I was pretty weary when the job was done.

Raymond and I worked on the Cub which has been trucked down the coast by two men on their way home to San Diego. The weekends in his hobby shop helped build me back. I might make it yet.[41]

---

[41] RLP convalesced from the injuries sustained in the airplane accident of 10-6-76 at Raymond Proenneke's home in Lynwood, California.

CHAPTER FOUR – 1977

REHAB AND RESTORATION AT TWIN LAKES

[Proenneke flew back to Alaska in early June eager to return to his life at Twin Lakes.]

[June 1977]

Glen came to Anch. on June 7 [1977] and his load in the [Cessna] 180 going home was me and a load of chicken feed. Fine weather and we started a clean up and repair campaign that very day. Clean out the goat barn loft and 1st floor to make room for feed. A small barn but two tractor loads of 30 years gathering of sacks, egg cartons, and other rubbish. We cleaned up the yard about the house and it looked as if some one lived there after we had finished. We repaired the top of the cooler well casing (of wood) so it could be used to cool that good goats milk again. Odd jobs too numerous to mention. Teen camp (teenagers) was in progress and of course I was expected to attend the religious meeting each evening. The sister of Mary's (Anna)[1] and I acted as judges to determine the winners of different craft projects. I was anxious to see Twin Lakes.

It had been blowing southeast and now calmed. Glen had a trip to Anch. the morning of June 10 [1977]. In the PM we would fly me in. Cody[2] the registered nurse at teen camp and sister-in-law of Glen's brother John wanted to see Twin Lakes too. No problem, Glen said! We are flying that super 135 hp. "T craft." It was two PM before we got my gear loaded for the trip. Cody climbed in on top of the load and we tried for take off and made it in good shape.

After we left Lake Clark I began to show interest in the surroundings. Not as much snow as I figured there should be. No ice to be seen where ice from seepage usually builds up. Across the Kijik and climbing. Glen wouldn't go around the lower end but over the mts. well towards the upper end of the lower lake. Over the top and both lakes in view. Little snow to be seen even on the north slopes. No ice on the lake shores and I have seen it there in late June and July. It had been a mild winter.

---

[1] Anna S. Benson (1914-1994) was married to Bennie Benson who designed the Alaska state flag.

[2] Cora "Cody" Bower lived in Anchorage and was an R.N.

A turn over my cabin and every thing looked in order. I had heard that Babe's neighbor Ken Owsichek[3] the guide had hunted bear from my cabin in late April and early May. He had asked Mary a couple times when I was coming back and she had said anytime now. Fish & Game had found his hunter (a non-resident with no bear tag) and one of his pilots acting as guide and he also a non-resident and not an assistant guide. Hunting from a non-registered camp too. Owsichek had also told the Fish & Game agent that he didn't have any bear hunters out. So he is in court.

I wondered how they had left my place and was prepared to write him a letter.

A light breeze down and Glen landed out from my beach. The windows still covered as I had left them. Everything looked to be in order.

On the beach some beaver cuttings. In front of the cabin some charred sticks of wood from the stove. Inside the floor leveled as I had left it. Everything neat as a pin. That pilot (Mark) [Lang][4] had done a nice job of closing up.

We uncovered the windows and packed my gear in from the beach. Across on Falls Mt. was a nice bunch of sheep. Glen counted 28 head and I counted nine good big lambs in the bunch. Cody took some pictures.

Now, when should Glen come checking on me. Better make it in two weeks the first time. I had picked up a very bad cold the day we left Anch. and had rapped my left thumb a good one with the back side of a hatchet the day before we flew in. I wasn't in the best of shape. He had another trip to Anch. before the day was done so they took off.

Just like it has been for nearly 10 yrs. Me alone at Twin Lakes once more. How would it go this time? Not in the best of shape physically not to mention the cold and sore thumb. Things started to take a wrong turn from the start. Where was my three doz. eggs? Mary had said "here is three doz. eggs for you." She had given me a batch of vitamin C pills and Contact capsules for my cold. "Come to Hawaii for the winter and recuperate," she said.

I came to my sourdough and it didn't look too good. Only eleven days since I had used it. I added flour and water and mixed it well.

I glassed the far side often hoping to see a bear on the slope of Allen Mt. No bear or any tracks in the snow patches.

Maybe an hour after I arrived I heard a camp robber and rushed out to greet my old friend. It was one of mine all right. I came in for a can of dog food. Only bird and it wouldn't come to my hand but came to the stump with me standing close by. A second bird came and I was sure that it was one of my welfare birds. They came back later but still shy and refused to show much interest in canned food.

Near the end of the day I went to the creek flats. Ice and snow long gone but I got some indication as to how much ice there had been. An ice flow had come from what appeared to be the direction of Jerre's point. It had hit our nice break water head on and

---

[3] Ken Owsichek, a pilot and big game-fishing guide who owned Fishing Unlimited, a lodge at Port Alsworth.

[4] Mark Lang, a hunting and fishing guide from Port Alsworth.

lifted and shoved it back. It is now a foot or more higher than before and shorter too. Many truck loads of gravel and rocks pushed high against the steep bank from the break water around the point towards Hope Creek. Where I had parked the Cub on its beaching rock a mound of gravel three feet high. No caribou tracks to be seen but a few small moose tracks. A big bear track in the sand where my trail hits the creek flat on the way to the cabin log timber. As large a bear track as I have seen near here.

I circled down to Spike's cabin. Someone had opened the door but rebolted it without putting the bar in place. Everything in order. Hope's cabin was as I had left it.

I wrestled the canoe out and paddled down along the beach. I was happy to learn that I wasn't uncomfortable pulling the paddle. A little practice and I could fast paddle again. So it was nine before I turned in after a can of mushroom soup compliments of Owsichek, the outlaw guide.

A breeze down the lake. The sky partly cloudy and the temp. 50°.

June 11

Overcast, breeze down and 50 degrees. I had slept pretty good having heard only one porcupine rasping on a moose antler. My sourdough looked really sick. I hated to think of losing it after eleven years. Boy, I would be in bad shape without my good hotcakes and biscuits. In Spike's cabin was some dry yeast. I would see if I could get something going.

I had canned bacon, lots of spuds, oatmeal rice and raisins for breakfast. Early I had heard my birds outside and later they came again. Still they didn't care if they went on welfare or not.

A busy day finding everything I had tucked away in a safe place. My Bolex in a sack of rice. The telephoto lenses in a sack of beans. Pan head in the dried sliced spuds. Tripods far back under the bunk. It was a morning of getting organized and watching the progress of the sheep on Falls Mt. and looking for bear directly across.

I set my time back to wilderness time. The sun directly over Cowgill peak at twelve. The day bright and warm with a breeze down Hope Creek. I would climb the hump for a look up to the moose rutting cottonwoods. The climb was a climb but not too bad. I stopped three times to enjoy the view.

Only one track on the snow patches up Hope Creek as if a lone caribou cow had gone up to calve. I heard a few squirrels and glassed the valley from behind a bank in the warm sun. I laid back and dozed off only to wake up feeling cool. The day had darkened by a huge grey cloud. I moved over to the knoll and glassed across. I counted 10 sheep on Bell Mt. and picked up a lone moose above the cottonwoods. It was feeding and didn't move very far until turning into the bush again. A cow with a small calf bedded there would be my guess. Still no sign of bear on the mt.

The dry yeast and I read: "for best results use before Dec. 1965." In a separate jar I mixed some fresh starter using half a packet. For supper I boiled a potato and used the water to boost my old starter.

Near turning in time I paddled over to the Farmer's landing. I saw Lofstedt's boat still on the beach where the new owner had cached it last Sept. Bud will take a dim view of his boat being moved from his cabin. He doesn't forget easily. I walked the game trail behind the cabin and saw only the tracks of the young moose going down country. On the beach coming back I picked up a section of the green fiberglass roofing blown from the over hang of the cabin roof. So the wind had blown hard from the high mts. last winter.

Batter for hotcakes wasn't looking to prosperous when I turned in at nine. Near calm, broken cloud cover, temp. 55°.

June 13 – Flat, Calm, Partly Cloudy & 45°.

Past three I loaded up and headed for the canoe. A light following breeze and a pleasant paddle home. I was well satisfied with my ability to travel and feel sure that a few more such tours will see me ready for anything.

Cleaned up and an early supper. A brown rabbit came to the clothesline to lick the gravel where I drained the salty water from my spuds. A rabbit as tame as those who spent the winter with me and I wonder if it is. The birds came for hot cake – just like old times. A nice calm partly cloudy evening. Temp. 50 degrees. A real good night's sleep last night and this morning at five I could hardly get my eyes open. Just a very long time since I slept so well. Frank Bell said "I feel better at Twin Lakes than any place I have ever been."

June 19 – Clear, Lt. Breeze dn. & 28°.

I half expected Bob Belous of the Park Service to fly in and so I would stay close. I had letters to write, always letters to be answered.

The day was going to be cloudy. Noon came and went...I heard a plane coming up the lake and it sounded low. It flashed by on its landing run headed for Carrithers' point. A good looking [Cessna] 180 and soon it came back on the step and turned to my beach. A young blond long haired guy climbed out and tossed me a line - he had shut her off to soon. He introduced himself as Jim Teegarden[5] from Telaquana Lake. Dick Straty had told him to stop and say hello. From the passenger side out climbed a small woman, a Japanese who he introduced as Tash. She was carrying a notebook. I invited them in and they stopped at the door. Run their hands over the hinges and examined the latch. Finally he said, "Do you mind, this is new to me." They came in and looked the place over.

---

[5] Jim Teegarden, pilot from Anchorage who had built a cabin on Telaquana Lake in the late 1950s.

I built up a fire for tea. He had built a cabin at Telaquana about the time I built mine and has spent a lot of time there winter and summer. Stays until he runs short on money and then goes north to the villages to fly float planes till he makes a grub stake and then its back to his cabin on Telaquana.

June 21 – Partly Cloudy, Calm & 36°.

A pretty morning for the longest day. Early, a cloud bank way down and after breakfast mares tail overhead. This might be the day to visit the sheep lick on the high ridge towards Turquoise. If the weather held fair I could make a long day of it and stay in Arlen's cabin for the night. I got away to a 7:30 start. The little kicker along in case the wind took over.

Looking back from halfway down my lake I could see a banner cloud from a high peak. It indicated a north wind up there. If it blew it would blow up the lake. Just before the stream ripples coming up and in the lower lake I could see dark water. Wind was coming. No more than a mile down and I put in at a sandy point to hang on the kicker. By now clouds were building fast. Big white cotton clouds but before I reached the lower end they had turned heavy and grey looking on the bottom.

It sprinkled a shower while I got organized. I hated to call off the trip after coming so far. I would make a try at it anyway. I had my rain jacket along and wearing my L.L. Bean tin pants. I loaded up and took off, 400 ft. of 16 mm film in my pack. Across the knolls and mosquito flat. They gave me a bad time until I climbed out at the foot of the ridge. It was going to rain sure enough. Solid grey with streamers over the ridge. I climbed stopping to glass the down country (where the sun was shinning) for the big caribou herd.

At about the halfway it started to hail – pea size chunks of ice. It came heavy and after the hail came rain. I was wet and dripping in no time. No problem I was warm and would dry again. It let up and I trudged on up and up.

I took a turn to the right to avoid crossing a canyon. The climbing came steeper but I wasn't hurting. Again more hail and less rain. Finally I broke out through a notch and was surprised I was high enough but still had a mile to go. Had I crossed the canyon and stayed more to the foothills I would have avoided this extra travel. More weather and it didn't look favorable. What a day to be on the Mt.

Now I was in the lick area but saw no sheep and was very close before I did. Sheep grazing up the ridge from the lick and from a favorable view point above the lick I could see a lot of sheep. Standing on the edge of the canyon I made a quick count of fifty odd and a few at the lick. Directly below me was four near legal rams. I had never seen rams there before but this was earlier than I had visited the lick after years. The clouds were heavy and the wind cold and strong. I was wet and barely through dripping.

Filming would be no good, I would go, but before I did I traveled up country for

a better view. More sheep and a rough count made it seventy or better. Many new lambs in the bunch. I headed down. Out of the wind it wasn't bad and I stopped. Maybe the weather would fair up and I would get some sun in an hr. or so. The sun was lighting the low country towards the Bonanza Hills. It didn't look promising and I took off down the mt. Halfway and it was looking better over head. Into the timber and brush below it was as wet as the rain above. I spooked a moose which I only got a glimpse of. I followed the trail and was surprised to find a young cow standing watching for me. Little more than sixty feet away but she stayed and watched me. I finally walked slowly towards her and she moved slowly away only to stop when I turned off and went on my way. Looking back I saw her go to where I had been. Nose to the ground checking on that strange looking creature.

It was four o'clock when I reached the canoe and sure enough the sun was on the ridge but not the sheep's grazing ground. The lake was calm so I would paddle. Good for my lower back arms and shoulders. Going around the bend and out of sight I could see sunlight where I wanted it but it wouldn't last. A few minutes later it was grey again. A quartering breeze against me but I paddled on. Two and one half hrs. to the stream. The stream is high and fast but the canoe lined through easily. The upper lake near calm so I paddled again. Just below and far off shore from Low Pass Creek a breeze came down so I fired up the kicker and motored home. Nearly eight o'clock when I unloaded my gear. A good fire going and the stove smothered with things drying. Down country it looked wet and not more than thirty minutes after I arrived a fair breeze came up the lake. Boy oh boy! This had been a day, 12 hrs. of canoeing and packing up the Mt. and down. I could feel it pretty good and I figured morning would find me pretty well shot down. It was ten before I turned in. The setting sun had lighted the misty lower lake and turned it to pink. Much blue sky over head the light breeze up and the temp., 46 degrees. So went the longest day. I wouldn't stay up to see it complete.

June 22 – Clear, Calm & 36°.

This was the day I should have gone but I wouldn't go again so soon. I slept like I haven't slept in a long time and was surprised that I felt better than when I turned in last night. Legs only a bit sore and hips the same. I could feel it a bit in my arms and shoulders. The trip had been worthwhile even though no film was exposed.

Hotcakes for breakfast and then my gear to get organized again. This would have been a perfect day for the sheep lick country. If I had stayed at Arlen's cabin last night I most certainly would have made the long climb again. But what a place to stay during mosquito season. Build a fire to dry things out and you must open the door and let the blighters in.

A nice little spruce covered knoll over looks the ponds and today the breeze made it down wind. A perfect blind. I set up the camera and sat down to wait. Who

would come to the pond today. A diving duck, the American goldeneye came to feed. A porkypine waddled by and that was about the extent of it. Mosquitoes and flies were a nuisance. I toughed it out till three and decided it wasn't the place to be. I would go to the lower pond and see what the fox was up to. Clouds were getting bigger, darker and closer together. I traveled the trench between the ponds and climbed the backside of a bank facing it. Who did I see? – not one but three foxes. The old mother and two pups. She was forty feet out on the flat from the den area brush, sitting on her haunches, straight as a fence picket and about as plump. The two pups were having a rough and tumble between her and the brush. Not a care in the world as they ran circles and wrestled as domestic dogs do. Nearly half the size of their mother and better color. All three had one thing in common – a white tip on the end of the tail. The pups heavy and clumsy looking.

June 24 – Clear, Calm & 40°.

A perfect early summer morning. An ideal day to start a grand tour but with the possibility of Glen coming in I had better stay home. Clouds started to form early and it would be a repeat of yesterday. After breakfast I got my mail in order and my grub list made out. If he came Glen wouldn't be coming until mid afternoon or later.

I had the tree to pack in and how would it go. Five trips with four loads and no sign of over load. I sawed and split a couple lengths to round out the pile. Noon time came and I was here to get a time check. By the sun over Cowgill peak I was thirty minutes fast. This afternoon I would neaten things up a bit. Cabin and woodshed got the business. Burnable excess started a fresh kettle of beans to cooking. Glass and tin was flattened for the metal pit. A fresh breeze came up the lake and the big clouds pelted the roof with a few big drops of rain.

Two of my birds got wise that I was at home. One I recognize by the way it enjoys its food. Dainty little bites with much relaxing in between. Sit and look around as much as to say this is all we have to do today. The sun swung around to the big pasture and it was time to think about supper. And after that the well soaked beans to be doctored and simmered until time to cool the stove for the night. No plane today and it seems to me that I remember other years and days of waiting.

Now at 8:30 partly cloudy a light breeze up and 62 degrees.

June 27 – Clear, Calm & 35°.

Clear, not a cloud and the lake like a mirror. A jet trail if moving at all was going south. Today I would try for the sheep lick again. I was up at 4:45 and away by 6:15. Enough gear along to spend the night if I did get storm bound.

A quick paddle down 1 hr. and 15 minutes to the connecting stream and 2 hrs.

and 50 min. to the beaching spot at the lower end. As I went around the bend of the mt. I could see a cloud bank in the direction of Whitefish Lake and as I sorted my gear and put the stay behind gear under the bottom up canoe the first fluffy clouds came over the high ridge from Turquoise. So, I might be in for a day such as last time. Clouds built fast as I crossed to the base of the ridge and started my climb. A cold breeze came and was welcome for it was too warm paddling down the lakes. Two thirds of the way and a hen ptarmigan with very small chicks. One little guy didn't make it to cover and froze in the wide open. I stooped down and picked it up. No resistance and the same when I put it back down but this time his head was tucked safely in the moss. The rooster appeared and both parents put on a big to do about my being there. I moved away very careful that I didn't step on one of those little hard to see midgets.

Hail started falling on my head and as is normal procedure it turned to rain. This time I was prepared. Besides my rain jacket I had taken a garbage bag along. Big enough that I could pull it bottom up over my head. By squatting down I could stay completely dry and there I was until the pelting of rain drops diminished to tolerable limits. Only showers that would cool the day and bring more sunshine. Caribou on the skyline and I had seen tracks on snow patches. A nice bunch of cows and calves and I could see some bulls in the bunch. Closer and I spotted a bunch of maybe 20 or thirty bulls under the crest of the ridge on a little patch of solid green. It looked like I would be in business. I got organized and headed on up. Below me a cow and calf flushed and headed for the bulls. A loner and I hadn't seen her. Her alarm was reason to move and the bulls started to climb. The best I could do was a skyline shot. I climbed on up. Down country on the ridge was many caribou – a couple hundred at best. I could use a hundred feet of film there. The bunch of bulls were no where to be seen and it was wide open.

I wanted to check the lick which was only a half mile up country. If no business there I would come back and follow the caribou. I was getting close and could see many sheep grazing up the ridge from the lick. With sunlight I could do some good. Just breaking over for a view of the lick when I saw something a few hundred yds ahead and to my right. A big dirty looking sheep was my first impression. Too big and then it hit me, bear, a good sized blond and moving up country. No filming light so I watched her. Only one thing wrong. The wind was sure to give me away and soon. The bear ambled on for a short distance and then stopped turned and tested the air. It laid down and there I was, pinned down as far as getting to the lick, so I waited. Up and on the go again. Headed for the grazing sheep. This was interesting. How would a big bunch of sheep behave and what was the bear up to. As the bear got closer the sheep began to move farther and higher. Not alarmed but just moving slowly and feeding. The bear crossed a canyon to their ridge and that moved them more. The bear came over a rise with sheep on top. Less than a hundred yds away, they hurried away but the bear showed no sign of seeing them. On it went across another canyon to move more sheep. The last I saw of it, it was standing looking down on Beatrice Creek from the top of very steep and rough sheep country. A few sheep at the lick but no filming light. A nice bunch of sheep on solid green that the bear had left undisturbed down country from its route. I would try for them so I headed on up country

to get opposite. Out of sight behind a rise for a few minutes and when I came out – no sheep, not one. In their place was another bear. This one smaller and very dark. Fooling around on some snow patches and finally working my way with two canyons to cross. Still coming good and only one to cross when it hit the tracks of the first bear. Sniffed around and got lined out and away it went on the track. All the way to where the first one went out of sight... it searched for a few minutes and then over the edge. So – the sheep were much higher but the sun was in and out. I could climb several hundred feet and be on their level. I did and from there could check on the caribou herd. Gone, not a trace of them on that big wide open ridge below. Today things had a way of not working out. Now the sheep were climbing out from the lick. My grazing bunch didn't mind the bear but I was something else. Sight of me above and they decided to put a canyon between us and over the edge they went. Then I spotted the dark bear back where I had first seen it. Again it followed its route to my side of the canyon and made it. I was far above and was interested in its actions when it crossed my trail. No alarm and it crossed over and down to where the caribou herd had been in the past few days. Just going it seemed. Wandering around and at one point swerved its course to

Making good time but soon my tail wind became a cross wind from Black Mt. I had never seen it like this before. At the halfway it became straight from the mt. and so strong I was being drifted to the far side. I wished for the kicker but it was too rough to wrassel it from forward and hang it on. So I paddle my best and finally it let up.

back track a few hundred yds...to sniff around and then go again. Now it was on my route coming down to the lake. I would follow that guy, staying down wind. Over and down I went. The bear had dropped down a bench and out of sight. I hurried to pick it up again. Watching right when I came to the edge and there it was just below me and traveling left. My down wind was now cross wind and soon to be up wind. Plenty close enough and I made a run or two before backing and hurrying to stay abreast or better. Anyway I did it I was going to lose the bear which close up looked like a 2 yr old and that big blond may have been its mother. Couldn't make it and I swung back and crossed behind the bear. It would wind me for sure. I doubted if I would see it again or if it was a fearless one I would see a lot of it and me in the wide open. On down and around a knoll and there was my bear hundreds of yds away and running hard, headed for the canoe. I headed on down and at my crossing of the brushy canyon I saw fresh bear tracks on a dirty snow patch. My bear headed for the timber below. It had been a day of very poor light and now it was building in the northwest. A fresh breeze on the mt. and the lake. An easy paddle to the upper end. 5:45 when I left the beach and headed up. Making good time but soon my tail wind became a cross wind from Black Mt. I had never seen it like this before. At the halfway it became straight from the mt. and so strong I was being drifted to the far side. I wished for the kicker but it was too rough to wrassel it from forward and hang it on. So I paddle my best and finally it let up. Nearing the upper end it blew out of Emerson Creek country and I paddled hard again. A mile to go and I spotted another bear and this one traveling

the beach. A good sized dark bear and I wanted to get closer for a better look. Doing my best all I could do was stay the same distance. Near the connecting stream it turned inland to the Emerson [Creek] timber. I made it – calm water for a change. I pulled to the beach at the mouth of the fast entering stream. Now I would have to arrange my gear towards the stern for better control in lining through to the upper lake. I had just started the operation when I heard a bellow across the stream. Here came a cow and calf moose on the run. This could only mean one thing, a bear was after them. Sure enough a bear appeared but a blond not the dark one I had seen on the beach. The cow and calf came to the bank at the lake shore and stopped. She stood looking back to see if the bear was coming. It was sure enough and no more than fifty yards away when she saw it.

Over the bank into the shallow water of the entering stream and the lake. The bear close behind. Belly deep and the cow turned on the bear and went charging for it. It turned and ran. She was right onto him when he reached shore. She stood him off as the calf proceeded down the lake, swimming. It came towards shore and the cow turned and trotted to it. The bear gave chase again and they took to the water. This time it was deep and the cow swimming. The bear close and gaining, the cow angled to shore and the bear followed and why I shall always wonder. Again both on the beach and the calf angling to shore farther down. Again the cow and calf took off down country in the shallow water. Again the bear gave chase. The calf swimming father out and the bear got by the cow. She whirled and charged into deep water after him and there was lots of water flying. Then I heard the calf cry and it continued to cry as the bear swam ashore and dragged it up the steep bank. The cow followed and I could see her circling about in the brush. Finally she spotted me in the dim light and came trotting up along shore to stop often and look to see if by chance I was her calf. Satisfied that I wasn't she trotted back into the timber.

So – that was the 2nd moose calf I have seen killed by bears. I feel sure that they get their share of them. In this case it was a sure thing for the calf to die. On land it had no chance. In the water the bear could swim faster. The cow couldn't fight in water where she was forced to swim. In belly deep water she could turn the bear back but it was determined to get the calf.

So I lined through the stream to find the upper lake nearly calm and so started to paddle. My arms were sore from heavy paddling and it was late. I hung the little gas paddle on and motored slowly up the lake. Nine o'clock when I beached. A fire going and water heating while I heated my supper. Ready to turn in at 10:30. The sky overcast wind calm and temp 45°.

June 29 – Partly Cloudy, Calm & 43°.

Last night at twelve I was awakened by rasping and it was on the cabin in front. I hurried to the door. A porky hurried towards the clothesline and beyond. Me, following with my walking stick. I was knocking a few quills and he decided to climb a tree. None of that so close to the cabin and I rapped him on the skull. Down he went in a heap and laid there.

Ok, Ok, now I would have to skin him out. I didn't think I had tapped him all that severe so stood and watched him. Pretty soon he came to and hurried away at porkypine double quick time. I see many porkypines and lots of young ones. What determines the limit of the population? Food supply is unlimited and no predators except me.

This morning early as I went for a bucket of water an American goldeneye drake came scooting into my little bite. A friendly little guy. Talking the language of his species and came very close as I stood watching him. Goldeneyes seem to the camp robber of the duck family – very gentle little ducks. Yesterday on Blueberry Hill[6] a robin nest low in a stunted spruce. She flew and scolded from a nearby tree. In the nest three robin blue eggs. So, it isn't time for the robins to hatch but I see young birds not long out of the nest.

July 1 – Partly Cloudy, Calm & 43°.

There sat a fox at the edge of the brush and me on the wrong side of the ridge. It was a red fox. The dog fox, the father one. Soon he trotted across the end of the pond flat, stopped to look back and then entered the brush. So now I got back to my camera and waited. 13:00 and no action. Cloudy bright now and I would settle for that if I couldn't have direct sunlight. 13:15 and suddenly I had foxes to throw to the birds. Four foxes. Three pups and the vixen. How come I had never seen but two pups before. The rough and tumble was on. If there is more fun than two pups its three. One appeared a little lighter in color than its mates. The mother one supervised and stood guard duty. Now and again a pup would dash for the brush as if danger threatened and she took a quick scan of the area. She showed no indication of suspecting I was there. The pups were out for nearly an hour. Playing, wandering in the pond and doing everything pups do including giving their mom a bad time. That third pup left the party early and didn't come back. Like the cub bears, fox pups are different. Some like to get out and explore, others prefer to stay close to the den. Another pup went in and now it was one with the mother who was gnawing on a bone. She would snap at the pup when it got to

> *Four foxes. Three pups and the vixen. How come I had never seen but two pups before. The rough and tumble was on. If there is more fun than two pups its three. One appeared a little lighter in color than its mates. The mother one supervised and stood guard duty.*

inquisitive. I wonder if the foxes have fleas. I saw the mother one scratching many times and a pup or two do the same. I got a little sunlight but only for a few minutes. I lost the last pup. The vixen went for a drink of water and then into the brush. I had exposed 145 feet of film. Pretty happy that I came today as I packed to leave. The wind was strong up the lake and I would have a fast paddle home. 4:30 when I beached. The beans done just right and I had a sample before supper. I cleaned up my gear and got the Exakta ready for

---

[6] RLP's Blueberry Hill was probably located near Low Pass Creek on upper Twin Lakes.

duty. If Rob Belous doesn't get that fancy Park Service camera and lens here soon I will waste some film without it. Supper over I sprouted my spud supply. A good supply and should last until potato digging time in Sept. if I don't get too much company.

Now at 7:30 it is overcast, the wind strong up the lake and the temp. 57°.

July 4 – Overcast, Calm & 43°.

I cleaned my fish and hung them under the roof eave to stiffen. Rain shower over the lower lake and at times it sprinkled pretty good here. I thought of taking the kicker along and going up the lake but didn't relish the idea of a possible wet trip. So I took a little tour up the beach past the Weiser cabin. I sat under a spruce during the sprinkles and checked on the blueberry crop and the moose situation when it wasn't. Spike has the best crop of fireweed greens in these parts and I loaded up on my way back. Why try to grow something civilized when fireweed, the best greens ever, does so well. A couple plants of huge dandelions came with Voight's strawberry plants. The strawberries have all but died but the dandelions high and healthy. With all the seed they produce I am surprised that I don't get more.

Back at the ranch I worked on my Parker pen. It broke and I sent it in and it broke again, same place. I have used it by dipping in the bottle but that is a pain. Now I have made a bending adjustment and maybe it will feed which it wouldn't before. This Shaffer uses entirely too much ink and ink is hard to come by.

My grayling ready for supper. Bite size pieces, no skin, no bones, seasoned well. Fried nice and brown. Beans and a big salad to complete the meal. To put on the dog a little bit I opened a can of GI fruitcake from a box of those super deluxe in flight rations. Canned juice, canned fruit, can opener in every box. Compliments of CAP (a full case). The showers stopped for the day and now at 8:15 partly cloudy, a light breeze down the lake and 50°.

This was a no non-sense 4th of July. The loudest noise I heard was the dishes rattling in the dish pan.

July 5 – Overcast, Breeze dn. & 42°.

The weather had improved but the lake was still rough. Earlier I had thought of paddling to Low Pass beach & check on my foxes and motor back. From the Farmer knob I could see it would have been a rough trip back. I went for greens and cut out my trail (closing in) along the way. Passing Spike's biffy[7] I smelled gasoline. Terry Shurtleff had 4 cans of gas cached there. One was a leaker and nearly half empty so I packed it back and will use it for kicker gas. Three or four years since he left it. Ketchum has two cans at Low Pass

---

[7] Biffy, a variant for an outhouse.

beach that are nearly that old. Lyman Nichols has 6 cans here in the brush on the point 4 or 5 years old. A Kenai boy, 3 cans out past the woodshed. Stu Silvers [of] Anch., 1 can – gas all over.

I got supper and fried my grayling. I was eating when here came a Super Cub on floats. He turned back and turned again and landed out from Hope Creek. A blue Super Cub with a Dept. of Public Safety decal – the game warden and me eating fish with no fishing license. David Cornwall[8] from Dillingham and his sidekick assistant. I invited them in and offered them some fish and fireweed greens plus a cup of tea. They wouldn't sit down – been sitting all day. Where had they been and what had they seen. They had done a lot of flying, saw a few moose and one bear – no caribou. Checked a few fishing licenses. Say now, did I need a license to catch a few fish to eat. Would it be considered subsistence fishing. The man said a net is used for subsistence fishing. Hook and line you need a fishing license. Would he sell me one. Didn't have any forms with him but he would bring one some time. Chuck Rodgers said the same thing and I never saw him again. He wrote down all the vital statistics and stuffed it in his pocket. He is from Michigan and he sidekick from Colorado. They stayed an hour or more and we hashed over the proposed park. He was against it. A park, and no planes could land, only a few with lots of time and energy would be able to use it. Ramstad[9] came to the surface and so did Owsichek [big game guides].

Well, they had better fly. They planned to camp at the lower end tonight. They wanted to wet a line in the river. So – they took off but said they would come again. They left me a book and sport fishing regulations but didn't have one on hunting. A change had been made in hunting he said. No more hunting the day you fly winter or summer. That will cull out a few of those winter and early spring caribou hunters.

My dishes and writing done it was 9:15. Still a good breeze down. Overcast with bright spots and temp 50°.

July 15 – Overcast, Lt. Breeze up & 43°.

I wanted a couple more grayling. The lake was calming but rain showers marched up the lower lake one after the other. I stalled till three and then decided that the only way to get to Emerson Creek was to make a start. I would motor down and paddle back. Good cooperation by the weather and only a few sprinkles. As I got close a young moose suddenly appeared on the beach just this side of the entrance to the connecting stream. I cruised on down wondering how close I could get. Not closer than three hundred yds. my moose trotted into the brush.

This would be a sure thing. All I needed was the casting rod and super duper. Don't pack a lot of extra gear. A good stream running into the lake. First cast and I had

[8] David Cornwall, a state of Alaska Department of Public Safety, Division of Fish and Wildlife Protection officer-pilot, stationed in Dillingham.

[9] Stu Ramstad, a pilot and big game guide who had a lodge on Fishtrap Lake about 20 miles west of Twin Lakes.

one on and a nice one by the feel of it. I wore it out and towed it ashore. A grayling about seventeen inches long and it had taken that treble hook down into the gills. Easier to take it out through the gills than the mouth. I had one, all I needed was one more. Next cast, nothing and third the same. Many times I flung the scrap iron out into the lake and nary a strike. Those grayling learn in one easy lesson. Then a light strike and then nothing. I hated to quit with one after traveling so far. A second stream entered the lake up the beach 50 yds. I would find a dumb one there. A few casts and I had a mate (for size) for the first one. I parked my fish at the canoe and walked the beach looking for the moose. Tracks where it had come out and gone right back in. This one was a young cow. Still tall and slender. Except for cows with calves all the moose I have seen appear to be young.

A very light breeze to help me along. The sun came out at the halfway and I shucked my rain jacket. To my beach in one hour and a near calm lake. True to form the lake was well ruffled by a good breeze coming up as I cleaned my fish. One grayling, beans, sourdough biscuits and a green salad for supper. Now at 8:45 partly cloudy, the lake near calm and temp. 48°.

July 17 – Partly Cloudy, Calm & 43°.

The wind came up the lake and with it an airplane. It looked like the Governor's good looking 170 Cessna. He circled, landed into the wind from off Carrithers' point...It was our whiskered Governor alright. Happy as always when he climbed out...[and]...his resource manager Bob [LeResche][10] (a younger guy) the other.

Jay showed his man Bob around and then we came in. I built up the fire for coffee or tea and we visited. I asked Jay, "Do the bears get many moose calves?" "A lot of them," he said. "Instead of working on a wolf control program, I think we should work on a bear control program." Bob used to work for Fish & Game. In the big fenced Kenai moose study plot they watched close and put radios on calves soon after they were born. They kept them tuned in and knew where they were when the radios went dead. 50 calves and bears got 20 of them. It had been Jay's experience while working for Fish & Wildlife to see a big moose calf crop and very soon only a few calves left. It was those calf hunting bears and not only browns but blacks too.

Tea was served and I unwrapped that chocolate cake. "Ah! My kind of cake," Jay said. So, we talked about most everything pertaining to the wilderness. I dug out my rock collection. Jay knows of that big rusty streak across Twin Lakes country. A very rich vein of uranium on the Kijik River but the old boy Brown Carlson[11] who with a geologist found it couldn't find it again many years later when Jay and another man went in with him. Jay has a few claims staked out the peninsula and has had for years. More tea but no more cake. They wouldn't eat up my good cake. The lake had calmed again. We talked of

---

[10] Robert LeResche, Alaska Commissioner of Natural Resources in the Hammond Administration.

[11] Brown Carlson (1878-1975) one of the first permanent Euroamerican settlers on Lake Clark starting about 1902.

fishing and the reds that come to Twin Lakes. Jay's wife and one daughter at least fishes commercially at the set net site at Naknek. Fishing was better than expected this time.

While here I think Jay forgot about Juneau and all the problems of being Governor. Now he plans to put a shake roof on the new log steam bath and laundry building. Thinking about a water powered generator to make electricity to run a refrigerator. Try to get away from the business of using fossil fuel, [it] is hard to supply Lake Clark.

Finally, he made a move. Let's take advantage of the calm lake and head for home.

July 23 – Partly Cloudy, Calm & 42°.

Across Hope Creek bridge and up the trail. No gun but my custom made walking stick which gives me a feeling of not being defenseless. Climbing the Cowgill benches I saw a few blueberries in the green and also a half dozen or so blue but not much for blueberry taste.

I headed back and this time on the game trail along the creek. Just leaving the bear hot spot when there in the trail was a big bear patty and not many days old. There may have or there may have not been a bear there now but there had been and no doubt about it. I went on keeping a very close watch on creek bottom brush. A big bear track and it would match the size of the tracks near my cabin when I came. Then little bear patties on the trail. A sow with new cubs. I walked quietly and watched closely. Don't surprise her and she will take her cubs and go. The people who claim to know say she isn't likely to harm you unless her cubs are in danger or she thinks they are in danger. What she thinks is the determining factor. What I think doesn't count.

July 26 – Overcast, Blowing dn. & 53°.

During the night I heard the wind strong in the trees. This morning was proof that a major storm had moved in. Heavy grey clouds moving fast and the lake a million white caps. As it is with a gulf storm about here. Grey with light rain from here on up and down country too later in the day.

Not safe to be in the timber when the wind is strong and the brush was wet anyway. I had plenty to do inside. Three packages to wrap and a couple order blanks to fill out. Write a check for my fishing license and mail it to the warden. I may not be home when he delivers my license, if he ever does. A few more letters to write. And then I had some clothes mending to do. Dwarf birch is very rough on anything but the moose, bear, and caribou. For them it is a stiff brush for a sleek coat.

Lunch time and the wind stronger if anything. I thought – you leave for the lower end with a good breeze down and clouds to match. Had it come like this while I was there

I would be caching the canoe and walking home.

After lunch a few tinkering jobs and I ran onto some old *Readers Digest*. Nothing better for wilderness reading unless it is old *Alaska Magazines*. They strike me as being more interesting than the present issues. I read till three and looked for employment. Two burls and neither struck me as being worth the effort. But, you never know. Really put some time in on a really rough one and it turns out to be the most attractive. The burl bowl graduation gift is a beautiful piece of wood. Brace and 5/16 drill bit to remove a lot of wood and make the gouge work easier. A stick of near iron hard spruce limb for a mallet. The block plane to form a flat base. It was 5:45 before I checked the time. An easy day, a light supper. Another batch of beans on to soak. This evening as it was this morning. Grey with light rain. A strong gusting wind down and the temp. only 2° warmer, 55.

July 27 – Overcast, Rain, Blowing dn. & 53°.

I would take another run up Hope Creek. Maybe this time I could see the bear. Heavy sweater in my camera pack sack. Big pistol on my hip.[12] The first time to carry it this season. Going up the creek trail on the far side and suddenly a familiar sound but I didn't see what made it. That momentary flutter of wings of a spruce grouse going from ground to tree. I wanted to see that guy. I hadn't seen one since I came. Slowly I circled a big spruce and there in the dead one a rooster grouse. Where had he been for the past two months. He would be good for a practice shot by a hunter. At Ketchum's camp (3 years ago) I saw one hanging by his neck from the crotch of a willow branch. Shot through the middle and not much left to eat.

August 1 – Partly Cloudy, Calm & 46°.

We was away about 7:30 with Sig on the bow paddle. Those two boys have really improved in the last couple years. It is hard to find a young kid who has the patience to pull a paddle for an hour without becoming more of a hindrance than a help. Both are pretty good but Leon the best. We stopped at first point to change paddles and glass across. Leon took her on to the upper end. I remembered that there is a way to climb out and break very little brush. Steep for maybe 20 minutes and pretty steep side hill for thirty, the remainder of the hr. and a half good going.

Right away after leaving the canoe a big and not too old bear patty. I thought of my .357 hanging on the bunk post and the two little guys along. We climbed and they were satisfied to follow instead of lead. More bear sign near the top and before we got to marmot country we learned that there were cubs too. I figured it was the same old mother and cubs from Hope Creek. Leon heard the first whistle and saw the first marmot. More

[12] RLP had a Western Marshal .357 Ruger revolver, apparently imported by the Hawes Firearms Company but manufactured in Germany by J P Sauer.

snow up there than I had ever seen and I feel sure that it won't be gone by the time snow comes and stays again. We saw four marmots, two young and two adults. Easy to locate for they lay on top of a big rock and pass the word by means of their one sharp whistle. You move too close and they quietly slip over the side and into the very coarse rocks that form their home.

Sig was interested in the pretty rocks of the big tailing pile. Leon and I glassed for sheep, bear and caribou. We prowled around on the huge glacier tailing pile and ended up on a moss covered ridge leading up to ram country. A perfect place to sit in the sun and admire the scenery if you can sit that long. Leon and Sig have to be on the move.

Eleven thirty and hunger was mentioned often. No, not a chance of eating before twelve. To do so only makes the afternoon longer.

It had been all up grade and now those steep snow patches provided fast transportation. Go skating down on the shoe pacs or ski down minus the skis if it was steep enough. They reminded me of cub bears. Run and deliberate tumble and roll down the slope. Finally we had to leave the snow for the steep side hill again. Rock to the edge and over looking upper lake and river, we sat awhile and looked for something to move. I remembered last trip to the rock pile and no tracks. It wouldn't be different now.

About 1:30 when we reached the canoe and I was happy to see a light breeze down. Leon and I took it to first point and Sig and I on down. Near Carrithers' point we bumped into an up coming breeze.

August 5 – Partly Cloudy, Lt. Breeze dn. & 48°.

Beached and on the slope picking when here came a Beaver up the lake. It circled, landed and went to my beach. A load of congressmen being guided by the Park Service was my guess. We wouldn't rush home so kept on picking. It stayed a half hr. or more and then took off and headed for Port Alsworth. The big party was staying at Glen Van Valin's. We got our gallon and small can full. Fired up my little jewel and motored home. Sig was very happy with the speed we could make in calm water. A note and 8 big red apples, three oranges and a big cucumber on the table. The note read "Here's a gift from the Van Valins. We were passing this way and dropped it off for them." Signed, "Chuck Gilbert, N.P.S."[13]

August 9 – Overcast, Lt. Breeze up & 45°.

It being blueberry season I would hunt blueberries. I took my big tin cup and headed for the down country. Cowgill benches where Sig, Leon, and I had picked first. I couldn't find enough berries to cover the bottom and crossed to the up country side of the creek. I

---

[13] Chuck Gilbert, an NPS writer with the Alaska Task Force.

scouted around and found a fair patch and filled the cup (½ gal.) A few leftover and I ate those. It was near eleven by the time I got back and still no caribou showing. I would take a hike up Hope Creek. A sourdough sandwich and a big red apple would be my lunch at the far end. I was looking for caribou and bear and wouldn't see a trace of either. The big sheep Leon, Sig, and I had seen was absent also. It was cool at the second canyon and I was glad to have my heavy sweater. I waited an hour and nothing came out of hiding so I came down the creek trail.

While I did my writing a plane came up the far side. It was low but climbing fast. A turn back at Glacier Creek and over the big pasture. It flew up Emerson Creek. A big white Beaver and the first time I have seen it here. As I started my hike up Hope Creek a light plane on floats flew the mts. along the lake. Tomorrow, Aug. 10 the first day of sheep season. From now till snow comes and stays "One Man's Wilderness" will suffer. Man, the worst predator of them all is on the prowl.

Partly cloudy, light breeze down and 52°.

August 12 – Overcast, Rain, Blowing dn. & 52°.

Another dark morning with a threat of rain. Till now the lake hasn't started to rise so rain must be light in the high mts.

Hotcakes and blueberries for breakfast and then I would get my fresh beans cooking. A day to work on that big green blow down. I didn't intend to get it packed in or even completely bucked for packing. A lot of fire wood there. I took my pack board, axe, and big bow saw. The back end was still two feet above ground, elevated by slivers from the stump roots. I set a chunk under the trunk twenty five feet out so as to keep it from dropping to the ground after my first cut near the break. From there towards the stump I sawed until the saw started to bind and then made another cut and so on to the stump. About twenty feet of the trunk, too big for the bow saw to reach through. So, at the stump I cut the slivers and dropped the log, rolled it over and sawed the remainder of way second cut from the opposite side. That made two stove wood lengths to the chunk for packing.

The day turned grey with light rain. A dampening rain but cool and no bugs. A perfect day for the job. The top length I had to fight. Laying on the ground with limbs pushed into the ground. Saw and chop – leave the top eight feet in one piece for packing. I hadn't taken a watch and came to the cabin. Eleven o'clock. I would pack a few loads. By my calculations the tree would make nineteen loads and I learned it was 640 steps to the load.

At noon the sun came out and I was tempted to head for the fox pond but soon it turned grey again. I went back to packing. I started packing from the wrong end of the tree. As the afternoon wore on the chunks got bigger and very much heavier. Rain came again and I stopped and read awhile. It quit and I went back to my packing. It was five o'clock when I came down the trail with the last one. An eighty pounder by my estimate.

Scrap wood came in too. Sawed out the pile. The day was done and I had a feeling that morning would find me feeling today's labor.

Fresh baked biscuits with my peanut spuds, with lots of oleo and beans. As I ate, it was raining a good rain.

August 23 – Partly Cloudy, Calm & 42°.

I was back down and rigging up my sorter on the beach when a Super Widgeon went up the lake at good altitude, then back down the far side to the lower end of the lake. Another turn and I knew he was coming to my beach. In he came, a good looking McKinnon Widgeon. He came till the wheels touched then opened the window and said "Richard how is everything?" I didn't know the guy but he knew me sure enough. Said he had some Park Service boys to see me. He turned around but I had to use the canoe poked out from the beach for them to get ashore. That guy was Charlie Allen, the real good bush pilot. If he had been wearing his polka dot cap and flying his old [Cessna] 180 I would have known him. The Park Service boys, one from Katmai and two from Anch. What [is] the deal on coming here was I never learned. Nothing for me, no message, just came to see my place it seemed. All young guys and all agreed that this place was a little extra special. My camp robbers came and it seems that they are wise to company. Beg like crazy while the tourists empty their cameras. They visited awhile and of course Charlie didn't mind. That Widgeon was drawing standby pay. Finally it was time to go and the canoe came into play again. Charlie says here "I've got something for you." A fancy box lunch like the airlines put out. "Next time I'll bring you some green stuff from my garden," he said. Riding light on the wheels the Widgeon moved out easily. He taxied well out and took off up the lake and then down. Charlie had said "I sure like that Widgeon."

Right away I dug into that box lunch. Fresh milk, ham sandwiches, an apple, green salad and pie for desert.

Now at 7:45, partly cloudy and clouds moving slowly right to left down country. The lake is calming for the night and the temp. after a near 70° today is now 65°.

Charlie told me that just recently he flew three beautiful back packers to Chakachamna Lake and they planned to hike through Merrill Pass[14] to Telaquana Lake. Good looking girls about 25 years old. I didn't think fast enough or I would have told him I always thought two 25's might be kinda nice but I hadn't thought of three.

August 31 – Fog, Calm, Smoke & 42°.

Today on the mt. I heard three shots in the direction of Bell Creek. Yesterday we saw smoke and tents there. Sheep hunters or maybe someone decided to open the moose season one

---

[14] Merrill Pass, a 3,180 ft. pass through the Alaska Range west of Chakachamna Lake and about 45 mile north of Twin Lakes; Tutnutl'ech'a Tustes is a Dena'ina word for "black water pass."

day early. Tomorrow is the day and this evening a Cessna 185 came to Emerson and flew away as if leaving a party there. I am thinking "One Man's Wilderness" is going to see more pressure now with moose added to sheep and caribou as a target for those who must kill something. Not that they need it or that it is cheap meat, just the urge to kill. Yesterday Geraldine [Straty][15] spotted my little framed bit of printing by the fireplace. She read it – "Is it proper that the wilderness and its creatures should suffer because we came?" And she said, "That's good, I like it."

September 3 – Overcast, Smoke, Calm & 43°.

I went to Hope's cabin for salt and on to Spike's to see if it was in good order. Bill and Pat had left a box of groceries on my outside table. In a sack there too was 12 rolls of 16 mm film and 10 of 35. Someone had delivered them for the Park Service. A note from Bob Belous saying the movie had been completed but no copies had reached Anch. as yet. No mention of that fancy camera and lens he was going to deliver personally back in mid June.

So – I spread the skin pieces on the beach and gave them a coat of salt.

September 7 – Overcast, Raining, Calm & 38°.

This time I had left the canoe open to the weather and dumped it before shoving out. Quarter past five when I headed for home full paddle against a light breeze. Quarter to six when I beached in front of my cabin. A record run from Glacier Creek.

Smoked caribou ribs smothered in good bean soup. What could be better for the main course. Now at 8:30, raining, calm & 42°.

September 10 – Overcast, Blowing dn. & 46°.

My hotcakes out of the way I got busy on my outgoing mail just in case Glen did show up. I had just finished when I heard a little airplane and operating at reduced power. He was making the landing approach straight in. I was at the beach to stop those precious floats from grinding on the gravel. Babe would never allow that to happen. He was always out and ready to step off and stop her before she touched. At first I thought he was alone and then the passenger door opened and out climbed a strange woman. Blond straight hair she looked to be the outdoor type. He introduced her as Lael Morgan[16] of *Alaska Magazine.* So this was the woman who takes the good pictures from who knows where in

[15] Geraldine Straty of Auke Bay, Alaska and wife of Dick Straty, they own a cabin on Telaquana Lake.

[16] Lael Morgan, writer, historian, chief writer of *Bristol Bay Basin* for the Alaska Geographic Society, published in 1978.

Alaska and does a real good job of writing. She didn't state her reason for being here but later I learned it was in connection with Alaska Geographic [Society]. Doing an issue on this area or some such deal. Glen says I brought everything but one – your mail. Didn't think of it until we were well on the way here. No problem, I wouldn't have any letters to answer. The birds came and put on their best performance. More business for Eastman Kodiak. We came in and had a cup of tea. Glen had taken Leon and Sig to the Bonanza Hills and they each got a caribou. Leon shot his at 80 yds. with Glen's scope sighted 300. One shot, right though the eye. A nice bull, real good meat. Lael told of a couple of her experiences traveling. Getting five cups of tea from a tea bag and eating lots of pilot bread while walrus hunting with the Eskimos. She told of an old man she had met, 87 years old, and still very active. He takes vitamin C, feeling it is good for his arthritis. She told him she had heard vitamin C was good for romance. He screwed up his hearing aid a bit and ask her to repeat it. After a couple repeats she said, "I hear vitamin C helps you out with the girls," "Oh! that is good to know in case I have to drop back to it." Babe knew him and used to see his trap line snowshoe trails all over that part of the country. See him miles from camp, land and offer him a ride, "Oh no, I'll walk," and he would go treading on.

I noticed she was busy with her notebook and Nikon 35 mm with flash. It didn't bother my birds. Head for the door at the flash but come right back in. She asked me how many copies of the book had been sold and I said that quite sometime ago the report was 50,000. She had heard a million. I told her the royalty checks didn't indicate that many.

Today before Glen and Lael flew away. She asked, "where is your outhouse, I want to explore the outhouse." In a few minutes she came back and said, "I judge a man by the kind of outhouse he builds – you rate pretty high." She inquired about the many ink bottles she saw stored there. "Is that where you do your writing?" Great sense of humor, that gal.

September 12 – Raining, Blowing up & 39°.

A third airplane, a Sea Airmotive turbo Otter was circling Carrithers' point. It landed and beached near Hope Creek. What was the occasion for all the activity aimed at my diggings.

I came to the cabin to find it full of people and some outside. Bob Belous of the Park Service was the spokesman. He began the introductions. Mr. this from ABC and Mr. that from ABC and here the cameraman and here the soundman and the producer and a pretty girl to carry and hold odd pieces of gear they would use. ABC was doing something on Alaska and would like to take some footage of my activities and also film with sound an interview. The man I would visit with was a big good natured man and a real narrator. He told me he has a book out *Monarch of Deadman Bay* by Roger Caras.[17]

---

[17] Roger Caras (1928-2001) writer, naturalist, and television commentator.

He hunted brown bear there with the late Hal Waugh.[18] The filming of the interview was done on the up country side of the cabin. Me sitting on the rounds of my short ladder leaning against the cabin. He sitting on a gas can box with his back to the camera. The sound man between us with his two foot long microphone. The producer standing near and coaching – managing the subjects he wanted discussed. The cameraman was using an $11,000.00 dollar camera (made in Calif.) and using 400 ft. reels. Bob had said, they wanted to ask me a couple things but when the producer said "make yourself comfortable this will take awhile" I figured we would waste some film and the cameraman did reload no less than three times. So much for sound. Now they wanted silent footage of us visiting and then footage of me doing things about the cabin, and then footage inside using a hand held flood light powered with a battery pack belt. Footage of me making an entry in my journal and of me pouring a cup of tea. Footage of the entire interior and of the door with wooden hinges. My birds used their fair share of film. All three came and made the most of the opportunity. Then Roger Caras retired to the work bench towards the woodshed. He said excuse me while I talk to myself. I have a little memorizing to do and so he started reading from his notebook. In no more than two minutes he was ready. They stood him beyond the clothesline with snow capped Allen Mt. for a background. He faced the camera and spoke his piece not once but three times and the same every time. Not a long speech but one that would require a half day for me to memorize and then I would get tongue tied when I looked at that 120 mm zoom lens.

Now some of me with my camera gear on my back. Going up the trail, coming down the trail. Following the creek out on the flat and with camera gear set up pretending to be taking a scenic shot. The producer was having a great time and we would head for the hump next. His superior stopped us right where we were. It was time to fly to Port Alsworth, and Glen Van Valin, Bob Belous thanked me for my cooperation and was there anything he could do for me in Anch.

He didn't mention the Nikon…camera and expensive lens – the louse, but did say the film is good. Both he and John Kauffmann had seen it and thought it real good. They would be getting their copies (last June he had told me about a hundred).

September 20 – Overcast, Rain, Lt. Breeze dn. & 40°.

Very early in the morning I heard the light sound of light rain on the chimney guard. It was 6:30 before I awoke to find it past time to go to work. No hurried phone call to say I would be a little late. No rushing around to get a bite to eat – just set the clock back and carry on as usual.

Soon after hotcakes I noticed that my Baby Ben had stopped. Not from lack of winding and I shook it. Five minutes later, stopped again. Now, what was wrong? I had only run for about twenty years without cleaning or oiling. I removed the cup like cover

---

[18] Hal Waugh (1910-?), Alaska big game guide who hunted brown bear on Kodiak Island and other game in the Alaska interior.

from the back and submerged the works in a tuna fish can of gas – shoot it around a bit and set it on the stove warming shelf to dry. It took off of its own accord and ticked like an Elgin. Next, I dunked the works in kerosene for lubrication – dried it out again and it ran. The back cover on, set to "Wilderness Standard Time" and except for gaining five minutes in ten hrs. it runs perfectly.

Rain, a nice gentle rain and yet the lake is falling. Down at least a couple inches in the past few days.

September 21 – Raining, Breeze dn. & 38°.

My bannock, the fire was a little hot and the two sides turned brown and black before the center was done. I did have my cake too thick to start with too. Next time it will be better.

Since when has autumn started on the 23rd of Sept. My Mercury outboard "kicker" says so. All of my calendar life it seems the fall season started on Sept. 21st. I have all of my calendars used here over the years. Only one other has it marked. In 1968, 1st day of Autumn, Sept. 22. Farmers Almanac 1972, Sept. 22 Autumn begins. 1969, Vernal Equinox Sept. 20. I believe it is as Henry David wrote "All any one really knows is that the wind blows."

Now at 8:45 blowing hard up the lake. Trace of moisture in the air and 34°.

September 24 – Partly Cloudy, Calm & 26°.

I would climb Bell Mt. and check out that possible bear den I had seen with the scope from Hope Creek flat. Located high on the slope and just under the rough stuff. Real close to the only big canyon coming out of the mt. and on the up country side of it. A big poplar grove was the start of the climb. Many high-bush cranberries grow there and I grabbed clusters of them as I climbed. Finally out onto the open slope and the long climb. Now and again I stopped to glass the river flat up at the head of the lake to see if I could spot some one butchering a moose. I looked for my three across but couldn't locate them.

Close up to the den area and I felt a little uneasy. One time I had tried to look in a den and heard the loudest closest growl I had ever heard. A big bear no more than six or eight feet away is close enough. Only a sissy bear would be in a den this early and I cautiously made my way to it from one side. No tracks on the dirt mound and no bear in side. A hibernation den sure enough and used last winter. Big enough at the entrance to crawl into and I did. Maybe eight feet to the back end and a nice big living room. I could live there pretty comfortably but not for six months. Four feet wide at the rear and at least that high. A nice hollowed out bed and lined with grass. All the other dens I have examined had no covering for the bed. I snapped a couple pictures from the rear looking out at the mts. across the lake. A rock had fallen from the side or overhead and I threw it out and pronounced the den suitable for this winters hibernation and I must keep close watch on it when snow comes deep. A trail leading up to it guarantees me a bear in hibernation.

September 25 – Overcast, Calm & 37°.

Who would be my visitors, two sitting on the beach. I thought that I recognized the dark complected one. Nixe Mellick from Sleetmute on the Kuskokwim River. A Native or part Native who had visited me the winter of '74 & '75. He had been here before that in late summer when Spike and Hope were here. He always asks about them. This time he said, "I met someone, not long ago, that you might know – Acheson, Bob Acheson." He had seen him not more than a week or two ago. Bob had been to or was coming from McGrath. I told him Bob owned the two cabins up on the point. "Why that son of a gun, he didn't tell me. Wait till I see him again." Nixe has a cabin on Telaquana across from Dick Straty's. Ketchum had used it without his permission and messed it up good. Just recently he had been fixing it up in preparation for trapping this winter. The man with him a tall grey haired man from Nevada, Jim Rock, Vice President and Manager of the First National Bank of Nevada. Up for a little bird hunting. They had hunted ptarmigan over near Telaquana today and bagged six. At Turquoise they had seen two planes that met with disaster. A float plane bottom up in the lake and in the process of being salvaged and a Lake Buccaneer amphibian that failed to clear high ground after take off. I had built a fire and they each had coffee while I had hot chocolate. Nixe is a good man, wise in the ways of the north country. He wanted Jim to see a copy of my book and then leafed through it himself pointing out his favorite pictures. The spring break up of the lake was a favorite – the singing time of year he calls it. He likes to see the birds come.

The sun was getting around and they made ready to turn that big bird tail to the beach and take off. Going back to Sleetmute yet this afternoon. Nixe said he would drop by again if I was staying this winter. He might be trapping at Telaquana. They taxied up around the point and took off down country. 4:30 I would have an early supper. Near six and sunset. Sunlight poking through broken cloud cover. Still a trace of smoke, calm and 40 degrees.

Yesterday afternoon the sun above the thin overcast was a very red ball. It looked like a smoke condition but with all the rain and being so late in the season I didn't think it possible.

September 27 – Partly Cloudy, Lt. Breeze dn. & 45°.

A check for game and none to be seen. The morning was becoming dark and the lake noisy rough. I wrote a couple letters and a couple checks which don't require as much time

but are more expensive. Everything under control and I took my wood packer to the back 40. 630 steps each way and I would pack in many loads before the rain came.

Much noise pollution by the intruders up the lake. Small arms fire as if target shooting at a chunk of wood floating in the lake. Yesterday afternoon the same and at times the fire was very rapid as if they had a light machine gun. Little chance that they will do any real harm except possibly to themselves. Any wild animal would stay well clear of 1st point.

A break for lunch and I went at it again. Two loads to go and it started to rain. A fire in the cabin all morning, burning punky wood. I have been wanting to make more bannock. This time I would use Bisquick and sourdough, add a little shortening and salt plus some clean berries, no soda or baking powder. The fire not too hot and it turned out much better. Some brown sugar and raisins would make it good. Maybe a shot of garlic salt instead of table salt. Much quicker and less attention than biscuits.

So – the day was about done. I had boiled more caribou front quarter and I wish I had known those lazy meat packers had left so much good neck and backbone meat plus the rib cage on the mt. Enough meat to last me most of the winter. Erv Terry[19] had said my book was the reason for him becoming interested in this country. The book points a finger at a few sloppy hunters.

It was a good supper, peanut spuds with butter, salt and pepper, good beans with smoked caribou shoulder, tomato, carrot sticks, bannock with butter and Canadian strawberry jam. Cold porridge pudding with cinnamon and blueberries for desert, followed by more bannock and a cup of hot chocolate.

Now at 8:30 raining, a gentle up the lake surf and the temp. 40°.

September 30 – Overcast, Calm & 24°.

This afternoon I would paddle down country. Go down the left and back up the right side to Jerre's cabin. A chance that Glen would fly in but if he did he would see me on the lake. It doesn't pay to sit in camp waiting for airplanes that seldom come.

The grebes are here. Some time ago a little one in my bend of the beach. Today I saw four. It isn't till fall that I see them and they stay until the lake freezes. I also saw a little white butterfly fluttering aimlessly about far from shore. Later than this I saw hundreds of butterflies up Hope Creek. The sun had dropped behind the mt. and every stem and branch had a slowly working pair of wings. It was too cold for them to fly. From the gravel banks I headed for Emerson Creek. I would check the Vanderpool cabin. I know that hunters had used it this season. I was surprised, they had left it looking better than years past. A carton of 8 eggs that would soon freeze and break. My supply down to six so I would take them along. Soda crackers that the squirrels had already been into.

---

[19] Erv Terry, Anchorage businessman and pilot who owned the Cowgill-Farmer cabin.

A plastic bag of cup of soup mixes and mixes of other kinds. No open ended gas can so I stashed them on the table and bottom upped the dish pan over them. The chimney pipe taken down and the roof jack covered. The bars to cover the window and I called it closed for the winter.

From across the lake I had seen what appeared to be a frame work of the A frame type covered with clear plastic. Below the connecting stream and back in the shelter of the spruce. The German hunters had camped there. A half mile down from the lower end and the canoe. I hiked down to check it out. It was intended for a camp. About seven feet up two poles nailed one on each side of two trees about ten feet apart. More poles on each side from the ground up to the ridge poles and set at an angle making it about eight feet wide at ground level. Covered with heavy clear plastic and more small poles for bottoms to keep the wind from pulling the plastic free. A spruce bough bed along one side. I can see where it would be a simple and satisfactory camp. There on the ground a little GI entrenching shovel (combination hoe and shovel). Just what I always wanted and I wondered why they left it. The locking device that makes it a hoe or shovel was badly bent and so it was neither and no good. I could fix it or fix it so it couldn't be fixed so I brought it back with me.

October 2 – Partly Cloudy, Lt. Breeze dn. & 35°.

My hauled in wood to saw and split and it took longer than one would think. Enough wood for a couple days at least. The skull to trim close to the antlers and I had brought back three lower legs to skin and salt. Coming back from Hope's cabin and my salt supply I saw my tame snowshoe rabbit. Closer than ten feet from the trail and I stopped and watched it closely to see if I could see a change in color showing now on Oct. 2. Very little, if any, the feet may be turning just a little but very little if they are.

The sun had set and I rustled around getting supper. I sliced a small steak of shoulder meat and fried it in a salted skillet. Tender like you wouldn't believe. It reminded me of brother Jake's and my big supply of moose meat from the over turned Cessna Skywagon. Two weeks old at least and after trimming it was very good. On leaving the lakes Oct. 12 we took the last of it to Babe. The next spring I had heard him say "That was the best moose meat we ever had." As Spike used to say, "Tender as a mother's love."

October 7 – Snowing, Blowing up & 27°.

It looked pretty wild when I looked out at seven. I had heard the surf during the night and thought of my poles at the waters edge. I had untied them and pulled the stake. A strong surf might work them up the beach and around the point. I got dressed and pulled

on my boots to go save them. This morning the ground was white and snow plastered the windward side of everything. It was storming a good Oct. storm.

Plane day coming up Oct. 15, this would be a good day to write letters and do small chores. Letters first and so I wrote and watched the churning of the green water. Since June 10 I have used nearly and very nearly two and one half bottles of ink. Paper nearly 500 8 _ x 11" sheets in the last two seasons at Twin Lakes. Envelopes, packages of them. I wrote till noon, took a break. The snow had stopped but visibility was very limited and I didn't look for sheep or moose.

No more square 5 gal. gas cans and all pilots are unhappy about it. No more good cans and no more good gas can boxes, they say! The new round ones heavier and won't stack as close in an airplane. Not tin plated, they rust out in no time. A good looking heavy round can with a good strong fold flat handle on top. What would they be good for. Today I would make a storage can from one. A real wolverine, mouse proof, damp proof storage can. With all the gas shook out I let it dry and then with my little hack saw, sawed three inches off (down from the top). With my 12" flat file I smoothed the two edges and with my patented corrugating tool I corrugated the top of the bottom section. Reduced it in size enough so the top would slip down over it. A real neat looking job and strong like you wouldn't believe. One filled with silver dimes would be worth quite a bit. I heard a rumor that Babe hand packed a bucket of silver to Hawaii and I wouldn't bet a nickel that he didn't. My mind satisfied on the usefulness of the new gas cans I went back to the drawing board to write more letters.

October 18 – Partly Cloudy, Lt. Breeze up & 14°.

I searched back and forth hoping for a glimpse of them some where along the lower slope. I trained the scope on the possible den I had watched from down Low Pass Creek way. Bear! big and very dark at the suspected spot. Moving slowly and I saw a rock or two roll down the mt. Falling my way so he wasn't digging. I watched and saw him using those front claws. Then I caught on. He was raking grass for a bed. Moving backwards he raked it towards the den then while slowly backing in I could see that front foot raking in the grass. I moved the scope in front of the cabin door for I could see it as well from there as the breakwater. Near sundown and I started stowing my new provisions and getting supper. It was a rush doing everything and looking through the scope every time I came close. The bear was out again and this time searching above the den entrance with that one front foot. Raking but evidently not getting much for he came back to the original site and raked more, dragged it back and into the den. Three times he repeated this. The sun went down at 5:30 and my bear didn't show again before dark. So I have a bear and one I can watch from the cabin door. One I can climb too – a good sharp ridge facing the den and just right for distance. No sign of the two bears on the mt. at dark. This one had to be in the den while I was glassing it from the lake and down country.

October 19 – Overcast, Breeze dn. & 20°.

My mail to read a second time and more thoroughly. A suggestion by Helen White that my journals be published in the *Anchorage Times*, Sunday edition, newspaper. A sort of continued story sort of thing. Of course the *Times* would have to be consulted about the possibility.

Part of the reason (bears for one) of my not sleeping well was thinking about the idea. I think it would be good and many people would look forward to reading about my observations in the wilderness where for 10 months of the year it is "As if man had never lived on Earth." If they could be content to read and not get the urge to come see for themselves it would be good. And then there is the fan mail problem. Some are bound to have questions and I would be on the receiving end and swamped with letter writing as it is. Maybe the wilderness would gain some respect if people approved of just looking and not touching. We shall see what develops.

It was time for supper and I stirred up a bannock, baking powder added this time and it was real good. The fresh kettle of beans with fresh bacon the best of the season. One good thing about my grub, I never tire of it.

Now at 7:40, 31°, some weak stars looking down and the lake not quite so noisy.

October 20 – Partly Cloudy, Lt. Breeze dn. & 32°.

Today I would climb to the sharp ridge facing the bear den. I didn't expect to see the bear out but that wasn't real important. I wanted to see how well the den entrance could be filmed from the ridge. But, just in case – I would take a full load of equipment. A paddle power crossing and a pleasure. I looked from the bare knoll for any sign of bears that I might disturb as I climbed. All clear and I took off towards a high bench with a couple stunted spruce to identify it as the one when I broke out of the timber. Many rabbit tracks and I crossed the tracks of the two bears still headed up country. Certainly not trail followers for they traveled the brush a few yds. from a game trail. A grey rabbit just below timber line and many high-bush cranberries just above. A cluster of ten was my prize pick. At the spruce and the crest of the knoll I could see sheep blocking my route. Seven head of ewes, yearlings, and lambs. One yearling ram in the little bunch. Only 20 feet of film on the roll in the Bolex. If I could get close I would use it up. I detoured back and around the bench and had cover for a spell but it ran out. That little ram spotted me and the bunch moved slowly over the ridge of the big talus slope. No loss and I climbed and headed that way. I hadn't seen them show on top of the big rock face or climbing the mt. They couldn't be far away and I approached the crest carefully. Just on the other side and feeding. No one had seen me. I backed up and set up the Bolex – inched up and planted the tripod and very slowly moved up to the view finder. I was in business at about 60 yds. I ran the camera dry and traded it for the Exakta and 400 mm. A full roll of 36 exposure

and I would shoot it all before they moved away. Three ewes above and they saw me but didn't spook for I moved slow like the lynx cat on a stalk. There should be some really nice sharp pictures in that roll. They slowly fed away to a point of rocks where they bedded down and didn't move until I climbed past not more than 150 yds away. A fresh load of film in each camera I was ready for bear. The climb long and steep but lots of grass and dry grass at that. I had picked the rocks I would check from . I had them pegged as directly across from the den and maybe a little more than 200 yds. I pulled up into the rocks and now what would I see. I was looking directly into the den. With a real strong flashlight I could have seen the bear. No bear in the den for the bear was 20 feet from the den raking grass. I hurried to get set up and when I moved into position the bear was gone. Only for a minute and its head showed in the entrance and then back out of sight. In a very short time it showed again and this time the bear came out and starting raking again. Carefully with that left and then the right. Above and below and in front, backing up and pulling the grass to him. This was something to see. A very big bear working so carefully to gather grass for a bed. Now he started picking grass and I wondered if it was for the bed too. All grass is dry now. Eating it, that's what he was doing. He left his little pile of bedding and fed out to the side and would go 50 yds. before turning down and circling back. Very slowly and feeding all the while. No hurry, I could wait. The afternoon was still young. I had only 100 feet of film for the Bolex and 36 exp. for the 35. I mounted it on the 400 mm lens and bedded it on the rocks nearby. I could rest my left elbow to steady the camera end so the set up was as steady as the tripod. One and then the other, I was recording a very important event of fall season. The dry grass. Now, it made sense. After the sow and cubs had left the den in 1975 I found the hibernation plug of the sow and it appeared to be dry grass. I have found the plug to be the remains of berries too – hard and dry. So – maybe this was the last meal.

The sun was getting around and a cloud bank was coming up down country. I could lose my light but had awhile to go. The bear continued to feed. One last bowel movement before turning in. The discharge appeared light in color and near liquid in consistency. Now, the sun was going behind the mt. as well as getting low. The den went in the shadow and the bear though working close didn't make a move to call it a day. I was down to a 25th and f4 with the 35. With the movie f4 and 12 frames per sec. and I doubted if I would get much at that. Finally the bear moved to the mound and started to rake in the grass. To the entrance and then above to rake more down. A pile of hay half as high as the entrance of the den. Light right at the bottom and the bear backed in and raked the grass in and I figured that was it for today. No light anyway and I tore things apart. I was surprised to see the bear out again but had gone in by the time I was ready to leave. In the dim light I could see that big head in the entrance of the den. I dropped down behind the ridge and headed down the mt. Not yet too dark but it would be before I got home. A good new route down and a minimum of brush. I will remember that route for the next climb. As dark as it was I spotted the tracks of the two bears in the heavy timber.

The lake was just below white cap stage and I would paddle. Warm and a fine

evening I wouldn't pollute it with a kicker.

Near seven o'clock when I came in the cabin. My gear stowed. Out of my climbing boots (L.L. Beans with new sharp Vibram soles). Supper on and good that I had a chunk of bannock saved for the occasion. Dishes and writing done by 9:15. Again stars are looking down and brighter than last night. The lake near calm but still the sound of water in motion out in the long run. Temp. 31°.

Today I noticed that the bear is lame in the left front leg. At times when he moved he carried that foot. Had he injured it in digging the den? Or was it arthritis. One thing for sure it will have a good long time to heal. A very beautiful bear. A perfect coat, dark brown in color with a narrow still darker stripe down the back from nose to tail. The bear appeared to be in very good shape for the six months

October 24 – Fog, Lt. Breeze up & 20°.

Along about two thirty it started to snow the kind of snow that comes with fog on a cold day. Before it did the fog had lifted to the peaks and the mt. slopes were grey with frost. I glassed for sheep but saw none and wondered where the spooky bunch would be today. No sign of moose making brown brush trails as it fed and moved in the brush.

All squared away for winter and I got the last six rolls of Park Service film ready for use (16 mm).

Another chore to be done – finish sawing and splitting the last two butt cuts of the big tough blow down spruce. It took some heavy splitting power but in due time it was of a size that would fit the stove. Another round gas can to convert to a storage can. This one I will give to Nixe Mellick for a Christmas present. A good storage container for dry stuff in his trappers cabin on Telaquana Lake.

October 25 – Partly Cloudy, Lt. Breeze dn. & 14°.

Nearly total overcast with fog over the lakes when I got up but within a half hr. it had opened up except for a fog patch over the lower lake. It looked like the perfect day. I wanted to make the long journey all the way down to the headwaters of the Chilly river and a mile beyond. A wonderful scene from the bend of the river and I had shot it in summer and fall but never with snow in the immediate area. I wanted to be there at 12 noon when the sun would be due south. I needed a blue sky and some white clouds would be desirable. I rushed around to get breakfast and dishes done, gear packed and loaded. It would take three and one half hrs. steady going to get there by paddle power. The kicker would go along to help me home in case the wind acted up. It was past nine when I shoved out so I would have to push it a bit. I was opposite Low Pass creek when I pulled into sunlight for the sun is very low behind the mts. at this time. A following breeze and that

Babe Alsworth at lower Twin Lakes with his "T-craft," the "little black bird," in 1968 • *Photo courtesy of Raymond Proenneke*

Doris Hagedorn, Pete Koktelash, and Florence Hicks at Nondalton circa 1974 • *Photo courtesy of Florence Hicks and Doris Hagedorn*

RLP filming at Snipe Lake 1975 • *Photo courtesy of Raymond Proenneke*

RLP overlooking Carrithers' point with Allen Mt., Spike's peak, Glacier Creek, Bell Mt., and Bell Creek in the background • *NPS photo*

Right:
Babe and Mary Alsworth in their garden at Port Alsworth in 1971 •
Photo courtesy of Mr. and Mrs. John Alsworth

Below:
Terry and Victoria Gill at their camp on Bonanza Creek in 1972 • *Photo courtesy of Raymond Proenneke*

Left:
Candice Downing, left, and Bea Van Horne, right on the Telaquana Trail north of Kijik in 1974 •
Photo courtesy of Walter Ward

Sig Alsworth, left, and
Leon Alsworth, right,
at Nondalton circa
1974 • *Photo courtesy
of Florence Hicks and
Doris Hagedorn*

Glen Alsworth with
his future wife, Patty
Elliott as students
at Palmer, Alaska in
1974-1975 • *Photo
courtesy Mr. and Mrs.
Glen Alsworth*

John Kauffmann,
National Park Service
writer and planner
in the Brooks Range
circa 1975 • *NPS photo*

Above:
Ted Swem, head of the NPS Alaska Planning Group and writer Mardy Murie at Proenneke's in 1975 • *NPS photo*

Right:
Keith Trexler, NPS interpretative planner for Lake Clark National Monument, circa 1974 • *Photo courtesy of Kris Trexler*

The Proenneke brother's J3-Piper Cub, the "Arctic Tern," on floats at Proenneke's in 1975 or 1976 • *NPS photo*

Left:
Chuck Hornberger at his homestead near the mouth of the Chulitna River on Lake Clark in 1978 • *NPS photo*

Below:
RLP kneels in front of the J3-Piper Cub on the ice near his cabin in the spring of 1976 • *Photo courtesy of Raymond Proenneke*

RLP and Margaret "Sis" Clum on the ice at Twin Lakes in 1978 • *Photo courtesy of Mr. and Mrs. Voight Clum*

Above:
NPS archeologist Harvey Shields at Telaquana Lake 1978 • *Photo courtesy of Michelle Aubery*

Right:
Ruth Koktelash picking blueberries near Nondalton circa 1975 • *Photo courtesy of Florence Hicks and Doris Hagedorn*

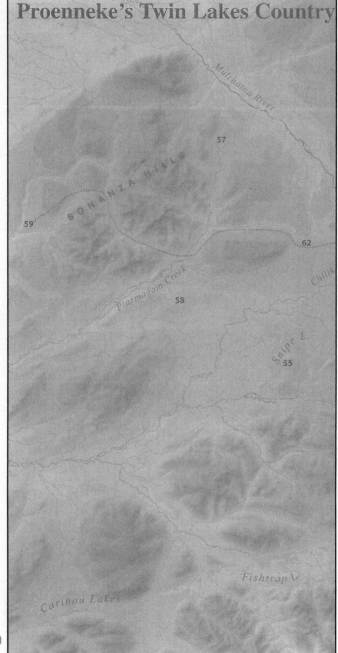

Proenneke's Twin Lakes Country

1. Proenneke Site
2. Carrither's Point
3. Hope Creek
4. Cowgill-Farmer-Terry cabin
5. Cowgill Creek and benches
6. Cowgill Peak
7. Cowgill Trail
8. Pup Tent Creek
9. Crag Mt.
10. Proenneke Peak
11. Gold Mt.
12. Low Pass
13. Low Pass Creek
14. Low Pass basin
15. "Eye of the needle"
16. "Old man of the mountain"
17. Connecting stream
18. Beech Creek
19. Dry Creek
20. Gatano's cabin
21. Volcanic Mts.
22. Pyramid peak
23. Skywagon point
24. Lake Trout Bay
25. Arlen's cabin
26. Frank Bell's cabin
    (Chilikadrotna River)
27. sheep lick
28. Beatrice Creek
29. Turquoise ridge
30. Black Mt.
31. Camp Creek
32. Camp ridge
33. Ram Mt.
34. Herb Wright sheep camp
35. Vanderpool cabin, variant
    of the O'Connel cabin
36. Emerson Creek
37. Falls Mt.
38. Falls Creek
39. Jerre Wills cabin (upper
    Twin Lakes)
40. Allen Mt.
41. Glacier Creek
42. Spike's Peak
43. Keith Glacier
44. Bell Creek
45. Bell cabin (upper Twin Lakes)
46. Bell Mt.
47. Waddell cache
48. Rockpile Mt.
49. Lofstedt's cabin
50. Lofstedt Bay
51. Lofstedt Creek
52. a white mountain
53. Big Valley
54. Pear Lake
55. Bell-Wills cabin (Snipe Lake)

Proenneke's Twin Lakes Haunts and Environs • *Photo courtesy of NPS*

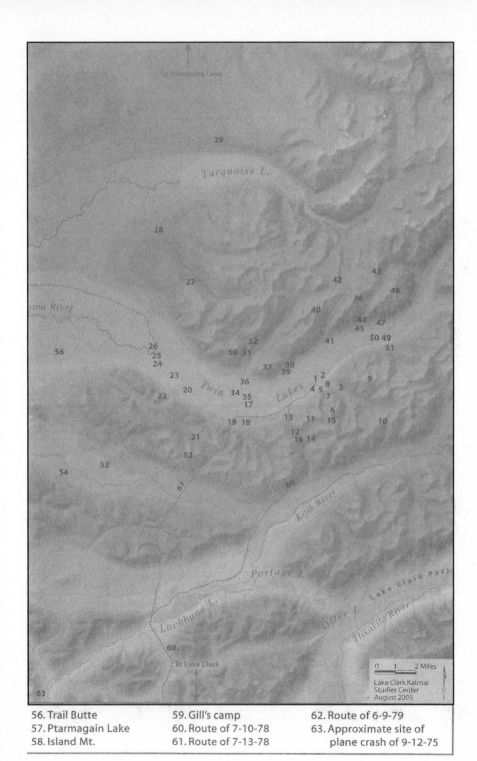

To Telaquana Lake

29

Turquoise L.

28

27

43
42
48
46
40
44 47
45
50 49
51

ma River

26
25
24

32
30 31
56
23

Twin 34 35
20
36
22

37 38
39

1 2
4 5 8 3
7
9

17

19 18

13 11
15
6
10

21
12
16 14

52

54
53

61

60

Kijik River

Portage T

Luchbuna L.

Otter L.
Lake Clark Pass

Tikakila River

60

To Lake Clark

63

0   1   2 Miles

Lake Clark Katmai
Studies Center
August 2005

56. Trail Butte	59. Gill's camp	62. Route of 6-9-79
57. Ptarmagain Lake	60. Route of 7-10-78	63. Approximate site of
58. Island Mt.	61. Route of 7-13-78	plane crash of 9-12-75

RLP in his loaded canoe 1991 • *Photo courtesy of Roy L. Allen*

Evan Vonga Bobby and Matrona Bobby at their home at Lime Village circa 1985 • *NPS photo*

RLP feeding a red squirrel circa 1985. Proenneke referred to all red squirrels as "Freddy." •
NPS Photo

RLP on his "Tom Sawyer" raft at Lachbuna Lake 1978. Proenneke and Branson built the raft
to cross the lake en route to Lake Clark. • *Photo courtesy of Raymond Proenneke*

RLP smokes meat on the beach near his cabin circa 1976 • *NPS photo*

An aerial view of Port Alsworth looking north across Lake Clark toward Kijik Mountain, center background, with Bee Alsworth's new landing strip under construction in the center foreground • *NPS photo*

Daniel Clum examines the wreckage of Proenneke's "Arctic Tern" near Sheep Mountain Lodge on the way toward Glenallen in October 1976 • *Photo courtesy of Mr. and Mrs. Voight Clum*

Laddie and Glenda Elliott in 1978 – 1979 at Port Alsworth • *Photo courtesy of Mr. and Mrs.Laddie Elliott*

NPS biologist-pilot Will Troyer in Katmai National Park and Preserve circa 1992 • *Photo courtesy of Will Troyer*

The upper reaches of upper Twin Lakes • *NPS photo*

Jack Ross building Van Valin's Island Lodge on Lake Clark near Portage Creek circa 1978. Proenneke referred to chainsaws as "Norwegian rasps." • *NPS photo*

Wayne "Bee" Alsworth at Twin Lakes salvaging an airplane circa 1980 • *NPS photo*

Woodenware carved by RLP • *Photo courtesy of Raymond Proenneke*

A hiker crosses Proenneke's Hope Creek bridge in 1982 • *NPS photo*

Paul Haertel, the first superintendent of, and a pilot for, Lake Clark National Monument on upper Twin Lakes in 1979 • *Photo courtesy of Mr. and Mrs. Paul Haertel*

231

Ranger Mike Tollefson,
the first chief of operations
for Lake Clark National
Monument • *Photo courtesy of
Mike Tollefson*

Proenneke's "eye of the needle" arch near Low Pass • *NPS photo*

Governor Jay Hammond
fishing at the mouth of Hope
Creek circa 1980 • *Photo
courtesy of Heidi Hammond*

was good for a speedy trip. Splashing a little with the paddle and it was freezing to my tin pants on the left side. By the time I reached the connecting stream I was well coated and beached there to beat it free and also to jog up the beach and back to warm my legs and feet.

It looked good for all the way. A few clouds over the high mts. A low cloud bank far down the Chilikadrotna-Mulchatna River way. I ran the stream which is low and no more than enough water to keep from raking bottom as I passed into the lower lake. A mile down and dark water ahead. A breeze coming up the lake and that was good for the return trip. A bit of a front moving in it seemed for it soon died and I had nice going to the lower end. A few scoter ducks still using the lower lake and I saw fish working along close to shore.

I was doing fine and I kept reminding myself that I would be there in good time but still I used more power than ordinary. A beautiful day as I beached. That cloud bank advancing but no problem. I loaded up and hit the trail down the river. Snow cover and trails stand out. Guides and fisherman have a beaten trail to my big red rock grayling hot spot. A lynx cat track on the trail and would be to my destination. It looked good, a few white clouds to keep the sky from being all blue. A few frames with the 35 mm and then I switched to the Bolex using a polarizer on the normal lens. A 10 sec. run from my best location and a seven second from an alternate location. Did it, and I was happy for the day. Then it happened – the light went out and the wind came very strong down the river. Clouds of snow rushed down the river flat and snow from the trees filled the air. Boy oh boy! now I was behind the eight ball. If it continued to blow I had no chance of canoeing home motor or no motor. The overcast had sneaked over the Volcanic Mts. and covered the sun. I had planned a tour of the Chili

A border of ice at waters edge and I could skid the canoe around the shoreline to a semi-protected spot. There I could get out and the kicker going if I was brave and foolish enough to try. I moved the canoe and packed everything else. The wind so strong it would blow the canoe away if I didn't park it on bare rocks.

River country for a shot or two down country but with no sky it was no use. I would head back. If I had to hike the eight miles I had no time to mess around.

At the lake a heavy surf rolling into shallow water and as far as I could see white caps. A million of them. Maybe after the front had passed it would settle down but I couldn't waste time on that possibility.

I had beached at the extreme end of the lake and exposed to the full force of the gale. No chance to launch there. My favorite beaching spot was blocked by new ice a hundred yds. from shore. I had paddled through a hundred feet of skim ice getting to the beach.

A border of ice at waters edge and I could skid the canoe around the shoreline to a semi protected spot. There I could get out and the kicker going if I was brave and foolish

enough to try. I moved the canoe and packed everything else. The wind so strong it would blow the canoe away if I didn't park it on bare rocks. If I could beat my way to windward for a half mile up along shore I could run with it on a stern quarter and make it to the other side into Lake Trout Bay. I could cache the canoe and motor in the spruce clump at Skywagon point and hike it up the lakes and home. I would give it a try. Everything loaded and the stern of the canoe on the shore ice with the tail end hanging over. I started the kicker and warmed it up. There would be no time for messing around once I left the beach. In no time I would be in the shallow water heavy surf. In hip boots I walked it out as far as I dared and jumped in – paddled out to deep water. The waves were big and the wind strong. It was as if I had sails. I was busy getting the "kicker" going and not directing my attention to the sea. First thing I knew I was in the trough and then on the front side of a big wave. It was good that I had a good load and a ballast of rocks or I think it might have rolled me. The kicker going and I had trouble turning into the sea. Made it and then the pounding started. With each big splash, the wind brought about a half gallon of water back into the canoe and on me. Three of them and I decided there must be a better way and I headed for the beach. Came in exactly where I went out. Jumped out and slid her right up on the shore ice.

It is said that the wilderness has unlimited patience – waiting for the brush rat to make just one good mistake and then when he has, he has had it. The law of average says it will happen if he stays long enough. Well, it wouldn't happen today, Oct. 25 [, 1975] for I was going to tie that raft to a little spruce – get under my camera gear and start walking. It would be dark before I got to the connecting stream and I could spend the night at the Vanderpool cabin there.

The canoe bottom up in a little swag protected by heavy brush. A rock laid of top. Everything I was leaving was under it. I took off up the beach and soon left it as it was a boulder beach and the wind terrific. I took to the knolls and inland to get away from it but it was everywhere. So strong that it was hard to face it and make head way. I had been over this route a few times, day and night. Stay close to the mt. till you near Emerson timber and then drop down into it and head for the mouth of Emerson Creek. Open going for a mile and then spruce patches. I thought of the old sourdough and what he had told Chris Crisler[20] when he went into the arctic barren land to film the caribou. The old man said, "Come back to the trees, boy." He had something there. I was making headway and would get through the mile long jumble of heavy rock at the base of Black Mt. before it got dark. At last I broke over a rise and could see Emerson timber. I had saved my double sourdough sandwich for the protection of the trees and the boost that honey gives one on the home stretch. It got dark in the trees and I began to stumble over the uneven snow covered ground. I could still see mt. landmarks and suddenly there was the Pyramid Mt. straight ahead. I was going southwest instead of southeast. As dark as it was I recognized the old Native blazed trail in the timber when I hit it and followed it a short distanced before crossing and heading for the big cottonwood grove and the cabin. It isn't easy to walk right to the cabin in the dark and I missed it by two hundred yds. but I

[20] Chris Crisler, was the husband of Lois Crisler who wrote, *Arctic Wild: The Remarkable True Story of One Couple's Adventures Living Among Wolves*, Harper & Brothers 1956.

knew where it was as soon as I hit the cottonwoods. It really looked good to me and now I was happy that a few years ago I had canoed a heating stove up from the lower end and set it in the cabin. The stove had been left on the beach by Oregon campers who had spent a month in a big GI pyramid tent.

Dark as all get out & I knew there was no lantern there. I felt around and got the stove going from fire starter brush and wood cut and stacked inside by the last hunters. Feeling around on the table I felt the form of a huge candle. I had a few matches and struck one. A big stubby red candle three inches across. Now I had light. I went to the creek to chop ice for the tea kettle. The full moon above the overcast was beginning to produce a little light. The hunting party had left odds and ends of grub. Cup of soup, instant oatmeal, hot chocolate mix, a couple cans of chili. Some tea bags had been there from years back. I was soon feeling well fed and warm. That down lake wind was a warm one as is usual.

The bunks, two of them. One had 2 inches of foam rubber and the other two heavy coarse, stiff blankets folded in half to make a pad. These I used for blankets with a folded up bunk mosquito net cover in between. There was even a feather pillow which the squirrels had worked on and liberated some feathers.

The lake roared loud and the wind sang a mournful tune in the bare branches of the cottonwoods. The tall spruce swayed heavily in the wind.

All of the strange sounds and the strange surroundings – I didn't do much good at sleeping. The cabin of logs and not tight by any means was drafty. I was up and down checking the heater and adding wood. I finally took my axe and saw that was there and went into the grove to cut wood by the dim light of the cloud shrouded moon. No time piece but I would know when daylight came. Finally I settle down to rest.

October 26 – The Wind Dying & Warm.

I noticed that the white caps were not as plentiful and the surf not so heavy. I climbed out of the wind and sat down to see what developed. In less than ten minutes no more white caps and then here came a breeze from Turquoise [Lake] ridge and up the lake. Well happy day. I could take the canoe after all and rushed to get things in order for travel before it changed its mind.

On my way. Still big waves coming down but no wind, in fact a breeze following. I made good time. At the halfway calm water and then a breeze still coming down. At the stream I lined her through and beached in calm water before entering the upper lake which was white capping down and plenty. I went for my gear and then entered the lake. I lined her up along shore to give me room to get the kicker going before thrown on the beach.

I was on my way. Big waves but not so much wind which is the deciding factor. The canoe splashes water and wind carries it in. Slowly does it, paddle speed and no more.

Quarter those big ones so you don't dig to deep in the next one. I headed for Low Pass beach and near there I switched to an up lake course and the protection of the points and finally the big one, Carrithers' point. I had it made and it sure tasted good to come in my beach again. Much snow had left the south slopes since I left yesterday morning.

My gear packed in I set up the scope to see if my bear was out. Sure enough and raking grass. It just has to be a mother one.

Squared away and water on for a hot bath. Beans, caribou steaks and some green stuff for supper. Sourdough biscuits baked two days ago, cold porridge pudding and hot tea. Now, I was living again. What a way to go to take a few scenery pictures and a few feet of movie film but I wouldn't have missed the experience for anything.

The up lake breeze arrive at dark and it is a cold one. 25° after being 38° when I arrived. It is overcast.

October 28 – Snowing, Lt. Breeze up & 16°.

Getting dark as I cleaned my lantern globe and fueled it. Wood and water for the night. A smoked caribou steak sawed and beans warming.

The breeze died and now at 7:30, 16° with a solid high fog overcast. From on the slope I could see out from under it down country.

Glassing across from my beaching site I could see fresh sheep trails on Falls Mt. but couldn't pick up the bunch. With solid snow cover one needs sunlight to see the white sheep which is not quite as white as new snow.

November 2 – Fog, Calm & 3°.

Last night in bed I was thinking of building a big candle like the stubby one in the Vanderpool cabin. If I could scare up enough candle wax I would mold one. In my survival bucket that I some times carry in the canoe was a bunch of small stubbies and I knew of a few more. The bucket needed cleaning out and sorting anyway. I came up with a bunch of them and put them in a stew pan to melt. For a mold I used a 2 ¾" pickle jar. Set it on a square of heavy foil and molded the foil around it. Wrapped it with string and removed the jar. For a wick I cut a candle the proper length, I would set it in the center of my mold and pour the wax in. The wax melted and all the short wicks fished out I poured it in. I did it outside on the table in 4 degree cold so it would cool quickly. Not quick enough for the candle was rapidly decreasing in size. Quickly I latched onto the wick with a clothes pin and suspended it in the center of the mold. Cooling rapidly and I was surprised how much candle wax shrinks when it cools. The center dropped considerably and I melted more to fill it. In fifteen minutes or so I removed the foil. A big white stubby 2 ½ inch high. The wrinkled foil had given the outside a cut glass effect that reflects light

and looks professional for rural work.

November 5 – Partly Cloudy, Very Lt. Breeze dn. & 1°.

Breakfast by candlelight and a close eye on the thermometer. I was sure that it would drop to zero just before the sun lighted Spike's peak. No such luck. It climbed and the lake began to roughen out in the long stretch. Partial overcast when I got up but it was clearing out. This was due to be a very beautiful day.

My snowshoe creepers – to make them still better I would put a rivet in each end of the inserts, 16 rivets in all. Sunlight came down the mts. across and I glassed for sheep. 4 head (3 rams) below the abandoned bear den where the twins were born. Trails, many sheep trails. It appears that they do a lot of looking before they are convinced that they will just have to dig for what feed they get. Another four head above the gorge of Glacier Creek and a trail or two below the rough stuff of Bell Mt. Just after mid-Nov. the last winter I stayed I found two big rams on Rock Pile Mt. above the upper end of the lake. They had just crossed the valley from right to left and were heading down country to join the ewes, lambs, and rams on Allen Mt. I climbed the slope above the old "Watts" Waddell sheep camp to film the big guys as they passed. The snow was a foot deep or more, dry and loose. How long would it take them to travel the three miles of mt. slope. Next morning I headed across to see if I could spot them. I had just climbed above timberline when here came the first of the two above the big rock face. Several hundred yds. back was the tail ender. That was the first and only time I have heard a ram make a sound that I could hear. A loud BAW BAW repeated several times came from the last one as he drew close. No fighting with the young rams present. A few clicks of horns and everyone knew where he stood. So – overnight the big rams traveled better than three miles of deep snow on the mt.

November 10 – Partly Cloudy, Very Lt. Breeze dn. & 8°.

What a joy to paddle in the sunlight. The sun still has some power and I felt warm with white coveralls top to bottom.

The connecting stream is low and will be much lower still by spring. Lots of gravel width to follow it without taking to the brush. I packed my crampons as I wanted to try them on the lake ice. How would it be to walk eight or ten miles with them. As I followed the stream I heard a familiar and welcome sound, one that had kept me company day and night for week and months. The lower lake ice was talking. Under pressure and growing in the cold. I have heard the lower lake ice groaning from my beach near the cabin. When it is active get an ear close to the waters surface and it can be heard plain enough. A distance of more than three miles. The ice looked good and plenty solid. I walked out onto its slightly ruffled surface. The wind had been blowing then it froze. I

sat right down and buckled on my spikes then took off down the lake for half a quarter, crunch, crunch, crunch, and as solid as walking hard dry ground. I could see that those crampons will pay for themselves many times over. Slipping and falling on slick spots is no fun. Good enough, a plane could land there no problem. The ice appeared to be at least 4" thick and probably more. I headed back.

November 13 – Overcast, Blowing dn. & 20°.

The breeze continued to rise and during the night it was gusting in the spruce tops. Freeze up had been delayed again. The lake was angry rough out in the long stretch.

After breakfast the weather puckered more and it started to snow. All down the line visibility decreased and I thought sure it would be a day of snow.

Sunday and nothing pushing. I put water on for a bath and laundry. Opened the barber shop and got a haircut and a shave. Tending the drying fire I sorted through my important for my last contract with the Park Service. It says, I shall get a copy of the edited film and a rough cut of all the best of the footage I have taken. That might amount to quite a lot of footage – depending who decided which was all the best.

The temp. climbed through out the morning. Please lord don't let it start to melt and it didn't, 25° was the high and the snow amounted to a trace.

November 19 – Overcast, Blowing dn. & 48°.

Dark comes early as Thanksgiving draws near. It was getting dark soon after three. Biscuits had been rising behind the stove today. Bannock is good but it doesn't take first place over my good sourdoughs. Two meals a day with a light lunch at noon, I would have an early supper and a cup of hot chocolate and a sourdough sandwich later. Boil a few small spuds and use some good bean soup for gravy. Fry the near last of my moose meat and have a few slices of carrot. A sourdough biscuit and my old standby for dessert. I could live on rolled oats, raisins, and rice three meals a day and never tire of it. Add some oleo or butter and some cinnamon, dry milk, and sugar. Dishes done without the aid of a light. So balmy out I pulled on my jacket and took a walk up the beach to the point to sit awhile and enjoy darkness settling down. The wind was backing off but I could hear it roaring on the mts. across. The temp. had dropped to 36° but now at 8 o'clock it is 38° and stronger. The moon more than half and building at 4:15. Now it is solid overcast again.

November 25 – Clear, Calm & 0°.

For my trip across I would wear my...pacs and crampons. The ice too slippery unless pushing the sled or with creepers. I was dressed warm enough for zero weather and it was 2 degrees. On smooth clear ice those crampons make a trail that could be followed from

the air. A trail of chipped ice. A great vibration is set up by all their crunching and I do believe it helps to keep ones feet warm.

Across and I followed the beach, going ashore now and then where there was good snow cover. Many seeps along the beach and ice is building up on top of the lake ice. Cold enough that in places the water congeals, not hard ice but not slush either. These I walked right across for there were many. Up as far as the moose rutting cottonwoods and that bruin was staying on the beach. He would probably follow it all the way to the upper end. One step hard ice and the next one hard slush and through I went. Close to shore and little over knee deep but I pitched forward and was in water up to my chest. I floundered around and got out. Jacket pockets full of water, mittens full, my pacs filling fast from water draining down inside my wind pants. Right about then I decided I would go home and see what the women and children were doing. I unzipped my down vest to get my binoculars out of the water and headed for the cabin full stride. The ice chips really flying. In no time my wind pants took on a white look as did my vest. I had a mile to go and could make that even though I might feel a little uncomfortable. Halfway and my mittens began to get stiff and my wrists cold. The cozy cabin looked pretty good and I opened the draft to get the fire into high gear. Zippers were frozen, plastic cuffs on jackets and pants were frozen stiff. Mitten cuffs were frozen. It would take a little time to get out of the frozen gear. Some warm water to soften the cuffs and the zippers down enough to get my jacket and vest over my head. The stove was soon smothered with streaming rags. Hot water for a bath and I was soon back to normal. A cup of hot vinegar and honey and I set about cleaning the logs of the cabins inside. Dust is a never ending nuisance and I would like to try some calcium chloride on my floor to keep it down.

November 30 – Clear, Calm & -24°.

I had dropped my tree and was bucking it up when I heard a plane and here came a Super Cub on wheel skis. He circled and I knew he wanted down. I hurried to the beach and headed for the cabin. He flew circles and finally a low pass. A long yellow streamer came down near me. A note "this is Will Troyer – is the ice safe to land. If so walk out on the lake. If not, I will air drop your mail. Glen will be in with grub and packages soon if the ice is good." I walked out arms out spread, the signal to land and he came sliding in along side of me. A skidding turn and the snow flew as he made a 180 degree turn in my little bite. Out he climbed and his partner too. It was good to see Will again. I had known him on Kodiak when he was refuge manager there. His helper put the motor cover on and we came to the cabin. They were on moose survey for the Park Service and staying at Glen Van Valin's at Port Alsworth. Been at it a few days and just getting into this area. Had they seen any moose near? Two cows and two calves along the lower lake both headed this way.

They had lunch, sandwiches and cookies and apples and a huge thermos of tea. I stocked the fire and would make a bannock. Well then they would leave the lunches for

me. I whipped one up and got it on the fire. Up ended the mail sack and what a stack of letters, big padded envelopes and a small package. Many letters from Alaska Northwest Pub. Co. concerning those wanted slides. The book *Monarch of Deadman Bay* by Roger Caras, the ABC narrator who interviewed me when the crew was here. Inside the cover "To Dick Proenneke, Who will understand, My Best Always, - Roger Caras." A note from Bob Belous. They would be screening my film soon and hoped to get me to Anch. to see it, but the note was dated Oct. 23. You will be hearing from us about Nov. 10th to the 15th.

That sounded typical of Park Service speed of operation. It also said that the Harpers Ferry crew have screened my recent footage and raved about the wildlife sequences. All of this is good to read but lets have some pay to rave about if it is so good.

I cut the bannock in thirds and thought I would eat with my company but got busy closing up my mail. I said, "you guys finish it." Boy! no second notice necessary. Will's helper snapped it up like a hungry dog.

The sun was leaving the mts. in shadow when they said they had better fly some more. Be going back to Anch. but would do much more flying in this area in Feb.

Will had a qt. of oil heating on the stove. "Only getting a couple hrs. to the qt.," he said. The cover off, oil in and fired up. I shook them loose on the cold snow and they took off up the lake and back down the far side. I got busy on my mail and the cabin got cool before I remembered that it needed fuel now and again. Gee those homemade cookies tasted good and cinnamon rolls when had I eaten a cinnamon roll last.

December 1 – Partly Cloudy, Calm & -10°.

A lengthy letter to brother Jake when I heard a plane and I knew it was Glen. Visibility not good down country but I learned it was local and better than it looked from here. He and his father-in-law Laddie[21] in the 135 "T craft" on skis. I pushed my sled out and greeted the boy to whom I had said on Oct. 18th give me grub enough to last for the duration and I could go a year without seeing anyone. The short span of freeze up would be no problem. Mail is the one item that takes priority. Some people could die or move away from the time my letters are written until they start moving. Glen – happy as usual and Laddie busy with a Canon 35 mm and a new something to 200 zoom lens by Vivitar. We loaded the sled with rolled oats, maybe 30 lbs. of it. 25 of brown sugar, 4 dozen eggs, 18 lbs. of rice, plus a lot of goodies like bananas, sweet rolls, a big jar of Smuckers strawberry jam. My packages that didn't come with Will yesterday. Many packages and by the time the light failed I would be well stocked for the Christmas holidays. First things first and I finished my mail.

---

[21] Laddie Elliott, father-in-law of Glen Alsworth, log builder, jack of all trades and master of them all, known for his "green thumb."

December 4 – Overcast, Snowing, Calm & 3°.

It was snowing lightly when I turned in at 9:15 after reading a chapter or two of the *Monach of Deadmans Bay* by Roger Caras. That Roger must be very intelligent and very well educated or did a lot of research or all three. A few things he had written as fact doesn't agree with my observations of the big brown bear but that is a small detail. If I ever see him again we will discuss a few things. I wish I had him, his camera man and sound man here for a tour of Twin Lakes country, Proenneke style, but I doubt if he could stand to climb 2000 ft. without hurting.

Still snowing lightly at daylight and the lakes country was a sight to see. 4 inches of feathers that fell in dead calm air and stacked up on everything in their path. Hotcakes and then my fresh beans to get going. I nearly over did them last evening, too much soda and too much boiling. They were nearly done when I turned in. Still the water to change and seasoning to add plus potato and bacon.

My pathways to sweep and the 4 inches swept like nothing. My roof looked perfect and I felt happy that I had leveled it yesterday. Now in the cold it will stay with only a hole for the chimney pipe. I would like to see snow come 2 feet deep and see how it stands up.

I finished reading the book and now must find a way to locate Roger and thank him. When he had said "I will send you an autographed copy" I figured it was just conversation like congressmen and such who shoot pictures like mad and say "if they turn out I will send you some" none ever came.

December 17 – Clear, Calm & -38°.

Packages. A couple from Helen White – good things to eat. One from Voight and Sis – more good thing to eat and two loaves of banana bread was part of it. Apples, oranges, nuts, candy everything imaginable. One from Brother Jake, many candy bars and peanuts salted in the shell plus two cans of nuts. A package from Tom and Marion Gregory more good things to eat. From Dick & Lila Fisher in Toledo, Ohio (readers of the book) a huge block of something good and when learning it could freeze I didn't open it farther, save it till Christmas. Glen, Laddie, and families – a big sourdough cake, candy, nuts and other goodies. All of this and more. Too much I wish that people wouldn't go to all the trouble. Evidentially they feel sorry for the poor miserable brush rat and like to bring civilization a little bit closer. Some how it takes a little something from the wilderness living with bannock and beans the accepted fare and happy with them.

Now the stack of letters and more than 40 letters and cards. Right away "saw you on the Harry Reasoner's – Barbara Walters show." People calling in from all sides and from coast to coast – tune in on this channel or that – the brush rat is on TV. And so it went. I was surprised at the number of people who had seen "One Man's Wilderness

[Alaska]." Coast to coast and Florida to Massachusetts where Sam [Keith][22] had two TV's going and then missed part of it. I read and read, lighted the upside down lantern and read some more. It was six before I got through them all and then it was a fast once over lightly.

I heated some beans and made a bannock using some graham flour that Glen had brought. Old stuff that had been in the store room for years. It made real good bannock but I won't use it in my sourdough starter.

When I went to empty my dish water I was really taken by the beauty of the night. -40°, clear, and calm. The sky as blue as indigo and the stars very bright. The moon half and over Gold Mt. Right then and there I knew I was going for a walk on the lake. I pulled on my mukluks over Mary's super socks and would wear her extra heavy knit stocking cap with my Navy foul weather cap over the top. My heavy Army shawl around my neck up to my nose. Sweaters a plenty, wool shirt and quilted jacket. My big mittens and I set the draft to zero and turned out the light. I had intended to cross to the far side and back but once there I headed down and didn't stop till I reached Emerson Creek and a cloud of ice fog coming slowly up from the stream. There I cut across to hit my broken trail coming up the center. The moon behind and over my right shoulder. 90 degrees to the moon is the bluest sky you can imagine. The mts. side lighted. The sky as if I was in a huge planetarium with every star in its proper place. I stopped often just to stand and look. The moon not yet full and I hope the clear, calm weather holds till Christmas. The most beautiful sight of all was the view of my cabin from the lake shore in the moon light. The snow covered spruce and brush the blue sky the stars, I just had to stand and look.

December 18 – Clear, Calm & -38°.

It was 12 before I turned in last night and I thought I would never wake up but it seemed that I slept very little – too much to think about. Had I done the right thing turning Jim Rearden's[23] letter back without accepting or at least inquiring more about the *Outdoor Life* deal. And the nation wide TV presentation, what effect will it have on Twin Lakes. I wondered how much they told – how was my short story introduced. *Outdoor Life* will wonder why ABC and not us. All that garbage and six thirty came too early and I waited till seven to roll out and get those deep tan hotcakes on the griddle. I had used half white and half graham flour.

December 19 – Overcast, Snowing (lt.) & +18°.

A session of letter reading before I started my journal entry. I learn that my welfare

---

[22] Sam Keith (1923-2001) friend of RLP from their Kodiak days, educator, writer, and editor of *One Man's Wilderness*.

[23] Jim Rearden, writer, historian, big game guide who lived in Homer. In the early 1970s Rearden was outdoor editor for *Alaska Magazine* and recommended to publisher Bob Henning that the Proenneke-Keith manuscript be published. In 1973 the book, *One Man's Wilderness*, was published by Alaska Northwest Publishing Company. RLP never signed a contract with Henning because he felt it was unfair, however, Sam Keith did sign the book contract. It is likely RLP did not want to be involved with the *Outdoor Life* deal because of Rearden's association with Henning.

birds and I were seen from coast to coast and from Florida to Anch. I wonder if foreign countries see ABC News. Now what? The best that I can imagine is that the Twin Lakes watershed will be made a sanctuary. Camera hunting and foot traffic only on all the mts. and streams feeding the two lakes. Too good to be true but I will mention it to Dave [Cornwall] the warden next visit.

Twenty till eight, snowing lightly (maybe an inch today). The sound of wind on Allen's Mt. and the temp. 22°. I hope it doesn't go higher than 25.

December 22 – Overcast, Calm & 31°.

Last evening I heard the great grey owl calling someones name and I wondered who it would be this time. I was up at seven to have my breakfast. I had planned to go back down to moose country again. I was thinking of hunters that might come and if they did they certainly would find my camera subjects from the air. Whether they would obey the law and camp one night before shooting is a good question. One thing for sure, I would know if they did or didn't.

December 23 – Partly Cloudy, Lt. Breeze dn. & 32°.

First thing after my spuds get some water on and cleaned up with laundry to follow and then write a few letters to go in case of something flying to the outside.

A long letter to that Vin Sparano, Senior Editor of *Outdoor Life* mag. Explain my decision not to furnish pictures for that priceless book promotion and give him a brief run down on the conduct of his head and leg hunter readers here in Twin Lakes country.

December 25 – Partly Cloudy, Lt. Breeze dn. & 22°.

"Merry Christmas." Again my Baby Ben quit. The moon full and bright in a clear sky and then it set behind Falls mt. peak and the night was dark until I could identify the roof poles over my bunk. A beautiful morning this 25th of Dec. and as it did yesterday the sun would touch Spike's peak at sunrise and then cloud cover would erase it for the rest of the day. My Baby Ben I would give another bath in jet fuel. The night had been to cool for the WD-40 I suspect. A bath and it took off and promised to keep good time this Xmas day if set at the correct time after it started. This I didn't know, so it was another blind guess.

The temp. climbed to 30° and reached a high of 33° with a strong breeze down the lake.

A few odd chores this Christmas morning. I went far out on the ice and with my new ice chisel I cut a hole to check the ice. Not more than sixteen inches and I was

disappointed.

I came down the long open blueberry slope and onto the ice for a cool trip up against the wind. 2:45 my clock said and I promptly stoked the fire. It was time to start Christmas dinner. The chicken a small one and I would fry it and make some chicken gravy. Boil some spuds and heat some beans. Biscuits had been rising since before noon.

My big square skillet on the fire. An ample amount of bacon grease. Some super seasoned flour to give it a good crust. I dismantled that little imitation turkey bird and soon had the sound of frying chicken. I chopped some onion on top and it would make the crust better. The door wide open and the birds coming often. How many Christmas days in Alaska are like this? It was a big meal. I did away with half of that bird. For dessert, my old faithful cold porridge pudding and an extra large helping. A good sized piece of Glenda's sourdough cake with good pink icing. The dishes done and everything squared away by five o'clock. I sat by the stove feeling stuffed and got sleepy. This was my kind of Christmas.

This was my kind of Christmas. A real no fuss no mess, no nonsense Dec. 25th. It is pretty amazing what civilization will make of a date on the calendar. How much money spent foolishly, how much energy (in short supply) used, how many accidents, how many deaths and here it is a day very much like yesterday or tomorrow.

A real no fuss no mess, no nonsense Dec. 25th. It is pretty amazing what civilization will make of a date on the calendar. How much money spent foolishly, how much energy (in short supply) used, how many accidents, how many deaths and here it is a day very much like yesterday or tomorrow.

December 31 – Overcast, Breeze dn. & 32°.

Here came the red "T-craft" sliding up the ice. A passenger along and it turned out to be his brother-in-law[24] whom I had never met.

Some spuds, eggs, chocolate mix, 50 qts. of dry milk and another item or two. Two big green mail sacks, which contained several packages along with my 36 letters and cards for this last day of the year.

I ask Glen about the weather at Lake Clark. Fine weather, no melting, about 25 degrees. It had been colder than here. Not much news from outside. Babe and Mary happy on Hawaii and Glen and Pat due to fly over for a visit later this winter.

I got my mail and packages ready to go. Took them out to show them my neat water hole maintaining system. Glen allowed there is just about everything in the world and there has to be a long tapered plastic tube with the small end plugged. He would

[24] Lonny Elliott, brother of Patty Alsworth.

keep his eyes open for one. They climbed in and I pulled the prop. In a very few seconds I was alone with my load of civilization. Packages from sister Florence, brother Raymond and Robt. & wife.[25] One from Spike and Hope and one from Lucy Benjamin and I knew what was in it. I had mentioned candles and she is a candle stick maker. A package from Porter's Camera Store in Cedar Falls, Iowa and that would be the new strobe light for my Exakta. A big brown padded envelope and in it the book *Island Between* by Margaret E. Murie, autographed and it read "To my good friend Dick Proenneke with every good wish" signed Mardy. The package that took first prize was one from bro. Robt. & Dorothy. A big box 14"x13" by 10" high and packed full of every thing from canned goods to chewing gum and writing equip. Very heavy and I wish I had totaled the postage. Glen's mother-in-law had sent in a big foil covered plate of

My cabin and cache have been full to overflowing for quite some time and each new load makes me wonder where I will stow it all. Till now everything has found a place but the place is beginning to look cluttered. Perhaps the season of giving is past, I hope so. I do appreciate everything but wish they would consider the poor miserable brush rat more fortunate than they and spend their money to beat death and taxes.

fancy sweet rolls. My three month old smoked caribou ribs and beans suddenly look very plain, but which would be better for the man climbing in knee deep snow.

My cabin and cache have been full to overflowing for quite some time and each new load makes me wonder where I will stow it all. Till now everything has found a place but the place is beginning to look cluttered. Perhaps the season of giving is past, I hope so. I do appreciate everything but wish they would consider the poor miserable brush rat more fortunate than they and spend their money to beat death and taxes.

Every box opened and everything stowed before I got the cards and letters. All afternoon I read letters and cards and learned that several new states saw "One Man's Wilderness" on TV. I was surprised not to find a few threatening letters in the bunch but this is the season to be jolly. Next plane will have some.

One letter was a little extra special. It rated more than just a once over lightly the first time through. It was from the old sourdough Mardy Murie. She had been to a Park Superintendents Conference at Estes [Park], Colorado. She wrote that they had a film evening and showed my film. "What an enchanting thing it is, I was so excited and moved to tears too." As soon as she got home she called the naturalist at Grand Teton Ntl. Park. One of the staff would be hand carrying a copy back from Harpers Ferry to Grand Teton.

[25] Robert (1910-2000) and Dorothy Proenneke, of Alexandria, Virginia, RLP's older brother and his wife. Robert was a civil service employee for the Department of the Army.

CHAPTER FIVE – 1978

MASTER AND AMBASSADOR OF TWIN LAKES

January 21 – Partly cloudy, Lt. Breeze dn. & 11°.

Coming back and I heard a plane and then saw the red "T-craft" coming in low and far out.

Not much freight, 25 lbs. of white flour and two half gallon jars of raisins. Inside I dumped the mail on my caribou rug. The volume down a bit and that is good. I ask them if they would have something to eat or drink. "Oh no, we should be getting back," Glen said. "I may have to go to Anch. yet today." Little Menda[1] (his daughter) is having much pain in one arm and may have to go to the hospital.

But today was a Twin Lakes holiday. Read about what the poor folks outside are doing. I was soon to learn – two brothers not far from home had died within 20 days of each other. A few dead and buried, an alarming number in the hospital. Colds and flu and no chance to avoid it. And then I came to the brighter side a letter from Sam [Keith]. He had received the Park Service film "One Man's Alaska" and had shown it at home and at school several times. Great! The only complaint was that 25 minutes was not long enough.

Now a small package from brother Robt., tape for my recorder and on the label "Audio portion of 'One Man's Alaska'." He had also received a copy of the film from the Park Service and had shown it twice a day for a few days. He wondered if it was my copy they sent to him and I certainly hope it isn't or he will have it worn out before I see it. He recorded the sound and sent it to me. I lost no time in getting it in the little Hitachi recorder and I listened to the music and the man's voice who introduced me and then I listened and tried to picture the exact scenes and sequences I was narrating. It is alright I guess but I would like it better if the introductory voice had done the narrating. And a short letter from Old Sourdough, Mardy Murie. They had a copy of the film which the

---

[1] Menda Alsworth, the oldest child of Glen and Patty Alsworth was 2 years old.

Grand Teton National Park had borrowed from Harpers Ferry. Ran it twice for young people parties in her home. Both times before the show she had read my description of the big brownie preparing its den for the long winter in hibernation. She thought that was a very appropriate way to start the show.

January 25 – Clear, Calm & 6°.

The plane circled right and came over the point and down Hope Creek. I waved and it came around again and lower. It was parked out front by the time I reached the cabin.

Roy Sanborn[2] of the Park Service, the man who had taken Keith Trexler's place. With him a smaller man, the pilot who spoke with a foreign accent. I greeted them with, "How do you expect a guy to get any sleep with all that racket." Roy grinned and had no ready answer except to say it was cold here. They had left Anch. wet and sloppy and it had been that way for a week. He had been trying to get over here for days.

Lake Clark had a lot of overflow on the ice and a plane had broken through and suffered much damage. That was the reason the pilot had made a touch and go here, testing the surface. "We came to take you to town," Roy said. I had suspected as much. "We want you to see that movie before we start showing it all over the place." "Why didn't you bring a small generator and projector along and we would show it here," I said. "Not enough length in your cabin," he said. "Show it small like a TV screen," I came back. "Take you in and bring you back Friday." I told him I wouldn't like to leave and have my perishables freeze. "Well then, we will bring you back tomorrow." "Gee, I don't want to go to town. I'll see the film sometime. I have lots of patience." "Well, I don't blame you for not wanting to go to Anch.," he said.

By now they were parked inside and I had poured each a cup of tea. He said they had ten copies of the film and it has been well distributed in the Lower 48. "When am I going to get my copy?" I ask him. "Give you one right away if you want it," he said. "No use for it here but I would like my brother Ray to see it." "Give me his address and I will mail him one today," he said. Allowed it wasn't all that important but he said no problem and fixed me up with note paper and ball point. I ask him if a film could be purchased. "Certainly," he said. "How much, $500.00?" "Oh no, less than $200," he said. (Mine free)

We had a long visit. It is pretty certain that Twin Lakes country will become a park and subsistence hunting by the Natives will be permitted. A surrounding area will become a game preserve and hunting will be allowed. Twin Lakes will be inside the Park boundary though. Next month they plan to do a big moose survey. The one in Dec. was to count bulls and the next will be everything for the bulls will have dropped their antlers. If I have it right they had counted 250 bulls in the Dec. survey. This one would take a couple weeks time and two Cubs would be flying.

Roy asked me about my Cub and the pilot said he had suffered 5 engine failures

---

[2] Roy Sanborn, NPS management assistant for the Alaska Task Force and pilot.

in the past year. "When she stops, isn't it quiet?" he said.

Well they would take a little tour of a few lakes and then go back. The plane a Robertson STOL [Cessna] 185 Skywagon belonging to the Office of Aircraft Services. (Gov't agency's plane pool.) I seen them off, had an early sandwich and prepared to climb again.

January 26 – Partly Cloudy, Blowing dn. & 26°.

How much activity will there be by the Park Service if Twin Lakes country is to become a park. I'm thinking the days of "One Man's Wilderness" as such are numbered and the numbers are leaking out much too fast.

Yesterday I said to Roy Sanborn, "I would like to see something tried that I have never seen or ever heard of. Instead of making this a park, make it a wilderness area. Put a small crew in here to film it in color year around. Edit the film and show it on TV spring, summer, fall and winter. Many times more people would see it and under the best of conditions. They would see much wildlife that they will never see if they come here. Weather can even prevent them from hiking for a week at a time. Millions of people could enjoy the beauty of the wilderness and it and its wildlife would be left untouched.

Very few families could afford to visit the Park anyway if they must fly and weather for flying is very uncertain. To come any other way would take days. Let them enjoy the wilderness while enjoying a glass of beer in their own living room." He looked at me and grinned but didn't say a word. He is a big wheel in the Park Service.

January 31 – Overcast, Breeze dn. & 28°.

Erv casually asked me what I had seen in the line of game. Had I seen any wolverine – no and no tracks. He doesn't know about the bear in hibernation or the better than full curl ram and its lessor buddies. I hadn't seen much, a few moose and a tame fox. I'm not forgetting that he is by his own admission hunter orientated and a leg hunter at that. Bee and I both related the outrageous behavior of the leg hunters. Bee had seen (in a past winter) eight caribou carcasses on the lower lake with only the legs taken. Bee said of Ken Owsichek (his guide neighbor) he shipped out a big plane load of moose antlers but didn't fly any meat back to camp.

From here they taxied over to have a look at Erv's cabin. I had asked him what he would do if the Park Service decided to buy or condemn his property if he wouldn't sell. He didn't know about that and would have to cross that bridge when the time came. He said the last report had it that the park proposal had passed in Congress. They took off after a spell and flew very fast down the far side. Wayne had said he cruises at about 135 mph at 2450 and climbs 1000 ft. a minute.

I started in on my few letters. I learned that I had been on TV (ABC) the second time in Wash. D.C. and that the movie "One Man's Alaska" is showing there on Public Service Stations [PBS].

February 2 – Clear, Calm & 7°.

Time to check the lake ice for thickness and while doing it I would see how much sun there would be. I took the 4 lb. pole axe, ice chisel, measuring stick and shovel. Went out maybe 150 yards or more and started a hole.

The sun touched the point and then Spike's cabin. On down the beach and Hope's cabin caught the very edge of the lighted area. Very soon they were both in shadow for the sun had dropped behind the Volcanics. I chopped and shoveled and chopped again to go as far as I could without the handle striking the edge. Only a little way with the chisel and I broke through. The hole boiled full of water and I used the measure. 22 inches and it didn't seem like enough if it is going to make 44 or better. 48" will go in a month when the sun gets high in the sky. Anything less could mean break up by the end of May or even before.

The temp. going down, 6° and the fog starting to move back again.

Sunset was near and I stayed to see the shadows reach the top. 4:30 exactly and my new watch should be very close. At the cabin I would learn from the book that Nushagak Bay[3] sunset would be at about 4:40. Already the daylight hours are about one hour longer each, morning and evening. 4° and looking good for a cool night. I had a green salad and some of my fresh beans and when I went to empty the dish water a dark overcast had all but covered the sky from the high mts. to the Bonanza Hills. The temp. 8° now at 7:40, 11° and complete overcast.

Dead calm and it appears that the first days of February have been robbed of a cold wave.

Fresh baked sourdough biscuits for supper.

February 3 – Partly Cloudy, Breeze dn. & 20°.

When I turned in at ten the stars were out and the temp. had dropped to 6°. Before morning I saw it 15° and a light breeze down. Partly cloudy but no light on the peaks as I removed the plug from the water hole at sunrise time.

Today I wanted to stay close for the big event. See the sun from my windows for the first time in nearly three months.

To waste away the time I would work up a blow down tree near the trail

---

[3] Nushagak Bay on Bristol Bay approximately 200 miles SW of Twin Lakes and the ultimate destination for Twin Lake's waters.

where it breaks out onto the creek flat on the way to the hump. It had been a green tree, hollow at the butt. The snowshoe trail ideal for the pumpkin seed toboggan sled. The tree had been down for a year or more so it was dry to the extent that it would burn good. Four loads cleaned it up including the limb wood. No chance to see the sun for the overcast was heavy and solid. So, I sawed and split until the pile looked well filled out. A real nice afternoon to work in the woods, the temp. 25°. Nice to have the extra hour of daylight morning and evening.

Still time to burn and I put some water on to get cleaned up for the weekend. Not expecting company but you never know. Probably wouldn't be home if someone did drop down. Another week and a half before the big moose count starts. Will Troyer will be stopping in for bannock and beans. He had told his observer when here the last day of Nov., "Dick can make real good bean soup."

The wind has increased since dark – blowing down and pretty good. Partly cloudy and 23°.

February 5 – Overcast, Breeze up & -10°.

I was hungry for some good buttered popcorn. I had been saving my corn for the visit of the mission girls as they are the popcorn eaters and asked me if I had plenty on hand. After nine years I have decided that Sam had it figured about right when he wrote "The coming of the mission girls rivals the second coming of Christ." I offered some to the birds and one did take a fluffy one to the spruce and picked it apart. They prefer hotcakes and the gentle one came along to enjoy a leisurely meal of nibbling and looking around while all of the cold from the outside rushed in the upper half of the door.

Second session and this would be letter writing. Hold them down to a respectable length and the outgoing basket fills faster. Biscuits had been rising in the pan. A heaping tablespoon of graham flour with one of white in my starter sponge makes real good biscuits. At full height and before the fall I put them under the oven and was pleased with the quality. A sugar cinnamon crust of course.

It was getting dark on a dark day and I was surprised to see it near five instead of 3:15 as it is in Dec. when the light goes out.

As I got in my wood supply for the night I noticed it -16°. A fine dry snow was covering my swept walkways. Now at 7 o'clock the ice is rumbling as if it is getting colder, the temp. is still -16, the snow continues and a light breeze incoming from down country.

February 12 – Overcast, Breeze dn., Snowing light & 28°.

This week should see some action by the Park Service moose counters, but the wind will

have to calm before they can fly low and slow. They will brag about how many moose they have seen and I will say, "And how about the snowshoes, spruce grouse, and ptarmigan." Tourists in the Park will see more of them than the wiley moose.

Tonight again, weak moon and stars and the wind strong blowing down. Temp. 30°. The high today 32°.

Two more days and Feb. will be half used up. If comparable to other winters I have stayed the coldest of the cold is past. Now it can only better after each storm.

February 14 – Overcast, Blowing dn. & 28°.

With saw and axe in hand and towing the pumpkin seed sled I headed up the trail to the cabin log timber. I passed two big dead ones – more wood than I wanted. Near my resting seat chunk under the spruce in the log timber was a ten incher, tall and straight. Fred Cowgill had used it for a parking place for his axe when he cut his cabin logs from the looks of the many scars. It had bled a lot of pitch and no more than a year ago it died. A good tree not completely dry which is better for holding fire. Three good sled loads when I got it all to the woodshed and my watch said it was 12:30.

The day was fairing up and the wind calming. Much blue sky down country. I would stick close to home. A sandwich and I took my little bow saw apart to set and sharpen the blade. It had sawed a lot of wood and was needing more set. The job done and I was putting it back together. A steel ring with ends not quite touching rotates through two holes in the frame to hold the outer end of the blade. On the handle end a half inch threaded rod two and a half inches long. The end that takes the blade is slotted. A hole drilled through for a pin to hold the blade. A very small $^3/_{16}$" diameter pin a quarter inch long. Easy to lose, that rascal. A wing nut is used to put tension on the blade and it must be very tight. The outer end locked in place. The blade in the slot and the pin in place on the handle end. Put the threaded end through the hole in the frame and put the wing nut on. Doing this on the table out front. The frame slipped over the edge and there she went. Like a sling shot that spring steel blade threw the threaded end and the pin. As luck would have it I saw the pin lite in the pathway to the lake but I didn't see the threaded one. No problem, it couldn't be far. I put the pin in the safe to make sure it didn't get away. I looked for a mark in the 18 inches of snow that would mark the entrance of the threaded one. No marks. I scratched along the edge of the pathway – got the broom and swept the snow carefully. Shoveled it away and swept more. What a deal – it might be May or June before the snow melted. A lot of searching but no finding. I went to work on the loose snow with the broom, sweeping it carefully into the path and shoveling it away. Two birds came to help. One perched on my head and the other on a shoulder. They had hotcake in mind, they wasn't fooling me.

Just as well forget the fool thing and park the little jewel. Use the big bow saw. One more time I would look. Sweeping along the edge of the path where the pin had laid

and I uncovered it under the deep snow at path level. Boy! I was glad to find it. Some warm water from the tea kettle to clean it up and then I put her together and tightened the blade. Two holes in the out board end and I broke one out to shorten it and get more tension. In the woodshed I sawed a few lengths to check it out before hanging it on its peg in the wall. All is well that ends well, but that was a close one.

February 15 – Overcast, Breeze dn. & 30°.

I was ready to get up at 6:30 and did. Everything worked to perfection and I was soon doing my last chore of the morning – watering up. By now it was clearing down country. The upper end closed in. I did a few odd jobs to give Glen a chance to get here if he was coming. 10:30 came and no red airplane. I would load up and head down country. The pin in the map and note on the table. If I was still on the lake he would see me. If I wasn't I would be there by the time he packed in my mail and grub, read the note and came looking.

Here came a little airplane, a red one, not very high and quietly. Glen had come at last. I quickened my pace as they flew by and turned to fly down the far side. They turned again and came up along the Low Pass side to land in close to my beach. Two climbed out – that would be Glen and his father-in-law. Both in the cabin when I arrived. "Boy, what a beautiful day," I greeted them. "Sure is," Glen said. I asked him if the wind had been blowing on Lake Clark. Sure has and how was it here the 11th. "Fine weather but blowing strong," I told him. Had it been windy here with the cold before the 10th. At home 20 below with a 20 knot wind – real bad. I told him that I was thinking it would be time for he and Pat to go to Hawaii before he could get in. "Going tomorrow," he said. "Be back about March five." Voight would be keeping the [Cessna] 180 and they hoped to fly in some weekend. Little Menda had an elbow joint out of place. She fell and accidentally put it back. Not much news from outside. He had brought me in a manuscript written by William Park[4] who had a cabin up the lake from Babe's bay (Voight and Sis own the cabin now). Park had spent a part of one winter on the Swift River[5] (beyond the Stony[6] [River] from here) with two men who were trapping. 33 typewritten pages of their activities from the time they were landed on a lake by plane until he traveled out with an Indian family to Lime Village[7] on the Stony River and on down to a trading post of the Kuskokwim River[8] and to civilization by plane. This was back in the nineteen thirties. He wrote of their building a cabin with the only material brought in being a few nails and spikes and a few panes of glass. Two axes and one man cross cut and I suppose

---

[4] William "Bill" Park (1892-1963), retired school teacher who lived on Lake Clark in the 1940s and 1950s.

[5] Swift River, a 100-mile long tributary of the Kuskokwim north of the Stony River; Huch'alitnu is a Dena'ina word for "flows up and out river."

[6] Stony River, a major tributary of the Kuskokwim north of Telaquana Lake; K'qizaghetnu is a Dena'ina word for "distant stream."

[7] Lime Village, a small Dena'ina village that dates from the 1930's and was formerly known as "Hungry Village." Hek'dichen Hdakaq' is the Dena'ina word for "lack of abundance mouth."

[8] Kuskokwim River, a 500-mile long river north of Twin Lakes that drains the Alaska Ranges into the Bering Sea.

a hammer but one axe was a pole axe which would serve as a hammer. He wrote of the caribou, the moose and the wolves. Of the Indians and how they lived. I had to read it all before I started my supper but after a once over quickly with my letters. Good news – a few reports on my movie "One Man's Alaska." Only one fault – not long enough. Helen White wrote of the private show the Park Service had put on for my friends in Anchorage and I thought that was real nice of them. How I wish I had been there to see it with them. "It was good and more than good," she wrote. Raymond gave me [the] report after seeing it with his airplane building friend Carl.

February 16 – Partly Cloudy, Blowing dn. & 30°.

So – it was noon and I had a sandwich and I thought of Mardy Murie. She wrote that she had just finished the first draft of the additional chapter for *Two in the Far North* – then added, "I may as well tell you now that you and your sourdough pancakes with honey and onion are in there." She had tried that combination when here for a few hours visit. I must write and tell her "don't forget the peanut butter."

Again I read the manuscript *The Land Beyond* by William Park. It starts "Let us probe the silent places. Let us seek what luck betide us. Let us journey to a lonely land I know." The experience took place in 1937. Park was a educated man. A forester by profession and a graduate of Pennsylvania State College and the University of Alaska. Before he died he willed his cabin (up the lake from Babe's bay) to Babe and Mary. Babe showed me the papers one time and remarked how simple a will could be written and still be legal and binding. William Park was a good man, I wish I had known him.

February 18 – Overcast, Blowing dn. & 31°.

It was near noon and I dragged out some maps. I wanted to see the Swift River country that Bill Park wrote about. The next river beyond the Stony from here. There it was just as he described it. The Rainey Pass Mts. to the south and then some lower mts. which the Indians called the "Dolikes."[9] Caribou and moose and wolf tracks as big as a saucer. He hadn't seen one but he had heard them howl and on answering them they howled again and again. I remember Nixe Mellick saying the south fork of the Kuskokwim has many wolves and big ones. Farewell[10] is on up from the head of the Swift and I had heard of big wolves, wolves as big as ponies. Ken Clark had told stories about the big wolves but when he mentioned 400 lbs. the stories became wolf stories and not much more.

Lime Village on the Stony River was the Indians home village. Hungry was the old name and in the fall the Indians fanned out from there to hunt and trap. 10 days,

---

[9] RLP's "Rainy Pass mountains" are the Teocalli mountains in the central Alaska Range north of Twin Lakes. The "Dolikes" probably refers to the Dena'ina word for the southern Alaska Range, Dzel Ken, "mountain base." It could also refer to Dghelay Teh, which refers to the central Alaska Range.

[10] Farewell is a locality about 24 miles E of McGrath on the Kuskokwim River.

it takes to make the trip from Hungry to Lake Clark an Indian boy had told him. One house along the way – not very far out, maybe four days. One girl had made the trip alone on foot in summer.

February 19 – Overcast, Blowing dn. & 30°.

A few small tasks and some straightening up to do while waiting for the weather to fair up. It refused to cooperate so I loaded up and headed for the Cowgill trail. Maybe I would get some pictures of the gentle one covered with snow. No sign of my broken trail on the lake ice but in the timber it was perfect. No tracks till I got up to the edge of the timber where the trail crosses the creek. There I saw tracks in a low brush choked draw on my right and opposite of the creek. I climbed on towards timberline to see where she had crossed. 50 yards before climbing the bank to the open slope her tracks in mine of last evening. I went back down the trail past where I saw the tracks in the draw and headed that way. I hadn't gone 50 yards and there she was, her back covered with snow. Standing in a bed so she had got up when she heard me coming. Farther up I had seen another bed so I suspect she lays down to rest and chew about two or three times during the night and the same during daylight. It was snowing hard and the wind strong. I crossed the draw and moved up the slope to see if I could get her in the clear. No good, the snow would coat the lens before I could make the exposure so I back tracked and moved in on the up wind side. In the lee of a shaggy spruce I waited for her to move to a better filming position. She shook her heavy coat and the snow disappeared but it wouldn't be long in collecting again. Completely gentle now. She doesn't hesitate to come within 25 feet of me if there is feed that she wants. I was shooting at 100th of a sec. and 250th of a sec. Stop every snow flake in mid air to better show the moose instead of the million oblong white spots. I only exposed a few to show the moose feeding in a snow storm. I could see it coming, she was going to lay down for awhile. Down she went and after a couple more exposures I moved away and down the trail.

February 21 – Partly Cloudy, Blowing dn. & 28°.

The day was about done and the wind getting stronger by the minute. My camp robbers all three here for a bedtime snack. One is a nuisance. I step outside the door and he promptly goes in to sweep the floor for crumbs. I don't dare go back in for fear of him trying to go out the window – so – I wait and wait and peek in to see if he is working or just killing time. Finally out he flies and I can continue my rat killing.

Supper of good bean soup, raw potato and carrot sticks. Cranberry, raisin sourdough bread and my old faithful for dessert. A cup of hot chocolate after dishes.

Now at eight the wind is blowing very hard and I am glad that I am on the lee side of the point. It is overcast and 32°. Today in the Cowgill jungle I saw a rabbit and it was

speckled with brown. Is it this very mild Feb. that is causing it?

February 26 – Partly Cloudy, Blowing dn. & 28°.

Behind the brush patches at the mouth of Emerson big drifted domes of snow eight feet high but the creek flat scoured clean. I was interested in the moose tracks I had seen two days ago. I found one track on the trail through the cottonwoods to the Vanderpool cabin. From the cabin it angled towards the stream & Dry Creek would be my guess for the feeding ground. In the cabin not much worse than last time for it was about as ratty as it could get. Everything edible had been eaten. The paper and plastic that the edibles came in was well scattered in little pieces. While I stood surveying the damage a scrambling behind me as the winter resident made a break for the outside. Where he came from I didn't learn.

From the cabin I took a turn back and then towards the falls. See who lives in Emerson timber. A few rabbit tracks and I saw one rabbit. The track of a lynx cat but none of a fox. My lynx cat had circled the cabin last night. Crossed the trail past the woodshed, coming from Hope Creek. Came out to the lake and down along my beach headed for the Farmer cabin. Very large tracks and brush marks from his long fur on lower legs and feet. The tracks deep in the very loose snow and I wonder who would win the race for survival – he or the snowshoe.

March 3 – Clear, Calm & -8°.

I wish that I knew more about the lake ice and what combination of forces it takes to make it active. Last night as cold as it was the ice was strangely quiet and today too. It can become noisy when the temperature is high (30°) and keep it up as a cold wave moves in. Perhaps air pressure has something to do with it and I wish that I had a barometer to check out that possibility.

Another beautiful morning and I was up to get the hotcakes started at 6:30. Spike's peak caught the first rays of the sun before 7:30 and the days stretching so fast that by my watch I can see the difference each day.

Today I would climb to the big pasture and see how many sheep there were up there and how they were doing. If a plane came, the Park Service exposed film would be on the table.

Carefully I topped the rise and saw sheep. Rams in the bunch but nothing legal. Down near the bottom of the slope and towards Emerson Creek a nice bunch of ewes and lambs. I set up the camera and moved slowly forward. No place to hide while getting in range so easy would have to do it. Of course there is always one to spot the predator. She decided I could stand watching. Heat waves rising from the rocky slope just in front of me

and I had to make the crest of the ridge. Close enough, I could see her thinking and she turned to go. Six went and four stayed and the four were rams. They looked good through that eight power lens. I shot half the roll and waited for the sun to move around to side light the scene. It was warm. No jacket needed the whole time I was on the big pasture.

I counted sheep and was surprised at the number. At least 38 head. A record number if they stay till lambing. Of course the rams will leave and that will make it near normal for May month.

Little airplanes are a lot like flies. Comes warm weather and bright sun and they begin to buzz and fly about. Little ones heading for the Bonanza Hills and little ones returning to the Kenai. One flew low up the lake and didn't return.

March 4 – Clear, Calm & -10°.

At the upper lake it came up the center. A red and white 180 Cessna with a "K" number, a STOL job and he dipped a wing. I knew it was Voight. A second time around before he decided its now or never and down he came. Voight, Sis, the kids and a green mail sack of mail. It was good to see them here. I commented on the good looking airplane. Voight allowed it should be as it had only 150 hours total time on it. An Anchorage dentist the owner. Sis babysits their daughter. Voight has the use of the new airplane for taking care of it.

You have snow here – no snow down on Lake Clark was their observation. Everybody packed something and the cabin was full of people, groceries, and mail. Sis had been shopping for my groceries and that Sis shops as if there will be no tomorrow. Apples, oranges, bananas, lettuce, tomatoes, carrots, onions, cheese, spuds and not just a few of each but enough to last one man a long time if he stayed close to home and spent most of his time to eat it all before it went to pot. A half gallon of ice cream, a full slab of bacon, 25 lbs. of beans, chocolate syrup and a frying chicken. And from her kitchen sourdough coffee cake and chocolate cake. Cookies, more than a gallon. "There," she said, "that should last you awhile."

March 10 – Fog, Calm & 14°.

Climbing higher and I looked back on my left. Sheep, a band of them watching me go trudging up the canyon. I counted ten and there was more. Ewe's and lambs. There I was on the wrong side of them – the sun in my face. A half dozen spooky ones left the bench and headed for Falls Mt. It didn't look as if this was my day in sheep country. I went on up and pulled out on to the big pasture country toward Emerson Creek. Circled down country and would come back at them with a side light. The spooky bunch had stopped to feed a few hundred yards from their starting point. They did a strange thing and with

me moving closer. They headed back to join the others and kept coming. Crossed in front of me and out of sight behind a rise. Slowly I moved forward and peeked over. Feeding, the whole bunch of about 16 or 18. I got down extended the legs on the tripod to clear the rise with the 400 mm and was in business. Plenty close and side lighted. Even the new comers who had seen me were busy picking groceries.

The breeze had come and straight up the canyon. It was cold like I wouldn't believe. My fingers got so cold in my buckskin fleece lined choppers that I was having trouble. Took two hands to work the cable release. I do believe it was colder on the mt. than at lake level.

Little more than a hundred yards away and going about their business. Finally a few took an interest in me and watched which was good. Then they got spooky and headed for Falls mt. again and took most of the bunch with them.

March 11 – Partly Cloudy, Blowing dn. & 26°.

Up to stay at six and it didn't look too bad. Maybe the sun would light the peaks but it never did. Some blowing and drifting. A good stack of sourdoughs for breakfast. Three birds here to get their ration. If they are not here and I call it isn't but a few seconds until two are ready and waiting. The third is usually a few seconds later and I wonder the reason for that. If one is a hen she would be wise to nest close and not miss one welfare check.

Chores done I put some water on for a Saturday nighter in the morning and then shuffled up for my caribou check. Snow was sifting across the benches and I stayed only long enough to make a check for caribou and sheep. I haven't seen a moose at Glacier Creek since January. For a change of scenery I came down the Cowgill trail through the timber and onto the ice. There was a big lynx track made since my last return by that route. The track headed up country.

My plastic water bucket dripping a bit so I mixed up a little epoxy, which is the one item more than anything else that holds "One Man's Wilderness" together.

Overcast began to take charge and the wind picked up. This would be a day to stay close. Write letters and do some small mending jobs. I noticed that my good choppers were beginning to rip at the seams. Some good L.L. Bean linen thread would fix them if I had a needle and I did until I broke it in half. So I repointed it and used half needle. My plastic water bucket dripping a bit so I mixed up a little epoxy, which is the one item more than anything else that holds "One Man's Wilderness" together.

The wind increased to a full gale and it was one continuous cloud of snow going down the lake. Again a large area of snow free ice from Carrithers' point towards Gold Mt.

No chance of outgoing mail leaving until Glen comes the 25th but old letters like old magazine are interesting if you haven't read them before. So I wrote letters and

wrapped a couple journals to go. Studied some from my book *A Field Guide to Animal Tracks* by Olaus Murie. I do believe that I have marten here, but if so, very few. Near quitting time I had a little session with the saw and splitter to round out the day and the wood pile. Boiled spuds with onion bean gravy for supper – lots of oleo, salt, and pepper on the spuds before the gravy. Spuds with jackets on of course.

The wind continuous very strong down and I am thankful that it is down instead of up. It is snowing lightly and the temp. 26°. A good night for sleeping. Listen to the wind until the sandman takes over.

March 12 – Overcast, Blowing dn. & 30°.

Scope and glasses along and I was down the lake buckling on my snowshoes when I thought I heard the lynx cat up country. Just the last of his call and weak but I figured it was his day to pass going down as he had passed going up two days ago. I went on my way to the old campground and took my trail to the semi open slope leading up to the benches. Just out of the timber and I heard it again and quite loud. It sounded that he was at Hope Creek below the gorge. Halfway up the slope is a crossing where he has crossed several times. I went on by to an abrupt rise and a few clumps of runty spruce. There I left my trail and headed up country a hundred feet and then a right turn up the slope behind a light screen of spruce. From there I could see the entire slope from the creek bottom to the mt. I had hopes of seeing my big cat and soon. The wind was perfect. Up country was right into it. Maybe I was there three or four minutes when here came that guy over the open rise a hundred yards away. No brush – a wide open view. I put the glasses on him. A real gray cat, tall and slab sided – hardly wider than the width of my hand. His head was as wide as his carcass. Long legs and straight (no taper) and feet that later on packed snow made tracks wider than my hand. Not exactly what I would call a well proportioned animal. On he came and directly towards me. As the many tracks I have seen indicated, he was walking like a lazy cat. He angled down a bit at a hundred feet and then turned my way again. Came to the point where I had made the right turn and stopped. Ten feet from me and he sniffed my snowshoe track. That stubby half moon tail twitching. For several seconds he smelled of the track, half raised his head and then back to the track. I was making like a dead spruce tree if there ever was one. He moved on six or eight feet and was now getting down wind of me. He stopped turned his head and looked at me but showed no sign that he recognized me as danger. For maybe three seconds he kept his eyes on me and then went on his way at his lazy gait. I stood there until he was out of sight and then some before saying as Babe would, "Now wasn't that something."

March 18 – Clear, Calm & -10°.

A bite to eat and here came a good looking Cessna 180 up the lake. He dipped a wing as he passed and then a turn down the far side. I was going to have company. A landing

up along the beach and then back down to park near my water hole. Three guys and Roy Sanborn of the Park Service was one of them. He carried a small jar and after greeting me with "How have you been?" said, "Here is that instant coffee you asked me to bring." Tasters Choice 100% freeze dried coffee. Net wt. 4 oz. and the price sticker said $3.05. If I was a coffee drinker that would be reason enough to kick the habit. With Roy a man named Paul of the Park Service[11] and the pilot from the Office of Aircraft Services.[12] We came to the cabin. They had been to Port Alsworth and now on their way back to Anchorage. Roy said Glen Van Valin is starting his new log home on an island at the head of Lake Clark and had a big crew helping. No more guiding fisherman for him. Fisherman are a pain in the neck according to him but I'm thinking hunters would be much more so. Now it is going to be float trips, hikers and picture snappers. Glen had sold his place on the island next to Babe's Bay (that is the lodge part of it.) and for an outlandish price. Then he broke the news "Where would be a good place for a large party of about 40 to camp on Twin Lakes?" He had been thinking of Turquoise Lake but it is a desolate place without a tree and being higher the ice goes out later. Early in June would be the time and would the ice be out here by then. "Very doubtful," I said. The 28th of May is the earliest I had seen it go out and June 26th the latest. The party – the [Secretary?] of Interior and other VIP's. Only be for one night which was a relief. I suggested the mouth of Emerson Creek with its good view up the lake. Good timber and the gorge and falls nearby.

They wouldn't have coffee but would have some tea. The water was hot and the order filled. The moose counters, what happened? "Scrubbed it because of little snow cover but they may do it yet." Well they wanted to go by Turquoise, Telaquana, Two Lakes[13] and Chakachamna so had better get flying. As they left the cabin here came a Super Cub – blue and gold – state colors the game warden. More airplanes parked out front than there has been since before freeze up. Dave Cornwall and Vanderpool. The Park Service was gone after a word of greeting. Dave said they could only stay for a few minutes. He inquired how it had gone this winter and had there been much hunter activity. "Real quiet," I said and asked if they had caught any violators. Not one but came close a couple times.

March 19 – Overcast, Lt. Breeze dn. & 26°.

Exactly the type of morning I would choose for this Sunday. I had letters to write and the fog down around the peaks would make it much more agreeable. Hotcakes put away and chores done I got with the program with hardly a thought of my caribou check. My birds kicked up a fuss so I set out a little can of caribou grease to give them something to work at. I wrote till noon without a break. The weather was looking better but I would stay with it. The temp. had climbed to 34° with a light breeze down.

---

[11] Paul Fritz, NPS planner with the Alaska Task Force.

[12] Office of Aircraft Services, aviation arm of the Interior Department supplied aviation support for BLM, NPS, and U.S. Fish and Wildlife Service.

[13] Two Lakes, a glacial lake in the Kuskokwim drainage that lies at the western end of Merrill Pass and was about 35 miles north of Twin Lakes; Tutnutl'ech'a Vena is a Dena'ina word for "black water lake."

Maybe it was thirty minutes later that I heard an airplane coming. A good looking [Cessna] 180 passed low overhead and back down for another circle before landing. This one on wheels and the bare ice an ideal landing area. Two young guys came walking in and I didn't recognize either one. One sporting a heavy reddish brown full beard. Bill Michael his name and later on his airplane I saw fancy lettering "Wild Bill."[14] The other smooth shaven and wearing a long stocking cap was Mike. A brand new Cessna 180 and Bill said he had just brought it up. "Are you the guy who built this cabin and wrote the book?," Bill said. Then he added, "We flew up this way looking for firewood and Mike here says there's that cabin from the book so we had to land."

March 27 – Partly Cloudy, Breeze dn. & 26°.

What bird is the first to come to the lakes in spring? The eagle. I saw a large golden eagle soaring along the edge of the big pasture. Too early for squirrels but in three weeks there may be some. The sun moved behind Falls Mt. and I [went] down the slope to sit and look awhile from the bench and my gear. Finally it was either get on those snowshoes and head down the trail or spend the night on the mt. so down I came.

Near sunset when I came up the path and it drops behind the lower end of the long slope of Falls Mt. at 6:30. It would be very near clear tonight. This afternoon had seen more melting than anytime since the first snows came last Oct. The eaves of the cabin roof dripping and in front the hard packed snow softened. My plastic plug in the water hole didn't freeze in. Spring has sprung just a little and probably only temporary. 8:30 and a few clouds. A very light breeze down and the temp. 24°. Checking just now finds the sky free of clouds. The light breeze down if it continues may hold it to the teens tonight. If it calms it could drop to 10° or less.

March 29 – Overcast, Calm & 24°.

A Cessna 185 came up the far side, turned at my place and came across. Down and around again and I headed for home. Three people waiting on the ice as I crossed. Park Service. Bob Belous, the pilot Bill and a young woman Paula.[15] They had a batch of stuff to pack in. They had come from Glen Van Valin's and they had sent green stuff for salads. They also had four airline box lunches. Bob brought all the slides I had taken since last June plus a batch of fresh film. 10 rolls of 35 mm and a dozen of 16 mm. He had been in Washington, D.C. for months, he said. Came back to find my two letters which I had written months ago. Figured it better to come see me than write. We visited and ate lunch. The woman a film maker for Public Service T.V. [PBS] stations and is making a film including footage that I shot for the Park Service. And she needed a bit more from

---

[14] Bill Michaels, bush pilot and resident of the Kenai Peninsula.

[15] Paula S. Apsell, a Boston based producer for the PBS documentary series Nova/WGBH.

here and of me. So – if it was alright she would come back in a week perhaps with a cameraman and sound man. Do a little talking and filming of me doing some of my usual activities. The completed film would be aired over 250 stations she said. What would we talk about? Oh, such things as what my opinion is of this country becoming a park, etc. I'm thinking the Park Service might not appreciate my point of view being aired over 250 stations. Take the wilderness to the people, millions of them, instead of bringing them to the wilderness. On T.V. anyone with any eyesight at all could enjoy the proposed park area. So she will be back with a crew. I asked Bob to take his film back and put it in the refrigerator. He told me to mark any slides that I would like duplicates of and that I can have a copy of any of the footage I have taken. Fair enough.

April 5 – Overcast, Snowing, Calm & 23°.

This time it [float plane] circled and landed. Only the pilot got out and came to meet me. He introduced himself as Stu Ramstad from Fishtrap Lake. He had been here once years ago but said he had been here when I wasn't here and a couple guys from Soldotna was staying here. He had questioned their right to be using my cabin and they had indicated that they were friends of mine (never heard of them).

We stood in the warm sun on the ice and visited. Stu in his shirt sleeves and wearing well worn out cowboy boots.

He asked me what I thought of the Park idea and said he approved of it whole heartedly. I was to learn later that he is afraid of what the state or the Natives may do if they get control of Fishtrap Lake country. He said that the proposed park boundary has been changed and Fishtrap Lake wouldn't be in the park but in the preserve that surrounds it. I was surprised to hear him say that he doesn't hunt anymore. (He was a guide and got caught with a bunch of illegal brown bear hides in his airplane at Juneau and again they hauled him into court for shooting wolves from the air.) I suspect the reason he is no longer in business is that they took his guides license. Anyway he is now a fishing guide and flies his fisherman around in the Beaver $1,000.00 per day he said. Fly fisherman and they turn them back except for one or two to have mounted. Many of his fisherman come back year after year – repeat business. He is highly unhappy with the hunters these days. Shooting cows due to calve soon and three German hunters shot one of his Labrador dogs for a wolf. Skinned it out, boiled the skull, a great trophy. Couldn't speak a work of English. He had quite a go around with them. He had turned in Dick Mall[16] of Kenai for leaving a lot of garbage at Snipe Lake (Dick had been using Snipe Lake as a caribou hunters camp). He told me the history of his family in Alaska. 90 years they have been here.

April 10 – Partly Cloudy, (Snowing), Breeze up & 18°.

The sun was still high in the sky when I got back and parked the tripod and scope where

---

[16] Dick Mall, a Kenai-based barber, pilot, and guide who was killed while spotting herring from the air in a mid-air collision over Togiak Bay in the late 1970s or early 1980s.

the path comes up from the lake. I trained the scope on the den area and would check again before sundown. I put some water on for a bath and to wash my light quilted jacket and wind pants and then sawed and split wood. No more night stick needs and I split most of them small for cooking. Cleaned up and laundry dripping on the floor I went to the lake for more water. Passing the scope I took a check. Something dark showing that didn't look natural but new rocks and bare spots are showing every day or two. Anyway it didn't move. Coming back with my bucket I looked again. Still there but while I looked it got larger. The bear, she was coming out. Slowly she came – head and shoulders showing. She shook her head and shoulders, I could see plain enough. She came on out and turned around and then worked as if cleaning out or enlarging the entrance. She all but disappeared in the hole and I finally delivered my water to the cabin and got a second bucket full before closing the hole.

Again I headed for Falls Creek with the scope and 40X eye piece along this time. I wanted a good look at her if she came out again. The sun had already left the dens slope when I arrived. I could see where the opening was well enough but she had come up through snow and I couldn't actually see the opening. No bear, she had gone out of sight before I got a fourth of the way across. I waited until the sun threatened to go behind Falls Mt. before I headed back. She didn't show and I doubt that she will before nine or ten in the morning.

April 11 – Overcast, (Snowing), Blowing dn. & 28°.

Now, I was at the same elevation and maybe 300 yards away. Still not much of last falls big den entrance showing. When she came out, she came up more than straight out. No sign of tracks outside of the den. She isn't operating as the last sow with cubs did. That one had a trail maybe a dozen yards long out to the side, same elevation as the den, where she walked slowly out to stand and then return to the den and back in. That would indicate to me that this one is in no hurry to go to work. Just wanted some fresh air and I can understand that. I imagine, 170 days in a den with the entrance plugged with snow. It must smell to high heaven.

I got set up and was ready for business. Still a gentle breeze down and snowing lightly. Some small fog patches that hid the den at times. No action but it only takes a second for it to start. The fog got worse and it was like looking into a bucket of milk. Closing in below too. I couldn't see Carrithers' point and then the shoreline below and then the timber. Socked in tight and there I was, blind on the mt. except for the rocks nearby. Next the breeze died to a trickle and now and again those snow flakes came from down country. That I didn't like. That could lose me a bear before the show started. I doubted that if she winded me she would come out. She would do like the bear did that growled when I got too close. She would wait and leave at night if she thought the cubs were ready. For a time I had a bright spot for sun and it was getting close to the mt. before the fog blanked it out completely.

I stayed and the breeze died completely. Dead silence and I would bet if the bear was out she could hear the camera if I used it. That up lake air came more often and I didn't approve. I was doing no good – better I should get off the mt. I figured it would break as soon as I packed up. It did and mostly above, I could see blue sky and now and then the den entrance across. I held up the operation thinking I might still do some good. More breeze and I called it enough for now. I was afraid I had done too much damage already.

I'm thinking I have a bear problem. Perhaps she knows she is early and won't be in any hurry to get going. Stick her head out of the den now and then. Just often enough to keep me on my toes climbing the mt. It will be worth it if I can be there when she is out for the den is under a snow patch and she and her cubs, if any, will really stand out against the white background. Some rare footage is at stake and I think it is going to take some doing to get it. Keeping the wind in my face is the only problem. The mt. is less than an hour of my time.

Again today only one bird came. I would give a lot to know where the other two are spending their time.

April 12 – Overcast, (Fog patches), Lt. Breeze up & 27°.

About to give it up when I heard a light plane coming and then I saw it descending after crossing the Volcanic Mts. Not Glen I hoped for he wasn't due for three days. The red "T craft" alright and after a few circles it landed just as I neared my beach. It was Glen Van Valin with Laddie the pilot. The first time Glen Van Valin had been here when I was as far as I can remember. They unloaded flour, brown sugar, vinegar, eggs, and raisins, plus some donuts and green stuff compliments of the Van Valin's. They had come to tell me that the Nova film crew would be in Friday morning, early April 14th. Nova the name of the outfit film for T.V. We packed everything in and I stoked the fire for a couple cups of tea. I gave my incoming a quick inspection to see if there was anything threatening. Glen [Van Valin] had been cutting logs for a new lodge and I asked him how it was going. Went fine for awhile and until he lost his little tractor through the ice into 600 feet of water. The ice safe enough but they were crossing a pressure crack. A chunk just the right size to fit the tractor settled slowly down and the driver jumped to the lake ice along side. He has little hope of hooking onto it but will grapple for it when the ice leaves the lake.

Laddie was having Cat trouble and brought his books along. Running fine he said. He closed the throttle to idle position and it went right on down and stopped and hasn't run since. Everything seems ok but no compression. A strange case and I would have to see it to make any suggestions for a remedy.

With all the visiting I didn't get my outgoing ready and would like to add a bit to those whose letters I just received. Glen said the filming crew was coming out to his place

on Friday so I would send it then. May 6th would be the next visit by the "T craft." They climbed in and I pulled the prop and saw them climbing to clear the ridge.

In my mail a letter from Paul Fritz of the Park Service. He will be in charge of this new Park I believe. He and Will Troyer would be in soon he wrote.

I packed my gear and waited for the hour and then headed across. The old girl was laying down at the den again and I figured she was good for an hour or more. The timber trail was soft and slower than two days ago even though more moss shows each day. On the lake a very light breeze down and I wondered what I would find. I didn't want it dead calm or even a very light breeze towards the den.

April 14 – Partly Cloudy, Calm & 32°.

I gave this place a good neatening up. Anything to take my mind away from the tragedy that was shaping up.

If they left Anchorage at 6:30 in a [Cessna] 185 they would be here by eight o'clock, no problem and even if they were a little behind schedule they would be here before I got to timberline if I started at eight.

I packed my gear and waited for the hour and then headed across. The old girl was laying down at the den again and I figured she was good for an hour or more. The timber trail was soft and slower than two days ago even though more moss shows each day. On the lake a very light breeze down and I wondered what I would find. I didn't want it dead calm or even a very light breeze towards the den. The high bench and no airplane. I heard a few but each time it was a jet high up. I climbed on gambling that they wouldn't make it today. To my filming rocks in one hour fifteen. The good load of junk made the difference. I got out from under my load before moving to where I could see the den. Still there and laying broadside to the entrance. Her coat looked clean and it must be a wonderful coat for when looking through the scope, when she shook herself it was three sizes to big. So far no good and I preceded to get both the Bolex and the 400 mm and Exakta set up. It was getting brighter by the minute. I was away from the camera to get my film lined up for a quick change when I heard whining towards the den. I had never heard a cub with such a small high voice. She was in shadow but

I could see a tiny cub spread eagled over her mid section. It looked very small to be the offspring of such a big bear. I was in business and only one run when I heard an airplane down the lake. Not a [Cessna] 185 but the sound of a Beaver. The show would end before it got a good start. I stayed to see how she would take it. The Beaver came low past my place and on above Carrithers' point before it turned back. I was happy that he didn't cross and fly down on the Allen Mt. side. She took it good but when the noise continued she got to her feet and turned to look for its source. Next pass up the lake the plane landed and I started taking things apart. The next time I checked she had gone in the den but I could see her. Before heading down I looked again and she was not visible but I felt sure that she was there.

I was away from the camera to get my film lined up for a quick change when I heard whining towards the den. I had never heard a cub with such a small high voice. She was in shadow but I could see a tiny cub spread eagled over her mid section. It looked very small to be the offspring of such a big bear.

I had left a note on the table outside. It read, "On the other side of the lake, be right back." To the lake in record time and the ice wet and slick where there was no snow. Halfway and some one headed out to meet me. It was Paula the producer. "Sorry we were late," she said. "The plane hadn't been fueled and we were late taking off." She asked me if I had seen anything and I told her of the big bear and twins. She was sorry for spoiling my good opportunity. On the way to the cabin she told me something of the program for today and about the film plus where and when it would be shown. Nova is the name of the program and it is scheduled to be shown June 28, 1978 (most places) on PBS – (the Public Broadcasting System) and these stations are in most major cities.[17] I asked her if I would realize any pay for my part today. I was unhappy to lose that good bear footage. They had said they would be here last week. Yes I would be paid and how much did I think it was worth. I had no idea and told her she was in the business and would know what was fair. "How about a hundred dollars?" I would think more than that in view of what I was losing. Well then how about $225.00 or $250.00. That would be better and how about a copy of the film. "Yes, that could be arranged easy enough," she said.

I met the crew. Bill Bacon of "William Bacon Productions" from Anchorage as cameraman. The sound man name I don't remember. Paul Fritz of the Park Service who took Fred Eubanks place and Paul Johnson pilot of the Sea Airmotive Beaver. Johnson I had met at Polar when he was pilot there. He was the pilot who would take skydivers to 12000 feet alt. and be on the ground with the engine dead when they landed. He was doing that with a Turbo Porter.[18]

They had brought a big sack of groceries and seemed in no hurry to get started.

[17] The Nova program was to be called "Alaska, The Closing Frontier."
[18] The Pilatus PC-6 Turbo Porter.

Paula gave me a briefing on what we would talk about in the interview and what footage they wanted of me packing camera gear.

They finally finished up with me packing my backpack across out front left to right and coming up the path. At no time did they include the cabin in the picture. I don't know how much footage Bill shot but suspect it was 2000 at least. Film seems the least of their worries. Shoot a scene and shoot it again and again to pick the best of the lot.

They climbed in and I put the scope on my bear to see how she would take the growl of the big Beaver. She was bedded down and didn't raise her head during warmup and takeoff. The last I saw of the Beaver is was betwixt and between the ground and the low ceiling. Paul Fritz had taken the Park Service slides and my outgoing mail along with five dollars for postage. So – my income tax deadline has been met – a good feeling.

The overcast lowered as I was sawing and splitting after cleaning up the leftovers. It started to rain pushed by an up lake breeze. The first rain this year and since the snows first came in Oct. My bear still on the mound before the rain started but no doubt she and the little ones are snug and warm in the den. Too bad those little guys can't enjoy the protection of that nice home for another month or two.

Now at nine the wind is strong up the lake, rain pelts the big window and the temp. is 31°. The moisture more snow and ice than rain I find on second check.

April 15 – Overcast, (Lt. snow), Calm & 26°.

The sun moved around facing the entrance and I could see in better. I could see her head and its sudden drop as bears heads do when they decide to sleep. Finally she was getting closer and I had my finger on the button and looking through that 200 mm lens. I wanted to get her coming out and out she came to stand and shake that heavy coat. It appeared that she has something in mind. She turned this way and that and went no place. Then she stepped into the snow leading to bare mt. side maybe forty feet away and across the bottom of the wash near the den. She turned hindquarters down the mt. and stood looking at the den. I knew what she wanted. She wanted the cubs to come with her. Two of them at the entrance but they wouldn't leave it and whined like little puppy dogs. She went farther and waited. They knew they were supposed to follow or they wouldn't cry about it. She went all the way to bare ground and stood looking their way. They moved to the snow near the dirt mound but no farther. She went back and climbed above the den and I could see that strong limp. They climbed a few feet but no farther. She came down and went to the side a second time. Then I saw something I had never seen before. I saw a sow pick up a cub by the nape of the neck and carry it a few steps and drop it, a few years back. This old mother picked a cub up by a hind leg and backed towards bare ground. The second one followed after a fashion. They seemed afraid of that steep snow patch. Now a surprise. I saw a third cub at the entrance. Triplets! for sure. It was the real scaredy cat. Always seems to be one in the litter who doesn't go for adventure. Now she had two of them

about twenty feet from the den but how about that last one. She left those and went to the den. She didn't touch him but evidently talked him into it for it followed cautiously. Now she had the three of them in a bunch. Again she picked one up by a hind leg and walked backwards with the little guy dragging its front feet. The other two followed and she soon had them on the snow free mt. side. I had been filming, winding the camera, changing rolls at a rapid pace and ran dry on the third roll just as she got them on dry ground. I hadn't missed much. Now all I had was the last roll for the Park Service, so I put it in. No time to use the Exakta and 400 mm.

April 18 – Clear, Calm & 10°.

Nothing until I saw a cub at the entrance of the den. She had taken them back for the night. And then I saw her where I had seen her last among the brown rocks. She was on her feet and moving up to the dirty trail on the snow leading to the den. All three cubs came out and went to meet her. She came to the edge of the snow and layed back against the slope so they could have their hotcakes. It takes them ten minutes or more to have a meal and she is very patient. All tanked up and she crossed the snow to the den and entered. One went in with her but the other two stayed out to play. Soon the third came out and not long after the mothers head appeared. "You kids get right in here," she said, and they got, and promptly.

April 19 – Clear, Breeze dn. & 26°.

I set up the Bolex just in case some action did come before the sun went behind the mt. Maybe I had been there ten or fifteen minutes when she slowly got to her feet and soon headed towards the den. The cubs trailing along behind. At the dirty path in the snow going to the den she hesitated and I wondered what she had in mind. I figured the cubs would head out for the den after sleeping out last night. She started to climb on up the mt. and then across a hundred feet above the den. Directly above it she started down but only came a fourth of the way before turning left and out on the ridge forming the edge of the den area slope. There she started to lay down for the cubs to suck but one was slow behind and she got up and stood waiting for the little guy. All three there and it was lunch for three. End of the roll and I changed. When I was ready to go she was heading across the face of the mt. – headed up country. Feeding now for the first time except just a very little from time to time. She rolled a few rocks down the mt. and used that lame foot to do it. They crossed one ridge and then another. Those little guys having a time on the steep patches. Clawing and scratching on the steep too smooth rocks but they made it. Of all the wild little ones I think they are about the most defenseless. Without the protecting by their mother they would be easy prey for wolf, wolverine, or a male bear which is their biggest threat. Out of sight and that was the end of the four bears. I felt certain that they

268

wouldn't return to the den again unless they come back to it next October. So – they left the den area on the 10th day after she came out the first time on April 10th. Two nights the cubs had slept away from the den and the mother one had slept outside almost as much as she had inside but always very close. Nobody, but nobody could get near the cubs while she was on duty. So – wasn't that something. Three different days I had filmed her coming out of the den and moving the cubs and now I had arrived just in time to film her leaving. The complete operation and it just has to be good or my camp robbers are going to find me pretty hard to live with.

April 23 – Partly cloudy, Breeze dn. & 30°.

I had just reached the far shore when I thought I heard a plane and as if it was on the ice. Sure enough one was just turning around over near my water hole marker. A white and cream Cessna 180 and only faintly visible on the snow white lake. I headed for home. Three were headed for the cabin. Who could that be. 33 Charlie the number and I didn't remember. In close I did. Nixe Mellick, the pilot from Sleetmute on the Kuskokwim River. He introduced the two guys with him – both from Sleetmute. They had just come from his cabin over on Telaquana Lake and going home. Nixe had a Nevada bird hunter here last fall and told me today that they had a hunting accident after leaving here. The hunter had shot at some birds – the shot glanced off a boulder to a second boulder and hit him (Nixe) in the side of the head. Five or six shot went under the skin and he can still feel one in there. The man had been back in January to hunt wolves but they didn't get any. Nixe had done good on marten trapping from his home. Sixty marten and the champion of the area. Very little snow at Sleetmute he said and they think the ice may go out in about a week. Very few April break ups of the Kuskokwim. I mentioned Glen Alsworth's manuscript by William Park. Hungry Village, Stony River and the Swift. Nixe knows that county and some of the Natives at Hungry Village. He would sure like to read that paper. I remembered the tape I had made and asked him if he would like to hear it. He sure would so I dug it out and got it going. He sat and listen, nodded his head and smiled when he heard a familiar name. Some of the Natives still lives. Ebonga for one and now past seventy. He made notes of part of it and would question old timers about people mentioned. He would like to play that tape and see how much they remembered. I told him I would ask Glen if it was ok that I pass the contents of the paper on and if it was ok I would mail the tape to him. Glen would agree I know but better to ask him first. Nixe told me a lot about Hungry Village. It was named right he said. A very tough place to live and they survived where very few could. Nearly a 100% meat diet. Where the white man would throw the lower legs of the moose away – they (the Natives), cooked them first. The marrow out of those big heavy bones was choice food. The big heavy hams of the hind legs that the white man prizes most they feed to their dogs. It's the bones and the meat and fat close to them that they want. Hungry Village is down, down and he turned his thumbs down. No more hunting and trapping on the Swift or anywhere. They are on welfare

now. Five years ago a school was built. Nixe says he has a good collection of equipment (hunting, fishing and trapping) made by the hungry Indians on the Stony. He is interested in learning all he can and recording it for before many years it will be gone forever.

April 26 – Overcast, Blowing dn. & 35°.

Three young rams still in spring training – walking towards each other on their hind legs. I laid back against that warm dry slope and took five before resuming my watch for a bear that I figured might have moved down closer to timberline and I couldn't cover that area, so, I would move to the bare knoll. I set up there and held rollcall of every rock face and grassy bed where I had ever see a bear. Nothing and I swung back to the den. There she was big as life, why that old hussy. Still standing in front of the entrance. How such a huge looking bear can get into a small den and still have room for three cubs is beyond me. She shook her blanket and moved slowly away. No cubs showing and how come. I should think those frisky cubs would be wild to get out. She had moved away fifteen feet or more before the first one showed and the other two were slow in coming out. They romped around and right to the edge of that super steep snow patch but not one went out to test it. She fed a little but very little and got no farther than twenty five or thirty feet from the den. Suddenly she turned and carried that lame left foot as she did. Marched right back to the den. The cubs in first and then her and head first. That was it for today as if there never was a bear on the mt. She was gone. Here it is sixteen days since she came out and she is lolling around doing very little and not eating in 16 days as much as I eat for breakfast each morning. The show was over. I headed across with the strong wind on my port side.

April 27 – Partly Cloudy, Blowing dn. & 30°.

I climbed out of the brush patch to go and was surprised to see those young rams at the base of the big rock face. The same three that was in spring training yesterday. I went that way and finished the roll as they climbed up around the end of the face.

In the protection of the timber I changed film and continued my rabbit hunt. I saw one but he wouldn't cooperate and I lost him. I headed down and ended up on Falls Creek – climbed to the game trail crossing, came down the other side. There in the timber the biggest surprise in years. Birch trees thirty feet tall.[19] Three of them growing from a common stump. Six inches or more in diameter. A porkypine had peeled a patch on one. I had seen no more than two birch at Twin Lakes and they were very small and no larger than willow brush.[20] I headed across to the creek to get located in case I wanted to find them again.

Past six when I got back and checked from here. She may be laying there on top

[19] Either paper birch, Betula papyrifera Marsh or Kenai birch, Betula Kenaica Evans would be exceedingly rare at Twin Lakes. Dwarf birch, Betula nana and shrub birch, Betula glandulosa are both common in Twin Lakes country.

[20] There are approximately twenty two species of willow in Lake Clark National Park and Preserve.

of that rock face. If not I'll hold roll call on all the rocks of the mt.

Two more meals of chicken and I hate to part company with that bird. Mixing my sourdough batter for morning and when finished I always lick the rubber scraper. Tells me if I forgot anything. Tasted nothing but flat this time so I added the sugar and dry milk.

Now at nine o'clock, the wind she is still blowing strong down. Strange that it feels warm in Jan. & Feb. but now it feels cold at the same temp. Partly cloudy and 32°.

April 28 – Partly Cloudy, Blowing dn. & 32°.

One more time I would go check. She was out and above the den. Two cubs with her. Cautiously I moved out for a clear shot. She waited for that third cub to come out and wouldn't go farther until it did. Little slowpoke finally came and they moved onto the slope. Now I was doing good. Facing the slope with a big brownie and three dark cubs. I noticed they all have white collars now and one cub is lighter in color than its mates. Looking through the viewfinder with film in the camera is much easier than fresh out of ammunition. She fed and the cubs romped about. I notice that she is hooking those big front claws and pulling back now. She is digging for food. Down to the last ten feet and I was sure she would nurse the cubs soon. If I ran it through I would have my head in that fool film changing bag when the action was taking place. I waited and waited. Finally it came and I wasted my film. It was a false alarm. I hurried to change and came back to find them nursing. I wanted some with the 400 mm and still camera after lugging them up the mt. So, I got set up and shot a few. Moved back and down and across again. Then I saw my way clear to get plenty close and too close if she came to the den. She was laying back to me and what if she got up and moved up the slope. My avenue of escape across the loose noisy rock would be cut off. I shot a couple frames and moved back. If it calmed too soon she would probably learn I had been there.

It was five and snowing like crazy while I packed to come down the mt. I came down by den no. 1 and looked at it again. I could easily reach the back side with my walking stick which is 4'3" long. Certainly it was no more than six feet to the back from the entrance when it was dug.

April 30 – Overcast, Breeze dn. & 35°.

I neglected my bears for a time and lost them so after lunch I took glasses and scope up towards the point. The glasses wouldn't find her so I would have to look closer. Set the scope up and trained it on the area and there she was without moving it. She had climbed higher than she had slept last night and was now just the smoothest brown rock on the mt. Resting and I could see a cub now and again. I noticed yesterday that when she lays curled the cubs are on the inside of that curl and sometimes one will be under her neck.

Today the last day of April. I would check the ice. A good distance out to clear any airplanes coming on wheels. I cut a hole. No more than three inches down I struck

water and couldn't chop without a lot of splashing so I used the chisel. The ice still in good shape and about 30 inches thick. At my water hole in close about 23 inches.

Letters to write, my bed to put together and outgoing mail to freshen up a bit. My bear to watch and she moved very little this afternoon. I'm afraid I couldn't have done much good on the mt. today. I saw a great scattering of sheep on both mts. and why they should be spread so thin I don't know. Another two weeks should see some new lambs.

This morning the sun tried to shine a bit but lost out to the overcast. The temp. reached 46°, the highest I have seen it this year.

A good bowl of popcorn late and a light supper. My crying nesters came but wouldn't give me a clue as to where their nests were. Today I saw for the first time a camp robber play with a red squirrel. The squirrel would come rushing out from the trunk of the spruce to the bough ends to chase the robber away. In turn the robber would dart at him when he was in the open. For several seconds they tormented each other. No sign of anger – just playing.

So now comes the month of May. The month of some greenery on the south slopes, the month of new lambs and caribou calves and possibly a few moose calves. The birds will return and I should see a robin soon. Sometimes they show on the south slope across the lake before here. Possibly the ice will leave the lake before June first. Twin Lakes comes alive in May. Sunlight unlimited. Soon it will clear Crag Mt. Now at 7:45, overcast, a breeze down and 40°. 40° the warmest evening temp. this year and on checking the record I find that April had an average morning temp. of 24, -2° the low temp. for the month. April was only a few degrees warmer than Jan. with an average morning temp. of 20°.

My bear is set for the night. Not at the base of a rock face or on top but against the lower side of a big rock on a scree slope in a steep swale.

May 4 – Fog, Calm & 30°.

Today had been declared a Twin Lakes holiday so there was no rush. To get up at five would be plenty good. It was like a morning in May after the shower of last night. Fog created a very low ceiling so there would be no searching for bears until near noon.

After my hotcakes I dug out a SOS pad and proceeded to brighten up my cooking utensils and my battered aluminum tea kettle. I would like to know the history of that old faithful kettle. I found it on the rocks of the lower lake shore a third of the way down the right hand side. Badly battered and a leak in the spout which I epoxied. I hammered out most of the dents and made a new cover which finally rusted out so I made a second and the present one.

Today I would write letters for part of the day at least. Plane day May 6th and I am expecting a good load of mail. April 12th was the last mail in. So – I wrote and

watched the fog slowly clear out. By one o'clock when I finished writing it had cleared the peaks.

I would have a special and good supper this holiday. I had baked some nice light sourdough biscuits and used up the last of my makings for a green salad. Opened a G.I. can of beef with spiced sauce and spiced it up more with chili powder, bacon grease, onion and corn meal. A generous helping of good beans and with my old standby dessert I would open Spike and Hope's fruitcake from Christmas time. Too full, I would save it. Two of my birds came and I'm surprised that I haven't seen a robin. I heard geese yesterday but none today.

It was calm and nearly clear while I was doing dishes but now at 7:30 a strong breeze is blowing up the lake. A few clouds over head and the temp. 36° after being 42° not more than 45 minutes ago. And so ended May 4th, the day of days and my birthday.

May 5 – Partly Cloudy, Calm & 28°.

The den I was anxious to see inside. It was larger than the hibernation den by quite a bit but not quite so deep. From the top of the entrance to the back wall it was four feet. About three feet across in the living quarters and about 30 inches high. The old sister had raked some grass and very light brush to make a fresh bed in it. Bears are pretty sharp but do have their weak points. Right in the middle of the nest was a big rough rock that stood up six inches or more. She can rake grass, why can't she rake a boulder out of the bed. I reached in and retrieved it. Also a heavy pointed rock protruding from the rear wall. It was a gouger for sure. Out it went. A timer shot of my crawling in and coming out head first indicated I could easily turn around inside. I set up the Exakta with wide angle and flash. Everything set and the button mashed – no flash. I had rotated the flash head plug in the camera socket to be sure of a good connection. I worked it more and wasted another one – no flash. I should have tested it with the lens cap on and saved two exposures. The sun was in and out so I waited for cloudy bright and made time exposures 1 sec. at 10. It looked good with fairly even light in the viewfinder. The flash I would get even with it when I got it home. A couple of me reclining in the nest and wouldn't it be something if that old girl came back for an afternoon nap.

Good enough and I packed to go down the mt. It was a pretty day with a good breeze from the upper end. Coming down I angled over to a point where I had seen her bedded down. There I found droppings from both her and the cubs, it appeared. Probably not the first since she came out of hibernation but probably the first after moving into den no. 2. The plug was composed of dry grass for half its length and then blending into a mixture of berries and probably roots and grass. So – I expect to get her system in operation she does eat a quantity of dry grass. Iowa farmers starting feeder lambs shipped in from the western states, fill them up on dry hay. The droppings of the cubs appeared to contain many berries and I wonder how she gets them started on solid food. I saw the cubs scratching and at other times they appeared to be eating mossberries. One time after

nursing the cubs I saw something that made me think that she may teach them to eat what she eats. It was on the slope facing me and I could see very good with the glasses. She had them all together on the open slope and climbed a few steps and layed down. The three cubs stayed with head in a huddle as if eating something and they stayed a couple minutes at least. Did she up chuck some food she had just eaten – I think she may have, I'll have to ask Will Troyer for he knows all about bears but didn't know that they usually back into the den. So – all he really knows is that the wind blows.

May 6 – Overcast, Blowing dn. & 35°.

In a letter sent out with the Nova crew I had told him not to land unless I gave him the signal. He knew it was good but came around again. Arms straight out to the sides is the land signal and it wasn't long until he came driving up the lake with the tail two feet above the ice. The wind was still strong out there. I directed him to the beach at the breakwater. The ice still hard and hooked to the beach there. Glen was alone this trip. 20° at 6,000 ft. he said. Part of Lake Clark is open and so is Babe's Bay. We packed in the groceries and mail. My movie "One Man's Alaska" had come to Van Valin's and they had a show. Good but too short he said. He wanted to come get me but the weather was bad for a few days. The film would go to Nondalton and then back to Anchorage. Glen said his mom is coming back this summer and if I remember correctly they have a cow on their Hawaiian ranch now. Working on the airstrip at home.

I was thinking that if they disturbed the soil by grading or dozing that it would blow, which it did pretty bad anyway. I ask him about that. "Well, we are trying to think of a way to sprinkle it," he said. "Would like to oil it but it would cost a fortune."

Bill Johnson, his neighbor, got part of a finger cut off cranking his airplane. His procedure was to prime it and then standing in front flip the propeller eight times (4 revolutions) then turn the mag. switch on and away she goes. This time he absent mindedly turned the switch on when he primed it. It started and chopped a finger. He won't do that again – at least not with that finger. I was licking my mail shut while we visited. We discussed the issue of when he should come again. Three weeks would be early I thought but the ice just might be out by June 1st. We agreed that he would come June 3rd. If I still have ice I will meet him at the lower lake.

I asked him about postage money. I was sure that Pat had used all I had sent. He didn't know and wouldn't take any. He would put it on the book. I had 20 letters and a half dozen parcels to go.

I seen him off – flipped the prop with him at the controls. Into the wind after taxing down the lake a quarter, he was off in no more than a hundred feet it seemed.

My grub – he isn't the good provider that Babe was. I had ordered onions he brought five and one of them bad. All they had he said. Rolled oats I ordered 30 lbs. or more – good old roll oats groats – oats for livestock – he brought 3- 2 lb.,10 oz. cardboard cans of quick oats. For quantity users it says on the can. A couple dozen eggs – I had 4

doz. A good supply of spuds and a big economy size box of soap powder.

My mail. A package containing peanuts, candy bars and a box of 35 mm slides from brother Jake. Two boxes from Helen White. One, another loaf of cranberry bread and this evening I tried some. It arrived in perfect condition and very good. In the other package envelopes and tablets which I had requested she get for me. In a little packet big needles with eyes for heavy thread. Needles to last for the duration and on the packet the price 10 cents. That can't be. Is there anything in Alaska costing only 10 cents? Letters from everybody – more than twenty, plus three or four from the bank of Kodiak. They finally have me up to date with the checking account but no letter of explanation which I requested. It was 10:30 before I got through the stack and looked at the slides. Very little of a constructive nature had been accomplished, but, so what. This was a Twin Lakes holiday.

I did have a job in mind that I wanted to do. Go down and dismantle that miserable German hunting camp below the Herb Wright sheep camp at the head of the lower lake. The big plastic covered contraption stood out like a sore thumb. Like a white wall tent pitched among the spruce fifty yards in from the lakeshore. The wind was up again but that would push me down. I could travel the game trail coming back if I didn't want to face it.

My ripping hammer and little double bit axe would do the job. Those Germans must have been carpenters and came prepared to build a permanent camp. The winter storm had wretched the plastic but the framework was still intact. Nailed with 16 penny nails and a big handfull once I got them all pulled. Trees limbed in a reckless fashion. Trees at two feet and more above the ground. Poles, I must have had a stack of a dozen and a half when I got them neatly piled. The plastic I wadded into a big ball and stuffed it under a shaggy spruce. Cans and bottles – one bottle, a huge wine bottle. The tall stumps I chopped close to the ground and piled the chunks for further firewood. It looked pretty neat when I finished and would be a good campground with poles ready to build a lean to. It was three when I bagged up the bent nails and got under my pack for the trip back. Again I tried for a trout but what trout would grab a mouthful of hooks on a windy day like this?

May 12 – Partly Cloudy, Breeze dn. & 42°.

The lake ice seemed safe enough but I wouldn't get caught because I thought it was and it wasn't. I went up to Hope's cabin and dragged out the sled and my homemade skis. The sled is a good rig. I can haul my gear plus an eight foot 2x8" plank. Pushing it I can put some of my weight on the handle bars and it makes enough noise on the rough ice to kill the squeaking. Nothing makes you feel so alone as to be out over 200 feet of water and have nothing to help carry your weight when you hit a soft spot.

I saw a Cub on big, big wheels flying around over the low country below the lower lake. That guy could land many places and where the bear was wouldn't be far from one of them. Bear season opened May 10th and I suspect that was the reason the yellow Cub

and the blue Cessna on floats were there. Strictly against regulations to spot bear but you can't fine a man for looking down when he is flying and sees a bear.

May 15 – Partly Cloudy, Breeze dn. & 40°.

No camera gear this trip and I headed for Low Pass beach to get out of the wind. Before I got there I checked with the glasses. Ah ha! one ready and waiting up in the rough stuff. I was glad to see one there. I had the scope along so promptly set it up to have a look. Sure enough one laying back in under an over hanging rock face. A gentle inclined ledge along the face of the rock face leading up to where she lay. A second ewe feeding at the start of the incline and I took it to be a yearling and her lamb of last year. Often they will stay with the mother for sometime after she has a new lamb. I went on down and picked a spot out of the wind. I could see two more ewes low down where the six head were yesterday morning. Two ewes not accounted for. My lambing ewe was a hundred feet or more directly above where I thought one might lamb and where I have seen them before. A tough spot to film for there was nothing as high and out far enough to see into her little hideout. She was back in far enough that the morning sun had not yet reached her. Laying there with her head up and soon she became active. Her head moving about and I wondered, what now? She got up and then I saw a lamb on its feet and eager for some warm milk. It had come last night for yesterday morning she was still a few hundred feet down the mt. and feeding. A tiny little guy and didn't show white as much as it will in a day or two. Its belly full and showing no more interest the ewe promptly layed down again and the lamb between her and the rock wall. She had made a wise choice for lambing. The golden eagle couldn't attack from above and the mother would put up a good fight on the rock ledge. I have never seen the eagles try to get a lamb but I don't doubt that they could and do occasionally. Babe came once and said he had just seen two golden eagles trying for a little caribou calf in the Big Valley beyond the Volcanic Mts. The cow was so frantic trying to fight them off that she fell. He had come on over the mt. and didn't know if the eagles were successful.

May 20 – Overcast, Calm & 30°.

As I traveled the beach I watched the slope to see if they were moving up. I saw something but not caribou. A big wolverine loping along high on the slope up country from the glacier tailing piles of Gold Mt. In the bright sun a beautiful sight. Dark brown with the broad cream wolverine stripes. The first wolverine I had seen during this last year at the lake. It traveled a crooked course as if hunting and finally concentrated on one small area. Then it began to dig and I could see handfuls of dirt fly. The wolverine with those long claws and powerful legs must rival the badger when it comes to making the dirt fly. As it twisted and turned that twin cream stripe flashed almost white in the sun. Its head was up as much as

down for Mr. Skunk Bear is a great one to be on guard for anyone that might surprise him. Who his natural enemies are I don't know. As the bear is, perhaps he is his own worst enemy. I thought of heading for home and the camera but knew he would be long gone by the time I got back. He dug and made progress and then searched around a bit as if he had lost the parky squirrel-at no time did it appear that he was eating anything. Probably it was ten or fifteen minutes before he continued on his way up country. Climbing as he went and finally into a scabby outcrop of rock choked with brush. I watched for another ten minutes for him to come out and continue on but failed to see him. If he had caught a squirrel and ate it, would he lay up for a while? He might, I figured so I hurried on and would be ready for him when he set out again.

May 23 – Overcast, (Lt. Rain), Blowing dn. & 42°.

Rabbits on the move at Spike's cabin. I saw three running around as if looking for some choice green stuff. On the beach the clear sharp print of a lynx cat in the sand. It isn't only in winter that the rabbit is hunted.

Now at eight overcast, blowing very strong down and the temp. 44°. The open pool out front is larger than at mid morning regardless of the acres and acres of ice that have move into it. By morning the lake should be considerably more than half ice free. From the mt. I could see that the lower lake was ice free to Gatano's beach. About 180 days from freeze up to break up.

May 24 – Partly cloudy, Breeze dn. & 40°.

I left the ridge and headed to the mouth of the dry stream bed coming out up country from the Pyramid Mt. This stream bed is always a source of wonder to me. Sheer walls of rock on either side and the bed wide and nothing but crushed rock. I have never seen water flow there but during an Aug. flood it comes wall to wall. I think that the mts. on that side of the lake at least should have been included in the park. It is like Glen says about the park area, "Nearly all of it is good for nothing except to look at." The Volcanic Mts. have scenery that can not be found anywhere else in the park.

As I did last fall I passed the scene of the tragedy that took the lives of several caribou. Broken bones, antlers, hooves, and hair covering a small area. A very steep chute coming down from the mt. wall. A snow slide had caught them there or was it rocks.

May 30 – Partly Cloudy, Lt. Breeze up & 35°.

On a big rock, a rock ptarmigan just starting to turn. Instead of brown it has black

markings on its head and neck. A very cooperatives bird and I got close enough to fill the viewfinder and used maybe 30 feet of film...There was a moose laying on the bank of the upper of the two ponds. Exactly where I had filmed the cow with twins in '76. Now! I was having a little luck. A light colored moose means its nearly sure to be a cow and calving time is close. I headed down the mt. with the high ground facing fox pond as my goal. Still laying down when I looked over the ridge. In a little opening surrounded by brush on three sides. The pond on the forth side and it was my side. I found a good blind and got set up. If she calved today I would be the first to know for I would stay till the lights went out. She layed there with her ears back as if something was on her mind. I waited and learned that my Kelty is the best of protection against mosquitoes. The light borderline and maybe a little weak. Much waiting and then I saw something dark at her side. A calf on its feet and nuzzling at her flank. A second calves head appeared from the brush nearby. Twins and very small and wobbly legged. She got to her feet and one searched for a nipple. So small that he could easily walk under her belly with his head high. She obligingly lifted a hind leg so that he could find the teat. The other one moved in on the other side and I was doing good business. Filled up they promptly layed down. She fed a little but very little and layed down too. I moved to a better location and waited. The light went dim due to overcast. Down to 2.8 and I was about ready to call it good for today and then I waited. I wanted to see how long it would be before they nursed again. It was a long wait, more than a hour at least. Finally blue sky began to move down the lake. First I was afraid they wouldn't suck again and now I was afraid they would before the sun came and gave me light. It came, the calves got up and went to the cow. She got up they nursed and I ran out of film just as the cow layed down again. The sun went back into hiding and I packed to go. While I packed the cow came down the bank and took a big drink from the pond and then climbed back up and started to feed. The calves still up and moving about. I came on up to Low Pass beach after staying well inland to keep my scent from her. I'll bet she is a tame cow and I will learn before she moves away. To show myself now might cause her to keep the calves more in hiding than she would otherwise.

June 3 – Clear, White Frost, Calm & 27°.

A very beautiful morning just after sunrise. The lake flat as glass, white frost on the cabin roof. This had to be the best morning of the spring season. I was up early for I didn't want Glen to catch me with a lot of finishing up to do. Hotcakes and a good stack. Oatmeal, I hoped he would bring some for I was running low. Dishes done and I got my outgoing mail ready, my cabin in order. Bright sun, this would be air bedding day. Raked my beach and still no "T craft."

I heard the "T craft" coming and he came in high over the glassy smooth water. Nose high she settled like a swan coming in to land. Dropping a little fast it splashed into the air again but only a foot. He made a step turn and came racing towards my beach. I saw that he had a passenger with him. Like his dad he hopped out and stopped her

from crunching onto the coarse gravel. "Boy! that water is smooth!" he said. Even from altitude you can't tell where the surface is unless you look at the shoreline. "What's new outside," I ask him. "Postage has gone up to 15 cents," he replied. My 20 outgoing would cost me $3.00 or more.

Glen said he would have been in early but had some flying to do. Ferried in a batch of gear plus a few cases of beer to Caribou Lakes[21] for the state geophysical group.[22] They stayed awhile and we visited on the beach. "Say! What kind of tracks are these?" he said raking his foot over my rake marks in the gravel. I told him I was dressing up the beach thinking he might bring some pretty tourists in. Vic wants to come he said and so does Doris & Flo [mission girls] and Glenda (Laddie's wife). I'll bring them in this summer sometime. He told me the Ntl. Park Service does want to build at Port Alsworth. They want 15 acres at Pike Bay which is in the far corner of Babe's bay towards Tanalian Falls. "Bee [Alsworth] is selling land like crazy," Glen said. Getting $16,000 a lot and nothing on it. I had heard he wants to sell his new home and the ground it sets on for $200,000.

June 4 – Partly Cloudy, Calm & 30°.

A very quiet night but porkypines running all over the place this morning. When I went to the beach for a bucket of fresh water I caught one rasping on my heavy rustic chair under the spruce. I promptly got a bucket of water and wet that rascal down good. During the past week I have been thinking that a well cooked porkypine would be good for a change.

I headed back over the top and down the long trail to the beach. It seemed good to get off the steep stuff and rocks to the park like area of the spruce. Going up I had watered up at the game trail crossing and coming back I hit it again. I thought of Terry Gill in his letter. He wrote, "It is nice here on Lake Clark. The grass tall enough to cut for hay, it is warm and no mosquitoes but the wood and water is no good and it is noisy." I wish he and Vic would come to Twin Lakes for a few days. Here the wood and water is the best and it is as quiet as the Bonanza Hills. I came on down to the beach to listen to the lake make its threatening sound and I wondered if it would calm come sundown. Banner clouds from the high ones answered that question. Just as well make this the first of quite a few to come so – I loaded up and pushed out. I knew I couldn't make my beach and I might do good to make one mile rock. One thing for sure I could make the far side and walk the rest of the way if I had to. She pitched and rolled but she took on very little water. I was making good course almost straight across and would hit the beach just below the Farmer's lower bend in the beach. Coming up along shore I noticed Hope Creek running a trickle of water into the lake.

Supper over and dishes done, I was writing when there came two rasping sounds

---

[21] Caribou Lakes are a group of small lakes about 30 miles SW of the Proenneke Site.

[22] RLP probably refers to the Division of Geological & Geophysical Surveys in the Alaska Department of Natural Resources.

loud and clear. On the corner of the cabin, that's where it was. I was out the door in a flash and with walking stick in hand I was around back a few seconds later. He was leaving but only started. I left no doubt in his mind that the cabin was off limits. Had it been earlier he would have been cooling his carcass in the woodshed.

June 5 – Overcast, (Raining), Blowing dn. & 40°.

Two in the morning and porkypines climbing the wall. I bounced out of my bunk and was around back in short order. No porky in sight. They are not so dumb. Rough one up a time or two and he remembers. Dislodge him a couple times as he tried to climb a tree and he will stay on the ground. As I came back around front there was one past the clothesline. It tried to climb but I wouldn't stand for it and so he went out of sight among the spruce without trying to climb another. Last fall I had them avoiding the cabin area and I will again or eat a few.

At that time in the morning no sign of rain real soon, but when I woke up at five it was raining a good rain and I was glad to hear it. I wanted to stay close today and get a few projects done. My little kicker had a minor crack in the plastic cover that I would epoxy. Glen's born again passenger was so fascinated with the door and latch on my cabin that he had to see how it worked. He broke the little night latch handle. It had been broken and glued a couple times before this time. I would fix it good. Make a wide saw cut in each of the broken ends and in the cut epoxy a thin strip of axe handle hickory. Still it rained a nice gentle rain and the lake was calming. Through the grey I could see my little lamb band back on the face of Falls Mt. The face greening up very fast now and they may use it for a week or more.

My wood pile was looking poorly so I sawed up a heavy length that had been standing by for a year or more. That and a couple sawed chunks put it back in shape.

June 7 – Partly Cloudy, Calm & 37°.

Back to glassing and now the high ridge across the river. I looked for sheep on the lower end of Black Mt. and the sheep lick area. I saw eleven but not near the lick. There! west, northwest over by the Chili River was something. Caribou! and a good big bunch. Much farther to go but no matter. I could make it back to my camp before sundown. Many objects of the same size and color. I watched to catch one moving and so be sure before going another two miles and more. Caribou sure enough and I took off after changing film. At that great distance I couldn't tell which side of the river they were on for I couldn't see the river for high ground. In forty five minutes I was seeing caribou with my bare eyes. In one hour I was slowing down and watching close for one to raise its head and look my way – they were feeding. A brush covered hump two hundred yards away and that was my goal and I made it easy enough. Many cows and calves and some very

small calves that no doubt had just joined the bunch. I had a full hundred feet of film to use and that would be enough if I picked my shots. It was past four and a good side lighting. Caribou and sheep look nice in a late afternoon sun. I tried to count them and came up with 150 as a bottom figure. Many more than that for they were bedded down. A big bunch of caribou don't spook easy and they paid no attention to me on top of that little hump. I came near the end of the roll and wanted to get a little closer. They began to get up and feed away. Many more caribou than I had counted. 250 or more would be my guess. She ran dry and I packed to leave. The caribou feeding slowly down country and many had crossed the river.

Head directly up country and pass the wolf den. I had been wondering if anything was using it. As I traveled I saw two new white objects in the distance. Something I hadn't seen before. Closer I saw it was the jaeger bird. The first I had seen. Now and then a ptarmigan flushed and I looked for nests and glad I didn't find one – too far from home. Foxes had taken over the wolf den but didn't appear to be using it this spring. It's a long haul to the bare faced knoll from far down the Chili River and it took me nearly two hours to make it. Less than a half mile from my camp three caribou. A cow and two yearlings. They let me get quite close before they trotted a half circle around me to get my scent.

The sun was getting low as I pitched my tent and built a little cooking fire in the edge of the gravel bank. I would see the sunset and not behind a mt. this day. It looked half good so I made a time lapse piece of footage (300 frames).

The day was done and I turned in at about eleven. A space blanket double under my GI sleeping bag. A few mosquitoes along the stream but the tent mosquito proof. It had been a good day. At last I had filmed caribou cows and calves and many.

June 8 – Partly Cloudy, Calm & ?

Hot water for tea and I cooked some instant porridge with lots of honey and raisins added. I still had a cold sourdough sandwich. Finally the sun came up in the vicinity of Telaquana Mountain[23] but it wasn't an impressive sunrise. Clouds were moving in from up country. Breakfast dishes done I broke camp and packed up – watered down my little fire and was on my way at five. Goldeneyes on the chain of lakes and no doubt they are nesting there. I have filmed them there before. About an hour and a half to the canoe and my clean up project. I dug a good big pit and in pure sand. I dug it close so there is no excuse not to use it. With the flat side of my little double bit I flattened all the cans on a rock, broke the booze bottles and burned the burnable garbage. It looked pretty neat when I finished and I'm thinking it will stay pretty much that way.

I had thought of going over to the Chili River for a grayling or two but it was raining up country and clouds moving fast enough to blow later in the day. I decided I had better head up.

[23] Telaquana Mountain is a 8,070 ft. high peak about 12 miles N of the Proenneke Site; Nduk'eyux Dghil'u is the Dena'ina word for "animal goes in mountain."

June 9 – Partly Cloudy, Calm & 39°.

Morning came at 5:30. I had slept as if I had died. No hurry I had planned this as an easy day anyway.

A pretty morning with the sun splashing down here and there. Clouds drifting slowly out of the southeast. Twin Lakes country is green again.

I checked my trot line before hotcakes and had no fish. After breakfast I neatened the place up a bit. My old cow barn lantern evidently has a very slight leak for I have been noticing a wet spot on the fireplace hearth. I set the old residenter in the fireplace while I scrubbed the hearth with soapy dish water. It looked so good there I lit it and was surprised that in a small way it takes the place of a fire. I must do that more often.

Today completes the last full day of my year at Twin Lakes, this hitch. Looking back I see it as the most productive (in many years) year ever. 6,100 feet of 16 mm and approximately 1,150 35 mm frames exposed. Miles hiked packing a load I can only guess and my guess would be 2000 or more.

Now at 8:30, Partly cloudy, breeze up and 34°.

June 12 – Clear, Calm & 32°.

At the lowwater fall [Emerson Creek] the ouzels nest looking real prosperous. In a cavity of the shear rock wall not more than two feet from the falling water. It looked round and dome shaped with a hole in the side. Like a round topped cake of damp brown moss. I wondered if there were young and after watching a half hour I decided there wasn't.

Probably one on the eggs but being covered over I couldn't tell. An ouzel came to the nest and went to the entrance as if to look in and then flew away. I waited and saw it a couple times but not near the nest. I climbed the winding trail up the rock face on my way to the high falls. It was there that I saw so many blueberry buds. The Emerson benches are always early. A good south slope and the snow leaves early. No sign of life up the creek or on the mts. I think the sheep have left Falls Mt. and the big pasture. Next I will see them at the lick and later scattered from the lick back this way to the head of the right fork of Camp Creek. Coming back down the creek flat I picked up all the pet rocks I could carry. Perfect for symmetrical is all I am interest in, round ones, eggs, round and flat, long and round. They come in all shapes and sizes. A million dollars worth of them from the lower falls to the lake. In Anchorage or the lower 48 they would sell like hotcakes and you name the price.

I went for the shovel which is rusty but shows little wear. It hadn't been abused, those Aniak[24] boys wouldn't abuse a shovel. Carved on a cottonwood tree at the camp site "Chas Barnett 1958." He and a friend had hunted sheep from there. Cans to smash

---

[24] Aniak, a village on the Kuskokwim River NW of Twin Lakes.

and bottle to break but one hole in the woods and one in the gravel next to it took care of them.

June 13 – Partly Cloudy, Calm & 40°.

I came down the Cowgill trail from timberline and near there along the trail a brand new bear tree. Hair rubbed into the bark and above more destruction of wood and bark than I have seen for a long time. This was no ordinary Alaskan brown bear. It looked as if a soft point bullet from a big caliber rifle had made a near miss and left a very impressive wound. The mark maybe seven feet above the ground and from the looks of the damage I would say the bruin wasn't reaching his best. I would have to look for tracks of that guy. I cut off and went up the game trail behind the Farmer cabin where I knew of wet spots and bare ground. Sure enough a good front foot print going each way. The size of those I saw climbing Low Pass and probably the same bears. Why the new tree I wondered for there was one no more than a hundred feet down the trail. It hadn't been touched but the bear had torn the old rotted chunk apart that stood next to it.

Raining lightly as I crossed my pole bridge and came to the cabin. Right there in front was my chair eating porkypine. Just time enough before starting supper to hang his carcass in the woodshed to cool. I would have porkypine liver for supper and they have a very large liver. In due time he was cooling and the camp robbers fleshing his quill side down hide before I burn it. Porkys can be so destructive. For no good reason they will start rasping on something , anything – transom of the canoe, cabin logs, saw buck, woodshed, table leg, okum chinking, gas can box – you name it, they have tried it. Let a few do some good for a change – give Jim Shake's big porkypine cooking kettle a job. It has stood idle under my bunk bed long enough.

June 15 – Overcast, Calm & 38°.

The porkypine just filled the Jim Shake big kettle. Lots of seasoning including a half packet of onion soup mix and some chili powder. While it bubbled on the stove and the rain came down I mounted the mirror. I drilled a very tight _ inch hole in the small rectangle of gas can box wood and taped it to the back side of the mirror with L.L. Bean super tape. The hole small enough that the camera mounting screw on the tripod would form threads. Oiled the threaded screw and put some 5 minute epoxy in the wood threads screwed it up snug and moved it a time or two as the glue set. Perfect, I am ready for the hatching of the robin blue eggs.

I wrote letters while the water bubbled and what an appetizing odor came from under the lid of the cooking pot. Still it rained a steady rain. Snowing on the peaks. The lake and creek rising steadily.

Porkypine and beans with sourdoughs, carrot and raw potato sticks. Enough meat to last nearly a week and much good broth after that.

Now at eight, raining from a low ceiling of fog patches. A breeze down and 38°.

Just a minute ago camp robbers came calling and for the first time a young one came to my fingers on top of the open door. He is hooked on welfare from this minute on.

June 16 – Overcast, Lt. Breeze up & 32°.

Here came a Super Cub up the lake and as it turned I could see the big [Alaska] Dept. of Public Safety emblem on the side. Dave [Cornwall] the warden. I headed for the cabin and he coasted into the beach as I arrived. He climbed out, a big smile on his face. "How have you been," he asked. "Fine, and where have you been hiding out so long." I hadn't seen him since February. "Oh, I have been around," he said. "Was here a couple weeks ago and you wasn't at home." I saw that he had a spotted bird dog pup with him. "Mind if I get my dog out of the airplane," he said. I wouldn't mind. My camp robbers would take care of him. Snoop was his name and he was well named. We came in and he had to investigate everything before disappearing outside. I ask him if he had done any good since he was here last. "Oh, we did some good during bear season," he said. "We collected five airplanes." And he went on to tell me how Federal men from the south 48 contacted guides in Alaska and passed as hunters wanting a bear hunt. Came up went hunting and then after the guide had made a big violation identified themselves. A bunch of Super Cubs and a Cessna 185 was the take. Till now it has been pretty tough to prosecute a violator – too many ways he could get out but this worked. Same difference as if the guide had taken the game warden hunting.

And then he said, "Have you been doing any fishing." He remembered last year I guess and figured I didn't have a license. I had to tell him about catching that big 20 incher and then said "Are you prepared to sell me a license today." "No, I don't sell them but I can get you one and will bring it in next week." Good deal and I wrote him a check for $10.00. When I handed it to him I said "I was 62 just a little over a month ago and I came to Alaska in 1950 so you won't be able to hang me for a license much longer." He grinned and I could tell what he was thinking and that was, I'll be seeing that you buy one until after 1980.

I asked him if he had seen any caribou. "Nope, flew up the Mulchatna and the Chilikadrotna [Rivers] and didn't see one." "The herd is in bad shape," he said. I ask him why and he didn't know why. Hunting pressure and predators he supposed. They are just not there. I suspect there are more there than he knows about.

I asked him about fishing in Bristol Bay. "They are expecting the biggest run ever," he said. Now that would be a lot of fish for there has been some pretty big runs in the past.

When he came in and I started to build a fire he said now no tea or anything for me I'm fine. Couldn't stay long – wanted to go by Turquoise and Telaquana Lakes yet

this afternoon. So we went out and he called Snoop who came from the direction of my porkypine skin draped over a stump, skin side up. I had noticed that my camp robbers had fleshed it clean so I had skinned out the tail and head so they could get more meat. Snoop probably ate the tail. Dave and Snoop took off down the lake and I went back to my irrigation ditch.

June 17 – Overcast, Breeze dn. & 40°.

At noon as I sat on my chair under the spruce eating my lunch the freshly educated young camp robber climbed all over me trying for a snack. At about the same time two were taking a bath in the lake and I wish I could have filmed it. A great splashing of water and then much fluttering of feathers to get them dry and in place again.

June 18 – Overcast, Breeze dn. & 42°.

The afternoon rains let up and now there appeared to be a blue haze and that would be smoke from a tundra fire some where. That would really foul my trip to the sheep lick for I wanted to look for caribou and visibility would be restricted.

The lake was calm as I paddled up and soon after I arrived a nice up lake breeze but it was entirely local. A half mile down was flat water. 5:30 when I packed my gear in. Birds waiting to be fed. This morning I had seen Freddy the squirrel searching for camp robber caches of hotcake. Out on each bough and search among the tips. She found one too. I called her and before she left the area she came to the stump and carefully took my offering from my fingers.

Overcast, smoke, a very light breeze up and 45° now at eight.

And now Labrador tea[25] is starting to bloom and so is chiming bells[26] and Boykina,[27] the bear flower. Star flowers,[28] miniature dogwood[29] and on Falls Creek I saw many wild currant blossoms[30] and also mossberry blossoms.

Again I visited the robin and she left and returned to the nest with me near by. Many fresh moose tracks in the garden yesterday but none have been added since.

[25] Labrador tea, Ledum palustre L., an evergreen shrub also know as Hudson Bay tea, with a white flower.

[26] Chiming Bells probably refers to the Bluebell, Mertensia paniculata, with a blue redish–white flower.

[27] Boykinia, or bear flower, Boykinia Richardsonii, with a white or pink flower of the Saxifrage Family.

[28] Starflower, Trientalis L., with a pinkish flower.

[29] Miniature dogwood, a variant of bunchberry and Canadian dwarf cornel, probably Cornus canadin Canadensis, with a white flower.

[30] Currant, the northern red current, Ribbes triste, with a purplish flower.

June 20 – Clear, Calm & 30°.

I woke up at 3:30 and found the sun just starting down the peaks of the Volcanics. It was calm and 30°. I decided the time is now, not 5 o'clock to build a fire and get started down the calm lake. I searched for frost and found a trace of it in the edge of the brush at my little holding pond.

A spud breakfast and all necessary gear packed to the beach. I would go intending to spend the night if the weather continued fair till evening. The water was burbling behind the paddle at 5:30. I was on my way. A beautiful, and very quiet morning for the trip. The only sound on the lake, my paddle and the streams and water falls. I was making good time. One hour after starting I was coasting into the lower lake. Early in the morning I was alert for a bear on the beach or the sight of a cow with calves. Rippled water halfway down and then calm again. Two hours and I was opposite Gatano's airstrip. Two and a half, I pulled into my little mutilated (by the Oregonians) clump of spruce. The best time I have ever made to the lower end with a load on calm water. I had made it to the head of Lake Trout bay one time in one hour fifty min. A light load and a wild lake, blowing down, I had to walk home that trip.

On the beach I sorted my gear and made up my pack. The 400 mm lens would stay. So would the big pistol and the sleeping bag. The lens I would wish for a few hours later.

Still a perfect day when I headed across the gravel knolls to my climb out spot from there to perfect hiking country, solid under foot and only a little patch of dwarf birch or two at the start of the climb. A cool morning and insects not a problem as I crossed mosquito meadow where they can be pretty vicious on a warm sultry day. The spruce and poplar timber and sign of last winters moose population. No sign of bear on the entire trip.

Climbing and the beautiful view of the big Chili River country. I stopped twice to glass for the caribou herd or even a good bunch for it is usually about this time that I found them below the lake. No ptarmigan this trip. Last year twice I saw birds and once a pair with small chicks.

Before it has always taken real close to six hours to go to the lick by either the lake route or over land by Camp Creek and over the high peak above the lick. I would beat that this time. I was getting close and finding the ponds still not completely free of ice and if they were, sometimes a big snow bank with a straight side over hanging the clear water bordered by the green of mt. avens and other wild flowers. Five hours ten minutes saw me ready to learn if my trip had been for scenery alone. I hadn't seen fresh sign of sheep but last year at this time many sheep were at the lick and I suspect the date they come to the lick has varied but little for a hundred years or more. Topping the ridge I saw a few sheep across the canyon on the green slope above the lick which was still out of sight and deep in the canyon. Fifteen I counted which wasn't much. On down grade to the high point

looking into the canyon. A few more but only a few. Two less than legal rams layed on the bare slope. Before I had seen some pretty good rams here. To the edge and I looked down onto a scene that was a sight to see. Sheep, just an awful lot of sheep. Ewes and lambs and a scattering of rams three quarter or less. Bedded down in a small area on the base slope of loose stuff. The small but noisy creek just below them and across the creek good feed, lots of it. They have it made there at their spring convention center. Sheep from far out and no doubt from here on Allen and Falls Mts. go there I am sure and how about those up the lake and the river. Perhaps they have a lick in the high country.

Now the few I had seen high up were trailing down in twos and threes. Maybe a ewe with two or three lambs would come running down the sheep trail. They were the tail end coming in after a night of feeding.

I was soon in business and so many are a problem to film. Where is the most interesting action. Lambs playing is good but I would see very little of it today.

Here is one place to hear sheep sounds. Ewes hunting for their lambs and lambs their mothers. It reminded me of a lambing camp in sheep country Outside. It seems that ewes and lambs couldn't careless where each other are until they get hungry or the mother wonders where the little tike is now, and then it is much running back and forth between bunches to find each other. Big lambs and some still quite small that would have to consume lots of milk to be ready for late October and the start of winter snow cover.

Sheep were crossing the creek and spreading out feeding on the green slope. In the bright sun it was a sight to remember. I tried to count all I could see and came up with 125 but later as I moved farther around the high half circle crest of the canyon rim I counted 150 and still felt that I was missing maybe 25 or 30.

There are about four or five areas where they eat the blue mud but two main and favored spots. Water is seeping out at each place and if it is the water that contains the preferred mineral or the clay I don't know but the mud is well churned and some place half knee deep. I saw ewes and rams down on their knees in front with heads back in a hole getting at the good stuff. Sheep jostling each other around to crowd in to the best places.

A small ewe with a small lamb came running. She waded in and a near _ curl ram already there butted her in the side. She turned and hit him back and stayed. Some very dirty sheep. Legs grey to the knees and faces a mess. At not a time did I see lambs eating the dirt but many in it.

I moved around the bend of the canyon rim to face the lick area and to get strong side light on the scene. Then after a time I started to move down for it was mid afternoon and they would be moving out for a night's feeding again.

I got the feeling as I moved closer that the sheep feel that the lick area is a sanctuary. A place where they are off limits to the predators. They showed next to no fear of me. Even the rams paid little attention to me at little more than a hundred yards. A choice location for the meat eaters to give the sheep a bad time but all I have ever seen there was two bears and they were passing through and paid no attention to the sheep even

though bears were hunting calves at the time.

Dave the warden says it is legal to hunt at a lick site but it is not legal to establish a lick by putting out salt or mineral. I think the lick should be off limits to hunting with a gun or bow. And if the lakes country becomes a Ntl. Park I feel that the lick should be included in the park. As the boundary line is now, it is questionable. The lick would be a great attraction for those capable of climbing to the high ridge.

I had used nearly 400 feet of film which is quite a lot of one subject at one location. Sheep were starting to trail out and I prepared to climb back up to the top and head for the lower lake. A high overcast had come from the south east and a breeze with it. Loaded and starting my climb when there on the skyline stood a bull caribou. Side lighted by the five o'clock sun he was a pretty sight. I was carrying the camera mounted in case I wanted to film the sheep feeding above the lick. I planted the tripod and trained on the guy. He knew I was a stranger in his land and he turned and trotted over the rise only to circle and come back to my side which looked good. Then he was gone. Where had he come from. When on top I had glassed the big open country for caribou and would again when I climbed out. He would be gone, no sign of caribou down country or towards Turquoise beyond the ridge, or the beyond on the big table land towards Telaquana.

Back over the edge and down for an hour or more before I entered insect land again. The lake was ruffled, but below the whitecap stage. A dark evening and I felt sure that tomorrow would not be bright. I would use the kicker and head up the lake – come back again when prospects for sunlight were favorable. Forty-five minutes to the stream and the breeze was quite noticeable there. The upper lake would be noisy rough and it was. A slow trip to one mile rock and then a strong finish. Ten o'clock as I packed my gear in and got my supper fire going. Later water to get cleaned up for tomorrow would be an easy day. Sleep later and bring my journal up to date. It was 12 when I climbed the ladder. This had been a 20 hour day and a good one. When I turned in the sky was solid overcast, the lake noisy down and the temperature 48°. No frost could come this night.

So now, I would like to go back again soon. Take the 400 mm and accessories to use it with the Bolex to get a few feet of real close ups of the sheep eating the blue mud.

June 21 – Overcast, Lt. Breeze dn. & 46°.

I slept but not as sound as I will tonight. It seems the second night is my sleeping night after a long day. It was six before I rolled out and splashed some cold water in my face to help open my eyes. I had started batter for hotcakes before turning in. It was 9:45 before I got my writing done for yesterday.

The day was improving as midday drew near. Partly cloudy and the lake calming. It would have been a nice day on the Chili River.

The overcast getting heavier and of a solid grey. The breeze picking up blowing down. I did some mending and it was six before I realized that the day was about done.

While I was getting supper it turned grey over the lower lake and by seven it was starting to rain here. Now at eight it is raining a good get wet rain and the lake whitecapping down. Now, I was happy that I had gone to the lick yesterday and came back last evening. There is nothing as wet as a canoe on a lake in a rainstorm. So now – the end of the longest day and the shortest night. It has seemed a very short six months since the longest night and the shortest day.

June 25 – Overcast, (Raining), Breeze dn. & 42°.

A grey morning at 5:15 and light rain speckled the lake out front. A new dusting of snow along the ridge down country from Spike's peak. This morning I would read my mail more thoroughly and also the four *Newsweek* – beg your pardon, *Time* magazines and one, outdoor magazine that I had never seen before, Mariah the name. Two months – six issues a year at 2.50 per issue. And a big brown envelope of machine copies of newspaper articles concerning the D-2 lands proposal[31] sent to me by Paul Fritz of the Park Service. Also a letter in which he said a writer photographer from National Geographic is coming and would be visiting the Lake Clark Ntl. Park area. And, he would be visiting the upper lake too. The Secy. of Interior and his posse can be expected after July 6th. Sounds like the invasion is shaping up.

June 27 – Overcast, (Fog), Blowing up & 34°.

I was up in good time to get my hotcakes put away and my house in order. I figured that I would be having company before ten o'clock. Things looking pretty shipshape and I heard someone coming from the woodshed and it turned out to be a middle aged man with a crew cut. I had expected it would be long hair and beard to match. Brant[32] something or other was his name and he looked cold in his little green wind breaker. I ask him where he was from "Santa Fe, New Mexico," he said. Oh! the dry one "Well drier and warmer than this," he said. I asked him in but he wouldn't now. Just came to tell me that he, his wife and another couple were camped across the creek. They had all read the book and if I didn't mind they would like to come for a visit. We talked and it turned out that he is well acquainted with Andrus, the Sect. of Interior.[33] It seems he is with the Sierra Club or some such and has been to Washington quite a few times on environmental issues. So, he left and I killed time by building up my split wood bank account.

They came, he, his wife Laurie, Mike and his wife whose name I don't remember.

---

[31] D-2 lands refers to Section 17d-2 of the Alaska Native Claims Settlement Act (ANCSA) of 1971 authorized the Secretary of the Interior to create up to 80 million acres of public land as national parks, forests, wildlife refuges and Wild and Scenic River Systems. During the 1970s the D-2 lands debate raged throughout the state and on a lesser scale nationally, climaxing on December 2, 1980 with the signing of the Alaska National Interest Lands Conservation Act by President Carter that protected some 131 million acres of land in conservation units.

[32] Brant Calkin, a resident of New Mexico and president of the Sierra Club in 1976-1977.

[33] Cecil Andrus, Secatary of Interior in the Carter Administration and former governor of Idaho 1970-1977.

I had a tea kettle of hot water ready for tea or whatever and we visited awhile. They had come here from Homer[34] and would be leaving Friday afternoon weather permitting. Brant and Laurie had the Klepper kayak and planned to tour the upper lake. Mike and his wife would do some hiking.

On the lake a strong breeze up. We came down by split rock and the teetering one. One of the wonders of the world. Brant said he sure wished that Andrus could take a good look at Twin Lakes country.

The weather had cleared to a partly cloudy day. The sun bright and warm, a nice breeze up.

Tomorrow, they would wait and see what the weather did. Brant and Laurie would tour the lake in the Klepper. I offered to take Mike and his wife in the canoe if they wanted to travel in the lake area. Go to the sheep lick if they wanted. Both are good with canoes and just ran a wild river. I'm afraid the mention of the lick has Brant and Laurie wanting to go too. A chance for me to shoot some 35 mm film with the 400 mm lens. So – they trudged for camp after inviting me over. Nice people, all of them.

June 28 – Partly Cloudy, Calm & 29°.

I was eating supper when there came a light rap on the door. The first time anyone had knocked on my door for a year or more. It was Craig Coray[35] from Lake Clark. They had come looking for me and found my note. Getting late and didn't know if I would be back today. Glen Van Valin had flown him, his brother[36] and his brothers girlfriend[37] to the connecting stream.

Last evening at eight I had gone to check my robins. Both gone from the nest but the hen appeared from nowhere to give me a fly by. Then the male with a load and those young necks reach high above the nest. Once around poking groceries in and he flew away. Soon the hen and she did the same except for doing her best to cover the flock. She rides very high on the nest. Craig's brother said, there must be a robins nest close somewhere. A robin really chews us out every time we get close to the cabin.

June 30 – Overcast, Calm & 38°.

One thing about the Sierra Club – they leave a clean camp and I mean clean. Anything not burnable went out with them. The campfire was well watered and fire starter and wood carried to a brush pile. Time to go and Mary Lee was nearly in tears. Both she

---

[34] Homer, a coastal town on the SW side of the Kenai Peninsula about 125 miles south of Twin Lakes.

[35] Craig Coray, long time resident of the Lake Clark whose parents were the first school teachers at Pedro Bay on Iliamna Lake in 1952-1953. Coray is a music teacher at the University of Alaska, Anchorage.

[36] David Coray, younger brother of Craig and resident of Soldotna on the Kenai Peninsula.

[37] Marilyn Garcia, a friend of David Coray from the Kenai Peninsula.

and Laurie had to give me a big hug. Brant gave me his card and said anytime I came to Santa Fe area, come to their place and stay and have some good green chili. His name is Brant Calkin and he is Southwest Representative for the Sierra Club. I paddled away as the Beaver moved out. It was pretty grey down country but the pilot said the weather had been pretty good coming from Homer by way of Pile Bay.[38] Weather report had Lake Clark Pass closed but it looked open as he passed.

Craig Coray, David and Marilyn – I wonder if they went to the lick. I think they probably visited the waterfalls instead. They had brought me a big brown envelope from Port Alsworth. It was from Paula Apsell the Nova program producer. She apologized for not writing sooner. They had been very busy working on the film and just finished the day she wrote (June 21). She wrote (among other things) "We wound up using quite a bit of your interview in the final film. It was really very good, and makes up some of the most meaningful moments in the program. We also used a lot of the Ntl. Park Service film "One Man's Alaska," although we were forced to cut it down a bit to include more information on the D-2 issue." So – it looks as if I am involved in the battle and I'm thinking some Alaska politicians in Washington are not very happy. Some nice wildlife footage can pull a lot of heart strings. The name of the documentary – "The Closing Frontier."

July 5 – Partly Cloudy, Lt. Breeze dn. & 50°.

And it rained again and did a good job of it at times. Hope Creek was on the rise and so was the lake but more from warm weather than rain. In *Time* magazine I read about the worlds problems of which Jimmy Carter has his share. I'm thinking that the good ol boy, brother Billy was the one who won in the election. Nothing to lose and everything to gain for him and he knows it.

I finally got around to reading, sorting and discarding old letters. Nearly seven for a dollar these days. Pretty expensive fire starter material.

Fresh cooked beans and sourdough biscuits for supper. This Twin Lakes job is like the man said – "She ain't much for pay but she is a good feeder." One more cooking of Quakers quick oats and then its goat feed again.

Partly cloudy now at 7:30. The lake still noisy from a down the laker. Hope Creek very loud and filling my ditches bank to bank. Temperature 45°.

July 7 – Partly Cloudy, Breeze dn. & 47°.

It was 2:15 when I heard porkypine talking out front. I couldn't understand what they were saying but I suspected they were getting squared away on who would rasp the stump and

---

[38] Pile Bay, a very small settlement on the eastern end of Iliamna Lake at the western end of the Iliamna Portage, about 90 miles south of Twin Lakes. The Dena'ina word for the Pile River is Tsayantnu which means "cliff river."

who would rasp on the antler. I thought here is your chance for porkypine in the cooking pot. I went to the door and was surprised to see three. One a very small young one working at the stump. The dark complected one of yesterday morning hadn't remembered his bout with me. While I watched he left the antler and went to the chair, sat up on his haunches and proceeded to eat wood. That did it and I quietly went to the woodshed for a good porkypine stick. At that time of the morning it was daylight and I was soon churning the carcass in the lake to wash the blood off – hang it from the ridge log in the woodshed to cool and dry. The big liver and heart I put to soak in salt water. Porkypine liver is very much like seal liver, very good fried. It was after three when I turned in again and didn't sleep much due to the fact that I got well cooled out butchering and washing.

July 8 – Partly Cloudy, Breeze dn. & 47°.

Read a few letters and listened to a tape of "The Closing Frontier" sent by brother Robt. in Arlington, Va. In another little envelope a second one from him. It a complete reproduction of the aud,io portion of the program. It sounded not too bad but for my part filmed by Nova. I was pretty terrified by the sound of it. A film report by brother Jake and he was critical which I want him to be. Only if I know how the processed film looks can I improve if it is possible.

July 9 – Overcast, Blowing dn. & 48°.

At Low Pass point big rollers were coming in. It was not canoe water. On down and we saw a string of bright tents on the beach near the head of the stream. Who could that be. River floaters wouldn't be starting from there. Closer and we could see the little nylon things whipping in the wind. Who would camp in such a windy place. Quite a group of people greets us. One was from Baltimore, Md. and names and places were coming thick and fast. They were Sierra Club members on a hiking tour and had started from Portage Lake. Came up the other side of the Kijik and crossed opposite Low Pass entrance – came on though the pass and ended up there at night. Bob Waldrop of Anchorage was in charge of the fifteen hikers. I knew Bob and soon he came still wearing long hair and a mustache to match. He said John Kauffmann and Bob Belous was along. We went to find John with his little hat and full beard hunched over a little fire fixing his breakfast. A bunch of plastic bags with his rations for the trip in them. John's baby was the Gates of the Arctic Ntl. Park and I ask him which was best, Twin Lakes or his land. "It's a toss up," he said with a big smile on his face. We didn't see Bob Belous, the big house dog, and I suspect he was still in the sack. We had to go if we would get back today. We had used up an hour and three quarters of our traveling time already. I had a mark on the bank where the shallowest place in the stream was. John [Branson] removed his pants and shorts and put on his basketball shoes for the trip across. It was a long cold trip but he made it. I had taken my rain pants to wear to keep the splash from cooling me more. I made it no problem but I doubt that I could have returned without warming up. The urge to just stop

is so strong that one could just cease to move. Back into our hiking gear and ready to hit the trail. We would follow the blazed trail to Emerson Creek, go up by the falls and then up Camp Creek to the triple fork and on up the mt. to the high peak. The hike was going well. John in his L.L. Bean shoe pacs was keeping up pretty well but he vetoed going down in the canyon of Camp Creek to climb to Camp Ridge and easy travel. He didn't mind steep mt. side travel one bit. At the triple forks we pulled our boots off and soaked our feet in the cold water for a minute. Nothing better for hiking feet than cold water. We started the long climb for the distant peak and hadn't gone far when we began to see sheep. 20 here, 5 there and two another place. We might not see many at the lick. On up to a high saddle and the first look of the Chili River country. John says, "Isn't the lick near here some place?" It was miles away and over that high peak. "Oh no!," he said and soon he complained of the wind on the mt. But it was an easy climb and we saw some sights that opened his eyes. Couldn't we go around that high peak? We could but it would be farther and no sheep trail to follow. Far below we could see a nice bunch of about 25 sheep. On the peak we took a break. We could see the lower tip of Turquoise Lake and the Mulchatna snaking down the big flat and edging in close to the Bonanza Hills. We could see Whitefish Lake, Snipe Lake, a bit of Lake Clark and many other unnamed small lakes in the big low country.

I looked for a big band of caribou but saw none. Time of decision, turn back and downhill all the way or go down the back side to the lick and come back by the low route along the lower lake. We could see a couple sheep in the lick area so John said lets stick to plan A. A steep west side from the peak towards the lick and it was solid snow cover. I would do straight down. John wouldn't, he would stay on the loose crippling along rocks. I was down on bare mt. slope before he got halfway, and eventually he got snow in his boot anyway. While I waited I glassed, discovered a nice bunch of caribou on top of the high rim surrounding the lick. A good bunch and I thought of the camera gear. The sun was in and out too. We went on down and sat on the point glassing about 30 head of sheep at the lick and about 260 head of caribou on the big green pasture. A pretty sight. A nice breeze and no bugs. The caribou taking it easy. We stayed maybe half hour before starting back. 25 till two when we took off. In one hour we was down on mosquito meadow and heading up the lake, taking advantage of the many gravel knolls and solid footing. John was doing good. It's a long hike the length of the lower lake. Many deep trenches to cross and climbs to be made. In three hours time we were near our crossing of the connecting stream. A record trip from the lick. No sign of the hikers. From up at the high waterfall we had seen them crossing the stream. Bob Waldrop had said they would camp in the trees and visit the falls today and then continue on to Turquoise Lakes. They had planned on Telaquana but figured Turquoise would be enough for everyone.

July 10 – Clear, Calm & 38°.

I was traveling light. A wool shirt and my nylon wind pants which I would wear at night in my sleeping bag liner and in my folded space blanket. John had a big lightweight

ripstop nylon tarp in case it rained. My little double bit axe would be good to make a roaring fire possible in short order. John was packing his usual too much and I would end up packing part of it. We got away soon after six and paddled to Low Pass Creek and the start of the trail to the pass. The sun was out and warm, the shade of the mt. felt good as we climbed into it. I was trudging along with my eyes on the moss and noticed a little long rectangular stone laying there. Strange that a natural stone should be so true and I picked it up. It was a knife sharpening stone lost by some hunters. Probably he had been sitting resting and sharpened his knife and layed the stone down. On through the pass and down the long grade towards the Kijik. John wearing his Converse basketball shoes and me my…hikers which turned out to be satisfactory for the long walk. On leaving the canyon we crossed the creek that drains the big basin and traveled the mt. slope to the right of the Kijik (going down). It was good except for the huge talus slope of loose rock that had to be crossed. Too much side hill is not desirable. At the first good stream we stopped to soak our feet in the cold water.

It was near twelve when we crossed the entrance to the Big Valley. Too much dwarf birch along the Kijik and the lower slope of the mt. facing the river so we would travel the north slope with solid footing and no brush – then climb over the mt. and down the same route that John, Craig, and Heidi had come up last summer. Trudging along and there laid a hunting knife. A Russell belt knife made in Canada. I was doing alright in the finding department. As we gained a little elevation after crossing the head of the big valley John spotted caribou back and to our right. Many caribou and we estimated their numbers to be more than a thousand. They were feeding in a green swampy area and it was just caribou as numerous as flies. Now we started our climb to the high ridge and we would see many more caribou in the highlands. From the top a view of the Kijik but still it was miles away. Down over a big hump to the fast small stream below. Those barren hills put out the best water. Crystal clear water flowing over stones completely free of algae or other growth. Here again we took a break and soaked our feet. I had calluses that were giving trouble so I sharpened my knife and trimmed them thin. Heavy thick stiff calluses pull the skin surrounding them when the walking is other than level.

On the go and headed for the lakes upper end we dropped on down staying clear of the deep canyon. Then the brush started and at lower elevation such as Lachbuna and Lake Clark brush can be a problem. John leading for he had traveled the route before. He was plowing right through and not taking advantage of some possible easier going. On and one we went struggling in shoulder high dwarf birch at times. Suddenly he dropped to his knees and said, "This brush really takes it out of me. It is very depressing, no end to it – I can see spruce a mile ahead and know it is that far at least to the lake." I told him that he was going to fast. I could hardly keep up. Let me lead and him tag along. I took advantage of every trail and opening and before long we broke out of it onto an old dry stream bed and spruce timber open as a park. This he remembered from last trip. On the lakeshore at last and again a foot bath before walking the beach headed for Jay Mueller's cabin[39] at the lower end. We had the mouth of the College Creek to cross so had to go to wading footwear one more

---

[39] Jay Mueller, an Anchorage businessman and his wife Barbara owned a cabin on Lachbuna Lake near where the Kijik River drains out.

time. It was six o'clock when we got to Jay's and no one home. Had he been there we would have asked him to ferry us across above the head of the river which is very near. His flat bottom aluminum river boat lays bottom up and chained to a big spruce. We would have to build a raft.

We left our gear on his beach and went scouting for raft logs close to where we hoped to cross. Luck was with us, a good blow down tree and a few dead ones still standing. I would chop out some raft logs while John got supper. The blow down still some what green and heavy. I doubted that it would carry much load. I dropped a good solid dead one to go with it. By the time he called "soups on" I had the logs ready for moving to the beach. A good meal ...Freeze dried stuff and two or three mixed together. After supper we went down and put the logs on the beach and would wait until morning to build the raft. The day had been fair but too warm. Now mares tails in the sky and a change was coming. We turned in but neither slept too good although each insisted that the other made the sounds of sleeping. I looked out from under the tarp at two and saw a beautiful sunrise in the making. A red sunrise isn't good and by three when we got up it was a grey morning. A big bowl of grape nuts and raisins was our breakfast and soon we were putting logs in place for lashing. I had brought my long canoe tracking line along for that purpose. So now[...]

July 11 – Overcast, Breeze dn. & ?

[...]we would try for a crossing a hundred yards up from the head of the river. The lake maybe 200 yards wide. We both wore our packs for I was sure the raft would be riding very low in the water if it didn't sink from our weight. Two long spruce poles to pole us out to deep water and then use them as paddles. We pushed it into deep water on the pole skids and climbed aboard. It floated but none to spare. Another hundred lbs. would have pushed it under. Slowly we splashed across to the far shore. There we used our poles as skids again and beached it high and dry. I would use it for my return crossing.

It was six when we left the beach and headed down the river to the mouth of the stream running up to Portage Pass.[40] There we would look for a tree across the creek to be our bridge. We had only started up the creek when it started to rain. Tall grass and taller brush, this was going to be a wet one. We found a good down tree crossing and then we had to climb to stay away from the canyon. And there was very deep and steep washes coming out of the mt. that had to be crossed. Water squishing in our boots, cold and wet we battled our way to an open valley with good caribou trails. We saw a few caribou mostly cows and calves but a few good bulls too. At the summit at last and now all down hill except for snow gulch. This one the deepest of all and a roaring stream. John missed the crossing and we ended up on a ledge high above the stream bed. A bit of scouting found a very steep route down. Boots full of water so why take them off – we sloshed

---

[40] RLP's Portage Pass, a pass about 8 miles long from the Kijik River southwest of Mueller's cabin SE toward Portage Creek on Lake Clark.

through and started the climb out. There had to be a better way and there was. A caribou trail crossed a half mile below our worst possible place. With so much high brush good crossings are not easy to spot.

Now the weather had faired up and there was Lake Clark. A beautiful sight after what we had been through.

There in the open just above brush line three real good caribou bulls and one small one. John found the trail going down to the Bowman gold diggings.[41] A blazed trail and worn smooth and solid by moose, caribou, and bear. A long trail down but a good one. One last wringing out of our socks before continuing on to Brown's Landing[42] and Coray's place near by. There we would pick up Mojo [Labrador retriver] who had been left in their care. We stopped a few minutes to have a cup of tea and a fresh baked biscuit with strawberry jam and then with Mojo we walked the beach towards Miller Creek[43] maybe four miles distant. We had made the trip in good shape and in a little more than a day and a half. Jay's lodge looked good to us.

John left me to get some supper going while he went up to Al Woodward's at Priest Rock[44] (on down the beach) to get his Labrador puppy which they had kept for him. Fresh cooked beans plus other odds and ends was our supper and then he fired up the steam bath. Nothing like a steam bath after a tough trip through the mts. I would sleep good and I did.

July 12 – Overcast, Calm & ?

Jay the governor was due to arrive yet this evening and I suspected there would be a delay. After supper we took the good boat Boston Whaler up the lake to see Glen Van Valin's new $100,000 lodge set up which is now being built. We found he and his crew of four having supper of grilled salmon on the beach. A few logs of the lodge in place, the floor joists in place and foundation piers for three cabins in place. A well partly dug too. We chewed the fat and had tea. Jay flew over as we were ready to leave to come back by Coray's and invite them to supper Saturday, July 15th. We arrived back at Miller Creek just as Jay was leaving his airplane and walking the short distance to his lodge. Just one of the boys on Lake Clark when he comes – nothing Governor about him. He had to take a tour and see how John's projects were progressing. The big garden which looks very good. His goat shed just starting and a new root cellar and the smoke house. He learned that I was starting back and offered to fly me all the way, I said that Lachbuna would be a big boost and so that's the way we left it before turning in.

---

[41] Bowman's Camp was the site of a small early 20th century placer mining operation on Portage Creek near Lake Clark named for Fred Bowman (1890-1959).

[42] Brown's Landing was the home site of Brown Carlson who is considered the first permanent Euroamerican settler on Lake Clark having taken up residence circa 1902.

[43] Miller Creek, a small creek that empties into Lake Clark 3 miles east of the Kijik River mouth and the site of Jay Hammond's homestead. The Dena'ina word is Nan Qelah, which means "mossy place."

[44] Priest Rock, a large 30-foot tall metamorphic monolith that is a prominent landmark on Lake Clark; Hnitsanghi'iy is the Dena'ina for "the rock that stands alone."

July 13 – Partly Cloudy, Calm & ? (Warm)

A good night's rest by everyone. Jay said he had slept straight through. I was elected hotcake maker while they unloaded the airplane. He had brought some hamburger which I doctored up to use as sausage. Jay ate two helpings of these hotcakes and thanked me for the good breakfast.

I was all packed ready to go and though it wasn't a bright and early start it wasn't late when we took off...We flew by Miller "cabin" Lake[45] and up the Kijik to the lake. The raft still there, and he landed coming down along shore as the water was glassy smooth. My pack unloaded, hand shakes and good luck, they blasted off and I was alone and a full days hike from home. I launched the raft and using one pole as a kayak paddle I paddled slowly across. With one aboard I had a dry raft and my gear could ride the deck instead of my back. I beached at Jay's [Mueller] landing and took the raft apart and rolled the logs up high and dry. I wrote a note telling him of our passing by and here was some fair firewood for him. It was nine o'clock on the nose when I got under my pack and headed up the beach. I would come back the route I had used about fifteen years ago. It was August then, Spike and Hope were here. I had gone one day by way of the Kijik and came back the next, cutting across and through the Volcanic Mts.

Brush, lots of it. College Creek[46] to cross but a down tree came just right and I walked right across. I was above brush line in two hours. Alpine country – high and solid, a good breeze – I headed north. In five hours I was crossing the creek in the big valley and there I stopped a few minutes for lunch. Then up a big dry stream bed next to a white mt. The stream bed turns to a trickle and then more, and more until it was a problem to cross. Then I entered the mts. and big boulders formed stepping stones as I switched from side to side as the creek channel directed. I knew I was on the right creek but where was the pass. I remembered turning sharp left up a canyon near the top. The creek got smaller and I got a cold drink where it was just a starting trickle. Then suddenly the pass came into view and I started the climb. Over the top and down a steep snow patch that remains in the canyon. Then I left the canyon to keep from going low and climbing again at the fork below. Around the mt. and it was 7 hours and 15 minutes after leaving Jay's [Mueller] place that I could see my cabin far up the upper lake. On down the mt. and I stayed in land crossing Dry Creek and Beech Creek. Nine hours and I was at the bend of the beach below the gravel bank. If I worked at it I could make the trip in 10 hours flat. At Low Pass point I dragged the canoe out and headed up the calm lake. It was going to be close and I poured on the paddle. Didn't make it in ten hours, but in less than 10 hours and five minutes. My birds were at the beach when I came. The cabin never looked so good. Someone had been here. Two gas cans under the clothesline. The lock lever on the door in a different position than I left it. A note on the table. Will Troyer, flying sheep survey. He would be back for the gas and would bring my mail.

---

[45] "Miller Cabin Lake," a variant of Miller Lake, a small lake that is the source of Miller Creek. The Dena'ina word for the lake is Vegh-deq Idaltin, "body of water above it."

[46] College Creek, a tributary of Lachbuna Lake about one mile NE from the Mueller cabin.

A fire going, beans and my porkypine kettle on. Water to get cleaned up after a bite to eat. My gear stowed and hotcake batter started. This was the ending of a good day. I had wondered how I would stand that long hike as compared to my previous hike from Lachbuna [Lake] and was happy to learn that I did it just as easy. It was after nine when I turned in. I would sleep well I was sure of it.

It looked like a fair day coming up. Partly cloudy, a light breeze and 50°. My lake up a couple inches since John and I left July 10.

July 19 – Overcast, Blowing dn. & 50°.

I hadn't started my days schedule when I heard the chopper coming and down past Carrithers' point. In close to the beach and low down he came. Out front he hovered and turned facing the cabin. He came closer and then backed up to go towards Hope Creek and land. A Bell Jet Ranger and it was Lofstedt's. Three came to the cabin. Vern Lofstedt,[47] one of Bud's boys and a man from King Salmon & one from Anchorage. One had come yesterday in the [Cessna] 180 to join Vern and the other. The [Cessna] 180 was due back soon to pick him up. They came in but wouldn't have anything to drink – just had breakfast. Vern asked where they could catch a fish on short notice. I allowed the Chili River would be their best bet. And did I know where the Lofstedt boat was. Yes, I knew and I was surprised that he didn't. I told him it wasn't far from here and I could see that he had a good idea where to look. His dad had been over a couple weeks ago and came home saying it was gone.

I could use a trout and I tried out front and at Hope Creek without a strike. Got my spinner hung up in the rocks and had to get the canoe to back it out. It rained and I retired to the cabin to write letters and study clippings that came last mail. A few on the Alaska land bill that I found real interesting and I must save them for ammunition in case an Alaska senator or congressman happens by. One clipping asks the question "Have we ever done wrong in the past by setting land aside as a Park." And another says "the Alaska land under dispute no more belongs to the state of Alaska than the Grand Canyon belongs to Arizona." Both clippings came from Washington, D.C. newspapers.

So the day was about done. The lake looking good and the wind calmed to a light breeze. Now at 8:40 a patch or two of blue and the temperature 47°.

This afternoon I saw a little sandpiper on the beach, a tiny little guy and what are his chances of living to fly out come fall. Just now a red throated loon cruises by out front.

July 20 – Overcast, Lt. Breeze dn. & 45°.

Today I would take a little tour so after hotcakes and cabin in visitor readiness I hung the little kicker on the stern of the canoe. A couple campsites that I wanted to take care of so

---

[47] Vernon Lofstadt, Jr, a pilot for Kenai Air Service.

I took my old long handled no. 2. I traveled slow to keep the splash down and beached at Glacier Creek. A nice little campsite and right on a bear trail. I wonder how many realize that when they camp there. On the same trail a bear tree with teeth marks higher above ground that any bear tree I know of and just beyond it no more than a hundred yards from the campsite the site of a bear kill done early this summer. Again today I went to see if a bear had been there since I had. I wasn't surprised to find the remains not as I had seen them last. A few bones, a little hide and a large area covered with moose hair. Sign that moss had been raked to cover the kill. The skull of a cow and I wonder just how the kill came about. It is swampy at the site and I can't imagine a cow being bedded down there. Perhaps the bear winded her coming along the trail and ambushed her from the brush nearby as she passed. Cans, bottles and plastic at the campsite and I buried the works. I motored on up the lake to Frank's cabin. At the rear corner a big porkypine half in and half out. I fanned him with an old pancho I picked out of the brush along the beach and he crawled in under the wall. A hole gnawed completely through between the two logs. Porkypines and the capers they pull are a mystery to me. One will work at destroying something just to prove for his own satisfaction that he can, or so it seems to me. The cabin just about empty. All furnishings of plywood have been devoured. A stove of a sort rests on the ground where I last saw Frank and the Indian Steve Hobson[48] building it from two gas cans. Nailed on the front wall outside a sign "Property of Jerre Wills Box 1111, Homer, Alaska." $1000 for Franks three cabins is what he paid. I had written to Frank asking for his lowest price on this one. I told him I would burn it, clean up the area and turn it back to the wilderness – he didn't answer my letter.

Again the afternoon rains came but not so much as yesterday. I see by my calendar that July has had two clear mornings and one nearly clear sunset – blueberry growing weather.

An early supper and dishes done by 6:15. Time to read a chapter or two from the good book *Reflections from the North Country* by Sigurd F. Olson.[49] The book loaned to me by Helen White. Will Troyer gave me a copy of the book and I read it. It's in Iowa now. Enjoying this one as much as the first reading.

Overcast, raining lightly, breeze down and the temperature 45° now at 8:30.

July 21 – Overcast, Calm & 42°.

A plane came up from the lower end – a [Cessna] 185 on floats. A red one with white trim. Up the center and that is a bad sign. He turned as he passed and that is worse. I was getting company and me dressed in my breakfast shorts. Down along the beach and nosed in to the gravel. Rust's Flying Service on the side. I hadn't seen that rig in a long time. A bushy looking guy climbed out from the pilots side and says I brought Paul Fritz

---

[48] Steve Hobson(1908-1983), a Dena'ina who was born on the Stony River but lived most of his life at Nondalton and a friend of Frank Bell's.

[49] Sigurd F. Olson (1899-1982), author, conservationist, wilderness-advocate who corresponded with RLP.

to see you. Paul of the Park Service and there was two in the back seat. Woody,[50] a Nikon shooter for the Park Service and Melody a young woman whose business I never learned. Paul had a garbage bag and started rummaging around in the litter for some good leftover garbage treats for me. Two small cans of Hood River apple juice and two pieces of cake. They had just eaten lunch at Telaquana.

Paul wanted to tell me that National Geographic would be in soon – probably Sunday or Monday weather permitting and would probably come in Rust's new (rebuilt) Beaver. Paul and John Kauffmann would be along. I stoked the fire for tea and we talked D-2, the Nova program and the park. "We certainly hope that Hammond gets busy in the campaign," Paul said. "Hickel[51] is way ahead and it could be down right dangerous if he becomes Governor." All the while, that Nikon picture snapper Woody was wading around in my delicate vegetation picking all the best shots. Melody fed the wise camp robbers and it was the thrill of her lifetime. From here they were going to Hornburger's on Lake Clark (Frank Bell's place at the head of Chulitna Bay). Boy that Sara Hornburger is a good cook Paul said and he looks so round as if he enjoys good cooking. They boarded in preparation for take off. The pilot last to ease the heels of the floats to the water edge. He said he would be back in August sometime and he would like to talk to me if it didn't imposition me too much. I wonder what kind of deal he had in mind. It had better not involve Hank Rust for he isn't one of my favorite people. That 300 horse [Cessna] 185 makes a terrible racket on take off. More noise pollution than Twin Lakes has known for a long time.

My last pair of good Mary Alsworth brindle colored wool socks have had it. More darned than not but I liked them for the good high tops. What to do? - I had a pair of L.L. Bean outdoor socks with baggy tops. I would scissor the tops below the ankle bone on the sides – toe and heel amputated and sew them on over the L.L. Bean top and bottom. Looks good, feels good and double the thickness over the ankle bone, which is the hurting point with L.L. Bean shoe pacs.

Grayling for supper and a light breeze came up the lake while I had it. Overcast with fog around the peaks. The lake ruffled up and temp. 49°. Anchorage has been having dark rainy weather too they said.

While they were here we discussed subsistence hunting. Who qualifies as a subsistence hunter. Paul says Lake Clark area people but it's up to the state to determine. The pilot allowed that hunters paying $800.00 to get in and out from Anchorage certainly couldn't qualify. Going to be battle there I'm thinking. Where to draw the line is a tough one. Paul says the lower lake will be in the park and a ranger station there. It will be in the park but not the instant wilderness, whatever that is.

July 23 – Partly Cloudy, Calm & 36°.

The day was clouding up with a light breeze down. The clouds not indicating any wind

[50] M. Woodridge Williams, an NPS Alaska Task Force photographer.

[51] Walter J. Hickel, Republican governor of Alaska in 1966, Secretary of the Interior 1969 and 1970, and lost the primary, the run-off, and the general election to Jay Hammond in 1978.

at altitude. I had another project or two in mind – set and file my wood cutting saws and file and hone my little double bit and the 4 lb. pole axe. That done I dug out a bright gas can of the old square type and would make a new four and one half inch deep wash pan. Ten years is a long time for gas can tinware and mine showing rust inside. This one a little different from any I have made. I rolled the sides and folded the ends two laps to stiffen them. When completed it was a good looking pan and I'm anxious to see what those Iowa cooks think of it. By the time I got the litter picked up it was time to build a fire. For supper I would have that big fish and I would cook it in the stove. A good fire going to have some coals. I went for the fish which I had buried under the moss. Temperature about 40° there. Chopped the head and tail off and would split the head and fry it separate. Inside my fish I doctored it good with bacon grease, oleo, salt, pepper, season salt and chili pepper. Also put in some onion soup mix but think raw chopped onion would be better. Double wrapped it in foil and shoveled it into the fire box. Twenty five minutes I left it while I got the rest of my meal ready. With the fire shovel and stove poker I brought it out and deposited it on the gravel out front. Undid the closing of the foil and there was my fish, looking very well done and juice a plenty. So good that I cleaned it up even though I was feeling a bit stuffed. After dishes I baited the trot line and tossed it out.

July 27 – Partly Cloudy, Fog, Calm & 40°.

I had finished my breakfast dishes when I heard the helicopter coming and then the sound of landing at the lower end. There it was parked at the mouth of Emerson Creek. Still too much fog along the mts. for them to hunt rocks. All four climbed out and one or two tried my grayling fishing spot. I watched with the scope but didn't see any fish come ashore. They messed around awhile and then climbed and came up the far side (Low Pass side). I was very surprised when he landed on the upper Cowgill bench close to the canyon. Everybody out and everyone but the pilot had a rock hammer. The girl also carried something white resembling a folded map. They started pounding rocks at the base of the steep slope and then the fog closed in. I waited and it didn't clear out. If I got going I could be up there before they took off. I was interested in the head geologists opinion of this Twin Lakes country. So – I pulled on my wind leggings and crossed the creek. Forced march on the climb and I was getting warmed up. I was sure they would fly away before I got in sight. The fog was clearing out. I got there to find them in a huddle on their knees beside the whirley bird studying maps. They said that fog was holding them back. It had been wide open and beautiful at Turquoise this morning. They were part of a U.S. Geological Survey team. Two helicopters and four geologists. A rush job for some unknown reason. Headquarters wanted to know what was in the proposed park in the form of rocks and minerals. The man said he figured the last big glacier periods covered the Twin Lakes area to a height of the upper bench and the foot of the steep slope of the mt. The many big granite boulders and humps came down from the high mts. on the ice. It melted and left them where they area. He figured the ice extended down country as far as the Mulchatna River or farther.

I went over the see what Hope Creek had done towards cutting the new channel and had only been there a few minutes when here came a Beaver. A red shiny one and I knew it had to be Hank Rust in his new Kenmore Beaver. By the time I got to the cabin it was taxiing down along shore. Red with brown and white trim, a beautiful paint job. Four guys climbed out. Paul Fritz, John Kauffmann, and that picture snapper who turned out to be Perry Riddle[52] from Chicago. A newspaper photographer and he told me this was a one time deal. They had asked him to take the pictures for this parks of Alaska story that I learned later is due to be out next May or June. A true shutter bug, he had two cameras hanging from his neck and a satchel full of equip. Hank tailed that purty Beaver into the beach and came in with the rest. Perry had an electric Nikon 35 mm that advanced the film and cocked the shutter as fast as he could mash the button. He started outside and was soon inside. No flash no nothing, just shooting and I finally ask him what kind of film he was using. Ektachrome 200 he said and shooing a 15th of a sec. Could he hand told at a 15th. "Well, shoot a batch of them and some are bound to be good," he said. I would hate to guess how many he shot here inside and out and of me. All the while I was visiting with Paul and John. Paul had brought me more garbage cake. John is going to do a story on the Lake Clark Park for National Geographic. I asked him if he would tour the park area for national and he said, yes, as much as is possible. Hank Rust planted himself in the doorway and everyone had to climb over him to get in or out. They had brought lunch and I made a couple sourdough sandwiches to give them a treat. Even Hank had to try a sliver. Perry wanted a couple more of me under the spruce with my rustic chair. I said and I want one of you there too. "Fine, "I would like that," he said. So – with his camera I shot a couple. Hank says, "How about taking one of the cabin and my airplane." If he could get them all in he would. So – it was full crew with the purty new Beaver and Perry on the breakwater and then he planted the camera on the break water and came running to join us before the shutter clicked. I asked him how many rolls of film for this assignment and he nearly bowled me over when he said 150.

I asked Hank if he ever wished his Beaver was turbo powered. "No, not really," he said. For the difference in price, this one is good enough. One hundred grand for this one against about 300 grand for a turbo. I asked him if three is a shortage of Beavers to rebuild by Kenmore. Not yet, he said. They just bought 15 used ones Army or Air Force surplus. I had been thinking about John and his story. Why didn't he come in and we would take a little tour of Twin Lakes country. "Do you really mean that," he said. I said yes I would like to help him get some material. When should he come. We settled for about August 15th. He would let me know before that date.

They climbed in and Hank cranked her up and taxied out. He is proud of that big bird. Lots of time to get her ready to fly and they took off. Paul had my outgoing mail and had brought mine from Port Alsworth.

A beautiful afternoon. Cotton clouds and blue sky, green of summer and a Turquoise Lake. I had asked Perry if he uses a polarizer and he said no. I told him that I didn't consider him serious competition. He smiled.

---

[52] Perry Riddle, a *Chicago Daily News* photographer.

Twin Lakes holiday for the rest of the day. About 25 letters and two packages. I sat on my chair under the spruce. The bundle in my lap and those read went in a heap on the ground. Some good news, some not good. Many had seen the Nova program. Some thought it was wonderful and some listed my faults – can't please them all as many people have learned.

The lake became restless. Swells starting coming to my beach. 'Something was happening at the lower end and before supper here came a fair breeze up. Now at 9:30, partly cloudy, a light breeze up and 55°.

August 1 – Clear, Calm & 40°.

Even at the early hour of seven o'clock it was warm as I trudged up the Cowgill benches and the trail up the creek. I was headed for my peak[53] overlooking the Kijik River valley including Lachbuna Lake.

The British Limeys have something practical. Seems that they are the inventors of shorts. Complete freedom of the legs and knees in hiking and climbing. They lose some of their popularity when there is wire brush (dwarf birch)[54] crowding the trail as it does up the creek in a place or two.

I kept a sharp eye for bear sign after I passed 1st canyon. August is the month for bears at 2nd canyon & the head of Hope Creek. The trail would be clean, not so much as an old caribou track to mark the trail. Up the Farmer trail[55] from the mouth of the canyon. Years back that trail had produced a few cans of GI rations that one of his hunters had declared excess baggage. All but buried in the moss and the markings weathered away. One can contained fruit as I remember.

Up at the head and the steep snow patch leading up to the high ridge. I buckled on my climbers and zig zagged up the steep pitch that was very soft where the heat of the sun was reaching the rocks below the snow.

The Kijik valley is nice country. The turquoise green white water river, a few beaver ponds. Much brush in patches along the lower slopes next to the river. No place for an airplane hunter to land unless it is on one of the river bars and I suspect some have landed there. Many nice side streams coming into the upper Kijik. Streams fed by many glaciers. Some very impressive rock formations too. Towards the mighty Redoubt Volcano one very tall stone chimney and I hope to see the geologist again and ask him if they had landed close to it. Both Redoubt and Iliamna Volcano in solid snow cover. Today the only time I have seen Iliamna when it wasn't putting out a plume of steam. Completely free of that trademark.

I traveled the ridge and up the steep pitch to the peak. No sign that sheep had

---

[53] "my peak," refers to RLP's Proenneke peak, a 5,200 ft. peak near the head of Hope Creek.

[54] A variant of dwarf birch, buck bush or wire bush.

[55] RLP's Farmer trail, not discernable on the ground but the most logical route from Hope Creek to sheep hunting area used by guide Marshall Farmer in the 1960s and 70s.

used the grassy bed there though I had followed old sheep tracks along the ridge. I was early – not yet eleven and past twelve the sun is 90° to the scene I hoped to shoot. It was cool with a nice breeze drifting by. I climbed into my wind breakers for the wait to film Redoubt. I felt sure that there would be moose and maybe a bear down along the Kijik. Caribou should have been visible on a snow patch or glacier. Directly below I spotted two moose and bulls. I was sure of it although it was nearly to far away to tell for sure. Far below me something white on a grassy point. I couldn't make it a sheep until it moved. Laying in such a way that I couldn't make head or tail of it. The moose fed and layed down. The sun moved around and I got my picture.

A very steep and precarious climb down the back side of the peak to a ridge leading farther west and a view into a big pocket that drains into the Kijik. I had gone over the top from Hope Creek and down through the basin a few years ago. I had gone on down the Kijik and up through Low Pass to this side and the lake. Now I climbed down and was making my way through some heavy loose rock to the ridge. It has always been on my mind, watch that heavy loose rock. One big one can tip or slide and trap you by a leg. This time one nearly would. I had stepped on a small one which was the trigger. Heavy rocks started to move. Off balance my left leg went down between two rocks, the rock above pushed me over. Something gouged me severely in the right hip pocket. Movement stopped and I pulled my leg out. It was hurting pretty good and after getting in the clear I discovered that it was skinned in no less than a half dozen place but only a trace of blood showing. I hobbled on down the ridge to look into the hole. Caribou some times use the big snow patches there. None there today and I headed back up to the peak. I was feeling pretty well beat up and had visions of riding slowly home on my good sturdy stick horse. Again I parked myself on the peak and exposed my skinned leg to the very warm sun of two o'clock. I saw my moose again and wondered if it would be worth a try to go from Hope Creek over the high ridge for a try at those big birds. I might be lucky and get them from the high ground but again I could be there for days and not see them.

The white object got to its feet. A young ram and was he alone? I wouldn't go that far down the wrong side of the mt. to find out today. I waited the limit before heading down. My leg was feeling better. My hip felt like I had been harpooned with a sharp rock. A very steep snow patch leads down several hundred feet from very near the peak. I buckled on my spikes and went over the edge. Slowly does it and I had no toboggan ride today. Down to the loose rock and I got off of the spikes. I was doing pretty good and would make the mouth of 2nd canyon in one hour. A sore spot under my right hip pocket was the offensive one.

Down the trail and when I arrived I felt as if I could run the course again (minus the scrapes and bruises).

5:45 when I crossed Hope Creek. I wasn't long in getting supper and batter for morning out of the way. A bath and my wounds licked I was ready to call it a day. It would be good to sleep in my upper bunk and not on my favorite peak tonight.

A fair breeze had been up the lake and in mid afternoon considerable cloudiness

but now at 9:15, almost clear, a light breeze up and 60°.

August 3 – Partly Cloudy, Calm & 45°.

Very few clouds but enough that I couldn't call it clear. The lake is rising because of so much warm weather. With so much calm weather I should be seeing sign of red salmon but as yet, none.

Today I would go to the far corner and get a good sunburn in the process. Go up the right hand fork of Camp Creek. Climb to the high ridge looking down on the head of Beatrice Creek. Sheep country in the summer time. Sheep leaving the lick climb to the high ridges and keg up on the ledges just under the crest of the ridges. It's a long haul, almost like going to the lick as far as travel time is concerned.

I was a long time making up my mind – too many far away places that I would like to visit. This one had priority because of the satellite or space station that had burned on re-entry to the atmosphere of earth. Some garbage separated from it as it passed over head. I felt sure that it was to high for any space parts to land this side of Turquoise Lake but I would keep it in mind as I trudged along.

I crossed at the mouth of Camp Creek and I thought of Roy Allen. He and I had come down Camp Ridge to the creek crossing after an unsuccessful sheep hunt. I had worn boots and offered to pack him across. He disappeared in the brush up the creek and after what seemed an unreasonable length of time he came back with a stout willow pole that he had cut and limbed with his hunting knife. "I didn't take pole vaulting in college for nothing" he said after pole vaulting across the narrow stream. Camp Ridge is a good place from which to check Emerson Creek for bear. A lush green patch far up at the eroded rocks waterfall and a sow with triplets spent some time there one year.

I was sitting down glassing the country and just got to my feet to move. Here came a nice ewe and lamb around that point of loose rock. No more than fifty feet away and she stopped to check me out. I stood still and she and her lamb passed me at twenty five feet headed on up the ridge. Here came another pair, a nice looking ewe molted clean and starting a new coat. The wind in my favor so she wouldn't wind me. She came a few steps and stopped to watch me. Closer still until she was no more than fifteen feet away. The lamb as close and off to the side. Me with the Exakta hanging around my neck and I didn't dare move. Those little sheep flies of the high country were biting me on the legs and still I didn't move. Could I move slow enough to get the camera up without spooking them. I would give it a try. Very slowly I moved my hand and they watched. The ewe moved back to twenty feet as I raised the camera. Ewe and lamb came together and I got them. The click of the shutter was too much and they moved back the way they had come. Another pair came and caught me moving and trotted away.

I stayed up there as long as I dared. 2:45 and it would take me at least three and one half hours to get home. It had been building heavy clouds and so I would have shade

for the descent. One last look around and I headed down the loose rock mt. Forty minutes that took an hour to climb. Two hours fifteen to Emerson Creek flats below the falls. A nice breeze up the lake and I wouldn't use the kicker. 50 minutes from Emerson Creek to my beach. The wind was calming while I had supper and now as I finish my writing it is near glassy smooth. The circles of a strong rise out front and it may have been the first of the red salmon. At 9:30 nearly clear again and the temperature 55°.

August 6 – Overcast, Calm & 51°.

I had beans to cook and got them on the fire. Sis and Voight had brought them in last winter, a 25 lb. sack and I suspect they got them in Anchorage. Last trip in I had asked Glen if he had small white beans on hand. "Lots of them," he said. This last sack very good. I could have them done by nine o'clock. Babe brought some that he had bought at a fish cannery when it went out of business many years ago. Like cooking gravel and I wonder if Glen is still selling them.

August 12 – Overcast, Blowing dn. & 48°.

Again yesterday Jerre had told me the story of the ten wolves closing in on him while still a mile from his camp at Snipe Lake. He had written me of it and I figured him to be a big windy story teller but now I believe it. It was two years ago in winter. He had started late and it was dark with a moon peeking through now and then. He was tired and perspiring and he figures the wolves sensed this and was taking advantage of it. He shot at one following at fifty feet but wasn't sure he had hit it. They backed off and he hurried on. Before he got there they were coming again and he hurried to the cabin. "They howled a lot that night," he said. Next day he headed back and saw nine which watched him from a half mile. Two blacks and seven greys. He found where they had torn the one he had shot at to pieces so he had wounded it sure enough. All this was strange because there was caribou, lots of caribou in the area. Experts say that wolves won't attack man but Jerre is of a different opinion. "And to think I nearly didn't take my rifle with me that trip," he said.

To finish the day I pulled on my rubber boots and went to tend my water in the ditches. Pitch out what rocks I could lift with the shovel and encourage heavy ones to roll with the current.

An early supper and my writing done. I would write another letter. This one to Will Troyer. I haven't seen him since last winter when he said I'll be back soon counting moose and then caribou and then sheep. I haven't seen him since but he was here the day I was at Miller Creek on Lake Clark. He had left a note "be back soon and bring you mail." No Will!

Now at seven the wind is increasing as it did last night at this time. Solid overcast and 52°.

So now I expect it will be next Saturday before Glen and then Long John Kauffmann may come for my $500.00 tour of Twin Lakes country. John hikes a great deal and I would be interested to know what he packs in the line of groceries. At the lower end of the lake with the Sierra Club hikers he had many plastic bags open while he fixed his breakfast over a little fire. I had thought a mixture of rolled oats, brown sugar, milk, salt, raisins, corn meal and rice would be good. Throw a couple handfulls in the cooking pot and boil it awhile. Maybe take a can of Spam or some G.I. ration canned meat. Quick and simple. I must try that, next overnighter.

August 15 – Partly Cloudy, Calm & 42°.

I had supper and then decided to go for a paddle across and up to Glacier Creek. See if I could spot a moose and maybe a sheep. From my big erratic granite rock I could see a bunch of nine head of ewes and lambs on Falls mt. Good decoys for the green sheep hunter. Sheep, and the mt. much easier to climb than the big rough ones. Climb and look at the mother ones with babies while the full curls lay on the high ledges three miles up country.

So, I paddled across and up the far side. I noticed clouds were now moving out of the southeast – weather was headed this way. I saw no game and headed back with a confusing pattern of ripples. Light swells coming across in the opposite direction from Allen Mt. Farther down a light breeze up. It was nine when I beached and found a nice dressed out red salmon in a little pool formed by gravel at the waters edge. Erv [Terry] had been here with his usual offering of friendship. He is hunting oriented and it bothers him to kill my close friends and neighbors. I told him one time that I didn't like to visit hunters camps for fear of recognizing some of my camera subjects there.

I put the red in a big plastic bag and tucked it in my deep moss cooler and soon turned in for what I expected to be a good night's sleep. The sky partly cloudy. It was near calm and 50°.

August 19 – Partly Cloudy, Breeze dn. & 52°.

The wind had changed during the night and when I got up a few minutes after five it was whitecapping down out in the stretch. I hurried around to get my hotcakes out of the way and diggings in order in case Glen flew in early. I didn't make it. Just finished eating and I heard the "T craft" on the water behind the point. Me dressed in my breakfast cooking shorts and T shirt. Too late now, he was at the beach and he wasn't alone. Out crawled his real nice looking mother in law, Glenda. He said she wanted to come see my cabin. For me she had brought a big round sourdough coffee cake with icing on top. "Had you expected me in last Saturday," Glen asked. It was blowing out there and he suspected it

would be here. We packed in groceries and mail. A 25 lb. box of small beans. The box looks very familiar and on it stenciled in black "Alaska Packers Association," Pilot Point, Alaska. California small whites. I'll bet they are 20 years old if not older. I'd have to think a head and soak them two or three days before cooking them.

"How was everything at the ranch?" "Oh fine." They have a good bunch of logs out for Laddie and Glenda's cabin. Didn't have to irrigate the spuds, lots of rain. Sig is coming home to go to school after spending the summer in Hawaii. Leon had been good help here this year. Glen Van Valin has his $100,000 lodge construction job well along. I can remember when he and his wife[56] were poor school teachers. When Jay Hammond became governor he sold Glen [Van Valin] his plane and guiding business. Glen had bought Frank Bell's property on the little island near the mouth of Babe's bay. After hauling sport fishermen for a few years he sold his lay out for a very high figure and is now building a fine big lodge up near the head of Lake Clark (on an island) inside the proposed Park boundary. Glen (Alsworth) has applied for an air taxi permit and is now in the process of getting the "T craft" legal. When it is it will be the first time it was since it came from the factory. I noticed that all compartment openings in the floats had covers on since the first time I saw it on floats. "Now, I can't tell how much water is in the floats without pulling covers," he said.

Glenda, a very ladylike person sat quietly and admired my view out the big window and door. I got my outgoing mail closed up and in the sack. I asked him how I stood on postage money in the post office. "Oh, we just stamp the stuff and add the cost to your grocery bill," he said.

Ready to go, I asked Glenda if she would like to climb the ladder for a look in my cache. She did and I remembered my uncovered blueberries just inside the door. I asked her to hand me down a can which I would send home with them in payment for the coffee cake.

When would he be back – we made Sept. 9 or the 16th the day. They climbed in, I flipped the prop and they were on their way.

The wind was picking up and continued as I sprouted my spuds and stored my grub in the cache. It turned grey as I started on my mail. I had thought of looking for another gallon of blueberries after reading a few. Packages, a bunch of them. Laurie Calkin, Brant's wife from New Mex. sent two. One containing four fancy boxes of instant coffee beverage. Swiss, French, Austrian, and Italian style. The other package a paperback *The Immense Journey* by Loren Eiseley and two big magazines *Sunset* [and] *Family Circle*. A nice letter saying Brant would be mailing me more stuff soon. A bundle of notebooks from Helen White and when I saw them I remembered that I hadn't wrapped Volume 22 for mailing. Sorry about that. One from brother Jake. Cloth backed adhesive tape, peanuts in the shell, canned snacking peanuts and candy bars. In a letter a good report on my last film 16 & 35 mm.

A letter from John Kauffmann asking – did I really mean it when I invited him to

---

[56] Sharon Van Valin, long time elementary schoolteacher in SW Alaska and co-owned Island Lodge on Lake Clark with her husband Glen Van Valin.

come for a tour of Twin Lakes country. My gawd-a-mighty John! With mail service as it is don't waste time writing for confirmation on the invitation come on in. Now I must try to flag someone down to send a reply to him.

By now the wind was strong and the day grey with rain. I would declare the entire day a Twin Lakes holiday. Paul Fritz had sent me four big envelopes of newspaper article copies on D-2 Land Bill news. Paula Apsell, the producer of the Nova program, "Alaska, The Closing Frontier" had written that she had heard from some Alaskans and politicians claiming that the film was biased in favor of wilderness values. One newspaper editorial started with the heading "Film deals devastating blow" (to opponents of D-2).

A letter from Brian Jones producer of "One Man's Alaska." He wrote that the film is very popular – more than 100 release prints already. It won a 1st prize blue ribbon in the nature and wildlife category at the American Film Festival in New York City. Also, the International Communications Agency is picking up the show for international distribution.

August 22 – Partly Cloudy, Calm & 38°.

Right away after breakfast I wrote a letter to Long John Kauffmann and told him not to dilly dally, but grab his pack sack and get flying. I wanted to get him in and out before the fall colors come for then I will be busy, weather permitting. No fifteen cent stamps but I found two self addressed envelopes with 8 cent air mail stamps on them. Two would be 16 cents and better than two thirteen centers. How to find someone going out soon. I figured the party above Bell Creek was due to go. Bad weather over a weekend always had someone anxious for that plane to come.

I neatened up their parking spot a bit and then down to Bell Creek to dress that one up a bit. They had said a party had come to Glacier Creek yesterday. That would be the red Beaver I saw but it was an Otter instead. So I paddled on down. A pyramid tent pitched just inside the brush. Someone pumping up a big inflatable raft with a foot powered pump. Again a party of three. As I came close the one idle said "Dick Proenneke" just as if he had known me all of his life. "That's right," I said, "who are you." He told me and said "I'm from New Jersey and read your book." Then he introduced a chubby 5x5 with frizzled hair and she didn't have the same last name as he. "And this is George Pollard from Kenai." Pollard the guide. I had never met him but had heard from Will Troyer that he was a good man. He said, "I have heard a lot about you." We chewed the fat there in the warm sun on the beach. It seems that this man is a repeat customer of Pollards. They have hunted a lot together on the Kenai and here at Twin Lakes and Snipe Lake. Pollard a likeable sort of guy, quiet and easy going. Said he thinks this area should be closed to sheep hunting. "Rams are trophy animals and I don't see many trophies here," he said. And he added, "This is tough sheep country to hunt." They would be here nine or ten days, do some fishing and maybe a little hunting. Mostly just playing around. I suspected that for the man didn't look like he would make it as high as the rough stuff and

his lady friend would have to lose fifty pounds before she could get very far from lake level. Pollard had floated the Chili river and told of one guy in the party who got caught by a sweeper which over turned his Klepper kayak, then it went into a log jam. He tried to get out and up on the jam. The water pulled him under and flushed him on through, pretty lucky. Since they had read the book I invited them to stop by sometime. They would do that. I prepared to head across and again I was asked about my Sears and row back motor. I told him I only used it when the paddle got tired. "I would use it until it got tired" he said and I thought about that time you would learn that the paddle was tired too.

August 24 – Partly Cloudy, Calm & 31°.

I skinned out the lake trout and had it for supper. Sliced fresh peaches with my cold porridge dessert. My sourdough batter mixed for breakfast and I was ready to write when here came a pretty airplane lowover head and next I knew it was coming down along the beach. It was Governor Jay's nice [Cessna] 170B. He and Heidi climbed out. Early in the morning I had seen an airplane come over the mts. and circled down country. Fog was forming after a clear sunrise. In fifteen minutes it had become full coverage and very dense. It was nearing that stage when the plane came. He said that he had been here and found the lakes well covered. The reason he came and he got right at it. He had the head gasket set for his Lister diesel light plant and would I come down and put it in shape. I thought of John Kauffmann coming but doubted that he would arrive before the 26th at the earliest. This job wouldn't take more than a half day. I said I would. Could I go along back and spend the night there. I could and how about my hotcake batter – could I take it along. "Sure thing," he said. We will have sourdoughs for breakfast. So – I grabbed a GI sleeping bag and a jacket. Told Heidi to pick up the coffee can of blueberries and we were soon climbing to clear the Volcanic Mts. and our course followed my hiking route from Jay Mueller's cabin at the mouth of Lachbuna Lake. That flight in calm air with the sun low was a nice trip. I relived every mile and every hour of that 10 hour hike. Lake Clark was near calm with a breeze from the beach. He landed head on against the trees. Something that Babe would never do. Always leave a chance for a go around in case you have to he said. But we came right in as if it was recommended procedure...The lake high enough that Jay could taxi up the creek and tie up to some scrub willows. Too late to do anything towards fixing the blown head gasket trouble so we visited for awhile before turning in. Jay said it looks very much like Wally Hickel would be Alaska's next Governor. Jay didn't mind losing the election so much but he hated to lose to Hickel and then too many of his crew would lose their jobs because Hickel would appoint his own. "So – I may come back to the country to stay" Jay said.

August 31 – Partly Cloudy, Calm & 46°.

The lake was now calm so I took a little paddle up to Glacier Creek and down along the far

shore. No sign of moose. I had seen one caribou below Low Pass Creek. I had just come across when here came a pretty red and white [Cessna] 185. Roy Sanborn of the Park Service out joyriding in the Park Service's new airplane. "Where is John [Kauffmann]," I asked. "Oh, I see him around the building," he replied. Evidently he hadn't got my letter. I told Roy to give him the word to come on in. Good news, Gov. Jay is now ahead by 341 votes in the election. The absentee ballots are running in his favor. We visited, had a bowl of blueberries and he took off packing a few letters I had ready. Bring John in I told him and he said he might just do that. I went out back and picked a half gallon with the picker and then tried for a fish. First cast a nice grayling. On the gravel and in the pan and it got off the hook. No more, that was the last one in the lake. Partly cloudy, light breeze down and 50°.

September 1 – Partly Cloudy, Calm & 34°.

A young caribou left the brush on my right and crossed in front of me heading toward the lake. Not spooked but it had seen me and that was no good for pictures. The sun in my face anyway. I hoped it would continue on up country but next I saw of it the very unfortunate thing had turned down country. If it continued on it would end up on the meat pole. The heavy man had turned and headed back towards the connecting stream. He sat down on a rock and was using his glasses. That caribou was getting too close. It was in the open not 200 yards away when a shot rang out. It didn't go down but it staggered and turned this way and that. More shots and still it stood. Another shot and I saw it was hit again but still on its feet. It was the heavy man shooting. The little caribou regained some strength after the shock wore off and started to leave heading away and up country. It was badly crippled and one hind leg was broken and painted bright with blood. It appeared lame in a front leg too and was making very slow progress. As slow as it was the hunters didn't follow. The man who shot headed back to his buddy and then I saw a third man. The caribou crippling along with its mouth open and tongue hanging out was angling up my way and climbing the slope below me when suddenly it disappeared. If it went down or just moved into a low spot I couldn't tell. I watched for it to reappear but all I saw was my hanky hanging on a dwarf birch. The hunters made no attempt to come look for the cripple and finally I headed their way. I would let them know where I had seen it last and help them finish what they had started. One saw me with his glasses and I motioned for them to come. The heavy one and blue jacket headed my way and slowly. Close I could see they were at least part Native and told me they were from Kenai. Bud Lofstedt had brought them. They were camped at the upper end of the lower lake and had caught nice lake trout. I didn't ask their names. Blue jacket was young and wearing a Trapper Nelson[57] pack board. He didn't strike me as being much of a backpacker and

---

[57] "Trapper Nelson" back packs were designed by Lloyd F. Nelson in the 1920s after a trip to Alaska where he had seen an Indian pack that he elaborated on to create a wood pack frame with leather straps and removable canvas bag. Nelson sold his pack design to the Trager Manufacturing Company of Seattle, Washington in 1929 and the pack went on to world-wide use.

especially after he asked me if I knew Don Stump.[58] Yes I knew him. "Well, he is a real good friend of mine," he said. "Don Stump is a born again bar tender" and doing pretty good at his new trade, I'm thinking. "Gee, this is a beautiful place. You have a wonderful place to take pictures in," the heavy one said. I thought, after the caper you just pulled and then comment on how nice it is. He had done all the shooting and he knew he had hit the caribou two times for he heard it hit. After they had rested we headed up country to be above where I last saw the caribou. I would climb the slope so I could see it if it moved. They should search the heavy brush on the back side of the slope below. I climbed as they headed down. No caribou, they kept going and finally out of sight below and I wouldn't see them again. Where they went I don't know but I presume back to camp. So – I went down and looked and picked up my bandana. I looked for blood but with so many red leaves it was a hopeless search. I looked and looked for sign of the cripple but couldn't come up with any evidence. Where would it go – it was climbing towards me. I wouldn't go back down to where it had been crippled. It would head on up towards Low Pass Creek if it could. Heavy brush and if it crawled in there I wouldn't find it. I hit a game trail going past the point of the heavy stuff and went through to search and then came back to look more where I had seen it. Again I hit a trail lower down and headed up country through the jungle. Through it and into a little opening and there layed the caribou against the brush along the side I had entered. I was no more than twenty feet away when I saw it. It was breathing fast and heavy its head laying on the ground. I wouldn't waste more time with those who had made the mess. I would kill it and stop the suffering. All I had was my Old Timer.[59] I figured it would be a big struggle if I grabbed its antlers. It was a two year old bull. If I had a big club I would strike it a heavy blow on the neck and maybe stun it enough to get its throat cut – so – I cut a heavy willow club about six feet long. When I came in view it raised its head as if to get up but how could it possibly get up with a hind leg broken and on the opposite side a front leg also broken. How it traveled so far, a half mile at least, I shall never know. Both big bones completely shattered in both legs. It laid its head back down and I moved within reach and dealt the mighty blow. It flopped over and I grabbed the antlers and pinned its head to the ground. My Old Timer was open and in my hip pocket. I cut its throat and held it until it was completely helpless. I field dressed it and dragged it in the deep cool shade of big willows. I knew the flies would be swarming before I got back with pack board and butchering equipment. Me anxious to get back to the meat before the blow flies carried it away or loaded it with eggs.

Flies a plenty as I skinned and quartered. I couldn't make it less than three packs and two of them would be heavy. First load was front quarters, neck, hide and antlers. Second would be hindquarters and last of the rib cage, liver, heart and tongue. 45 minutes from the gravel bank and back again once I got packing. It was five when I came to the canoe with the last load. Had I more time I would have paddled up the still calm lake but it would be late enough by the time I got the meat hung and cleaned a bit.

---

[58] Don Stump (1918-2004) was a missionary from Washington state who first moved to Pile Bay on Iliamna Lake in 1945. He was a founder of Tanalian Bible Camp at Port Alsworth in 1965.

[59] A Schrade Walden "Old Timer" belt knife.

My birds met me at the beach and would work overtime to keep the small scraps packed away. The sun was behind the mt. when I called it good for today.

How would this meat be, I was anxious to find out. A crippled animal that is slow in dying can be very tough meat. We shall see.

A cloud bank loomed up down country and a fresh breeze came up the lake for a couple hours and then died. Now at 10:30 partly cloudy, calm, and 38°. The meat will cool out good by morning.

This evening the most colorful sunset of this year. Very red from the lake level on up.

I wonder, how many times during a hunting season does the worst predator of them all (man) perform as those did today. Of the three only two came to search. They walked through the area and disappeared. With them I would do as we did turkey killing sheep dogs in Oregon. Tie it around their neck so close they couldn't bite and just let them pack it until it fell apart. They killed no more turkey.

September 2 – Clear, Calm & 30°.

Here came a [Cessna] 185 flashing by. A climbing turn and then back down to land on the glassy water, coming towards my beach and I should have known because of the jazzing of the throttle as he came close to splash a bit. Bud Lofstedt again and he said he had brought two old guys to his cabin. He didn't think they were hunters. I thought of the last couple and the tragic end. Why did he stop to tell me he had brought more. He asked if I intended to stay this winter and I said I didn't know for sure. Would I build a new cabin for him. I told him I had better not start one. "No way will you do it," he said. He says, "I have one but it is looking pretty ratty and I would like a pretty nice one." I told him I didn't think BLM would allow him to cut logs for one and I doubted that the Park Service would let him build one. "Oh, I think I could build one up there," he said. Better check first, I advised him. He said he has had logs cut for four or five years. I haven't seen them and he said they hadn't been peeled. We visited on the beach a few minutes and then he took off to check on his party at the stream. From there I saw him flying a crooked course along the low country bordering the lower lake as if looking for caribou. If flying would get a job done I think Bud could do it.

I was putting the canoe in its resting place when suddenly Long John Kauffmann came around the point from Hope Creek. A big grin on his face. He had come in that [Cessna] 206. Yes he had received my letter but couldn't come right away. A young man, a relative of his had been severely injured in a very bad auto accident in Anchorage. Three hours of surgery to put him back together. Then arrangements with lawyers to get the insurance straightened out. Now he is out of danger and John could come. We came to the cabin and in front was three big boxes plus a rubberized pack sack full of food. Enough food to last a month and I had only suggested he bring some green stuff for salads.

He guessed that he got a little carried away with his buying.

I set up the sorter and we ran the blueberries over it and did end up with a gallon and a half. Now, we would get him located for the night. Would he like to stay in Spike's cabin – he sure would. 6 foot 4 inches, he was pretty long for my lower bunk. We paddled up and took his gear. He liked the looks of that big double bed.

The sun had dropped behind Falls Mt. It was getting close to supper time. Caribou liver, beans and a big salad would be our supper. John made the salad and what a salad. Lettuce and cucumbers only with a dressing mix he had brought along. Trouble was he didn't do his share of the eating. It was nine thirty before we got the dishes done. He wasn't sure he would wake up at five so took my Baby Ben along when he trudged the beach to his sleeping quarters. I got with my writing after storing the groceries we had scattered outside.

Again it was going to be a clear calm night. The temperature 40° at 10:30.

September 4 – Overcast, Blowing dn. & 50°.

The day was fairing up and we headed up Hope Creek more to see the country than anything. The colors not yet bright but after returning John would remark that it was the nicest hike of his life and the colors out of this world. We climbed to my high lookout at the mouth of 2nd canyon. Our bull caribou was feeding on the slope directly across. A pretty sight in the colors when the sun broke through. Every time we sat down John dug out his notebook and started writing.[60] He was getting material for his Lake Clark National Park. I glassed for game but the bull was the best I could do. He finally came down and crossed Hope Creek to our side but on the opposite side of 2nd canyon from us.

We headed back at quarter past four and it was none too soon. Rain came to upper Hope Creek and to us as we pulled out on the Cowgill benches. An hour fifteen to the cabin from the far end.

Time to start supper and we had better fry up the package of chicken thighs and the lamb chops John had brought. I smelled of the package which had been in the cooler box since he came. It didn't smell too purty good to me and John sniffed and said bury it or feed it to the birds. We hashed it over and decided to give them the heat treatment. After frying well done if they didn't pass the sniff test we would deep six them.

I doctored them up real good and covered the big square skillet over a hot fire. They sizzled and fried and grease dripped from the lid onto the stove. The chicken golden brown and we would save it to eat cold. The lamb chops got the same business and turned out as fresh as today's market. If we got sick I would drink a big shot of vinegar and John allowed gin would be better.

---

[60] John Kauffmann was researching a chapter in the National Geographic Society book, *Exploring America's Backcountry*, entitled "Lake Clark the Essence of Alaska: Tundra, Glacier, Mountains."

Dishes done and we would build a fire in the fireplace. John says that every evening winter and summer he has a fire in his fireplace. He sat on my caribou mat on the floor resting his back against the lower bunk and had a hard time keeping his eyes open till the fire burned down. It was raining and had been off and on since we came down the mt. I wanted him to stay and use the lower bunk but he wouldn't. Pulled on his little rain jacket and took my old cow barn lantern up the beach. I did my writing while the coals died and time to cover the chimney. A good day and if it was storming in the morning John might sleep in a little. Still places he would like to see if the weather faired up. Go up the lake and the right fork to get close to the high ones and climb to my peak for a view of the upper Kijik. Redoubt and Iliamna volcanoes. I doubt that the weather will cooperate.

Now at 10 o'clock. Blowing down, still raining and the temperature 46°. I suspect that daylight will see new snow on the higher peaks.

Today near split rock we saw a half gallon of blueberries waiting to be picked. Still firm and a picker would get them quick and easy.

September 6 – Partly Cloudy, Calm & 35°.

We headed back and again spent a little time over looking the valley while he wrote notes. His notebook was getting well filled. He would be limited to about three thousand words for the National Geographic story he said and he was thinking that to write about the whole Lake Clark Ntl. Park would be a chore. To float a river or hike a trail would be easy to write about.

While up the canyon we had seen Lofstedt's Cessna circling below in the vicinity of his camp. No plane there now and I spotted the moose packers a mile up the river flat and still trudging towards the forks. I'll bet they will think twice before they kill a moose so far away again, that is, if they pack all the good meat out.

Just here and a C-130 [Lockheed Hercules][61] search and rescue passed headed up and soon passed headed back down. Someone must be in trouble. Then a big military helicopter came down Hope Creek and low down the lower lake. The C-130 [Lockheed Hercules] continued to fly back and forth over the lakes. I built a fire and popped some corn. "Two things I can't resist," John said, "Popcorn and peanuts in the shell."

I waited before starting supper in case his pilot came. We finally decided he would wait till morning so I opened a can of corn and spiked it with bacon butter and chili pepper. I cut a chunk of caribou backstrap to fry. We had salad ready for dressing. Nearly through with our meal and here came the [Cessna] 206 low over the cabin. It was Tim[62] and he was soon at the beach. A front had just passed Cold Bay[63] headed this way and

---

[61] The Lockheed Hercules, C-130, a four engine cargo plane.

[62] Tim LaPorte, bush pilot and owner of flew for Iliamna Air Taxi who lived in Iliamna.

[63] Cold Bay, a small village on the SW end of the Alaska Peninsula.

the ceiling was lowering at King Salmon. He figured he had better get John out. Looks like a village at the lower end of the lower lake he said. Tents a bunch. A [Cessna] 185 or [Cessna] 207 bottom up in Lake Trout Bay. The tail broken off so it must have hit pretty hard. A big helicopter there. The C-130 [Lockheed Hercules] overhead to keep in contact we figured.

Tim runs a hunting and fishing air taxi service and says there may be some sportsman hunters left but he sees very few of them. Some he refused to fly out unless they haul more meat. Said he told two guys, "You boys have some work to do before I will take you out." They did and he did. He had been going full blast today. I offered what was left of our supper and he sat right down and went to work. John had gone up to Spike's cabin for his pack and lost no time getting back. He thanked me for the fabulous tour and he would write. Left me with fifty or more dollars worth of groceries and flew away. The dry and canned stuff will keep but the perishables, I can never use it all before it goes to pot. Glen is due in three days. I'll see if he can use some garden trash. I know what he will say, "We have a garden full of it."

September 7 – Partly Cloudy, Lt. Breeze dn. & 40°.

It seemed good to wake up this morning and plan my day with no one else to think about. This was going to be a busy one. After my hotcakes I promptly canoed up to Hope's cabin and hauled my smoke equipment down – dug a pit in the sand bank at the holding pond for the fire box, a trench for the 4 inch pipe and elbow. Set up the tripod and got a smoke going with balsam poplar for fuel. I stripped the meat sacks from the six large pieces and hung them from the top and the three legs being careful that they didn't bear against each other and leave unsmoked spots. I also added a part slab of bacon and my moose sausage from Dick and Geraldine [Straty]. Everything hanging free I put the cover over and used clothesline to snug it in around the top. I was in business and I would give it a good smoke.

The day was fairing up. Blue sky and a fair breeze down the lake. It would have been a good day but not on the lake for the breeze increased and the lake rough.

I had water on the camp stove for a bath and a big washing. Wood to saw and split for I had neglected everything to give John the best tour possible. My smoker was doing a good job and I had little trouble with it burning hot with little smoke.

Airplanes flying again today. One that I didn't know about took off from Jerre's point. Jerre had put a padlock on the door and showed me where he hid the key in case I wanted in. "Only a very few would know where it was," he said.

This afternoon I got with my letter writing and kept it going until three and then decided to go cut some alder to fuel the smoking fire. Up the creek trail on the far side was a patch and I went for a pack board load. Green, and I burned everything for a good dense smoke. A blue and white swept fin Cessna came to Emerson Creek and I saw three

out on the beach but after it flew away I failed to locate anyone. It was slow in becoming airborne so perhaps everyone was aboard.

The weather thickened and a few drops of rain came near supper time. A big salad, the remaining piece of chicken, beans and sourdough biscuits would be my supper. My smoking fire I would fuel for the last time today at 8:30. Usually one good days smoke is about enough. Smoking is a sure cure for fly problems. They can't stand that smokey flavor.

Now at 7:45 heavy overcast, blowing down and 44°.

1978 is a spruce cone year and today Freddy the squirrel was busy cutting cones. Working very fast she could have two in the air on the way down at one time. The ground near the young spruce by the bone pile is well covered with new cones. How many will be put into storage is a good question.

September 10 – Partly Cloudy, Calm & 30°.

It rained a light shower and the lake calmed. The creek very low and I saw where I could work in my ditch. Get those boulders, too heavy to lift, lined up so they wouldn't slow the flow too much. Pitch out those that fit the shovel. Sunday and airplanes going home. Two Cubs on floats flying formation, a Beaver very high and above the scattered clouds. A big Cessna took off at the lower end. The Park Service says airplanes will be permitted if it becomes a park. Subsistence hunting only and who qualifies – me for one.

September 13 – Overcast, Blowing dn. & 42°.

It was after lunch when two big Cessnas on floats came up the far side. One a white one and the other light brown and white. They both turned out to be Lofstedt's. Dealing with the oil companies I suspect he passes out a hunting trip to Twin Lakes now and again to cinch a good deal. His white one came down to Jerre's and the next move was to try to tow the river boat up the very rough lake. Full power and it appeared he was trying to get on the step or to fly just clear of the water. That would have been a good stunt if he could do it which he couldn't and gave up. Back to the beach with the boat and he flew up. Soon the brown one came down and let a man in a bright orange cap off at Jerre's. Soon he was snailing up the lake propelled by more horse power than Jerre's little Chrysler. Now it soaked in – it was Lofstedt's white Cessna with landing lights turned on that circled the two bull moose. Was this guy going to try for the second one. There would be little need for the boat up at Bud's cabin. Sure enough up and around the point to Glacier Creek beach he went and stayed. It is sad. There is no safe place for the bull moose these days. Airplanes flying low are sure to see those white palmed antlers. The only half safe place is miles from water for float planes and then the Super Cub with very big tires takes over.

To forget my unhappy thoughts I gathered up my wood cutting tools and went back behind Spike's 40 to drop a lodged dead spruce, limb and buck it for packing. Seven days and moose season closes until December 10. September 20 can't come too soon. No track sign that the moose are moving yet but any day now they will show.

Now at seven o'clock. 44°, blowing down and overcast. Low clouds moving as if tomorrow will be another rough one on the lake.

I wonder if there is a salvage crew working on the overturned Cessna. Pretty tough row to hoe when the lake is rough. I am thinking of riding down with Glen when he comes and see how they are progressing and then walk back up.

This afternoon as I went back to cut wood a spruce grouse flushed from the moss to a tree. A little farther and another one. Good to see them near.

September 14 – Overcast, (Raining), Lt. Breeze up & 38°.

The rains came in earnest and I was glad I pulled on my heavy GI sweater and nylon Kelty before heading down. I headed for the camp at the perfect beach near Arlen's cabin. I had cleaned it up good early and wondered how it was now. Litter laying around but not one can added to those I flattened and put in the deep pit. All of the lower legs of two caribou with hanging strings still tied but cut lay on the beach. Chunks of caribou skin laying at the edge of the campground. It struck me that people are no more educated this season than last. I cleaned it up again and paddled to Arlen's cabin. Twice as bad as early spring if twice as bad is possible. The door standing open and somewhat of a trail from it to the back wall. It would take a very big pit to hold all the empty cans, boxes, bottles, and other refuse. I wouldn't attempt to clean it up for the cabin is in terrible shape from vandalism.

A great supply of Morton's salt and I picked up a 26 oz. pour spout can to refill my salt cellar. A one lb. carton of oleo that the squirrels had already opened joined the salt.

September 16 – Overcast, Breeze up & 35°.

The lake rough they landed above the point and taxied down. Laddie was pilot and Glen riding shotgun. "I'm late," Glen said as he climbed out. "Couldn't make it the 9th." The three of us gave her the old heave ho and put her high and solid on the beach. They started unloading and out came that great big sack of rolled oats groats. If I ran out of everything else I would still have my porridge. 2 dozen eggs and 25 lbs. of brown sugar. 25 lbs. of flour and lots of mail.

What was the new outside. "Well, it looks like Jay Hammond is going to be governor." Doing a recount now. When is spud digging time? "Hasn't frosted yet." Glen had applied for his air taxi permit. He asked me about the wreck in the lower lake. Was it worth bidding on. $2,500 he would bid but I doubt if he could get it for that as the floats

are probably worth $12,000. Would I help him get it out. I allowed the way to go would be to have a big helicopter pick it out of the water and fly it to Port Alsworth, no muss, no fuss.

I got my outgoing ready and Glen allowed they had better head back for lunch. They hadn't had breakfast yet. A hop skip and a jump put the "T craft" into the air and it stayed after a fashion. I stored my groceries and dug into my mail. Many letters and one from Sam sounding pretty friendly again and forwarded a letter from a guy in Pennsylvania. Went to the hospital with a bad back and they learned he has heart problems too. But he is determined to come to Alaska and wants my permission to come to my place. I don't think that I would do anything as dangerous as that and plan to tell him so. He smokes, is 6 feet tall and weighs 243 lbs., is in the hospital and has been told with proper diet and to get in shape will erase his problem – so – he wants to come visit me at my home. As Babe said when the engine stopped while on the way to Nondalton and we coasted up to the shore on the far side of the little lake, "Now! wasn't that something."

I gave my stack of letters a fast once over lightly. Some nice reports on the film "One Man's Alaska." It has been recommended that every school child in Havana, Illinois should see it.

September 20 – Overcast, Calm & 33°.

More of the same – the ceiling right down along side the mts. Fine weather for the closing of the sheep and moose season. The poor caribou will have to tough it out until next March 31st.

A good lake to travel. A little tour to the upper end was in order. See Cowboy Bud's pretty nice predominately blue Widgeon. I wanted to visit the site of Jerre's moose kill too so paddled across and bumped into a big raft of ducks far out in the long stretch. Ravens talking so there was something to eat up in the brush. I thought that I knew right where it was but I circled and crisscrossed the area. Down near the beach and I decided one more go round and this time 50 yards higher. There it was, head, part of the neck bone attached. The antlers chopped out of the skull. Part of the backbone too and some litter which I picked up and tucked in the belly pouch of my Kelty. Plastic ribbons tied on the spruce and was surprised that the great guide Jerre Wills would need a blazed trail to find a dead moose little more than a hundred yards from the beach. I paddled on up past Glacier Creek and angled for the cockeye Widgeon (one wing pointed at a 45 degree angle). I found it parked near the old river bed outlet and a hundred feet from the lake. Both wing floats torn loose and the right aileron dinged up from the float striking it. Just standing and looking at it appeared to me that Bud was in a hurry and didn't go down the lake quite far enough for an up the lake take off. She was ready to fly and should have but the beach came too soon. Bud seen he wasn't going to make it and chopped the power – too late – the keel of the hull cut a groove in the ridge of the gravel, jumped a few feet

and then settled down to slide and veer to the right. "I'm not very good yet," Bud had told me before it happened. I took a couple pictures of the dry ground wheels up poorly looking bird and paddled on around into the bay. Moose bones where someone had boned out before loading. Plastic laying about and I picked it up and put it in the cabin. Again it looked as if everyone jumped up and ran. Water bucket full, groceries left outside. Kosher pickle jar cooling in the creek. What a way to go.

I paddled down against a light breeze and home by one thirty. A bite to eat and I climbed Cowgill Mt. to look down for moose. Nothing moved but I saw the wrecked [Cessna] 206 has been taken out and away. A beautiful view and if the sun would shine I would climb for pictures. A pretty Beaver flew up as I came by [Erv] Terry's.[64] A porky rasping under the floor of the tent frame. I was home when it came down flying very low and slow.

A little time still standing so I bucked several chunks from my feather light wood tree.

Blue sky showing now at 7:30. A breeze up and 36°. So now – I know of five moose that died and I wish that I knew how many more. The start of the deadest moose rutting season till now.

September 24 – Partly Cloudy, Calm & 25°.

The little kicker along for the ride and I was paddling by 8 o'clock. A nice quiet morning and I watched above timberline for the mother one with triplet cubs. To the stream in 55 minutes, which is real good time. Always enjoyable to run the stream. How many times have I wished the scenery would go by that fast on a calm lake. In the lower lake and on the right hand shore below where I beached the Cub before break up, a frame work on the beach. The two guys from Anchorage hunting sheep and seeing only ewes and lambs had camped there. It appeared that they had a tent with aluminum poles but the wind demolished it. So – they had a combination of spruce poles and metal ones lashed together. And they left the frame work. Not too much litter and their fire pit heaped high with gravel. I kicked into it and all sorts of garbage began to show. A terry towel, tin cans, foil, half burned plastic and some vegetables. I tore down the frame and sorted out the fire place. The spruce poles went back up the high bank to the German carpenters campsite for that is where they got them and they burned the rest for firewood. There under a spruce was three big garbage bags. Two of heavy plastic sheeting and the third of garbage from camp. So many Coors beer cans I have never seen in one sack. On top a part can of Hills Bros. coffee and a half can of Hi-C peach flavored drink mix. Those I held out and the camp fire garbage went in.

Ready to continue down and here was a fresh breeze coming up, so I put the kicker on and motored down. Getting there and I saw no sign of life at the wreck so I

⁶⁴ Terry's refers to the Cowgill-Farmer cabin owned by Erv Terry.

followed the right hand shore line to check campsites. I cleaned up two near the mouth of the lake. At one all cans were burned in the camp fire and then put into a cut open gas can and left setting by the burned out fire. Beer cans, foil, and what have you was scattered down the beach. I crossed over to check the river floaters campsite. A long string of tents on the bare ridge up from the lake shore when Mike, Mary Lee and I had gone to the lick. A clean camp. Not a trace of litter. All that I found was dozens of heavy rocks they had used to anchor their tents. River floaters are a good bunch, I think.

September 29 – Fog, Calm & 28°.

Nothing pushing so I didn't get up till six. This was another foggy morning. Spuds for breakfast and I had them and my porridge on the fire when I heard a little airplane coming up the lake. It had to be Glen I figured. I went outside to listen to it pass. It sounded only a little higher than the spruce but I saw no trace of it. I went back to my breakfast and was ready to fry the egg and caribou steak when I heard it again and this time coming down along the beach. The red "T craft" alright. He had found it open at the upper end landed and taxied on the step the three miles down. So foggy he was afraid he might hit a point of land that he didn't remember. Head out of the window to see the best possible. "We are a little short handed out there and want to dig spuds," he said. Figured on doing it today and tomorrow. Leon and Sig could help tomorrow.

He hadn't had breakfast so I set another plate and he had fried spuds with me. He thought that was a pretty hardy breakfast topped off with a big helping of porridge.

By the time dishes were done a trace of blue overhead. We would taxi back up the lake to get out of the soup. "You watch the shoreline and I'll drive," he said as we shoved off and headed up. I had left my cabin in good order right down to leveling the floor and tucking my camera gear and 06 ["aught six," .30-06 rifle][65] under my sleeping bag.

The first time since June 10 of 1977 that I had visited Port Alsworth. It looked as if a lot of action had taken place. Many logs on the beach. The runway freshly graded and widened. Paul Carlson[66] had put up a new house on the teen camp land and later I was to hear that he and his wife can live there the rest of their life and then the house belongs to the property. A nice looking two story house that cost something like $40,000.

A big white dish antenna erected near the woodshed at Glen's. Part of the new worldwide telephone system. Laddie and Glenda had talked to their son in Italy and Glen had talked to Babe and Mary. Four satellites spaced at equal distances above the equator around the world makes it possible. To talk from Port Alsworth to Rome, Italy for 17 minutes cost $3,700.00. To talk to Pedro Bay just over the mts. to the south the signal goes from Port Alsworth to Talkeetna to Anchorage to the satellite over the equator and back to Anchorage, Talkeetna and Pedro Bay. Good rig but it was out of order. Before

[65] RLP's 30.06 Springfield rifle.

[66] Paul Carlson (1916-1996) long time resident of Iliamna and Port Alsworth, guide, and heavy equipment operator. His wife, Irene Carlson (1915-) was a retired school teacher.

noon the trouble shooter flew in and found a circuit breaker had kicked out. Power surge from the portable generator the cause.

I got my outgoing mail licked shut before the mail plane brought the incoming and took the outgoing.

Glen, Laddie, and a full bearded boy named Doug,[67] were pouring concrete – six sided open ended boxes. More than three feet tall, twenty seven inches on a side for width and the wall five inches thick. Going to use them as casing in a new well for Laddie and Bee. With the dozer, doze out a trench about 14 feet deep. Then get down in the trench with the John Deere backhoe and dig as deep as they could go and hopefully hit the water table from the lake. Stack the concrete tubes and backfill around them. So – Glen and I went to the river flat with tractor and trailer for a load of sand and gravel. We had the concrete mixed and poured by noon and Glen pronounced it the quickest pour till now.

A good dinner and we went at the spuds. Red ones first and they turned out pretty good. That was all they had intended to dig for the day but I didn't learn of that and plowed out two rows of white ones. We picked them up and decided to continue. White socks a real nuisance. Those things are terrible at Lake Clark from now till snow flies. Bug dope does little good and I wished I had thought to bring my head net. Didn't bother little Leon at all and Sig very little. They helped after school. By the end of the day we had more than half of the garden coverage in the bin. The white ones not turning out so good. Some nice very large potatoes but quite a few had split wide open as if growing too fast.

Bee and family are visiting in Hawaii and Doug [Butler] staying in their house. He wants to hike to Twin Lakes before going back to work in the oil fields on the north slope. The boy is from Montana and a driller in charge of a crew for Husky Oil. He and I went to Bee's house to look at maps of the Lake Clark, Twin Lakes area. He had to go back to Anchorage by October 10th so wasn't sure he could make the hike this way. Intended to fly back out with Glen when he comes next trip but Glen isn't coming until the 15th of October or later.

It was dark when I trudged the road back to Glen's. The night clear and it would frost during the night.

October 2 – Overcast, Lt. Breeze up & 23°.

Since I had left the beach a fresh breeze came up and it was clearing down country. The lake was plenty rough enough. A heavy surf on the beach and a big one threw me back and put a gallon of water in the canoe. Next try I made it and paddled into Lofstedt Bay before getting organized for the trip down. Wet and cold was the trip and after a mile at low speed the little kicker showed signs of fuel starvation. Pumping the carburetor full with the fuel line squeeze pump helped but didn't eliminate the trouble. I limped along to

---

[67] Doug Butler, a North Slope oil worker from Montana who built a log house at Port Alsworth.

the protection of Carrithers' point and then let her die.

I removed the suction line from the tank and pulled the felt type filter from the end of the line. I puckered up and blew hard on the discharge end of the filter. I had noticed that the squeeze pump was very slow in expanding after I squeezed it flat as if the suction end was plugged. The reverse blast brought results like blowing your nose without a hanky and suction seemed free and easy. I put her back and fired her up. Ran her fast to the point and rough water again. No problem and that may have been the trouble although I had checked the gravity flow sometime back and pronounced it enough.

Coming down ice formed in bits and pieces where it splashed on me and my gear – the first of the fall season. Good to be back and a noisy fire to dry things out. The filter I pulled from the line again. Removed the felt and washed it in hot soapy water – dry it good and I'm thinking I have solved the starvation problem.

At sundown the temperature read 26° and the surf was noisy on the beach. Now at 8:30 still a fair breeze up. It is clear and 24°.

October 3 – Clear, Calm & 14°.

The lake nearly flat – just a trace of a breeze up. I had an early lunch and loaded to go hunt moose. I would go to Glacier Creek and check the game trail crossing and then work back into the big cottonwood grove. Halfway there I drifted and glassed. Somewhere there should be a moose. I suspect it is the wise cows who learns that to stay alive you must stay under cover. It wasn't always so. Back in the early sixties when there was little hunting pressure on moose here – cows and bulls could be seen in the open most anytime during rutting season.

Just as well go and I headed for the canoe a half mile up the beach. Not a cloud in the sky and the lake really flat calm as I headed for Carrithers' point. Halfway and the Cessna pulled out and took off down the far side. At the lower end it turned and came back up. Dipped a wing as he passed and turned back down at Bell Creek. Going to land and I heard him splash on the calm water. I waited as he taxied to me. "Rust Flying Service" painted on the vertical fin. Hank Rust or one of his pilots. His Beaver was trimmed in a rust colored brown and this Skywagon the same. A young guy climbed out on a float. "Just stopped in to say hi and look around," he said. Turned out he was with BLM and connected with timber sales. Staying at Iliamna and working Nondalton, Port Alsworth, Lachbuna and Currant Creek.[68] Why he came here I don't know. Evidently he scouted Carrithers' point for he mentioned the name Carrithers' and I had taken the sign down and put it in the cabin. He had read my book he said and he thought this was about the most beautiful spot he had seen. Two more in the airplane besides Hank, one of them a woman. We visited while Hank was collecting plenty in standby time. Tomorrow they would be going back to Anchorage. Carl was his name and "It was good talking to you,"

---

[68] Currant Creek, a major tributary of Lake Clark. The Dena'ina word is Nuch'tnashtnunhtnu,"we overdrank stream."

he said. I never did learn just what was his reason for coming. I figured that maybe I was going to be charged stumpage for the logs I cut to build my cabin. So – he climbed in and they took off down the lake. I had no more than reached the cabin when a fresh breeze came down the lake. Out in the stretch it was nothing but whitecaps.

October 15 – Partly Cloudy, Lt. Breeze dn. & 20°.

Getting there and just out of a cottonwood grove I looked up the slope and there high up was a moose calf at the head of one of the open swales. With the glasses I could see the cow laying broadside chewing. She hadn't seen me which was strange as those old cows see anything that moves. How to get near enough and have an open shot was a problem. Up the swale would be out of the question. A ridge on both sides but brush would hide the moose. A big rock above might do it but doubtful. No greater failure than not trying so I eased back into the timber and started my climb with a ridge between me and the moose. Finally, high enough I figure and I came up the backside of the ridge. On top and the country looked strange. No big rock where it was supposed to be. Slowly I headed down and things began to shape up. I could see a dark object and made it the calf. Brush was still a problem and the best I could do was sit the tripod on top of the big rock. What a set up that was. Just as well stand on top of a step ladder. A nice open spot just below the moose but heavy brush hid them where they layed.

The wind was strong and I couldn't put up with it for long so I crawled into my Kelty. I waited and the calf got up and picked a few bites in the clear before laying down back of the brush blind again. The cow moved and layed down. The sun was getting around and an overcast would soon rob the light. I would have to encourage them to get up. So – finger on the button I began to talk to her. If she was a tame one perhaps she wouldn't move out too fast. I was talking but getting no action. Suddenly on her feet and into the open. Not one but two calves followed. Twins! that was a surprise. The old girl had saved both of them. Twin calves are not plentiful in the fall. A pretty shot as they moved out and headed down the swale. She stopped below to look back. She had only heard me. A caribou would never spook from my voice. Into cover and I waited. Out she came again to stand and look. The sun went into hiding and the light not good enough. I watched her awhile and then started to pack up for the trip down. They moved slowly away heading down country into the cottonwoods.

I followed their tracks and suddenly and not too plain I saw a boot track in the snow. Now who would that be in moose country and the season long closed. I looked around and saw a good print. Mine! I had been there before starting the climb. It's a big country with many groves and brush patches.

Following their tracks and I hoped to see them again. If she was an old friend I might find her waiting. It must be quite a puzzle to the cow moose. Winter and spring man is no threat and then comes late summer and man is out to kill. Trust no one and I was happy that she was teaching the calves to do just that.

The lake was roaring mad when I came out of the brush. Plenty rough enough but I would be running with the seas as well as across. An extra big stone behind the front seat and I slipped her into the water and shoved out. Got the kicker going but didn't see my long tiller handle. On my way and it wasn't long until I decided this was just about rough enough. That seventh wave and the next two or three following were enough to cause me to tend my knitting pretty close. Don't let her get in the trough and don't run to much with it or I wouldn't make the shelter of the point. Doing ok if they didn't get any worse. Carrithers' point seemed a long time coming. Taking only a few drops of water so no problem. Just out from the point in the biggest waves and I was a hundred yards down. Made it just like I figured and I pulled the fuel line to burn her dry before reaching the beach.

Things to do before supper. A fresh supply of lantern fuel from my jet fuel cache under the spruce. Dry milk from the cache. A fresh kettle of beans to get cooking. My camera gear to clean and stow. Four o'clock and the light was failing. A good salad with my beans and caribou. The end of a pretty good day. Now at seven the wind strong in the spruce tops blowing down. A solid grey overcast and the temperature 32°.

October 25 – Overcast, Lt. Breeze dn. & 32°.

In one letter a good clipping that I had missed when it came. A picture of the smiling boy Ralph Waite narrator of the Nova program. *Alaskan Battleground* by John Voorhees[69] television columnist. "One can recommend that Congressmen take a look at this weeks excellent Nova – 'Alaska, The Closing Frontier,' " he wrote and after describing it in some detail he finishes with – "One comes away from this important hour more doubtful than ever that man has any kind of right to destroy his planet so willfully as we have done in the past. It would be nice if a small portion of it could remain unharmed." I agree, Mr. Voorhees, I agree.

November 2 – Overcast, Blowing up & 10°.

For log bucking I took the big bow saw. With a good sharp blade it cuts very fasts and will work in wood that will stop the 4' one man crosscut.

This morning I noticed a blow down a hundred yards closer than where I had been working. Mostly dead but a few green boughs. The wood poor for quality but many heavy limbs which make the best of wood. Coming back I stopped by – limbed it and then bucked it with a total of 15 cuts. Wood to burn and all for the packing. Towards the end my ears and hands began to indicate a temperature drop. The sun had dropped behind the mt. At the cabin 6°. I wanted to try some of those good heavy limbs so took the pack

---

[69] John Voorhees, television critic for the *Seattle Times*.

board and brought in a load to be made ready for the stove before I called it a day.

Dishes done and now at 6:30, 6°, a cloud bank way down and a fair surf on my beach. Compared to last year today was about normal. A real nice day back in the timber where it was calm.

November 4 – Overcast, Breeze dn. & 25°.

Saturday and this would be cooking day. Cook a pot of beans and bake a pan of sourdoughs. I wonder if some food value is lost in my par boiling beans in soda water until they show sign of being half done before draining the soda water off and starting fresh. I tended the fire and did small jobs about the cabin and woodshed. The big bow saw to touch up. Since last sharpening it had cut faster and pushed harder using one end as the handle than when using the opposite end as the handle. On checking it I found that the drag teeth were longer on the hard pushing end. Now she will do better I'm thinking.

Noon time came and the beans still chewed like raw peanuts. The weather had turned dark and it did a nice job of snowing for a hour or so.

The temperature 30° and what better weather would I find to dig deep into the cache and get out my cold weather gear and fill the boxes with things unused and tuck them back in the corner. The snow white coveralls was one item I wanted and the down detachable parky hood and the chest high very warm Navy wool lined pants, and my Mary Alsworth super socks and Air Force mukluks and mittens. In due time I had the full outfit on the lower bunk.

November 7 – Partly Cloudy, (Snowing), Blowing up & 11°.

This morning was wash day and then I would go pack in a few loads from the jungle wood yard. The limbs, stump wood, plus other odd bits and pieces. Keep my ready line wood pile looking well fed. I couldn't operate as Jim Teegarden of Telaquana told me he does. Never a stick of wood in reserve. Winter or summer when he needed wood to feed the fire he cuts some.

November 18 – Overcast, Blowing dn. & 30°.

For a change of pace I went to cut a little wood this afternoon. Dropped one and stood the packing lengths against a big tree and then worked up two that had been down flat for many years but still good wood. Nearby leaned a nice one lodged against a green spruce. With the wind I saw it working at ground level and knew it was rotted off. After a couple loads of little stuff I decided to see if I could pull it free and fall it for wood. With 60 feet

326

of rope and my cache ladder I tied to it as high as I could reach and 40 feet to the side took a block and tackle hitch around another spruce. It was well tied by boughs of the holding tree and I doubted if I could free it. With the rope tight as a fiddle gut she showed signs of moving. A good old heave ho to the side and down she came across my timber trail. A job well done and the light failing I called it a day and came back to work up my packing for the day. Out front in my little bite the small grebe was diving for its supper. A gentle little guy, goes about his business quietly without fuss or muss. An example for all of us.

> *For a change of pace I went to cut a little wood this afternoon. Dropped one and stood the packing lengths against a big tree and then worked up two that had been down flat for many years but still good wood.*

The last of my lettuce and celery brought by John Kauffmann Sept. 1st went into my salad this evening. Only carrots and a little cabbage left and then I must depend on real live spuds, carrots, and one-a-days to fight scurvy.

Now at 6:45 rougher still, blowing down, overcast and 32°. Last year on this date it was 42° and in the morning of the next day 45°. A week later it was -2° and for the last two days of Nov. -20° was the high and -24° the low.

November 22 – Overcast, (Misting), Blowing up & 23°.

After lunch I started to read the book *Never Cry Wolf* by Farley Mowatt. I had read it once years back and wanted to refresh my memory on his observations of wolves in the Barren Lands west of Hudson Bay in Canada. It didn't last, I wanted to do some work so broke the crust to the jungle and cut another tree. A dead one and it had been a sharply leaning tree growing not round but egg shaped. A freak and had forked three or four times ten feet up to make many pole tops. The best of wood and the heaviest, hardest dead spruce I have cut in a long time. I packed in the small stuff and worked it up for the stove. Three good loads stand against another tree. Now I have wood waiting to come in from about seven locations. Instead of a pack horse I need a pack string.

> *A job well done and the light failing I called it a day and came back to work up my packing for the day. Out front in my little bite the small grebe was diving for its supper. A gentle little guy, goes about his business quietly without fuss or muss. An example for*

The temp. failed to rise and at sunset it started down the lake was calming and the overcast had bright spots. It might cool pretty good tonight.

Now, tiz the night before Thanksgiving and the wind had just returned, blowing up and the temp. 20°,

the sky overcast. Is this the same mild temperature wind of today or is it one from farther around to the north – morning will have the answer.

December 1 – Overcast, Calm & 25°.

The light breeze held coming down, a real joy to paddle and I made the run from the head of the bay in one hour fifteen. It was near two o'clock when I beached. Biscuits to get into the pan and a bite to eat. I sat down to read a chapter or two from the book *A Sand Country Almanac* by Aldo Leopold. The author was born in Burlington, Iowa, only 40 miles from home. As a writer he compares with Henry David Thoreau and the book review by the *San Francisco Chronicle* reads, "We can place this book on the shelf that holds the writing of Thoreau & John Muir."

December 5 – Overcast, Breeze dn. & 26°.

This morning I would start a kettle of small white gravel cooking. No soda this time but vinegar to see if it has an effect on cooking time.

While I was trying to make soft beans out of hard ones I dug out an SOS pad and gave my aluminum cookware a good polishing.

I came in to find the beans still not completely tender. Eight hours of boiling wasn't enough. I shoveled in a half teaspoon of soda and left them uncovered a crack to keep from foaming over. Tossed in a small handful of egg noodles to make them bean noodle. By five they were good enough and a pretty nice treat for supper. If Glen doesn't come until Christmas I will get used up some of the many items I have been holding in reserve for years. Some are near 20 years old, no doubt.

Now at seven, breezing down pretty good. Overcast and snowing lightly, temperature 30° In 1968 it was -35°.

Time to freeze this morning 40 minutes.

December 13 – Overcast, Lt. Breeze up & 20°.

Another kettle of beans to cook. Only two cup batches these days and they don't last long. This time I put in a half teaspoon of soda and wouldn't change the water. Toss in all the fixins and cook them and see how long it took. Everything working to perfection I finished my candle holder. A curled ring for a handle and a reflector to stand behind the flame. Makes good light for getting supper and washing dishes.

Supper over and dishes done. Now at seven, overcast, snowing lightly, blowing

strong up and 8°. How long will it blow? no telling but freeze up will come quickly when it calms.

December 17 – Overcast (Snowing), Blowing dn. & 27°.

The complaining by the ice gradually ceased and all was quiet except for the wind in the spruce and the roar of the surf against the edge of the ice. I wonder about the groaning of the ice. It can come and go with the temperature mild or cold as if it might be air pressure that causes it.

I looked out a couple times during the night to see that it was still snowing and building up. Soon after six I was up for hotcakes and used one of my last two eggs in the batter. I still have a good supply of dried egg powder but in batter it doesn't compare. To use it makes me think that I have lost my touch with sourdough.

By lantern light I read awhile after dishes were done and daylight began to show. A good book for the winter wilderness is Sigurd Olson's *Reflections from the North Country.* This makes my third time to read it and have received two copies as gifts.

Coming back it happened. I stayed farther out from shore to get more solid ice. From light snow cover onto bare ice with snow on my shoe pac soles. Out went my feet and both at once. There was nothing to break my fall but the ice. I hit the back of my head so hard that I was dazed for a few seconds. All I can say is that the human skull and brain is pretty durable. Now I have had it both front and back. My face and forehead making a complete wreck of the Cub's instrument panel and now I try to break three inches of solid ice. No further mishap on my way to the cabin.

December 20 – Overcast, Blowing up & 18°.

I'm thinking that I shall forever feel thankful that I stayed this winter and that I severely bumped the back of my head. Since coming in June 10th of 77 I have noticed that my sense of balance was not up to par by any means. I noticed it more in the cabin than anywhere. Forever making a step to regain my balance. Worse by far at night. Get out of my bunk at night and rest my forehead on the edge of the bunk a few seconds until my compass stopped turning and I could walk a half straight line. Crossing my pole bridge was a hit and miss proposition and if the water was high I used a pole to make sure that I got across. Now! no comparison on an even keel anytime and all the time. How many brain surgeons, I am wondering, would have used a black jack on the back of my head to erase the damage done by a severe blow to my forehead more than two years ago. If I ever have the opportunity I must ask one just what took place inside my pumpkin head.

December 26 – Overcast, (Snowing), Calm & 16°.

Mail, a batch of it. Later I counted more than 75 cards and letters and fourteen packages if you count big fat padded envelopes as packages. I got busy closing the last of my mail while Glen gave me a news briefing. Jay Hammond is still the governor and Hickel is begging his friends to chip in to pay for his campaign expenses. Again and again they took a poll and he lost some each time. And, "You are now living in a National Monument," Glen said a temporary deal hoping to convince the public that it should be a Park.[70] Far out on the lake two dark objects coming from Jerre's cabin. At last he was coming over. A message to send out no doubt.

I ask Glen about the radical postage fee of $2.20 on a 6 oz. 4th class package. Something wrong there and he agreed. A couple packages had come back for more postage. His guess was that Pat had weighed a heavy one or two and a light one and put the heavy postage on the light package!

Now, the man Tom[71] made his business known. He is with National Geographic and would like to come to spend a few days now or in March and preferably March. He too is working on that Alaska book by National Geographic. He wanted to be here to see what a typical days activities consisted of. So we agreed on March, and Glen would come again soon with my big grocery order on January 13, weather permitting.

Packages, I hardly knew where to start. A big box of goodies from Helen White in appreciation for letting her read my journals. Things I can use, seasonings and such and I appreciate them but wish she wouldn't for I'm thinking her income isn't all that great. Brothers Robt. and Raymond with good things to eat, candy and nuts fruitcake and heavy stick of lunch meat 20 inches long. And Eve Gelmer of Kansas sent me some metal chimes so I can have music when the wind blows. From L.L. Bean 66 feet of neoprene filling for my snowshoes.

The light failed as I read into the huge stack of letters. Once over lightly and more later. I hit the lantern and read till past six before having my cold porridge pudding. I had been sampling and didn't feel the need for more. Fifteen to go and I had to knock it off and get my writing done. The night overcast and dead calm after a sudden blast up the lake. Temperature 22°. What a Christmas this turned out to be.

December 27 – Partly Cloudy, Blowing dn. & 31°.

I still had mail to read. A bundle of copied clippings from Anchorage papers sent in by Paul Fritz of the Park Service. There is one guy in quite a batch that is on the ball. I wish that I had him for a contact when I was filming, writing letters begging for answers and

---

[70] As a deadline set by the Alaska Native Claims Settlement Act approached President Jimmy Carter invoked the Antiquities Act creating 56 million acres of national monuments in Alaska, among them Lake Clark National Monument.

[71] Tom Melham worked for the National Geographic Society and was an assistant to the managing editor for the book *Exploring America's Backcountry*.

getting none. My man was in Washington and they didn't forward his mail, or so the story went.

I lined up Paul's five big brown envelopes dating from August to November. Roughly 85 sheets 10½"x 8". Copies of clipping pertaining to the big hassle over the D-2 land issue. Some mud slinging there I tell you. Now as I get it there will be no chewing up of the wilderness in question for three years at least. I read and read and started picking those that looked the most interesting. Lunch time and still it blew clouds of snow down the lake. I looked for sheep on Falls Mt. as well as Allen's but didn't really expect to see any, but did. Seven head working above bed ground rock up from Jerre's cabin.

CHAPTER SIX – 1979

CHANGES IN THE AIR

January 6 – Partly Cloudy, Calm & 21°.

Gee! I was happy to see the winter shaping up a bit. Clear calm and cold is ideal. I was sure that it was clear at first light. Early in the morning the lake ice started talking and I figured a change was taking place. Four days running I had battled the wind and walked a total of maybe 36 miles. Now it was dead calm and the caribou gone. I would feel good about that later in the day.

January 7 – Clear, Calm & 10°.

I sawed and split a few to make the pile look unused and packed in a good supply for the night. That big white moon came out from behind Crag Mt. It's a cold moon, I'm thinking and hope it doesn't disappoint me. A little airplane flying very high passed on its way to Kenai after a caribou hunt no doubt. Two evenings ago three flying as a group passed going in the same direction. Still more than two months of caribou season before the close. For three months and ten days they will be legally safe from the greatest and worst predator of them all and then the shooting starts anew.

January 9 – Overcast, Blowing dn. & 36°.

Now, I believe that I can safely say that I am out of the woods with my battered brain. Soon after cracking the ice my head began to give trouble. To cough, sneeze, use the heavy splitter or even bend over caused pretty intense pain as if there was a severe pressure build up in my skull. It was momentary for the most part but to sneeze left it hurting for some time. Hardly noticeable in the morning but by evening it could make me wonder if all was going to be right in the end. Nice to have my sense of balance back but this was something more disturbing. Then, came the turning point and day by day it became

less noticeable. Now it is not noticeable except in rare instances when I can be reminded that not so long ago my head hurt. Sprains and bruises, cuts and burns can pretty well be doctored in the wilderness but the cranium in trouble leaves you thinking the worst and hoping for the best. Now that we are on an even keel and feeling real good let us think as Robt. Service wrote, "There's a whisper in the night wind. There's a gleaming star to guide us. The wilderness is calling, calling, - let us go," – and go we will.

January 14 – Overcast, Calm & 25°.

The storm was a short duration. The second half of the night was quiet. Looking out at past twelve I could see that the ground under the roof overhang was solid white. A good night's sleep and I was up for hotcakes in good time in case Glen decided to fly. About an inch of new snow and part of it had fallen after the calm for the lake was solid white. Visibility was limited to the lower end and I was soon to learn why. A light breeze came and with it snow. By the time my chores were done it was calm and opening up to be a fair day.

Church morning at Port Alsworth and so no Twin Lakes flight. The only time I have ever seen Babe's house empty and locked was in 1976. I flew over and after tailing the Cub onto the beach I went to the house to find a padlock on the door. No one in sight and I wondered what tragedy had occurred. I finally headed for Wayne's [Bee] house and it too was empty. Coming back it suddenly became clear. Everyone in the area came pouring out of the church (was the airplane repair shop and now the school house and church). So – maybe this afternoon would see the "T-craft" headed this way.

January 18 – Clear, Calm & -17°.

Snow was curling over the ridge of Rock Pile Mt.[1] A north wind up there but dead calm below. I stayed a few minutes glassing the brush patches along the slopes and then headed down. It was 2:30. I back tracked the lynx track to see what had taken place. At the start of the drag trail a couple tufts of hair but not of a white rabbit. No other tracks but rabbit and the lynx so I guess the lynx cat snagged on the dead branches of a small down tree he had dived into. No sign of blood or a struggle but tracks coming in, of a lynx on the run. Jumps six feet apart and I back tracked. A couple hundred feet he had been on the move making the chase. I was a little surprised. I figured the lynx cat made his kills by stealth and a pounce. I had seen one stalking caribou years back and he moved so slow and close to the ground I could hardly see him move.

At the beach by 3:40 and I should have been there earlier. Tracks of the wolverine in mine and he back tracked me a hundred yards before turning to Lofstedt's Bay. I came

---

[1] RLP's Rock Pile or Rockpile Mt. is probably the 6,070 ft peak located NE of the head of upper Twin Lakes. Named for a huge rock pile lying at its base.

on as the sun climbed the peaks. About three quarters of a mile down there was his tracks in mine again and back tracking. This time he forked off towards Bell Mt.

I thought I could feel it getting cooler on my face after the sun was long gone but when I came up my path after 1 hr. ten minutes of travel I found it -17°. Still good coals for a quick fire and supper was soon warming. I made a small bannock using Bisquick mix, added some raisins, butter and Wesson oil. Had the last of my cooked beans so after supper I promptly got three cups of dry ones in the kettle to simmer over night.

How cold will it get tonight, I wonder? Now at 7:15, -18°, clear and calm. Two more days and the moon goes into its last quarter. Dark of the moon is normally not cold weather time but all signs fail at Twin Lakes. Winter just might go on and on and on till April.

January 21 – Overcast, (Snowing), Blowing dn. & 24°.

Folded and in a large brown envelope six large maps stapled together Lake Clark National Monument and a bold line laying it out if I pulled the staple and spread them on the gravel. No need for that. This west border was of most interest to me. And in another envelope the Federal Register dated December 5, 1978. About three eights of an inch thick and describing all of the Alaskan National Monuments. 17 in all. The last page for each carried Jimmy Carter's signature. In the clipping copies I ran across a letter to the editor of the *Anchorage Times*. Quite a letter speaking of the wilderness. I came to the end and whose name did I see John Branson, Lake Clark. "Moose" John! Boy, he was a brave one. If the opposition knew he was caretaker of the governor's lodge he might get a lot of fan mail. Later I ran across a reply which said he might feel quite different if his property was taken over. And then another from the Kenai praising him for speaking his mind. I'm a little surprised that I haven't received a few letters about my part in "Alaska, The Closing Frontier." Till now no threatening letters. It was twelve thirty and my fire getting cold before I quit for a bite to eat. Still snowing which made reading easier. It had calmed though and the lake which had been scrubbed clean took on a solid white look again.

January 22 – Overcast, Calm & 21°.

A quiet night and a good night's sleep. I had let the fire die out and missed the instant warm water when I got up soon after six.

Some how I figured the Park Service might come in today. In the last mail a letter from Bob Belous saying they would be in as soon as they got word through Glen that the ice was safe. His letter post marked January 5 – so – he may be back in Washington, D.C. by now.

I had my spuds, and a real live egg on top. Got my chores done and then proceeded to get my cabin in real good order. I'm living in a national monument now and things must be regulation. Scrubbed and scoured, dusted and leveled. A few items to go to the woodshed and the camp lite to go to Hope's cabin. It was near noon before I was ready for inspection. The day was improving. Entirely flyable with a light breeze down and the temperature would climb to 26° today.

Before lunch I put on my snowshoes and climbed the Cowgill trail to the benches above timber line. The fresh tracks of the wolverine coming down and heading off down country. I could see no sign of sheep and I keep watching and listening for ptarmigan but for some reason they are silent.

Two weeks since I checked the lake ice and I found it 12". Gained four inches. It is less than half as thick as it should be on this date.

January 23 – Partly Cloudy, V. Lt. Breeze dn. & 4°.

16 degrees when I arrived at the cabin. It was near four o'clock and my birds were on hand for their bedtime snack. I'm thinking that if they could read the rules they would be as unhappy as many Alaskans are about the national monuments for it says loud and clear, "The feeding, touching, teasing, frightening, molesting, or intentionally disturbing any wildlife or their nesting, breeding, feeding, or related activities, is prohibited in the Alaska [national] monuments."

A couple sticks of wood on the fire and a bite to eat before I headed up and across towards the moose cottonwoods. More for the exercise than anything. I was quite certain that no moose lived there. A light breeze down the ice and the setting sun painting a few fringes in the slightly brown cloud cover pink. I was back by 4:45.

This evening was green salad evening. Odd number days are salad days. Lettuce, diced raw potato and onion. Easy on the real live onion for I see Glen has them down as 25 cents each. A slice of tomato on top.

Now at seven a few stars faintly showing. It is calm but I can hear air in motion on the mt. across. The temperature 16°.

Finishing my supper and doctoring up my cold porridge pudding when I caught the cook sprinkling Tide on top of the brown sugar (they were sitting side by side and shouldn't be). God almighty, what a mess but maybe I could salvage my good rolled oats groats. I scrapped off all of the white stuff I could see and put on plenty Carnation. Tasted a trifle soapy but not too bad I figure. About midnight will tell if it was.

January 25 – Overcast, Lt. Breeze dn. & 12°.

If the fool flying machine came at all it would be when I was as far from the lake as my travels would take me. I had climbed to the high bench looking down on the upper falls

when I heard a big Cessna down country. For maybe a half minute I heard it and then it faded. Caribou hunters over the low country. Now, if the caribou have read the paper they will head up into the big valley and the hills between here and Lachbuna Lake. Not many would risk losing their airplanes by crossing the line into the monument, I'm thinking. That purty blue and white Super Cub that I saw land at my place last week was Fish and Game according to Glen. I wish that I could have talked to them and learned who will ride herd on this country, Fish and Game or Park Service.

January 26 – Overcast, (Fog), Calm & -3°.

Dressed light for the climb. I was on my way. If the "Van Winkle boys"[2] came they could relax, which they do more and better than anyone, until I came down the mt. Those stick climbers are the real deal on the mt. Walked right up without spinning a wheel. I poked them in the snow by a spruce and buckled on the spikes. Holes in the fog above and I left real sure that I would have a good climb. No camera gear for I had seen no sheep. This way I could have the fun of climbing again. Soon it was a sea of grey cotton covering the lake below. I was up in the clear and climbing easy. Everything frost white and the mts. never looked more beautiful. I saw the tracks of the white weasel and what does he hunt so high on the slope at this time. Tracks of a few ptarmigan and high on the point sheep tracks. I would climb Falls peak and it appeared to be a snow free climb. Some snow patches but few and hard as the road. Checking the big pasture as I climbed the ridge I saw no sheep but there were many tracks and fresh along my route. Many droppings so they must be feeding good. What feed I could see appeared to be very short and I suspect that the wind blown granular snow cuts a lot of feed and it is blown into the next valley.

From a few hundred feet above lake level it was noticeably warmer and a really beautiful day high up. I tucked my L.L. Bean super mitts in my pack sack and wore my monkey face gloves. On every projecting point I walked out to look below for sheep. Some where there had to be quite a bunch. Maybe two thirds of the way up the high ridge I moved to the edge carefully for there were many tracks. There just below me was a ewe and lamb. The ewe had one horn and a nub. Both her and the lamb looked to be in real nice shape. Coats long and so very clean and white. Why is it that sheep don't suffer from snow blindness. Close and using the glasses I noticed a dark patch under each eye of the ewe. These would serve the same purpose as a charcoal smudge around the eyes of man. I had never noticed this before and wondered if other sheep have the same built in protection. I stood quiet and watched them scratch with a front foot, feed a few bites and dig again. I backed away and continued my climb.

On the peak and just a trace of a breeze from the north. The fog had cleared out below and it was totally clear in any direction. Redoubt and Iliamna volcanoes poked up above all other peaks. From the peak Redoubt is directly over the head of Hope Creek valley and Iliamna farther to the right and putting out a good big plume of steam from its

[2] "Rip Van Winkle boys," RLP's characterization of NPS law enforcement efforts during the early days of the National Monument.

east flank below the peak. I was looking right down into Emerson timber and looked for the moose of yesterday. Small chance with me so high. I would never spot them unless they were in one of the small dry ponds. I looked for a herd of caribou and I believe I could have spotted a herd tightly bunched if they had been in the first few miles below the lower lake. No sheep to be seen in Emerson valley or up Camp Creek. I folded my GI wool scarf for a cushion on the snow and perched on the peak for quite awhile. I layed my good walking staff to the side and nearly lost it. It rolled and started to slide, hit a small rock and stopped. Had it missed the rock it was due to have gone a long way and possibly to timberline for there was a snow filled chute from top to bottom of the mt.

I saw all there was to see and several times over so headed back. A Beaver had come from the direction of Redoubt and perhaps it was from Homer and hauling caribou hunters to their happy hunting ground in Whitefish Lake country. Again I watched for sheep for I figured they were below some where. On the point of the mt. above waterfall canyon I took one last look at the big pasture and there, across the canyon and towards my lookout peak was a good bunch of sheep. I sat down and used the glasses. By the time I got them all rounded up I had 33 head but not one noticeable ram did I see. So I had seen 35 sheep which is a good number for the big pasture at this time of year.

In the lee of a hogback I picked a long, long snow field going down. Without crampons I wouldn't dare try it but sharp shod I would give her a go. Steep and if I tripped up I wouldn't stop for hundreds of feet. Using my staff as a stabilizer I made short work of a few hundred feet. A jog to the left and I was on my trail to my snowshoes. The sun was very bright and from the peak I estimated that at least three fifths of the lower lake was in sunlight. Less than a fourth of the upper lake but along the side below me, continuous sunlight for four miles or more. At its best the point of sunlight came within a couple hundred yards of Carrithers' point. Two days more than a week till it reaches my cabin.

February 1 – Partly Cloudy, Calm & 24°.

In one neatly packed box I came onto a book Raymond had mentioned he would send up and I hadn't received. The story of Bob Reeve, *Glacier Pilot* by Beth Day. That would be good for hours of entertainment. First I had a couple packages to wrap and a few letters to bring up to date. Noon time had come and gone. I popped some corn and settled down at my table to read and enjoy the weather. The temperature had climbed to 28°. Clouds were moving up the lake and eventually a fair breeze came and with it light snow. What would tomorrow, Ground Hog Day, bring. Judging from the past few months I would guess that he won't see his shadow.

I read and was surprised to learn that Bob Reeve spent considerable time flying in South America before he came to Alaska. And think as Raymond did. It's a wonder he didn't kill himself. Guess he is still with us for I haven't heard otherwise. With him as with many others, extraordinary skill plus a very large helping of luck has kept his name out of the big book, I believe.

February 4 – Clear, Calm & -44°.

Paul Fritz is still on the ball. I wish that he had been my contact while I was filming. This mail again, a half dozen big brown mailers with copies of clippings pertaining to the parks proposed and the monuments that suddenly became a reality. In one mailer a beautiful magazine type book, *Wilderness Parklands in Alaska,* 83 pages of text and pictures of all the monuments. The text for each by a different author. And in a second envelope a huge map of Alaska with all the monuments' outlines. I was busy till noon and then got a time check by the shadow of Cowgill peak against the mt. across.

February 5 – Clear, Calm & -40°.

What to do about that cold sleeping bag. I laid my strap iron anvil and one of my pet rocks on the stove while I studied the new *Parklands in Alaska* book. Good and warm I tucked them under the covers, just like we used to do with flat irons in Iowa in the good old days (in the twenties). Cozy warm when I turned in and I slept more and dreamed less.

I doubted that it would drop to a -40° judging by the way it was dragging its feet. A beautiful morning, just like April except for the cool. Things squared away I looked for my sheep but failed to located them. A trail leading across the canyon from where I saw them last but I failed to find them at the end of it, so I shouldered the scope and went halfway across. That good ram was still on top of the big rock face and another was still where I saw the bunch yesterday. Trouble with the scope. Every time I moved my warm eye close to the cold eye piece the lens frosted over. By working at it I finally found the bunch above the good ram directly across. Today I would have another go at the mt. and this time I would be sharp shod for that iron hard snow pack. I wondered how my…boots would stand the -35° which is cold for leather shoes and close fitting shoes at that.

Down the trail followed by that cool north breeze. The trail hard enough that I didn't switch to snowshoes. It was cold enough. Those neoprene rubber and nylon crampon straps were very stiff from the cold when I took the crampons off. The second dose of sun was still on the cabin and in a few days there will be a couple hours and more of afternoon sun.

Again that cold up the lake breeze and shadow when I got close. -26° at the cabin.

A hot cup of something and I dug into the cache for a refill of "Tide milk" and "Carnation soap powder."

The temperature headed down as if it means business tonight. My wood supply in the box I called it the end of a pretty good day. I was surprised at how easy it was to travel the mt. slope. Those crampons, I wouldn't take quite a bit for them.

Now at eight, clear, calm and -34°. After my wood was in I dug out two of my

good smooth pet rocks from out of the snow along the cabin to hotten up my dog bed.

February 6 – Clear, Calm & -40°.

My king size pet rocks went to sleep with me and I have never slept more sound or comfortable. A time or two I nearly failed to wake up for my fire check. My big window showing as much ice on the inside as I have ever seen in winters past. The fireplace sparkling with frost and this evening I would find my cooked beans slightly slushy on the side of the kettle next to the stone work.

Hotcakes and I had no more than finished my dishes when the sun lighted the peaks. My birds came and a second time and I wouldn't see them again today.

This afternoon I wanted to go down country. See what was doing at the connecting stream. See if the land otter had spent some time there. See if I could spot a lake trout flipping stones on the bottom for the feed hidden under them. Biscuit sponge rising so I had an early lunch and put it in the pan as a small single loaf of bread. I prefer it that way now that I tried it a few times. Slice as needed with the very sharp Denver butcher knife. It was -34° when I headed down in the shadow of Cowgill Mt. Soon I was in the bright sun and would have only one spot of shadow in the three miles. I saw where a rabbit and a white weasel had crossed the lake. Where a fox had followed the land otter track. The otter, I learned was going to Low Pass Creek and what would he do there? Did he intend to go through the pass to the Kijik. I would like to see his trail on the mt. Run and slide on the lake. Give him a long down grade and he would generate some speed. I learned that he had been at the stream but had only traveled its length. Only a couple places where he came out on the snow. Here two wolverines had followed the stream before using the lower lake to get to the Emerson timber.

With all the cold the stream is still running merrily. Pinched in to a width of no more than ten feet in a couple places but still open. Traveling against the bank on a narrow shelf of ice I went through with one foot. Just in and out but that mukluk iced over in no time. I stood on the beach of the lower lake to glass the country. The only track I saw on the mts. were up Camp Ridge in the rough stuff where the snow is not so deep. A little water ouzel was working the stream hardly more than 40 feet from me. Hop off of the shelf ice and under the surface. Gone for two to three seconds and then bob to the surface and onto the ice with a tidbit. Many, many times it dived under and seldom failed to come up with something. Several times the catch appeared to be a very small fish for I could see if flopping on the ice as the dipper worked at dissecting it. Me all frosted up about the face and that little guy in and out of the water as if it was August. I wished for the Bolex and suddenly it flew away. I headed back up the three mile trail. I could feel it getting cooler and now no more clouds to be seen. The sun still on my cabin when I reached halfway but would be in cold shadow before I got close. Only three sheep had stayed close to the high waterfall. I had seen four head pulling into waterfall canyon before I headed down. I found the temperature -36° and

this was not yet before sun left the peaks. Tonight would be a record breaker. I stoked the fire and got my bread in the oven. Split a few chunks and packed in a couple good loads. Before calling it a day I went out on the ice for a last look at the sun leaving the peaks. I could feel that cold seeping in as I stood quietly watching. -38° when I came in and after supper a -40°. It could come close to -50° tonight. Now at 7:20 a blast of fog hit me as I went out side to check. -43° the heat gauge said. Clear with the moon very bright. Calm as only it can be at -43°.

> *Tonight would be a record breaker. I stoked the fire and got my bread in the oven. Split a few chunks and packed in a couple good loads. Before calling it a day I went out on the ice for a last look at the sun leaving the peaks. I could feel that cold seeping in as I stood quietly watching. -38° when I came in and after supper a -40°. It could come close to -50° tonight. Now at 7:20 a blast of fog hit me as I went outside to check.*

February 8 – Clear, Calm & -46°.

Again a tour across to see where the sheep were and if there was any sign of wolf or wolverine on the mt. Only two times in the four winters that I stayed did I see wolf kills. One at the high waterfall on Emerson Creek at 45 below and one directly across the lake at about the same temperature. And I know of three kills by the wolverine during the same period. This morning I failed to find sheep on Falls Mt. One fair ram on top of the big rock face across from Carrithers' point. In a good spot, I could get pictures of that guy but as I stood in the sun watching I saw four more sheep along the route I must take to get there. I wouldn't bother them. They have problems enough without me moving them. I stayed until that long wedge of sun was in line with my trail across and then came to find it won't be long until the before noon sun touches Spike's cabin. -38° when I arrived and not long before noon.

Now at seven the usual, clear, calm, and -42°. This makes one week of below zero weather and six of the seven mornings have had a temperature of -40° or lower. For the first eight days of February a -27° and for the seven below zero days the average morning temperature of -35°. The coldest one week I have ever experienced.

February 9 – Clear, Calm & -43°.

I would take a tour down. Leave the lake below Gold Mt. Climb and travel timberline to Beech Creek or maybe Dry Creek. Packing my snowshoes on the pack frame I headed down. Shuffling along with my head down to protect my nose from the cold. A quarter mile down I took a look at the slope of Cowgill Mt. to see if by chance a moose was above timberline. What I saw surprised me. A very bold series of tracks, pinched in here and spread out there. I couldn't believe that it was caribou for I had been above timberline

along Cowgill Creek late yesterday afternoon. Then I saw them, caribou! lots of them on the Cowgill benches next to Hope Creek gorge. Maybe a hundred or more if I could get a count. I turned back. This was something that doesn't happen often. Not in all the years I have been here, has caribou in such numbers come in early February.

As I came back a small bunch ran up the slope towards the bunch as if something had alarmed them. I looked for a predator but saw none. Later I decided that it was I that moved them. Some spooky cow had seen me traveling the solid expanse of snow and cried wolf.

To get a better look at them I headed up the creek trail to the cabin log timber and then to keep from being too bold in the wide open I stayed in the timber and would climb the hump where they couldn't see me. A half mile and more away but again there was excitement and a cow grabbed her calf and started to run for their crossing on Cowgill Creek. Others fell in behind and in no time I had a string of caribou heading for points west. Very spooky, in summer there would have been no problem. From where I stopped I could see many trails going up Hope Creek and felt sure there must be a good bunch up there. I came back to the cabin to put an extension on one strap of my snowshoe binding. Too tight and making my toes cold. From the cabin I found that the bunch had stopped below Gold Mt. and were now feeding. On down and up from the long blueberry slope another good bunch at least equal in size. I hadn't seen them. So now I had at least 200 this side of Low Pass Creek.

February 11 – Clear, Calm & -34°.

It was 3:45 when I rolled out to check my fire. The full moon was very bright and getting around towards the west. I checked the temperature too and found it only -34°. Right about then I decided that winter has seen its best nights. Now it would gradually warm, maybe. I crawled back in my bunk and lay there thinking. I wanted to shoot some time exposures, while the trees were still decorated with snow. And while I still had good snow cover out front. This would be the time to do it. Tomorrows moon would be later and near dawn. I knew I wouldn't sleep for thinking what I should be doing so I got up and started the day by frying some spuds, bacon, and egg. The moon still not around quite far enough so I loaded my bean kettle and soon had them drinking water. Glen must be out of Pilot Point beans as the last 25 lbs. came in plastic bags. 4 lbs. to a bag. Store bought beans and bound to be good.

The beans were done on schedule and a fresh loaf of bread was in the pan rising. A little airplane came down the far side and cut across to the left side at the stream. I expected him to turn and give the caribou a good looking at but he continued on down the lower lake. Glen had said that they are not enforcing hunting regulations in the monument this year and I wonder if that is true. At any rate no one seems interested in making a kill here along the lake.

February 14 – Clear, Calm & -45°.

It was -40° when I climbed the ladder to my bunk at 8:30. This morning, right back where we started from. Now if it doesn't make -50° I will be disappointed. The moon had no more than dropped behind the last mt. in the Volcanic string when the sun lighted the peaks.

I had nearly lost my fire due to sound sleeping and so I tossed in some chips with fine split stuff on top. Opened the damper and the draft and whacked the stove pipe a few licks with the hammer handle to drop the build up of creosote & soot. Smoke started coming out everywhere but where it was supposed to. Again I battered the pipe and still it smoked. I ran outside and set the ladder up to beat the pipe above the roof. And still she smoked. My oats wasn't bubbling and the hotcakes looking poorly. Hardly a sizzle from the griddle. The cabin so full of smoke I opened the door. Something just had to be in the stove pipe. If I had neighbors I would say some one stuffed a sack down the chimney for a joke. Finally I went to the woodshed for a six foot spruce sapling stick. I climbed up on the roof, pulled the chimney bonnet off and rammed that pole down to the stove and rattled it around. That did it, out came a puff of soot and a healthy cloud of smoke filled the cold air. The pipe was plugged where it passes through the roof jack. In the blind there and me beating above and below. Hotcakes started to brown up in good shape and the porridge came to life.

February 15 – Clear, Calm & -35°.

A good night's rest. Those hot pet rocks makes turning in a pleasure and it is surprising how long they will stay warm in a sleeping bag. Sun rise before moon set and the temperature refused to drop as I had expected. Jets were making long contrails which drifted very fast south ward.

I failed to see any caribou this morning and I figured they had moved down country. The moving trend is down and now it was from fox pond to Beech Creek. A good bunch at each place and a scattering of singles in between.

February 16 – Clear, Calm & -32°.

What would it be like to wake up in the morning and find it snowing and blowing a gale – I can hardly imagine. This is finest kind of winter weather. What will the weather be when the big change comes. I was up at six to find the moon still high and due to become last quarter February 20th. Mild weather sure to come with the dark of the moon.

Spuds two mornings in a row due to a surplus of leftover hotcakes. Spuds are cheaper than flour, sugar, syrup, butter and caribou grease anyway. Jet contrails and

drifting south but slowly. A check for caribou showed a good bunch of about 70 had returned to the Gold Mt. area. Not moving much but heads mostly on the up country end of the caribou. I would bet they were headed for the Cowgill benches and if so I might have another session with them in the afternoon sun.

I chopped out my water hole as the plug refused to go down much over halfway yesterday morning. 30 to 45 below is a good test for most any thing. If there is dampness there is ice and instantly. Clear lake water in my dipping pan will lose its shine in less than ten seconds and slush on the pan just sticks fast and doesn't come off until I turn it bottom up on the stove. The wooden handle of my ice chisel will coat with ice instantly even though it has been inside the cabin overnight.

I was in the mood for more letter writing and I wanted to stay under cover anyway. Let the caribou band get by to the benches if that was their intention. Later I checked and sure enough they were single filing along the slope of Cowgill Mt. And later still I counted 47 on the slope between Cowgill Creek and Hope Creek. I wrote and wrote and the temperature climbed to 20 below. Suddenly the sun and at one o'clock. Tomorrow it will make its appearance over the last shoulder of Cowgill Mt., below the peak. As soon as the sunlight strikes full force the temperature starts to climb with a vengeance. I would see it a -4° before it started down again.

A Cub had gone up the far side and back down. Now as I reached the cabin a Cessna came down and angled my way only to swing back and continue on down and out of sight and hearing. I'm beginning to think this Monument is a pretty good arrangement and will tell anyone who lands that the caribou never had it so good in these parts.

Dark and the temperature is slow in making the plunge. Supper over and dishes done by daylight and now at 7:15, clear, calm, and a tropical -20°. Maybe now we have winter by the tail and a down the hill pull!

February 20 – Clear, Calm & -16°.

The sun was bright and warm when I left. This would be a warmer day than yesterday though I wouldn't be here to check. Just a good start and I saw a blue cloud against the spruce this side of the bend in the beach above the mouth of Emerson Creek. It had to be a camp fire but I knew of no one on the lake. I watched it as I traveled and sure enough it was wood smoke. Then I saw two people on the lake ice. There had to be an airplane behind the little point of land near the smoke. Now I knew why I hadn't seen caribou when I checked at noon. Not one and I thought it strange. The two headed out to intercept me on my trail down the middle. I angled their way. Tim and Mike from the other side of Palmer. They had two friends over across the lake. They had seen a wolverine at great distance this morning and also wolf tracks across. I questioned them about the tracks as I had been close to their sighting yesterday. I doubted that it was a wolf, maybe a porkypine. No! they knew it wasn't a porkypine. From their camp they had seen the

caribou spook. A big bunch climbed through Low Pass and the rest went up Beech Creek. Maybe it was the wolf that moved them. We headed for their camp. A Cessna and a Champion Scout were tied down there. Two tents and much sawed wood on the ice. They told me of a disastrous wind at Palmer. 100 mph and more wrecked many airplanes even though they were tied down. The low temperature there about a -10°. The wind had come the first week in February. -75° chill factor.

February 21 – Clear, Calm & -20°.

I was up early so as not to be caught napping in case Glen came in first thing. Such weather I have never seen the beat of it. -20 seems like zero or higher back in the Midwest.

My chores done I would wait a little while but no longer than it took to get organized to go get the caribou bones. Take my little pumpkin seed sled,[3] meat saw and axe. The saw and axe would ride in a big paper feed sack and it would keep my load together coming back. Dressed cool for I would be pulling a load together coming back. I headed down my beaten trail for Low Pass beach. They has said go on down until you see where we dragged meat down the bank and then back track. Sunlight was already on blueberry hill and on the little orange & white [Bellanca] Scout parked across the lake. No sign of the boys and I figured they would stay in their sleeping bags until the sun knocked the sharp edge off.

I found where they came to the lake and climbed on the back track. They hadn't used snowshoes but allowed they would have been good in the timber. They had moved the meat in relays and dragged quite a bit of it. The first evidence of meat was a camp robber. No ravens flew and that was strange for they seldom fail to find a kill. The boys hadn't left a lot of meat but I would have a nice load. Head, neck, and backbone was at the kill in the edge of the timber. Tenderloin and back strap had been taken as well as the four quarters and rib cages. Even the hides were gone. I continued on up the slope following their drag trail. Not as much neck meat on that one and it was good that the unfortunate animal had been put out of its misery after being hit. A bullet had all but severed the lower jaw about four inches back from the nose. The tongue also had been cut nearly off. It would have been a terrible thing if that caribou had managed to get away. The heads I would bring back and remove the tongues here. The birds could have the rest. I was no more than fifteen minutes collecting my load. There would be scraps for the birds there too.

Coming back I cut across and would come out on the lake at Low Pass Creek. Not a heavy drag but I was plenty warm and frosting on the outside. I had never taken that sled down a steep bank and I had one to go down. My plan was to use my tow line to hold it back as it would really go if I turned it loose. If it hit a spruce, no more sled. So – I stepped over the edge and would catch it as it went by. In about a second we would both be going down the bank. The sled swerved a bit and hit my right snowshoe and leg.

[3] Pumpkin seed sled, a thin molded plastic 2 ft. by 4 ft. object that was shaped like a pumpkin seed and used as a sled.

I fell on the sled and look out below. We didn't go more than ten feet when a runty spruce stopped us with a thud. No damage done to me but my good sled had a broken nose and I hated that. I had to get off of my snowshoes to push the thing back in order to get by the tree. Right there I learned that the way to go is not forward but backwards. The square tail end would dig in and slow the load if it didn't stop it. I could follow and keep it out of trouble with the tow line.

Still no sign of life across as I trudged up the lake trail with my load. -6° when I arrived and not yet noon. Unpacking I took my axe and saw out of the sack and was not happy to see my meat saw had a broken handle. That collision with the spruce had done it. This afternoon I would spend as much time repairing my gear as I would taking care of the meat.

Right away I used one of my 30" bow saws on a backbone. Fill that Jim Shake kettle and get it on the fire. The heads frozen so I used the axe to open them up to remove the tongues. The damaged one I started to simmer. Nothing much better than caribou tongue boiled in salted water. Add a bit more salt and pepper and maybe some catsup or mustard when eating it.

My big feed sack I filled with sections of backbone and neck meat, sawed and ready for the kettle. My birds had come soon after I arrive and would be busy all afternoon. When I called it finished I had enough good bones and meat to last me until it starts to thaw. If that National Geographic writer, Tom Melham, comes in March, we will live on caribou like the Natives did years ago. Nothing fancy just grab them bones in your paws and gnaw on them like a hungry sled dog.

My meat saw I could make a new handle of wood or epoxy the plastic one and beef it up with super tape. That I would try and if it failed I could always make one. The sled got a hard nose, a reinforcing with gas can tin and the fiberglass sandwiched in between. The sun had dropped behind the mt. before I got every thing done. The little airplane had taken off and disappeared down the lake. A good looking Super Cub had flown by low and slow headed down. I was happy that the caribou had gone beyond the mts. And I wonder if these caribou were killed legally. Glen would say yes but according to the material I have read December 1st saw the subsistence hunting only regulation in force. Sensible hunting wouldn't hurt the herd. A clean kill and a good job of butchering is fine, in season or out as long as it isn't near calving time. Better that was than taking only the legs or killing caribou from the air with buckshot for bait.

Still daylight at six fifteen when I finished my dishes. Now at 7:45 again it is just as clear as it was for the last eight days – not a cloud. Dead calm and the temperature after a high of ten degrees is now -14°.

Some of that backbone meat for supper and it was very good. They can have their big slabs of meat. I'll take the bones.

February 24 – Clear, Calm & -20°.

I had just sampled that ice cream when I heard another airplane and went out to check. The red "T craft," Glen had came after all. They came sliding in and Laddie the pilot. "You're not going to Hawaii," I said. "Nope, called it off," Glen said. "Rain, I couldn't believe how much they have had over there. Sis had wrote Mom is ready to come back to Alaska. Roads washed out and she had to walk four miles to the post office to mail the letter." We unloaded the "T craft" of mail and my order. The last item out was my 100 lbs. of rolled oats groats. "Boy! we will eat again," I said. "No! this is not for people eating. The lady asked me," Glen said and, "I told her no its for goats." We laid it on my sled and towed it to the edge of the lake ice. A small tear in one corner and oats spilled a trickle.

It was a beautiful day out and me deskbound, opening and reading and getting things squared away. It was past four when I got things tucked away in corners in the cache and fireplace (a half gallon of goats milk from Glen). His air taxi hearing had gone well he said and he was hopeful of a permit. I'm thinking he will have a lot of business with the Park Service building there. If I got it right 40 people of the Park Service will be coming to Lake Clark Ntl. Monument. A ranger station is scheduled for Twin Lakes and right away I wondered, where! He had brought me $15.00 worth of stamps to stamp my own letters which will take a load off of the post office. Glenda sent me another heaping plate of sweet rolls. That Ntl. Geographic writer had called and will be here about mid-March so that would be our next plane day.

February 26 – Partly Cloudy, Lt. Breeze dn. & 22°.

I wondered if again this winter there was a big ice build up in waterfall canyon at the first forks. I had never been down over the steep face to get there from Falls Mt. but I would give it a good try at least. Steep, rocky and lots of snow. I would never have tried it without crampons. No ice build up this time and why should that be. Lack of water would be the only reason.

Down the canyon which is always wind packed hard. Hold to the right and come out on to the slope facing the lake above the high waterfall. Just broke out and there below me was a young ram not yet quarter curl. It moved over the edge into the canyon and I climbed back 50 feet to look down on the little guy. He crossed to the far side and started to feed among the rocks. Feed so scarce you would think there is none but they pick away at it and seem content. A real close look with the glasses. I could see a coat of very fine long hair, at least two and one half inches longer than the usual winter coat. It looked very much like guard hair on a fur bearing animal. On the top and back of its head a real top knot of long hair at least four inches long and what is the reason for that. It serves some useful purpose or it wouldn't be there. Old mother nature doesn't dress for looks alone.

I left the little guy and continued on down. Where the sheep had dug and fed I found that the feed was the little bunch grass of this country. Very much like the bunch grass of Oregon but much shorter and finer. In every case they had clipped it close as if done with shears.

February 27 – Clear, Calm & -12°.

Caribou trails and airplane trails crossing the lower lake in several places. Farther down more airplane tracks made before this last wind. Tracks coming out of and back into Lake Trout bay. I had seen no fresh sign of caribou along the lower lake. A lot of snow still lies on the high ridge towards Turquoise Lake as if the wind couldn't get to it due to the mt. to wind ward.

Airplane hunters had camped at Arlen's broken down cabin again. Empty aviation oil cans and Pepsi cans on the lake ice. Tie down ropes for two airplanes still in the ice and to one was tied a five gallon can of gas. The cut off lower legs of a caribou completed the litter. I bunched it up and brought a box from the cabin to haul it up to the rest of the garbage. The carcass of a red fox hung from the corner of the roof. The wood supply had been worked up near the cabin door. Some of the garbage from inside had been thrown out to make room for more. A GI mummy bag had been left plus some odds and ends of groceries. A five lb. sack of self rising flour standing open so the squirrels wouldn't have to open it. More salt and this time in round pour spout cartons. A brown paper sack of potatoes, frozen hard of course. But! here was a new wrinkle. It appeared that they had been cooked with the jackets on. I had never seen potatoes carried in freezing weather without the problem of frozen spuds. How would this system prove out. I added a few of the better looking ones to my gear to try for breakfast.

I doubt that they got more than the one caribou as I saw no sign of another. The red fox they shot from the cabin I suspect. Such a mess and will the Park Service clean it up. I may do it myself some day when I am wind bound at the lower end.

It had taken me just two and one half hours to make the trip down. The flour, spuds and salt would go back with me. The flour I wouldn't add to my starter but I would like to see what kind of bread and hotcakes it would make.

March 4 – Overcast, Calm & 5°.

Daylight was slow in coming but by sunrise there would be a good showing of blue sky up Hope Creek. Spuds two mornings in a row and 25 lbs. on order Glen had said. "We sort as we use and feed the little and the bad ones to the goats." I would be considered an old goat by some.

The plan for the day was set. Heat some water and wash my perma press trousers

and dress whites. Be looking half civilized when the book writer comes. I'll have to ask him if he wants it true "One Man's Wilderness" style and he had better not say absolutely or he will get beans caribou bones and broth with cold porridge pudding for dessert everyday.

March 5 – Overcast, Lt. Breeze up & 5°.

Eating my porridge I had chewed on something that didn't go down. Like chewing a small piece of brown leather. This morning the same thing with my hotcakes. It had come out with the last of my brown sugar syrup. Pieces of brown paper from the lining in the sugar sack. I had torn it when pounding the edge of the sugar lump. What a relief that was. Maybe that lady was right when she told Glen the oats wasn't for people eating, had been my thinking.

March 6 – Partly Cloudy, Lt. Breeze dn. & 31°.

Like a spring morning when I rolled out at seven. I hadn't slept the best and I blamed it on my over eating at supper time. The saying, "For breakfast, eat like a king, for dinner, eat like a Prince, and for supper eat like a pauper" is true, I think.

So – if it is going to be spring I would take my storm windows off and use vinegar and newspaper to shine the windows. One thing led to another and soon I was cleaning logs and dusting storage can tops.

March 7 – Overcast, Calm & 22°.

The plane went down and came up next to Gold Mt. It landed and I thought it had stopped at Erv Terry's. Soon, here it came taxing around the point. Two aboard and then I saw the name Hank Rust on the vertical fin. A little guy wearing a fur hat climbed out on my side. Brandenburg was his name, Jim Brandenburg[4] from National Geographic. Hank came around the nose and handed me a big paper sack. A gift from the Chuck Hornbergers where Jim was staying and possibly Hank too.

I had stoked the fire for tea water and we talked awhile. Jim says, "I guess you get pretty tired of people pestering you." No, I hadn't been pestered all winter very few had stopped. Well, he would like to take a couple pictures, with my permission. I asked him if Geographic paid pretty good for picture material. 20 cents each he came back and grinned. We talked about film and filming and he said I'll give you a few rolls of film to try.

Tom Melham wouldn't be coming and maybe it would be John Kauffmann in his

---

[4] Jim Brandenburg, a Minnesota based photographer for National Geographic Society.

place. Tom had suffered an accident while working on his house. A screwdriver slipped and poked him in the eye. He wouldn't lose it but caused him to possibly cancel his trip north. John Kauffmann's writing for the magazine may be transferred to the book, *Exploring the Back Country,* John might be here within the next two or three weeks if he comes.

Jim went for his camera gear and came back with his pockets full of film. 6 rolls of Kodak Ektachrome 64, 36 exp. Two rolls of A.S.A. 200 and one of A.S.A. 400. Boy oh boy I was making out like a burglar but was I? How much could I have held out for and not stop the show dead, as far as Twin Lakes was concerned. What I need is a tough business manager. He wasn't a writer but a picture snapper and he started with me feeding my birds. He wanted that purty dutch door so I had to stay inside. Then a round of shots of my cache and me on the ladder then inside and outside on the path. Snowshoes in the scenes and I told him it looked pretty goofy me leaning on snowshoes in the cabin. "You don't know the editors," he said. They want something that you neglected to shoot and you hear about it, so you shoot plenty. The film is the least expensive part of this trip no matter how much I shoot. And how many rolls does he shoot. One thousand rolls last year he said. Two cameras, Nikons hanging around his neck and a gadget bag full of lense and film. Lenses from 15 mm to 35 mm. Instead of a couple pictures it was running into rolls of 36 exp.

He wanted to get back before sundown for there was a sunset shot he wanted from Lake Clark. While he shot he would mutter this one they will use and then fire away five or six more times. He wanted pictures of that waterhole operation so I had to do the whole bit, tea kettle, water bucket, stew pan and all. It was covered from the time I left the cabin till I got back.

From Chuck and Sara Hornberger seven apples, four oranges, a big juicy pear and a jar of homemade raspberry jam and a note, "Hope to get up to see you one of these days. Meanwhile, here is a winter treat from last summers raspberry patch. Happy March, Your Lake Clark friends, Chuck & Sara."

Nice people and they have the nicest location I have seen on Lake Clark.

March 10 – Partly Cloudy, Breeze dn. & 26°.

The plane took off and circled high to go over the big pasture. They had located me by the pin in the map. I was out on the ice when they landed again only to take off and head down country. I could see one still at my beach. I lengthened my stride and crunched right across to find Bob Belous waiting and saying, "I hope we didn't pull you away from your filming." The other two had gone to look for caribou.

Inside I got my rising bread dough in the pan for rising while he emptied his briefcase and told me how busy he had been. He was terribly sorry for the way I had been neglected. The fault of two or three really and he one of them. He had approached the

new boss John Cook[5] with the details and the man had said, "Make a fair settlement and do it first thing."

My 16 mm footage and there was about 25,000 feet of it they would have copied, all of it instead of sorting out the very best as the deal had called for. Harpers Ferry has been cut back and working shorthanded. Too much time and expense to sort it. The slides, about 400.00 dollars worth of duplicates or the originals in case they didn't need them in the master file. The govt. can't give you anything but they can raise your pay to cover the extra expense. And they would pay me a satisfactory amount for my last filming. They would get busy on it first thing next week and it shouldn't take long. Good enough, I was happy to get some action at last.

Bob has now been made assistant to the big chief of the "Rip Van Winkle Tribe" of Indians. He wants to bring [John] Cook in to meet me. He had flown over once but for some reason – didn't see me or the weather wasn't good or some other excuse.

I learned from Bob that sport hunting is and was illegal when the Palmer boys butchered. And me as guilty as they – illegal meat (bones) in my possession.

March 11 – Overcast, Breeze dn. & 28°.

I wrote till noon and past. Had a bite and went at it again. A plane came up the left side and circled back only to come around again and on up. A good looking Super Cub with droop tip wings and belly tank. I went out to see who it was when it pulled up and stopped. It was Hank Rust again and he had Jim the Ntl. Geographic photographer. They had been flying for aerial shots and had seen a small bunch of caribou next valley beyond the big valley. They came in but would have no tea today. Jim said he would like to take a couple shots of me with my camera gear. Both Bolex and Exakta and the 400 mm on the Exakta. He would like to have me out on the ice so he could get those impressive mt. peaks in the background. What to wear for this operation – my Kelty green would look good in color.

Hank lugged the 400 mm and we trudged out to the slick ice and a little beyond. A real good place for a tripod leg to kick out and bash my bread and butter on the ice. I found a little patch of packed snow and set up with relative safety. He slipped and slithered about from one foot to thirty feet back and it was a repeat of the last session. Pictures, pictures, pictures. I would see him reload twice before he would say, "That's it, I'm through with you." He liked to shoot real close with that 400 looking just to the side of him. "Why that lens looks as big as a gallon bucket," he said. Finally it was, "Now tripod over your shoulder and walk towards the cabin while I shoot on the go." Hank was impatient to get going as they had to go to Chuck Hornberger's and then to Anchorage yet today. At the cabin another roll was wasted and all from one area. "You can't take too many," he said. The editor will look and say, "Why didn't you shoot one

---

[5] John Cook, an NPS manager who oversaw the Alaska Area Office, first Alaska Regional Director.

from this angle." He intended to have one from that angle.

I ask him when this book would be out – this fall he thought. It would have lots of pictures and I might get a letter or two because of it. If a letter or two is comparable to his picture or two that turns out to be dozens. I have had it. He was happy to learn that Ntl. Geographic has a few of my wildlife slides to go with todays shooting.

Now he was done in Alaska and would be flying to Washington, D.C. real soon. "Where to next," I asked him. "India, and I would rather work in Alaska winter at 50 below or insects in summer than India." He would like to come back and take a tour with me sometime. He is from southwestern Minnesota originally and well acquainted at Fairmount where Babe's brother Lloyd[6] lives.

As they prepared to climb in the Cub he said "John Kauffmann will probably be in within the next two or three days for more material." They flew away and left me wondering just how much of a part "One Man's Wilderness" is going to play in the book, *Exploring the Back Country*. When and if John comes in I intend to ask a few questions.

March 13 – Partly Cloudy, Calm & 5°.

Surprise! Surprise! Maybe an eighth inch of new snow covered everything and I hadn't expected the 5° either. It was stuck tight at 21° when I turned in. The breeze had come up and died soon after.

This was another good morning to travel but first I wanted to clear my lower bunk a bit in case Long John Kauffmann came. Some winter duds that could as well rest in the cache. Wash my heavy knee high socks and get them dry while I went on patrol.

I wanted to check out Hope Creek again. See if the ptarmigan birds were still there and maybe starting to turn. At the woodshed I saw little Milo again. Fighting some heavy chunks of caribou bone that I had tossed under a spruce. Pretty heavy work for such a little guy and I crushed a heavy bone that had marrow in it. He nearly took it from my fingers and promptly wressled it out of sight behind my odds and ends stack of stick and boards.

Chuck & Sara Hornberger had sent me the apples, oranges, and raspberry jelly. I had been thinking the raspberries were wild but now I think not. In their perfect south slope garden they must have a patch of tame ones.[7] Old Frank Bell owned that place before they and Frank had a green thumb. He could grown anything and I wonder what the old boy is doing now. I wonder if he ever got the time to clean that place up. I transferred the jelly to a mayonnaise jar so I can return their canning glass. Wrote a note thanking them and inviting them up. They have never been here and wrote that they hope to get up to see me one of these days.

---

[6] Lloyd Alsworth, (1906-1992) farmer and air taxi operator from Minnesota, older brother of Babe Alsworth.

[7] Koksetna Lodge on Lake Clark was owned by Chuck and Sara Hornberger. They purchased the 5 acre property from Frank Bell in1969. Q'uk'tsatnu is the Dena'ina word for the Koksetna River, meaning "rock river."

March 17 – Overcast, Calm & 10°.

Not much doing at Lake Clark. Having a little problem with the air taxi operators. They, Glen and crew, had spent a lot of time and money improving the airstrip. It's a private strip and he can charge for the use of it. Private use non commercial it is free but a fee is charged for a commercial operation. Laddie is the airport manager and they can't argue with him. Like the game warden, he doesn't make the laws he just enforces them. The air taxi operators have tried to prevent Glen from getting a permit to operate but they want to use his strip for their operation for free. Glen is a born again high Christian but not that high. Babe used to say, "I'm not laying away treasures on this earth."

From Paul Fritz of the Park Service a bundle of stuff. Three copies of *National Parklands in Alaska*. A half dozen very large Alaska maps showing the monuments, wild and scenic rivers, refuges, etc. The Dept. of Interior yearbook 1977-78, *Living With Our Environment,* September issue of *Audubon* magazine plus all his usual newspaper clipping copies. In *Audubon* "Lake Clark: One Park, Four Alaskas" a story by John Kauffmann. Part way through it and I came to Twin Lakes. He had visited my cabin to leave some apples. I was away on a trip to Lake Clark. He wrote in detail about my cabin, cache, woodshed, and view. That famous cabin he called it. And in *Living With Our Environment* on page 25, "Faces of the Greatland" – darned if I wasn't one of them, inside the cabin leaning on my dutch door. A 180 page book in color 9x12". The back inside cover picture, a very pretty girl Melody Grauman, Park Service historian feeding my welfare birds. One on her hand, one on the roof and the third on the spruce buck horns. It had to be late spring for one of the birds was still a black bird with a light colored beak. And in all the garbage a copy of a letter from the assistant to the director for Alaska to the Alaska Area Director of the Park Service concerning building Ranger Stations. In part, he wrote – I suggest you make use of two marvelous craftsmen you have available in Alaska. They are Harold Eastwood, a carpenter in Mt. McKinley Ntl. Park and Dick Proenneke of Lake Clark fame. Both are superb craftsmen with the most acute sensitivity to doing things in a way that does not disrupt the natural scene. We could all take lessons from either of them and he goes on and on and on. He outlined facilities such as I have and ended with, "You will let it be known that any Park Ranger who doesn't want to spend the summer under such circumstances needn't bother to apply for work in Alaska," signed Roger J. Contor Assist. to the director for Alaska.[8]

I'm thinking that with Twin Lakes country due to become overpopulated maybe it would be wise to sell them my ranger station (only a thought but a thought to consider).

[8] Roger J. Contor, assistant to the Director of the NPS on Alaska issues, later NPS Regional Director for Alaska.

March 18 – Clear, Calm & -15°.

Now the breeze was up the lake and cold. Five miles to the Chili River and solid white all the way. The chance of success not good enough so a half mile down I climbed the right bank and headed back toward the Vanderpool cabin. Check to see if the cow and twins were there or if they had moved because I had followed them in such a determined manner. Not a fresh moose track and very few rabbit tracks since the snow. At the cabin I circled up through the timber in hopes of seeing a giant rabbit again. Rabbits but all snowshoes. Building a ranger station of logs was on my mind. Every thick stand of spruce I found myself sizing up the tall straight ones. The man in the letter said, "They will cut dead trees for cabin logs." He could search all of Twin Lakes country and not find enough sound dead ones that are long enough, the right size and straight.

I came out onto the creek flat at the mud banks, crossed, traveled the spruce timber toward the bend in the beach above Emerson Creek mouth. In that open poplar and scattered spruce park would be a nice site for a cabin but the wind blowing down would require it stay back in the trees. No protection for a plane at the beach either.

March 21 – Overcast, (Snowing), Blowing dn. & 30°.

A bite to eat and I got my digging back in order before taking a look at my woodshed. A high rick of three chunk lengths between two trees directly in front. Many winds have moved the trees enough that the stack was tipping towards the woodshed. Tear it down and repile it was my plan. A lot of wood there and across Hope Creek. It looked 100% better when I finished, something tells me that this summer and fall is going to see more people at Twin Lakes than last. The Park Service has made it known that they expect 15 to 30 thousand visitors to the Lake Clark Ntl. Monument per year. Given Arizona weather they might do it but not with Twin Lakes weather. Mid-June to mid-Sept. will be the snow free season and the last half of that can have a lot of foul weather.

During the winter I packed my pathway to the lake to keep from having a shoveled path drifted shut with each storm. Now it was getting soft. My long handled no. 2 went to work on that and soon I will have bare gravel to the lakeshore. Much water on the lake ice and a plane landing would throw a lot of spray. Till plane day I was expecting John Kauffmann in but a letter came from him. Back in Chevy Chase, [Maryland] at his town house. Plans to come up with friends this summer and either go to the Brooks Range or to Lake Clark and maybe float the Chili River. Ntl. Geo. has too much Park stuff for the magazine so his writing is being transferred to the book, which makes him happy.

March 31 – Overcast, Calm & 22°.

I slept as if I had died even though I wasn't feeling any special effects from the climb when I turned in. Quite a few miles in too few days the reason I guess.

Today Saturday and it was cut and dried that I would stay home today. I would cook some caribou neck and write a batch and wrap a few.

Spuds, moose steak and egg for breakfast and after chores I took my butcher knife and meat saw to the woodshed. The meat still frozen in good shape so no need for the knife. The saw cuttings make the best of camp robber feed. A little later I went back to find little Milo the weasel busy cleaning up the crumbs. The camp robbers close but not too close. It was an ideal opportunity to study that little guy close up. No sign of color change unless it would be a slight yellowing just forward of the black on the tip of the tail. Milo was afraid of the birds and they of him. The hawk is his enemy and any bird that flies near puts him in the wood log pile. They know what the little blood thirsty guy could do to them so there is great respect shown by both. Milo got his share of the saw dust.

April 4 – Overcast, Lt. Breeze up & 29°.

It was good to see the ground white out front and snow falling instead of rain. A chance yet that the slush on the lake would freeze before plane day.

After breakfast and chores I went to check the creek. Still flowing quietly and not very much. All that snow up Hope Creek had absorbed a lot of water.

This morning I would saw more neck bones for cooking. Little Milo the weasel was on hand soon after I started and I got a real close look at that little guy. His face is beginning to show the change. No longer snowy white. A few little smudges as if he hadn't washed his face this morning. Pretty wise, those little scraps of meat went into the wood log pile about as fast as they fell. The camp robbers were there but content to just sit and watch and wish that rascal had never lived. The bones cooking, I removed the meat sack from the moose meat to soak the blood out and bleach. A garbage bag with a few ventilating holes in it took its place on the hindquarter.

The breeze from down country was cool and picked up a bit to start the temperature slowly down. Snow would fall now and again throughout the day.

Today I would finish the ladle I had started two days ago. More gouge chisel work and then a heap of elbow grease and sandpaper. If it turned out real nice I would give it to Glenda [Elliott], in appreciation for all the sourdough pastry she has never failed to send. She is an artist with a brush, I will let her finish it to suit her taste. White spruce takes a lot of sanding. Chisel and coarse rasp rips and tears much worse than when working with birch. I learned quite sometime ago that sandpaper will last much longer in use if you cover the backside with masking tape or better still cloth backed adhesive or aluminum coated duct tape.

My boiling meat was done and I had a fresh kettle of beans on the fire to simmer as long as necessary.

The afternoon was near shot when I decided the ladle was getting close to good

enough. A few small blemishes to fill with epoxy and in a day or two sand it again.

My spoon of green birch had been drying and I was surprised to find that it sanded good. It hadn't looked too promising but after altering the shape and giving it some pleasing lines, I have hope.

The temperature had lowered from 35° to 26° by the time I scattered the dish water. A few patches of blue down country. I expect a light crust on the slush covered lake in the morning. The worst that could happen would be a few inches of snow. In that case it would never freeze. Now at eight 26° and calm.

A letter to Terry and Vic. I plan to go to the Bonanza Hills and fix the brakes on his John Deere [bulldozer] when they go in for the season. Maybe in early June.

April 5 – Overcast, Calm & 23°.

After chores and a close inspection of that ladle for the artist Glenda, I decided that it need more sanding and it took a lot of it for the epoxy had stained the wood and I wasn't absolutely sure that a clear finish would match it – so – I sanded it down to clean wood. While I was in the business I finished the birch spoon and you can't beat birch for beauty. White as bone and just as smooth.

Now I could see the big pasture and it was solid white. A few inches of snow up there and no sheep or trails.

With nothing more important to do I took my little double bit axe to the woodshed and squared up the birch sticks for future use. Get them in shape to dry a bit before I start whittling. A couple small burls there too. One had been worked on last fall. Gouge chisel work of the toughest kind. Hold the burl steady with my left and push, not drive the gouge with my right.

Little Milo either sleeps late or goes on tour. I had worked an hour or more before he showed up. I do believe he would become as tame as camp robbers and in a very short time. A dozen times he ran from the wood pile to the stack of wood logs where he would show himself as if expecting a hand out. I finally cut a scrap of moose meat and tried to deliver it hand to mouth. One thing I knew – let go of it if he takes it or your fingers will suffer. He wouldn't quite come to it so I laid it on the tree root. That did it. Into the wood log pile it went and I saw no more of little Milo.

April 8 – Partly Cloudy, Calm & 20°.

I had just got my caribou skin seat on the steep gravel bank near the lake ice in preparation to finish the sanding of my burl bowl when I heard a plane. A little one but coming down the far side. Blue and white Cub and I didn't recognize it. He turned back to fly by.

Another circle and I went out on the ice. He came down by Carrithers' point and dropping too fast. He started to flare out but not strong enough. She hit pretty good and bounced. I directed him in close away from the slick ice and as he came along side I saw who it was. Hugo! Hugo Dietrich the Wein Consolidated Airline mech. from Anchorage. Hugo is from Switzerland, a husky guy and likes to climb mts. He had brought his visiting sister from Switzerland here on a camping trip in 1975. They had camped across Hope Creek. "How did you like my nice landing," he said as he crawled out. I had received a Christmas card from him and wrote inviting him in. "I brought you a little something," he said and starting fishing out his pack sack which he always carries. We came in and he fished out apples, oranges, and newspapers. Was it good vetter here yesterday? In Cook Inlet country it was lousy. When he heard that I had lots of Park Service coffee he would sure have some. He is not very happy with any agency of the Dept. of Interior. Not a hunter but he likes to fly and fish and climb and he doesn't like anyone to tell him where he can land his airplane and where he can't when you couldn't see the tracks the next day if he did. He told of McKinley Park where you must reserve a camping spot two years in advance. Do this and you can't do that. To H--- with you, I can have more fun outside the park. Hugo could go on and on and it would spoil his day, so I changed the subject and his blood pressure dropped to safe limits. Hugo had a short story "Aircraft Salvage & Repair" in February issue of *Alaska* (page A-28). "That black bear didn't wreck any tubing but it sure ripped a big hole in the fabric" he said. I had expected him to spend the day and was thinking about lunch when he said, "I had better be getting back, I have to go to work at four o'clock." We had a sourdough sandwich anyway and then I flipped the prop to get him started. I invited him to come spend a weekend. He would just do that sometime after the ice is out. No good ice on Lake Hood in Spenard. He took my ready to go letters. The packages could wait for Glen.

April 12 – Clear, Calm & 6°.

Such weather – if it was February it would be 40° below. How can this be with the sun so high in the sky and the longest day only a little more than two months from now.

Hotcakes and good ones. No birds came for breakfast and where have they gone. Little Milo was out at the stump trying to salvage some moose meat scraps that were frozen tight. He may be a blood thirsty little guy but he is also a scaredy cat. He makes sure that the coast is clear before he takes off from stump to bush to tree and when he goes its like a white noodle with a tip of black slithering over the snow. Freddy the red squirrel is a bold one compared to the white weasel.

April 16 – Partly Cloudy, Calm & 6°.

No good, better I should come back but the day had only started and I hated to miss a chance. I would follow the shoreline down country and see how things appeared from

there. I chose to stay on the snow pack of the lakeshore to avoid the solid white. Good going but by now it was flat light due to a solid grey overcast. I came to a glaciated area which had a good build up of ice at shoreline. There would be a good spot to get off of the ice when break up is near and a border of water along shore. I marked that spot in the back of my head and then it happened. Both feet kicked out towards the lake and I came down with a terrible thud on my right side. Evidently my right arm was at my side with elbow bent. Unfortunately, I didn't hit my very durable head. My arm and my lower ribs hurt so bad I could hardly get my breath. I managed to get out of my pack and lay there moaning and groaning and gasping for breath. This just had to be the worst ever on ice. The day on that side of the lake was finished I was sure of that. How long it would be before I felt no pain I had no idea. After a few minutes on the ice I decided the thing to do was head for the barn and I figured it would be a long trip for it looked like a long ways to Carrithers' point. With great effort I managed to get to my feet and the next big chore was to get under my pack again. It had contributed a lot to my striking force. I looked to see what had dropped me and found a little patch of sloping ice covered by a dusting of snow. My hikers had snow on the soles and between the two it was too much.

> *Slowly I made my way across and the cabin looked mighty good. If this had happened at the lower end or the upper with tough going and 40 below I would have earned my right to be here.*

Slowly I made my way across and the cabin looked mighty good. If this had happened at the lower end or the upper with tough going and 40 below I would have earned my right to be here.

Right away I took a couple aspirin and set down by the stove to rest awhile. My arm was paining pretty good on the inside but not out. My ribs had no point of source pain indicating a broken rib. Just very sore and much spasms made any movement a stab of pain.

I would lay down awhile, something I hadn't done during the day for a very long time. The upper bunk was mine so I climbed the ladder and slowly rolled in. It was about 9:30 and I rested till near twelve and may have dozed a bit. When I decided to get up it reminded me of my hernia surgery and trying to sit up in bed without aid. After a few trys I managed to roll over and down the ladder. I put one of my big gas can tubs on the stove and emptied the tea kettle. Hot towels between my rib cage and arm for an hour helped my arm considerable but the spasms were still there. Somewhere I had two or more elastic bandages but could only come up with one small one. On the shelf over the door two chocolate mix cans containing first aid supplies left by Navy doctors who hunted from Lofstedt's cabin years back. They had come equipped to perform surgery if necessary. In one can a small bandage and in the other a big body bandage. Brand new and in plastic. I unrolled that dude good and snug around my rib cage. That helped a little but only a little. Moving like 95 years old I could manage after a fashion. Boy I was glad that I had my

wood pile rounded out. Without it I would be sawing blocks short enough to go through the stove door vertically.

Better I should get another bucket of water just in case tomorrow ruled it out. A bucket of water and a load of wood or two was a project.

The weather was thickening down country and before long snow came. My arm not doing too bad and maybe I could write a couple letters. Sitting still was fine but boy that moving after a period of inactivity. I managed and come supper time had my carry boo and beans. Good Sara [Hornberger] bread and she complained of her bread not being good. The purtiest loaf of bread I have seen in years and I'm thinking Sara knew it.

> *Today's escapade reminds me of what I once knew. "Shoulder to shoulder we have fought it out, yet the wild must win in the end," but not today. Robt. Service*

Supper was early and now at 7:30 sitting quietly writing I'm not hurt'n but to cough would be like falling on my dagger.

The ceiling low and dripping a few flakes. Still a light breeze down and 27°.

Today's escapade reminds me of what I once knew. "Shoulder to shoulder we have fought it out, yet the wild must win in the end," but not today. Robt. Service

April 22 – Overcast, (Fog), Breeze up & 31°.

On skis and it came in for a landing. One man and heavy set. He stopped quite a ways out and came churning through the loose stuff. It wasn't till he got close that I recognized him. Nixe Mellick from Sleetmute. He comes once a year at least and this was his spring visit. Part Native at least and quite a business man. A trading post and owns three airplanes. The Cub, a [Cessna] 185 and a 206 Cessna. Does all his own flying. "I took the day off from a lot of flying to come over," he said. Eight or ten hours a day is too much flying. A guy gets run down. He had just come from Lime Village over on the Stony. I had mailed him a tape I had made of Bill Parks story *The Land Beyond*. He had taken it to Lime Village to see what the natives could add to the story for it was they that Bill wrote about. Ebonga[9] in the story still lives and remembers the times of 1937. In the story there was a man Chris. A good natured guy who was forever getting lost. He did again later and when they found him, his clothes were nearly worn out from beating the brush. Nixe had taken a Native and flew to look for the S shaped lake and the trappers cabin that Henry, Chris and Bill had built. They found the lake but the cabin is no more. A hippie has built another and it is a dirty mess, according to Nick.

I got out my maps and we looked at the area. He pointed out the location of the lake and much more. A long open ridge where wolves den and there are lots of wolves. They had seen several kills of moose along the Stony. Another area far up the Swift

---

[9] "Ebonga" is RLP's rendition of Dena'ina elder, Evan Vonga Bobby (1905-1995) chief of Lime Village for many years.

River where there used to be many grizzly bears and wolves too. He pointed out sheep country that was real good years back but no more. Another place in that area that would be a beautiful place for a cabin. Good timber and lots of marten. Nick says he approves of the land or some of it being set aside and out of reach for guides who make a fortune working only a couple months per year – selling game that belongs to everyone. He says that he owned the first 150 hp Super Cub in this country and for a long time it was his private domain. He knows what the game situation was then and now. He doesn't see it anymore.

He went out to the Cub to get a 1936 newspaper that he ran across at Lime Village Alaska Weekly but printed in Seattle. On the front page a picture of two Lime Village natives (one still lives) holding up a wolf skin. The nose as high as they could reach and the tail touching the ground. All of eight feet long we figured. At that time the Natives considered it bad luck to kill the wolf and that was what the story was about.

Hungry was the original name for Lime Village and it was a hungry place. Always a question of where the next meal was coming from. Now it is different but not better. Welfare has erased the will to work at making a living. Kids go to Anchorage to school and come back wanting bacon and eggs when all their parents ever had was caribou and moose.

Nixe told me his family got quite a lot of money from the Native claims settlement and, "We still have it and its working," he said. This past February again they went to Hawaii on vacation. Let the kids swim in the ocean. He caters to fly fisherman in summer. The same ones year after year and mostly elderly people. Fish mostly from a boat, a little wading but not much. He can handle six but often it is only two that will buy his full time and fishing spots. He would like to show me his place at Sleetmute and said I will come take you over there after breakup. He has a cabin at Telaquana Lake and says he plans to build his retirement home there. It was getting near nine when he said, "I had better be going. One hour twenty minutes to get home but lots of light now." I went out to see him off and felt that it would be pretty dark by the time he reached the Kuskokwim and Sleetmute. The ice may go out of the river in about a week he said. Birds are coming, fish ducks first. And he had seen a swan.

I lit the old cowbarn lantern to get squared away for the night. It was nine o'clock and the sky overcast, the wind calm and the temperature 26°.

April 23 – Overcast, Calm & 26°.

Doing better but slowly. My ribs feeling like the first days after surgery. I remember them insisting that I cough and now I can. At first, to cough was on the last page.

Breakfast and then to my hot two towel treatment. Again I could see a turning

point after one hour and stopped. Given time and my own pace I could do pretty good. It wasn't to go that route. Along about ten here came a little airplane with wide blue bottom skis. A Champion Citabria, yellow and white. He circled and landed stopping a couple hundred feet out. Here came a big guy trudging in with a "Hi, Dick, I finally made it." Will Troyer, of the Park Service. "I came over to see you and thought I would stay overnight," he said. Naturally I was glad to see him. Knew him on Kodiak as Refuge manager with Fish and Wildlife. He had been in here a couple times and promised to come a few more that didn't work out. Now my only wish was that I was in better shape to show him around. He brought me up to date on his family as we enjoyed a couple cups of tea. Just today his wife was going back to work after a very bad auto accident that wrecked her VW completely and broke a leg so badly that the bone is now wired together and a rod to hold it in alignment. $10,000.00 was the Dr. bill and luckily she was insured. Eric, his son had also totaled his car and now his insurance premium is up 25%. Will, happy as ever intending to retire in a couple years.

He asked me about open water up the lake and I couldn't believe it. He insisted and after a sandwich we would walk up and take a look. I wasn't prepared for what was coming but would come back feeling better than when I started. I had told him of my escapade and he allowed we had better not but I wanted to go.

We turned back and the breeze at our backs. Much better and it was an enjoyable hike down the far side past Glacier Creek, checking for rams as we went. Ten head of ewes and young stuff across from Carrithers' point on top of the big rock face. The weather started closing in soon after we arrive back at the cabin. He turned his flying machine around and tailed it in close to the beach. We packed planks and my short ladder out to make rock holding platforms under the wings. He loaded them with rocks and tied the little bird down for the night.

April 24 – Overcast, Lt. Breeze up & 31°.

I had mixed batter for hotcakes and set it on the stove shelf to rise. The starter in the mitten drier above. Both looked very flat and how could that be. I tried to remember putting in some thing that is forbidden. This morning and Will here would be the dead batter. Give her a go anyway and I added a little extra soda. They turned out fair and Will had four. More than he ever eats at home but that's what they all say. Too dark complected so a little too much sugar had been added. Two eggs instead of the usual one had gone into them. A small venison steak joined them and later some good porridge with lots of raisins and rice and real live butter. Not too bad and after I got the dishes done I started a fresh kettle of beans. A little blast of wind came now and again and Will watched the weather. His flight plan expired Wed. evening. He wanted to get out today if it improved a bit at the lower end. He wanted to take a little walk and did I want to go. I had better stay and water those thirsty beans. So he went and I fussed around straightening up the cabin a bit

and getting my wood and water, cleaned things up.

At ten it was looking pretty good. Here and there a trace of blue. He would go but not until he sampled those beans. He had brought some very dark and coarse brown bread. We had buttered bread and a good helping of beans. Seconds were in order. "Never have beans at home and I like them," he said. Did I have some letters he could take? I did, and after dishes got them ready. He returned the rocks to their previous location on the beach and got his little bird ready to fly. The weather looking good. He would fly around a bit down country looking for caribou. He hoped to be working in this area this summer. He would stop again and we would hike to the sheep lick. He blasted off straight down the lake and I went about getting things back in order. Better not load that top bunk for he might find it no good and come back for more beans and more of the good life.

More heat therapy was in order and in one hour I felt much more comfortable. The effects of that long hike on the lake yesterday were beginning to show. I still had my writing for yesterday and today to do and that would use up most of the afternoon. The wind had come quite strong up the lake and had Will been here I doubt that he would have taken off. Later it decreased to a light breeze and the overcast became broken. I got in my wood and fire starter and prepared for an early supper. I would sleep tonight. There would be only the sound of my Baby Ben to disturb me.

April 29 – Overcast, Calm & 36°.

Slowly I am improving. I notice it most when it comes time to roll out. Two weeks today since I cut that caper.

Breakfast and water fetched. For the first time this spring I boiled my water from the long pool next to the beach. Creek water feeding in and the best of water.

This morning I had a chore that had caused some thinking last night. A letter had come from a Kathleen Teter of Ntl. Geographic.[10] She is a researcher on book material and had sent three black and white prints of pictures they intend to use in the book. A picture of me in the door way feeding a camp robber. Her questions. Is that you in the doorway? Is that the front and only door to your cabin? Are you feeding a bird? What kind of bird and what are you feeding it? Of what kind of wood is the cabin constructed? Did you build it yourself? Can you describe the object circled on the door? Is it a type of lock? And a picture of me with tea kettle and water bucket going to the lake for water. Is this a picture of you walking from your cabin? Can you describe the location of the cabin? Are you going to the lake to get water? How far is the lake from your cabin? What is the building that is elevated to the right of your cabin? Would you describe what is kept in there and why it is elevated? Do you live here year round? When did you first come here to live? What kind of trees are in the background? And

---

[10] Kathleen F. Tetler, was a researcher for the National Geographic Society working on *Exploring America's Backcountry*.

of the moose picture. What kind of a moose is it? Where was this photograph taken? What is the moose doing? Is there any particular significance to this picture? Any other comments on this picture? And on all three pictures. "Any other descriptive details that you can offer will be appreciated." My god amighty, woman, you are a nosy one! She wrote April 5 and I got it the 28th. Time is critical she says and she would like to have the information as soon as possible. If I have any questions please phone collect. She is about to get a lesson in the manner in which the wilderness does business. Laddie and I had agreed on early June for the next trip to Twin Lakes. I expect she will be a mental patient by then.

> *Time is critical she says and she would like to have the information as soon as possible. If I haave any questions please phone collect. She is about to get a lesson in the manner in which the wilderness does business. Laddie and I had agreed on early June for the next trip to Twin Lakes. I expect she will be a mental patient by then.*

April 30 – Partly Cloudy, Blowing dn. & 40°.

Again I heard a trace of a call and still a couple hundred yards up. A pretty good view up the creek and on both sides. My head was on a swivel like a fisherman watching for jumpers. Suddenly there it was on the far side of the creek coming down. Not as big as the best I have seen but a nice kitty. I had my predator call along but hadn't used it. The cat was traveling in a walk as all cats seem to do and what would it do if I sounded the call. A couple weak calls and that cat stopped, looked and headed my way. No more than seventy feet away and coming head down and slower than its usual gait. At about fifty feet it stopped to look and then came on. Me up on the bank behind the willow clump and it stopped no more than fifteen feet away and in the creek bed. That stubby tail had been twitching as it came and now it stood looking up at me. It didn't act at all suspicious or as if it was looking for a meal but just curious as to what made that sound. I didn't dare move or it would be gone in a flash. I have heard that a lynx cat when surprised at close range will jump straight up about three feet before it heads for cover. Light brown eyes watching me and the down creek breeze rippling that silky coat. There was hundreds of dollars worth of fur, at today prices. A little tuft of hair more than an inch long on each ear tip. It turned its head to look down the creek and then back to me. Now and then a puff of wind to move the tails of my wool shirt and if anything is foreign to the wilds it is something flapping. At least two minutes passed and that cat still watching and wondering. I expect it to get my scent even though it was a cross wind. Finally it acted as if maybe a trace of scent did reach it for it turned quickly and walked back to the far side of the creek. I used the call again and it turned to look before sitting on its haunches facing up the creek. A pretty sight there in the wide open and I thought of the 400 mm and Exakta. The Bolex didn't have film in it yet. The cat opened its mouth wide in a big

yawn and I wished that rascal would give forth with the call of the lynx cat. The morning was wasting and it finally got up and headed for the timber. I called again and it stopped to look back and then on and into the trees. Maybe a female, I don't know. Certainly not as big as a couple I have seen and not as much contrast in its markings. Had I been set up and alert I could have filmed that cat but I most certainly wouldn't have seen it come so close or stay so long. I came back thinking I might go to the upper end today.

May 2 – Overcast, Calm & 34°.

No pills and lots of sleep. I woke up at five to find the ceiling very low and it was raining. I didn't roll out till six.

    This would be a good cooking day, so as soon as breakfast was out of the way I dragged out the bean kettle. This morning too I would boil what was left of the hind leg of moose. Many scraps from heavy trimming and I tucked a few good heavy ones in the wood log stack. A couple chunks of heavy bone went under a spruce where Milo and the red squirrel have gnawed on bones in the past. A little later I was passing that way and noticed the heavy scraps and one bone already gone. Who did I have that was big enough to pack them away and so bold to do it in broad daylight. A short time later I went for wood and saw little Milo the weasel in the woodshed. I was anxious to see what progress he had made toward his summer brown. With a meat scrap I coaxed him out. Saw him as close as if I held him in my hands. The change may be starting and then again maybe he had a dirty face from wrasseling with those heavy meat scraps. Later I saw him pack a chunk that would weigh every bit as much as a least weasel and more. Took it to a hole under a spruce root. Too much spread to go in so he parked it at the entrance and then from the hole yanked it in and out of sight. Freddy the squirrel came bounding down the path and I was surprised to see her examine the den entrance. Milo appeared and for a second I had squirrel and weasel no more than a foot apart and neither acted aggressive or afraid.

May 4 – Overcast, Lt. Breeze dn. & 36°.

I woke up near eleven feeling the full effects of the day so one ascription (aspirin with Maalox and used by the Providence in Anchorage) went down the hatch. Feeling the best yet at five so rolled out and got the griddle hot. A nice morning with new ice on the open water along the beach. Lake level still coming up and stands at about four inches above winter low water.

    My birthday and I was going to treat it like Sunday and a day of rest. Another hour at the hot springs and then I stretched out on my sleeping bag. It was eleven before I woke up.

An early supper so I sorted and stomached real live strawberries. I would check the grocery list and see how much Glen had charged for them but am afraid it would spoil my appetite. Better to enjoy the novelty of having some a few days and then check. A good chunk of fruitcake from the cache. A green salad and wheat berry bread left by Will Troyer. A small helping of my good fresh cooked beans. Goats milk for my porridge. Too much! I feel better with the waist band of my trousers unhooked.

The nicest part about being 63 was that I felt better than I did at 62. A real comfortable day. A good experience. Now I have an idea just about how long it takes to come back some wheres near after a real shatter. About three weeks if there is no sign of bones sticking out.

Tonight I will move back to my upper bunk – a more healthy climate up there, I am sure. My nose senses the difference – dryer.

May 7 – Overcast, Calm & 32°.

Eighteen inches of heavily candled ice. I had better push my big sled if I crossed. While I was dragging it out of retirement I noticed my seven foot, five inch wide skis standing in the corner and a life jacket hung from a perlin log. Take them all just in case. Glasses and scope would go. No camera for I wouldn't be climbing the mt. today. The sled made just enough noise to drown out the squeak of the ice. I could use the sled handle bars to support some of my weight. A few times I have dragged the canoe but it makes so much noise that one time I spooked a sow and cubs over the top by using it. Doing fine, a few soft spots but not too bad. About 200 yards from the far shore and the bare knoll the ice was no longer half white but blue and I found it to be of fine texture. Well onto it and it got soft and softer. The ice under me turned even more blue. It was sagging and water was coming up through. I climbed onto the sled and slid my skis out behind. That did it but even with the skis I was leaving a blue trail. White ice and solid near the beach. A border of water but the sled takes care of that. Push it in and use it for a bridge.

From the knoll a good view of the four bears. That third cub was very dark and chocolate in color. The sow very blond and I have never seen a yearling cub as blond as this one. Now I would watch for that limp. I saw it a few times but not nearly so much as a year ago. A bob of her head when she walked at times or in turning she would favor that foot. One cub curled up for a nap. A second one was high up and digging. Always a mamas boy in the bunch and the third was with its mother. Finally it layed down and then the old mother one. The second one above came down and then the high one came romping down. All three right in close and I knew for I have seen it happen often. Lunch time. She layed back against the slope and the table was set. I wished for my watch so I could tell close how long they nurse at this age. More than three minutes and maybe more than four when she raised to the sitting position. The cubs are real good size and it would take a big den to hold all four.

May 9 – Partly Cloudy, Calm & 25°.

About midnight I woke up feeling the effects of my hard labor but by five I was much improved. It had been good for what ailed me. Now it could be full speed ahead to full duty.

Calm at lake level but clouds over the ridge across were moving at a good rate towards the west or northwest. Breakfast and my treatment before I looked for bears on a very white mt. It seems I could have spotted them had they been there. She would bed down either real close to the wall of a rock face or on top of a rocky point having a grassy sheep bed. The cubs might be cuddled up against her or in a pile by themselves. No bears and I prepared to take a hike down country.

Now, the snow on the lower half of the mt. had melted. If the bears were still there they would be digging roots in the loose stuff of the scree slopes. Every now and again I stopped to glass that mt. good. A good scatter of sheep on Falls Mt. so little chance of seeing bears there. I was below one mile rock when I spotted the big blond. Directly across from my cabin and headed towards my last April climbing trail to the bear den. So, she was still on the mt. Right away when I reached the cabin I set up the scope. All four of them working on the scree slope. Many marks where they had dug.

After a bite to eat I checked again and just in time to see the cubs in a big free for all on a long snow patch. Two wrasseling and sliding down. Little chocolate drop was running along side. Down & on down they went and finally to an outcrop on the up country side. A good two hundred yards from the old mother and it is not common to see cubs, even yearling cubs ranging so far out. Like dogs feeling good they ran circles just for the fun of running. Sometimes one would run to get clear if it saw another coming. Not chasing each other, just running. The old mother went on about her business and ignored them. Now, supposing I was on the mt. and those fool cubs went on a crazy running spree and ran into me. Chances are they would head up the mt. and pick mom up and take her along as they went by, but, let one of them holler and she would be there pretty quick to see who pinched my baby.

They climbed back and dug roots while I spread my chunk of caribou hide along side of the cabin and stretched out to expose my rib cage to the greatest heat lamp of them all. A few scattered clouds and one eventually put me in the shade. My bears had bedded down for a nap on a little rock outcrop next to the digging grounds. Later I saw the cubs wrasseling and later still scattered and feeding but mom snoozed on. To me it is really amazing that she can supply milk for those three big lummox when on a diet of root and not an abundance of roots at that.

May 11 – Clear, Calm & 25°.

Raking was good for what ailed me. I could feel my sore spots more than when using the shovel. I moved my raked up rocks with the sled and called it good.

The sun bright and warm. The parky squirrel[11] would be out and I wanted some good close ups with the 400 mm plus two short lengths of extension tube. With that combination I could fill the frame with a parky squirrel. The squirrels were out and I learned that a squirrel will cover a very large area. A half dozen holes and he will stick his head out of any one or all of them. Stand quietly and eventually he will come out and feed or run to another group of sheltering holes. I finally found one with a burrow in the wide open. He was slow in taking cover and I picked him for a tame one and set up at about 12 feet. Magnified eight times at 12 feet makes a parky squirrel pretty close. He was the most cooperative squirrel I have ever seen. I did pretty good but wanted a few more. He called it enough and ran over the edge into Hope Creek gorge. I came for lunch but would go back later and try him again.

My bears were staying good. At one o'clock they were below where they had spent the night. Cubs have no respect for each other. One laying sleeping and another above. It comes bouncing down on the sleepy head and they wrassel and roll. I saw the old mother turn and she carried that left front foot just as she did a year ago last Oct. She is the same bear and no doubt about it. Now I had hopes that they would stay on the face of Allen Mt. for they were working slowly up country.

Parky squirrels like hotcakes and I would take a treat for my little friend. No sign of life there at his burrow and I planted the treat and waited. The sun was warm and I layed back on the moss to listen to the skeetos sing. A plane and here came a big canary yellow Beaver on floats rumbling up the far side. What would the old mother one think of that. I put the glasses on her. She and the cubs were taking a nap at the base of a small rock face. She may have raised to her feet but she didn't leave. The Beaver didn't come back so must have climbed over the top. I climbed too, looking for squirrels but could get no cooperation. I came back down to the tame ones house and there was that little guy about twenty five feet away and laying low in the mossberry growth. Headed towards the burrow as if he wanted in. I planted the hotcake bits and backed away. The little rascal ran right in and sat at the hole. Sniffed of the hotcake but didn't sample it. I was on the wrong side and shooting against the sun so slowly I picked up the tripod and moved around. My squirrel stayed. Layed down and rolled in the dirt as if grooming its coat. I had never seen such a performance and with me so close. He went out and picked old mossberries and came back. Sampled my hotcake and pronounced it garbage. I got all the pictures I wanted and he went on his way down the slope.

May 14 – Partly Cloudy, Calm & 30°.

I remember hearing a porkypine rasping on a moose antler sometime during the night and that was all I heard. It was 5:30 when I opened my eyes. The best night's sleep in a long time. My fresh made bed was solid comfort.

Hotcakes this morning and then a look at the mts. No bears but I could still see

---

[11] "Parky squirrels" is the colloquial name for ground squirrels, Bristol Bay area Natives used the fur for parkas.

the lone ewe with new lamb. New ice on the open water along the beach and I noticed last evening that the new ice starts next to the old and spread towards the beach.

Not a bright morning and small chance that the sun would be out for awhile. I wanted to go check for the swans and maybe see a fox. A few frames left on the roll in the Exakta and I figured maybe five, so, I would take it and the 400 mm lens today. I thought of taking an extra roll of film but if I took it I might waste it on white swans in less than good light.

I had just started down when here came the two swans from down country. Flying low and slow headed for moose pond. A beautiful sight as they passed at my elevation. They set their wings and went in for a landing.

By now the day was cloudy bright. Not as nice as bright sun but good for the few frames left on the roll. I headed for moose pond. Getting located was no problem. Swans with their heads under water don't see very well. Swans do have a memory. Their heads come up and there you are but motionless. They watch and if you don't move down goes the head. If it comes up and you are gone they show just as much interest and watch for a few seconds before feeding again. In shallow water and it appears that they are doing the hula. They are scratching with those big web feet to uncover feed and then down goes the head. I picked my shots and was surprised when the camera locked up after two frames. End of the roll. So, I just watched. A pair of green wing teal came to feed along the waters edge near the swans.

The feeding period ended with much dipping of heads and necks very deep and raising them for water to drain down over their backs. A pretty sight and would be beautiful on film for they did it many times. There in deep water the male whistler grabbed the female by the neck and there was hanky panky on the pond with her completely submerged. A great commotion and when they were both on the surface again they came breast together and there was a great honking and flapping of wings. Needless to say that if I had a few extra frames I would have used them. They went to the waters edge and did a great job of preening those feathers until each and every one was in its place. The gyrations they can go through with those long necks can only be imagined. And then it was back to feeding again. I backed down out of sight and packed my gear to travel. It was near 1:30 when I arrived at my beach.

After a bite to eat I tried my hand at splitting wood. Found some muscles that hadn't loosened up yet but I got the pile looking better.

I heard swans. It was the pair headed up the lake. About thirty minutes later I heard them again and saw them going down. I rushed for the scope to see where they went. Curving to the left and finally headed back up and into the wind like big airliners coming in for a landing. They set those wings and disappeared behind the gravel banks.

Supper at six and now at eight nearly solid overcast, snowing against Allen Mt. A light breeze down and 37°.

How many more times will I travel the beach. Fox pond country is a real hot spot.

May 17 – Partly Cloudy, Lt. Breeze dn. & 35°.

This morning a big Cessna on wheels had gone up and stayed a half hour or more. It landed I am most sure. Later it took off and climbed out over the mts. towards the Kijik. The plane had stayed about long enough to put someone off. Bear season is open until the 25th of May but certainly not in Lake Clark Ntl. Monument.

I sensed that it was getting late when I packed my gear in. My god-a-mighty! 6:45 when I came in the door. If my watch had been along I would have said I shall return long before the fox showed up.

With beans and meat cooked supper is quick and easy. Now at 8:30 it is overcast. The wind is strong down and the temperature 40°.

May 23 – Partly Cloudy, Lt. Breeze dn. & 37°.

It did nearly calm but the sheep had moved up into the rough stuff. There would be no chance to film them today.

"Many cows and calves," Stu [Ramstad] had said and that bounced around in my head during the night. "Caribou on both sides of the trail butte," he said. Stu is a great one for a ready answer to any question. It doesn't always correspond with the facts. Fly from Fishtrap Lake to here might or might not put him close enough to Trail Butte to see caribou unless he was looking for caribou. It would take nearly six hours steady trudging to find out if they were there and just because they were there on Tuesday wouldn't mean that they could be found within sight of Trail Butte on Wednesday. I knew while I was thinking that I would be heading for the low country come morning. So – I was up at five and all packed up and ready to travel by 7:30. The ice hadn't moved far enough to make using the canoe worthwhile so I would leave it parked bottom up by the breakwater. I was packing 400 feet of 16 mm film and the old big pistol which doesn't take good pictures unless the going gets very rough.

Fog moved in over the Low Pass country and a few flakes of snow came down. The day was getting darker instead of lighter as I had expected. The beach, the bank along side of the high ridge when I got to the lower lake would be my trail. Eleven o'clock when I got to Arlen's cabin. I was anxious to see how [Terry] Hamilton had left it. Litter and cans along the beach and he had said he had it well picked up. At the cabin I half expected to find someone there. A brand new camp axe laying on the ground and the same for a new GI shovel and an expensive ice auger. The cabin was once surrounded by spruce but no more. If he stayed a summer and a winter it would be a little house on the prairie. Still a lot of litter scattered about. What he had picked up was stacked against the cabin on the back side. Inside, a cup of tea still on the table. A kettle of meat on the stove. Coffee percolator loaded with coffee and grounds. Water in the water bucket. One corner curtained off and behind it his dirty clothes hamper, a garbage can. If you don't

like to wash clothes, keep them out of sight. A sleeping bag on the bunk, which was a piece of plywood on two gas cans boxes. It appeared that he left on very short notice which I understand he did.

I ate part of my lunch and hit the trail again. Down along the chain of small lakes to a high spruce knoll which is the first observation point. I saw no sign of life from there so headed for the bare faced gravel knoll in the direction of Trail Butte. A fair breeze behind me and any game ahead would know I was coming. Out went a caribou cow with a very young calf. It was very young. Like a fox without the brush and with long legs. As little as it was it was pretty fast but a brown bear would be able to catch it.

From the bare faced knoll I could see caribou across the Chili River, miles away. So far I couldn't begin to estimate how many. Two or three single caribou a half mile and less away. A good scatter and probably ready to calve or with a very young calf. I didn't want single cows, not after I had heard of hundreds two miles farther down. I went on, headed for Trail Butte. Maybe I had gone a mile when I came to a low spot, brush choked and with a high bank on my side. As I came near I saw the back of a caribou. A very light colored cow with one antler. That was a good sign that she had calved and not many days ago. Just far enough to my left that she hadn't got my scent. She was feeding. A ditch led into this low spot and I backed up and got into it. A point of the bank hid me as I moved to the mouth of the ditch. There she was and no more than sixty yards away. Too close, she would hear the camera for sure. I couldn't do better so I would risk it. Only one caribou lost if she spooked.

Very slowly I planted the tripod within plain view of her, and just as slowly I moved in behind it. She looked a few times but didn't spook. No action at the time she looked. She layed down and I was about ready to shoot and let her go. Get on down to Trail Butte. Not another caribou in sight and she might be all I would shoot. I looked for a calf but saw no sign. She dozed and I ran the camera. Up came her head and she looked right at me but didn't get up. Now, I felt that I had it made. If a caribou doesn't spook at the first running of the camera they are pretty sure to ignore it the next time it runs. I would wait her out and see what happened. She dozed, scratched an ear with a hind foot and her back with her nose. Time was wasting. She just comfortably filled the frame. A good close up. Maybe it was 30 minutes later that she got up and there not very far away appeared a little brown calf. It moved in along side and grabbed a faucet and butted her a couple good ones to get things going. She stepped ahead a couple steps and that put the calf in line for my side. He filled up and together they moved away. Boy! that was a good one. If I didn't see another caribou I wouldn't feel cheated. I continued on. I began to see a few caribou on my left and so stayed right to get by and to the high ground of the butte. Three or four cows crossing the ridge right to left and I waited for them to get out of sight. Climbing the butte and I was seeing many caribou on my left. High enough to see down to the right and forward. There, were hundreds of caribou 5- 6- 7, I don't know how many hundreds and on the move up country and towards the Chili River. Maybe a mile away. Stu was right, many cows and calves on both sides of the butte. The sun was in and out. I was in business with a couple shots of the big bunch and then with those nearby

on the opposite side of the ridge. More came streaming by below me and they doubled the number. I was soon changing film. Now they had moved to my back trail and would start to cross it towards the Chili River. I headed back and picked a ridge to my left for the next station. As I climbed the back side a red fox bounced out to stop and look. It was in no hurry to leave and I figured a den in the area, maybe. On top I walked right into an area of dens. A lot of dens and from the looks of it this had been a denning area for hundreds of years. Always lots of brown red top grass growing at den locations and there was plenty of it here. No place close to watch the den from. The best would be a gravel knoll a quarter mile away. Again I was in the caribou business and would shoot another hundred feet before I called it good. The bunch headed for the big valley behind the Volcanic Mts. I headed back and was soaking my tired feet in a cold mt. stream at six o'clock. My load of gear got heavier and the distant landmarks seemed a long time coming. I would stop and rest at Arlen's cabin for awhile. It looked pretty inviting down there at the head of Lake Trout bay when I came over the last rise.

More of my granolas bars, peanuts and raisins. My "stick of dynamite"[12] I was saving to push me the last three miles. I decided to stay and head on up early in the morning. It would be a long three and a half or four hours if I did it today. So – I pulled my hikers off and covered up with Hamilton's sleeping bag. Mosquitoes sang so I put on some "punkie dope" (Cutters) that I had along. That kept them at a quiet distance. Late at night loud rasping on the corner of the cabin. I hollered and it stopped only to start again. Soon I heard his bristly hide coming through a hole that Hamilton hadn't plugged or had been made since he left. There in the very dim light was a porkypine walking across the floor. I gave him the word and he crawled out but didn't leave until I went out and bombarded him, on the garbage pile, with an old gas can. I slept some and it was three when I decided it was time to start the day. I wanted to go bail out Stu's boat and turn it bottom up above high water line before I left. This little half mile hike would get me in trim to travel under a load again.

I had a cup of tea and more of my raisins and peanuts plus a granola bar and took care of the boat.

It was 4:35 when I prepared to head for home. A very calm peaceful morning with only a trace of broken cloud cover toward home and the high ones. Two hours ten to the bend of the beach below the gravel banks. It was there I sat on the bank and had my stick of dynamite. I could see my lamb band just below lambing rocks and heading for the point of the mt. overlooking Emerson Falls. I could count 8 lambs for sure and maybe nine. I headed on up the line and learned that the water advanced another half mile yesterday. This morning the lower lake had about a half mile to go to complete break up. One hour twenty to my beach and there was fresh moose track marching right on by. At Hope Creek I had seen a caribou track. Hope Creek running a small stream into the lake.

Putting my gear away and here came a light plane on floats. Will Troyer and he

---

[12] "stick of dynamite" was RLP's favorite hiking treat that he used late in the day when his energy was ebbing; it consisted of a cold rolled sourdough hotcake smeared with peanut butter and honey and topped with a slice of raw onion.

was soon at my beach. Just came from Lake Clark and didn't think my lake was open or he would have brought my mail. Showed me on the map where he had seen lots of caribou. At the mouth of Turquoise Lake many many cows with calves. In the big valley behind the Volcanics many more - the bunch I had seen headed that way yesterday evening.

Such a perfect evening I should go for a little paddle before turning in early.

It sure tastes good to be back home again but I'm sure happy that I went to the land of the caribou.

May 30 – Partly Cloudy, Lt. Breeze dn. & 43°.

I was eating supper when rasping came loud and clear from in front. It had to be on the cabin to be so loud. I fairly flew out the door to catch a porky just leaving. Not educated yet for it started up a tree. I have a long pole laying along side the cabin that teaches them not to climb trees. Poke them out and ker-plunk to the ground. They soon learn to just take off and keep going. Flail a few "quails"[13] out of them as they go and they forget to come back. This morning one took off in a high lope – the fastest I have ever seen a porkypine travel. He had been educated by that porkypine pole.

Nearly clear now at 8:15. A breeze down and 46°.

I can't locate the bears. They are still in the brush I hope, but may have moved on.

June 5 – Partly Cloudy, Calm & 31°.

A plane and I knew it was Will or Glen. Closer and I knew it was Will [Troyer] by the exhaust sound. I headed for home full paddle. He circled and landed close to the beach for it was glassy smooth. I found him sitting on the beach when I arrived.

Clouds were building and it would thunder later in the day. I ask him what the forecast was. "Good yet tomorrow for Anchorage anyway" he said. He had just had himself a lettuce, tomato and cucumber sandwich and invited me to have one. Boy! that was good. He came prepared to go to the lick but he would check from the air first to see if they were there. In Pear Lake country he had seen many cows and calves and he wanted to land there to get a check on the calf to cow ratio. "Can't hardly find a calf in McKinley Park," he said. Many calves here.

We sampled the beans and had some sourdough bread and butter topped with Sara's raspberry jam.

He would have to go to Port Alsworth to close his flight plan and gas up, so, a chance to get my outgoing mail out and mail from there. I would stay here and get

[13] The term "quails" was Sig Alsworth's idiosyncratic term for porcupine quills.

organized to go to the lower end tonight after supper. Pull his plane up tight behind the breakwater and leave it. He took off and I cleaned the lake trout before getting on to other chores. Clouds were looking big and grey. Would it fair up near the end of the day as it often does in June.

Be back at six he said and I didn't give it a thought that he was on daylight savings time. Promptly at five here he came up the far side and back down along the point. He had brought the few things I was short of and a green mail sack that looked well filled. "Brought you about as much mail as you sent out" he said. I had sent quite a number of packages, fruit jars, and such. I emptied the sack and out tumbled two large packages. One each from Raymond and Robt. I suspected Raymond had sent the new 300 mm lens and promptly dug it out. A nice looking rig and heavy but that's alright. A heavy lens is a steady one. I had mentioned Jeep caps[14] to Robt. and here comes two. I have two so am well supplied. Also a "Cat" diesel power cap[15] in bright yellow. A "Peterbuilt" cap of the same style and red. Those plus a batch of yellow lined writing tablets, peanuts, candy, etc. Letters, a batch of them and a big brown envelope from Ntl. Geographic. Mrs. Teter again and this time with a copy of the Lake Clark portion of the book material. They want to be very accurate and request that I read it and list anything that isn't correct. Still in a hurry and would I get it back to them as soon as possible. I didn't have time to get into my letters. Get a fire going, beans hottened up and the lake trout in the skillet. Will had brought more venison steak, frozen, so it went into the cooler box to thaw slowly.

The evening weather got worse instead of better but we figured it would improve later. We would paddle to the lower end of the lower lake tonight. Dishes done and getting organized when it started to rain lightly and fog was in streaks and patches along the mts. No good, wait till early morning. I lit the Coleman and read a few letters, soon sawing knots and clear lumber. I would listen to him till near twelve and think about the important events of the day.

When I turned in it was 52°, raining lightly and a light breeze up.

June 6 – Overcast, Calm & 40°.

I was up at 4:30 to read more letters and watch the weather. It didn't look promising. Will finally came to life and I got the fire going for hotcakes. During breakfast blue appeared over the Volcanic Mts. and Hope Creek country. The fog started to clear out. It didn't take us long to get ready to canoe down. We had put his plane on my Cub beaching rack and tied it down in good shape. Away soon after eight and we would make it to the connecting stream in 45 minutes. Will is a good strong man on the bow paddle. Everything along the way is of interest to him. All water birds have to be identified and shorebirds, he knows all the calls. Two hours and five minutes from my beach to the Chili

---

[14] Jeep caps refers to RLP's knit cap.

[15] "Cat"refers to a Caterpillar diesel bulldozer, RLP was a diesel mechanic.

River campsite which is real good time. Alone I can make it in 2 hours 30 minutes.

In flying the evening before he hadn't seen many sheep at the lick but many caribou on the creek flowing to the Mulchatna. We made up our packs and started that two hour climb to the lick. Camping gear we left at the canoe and might camp at the lower end if the weather blew down. Good time on the climb with a stop to film a rock ptarmigan in its changing plumage. A dirty white color now. Flowers a million and they had to be identified. Over the top and it didn't look very promising. We found no more than 15 sheep at the lick and they were spooky. Molting now and looking very ratty. Considerable snow in the lick area and the main lick area still buried. So – we would look for the caribou on down Beatrice Creek. Real good hiking along the edge of the high ridge. Will kept remarking that this was ideal hiking country. Past the upside down Cessna 170 and we found that a parky squirrel lives in the wing. Much scolding and its voice much amplified by the hollow metal wing. Circling down and left to higher ground for a look into the big low country. No caribou and Will was determined to spot them. Finally he did and miles away across the Mulchatna River. Too far, let them go. We circled back towards the Chili River and stopped at the break over point to glass the country. Will took his shoes and socks off, layed back and took a nap. This much hiking was beginning to show. His right foot began to cramp and required soaking in cold water when some was handy. We could see the lower lake whitecapping down so it looked like we would camp tonight near the Chili River. We headed for the lake and discovered we had hiked seven hours with a one hour rest stop. Maybe close to 14 miles we had traveled over hill and dale.

I built a little camp fire at my runty spruce clump on the beach and we had toasted moose wieners, cheese and drank many cups of Labrador tea. Will stretched out in a brush surrounded comfortable spot and took a long nap. I tended the smoky fire and drank tea.

The sun went down and still the whitecaps were too many but it should calm in an hour or two. The day time clouds had not indicated wind.

We had taken the spinning rig along and to give the lake a chance to calm we went down to the big red rock hot spot for grayling. Will had two nice ones with in a few minutes – that was enough.

On down to check Jerre Wills' ratty Frank Bell cabin. The door stands open for the cabin is leaning and the door opening not plumb. Squirrels had packed in and shucked a bushel of spruce cones plus a huge supply of mushrooms. What will the Park Service do with such an eye sore. Be accused of burning a cabin I suspect but that purty stretch of the Chili River would sure look better if it was removed.[16]

I put the grayling on a fish stick as we headed back by the fishing hole. Our tracks the first ones there this year.

---

[16] By the early 1990s the Bell cabin had collapsed and one solstice RPL dragged the logs to a Chilikadrotna River gravel bar and burned them. He completely cleaned up the cabin site, however, the burning of the cabin remains were not sanctioned by the NPS.

The lake was very near calm and we would head up promptly. Before we got the canoe loaded and floating a light breeze was rippling the lake from the lower end. 20 past eleven when we started. The coming full moon could be seen from the lower end. Big and yellow in a partly cloudy sky. We didn't need its feeble light but the sight of it was nice to watch as we paddled. We soon lost our trailing breeze and picked up one on the bow. Paddling at night seems slow. Landmarks ahead can't be seen clearly and seem a long time coming. 1 hour 30 minutes to the stream which is good time against a breeze. Will complained of being tired of sitting and that the bunk was going to look mighty good to him. I lined her through and we found the upper lake also with a light breeze down but an easy paddle. The day was getting lighter instead of darker when we came to my beach. There would be no 4:30 reveille this…morning.

June 7 – Partly Cloudy, Calm & 33°.

Will lost no time in crawling into that lower bunk. I made one last check outside and found a nice breeze had followed us up the lakes. The big educated porkypine headed up a spruce by the clothesline. Climbed four feet and remembered that climbing trees is forbidden. He hurried back down and for the brush while I hurried for the porkypine pole. The canoe still loaded was pulled up high and solid. It could wait till morning sunlight for unloading.

I didn't sleep well and I knew that I wouldn't and I suspect that is one reason that I didn't. A big day and I hadn't simmered down yet. Will was soon sawing wood.

It was near six when I got up to build the breakfast fire. Spuds, eggs and venison steak for breakfast. Will had his cup of coffee and later we had a cup of hot chocolate which really tasted good.

Today he would check on caribou and probably spend the night at Port Alsworth. His plane free and afloat. My grayling cleaned and hanging I invited him back for a fish fry but he wouldn't today, but later. Took my last package of seven rolls of 16 mm film to mail. He took off and I got things looking more normal before settling down to bring my journal up to date. Today would be a Twin Lakes holiday. Many letters to read and that Ntl. Geographic story book material to study and comment on. She [Kathleen Teter] had written the letter that came with it May 1 and asked for an immediate reply. Will told me that Glen was coming in tomorrow so if he does the material will be on its way. In his writing John had mentioned *One Man's Wilderness* as being an Alaskan classic which should make my partners very happy. In this batch of mail a royalty check from Alaska Northwest [Publishing Company]. January 1st to April 1st so it appears that they will be paying at the end of each quarter now. I read and the longer I read the more I wondered if Stu had mailed that big batch of letters within a couple days as he indicated he would. Nearly 40 letters came this last time….

June 9 – Partly Cloudy, Calm & 30°.

It wasn't long after breakfast that we heard the little "T craft" coming up the lake. It was Glen and little Leon who isn't so young in years any more but still small for his age. His voice has a more grown up tone to it now. Glen did have that important letter from the Park Service for me to sign so I could get paid sometime. A letter from Bob Belous. So sorry please – he had been away to Washington, D.C. for two mo. and no one at this end had made a move on my paperwork. Glen mentioned flying me to a lake in the Bonanza Hills so I could get to Terry & Vic's camp to work on the John Deere. John [Branson] had said he wanted to go. Seems he had told Terry once that he wanted to come down. So – we would hike it – stay a day and come back over the trail. A fine morning and just as well get with it. I hurried to get a pack put together and a few of my treasures out of sight. It was 9:25 when we shoved out for the two and one half hour paddle to the Chili River. Twelve o'clock when we turned the canoe over in the dwarf birch and took out across the gravel knolls to climb above timberline and follow high ground to the Island mt. and the Ptarmigan Creek beyond. John is a strong hiker and we made it to my erratic Hilton rock[17] by six o'clock. It's one long trek across that high dry (nearly so) country to the Island Mt. We figured we could make the Painted Mt.[18] before laying down in the wide open to sleep a few hours. Wading shoes for both the Ptarmigan and Beaver Creek[19] which drains the valley we would travel. We had bucked a head wind along the way but now only a light breeze. Mosquitoes soon found you if you stopped. John said lets camp while we were still in the timber bottom but I wanted on the mt. side where a good breeze kept the bugs away. At a cluster of beaver ponds we climbed and John wanted to go higher. We ate a bite, he opened a small can of tuna fish and insisted on taking the can down and submerging it under water to keep from attracting every bear in the country. I ate half a can of boned turkey and tucked the remainder back in my pack. We had seen no sign of bears and very few moose tracks. No rabbits at all and I was surprised for Twin Lakes has many rabbits.

John snored awhile but later said that he hadn't slept. Mosquitoes gave me a bit of a time and every time I looked John was sitting up watching the beaver ponds or snoring. Sprinkles came but not enough to chase us to cover. We had traveled eleven hours and it would take three and one half more to reach Terry's camp.

2:45 came and John complained of being cold. Just as well be walking as suffering so we hit the trail. Fog and light rain by now and it was very wet in the brush. Up the valley to the yellow faced mt. The climb to the pass and then all down hill to Terry's camp. Fog and the best I could do was follow the sound of Little Bonanza Creek from the mt. side. A little further but in due time we stood above Terry and Vic's cabin. 15 hours it had taken us. While we stood there looking down Vic came outside and I hollered. She waved and went in. Later we learned she had told Terry of two men on the mt. and he had

---

[17] RLP's Hilton rock, a glacial erratic boulder with large overlaying shelving rock that provides a traveler with shelter from the rain.

[18] RLP's Painted Mountain, a mountain in the Bonanza Hills on the way to the Gill's camp.

[19] RLP's Beaver Creek, a small tributary into Ptarmigan Creek on the way to the Gill's camp.

muttered Park Service and didn't even go out. The mining engineer and helper was there drilling test holes on Little Bonanza. Joe Fisher and Clyde Cooper their names. Terry was surprised to see me hike in as he had said he would pay Glen for two trips to get me in and out. The miners had breakfast and went to work. We fixed us some hotcakes and eggs. It tasted real good after our traveling fare of granola bars and peanuts.

First thing on John's schedule was to take a nap. Then he would split wood. Terry and I went up to see the drill in operation. Drilling in gravel at less than thirty feet and getting a color or two with each boiling. The John Deere was there and not in use so we took it down to camp. That right brake, what ailed it? The brake was being applied before the steering clutch was released. Adjusted according to the book and still it refused to act normal. I pulled the cover from the good one to see where the difference was. Ah ha! There it was. The brake actuating lever was frozen to the shaft that the clutch release lever operates. All same as no adjustment to get the delay between clutch release and brake.

Penetrating oil, a gentle application of the hammer and much working got it freed up. Now we had it working much better. Cover on and we gave it a try. The drillers wanted to move the drill so that would get things in line for a fine adjustment. The day was about done and it looked like rain. Vic had prepared a real good supper and I was ready to turn in soon after. John and I sleeping in a tent from under a white wall tent. I was weary.

June 11 – Partly Cloudy, N.W. Breeze & Warm.

It looked favorable for a start on our long hike back. The grass wet but it would dry. Again a hearty breakfast and Vic made us some ham sandwiches. Together Terry and Vic told me they intended to have Bee (Wayne) fly them to Twin Lakes when they got back to Port Alsworth. Maybe they would return to their camp in July. Still a lot of snow where they wanted to high grade with the suction dredge. I had been there on Synneva Creek[20] the evening before.

7:30 when we said goodby and climbed to the high table land behind the cabin. We didn't intend to go all the way in one day. Going was good. Cool, a nice breeze at our backs. 3 hours and 50 minutes saw us at Ptarmigan Creek. Noon saw us well up on the Island mt. It looked like we could make the lower lake at least. Across that terribly long three hour straight stretch and we took five before dropping into the timber and the last hour before the lake. Across from us on an open ridge was a pretty good sized brown bear and he came our way. We watched him working in the heavy brush on a slope facing us and suddenly he took off on the run down into the timber where we wanted to go. John has packed his .30-30 Winchester to the Bonanza Hills and back. Now he was glad that he did for he would rather not see a bear.

Time to go and we barged down over the edge and into the thick stuff. Should

[20] Synneva Creek, a small tributary of Bonanza Creek near the Gill's camp.

we talk loud while we traveled. Little chance that you will see him if you do was my prediction. No bear but we did see fresh droppings.

At the canoe and I was in better shape than I had ever been before after making that long haul from the hills, 11 hours since we left Terry and Vic. 10 hours and 35 minutes travel time. We would paddle on up with a nice following breeze. We collected the two inner tubs Stu Ramstad had given me. A straight shot from the extreme lower end to my beach and we made it in 2 hours 20 minutes. Who was at my cabin. A porkypine was sitting on a table out front and I feared the worst. After beaching I ran to the cabin but the culprit was gone. No damage on the table but my door sill and the log under had suffered. Right then and there I decided that the porkypine business does not pay and I would liquidate the company. Before I turned in the grey faced one was back and ended up on the brush pile.

June 20 – Clear, Calm & 31°.

A big Cessna and it came my way. Again the lake was glassy and we met on the big pond. Hank Rust and two with him. Paul Fritz, the park planner, was in the back seat and the passenger in front a "tourista," Paul is a talkative one. They had been at my cabin for about an hour he said. Saw my pin in the map and intended to fly up that way. Now, we could just drift and visit a few minutes. No doubt that 300 hp Cessna was drawing standby time for time is money to Hank.

They had brought my mail and some goodies from Hornberger's. Will Troyer had nearly lost his life by drowning since he was here. On a float trip down a river [the Alagnak River] on the peninsula with two others and their raft turned over. One member was under the raft for about 30 seconds. Will had a hard struggle to keep on top. His new Nikon camera gear got wet. Lucky to be alive those three. They gave me cookies and apples that were left from their lunch and fired up to go. Going to Turquoise and then back to Portage Lake and the pass...They took off and I glided on down the last half mile.

Sarah sent me another pretty loaf of bread plus a sack of cookies, green onions, radishes, an orange, apples and a couple grapefruit. Letters a few and one small package from Helen White. Books, and what kind? On opening it I was never so surprised in my life. The last two journals I had mailed to her. They cover from April 12 to May 29th. There just has to be a misunderstanding along the line somewhere. I declared the rest of the afternoon a Twin Lakes holiday and read my mail. Good to hear that the boy pedaled his way to fame across the English Channel in the man powered flying machine.

Late in the afternoon I crossed Hope Creek on the skinny bridge and checked out the Cowgill jungle. I climbed above timberline to check on the blueberry prospects and to look down on the nice lake scene. The lake still very blue and that is strange with 30" of new water. Partly cloudy calm and 42° now at 9. It could frost, it really could.

June 21 – Clear, Calm & 31°.

Tents on the lower shore where the river floaters camp before heading down the Chili River. Five tents of various colors and I thought of a similar tent village a year ago. Not far across from my beaching spot I would paddle over and see who it was. I could see three people as I came in range and a blond headed guy met me at the beach. I told him of a similar camp last year. "Same outfit," he said. He and a friend from the Palmer area were working for a guide who takes a couple float trip parties each summer. Fifteen people this time and at least some of them from back east in Connecticut. They hadn't arrived but would today. Four large rubber rafts were pulled up on the beach.

They had trolled last night and caught some nice lake trout and one big dolly. A five pounder he figured but from experience I have learned that fish caught can grow after they leave the water.

It doesn't take long to come down the mt. and in an hour and a half I was at the canoe. Again I paddled over to see what had developed. Quite a bunch of people there now and they came stringing down to the beach. Many cameras in action. Nearly everyone said they had read the book and would like to see the place. Well, why didn't they hike up tomorrow as they wouldn't be leaving for the trip down the river till Sunday.

Some were game to give it a try. Row one of the big rafts across to Skywagon point and start the hike from there. One had painted a few pictures from those in the book to help himself through school in Oregon. Some fancy camera gear in the bunch and one had a Hassalbald with lenses that would make me think that he knows how to use them.

I had to be paddling if I would make it home before sunset and so with "I'll be watching for you guys," I shoved off.

Gee, it seemed like a long haul to the stream. It was warm and I was getting sleepy, so sleepy I closed my eyes and paddled a few licks time and again. Made it finally and ate a stick of dynamite before lining through. A ripple up on the upper lake until past the halfway. The sun went behind the mts. and the cool of the evening took over. That helped and I felt more my usual self again. It was 8:25 when I beached. I had wondered what I could have for supper that would let me sleep soon after. I decided on a huge milkshake and a Sara Hornberger cookie. Tired but not too tired to go to Hope Creek for a fresh bucket of mt. creek water. Lots of dry milk, cocoa mix, sugar and honey went into my big shaker. Boy! that was good and I finished as the sun left the peaks down country. So, I had seen the sunrise and set on that longest day. Paddled maybe 16 miles and hiked 12 with a heavy load. My best count on the sheep was 150 and I felt sure there were a few more near but not showing. So, perhaps 160 or even 175 use the lick and this area of the sheep range.

It was clear calm and 45° when I turned in at ten.

June 28 – Overcast, Calm & 42°.

Emerson Creek is also running much less water and fishing might be better. I wanted a couple frames of me in the foreground fishing and the high up country for a purty back drop. I saw a trout break water as I got set up but caught no fish. I headed for the falls and knew I was early. The sun has to be near noon before it lights the lower falls completely.

What a disappointment to find the ouzels nest unoccupied this summer but as I stood looking an ouzel came near the nest but only to capture something and fly on up the canyon. Soon it was back and I noticed it went under the high grassy lookout point where I was standing. I stayed and tried to keep track of its comings and goings. Somewhere near was a nest. I moved back down to the fast water below. Climbed out onto a huge boulder for a look up along that wall with the water bouncing down along side. Ah ha! There was the big cake shaped clump of moss that is the ouzels home. On a ledge under the overhang and a dark place to see into much less film. The dipper came and went. The mate was in the house and so were young ones for I could see red mouths opened wide when the groceries came. Just opposite and across the spill way of the boiling pool a big smooth rock. That is where I wanted my ouzel bird – at home along side the churning water. I got set up and waited. Sooner or later that dipper bird would lite there. The distance a little more than I would like but nothing could be done about that as it was churning white water in between. I got a few frames but I wanted the sun around more so hung tough. Just opposite me and hardly more than 20 feet away was a huge rock and the bird came there at infrequent intervals. Often enough that I figured I could do some good if I trained on the top of it and waited. Now the bird used the rock up by the pool but I hung tough. That bird would come there or anywhere if I had the patience to wait. It finally came and posed for a few minutes in the bright sun. The camera dry and that was my goal – finish the roll before plane day. Another fine day soon I would be back and with me would be the Bolex and 200 mm plus my big truck rear view mirror. At 2 P.M. I could put that very dark nest in bright sunlight.

June 30 – Partly Cloudy, Calm & 30°.

I spent a lot of time awake and I blamed it to the big heap of fried grayling on my plate at supper time. By morning I would be ready to sleep. I did doze off and woke up to sounds out front. Porkypine or squirrel I couldn't tell which until the rasping started on the cabin. A little of that is great plenty and I was at the door in a flash. The porky was perched up among the rounds between the legs of the burl table and just getting started on a log. Scratch one porkypine and I would pick up the quills after breakfast. I had asked Paul Fritz of the Park Service – "What does the Park Service do when they have a serious porcupine problem?" "Well, the porkypine was here first. He may kill a few trees but others will take their place," he said. "Now sposin' the porkypine is chewing on my cabin," I asked. "Knock him in the head!" and that was settled.

Hotcakes and the weather was going from partly cloudy to overcast. Sometime during the night it was totally clear or the temperature wouldn't have been 30° at 4:30. I could find no frost or ice which was strange. This morning I would work on my mail and then if it was bright and sunny I would go to Emerson [Creek] again but first I must plant the porkypine near the rhubarb.

July 3 – Partly Cloudy, Calm & 49°.

All this messing around was to use up time till the sun got around to Cowgill Mt. I wanted to paddle to Low Pass point for that picture I had in mind and the sun needed to be some where near 90° to my line of fire. From there I planned to go to Emerson Creek and have another go at the little dipper birds. If only the clouds would stand back and let the sunshine in.

At the falls a few patches of blue and I waited for the sun so as to get a couple 35 mm shots before crossing. That done I went back down the creek 200 yards where it is fairly wide not to deep but very fast. I looked it over good and decided I had better go farther down but how far to find a better place. I knew of none closer than three quarters of a mile. Getting wet I didn't mind but I hated to dunk my good camera gear. I headed on down and then turned back. I would give it my best try and figured that would be good enough. Wearing my bobbed off Lee riders so no pant legs to roll and get wet even if they were. My good rib cracking walking staff to keep me on an even keel. I eased into it and angled up and across. The water was fast and the cobbles on the bottom large. Water was filling my pockets before I started to climb out on the far side. All this and I was gambling that the sun would come. I shot a few frames in cloudy bright and then over the trees a big patch of blue. I waited for it to uncover the sun. Sunshine for all afternoon it appeared and I took my time and enjoying the wildest of white water that I know of in Twin Lakes country. I was in the creek and out looking for the best angles.

Working up to get opposite the ouzels nest and it took some doing. I had my rope along but found that I wouldn't need it. I ended up just across the big white water chute (that is the outlet of the pool below the falls) from the nest on the little ledge. Hardly more than 20 feet away.

The light suddenly went out and I looked up to see those big grey clouds again. From then on it was birds at the nest and no sun on the mirror to light them or it was sun and no birds or it was water slopping over the big rock wall between me and the pool. I waited and watched the system of the ouzels. Not always are they both feeding the young. I saw them both in the house at the same time and I saw one stay and the other pack groceries. I saw the housekeeper pack out droppings and leave them to be packed away by the grocery fetcher when he came. Just to fly out and drop them on his way for more food wasn't good enough. Always it was land at the waters edge and deposit them in the stream.

I had climbed down using willows and brush as hand holds. If I couldn't climb out loaded I could climb empty and attach my rope to a spruce before going back for my load. Made it and was soon making my way down and away from that roar. No wonder the ouzels sing so loud and shrill. Not wanting to ford the creek again I climbed the game trail so as to follow the crest of the high mud banks. On the trail tracks of moose, a big bear and a little one. A sow with cub or cubs.

Again I recrossed the stream a mile down and found it much better. A light breeze up the lake and the creek showing the rise by dumping in drift wood.

50 minutes from Emerson which is good time breeze or no. Past six when I entered the cabin. My gear stowed and a quick supper. Laundry in and writing done by nine. A moderate surf on my beach now and heavy grey clouds level the peaks down country. Temperature 59° for the warmest evening temperature this year.

Tomorrow the 4th and it doesn't look promising for a bright day and it just may turn out to be a real no nonsense 4th of July.

July 4th – Overcast, Lt. Rain, Breeze up & 50°.

Today the 4th was a special day. I splurged and drank one of my remaining three cans of 7UP. Six cans in my cooler box over winter and no sign of bulging from the cold. And I would have a chunk of Spike and Hope's fruitcake if I could find it in the cache. I did but it took a second try to locate it (under my lard pail in a box with the Wesson oil.) A good green salad of lettuce, fireweed, radishes, green onion, and carrot. A good helping of cooked this morning small Navy beans. A slice of Sara's fancy bread topped with butter and Sis's strawberry jam brought down from the cache special for the occasion. Cold porridge pudding with lots of Carnation dry milk, sugar and cinnamon. A cup of hot Swiss Miss and my size 34 waist band was snug enough when I finished.

A very stormy looking late afternoon. A rough looking cloud deck lighted by the sun. A heavy surf climbing higher but would diminish by eight.

So now, it is overcast with a trace of blue. A breeze up and the temperature 45°. A very enjoyable 4th of July. It was truly a no nonsense holiday at Twin Lakes.

July 8 – Partly Cloudy, Calm & 35°.

I paddled on down and found the creek down a bit. No grayling working but I started with the fly rod. Not doing any good and about to try the spinning rod and bucktail mepps. I was keeping an eye on the flat, thinking of the sheep but not expecting to see any, but suddenly there they were up near the Vanderpool cottonwoods. I had the glasses and learned they were both rams. One maybe a two year old and the other a yearling. They hadn't seen me so I worked my way back to the canoe and set up the 300 mm. None

to soon for here they came to the mouth of the creek. Still acting very restless and it appeared the 2 year old didn't approved of the yearling – time and again it chased the little guy who trotted away but came back first opportunity. I was doing some good at decent range. The larger ram finally waded into the lake as if wanting to swim across and I wondered if he would try it. Close to a half mile to the gravel banks from Emerson. Belly deep and he chickened out. Soon he waded in again and this time it was for real. Deep water and headed across. The little one splashed in and followed. The first time I had seen sheep swim. Standing high out of the water at the shoulders as if standing on their hind legs. Making pretty good time but I could overtake them easy enough. I hurried to the canoe and tore my equipment down. I would hand hold the camera with the 58 mm lens. Maybe it was three minutes before I was on my way. They were out more than 200 yards and looking small with only heads and shoulders showing. I paddled and was surprised to find they were coming back. What had changed their minds? Farther than they figured perhaps. I wouldn't turn them so let them pass and then followed. Strange swimmers but nothing compared to a caribou. I got right in close but it is a chore to paddle and use a camera. Stop paddling and they move away too fast. I got to the beach just ahead of them and that didn't turn them. Came splashing nearby and didn't seem at all tired or frightened. They trotted to some brush and grabbed a few bites before moving on. So, they did want to cross. If they only knew, they could go down to the connecting stream and cross in a twinkling.

> *The first time I had seen sheep swim. Standing high out of the water at the shoulders as if standing on their hind legs. Making pretty good time but I could overtake them easy enough.*

Next I saw of them they were up near the Vanderpool timber again. I went up that way but got too close. They crossed the flat and went up the beach along the open park like area.

My fish cleaned and hanging to firm up. Everything under control, one more time I wanted to look for that camera case screw. Satisfy myself that I had made a good try to find it. Go slow and look close I went slow and looked close but I didn't see it so let it stay forever in the country where it has spent a lot of time and miles on the past eleven years and more. Coming by Spike's cabin I cut another mess of dandelion spinach.

The lake had calmed and now came a fresh breeze up the lake. Grayling, beans and dandelion spinach for supper. Now at 8:30 it is calming again. Overcast and the temperature 48°. Raining lightly.

July 18 – Overcast, Lt. Breeze up & 45°.

From my bunk I saw that the morning was another with a very low ceiling but it was time to roll out. Then I heard an airplane, a Super Cub from the sound of the exhaust and right

away I guessed it to be Will Troyer flying that brand new Super Cub he had talked about. A bright shiny red and white Cub and he dipped a wing as he passed. I hurried to make it look as if I had been up and dressed at least. Surprising how little time it takes a plane to be down and coming to my beach. "I thought I would get you out of bed," he said as he climbed out. "Fine weather as close as Lachbuna Lake but from there it is overcast as far as you can see." He had stayed at Hornberger's last night and took off at 4:30 without breakfast. He fished out a sack from Chuck and Sara. Lettuce, a cucumber, bananas, an apple and a small jar of jam. Will had intended to do sheep survey over this way but he could hardly see the mts. much less the sheep.

I got the fire going and water on for his Park Service coffee. From the cache a can of corned beef hash. A couple eggs and that was it for the main course. Rolled oats groats after the dishes were done. Will is happy with that new Cub. Leased by the Park Service for two years from a company in Anchorage. Assigned to Will Troyer personally so it's his Cub. He had heard at Port Alsworth that Babe and Mary are in Anchorage. What was new on this end. I told him that I had located a fox den with pups. That, he wanted to see and get some pictures. He would be back in filming weather and we would fly to the lower end or the chain of lakes and hike from there. He reported that Sky Lab. had tumbled in and parts of it hit in a little populated area of Australia and some garbage fell in the ocean near there. Will lost a friend at Naknek. A fisherman Martin Seversen.[21] Just completed a $100,000.00 year and then got his net caught in the propeller. He brought it to shallow water where it would dry up when the tide went out. He was under working at freeing the net when the boat tipped over and pinned him down. So its like old Nessmuck[22] said, "Wait is all the wurrled to a man when his wife is a widdy."

From here Will was going back to sunshine and Lake Clark. Probably fly sheep survey in that area today. "I'll show you how quick this rig will break water," he said as he climbed in. A good guy that Will but I wouldn't pay him what he is getting for the good he is doing.

July 21 – Partly Cloudy, Calm & 40°.

I was ready except to close up two letters when I heard the "T craft" coming. Who was it flying a little higher than normal for the down wind leg. I went out to the beach to see the landing. I didn't have long to wait. It came out from behind Carrithers' point headed down. Then, a rather steep turn for so low. Descending at a good rate and then it leveled off and was on the water. A shot of power to keep her high on the step. It had to be Glen who has been doing a lot of flying and feeling pretty confident. He chopped the power and she reared back on her heels like a mallard duck. Coming straight in to my beach and

---

[21] Martin Severson (1925-1979), a Dena'ina born in Old Nondalton and a Naknek fisherman, air taxi operator, village leader, state representative.

[22] George Washington Sears (1821-1890) author of the Nessmuk books on camp craft and woodcraft. RLP was familiar with Nessmuk and his advocacy of canoeing in the wilderness. RLP had a copy of Sear's *Woodcraft and Camping*. Nessmuk's championing of inexpensive light-weight canoe travel would have been appealing and perhaps helped inform RLP's basic philosophy.

getting close. Who was flying that rig anyway? Then I saw that old dirty Cessna cap and those solid grey eyebrows above a grey mustache. It was Babe, no doubt about it. I couldn't see a passenger. He hadn't forgotten the final item in landing – he was out and in the water to keep her from touching even my fine beach gravel. He told me one time – "I don't like to patch floats and this is the best way to keep from it." I said, "Boy that was a flashy landing." And he replied – "It's pretty hard to make a bad landing on floats unless you really work at it." I think the old boy was trying to impress me a bit with his flying after being ground bound for more than two years. By now he had the red bird tailed in to the beach and who climbs out but Mary. Little Mary didn't show above the panel as he came in. I expected Babe to be brown as a local boy in Hawaii but he looked the same as he did when here. He looked real good and I told him so. "I feel better than I look, too," was his reply. Babe fished out the mail and groceries and we each packed a load, cleaning the beach. 25 lbs of beans but where was my 25 lbs. of sugar. Will had said I told them to add sugar to your list. I was to learn that it didn't get added. "Too much going on there," Babe said. The order for sugar didn't get to the shipping dept. A big sack of lettuce, carrots, cabbage, peaches, apples, muskmelon, cherry tomatoes, pickles and cheese. "A gift from us," Mary said.

In the past Babe was always in a hurry to get back to Lake Clark but not today. He was content to set and sell me on the big island of Hawaii.

Mary came back and I offered to build a fire and we would have some lunch. Oh no, they would be heading back. They wanted to stop and see Van Valin's lodge. I asked Babe if he had flown as a pilot since he left in June of '76. "No, and I didn't miss it a bit," he said. "Now, I don't wake up at night wondering which way the wind is blowing on a little lake where I am due to pick someone up today." They invited me over and promised that they had plenty of work to keep me happy. All aboard and I pulled the prop. Babe didn't know how many shots of prime to give the engine. After three shots she came to life. Same old Babe on take off. On the step and then lift that right float to decrease the drag. It was as if he hadn't missed a day of flying since he left two years and more ago.

July 22 – Partly Cloudy, Breeze dn. & 54°.

I read till ten o'clock and still had a stack ahead of me. Paul Fritz clipping copies amounted to near fifty sheets. A real nice morning and a burbot to match. Lots of good spuds for frying. Potatoes harvested last September and little sign of sprouts unless Mary had sprouted them. She said she had sorted out the best.

Today, Sunday I would stay home and digest my mail more thoroughly. A great collection of clippings on Sky Lab, the Gossamer Condor, the DC 10s and other items of interest sent by the back east clipping snipper, my brother Robert.

About noon I took a walk up to see how my garden was doing. Spuds coming right along but lettuce and beets only a trace. It appeared that spruce grouse had been dusting and made salad of the two. Some miserable porkypine had pulled just a lot of oakum chinking from between the logs of Spike's cabin. More pulled than ever before and some chewed. Before breakfast I had chased one away from my door and it hurried up the beach. Porkypines look pretty dumb and act it sometimes but I swear it seems that if I give one a bad time he gets even at Spike's cabin. It is as if he is practicing Sen. Dirkson's[23] law which reads, "Get elected, get reelected, don't get mad, get even."

July 24 – Overcast, Blowing dn. & 56°.

The wind strong throughout the night and clouds still moving at a good rate when I got up at five. Today, I wanted to travel but it most certainly was too dark for pictures. Hotcakes and a few odd jobs to see if it might brighten up a bit. No fish on the line so I went to Hope Creek and soon gave it up.

It was breaking down country. The lake still churning but I could run with the sea as far as the good beach below Gold Mt. The little kicker would get me back past one mile rock and better water. The pin in the map said I would go as far as Beech Creek and from there I would come back against the wind along the slope above timberline.

There was my moose calf on its feet and where I had seen it last. Still no sign of a cow. It started to feed and I wondered if I had an orphan. It certainly looked that way. A calf less than two months old – could it survive without a mother. It worked to the edge of the brush and down the bank onto a little low land with a few willows and dwarf birch. I could see it better now and it didn't look too bad. It spooked a bit from the porkypine behind some brush and then stood and watched it pass before moving close to the edge of the running stream. The porky turned back and was getting close. This time the calf stood watching with ears forward. Suddenly back went those ears and it charged at the porky which I couldn't see for brush. Those front feet flailing the brush and then into the clear. The right front leg had a big patch of white below the knees, quills. There must have been a hundred of them. A white patch six inches long or more. The calf limped and held that foot clear of the ground at times. I didn't see the porky again so don't know if it was injured. The calf went back to feeding and came my way into the shallow water along the main channel. A small grassy island farther out. It came to that. Another larger one and it came on to that one where it fed on willow. In good range now. It worked up stream along the deep channel and then decided to cross to my side. In it went and had to swim in mid channel. The current carried it closer and it came out less than a hundred feet up stream from me. Now I was doing business. It saw me but when I didn't move it started to feed. Gradually it worked up stream and out of good range. I had shot at least 25 frames.

The weather had closed in and now it started to rain. I waited until the calf was

[23] RLP is probably referring to Illinois Republican Senator Everett McKinley Dirkson (1896-1969).

386

in high brush and then circled inland and towards the gravel banks.

If only the calf had left that fool porkypine alone. Now it will have one very sore leg to go with its problem of making a living without milk and a wise mother to teach it the do's and don'ts of the very cruel world that is nature. It would be interesting to keep track of this calf if I could. See what kind of shape it is in by the time snow comes and stays. I doubt that it will survive the winter.

Now it was raining and the brush was wet as a shower bath. Good that I had my Kelty along. Something nice had happened, the wind had died while I waited for the calf to show. Now the lake was near flat and glassy. I paddled instead of using the little kicker. Five past six when I came in the cabin. A fire going and the stove smothered with rags drying. For a day that promised nothing this one turned out to be a winner. If only that fool calf had left that miserable porkypine alone it would be more comfortable tonight. I wish Will [Troyer] would come with his dart gun. We would try to immobilize it and remove the quills.

Now at 8:30, overcast, calm, and 50°. Weather permitting I must look for the calf again to see how it is doing.

July 25 – Overcast, High Fog, Blowing up & 44°.

I crossed and decided to check out the brush on that side and also go to the scene of the porkypine fight. See if that calf moose did flatten him. I didn't think so. The calf had struck over the top to get that patch of quills on the back side of its leg. Halfway down and I saw the calf just leaving the lower lake headed up stream on the other side where I had been thirty minutes before. I hurried on to get a spruce in line and be as close to the stream as possible. The calf decided to cross to my side and I saw it carry that right front leg as it entered the water. That leg was giving it some trouble. Across it came a hundred yards down stream and then up the flat along the bank. Closer and closer, stopping to grab a bite or two along the way. Finally it could hear the camera and would stop to look before moving closer still. Less than a hundred feet and me in the wide open, it stopped and held that quill loaded leg up for me to get a close up. Then it climbed the bank and moved back into the brush a hundred feet to lay down. I had used a hundred feet of film and hadn't brought the extra roll from the canoe. The calf out of sight I headed back up to change film. The calf was bedded near the little flat where it fed and thrashed the porkypine. Next feeding period it would go there again. I went back down and stationed myself far enough away to keep the camera noise from alerting the calf and waited. I knew it would be a couple hours as it had been yesterday.

The calf moved out and fed on willow. Not in as good a shape as I thought. With the light right I could count every rib. But the little guy was working at it. Right now if a bear came along it would be a goner for it is lame in that front leg. A little bull calf I noticed as he added water to the stream already running bank to bank. Me on the bank

behind a low willow and shooting slightly down. The calf fed my way and nibbled at feed in shallow water half way to his eyes. For being an orphan he was doing pretty good at acting like a full grown moose. He fed in my direction and again he would come within a hundred feet of my 6x lens. That camera noise again and he stopped to look every time it ran. Another 100 feet exposed just as he finished feeding and headed for his bed ground in the brush again. Out of sight and I could walk away and not disturb him.

August 1 – Overcast, Lt. Breeze up & 49°.

A nice view of Kijik country from its headwaters to Lachbuna Lake. A lot of moose, caribou, and bear country and I settled down over the crest and out of the very cool breeze. Wisps of fog would scoot by. One minute I had a clear view and the next it was misty. Lake Clark country appeared to be having a high overcast and fair day. The Kijik noisy and Lachbuna flat calm. I glassed the country many times over and figured a bear would be my best prospect for there was many bright green spots that bears like to graze on. Lots of clean gravel bars along the fast water and I could easily spot game there with my bare eyes, but I didn't.

An hour and time I was heading back down. I had left my pack at the bottom of the last climb. Downhill all the way and I took advantage of the long deep snow patches on the down grade. Fog had cleared out and it was a fair day in Twin Lakes country. Again I stopped on the big erratic rock of granite to glass the connecting stream before dropping down to blueberry country and dessert for my stick of dynamite.

A light breeze up the lake and how lucky I have been the past couple weeks. Calm going and a breeze to help me home.

At my beach I checked the trot line first thing, nothing. Strange tracks on my beach and the door latch handle not at the angle I had left it. Going up Beech Creek I had heard a big Cessna over the lakes.

On the table a big package and a few letters with a note on top. It read –
"Dick:
Brought your mail from Port Alsworth. Sorry I missed you. Do want to meet with you. I am temporary National Park Service Ranger assigned to Lake Clark this summer.

Will try to stop back at a later date.

Stu Coleman[24]

I am staying on the island at Port Alsworth – in the old Van Valin house."

---

[24] Stu Coleman, NPS law enforcement ranger assigned to the fledgling Lake Clark National Monument at Port Alsworth, he was detailed from Great Smoky National Park in Tennessee.

So, the ranger was here. I would like to hear what he has to say but to catch me home he had better come pretty early or late if it is a day to travel. Such days are not plentiful and I must take advantage of them.

I fried my big grayling and opened a can of spaghetti and meat balls. One given to me by Marshall Farmer before he quit the business. I noticed it rusting badly on one end. It had survived the winters freezing better than most canned stuff. In fact I couldn't tell that freezing had effected its quality more than slight. By the time dishes and writing was done it was 9:15. The sky more than 50% clear, a trace of a breeze up and 52° .

August 4 – Clear, Breeze dn. & 40°.

Spuds for breakfast and last thing on the menu was my rolled oats after dishes were washed. A plane, a little one and low. Who would be coming so early. It was the red "T craft" and I saw two aboard as it came to the beach. Glen and he had a young guy from Anchorage with him. The boy that figures his income tax and other paperwork. From the south, Tennessee or some such foreign state. He had promised the kid a look around in Lake country and this was part of the tour. One letter, a dozen eggs and 50 lbs. of sugar. Didn't have it in 25 lb. sacks so the 50. Two brand new still in the wrapper, copies of *One Man's Wilderness* for me to write my name in. Had to hit three book caches in Anchorage before he found them. "Ask them for the book and they go look – come back and say sorry guess we are sold out again." The books are for the couple and their daughter camped at the lower end. It was because of the book that they came from California to Twin Lakes. Weather permitting I must go down and see them.

The visitor was busy taking pictures and my welfare birds were taking advantage of the opportunity to load up on hotcake. While Glen and I sat visiting at the big window little Milo the brown weasel was scampering about the breakwater where the parky squirrel lives.

Mary had gone over to Sophie Austin's[24] across the lake to pick blueberries. Sophie had a good patch staked out. They found that a bear had cleaned up the patch. Babe was busy filling the woodshed with birch. He (Glen) had heard that Terry & Vic wanted a helicopter to take them to Anchorage and that I didn't like to hear. It means that something is not right on Bonanza Creek. Glen had met the new monument ranger, Stu Coleman. A young guy from state side and imported for the summer. Not a pilot but has a big Cessna standing by ready to go. Boston Whaler pleasure boat with two 85 h.p. Johnson outboard motors hanging on the stern. Had to have a mechanic out from Anchorage to adjust the throttle. Sounds like an expensive way to go.

August 10 – Partly Cloudy, Blowing dn. & 50°.

I found them at the woodshed and it was Stu Coleman and another ranger and their

[25] Sophie Hobson Balluta Austin (1911-2002) Dena'ina elder who was born on the Stony River but lived most of her life on Lake Clark. In 1979 she was living on Lake Clark north of Port Alsworth at the bay, Chaq'ah Tugget "one is kept in the corner."

pilot "Brought your mail again," Stu said, "And thought we had missed you again." He remarked about the windy day and the rough ride. I learned later that he had gotten air sick. A one sack trip he called it. We came and got acquainted. This being opening day of sheep and caribou season he thought I would be hunting and how come there were no hunters camped on the lakes. I told him I doubted that there would be any now that this is a monument. Hadn't I heard of the "Great Monument Trespass." Everyone makes it a point to go hunting in the new national monuments. They hadn't seen any camp except one at Snipe Lake and it was a recreation camp and outside of the monument at that. How did I feel about this thing. I allowed it would be a better deal to educate the hunters and let them hunt. Make it tough like it is in the old country. Take a two hour exam plus a demonstration of marksmanship. Prove that you can make a clean kill, do a decent job of butchering and be able to pack it out. They allowed that would be a pretty big order but didn't doubt that it would weed out a lot of would be hunters.

Stu Coleman spotted my Exakta and I knew right away that we would get along. Did he have one. "I have five," he said, and he named all the models and accessories. So much Exakta equipment that he couldn't afford to change to another brand.

I ask him about the Park Service policy in regards to neglected cabin camps – did they intend to clean them up or talk to the owner about cleaning them up. And what would they do or could they do if he didn't. Stu said, "I really don't know." It's pretty touchy to do anything unless it's a case of abandonment. If after a determined search they couldn't locate anyone to claim it he supposed they could do something.

Stu is from Tennessee and spent a lot of time in the Great Smoky Mountains [National Park]. He was borrowed from there to spend the summer here. Evidently he didn't have to fly there – this rough air he couldn't take.

August 14 – Partly Cloudy, Blowing dn. & 48°.

On the lake it was a nice afternoon. The lake very green and crowded with whitecaps. Light showers along the mts. down country. I looked for moose at the cottonwoods across near Glacier Creek. This year if things go according to plan there will be no Bud Lofstedt to fly a tight circle over the good bull moose and no Jerre Wills to chop him up and take him to Homer. It will be as it was about fifteen years ago. No airplanes flying and no shots fired during moose season. Moose could be found much closer to home than Twin Lakes.

Coming down the slope I picked three beefsteak mushrooms. Only once till now had I tried them. Tony's wife[26] had fixed some a couple times while here. Salt, pepper and enough garlic was the seasoning. She fried them in oil. I did mine the same and then stirred them into my small Navy beans – not bad – in fact pretty good. Again trout for supper and the trap set for more.

[26] Tony and Lucille Sardegna (1938-1994) were from Los Angeles and had read *One Man's Wilderness* in the mid-1970s and came to visit RLP and eventually moved to Port Alsworth.

August 17 – Overcasts, Lt. Breeze dn. & 44°.

While I was having supper a Super Cub came up the far side and came across and then back down. While I was writing two planes, the Cub one of them, came up and landed at Jerre's. Evidently they couldn't find the key to the padlock. One soon taxied over to my beach. A young kid named Alan asked where Bud Lofstedt's cabin was. They had come to do a little sheep and caribou hunting for a couple weeks. I asked him if he knew this was national monument country now. Yes, he knew but Bud told him they weren't enforcing the regulations this year, but added you are on your own in case they decide to enforce them now.

Today while I was with the moose the Park Service [Cessna] 185 flew up the left fork and back down again. I told him they had been here earlier and indicated they were checking for hunters. He had better fly to Port Alsworth and check with them if he wanted to be safe. He allowed maybe it would be safer to hunt caribou from Snipe Lake or the Bonanza Hills. He talked awhile and his buddy drifted around on the calm lake. Finally they took off up the lake to spend the night in Bud's cabin.

Now at 8:45 lots of clear sky, dead calm, and 44°.

A fresh kettle of beans about ready to leave the fire.

August 22 – Partly Cloudy, Calm & 34°.

I hadn't been there five minutes when I saw a big Cessna landing at my place. It didn't stay long and I figured it was the Park Service and Stu had brought my mail. It took off up the lake and when it didn't go back for a half hour I figured it had landed at the upper end. When it did go down it climbed and went through Low Pass.

A breeze from the south on the peak. The sun very warm and I would get somewhat of a sunburn which I didn't think possible.

The sun marched around to the side and I got my pictures I had climbed so high to get.

Downhill all the way when I finally decided to go. I had glassed the country good for the big rams and saw none. I didn't realize it until today that the huge mt. with the high sharp peak to the northeast of me was Telaquana Mt., which is the big mt. seen from Turquoise Lake.

Down the mt. and I do believe that if I was in a hurry I could drop to lake level in a hour and a half but no hurry – blueberry picking to be done on the point of Bell Mt. There they are the small dark blue ones and tasty.

Sure enough a shopping bag on my table and on top a note. It read – "Dick – There are two rangers camped across the lake and near the outlet of the upper lake. They

would like to talk with you but may not be able to wade the connecting river to get to you. Feel free to go across to meet them. They will be camped for a time at Twin Lakes to keep an eye on the sheep during hunting season. Your mail in the bag. Stu Coleman

P.S. Rangers across lake – Terry Pentilla

Larry Van Slyke."[27]

August 23 – Partly Cloudy, Lt. Breeze dn. & 44°.

From the half mile I could see their little tan colored igloo shaped tent but couldn't see anyone stirring and figured they might be up and gone. As I came close they appeared out of the willows. Each scooped up a camera and I was shot a few times before a word was spoken. Terry & Larry their names and friendly like all Park Service boys seem to be. They seemed glad to learn that the native of Twin Lakes was friendly too.

Both from the "south forty-eight" and came here from Mt. McKinley. Come moose season they would be going back to that park. I hadn't been there long until I was asked what I thought of this monument business. I allowed we shouldn't let them chew the place up, that I wasn't strictly against the sport hunting but feel that if you must kill it, eat it.

They told me the story of the Cub parked on the strip at the upper end. Stu Coleman had talked to the man. He claimed to be a guide and he was using that strip as his base camp to hunt caribou outside of the monument. It wasn't long until that Cub on very big tires flew by headed down country. And throughout the day it would fly regular trips down and back as if ferrying gas, people or gear or all three to the low country. A Cessna 185 had made two trips in to supply the operation.

I said, "What you guys need is a big two man Klepper kayak, a Zodiak or Avon rubber raft with motor." They agreed and had requested that some form of water transportation be sent in. They felt very ineffective camped on Emerson when all the action was at the extreme ends of both lakes. A plane and tent on the old Gatano airstrip and a float plane at Arlen's cabin.

They had taken a hike up above the falls yesterday and saw a beautiful black bear on the Emerson benches plus a few sheep on the skyline up Camp Creek.

Each carried a walkie talkie radio and they pack a big rifle. Stu Coleman was due in and soon we heard the [Cessna] 185. It flew to the upper end to check on things and then back down. One lemon and a little circular wire grate for their campfire was the delivery. They held a little powwow on strategy and decided Terry and Larry should be camped at the airstrip at the upper end. They would make the move this afternoon.

I had camera gear along and wanted to go see if the black bear was still camped in the blueberry patch. So, I left and paddled to the down country side of Emerson to beach

[27] Terry Pentilla and Larry Van Slyke, NPS law enforcement rangers detailed to enforce NPS regulations at Lake Clark National Monument. They had been detailed from Mount McKinley National Park to patrol Lake Clark National Monument.

and head up the flat.

Airplanes were flying thick and fast. A Cub circled their camp and I recognized it as Alaska Fish and Game. Two more Cubs flew by and I thought this quite a contrast to the very quiet opening of the hunting season.

He [Terry Pentilla] talked Park Service and of the many things a ranger must learn, first aid, fighting fire, search and rescue, public relations and much more. Rangers like to work with people, he said. In Alaska at the present time they are finding that a bit difficult.

Larry came back looking as if the heat was about to get him. As we sat there on the beach, who charges out of the brush not 30 feet away. None other than that bull caribou. He ignored us and took to the shallow water along shore. Up along shore he ran making the water fly. Stop and stand, shiver and shake and take off again. We had seen two other caribou doing the same in the lake and a little spike running up Emerson Creek. Why don't the fool things get out in the deep water and swim they are very strong swimmers.

I left the boys and headed up the calm lake. At halfway who passes but the red "T craft" heading for my place. I poured on the paddle so as not to make him wait so long. A half mile to go and it took off up by Carrithers' point and dipped a wing as he passed headed home. What was the reason for that unscheduled visit. I came to the cabin to find not even a note on the table. No sign that they had been here. I'll have to question him about that foolishness. 5:30 and 76°, too warm to build a fire so I had vinegar and cold beans. A big green salad and my usual dessert with blueberries.

Getting dark and a powerful big Cessna went charging up the lake. Terry and Larry would be there to greet him.

Clear, calm, and 52° now at 8:30. A beautiful quiet evening. That big wheeled Cub flew over the big bull moose's hideout a half dozen times today.

August 24 – Clear, Calm & 37°.

Now that rangers Larry and Terry had moved to the upper end the Cub wouldn't fly. I suspect he had been busy ferrying hunters gas and gear into caribou land. He had used the strip because the lake was near and the [Cessna] Skywagon could get close. A few little airplanes landed at their end. Next time I see them I will ask them how much such a vacation is costing them. Department of Interior pays for board and room even if it is living in a tent. To enjoy Twin Lakes and get paid for doing it seems not right.

August 25 – Partly Cloudy, Calm & 48°.

In my last mail another letter and material to be read and corrected from Kathleen Teter of National Geographic. She ended with, "Time is very critical and I must ask that you

phone me collect on any changes you see fit to make in the manuscript as well as returning the copy with changes written in." My god-a-mighty doesn't she know by now that Twin Lakes doesn't communicate by telephone? I'll have it ready and Glen can phone it in after next trip.

A letter from Chuck and Sara Hornberger. I had given her a start of my good sourdough. That sourdough is the best she has ever had, so alive, a joy to use. They had seen Babe and Mary away from Port Alsworth. She, (Sara) had cried, - just couldn't help it.

I was outside and heard a big Cessna coming. Long lines trailing it made it the Park Service. I was surprised when it came taxing down the beach. It was Bill the pilot[28] hauling Terry & Larry. As they came in to the beach one on each float. I ask them, "How much does it cost you guys for a vacation like this?" Terry was ready for that one. "Plenty! I've worked ten years for a chance to take it," he said.

I put up a sign "Please use the gravel walkways – fragile vegetation," and who is the worst offenders? Park Service that's who.

Those two guys as excited as Japanese shutter bugs in a new land. Shooting the cabin from all angles and then each of them passing in front while the other took the picture.

Here was a chance to get Kathleen Teter's material on its way. Bill the pilot said he would mail it after calling her collect as she had requested. Going to Anchorage yet today or tomorrow and would take care of it. And I had more letters to go so licked them closed and put a rubber band around the bundle.

August 26 – Overcast, Lt. Breeze up & 44°.

Fog clouds halfway down the mts. and that was something new after so much fine clear weather. I was up at five and it was fortunate that I was. Just got my hotcake dishes done when here came the Park Service [Cessna] 185. First it landed next to the gravel banks and pulled in at the bend of the beach. One man headed down the beach towards the stream with a pack sack. The Skywagon took off and came on up. It was Bill the pilot with Stu and Larry. They had come to visit the party that had the fly blown birds in camp. Terry was the one elected to go talk to them and he was coming into camp from the brush nearby. They could have landed and pulled into the beach directly in front but he wanted to study them first and see if they were hunting, fishing, hiking or reading paperbacks in camp. Pretty sneaky those rangers.

So – my three came in for a cup of tea and a good visit. Stu asked me if I wasn't a little concerned about the possibility of a grizzly climbing in through my big window. "With me here or away," I asked. Either one he replied. Down in the [Great] Smoky Mts. [National Park] they have a terrible time with black bears. Bears chasing back packers

---

[28] Bill Belinsky, an OAS pilot who flew regularly in the new national monument.

who dump their packs and flee. That is what the bears want. They tear into the packs for the good lunches they carry. They have a big problem of keeping packs out of reach for the bears at campgrounds. He claimed they could climb a 4 inch iron pipe by hugging it as any two legged pole climber would do. That, I would have to see. Now and again he tried to get Terry on the walkie-talkie and I made out that two people were hiking the beach packing fishing poles.

Stu asked me if the Park Service had told me what my status here in the monument would be. I said that all I knew was what they told me when it was being proposed as a Park and that was – If it became a Park, me being here created no problem. He is of the opinion that they will issue me a long term permit to stay here, and it may be soon.

About the German who fell into the crevasse. Ken Owsichek the Port Alsworth big game guide was his guide and when informing F.A.A. of the accident and asking for a rescue attempt he insisted that the Park Service not be notified. Now there will be an investigation to learn just what the German fella packing a fancy rifle in sheep country up the South Fork of Currant Creek was intending to do. He isn't saying as he doesn't speak English- not since the accident anyway.

Stu headed for the powder room and came back all excited. Come see the weasel, he said. Little Milo put on a real show for the boys. So many places at once that they asked if there was more than one. And a red throated loon drifted and dived out front. Larry had heard one call a few days ago and thought it was someone across the lake calling to him.

August 28 – Partly Cloudy, Calm & 31°.

Halfway down the lake and here came the Park Service [Cessna] 185. They turned over me and went back to land on the upper end of the lower lake. I ran the stream and found them about a mile down on the right hand side. A camp there. I intended to go on my way but someone waved me over. It was Bill the pilot and he got some potatoes out of the plane to give me. "From the Hornbergers," he said. Stu had been over there yesterday. Now I learned that this was the dead duck camp and the campers still there. Three Austrians and the man who brought them said they could hunt here. Only one of the three could speak English. They had been waiting three days for the plane to come and take them to Two Lakes where they could hunt legally. They wanted a caribou.

A new man with the Park Service, Jim from the Grand Canyon [National Park].[29] Larry had been sent back to Mt. McKinley's new addition to help save the moose from those who don't know the lines and the rules and those who don't care.

Bill said they had intended to stop at my place next and he had brought his camera to get a picture of little Milo.

---

[29] Perhaps Jim Berens, an NPS administrative officer from Anchorage.

The Austrians, big, well built men and looked able to pack a lot of caribou. Too bad they must spend so much time waiting for a plane.

I asked Bill if that German who fell into the crevasse finally learned to speak English. He thought not. The guy refused to be taken to a hospital in Anchorage and ordered the rescue party to take him back to Port Alsworth after they fished him out. So, they flew a doctor out to take care of him. He had got banged up a bit in the 40 foot fall and suffered a little frostbite while waiting.

A twin engine Widgeon went up the far side and was gone for maybe 20 minutes before it came back. Next a big Cessna went up and landed at Lofstedt's bay. Had he flown in hunters too. He was the one who said the Park Service wasn't enforcing regulations this year. It stayed long enough to unload hunters and gear and took off back down. The high mts. socked in tight.

It was near eight thirty when I came to my beach. Gear to put away, fish to clean, supper to hotten up. It was nine 30 before I got the dishes done. At that time it was calm, overcast and 46°. Now it is 42°, overcast, and a noisy surf on the beach.

I came back to find fresh tracks on my beach. Things rearranged on my table out front. The door latch not as I left it. Park Service Bill, Stu and Terry had given the new boy Jim a tour of my diggings. I don't mind. They are a good bunch. Good boys but I would hate to pay them the wages they are getting for the good they are doing.

August 31 – Clear, Calm & 26°.

A good two thirds full and here came a [Cessna] 180 on floats. I didn't recognize it because of the paint on the float bottoms. It circled and landed so I headed for the cabin. Two men on the beach and one a senior citizen. Al and Earl Woodward from Lake Clark. Earl is Al's father and lives in a nice log house[30] on the point at the mouth of Babe's bay. The Park Service wants to buy his property and make it headquarters for the Monument. They had threatened to come see me sometime. Al, a retired F.A.A. employee and a good man with an airplane. Out looking over their old hunting grounds they said. They used to hunt sheep here back in the fifties. "I won't shoot another ram," Earl said. Can't see anymore. Cataracts, both eyes and now he wears very thick glasses. They came in and we visited. Earl bragged on my cabin and told of seeing me twice on TV at Prineville, Oregon where he and his wife spend winters these years. They wouldn't let me built a fire for something hot so we had a bowl of blueberries. It finally came out that they may sell to the Park Service. Earl wouldn't be needing the place many more years anyway. Al has a new cabin across the lake by Priest Rock near Jay Hammond's lodge.

Near one o'clock when they decided they would see some more of their country. Earl said he would be going to Prineville again this winter but would be back on Lake Clark next summer, "I hope."

[30] The Dr. Elmer Bly House was purchased by the NPS and has been used as offices and NPS residences, and is to be nominated to the National Register of Historical Places.

I grabbed a bite and went for more berries. This time up the Cowgill trail. Good picking and I filled the gas can bucket to over flowing. Back at the woodshed I set up my burlap sorter to get them reasonably clean. I lined a big double thick grocery bag with plastic and poured them in.

Twenty five pounds would be my guess – enough to make a lot of mossberry jelly.

Getting back on schedule. Now for some supper and then get at my mail for Glen might come before breakfast. A red and white [Cessna] 185 went up the far side and I heard it on landing approach. Later it came back down over Crag and Cowgill Mts. – turned at the lower end and landed coming up. Park Service, Bill the pilot and Paul the passenger. Bill had my mail. "You get more mail than all of us put together," he said. "Maybe I write more than all of you put together." He agreed that I was probably right. What had they seen at the upper end? Saw some rams on the Rockpile Mt. directly across from Lofstedt's cabin and someone was using the cabin and they (Park Service) had put two men off with a camp outfit at the old "Watts" Waddell sheep camp. So – the law is between the tourists and the rams. In the Brooks Range they had picked up a dentist from Anchorage. He had killed a full curl ram in a monument and took only the cape, horns, and the good backstrap meat (along the back bones top side). A black eye for the hunting fraternity. They stayed and visited while my supper was getting later and later. Bill had to go look for Milo the weasel and to check the trot line and look for sheep up Glacier Creek. They had more flying to do but it would be light later due to the partly cloudy evening.

September 1 – Clear, Calm & 28°.

Hotcakes and I got with the program figuring Glen would be in early. My mail was all sealed and ready to fly. I had my dishes washed but hadn't eaten my porridge when I heard the "T craft." Low and slow and a long ways down the calm lake. It must have been a half mile from my beach when it touched the water. Slowly it taxied in and Laddie climbed out on the pilots side. Glenda, his wife, was the passenger. She no doubt has a lot of faith in her husbands flying. I doubt that he has received instruction from anyone but Glen.

"Just couldn't find the water," he said. They had come before breakfast but wouldn't have anything but a cup of tea. I ask him when they would dig spuds and he thought about the 21st. Potatoes had done real good the last few weeks and they might have a fair crop. They told me about the German (really an Italian) who fell into the crevasse on the glacier. His hobby is skydiving so he was in good shape for this adventure. A snow bridge broke with him and he fell to a ledge 40 feet down. He didn't know that the boy with him hadn't fallen in too and gone much father down. Twice he tried to climb out and fell to the ledge again. He saw the airplane cross overhead but there was no way he could signal to it. It was a very long night. He dared not go to sleep for fear of falling off of the little ledge and going on down to the green depths. He couldn't see the bottom. At Port Alsworth, when they saw the helicopter coming they was sure it was carrying the body if they had

found it. After it landed out jumped the Italian. A little banged up but not too bad. He didn't want to go to Anchorage to a doctor so one was flown out to check him over. Maybe a little frostbite on the finger tips was the extent of his injuries.

Glen doing a lot of flying and Laddie working on his new log home. The largest logs in the back wall and they are 32 footers and big. He is cupping them too which takes a lot of time. Some days only one log goes into place. Glenda thought Babe and Mary were a little anxious to get back home[31] and see how everything was. Babe had spent a lot of time flying while here as if he was really enjoying it.

September 5 – Partly Cloudy, Blowing up & 29°.

A Beaver came over the high ones and was descending. In a few minutes it came back up the lower lake, circled over the connecting stream and landed above Emerson Creek mouth. Three besides the pilot and they unloaded a batch of stuff. Several big boxes of the same size. It took off and flew down the lower lake. Now, here came the good guys (Park Service) with all the Irish pennants trailing out behind. Up the lake but they didn't land. Soon they went by turned and landed. The lake very near flat calm. Stu Coleman was back and a ranger Doug from Teton Ntl. Park.[32] Stu had gone to Anchorage with an impacted tooth. They had made an emergency appointment for him, he said. He got there and when the dentist learned he was Park Service he refused to treat him. Said he was emotionally involved with the D-2 land bill and wouldn't doctor Park Service employees, upper class at least. So – Stu had to look for another dentist. He said, "I didn't do too good in Anchorage." Jim and his partner at the upper end had been moved to Chakachamna Lake where they caught a hunter butchering a moose. A man and his wife in a Super Cub. I asked Bill if the man knew he was in the Monument. "Didn't have the foggiest idea that he was," Bill said. They took the moose and today a helicopter was coming to haul it out. Doug took some pictures of my layout and Stu said he heard I might go out this fall and if I did how soon would it be. Not before October 10th if I went, I told him. For some reason they are showing a lot of interest in my going or staying.

From here they headed for Emerson Creek to talk to those guys before they got all set up cozy like.

My cache roof – just as well get with the program and fix it. I had small poles to replace the broken one so got them cut and notched before lunch. I would get this project completed before the Park Service told me the regulations on gathering moss for construction and repair. Probably it would be "The moss will not be cut within one half mile from the lake and in such a dispersed manner that the scar will not be noticeable."

I used the mattock to cut the outline and then the big sharp bacon slicer to cut the under side. Worked good – roll it and cut along the up turned side. Big rolls and a

---

[31] Babe and Mary Alsworth had retired to Hawaii in 1976.

[32] Perhaps Doug Warnock, a Deputy to the NPS Regional Director.

half dozen covered it. For a scaffold I had tied long poles to the cache legs, up under the cache proper. Then my 2x8 planks on the extending ends for catwalks. I assembled the hold down poles on the ground and unfolded them over the roof. This time a rock on each corner to snug them down. The job was complete and my cabin roof neatened up around the edge and the tools put away by five. Glad to get that job done in good shape.

September 7 – Clear, Calm & 28°.

It looked like a calm day so I paddled to Low Pass beach and then climbed blueberry hill. A blue and white Super Cub had gone up the far side and now it came back down the middle. Fish and Game colors and I could see the Department of Public Safety emblem on the side. I was surprised to see the state on patrol here at the lakes.

Past fox pond country to check for moose and then I headed inland and up the long slope to the game trail headed around the point of the mt. into Beech Creek country. Bugs were bad. No mosquitoes but those yellow flies that make a steep turn in your ears and like to sit on your temples and forehead. Above brush line I got out of my wind pants and black sweater. I would be warm climbing but it would be cool and no bugs at my destination.

September 9 – Clear, Calm & 30°.

It is his [Jerre Wills] little yellow P.A. 12 Piper [Cub] at the upper end. I had missed seeing it a few days ago but they had seen it since and it was ok. Bud had offered the use of his boat after his hunters got through with it. "Hunters!" I came alive on that one. "How can they or you subsistence hunt here and fly in," I ask him. "I feel like a lot of others," he said. "Ignore the Park Service regulations and hunt as always." "Have you talked to the Park Service about this," I ask him. Yes he had, but I doubt that, very much.

We talked fishing to let things simmer down a bit. A complete flop in the [Cook] Inlet this year. Fish and Game is running it in favor of the sport fisherman. He had taken his boat to the Bering Sea herring seining this year but it was a long rough trip out to False Pass and through the Bering.

Finally – "Did you see that big bull moose?" he asked. Yes I had seen him a few times. I figured he had seen him from the air but maybe he baited me to see if the bull was there. "Well, we probably won't get him but we may give it a try." Boy! that was a shocker. Here he is hunting in a completely closed area as far as sport hunting is concerned or even subsistence hunting, coming from Homer and flying to boot.

"Those big old bulls should be killed, probably die in a year or two anyway." I didn't agree and cited the fact that we have a lot of old people who will probably die in a year or two. The moose population isn't creating the problems that the human

population is. I agreed that the regulations as they are can cause a lot of ill feelings but is lawlessness the way to correct it. About the next thing that will happen will be to close it all together.

September 10 – Partly Cloudy, Calm & 32°.

Where is the Park Service? Probably they have been moved to a hot spot. A lot of hunters ignoring regulations could make them look very ineffective.

A real pretty evening. Many yellow clouds in various shapes and sizes. The lake is rough out in the stretch and I expect a good wind down again tomorrow. The temperature 50° now at seven o'clock.

September 13 – Partly Cloudy, Lt. Breeze dn. & 51°.

A plane coming and I figured it was the [Cessna] 185. It was a twin engine Goose and circled over my cabin before coming in for a landing. I headed down and soon heard the mighty roar of a Goose stuck on my beach. It is never solid and if they try to come to far out of the water they sink to the hubs. Good thing I had the canoe by the breakwater or that blast would wrap it around the trees out front or into the side of the cabin if it got by the trees. Quiet and then another blast. He was stuck for sure. I arrived to find people walking around looking. Paul Fritz on the beach with my shovel and they had one. The water too deep to even see where to dig. My canoe was gone and then I saw the nose of it pointing out of the brush. I figured they have moved it before trying to blow the break water away. The pilot had come in to turn left instead of right as they always do. That put the canoe dead astern when he got stuck. I ask someone if they moved the canoe. "No, the Goose did." Had it been damaged. They was afraid to check. It had gone over the top of the breakwater and down the beach thirty feet or so. I feared the worst and didn't want to go look either. Four guys and the pilot. I ask them if they had any rope in the junker. We could tie onto the tail and the inboard wing and help pivot it around and headed out. No rope so I got mine out of the cache. Three of us pulling broad side on the tail and one on the wing turned it easy enough with those big engines blowing the fall colors away. He taxied out, raised the gear and came in easy, tailed the big bird around and snugged her against the beach. That is the best way on my beach (our beach).

We came in to sit and chew the fat. Nothing special, just a loafers conversation. Stu Coleman was along and asked me if I saw the [Cessna] 185 today and if it has stopped at Jerre's. I said I was sure that it hadn't as it was up and cruising at Glacier Creek.

Later he told me that they would be stopping to see Jerre this evening or in the morning...Later we were all out front when someone said, "I heard a shot up lake." I thought oh, oh! There went a moose...I said, let's go look at my canoe while I have lots of

witnesses. I may need a new one. We dragged it out of the brush and found the gunnel forward of center shoved down about an inch. Back farther a little kink in the combing. One rivet popped and the side kicked in at the severe bend. I figured I could iron it out in pretty good shape. Paul Haertel[33] was their spokesman and a wheel in the Park Service. He said if there was anything I needed to make it right to let him know. No other dents and I was really surprised. It could have been a junker.

Paul Fritz got me aside and told me, "I'm going home, back to Utah. I'm taking early retirement (25 years). Going to raise peaches and vegetables among other things. I want out of the govt. service." Paul wasn't happy in Anchorage. Summer and winter were the only seasons. No spring or fall to speak of. Will Troyer was his best friend in the Park Service and Will plans to get out in a couple years.

September 15 – Overcast, Lt. Rain, Blowing dn. & 49°.

To write letters has been nagging me for a week or more. Plane day coming the 21st and few written. I would write today rain or shine. It was 8:30 or later before I got at it. The wind roughing up the lake good and one time I thought that I heard wild geese in the sky but on going outside I didn't hear more. Saturday, would the Park Service come today. Stu [Coleman] and Bill [Belinsky] both said they got no overtime pay. Just work the hours necessary to get the job done. How can that be when the Labor Dept. says you can't work a man more than eight hours per day or more than forty hours per week without paying him overtime.

September 16 – Overcast, Blowing dn. & 48°.

I had beached below the cottonwoods so angled up through the spruce towards the game trail...A real neat operation completed while the Park Service was attending Sunday school. I crossed the creek and climbed the steep loose dirt trail...No trouble to find the kill site for a magpie was sitting in a spruce top next to it. There in a little hollow layed the paunch, four lower legs, back bone, and head...it was a big moose. The head told the whole story. Even with the skull chopped away to get the antler intact I recognized it. The bell (as I had seen it with the scope from this side) was not long but very wide as seen from the side. This one was like that. A big head too...Jere had done a real good job butchering. The backbone there in two sections but it had been boned very close...The big tongue was still there but I wouldn't take it—too hot to handle, an illegal kill.

I arranged the mess in a neat display and took a couple of pictures. I had told Jerre that if I got a real good picture of that big guy I would send him one.

I collected some nice scraps of suet and lashed them to my pack. My birds would think it Thanksgiving.

[33] Paul Haertel first superintendent (1979-1989) of the Lake Clark National Monument.

September 18 – Overcast, V. Lt. Breeze dn. & 46°.

Camera on the tripod, I was ready to travel when I heard a big Cessna coming. I figured it to be Bill and Stu. Sure enough he was letting down for a straight in landing off of Hope Creek. Bill said later "This is a nice place to come too. Come in close and you have smoother water."

Just the two of them and when they climbed out Bill said "We brought your new carpet." I had told them not to bother as Glen could bring it at spud digging time. He wrassled out the big bundle that when unfolded and laid out would be 12x16 feet. I said "If you will give me half what I paid for it you can have it." He said "I like it, a nice color, but I don't like it that much." Stu had my mail. I'm going to miss those boys. A loose corner of the carpet showed it to match the fall colors perfectly. A fine pattern of many colors from yellow to red. So new and clean, I am afraid it will make my cabin look old and dirty. A ten dollar cabin and a $121.58 rug. I would put it down but do no cutting for the fireplace hearth. If I can't get used to it I will put it up for sale at a low, low price.

Well, what was new, where had they been. Bill was having a cup of Park Service coffee and Stu ..., [Constant] Comment and a sprig of Labrador [tea]. Not much was new and they had been on the coast. Saw many bears fishing in Iliamna River over at Pile Bay. Weather had been pretty no good and today it was better here than anywhere.

I was surprised to hear that they had talked to Jerre and at the site of the kill. They had seen his boat on Glacier Creek beach so flew the area. Bill said it was easy enough to see that big moose in the butchering stage. They landed and hiked up the trail. Stu said, "I see you shot one." "Who said I shot it," Jerre came back. They had a little chat about whether he was eligible to subsistence hunt and Jerre hollered discrimination. Stu allowed it sure was because he or Bill couldn't qualify and they figured they should be legal if he was.

That Stu is no dumb one and I'm not surprised that he was picked for this area... He wouldn't be easy to give a snow job.

Bill said it was a good big bull with a perfectly symmetrical rack. Seven points on a side (as I remember) and might go 66 inches which I wouldn't doubt. It had looked wide over there and through the scope from here but on Jerre's beach it didn't look 60 inches. Trouble was his first shot had hit the antler and damaged it badly. Jerre said he was aiming for a head shot so as not to damage any meat. "This is not Dick Pronneke's moose," he said. No one had said it was.

Anyway, headquarters had decided not to cause trouble for the killing of it or the caribou due to the present controversy but before he can hunt here again he must get a subsistence permit because of the fact that he isn't a resident of the area. Port Alsworth and Nondalton are considered resident areas to this monument. So Jerre got his caribou and moose and I'm happy about that. He worked hard and saved more meat than most hunters would. As for next season I feel as Stu does – have it open to everyone or closed to everyone and no exceptions.

Stu is going back to the Smoky Mts. of Tennessee in a day or two and he had a big grin on his face when he told me. I ask him if they still have "hillbillies there." "We call them mountain folks," he drawled. "And do they still run stills?" "Yes, they sure do I known of a few places I could buy some right now, today."

So they prepared to board, - Terry & Larry would be here and Bill to fly them around "Might be flying a different [Cessna] 185 next time," Bill said.

Had they seen any caribou. "Yes, over along the Kijik [River] and Fishtrap Lake." "Bulls all of them." And bears too, blacks and browns. Browns on the upper Kijik. "So, I'm convinced that the bulls summer over in that area more than here." Stu shook hands and thanked me for autographing his two copies of *One Man's Wilderness*. A good man that Stu, I would like to see him stick around if we had some regulations fair to everyone. They took off up past Carrithers' point. Flew up the lake and came high down the far side and were soon gone. I came in to read my mail. Only five this trip and I still had time to make the day pay a little bit. I got under my pack saddle and went to fetch in the rest of the down tree and a load of fire starter spruce tips. The weather had cleared to fair but now it was raining over the Volcanics again. A good shower came down from Low Pass.

September 20 – Partly Cloudy, Lt. Breeze up & 39°.

I kept my birds occupied by nailing a good chunk of suet to the stump. That wasn't enough, they came knocking many times and as often as not four would appear suddenly from out of the forest. I wrote till noon and after before knocking off for lunch and then back to work. The Park Service welcomes comments on the proposed regulations for the Monument. I had a couple – subsistence hunting. Open it to everyone or close it. The line between the legal and illegal is too fine. Limit the use of airplanes to flying in and out only. If they must kill it they must pack it out, all edible meat. Pretty tough to enforce I know, but, collect a few airplanes and eliminate the privilege to hunt for a few would be a good start. On motor boats. A motor can mean the difference between life and death on the lakes when it is rough. The Hawaiian couple for example.

Does it make sense to prohibit the use of a small outboard motor and allow large airplanes to use the lakes. I think not.

> *The Park Service welcomes comments on the proposed regulations for the Monument. I had a couple – subsistence hunting. Open it to everyone or close it. The line between the legal and illegal is too fine. Limit the use of airplanes to flying in and out only. If they must kill it they must pack it out, all edible meat.*

September 21 – Partly Cloudy, Lt. Breeze up & 34°.

Back at the cabin I pulled the film out and was making up a box to mail it in when a plane came heading for my beach. It was Glen in the [Cessna] 185 that he has been hauling fishermen, for Glen Van Valin, in all summer. With him two young guys Phil and Mike. Turned out they were surveyors and surveying a headquarters site for Jay Mueller's wife Barbara, at Lachbuna Lake. Staying at Alsworth's and Glen flying them back and forth to the job. He had come to pick them up and then on up to get me to help dig spuds. Tomorrow (Saturday) would be the day. I rushed around getting a few things out of sight and gathering a few things to go. The floor leveled a bit and the door closed we took off for Lake Clark and Glen's. The trip a little turbulent for a wind storm was on the way. I hadn't seen Port Alsworth for a year and was surprised. It looked like a village with all the new cabins and houses. Wayne [Bee] Alsworth's new airstrip 200 feet wide and 4000 feet long was a site to see. He had material flown in to build a new home along side the strip but talked his wife Betty into letting him use the material to build a new hanger and they would live in a small house that he had been using for a shop. He moved it to high ground along the new strip and on high ground wasn't enough. He put it on posts maybe five feet high. A real nice view of his new air field. *[RLP spends the night at Port Alsworth].*

September 22 – Overcast, Blowing & Mild.

During the night the wind blew very hard. Hard enough to shake that big solid house. Glen says it takes a 50 mph wind to do that. Rain pelted the window and I wondered how many days I would spend away from my cabin. In a strange place I slept very little.

After a good breakfast we took a close look. Not too wet and the wind had let up some – we would dig. Glen and I mounted the spud digging plow on the Ford tractor. A good big crew was standing by. Must have been ten or a dozen picking up potatoes. The surveyors took the day off to help.

A better crop than last year and better spuds too. Very few that had split from growing too fast. Three rows of new seed from a truck farmer in Palmer and Hawaii produced as many and better potatoes than three times the number of rows of three old year after year home seed. We didn't stop until the job was done at 2 P.M. Then the big celebration. A big dinner for the crew. A dinner like they used to serve at thrashing time back home. Terry & Vic were there. They had just returned from Bonanza Creek and their gold diggings. Now, where to spend the winter. Vic would like to stay at Port Alsworth in their log cabin. Terry doesn't agree. Winter in the cabin he doesn't mind but that outside plumbing swings his vote towards Anchorage and a house sitting job.

Glen had a radio antenna job to do. Tear down a couple and put up a new one that required four poles or trees spaced about right. The old RCA telephone antenna to take down. A complicated rig of heavy water pipe, pipe cross arms and cross arms on the

cross arms. A lot of climbing and unbolting. It was evening when we got everything done. Tomorrow Sunday and a day of rest.

Supper was another meal such as I have seen few of in a long time. It is easy to see how Laddie and his wife Glenda got that very well fed appearance.

Tonight I would sleep better. The spuds were in and it was raining a corn growing rain.

October 1 – Partly Cloudy, Lt. Rain, Blowing dn. & 41°.

I saw the [Cessna] 185 before I heard it and figured it was Bill for the Park Service. Caught in the act – I would be motor boating in non flying weather and get caught doing it. Around he went and was on my beach before I arrived.

Bill and Paul Haertel and I told them I figured I was safe enough in motor boating on a day like this. They hadn't noticed that I was using a motor and helped pack it and my gear to the cabin.

More of a social call than anything. Bill's last trip and soon out of a job. Have to start looking for another and at this time of year flying jobs are scarce and I suspect they are even more so if you have been flying for the Park Service. Park Service is a bad word in Anchorage and Alaska.

Paul wanted to know when I would be in Anchorage and be sure to visit his office when I came out. They want to fix me up with a five year permit, renewable but not transferable. I asked him about Bob Acheson's cabins and he said Bob would be eligible for the same. I'm thinking Spike & Hope and Bob will be pleased to hear that bit of news. Will Troyer will be doing some flying here on moose survey after snow comes and will keep an eye on my cabin. Other Park Service personnel will do the same when flying this winter from time to time.

I had the fire roaring for a cup of tea and a wedge of sourdough sandwich. Bill told me where there are a lot of moose. A long way from here though. Between Port Alsworth and Pile Bay (upper end of Iliamna Lake – Tazimina Lake country).[34] About six miles in from the nearest lake and no place to land Cub on big tires. Seventeen moose he saw there – two real good bulls. He said "Nobody is going to pack a moose six miles." I would agree but feel that Ken Owsichek the guide at Port Alsworth would think nothing of telling his packer to pack out a real trophy rack. The area is in the monument so that might influence his action a little but no more than that.

When they came, they couldn't stay long. The weather was borderline but now it was improving fast. Paul told me he had talked to Bob Belous about my slides and 16 mm copy. The duplicates they have but not the copy yet. Something about making up a work order. And again they asked for an address to send them to. More than a year and a half

---

[34] Tazimina Lake country refers to Upper and Lower Tazimina Lakes that lie south of Port Alsworth and north of Iliamna Lake. The Dena'ina word is Taz'in Vena for "fishtrap lake."

now, but maybe soon we will have it squared away.

Getting late, Bill wanted to show Paul those moose yet today. The sun in and out and ready to set soon. I set up the scope to count 35 head of sheep from directly across to Glacier Creek.

Bill shook hands "See you next summer maybe if I don't crash," he said. They climbed in and taxied down towards Erv's cabin to take off close in as they came by. A big climbing turn and they went through Low Pass. Bill had seen two big bull caribou plus some cows and calves in the pass one trip recently and nearly turned back to let me know.

I cleaned my grayling and had half of it for supper. Bill gave me a huge head of cabbage. One of two that Glen gave him. Supper and dishes and now at nine blowing strong down again and 42° with a partly cloudy sky.

October 3 – Partly Cloudy, Breeze dn. & 38°.

I looked at my carpet, folded three times, resting on the hearth and decided right now would be the time to put it on the gravel. It would be late in spring before I could do the job. Now, today the beach would be dry to spread it flat, mark the center of both ends so as to get it well centered on the floor doing only half and loading everything that belonged on that side back on. There would be no shifting so it had to be close. I marked the center on both ends and marked the center of both ends of the cabin. I rolled it up but 16 feet long instead of 12 feet. Right side first so I unloaded the book shelves and packed the rack outside. Table too, and storage cans under the counter surrounded the stove. Half of the floor cleared I leveled the gravel and covered it with clear plastic. That would be a vapor barrier in case I had a problem with moisture dampening the carpet on the bottom side. If I dumped a pan of water on the carpet I would have a mess. Plastic in place and large enough to stand up around the edges a few inches as the carpet would do the same. I dragged in that 16 foot roll and proceeded to get it lined up. Too long for the cabin floor so it was stubborn to unroll. I soon had the floor half and half and it didn't look too pretty fancy to me. Many bulges and kinks due to the roll being folded. It appeared to have stretched the carpet at the kinks and I was wondering if in time it would flatten out.

The stove still had a low fire in it so I shoveled it out and removed the pipe above the roof. Smoke still poured out the opening while I cleared the bunk both under and on top. My storage cabinet I could move to the carpet side. My god-a-mighty what a batch of garbage I have collected. The cabin was full and the overflow was stacked out front. The stove would be a monster to move outside and the bunkbed would never go. The stove I swung around close to the wall and after moving the bunk out and cleaning and leveling I moved it back but far enough from the wall so I could get in between. More plastic rolled and the edge under that already in place. As I unrolled the plastic I unrolled the carpet. The protruding fireplace jams caused trouble so with my sharp Denver butcher knife I cut the big notch. Cut it a little small so I could trim as necessary to get a good fit later.

About now I was beginning to wonder how the ends would fit. One corner of the carpet might be inches from covering and the other a foot up the wall. More than chimney smoke would be pouring out if that was the case. Now I moved the stove over the roll and onto the layed carpet. Inched up the near side of the bunk and rolled everything under. Raised the back side and flattened the rascal out. The fit, pretty good. Higher on the wall behind the bunk than in the front end of the cabin but just right in front.

I trampled and kicked and stretched the wrinkles and kinks out best I could before loading it down with everything for that side. More sorting, cleaning, and returning garbage to its rightful place. It didn't seem possible that there would be room for it all but it went back and didn't look too cluttered. I got things pretty well in place and the floor cleared. It looked better now but the real test is your first impression when opening the door and looking in. Does it look good or no good? Coming back from the woodshed I thought of that. Pulled the top door open and Well! how about that it looked real good. A very neat and clean floor. The Swedish copper tuffy carpet looked compatible with the interior and I dare anyone to say otherwise. Short nap it would sweep easily. Rough soled shoes are bad at packing in gravel. The cut out chunk at the fireplace would make a throw rug at the door (inside).

I needed a new section of stove pipe to replace one badly rusted. Maybe it was a year ago or more that I found three joints of brand new galvanized 4 inch heavy pipe in Spike's cabin. Evidently someone had come intending to use that cabin or mine and thought they might need some pipe. The seams still open and the three nested and standing inside an old section of 6 inch. I went for a section of new 4 inch. Now it would be galvanized from stove to chimney cap and I must remember to get a new 4 inch adjustable elbow. Late in the afternoon the sun looked down a few times and would set behind scattered clouds. It had sprinkled many times so it wouldn't have been a good day to film. I was happy to have the carpet laying job done.

It seems strange to walk on carpeting and not have that crunching of gravel at every step. The cabin looks neater and certainly much cleaner. I'll have to thank Sis for buying that miserable carpet before I could get word to her to forget it. It was time to start my supper fire and get cooking when I finished with my project. Bill the little pilot would be happy to see it in place after going to the trouble of flying it in. Yesterday the first thing he said was "got that carpet down yet."

As the light failed the mts. to the south were smothered with moisture on top. Last evening the coming full moon showed itself for a little while. (Full moon on the 5th).

Now at 8:15 the wind is strong down again, the sky overcast except for a very few breaks and the temperature 40°.

Tonight there will be no need for my round mt. beaver (caribou) rug along side the ladder. Carpet wall to wall and up the wall just like the Waldorf.

Before dark I went to check my trot line. Nothing, the bait still on both hooks. I could see eleven head of ewes and lambs on the slope of Crag Mt. that faces the lake. They

have spent a lot of time on that slope this fall – good to see them there.

October 6 – Overcast, Lt. Breeze dn. & 34°.

It would be time for supper by the time I got to my beach so headed back over the trail. A very light breeze down but no whitecaps as I made the 30 minute paddle. The sun ready to drop out of sight as I dragged the canoe up and turned it over.

This evening I would have a green salad again. Split the lettuce supply and add some cabbage. Lettuce chopped carrots diced in and I was wrasseling with the cabbage sack. All this operation was out front on a table. Off on the ground went the plastic salad bowl and scattered salad far and wide on the gravel. My god-a-mighty, what a mess. Salad material doesn't grow on spruce here at the lakes so I picked it up and washed it in the lake. Using bowl and kitchen strainer I cleaned and recleaned. The proof of the pudding is in the eating. It was never better.

It may frost tonight as the temperature was 34° a half hour ago. It was partly cloudy and calm. Now at eight more clouds and 36° so the frost prediction is off.

October 9 – Partly Cloudy, Breeze dn. & 40°.

Before first light I heard the whistling swans, the first of the season, and not long after, the rains came. Only a light shower and when I rolled out to greet the new day it was a morning more like summer than early fall. No sunlight on my cabin now till after twelve noon.

Hotcakes and then another session of getting things in order to leave them for a few months. My decorations on the fireplace mantle would be considered souvenirs of "One Man's Wilderness" to some people, so, I wrap them in newspaper, box them up and store them in the cache.

The lake was soon whitecapping in grand style so I would stay off of it. If it was an easy trip I would go to the upper end one more time.

It was four o'clock. I could still go for the down tree I had looked at. Two good loads cleaned it up and the fire starter spruce tips stand under a thick spruce. I sawed and split a few lengths and stacked the rest on top of my wood log supply. If it's a mild winter someone could heat the cabin for a good long stay and not go to the woods for a single stick. I would rather they burned from the pile than cut trees close to the cabin as Hamilton did at the lower end [lower Twin Lakes].

October 12 – Partly Cloudy, Lt. Breeze dn. & 37°.

There [near RLP's cabin] I found all three of them [moose] and the bull much more

gentle. I stood and watched as the cow acted as if she was a brave one and fed towards me with her calf. The bull hung back and circled a hundred fifty feet away. Not often did he stop in the open—always behind a spruce with one eye showing. They went by me headed up and I came on to the cabin. It was time to build a fire.

When Babe and Mary came they brought a box of groceries and among them a roll of ready to bake cinnamon rolls from a dairy case. I put them in the cabinet outside and forgot about them. "Keep refrigerated" it said. Use before Aug. 9 for best results. The fire hot, I would bake them. Four at a time in my two little bread pans. Not crowded so they didn't rise a lot but light and good. A small container of icing in the roll. A real treat.

Tonight it may freeze a bit. Now at 7:30 partly cloudy, a very light breeze down and 34°.

Now I must get with the program. Only two days to go until its time to cover the windows and take down the stove pipe. Many things to be taken care of before then. The kicker to winterize, the canoe to put away. A hundred other small details to take care of to make it a proper close up. If I have to go I like to leave the place looking perfect. Others finding it looking that way are more apt to leave it that way.

The bull is young, maybe four years old. The antlers not the greatest, maybe 50 inch spread. The tines, very long, a real nice looking bull with a very long bell. He is a lucky guy – no competition.

October 18 – Partly Cloudy, Calm & 24°.

The wind calmed during the night. Many stars out at nine when I turned in so I wasn't surprised to find the temperature 24° at six o'clock. A real fine morning with a white frost on the cabin roof.

I had my spuds, the second to the last real live egg and all of my remaining bacon. All four birds came for breakfast and I wonder why they are working at it so hard these days. What a let down it will be to come time after time and no welfare.

I took a pan of ashes up to Spike's garden and then collected more dead willow to see me through the day. I guess it was about nine thirty when I heard a plane and knew it was for me. Not the "T craft" that was for sure. It passed overhead and I recognized it as Glen Van Valin's 185 Cessna. A turn down and back up straight in to my beach. Glen Alsworth climbed out on the passenger side. It was Glen Van Valin at the controls and his wife Sharon was along too. She had been wanting to see Twin Lakes for a few years and Glen allowed she had bugged him long enough. They had come prepared to leave me at Twin Lakes. Some groceries and two dozen eggs plus a lot of mail.

They made a big fuss about my carpet and Van Valin allowed as how I would now have to get a diesel generator to operate a vacuum cleaner. While they visited I flew around getting packed and doing my best not to forget anything. The ladder to the cache went out

to stand with the ladder by the meat hanging tree. I tacked the last big chunk of suet to the stump for the birds. That would have to do for Thanksgiving and Christmas at least.

The last two covers over the windows and now it was very dark inside. The stove pipe came down and was stored under the rear overhang of the roof of the woodshed. I had intended to put part of my sourdough starter on the stump for the birds and carry only a little to be added to when I thought it necessary. Sharon said, "Please give me a start, I would like to try your brand," so now it has spread to their new fine lodge and will be enjoyed by many clients. She asked the history of it and after learning I felt sure that she will make an extra effort to keep it alive and well.

I close the door and turned the lock lever to lock. Close up was complete. A beautiful morning to leave and to fly. One last look at the gorge and waterfalls up Emerson [Creek] as we passed a half mile below. At the crossing of the Kijik, Glen [Van Valin] headed through a pass to our left that would take us down Portage Creek and to their lodge on a small island in Lake Clark. I hadn't seen it since it was completed. Lake Clark was smooth and we were soon entering the little bay in front of the lodge. It's a beautiful log structure with a green aluminum roof. Glen is afraid of fire. They had just put down new carpeting and under it was a soft pad that made it seem like walking on the moss of Twin Lakes. A floor to ceiling (upside down V) shaped window looking up the lake to the rugged mts. and Little Lake Clark[35] country. I was busy examining the log work of Jack Ross[36] the master log man. Real nice work and hardly a notch that didn't fit real close.

It was past one when the two Glens and I headed for Port Alsworth. That [Cessna] 185 is a joy to ride when cruising fifty feet above the water.

At Port Alsworth I learned why they had come in Van Valin's airplane. Glen Alsworth had taken his floats off of the "T craft." After Laddie had undershot while landing on a small lake out Pilot Point way. Hit the tundra and bounced into the lake. It took sometime to get the rig in shape to fly back to Port Alsworth and it still isn't completely healed.

The remainder of the afternoon was spent getting beaching gear ready to remove the floats from Van Valin's [Cessna] 185 and examining the log work of Laddie on his and Glenda's log home under construction.

A good supper and then I sat on the floor in the post office and read my mail. The last entry was still to be made in my journal. More than two years and four months of everyday writing. I do hope that the reading by others has been as interesting as the living and writing. I'm going to miss Twin Lakes and the writing.

[RLP spent part of the winter of 1979 and 1980 in the Lower 48 returning to Twin Lakes on March 24, 1980.]

---

[35] Little Lake Clark was formed by the alluvial fan of the Tlikaklila River that drains Lake Clark Pass to the W almost cutting off the eastern end of Lake Clark by nearly forming two different lakes during low water. The Dena'ina word means "stream where salmon are."

[36] Jack Ross, first came to Alaska in 1937, master wood worker, first maintenance man for Lake Clark National Park and Preserve.

CHAPTER SEVEN – 1980

ON TOP OF HIS GAME

March 24 – Partly Cloudy, Blowing & 35°.

March 3rd I started the long journey from Primrose, Iowa to Twin Lakes and my cabin. It would be a long trail by way of Los Angles, California. Three weeks later, and $485.00 spent for buses, train, and plane fare, found me sprouting and sorting spuds in the cool spud locker of the bush pilot's home at Port Alsworth about 40 miles from my destination. Yesterday we would have made the trip but a very strong northeast wind was blowing out of Lake Clark Pass. This morning it was still too strong but Glen [Alsworth] felt confident that it would calm. It had better for he had two trips to Anchorage scheduled for Tuesday the 25th. By noon it was calming and after lunch I got my gear together while he gassed the "T craft."

A pilot landed after coming through the pass and reported it still blowing and snowing in the big trench [Lake Clark Pass]. Miller Creek, the Kijik, Pear Lake and the Volcanic Mts. would be our route. Weather in the pass wouldn't concern us too much.

We took off and climbed to 5000 feet. Only light turbulence and with the sun in and out it was a pleasant trip. I watched for moose and caribou trails but saw no sign. We broke over the ridge and looked the length of Twin Lakes. "Looks like it hasn't changed much," was Glen's remark. Lots of snow on the lower slopes but from there to the peak the mts. looked as if swept with a giant broom. Spring would come early above brush line.

The upper lake more than 50% snow free. Shallow drifts covered the lake surface. Too long away from the lakes and their traps I guess for I never gave it a thought that some of those drifts could be a foot deep. Glen came up the lake low and slow before touching down a quarter mile from my beach. Touch down and then crash! We bounced high and came down to hit another one but not so hard. It was a very rough landing. In close we found it smooth and to have landed along the shoreline would have been the way to go.

I noticed two or three old tracks made by planes on skis as we coasted in. Someone had visited at least. Snow, lots of snow on and around the cabin. It appeared to be about three feet deep.

Solid enough that we had little trouble packing my gear to the cabin. We found my night latch in the unlocked position but no sign that anyone had been inside. As neat and clean as I had left it on October 18 of 1979.

I would have a heap of shoveling to do before I got settled. More than two feet of snow covered the stove pipe roof jack which I had covered with a gallon can weighted down with a stone.

First thing I went to the back side of the woodshed to see if my stove pipe was still there – it was. Glen was free to fly away now that I could set things up for a cooking fire.

March 26 – Partly Cloudy, Blowing & 35°.

Morning came too soon. I had no more than closed my eyes when it was daylight again. Batter had been rising for my first batch of hotcakes. In my hotcake locker I found a small one held over from last Oct. 18. Curled and dry as a bone but no sign of mold. Plenty good enough for the welfare birds.

Evidently the calm came near dawn or the temperature would have dropped. In '79 I had a -20° on the morning of April 15th and I may have some minus reading this spring before the water starts to run.

A good kettle of beans and I got them going soon after breakfast. Tending the fire and the water while I did small chores about the cabin. I had discovered that I had a floor problem. My storage cans under the counter were frozen tight to my new carpet. Empty cans and jars in the right rear corner under my storage shelves were frozen fast also. That would mean that water had come in from the outside. It happened once before in winter while I was away. A build up of ice on the outside directs the water in if it rains more or snow melts. If the cabin had been in use and warm the water would go down but frozen hard as 40 below the water forms ice on the surface. I broke the cans loose and finally got the carpet turned up so the heat could work at the ice. Many times I sopped water with a big sponge.

I took a little tour to Spike's and Hope's cabins. Both as I had left them and the gravel floor dry. Both drain better than mine.

Out near the woodshed the fresh track of a porkypine and up the beach the fresh track of a big fox or coyote.

Again this March I heard that coyotes are becoming plentiful on Lake Clark. That will be the day when I hear the song of the coyote at Twin Lakes.

March 30 – Partly Cloudy, Lt. Breeze dn. & 30°.

I had noticed Emerson Creek flat was nearly free of snow so I would go up and into the cottonwoods where the Vanderpool cabin stands. See how it had stood the winter. Huge

snow banks in the cottonwood grove. Snow that came from the long run of the lake and the creek flat. Some drifts may be seven feet deep.

I had just entered the grove when I thought of the big birds nest to my left. Last fall I found it and wondered if it was an eagles nest. A big nest constructed of heavy sticks such as an eagle uses. Now, showing above the nest was two pegs – something was in it. A great horned owl was my guess. Who else has horns and sits on a nest. The glasses made it an owl sure enough. That big round head and yellow eyes was facing me. Never had I seen the great horned owl on a nest and very seldom sitting in a tree. Always it had just left its perch when I first saw it. When does the horned owl nest. I had never thought of it being in March. I watched a few minutes and then went on towards the cabin. Another big owl, and the male I suspect, flew from a spruce. More and more I was thinking the time is now for the horned owl to sit on eggs.

Lots of snow on and around the cabin. I had to go to snowshoes a hundred yards before I reached it. Some red squirrel damage inside. A few items of cloths and towels hanging from the perlin logs had been badly cut up. I headed back and this time I would go near the owl tree. One hundred feet she stayed and I was surprised for they are a very shy bird. At fifty feet she stayed and it was near thirty when she stood up and flew away. I promptly moved away a couple hundred feet and waited to see if she would come back. If she did the chance was good that she had eggs to keep warm. More than five but less than ten minutes passed and here she came to lite in a tree about forty feet from the nest. A hawk came and made diving passes while it screamed at her. Each time it passed her I could hear a clicking sound as if one or the other was popping its beak. The hawk flew away and she promptly came to the nest. Did a short hula dance as she settled down. Eggs in the nest and I would make a little wager that there are. One tree thirty feet away that I could climb and see into the nest but I wouldn't keep her away long enough to climb it. The nest no more than maybe twenty or 25 feet from the ground. I must take my 16 foot ladder and try for a good picture of the only horned owl I have ever seen on the nest.

I left her and headed back. Slipped and slithered across to Low Pass beach and on up. The wind was calming. Three o'clock when I came in the cabin to find coals for a

quick start and a hot cup of chocolate.

40° and the ice in front of the cabin coming loose from the gravel. A little effort with shovel and rake put it in shape to go quickly. After freeze up rain had come and drained into my woodshed. No problem now but when melting comes it will be a pond. With the old Jim Shake splitter [maul] I worked at removing some of it and found it nearly 4 inches thick in places. And so ended the holy day of March 30th. One more day and it will be April month. Will half of the snow be gone by early May. One year about eight years ago I came back May 11th and found a good two feet of snow about the cabin. Lake ice was 48 inches.

31° now at 8:30. Bright spots but no blue showing. A down lake breeze to be heard in the spruce tops.

I have a feeling that if I play my cards right the great horned mother will cooperate.

March 31 – Partly Cloudy, Lt. Breeze dn. & 29°.

The ladder, I fastened the top end to my pumpkin seed sled and would let the tail end drag like sled runners. My hiking boots and crampons for a down the middle course. My Kelty in case the wind came strong. Crampons can't be beat for dependability. Every step is a money maker even if it does take a little extra power to chip the ice. The trip, the sled, the ladder no problem and in due time I was moving in close to the cottonwoods. With the glasses I could see that she was glued on the nest but she came unstuck as I entered the grove. The ladder was too much of an attraction I guess. She flew and I didn't see her lite so promptly left the ladder and went back out and up the creek flat for a few minutes. When I came back she was there and headed my way. Slowly, a few steps at a time I moved forward. She watched me and sometimes her attention was attracted to something off of my right. Slowly I moved in and stopped at about 40 feet. I didn't want to force her off the nest as by now the breeze was cool and strong. I stayed a few minutes and then backed up to come in by a different route and hopefully a better view. Again I got as close or closer than before and she stayed. With the glasses those big brown (not yellow) eyes blinked slowly about every eight or ten seconds. Close enough that my 300 would get a good picture of her and that heavy duty nest. Again I backed away and left her. Never have I felt that I could get so close to the great horned owl.

April 1 – Partly Cloudy, Breeze dn. & 34°.

Snowing came again for awhile and I doubted that I would go see the great horned one today. Along towards noon I added another letter to the outgoing.

Cloudy bright and a fair breeze down after lunch. I would take the heavy tripod,

Exakta and 300 mm lens to see the nesting owl. I wore my new hip boots and good that I did. Dodging around to stay away from slick spots I found deep slush under the snow up country from Emerson Creek.

She was there, the old sister, but, she left the nest before I entered the grove. I moved across the flat and waited. The sun warm and she was in no hurry but did come back and wiggle down on the eggs. Slowly I approached and she left again. I had given her time to get the eggs warmed up. I moved back and soon she returned. I was thinking I had better call it off for today. Pick a chilly one so she would sit tight. One more try and by my route of yesterday. She stayed and after awhile I started moving in. I ended up less than 30 feet away. Close enough that the nest nearly filled the frame. Pretty good that was. Only problem, the sun was back lighting the nest so I waited for small clouds to cover it up. Would she stay if I brought the ladder. Slowly I carried it forward and leaned it against a tree closer than 25 feet. Climbed to the top, not much below her level. She stayed and blinked her eyes slowly. I learned that she can do something I can't. Close one eye and either one. I packed the big lens to the top for a head on shot. A side shot would be nice so I moved the ladder around to another tree. No good, limbs in the way so I moved it again. Good shot and I left her there inkybating. I have really got something going. It will be a cinch to check on the young ones.

April 2 – Partly Cloudy, Calm & 18°.

I was away in good time and the snow ideal to travel. I wouldn't find any slush this trip. I took my time moving into the grove and she stayed. Sitting on the nest with those horn feathers up, she looks exactly like a big fat cat with tufted ears. The camera set up I moved to thirty feet. She was in the shadow of a big limb and I waited for the sun to move around. A shot from there and around to the sunny side and the ladder. Good shot, as easy as shooting fish in a barrel. Another tree about 10 feet from the nest would she stand for that, she did. Another one farther around and about ten or twelve. Slowly I moved the ladder and poked it up the tree trunk. That was a little close and she took off toward the Vanderpool cabin. I climbed up to see how many eggs. Two, near white and about the size of pullet eggs. I left the ladder and moved away. Soon she was back but would leave again five minutes later when I entered the grove to get my camera gear. I wanted a shot of her coming to the nest and settling down so got set, finger on the button. Soon she came and it looked good. Enough, 50 feet exposed I packed up and left her looking like a fat cat on a big nest in a cottonwood tree.

April 3 – Overcast, Breeze dn. & 29°.

This afternoon the wind was noisy on the mt. across and if I had guessed how strong it was I would have stayed in the shelter of Carrithers' point. I needed some exercise and the

lake was the only place to get it. I would take the Exakta and 300 mm for a look at the "sittin" hen. I wanted a good close up and I mean close up. Fill the frame with a great horned owl.

The lake was good for travel. Bare spots not as slippery as days back. I noticed the wind getting stronger as I went. Sometimes it tapers off the farther I go.

I entered the grove to find her on the job and what a place to be when it is blowing a gale. Those bare cottonwood trees swaying and moaning as they do in mid winter. Back beyond the Vanderpool cabin would have been a more sheltered spot. I didn't go close for I didn't want her to leave the eggs today. Not like the robins, grouse, ptarmigan or numerous other Twin Lakes nesters who set rock solid. She sits up there with her head on a swivel. I wonder when she sleeps, if she does. Broadside and the wind ruffling her feathers – seems she would be smart enough to sit facing the wind.

About now I wished that I was three miles up the lake. In one hour fifteen I could be there so I pulled all the strings to snug up my Kelty and took off. It must have been blowing thirty and maybe close to forty at times but at 35° it wasn't too bad. The wind was eating some snow today and I would find that the snow outside my big window is down about one foot from it high mark after the six incher.

April 5 – Partly Cloudy, Calm & 20°.

The old girl was on the nest but pointed in the wrong direction. My ladder was at the tail end. She stayed when I entered the grove and that's a good sign. The camera hooked onto the 300 mm I crept slowly closer. As I moved around that tail end to the ladder her head turned 180°. Now I would see if she could do better than that. The ladder was still a quarter turn away. I expected her to do a reverse twist and get me coming on the other side but she didn't. 180° was the best she could do and from there it was one eye watching me. I reached the ladder and slowly started to climb. About fourteen feet away and closing. About high enough and I focused the lens. Just under 12 feet the scale read. I aimed and tripped the shutter – she stayed. One more step for a better shot. Just made it when off of the nest she went. Too close and I don't blame her for leaving. I climbed to the top and saw the two eggs still there. Quickly down and I moved the ladder back fifteen feet. The sun was warm and I figured I must clear the area or she might stay away a good while. From out on the flat I heard an owl hoot several times and finally she came to settle down again. I gave her time to warm things up good and then started her way. I hadn't gone 20 feet when she left. More than a hundred yards away and she flew the coop. So I went up the creek and found her back when I returned. Again she took off before I got to the grove so I packed up to go look for caribou along the lower lake. Not far from my lookout knoll when I came onto a big wolf track made since the snow last night. Crossing from right to left and into the area where I had seen the caribou. A big track and with my Old Timer I notched my walking stick to get length, width, and stride while trotting. Back at the cabin using the tape I found the print to be 5 ½ long, 4 ¾" wide and distance

between tracks about 29 inches. A real impressive string of tracks and I would sure like to see the guy at fifty yards. The tracks left the ice and climbed the bank headed for Dry Creek brush patch.

April 8 – Partly Cloudy, Calm & 30°.

I found the old sister on the nest but went on up the creek to see if anything had crossed since the snow. Not one rabbit track but the track of a fox crossing right to left on the game trail crossing at the big mud banks. I came down to enter the timber where I had before. She sat tight watching me. Slowly does it and I took my time getting ready. She was pointed the wrong direction but a tail end shot would show that very grey brown plumage. I made it to the ladder. It looked like I had it made for I had shot from there with the Bolex and no problem. Two steps up and off she went. Away towards the big spruce near the Vanderpool cabin. I moved out on the flat and she came right back. I gave her time to forget and tried it again. Didn't make it to the ladder. I wanted to see if she was still warming two eggs or if they may have hatched so – I hurried to climb the ladder and into the branches above. Two eggs it was and here came the old sister back to raise quite a fuss hooting and snapping her beak. Had I been on the snow and the lens tripod mounted I could have shot an owl in a cottonwood for she was brave enough to move in close, but only while I was up the ladder and the camera on the ground. I left her and headed for the stream and the lower lake to see if any water birds had arrived. I'm thinking that some will show before the week ends. I stayed awhile and then came back for one more try. Didn't get as close as last time in fact I was a hundred yards away when she took to the trees. She isn't the wise old owl for no good reason. She knows that the way to keep me away from the nest is for her to leave. How will she perform after the eggs have hatched. And how soon will they hatch. Two weeks now since I came and she may have been setting at that time.

April 9 – Clear, Calm & 15°.

Crystal clear, dead calm and a very beautiful spring morning. The sun lighted the peaks down country at 6:05. I know that today was the day to climb the mt. so I got busy with my breakfast.

By the time I got away it was straight up eight o'clock. How many hours and how many minutes to the top of Falls peak 4,730 feet above sea level. I wouldn't push it but I wouldn't loaf along either. The snow frozen hard and I wished it would be on the return section from timberline to the lake. Nearly 20 minutes to the far side another twenty to timberline and it was real good climbing. A good look at a big snowshoe rabbit and I decided it had started its color change. From timberline to the point of Falls mt. above the waterfall was a no snow climb and took 40 minutes. Right away I saw sheep and as I

climbed I would get a close look at a ewe and a half curl ram. Looking pretty gaunt and thin as if it had been a tough winter. More sheep and they left my side to cross the saddle to the far slope. I would count 21 head but there may have been a few more. Sheep blend well with thousands of little snow patches.

Some snow patches on the way up to the peak but only a few and they mostly hard packed. 2 hours 5 minutes from my cabin to the peak. A beautiful view from up there – not a cloud and only a very light breeze from the southeast. I could see Redoubt and Iliamna Volcanoes. Iliamna had a plume of steam pouring over the top as if there was an east wind there. I went to work with my glasses looking for tracks or trails. I could look right down on Emerson Creek country and if there was a fresh line of moose tracks I'm sure I would have spotted it. No caribou on either side of the lower lake. No sheep across Emerson valley. Just an awful lot of snow on this side of the valley. Hope Creek country looked the smoothest of them all. Give me a good cold night and I will try it next morning – going by way of the hump and then down into the creek bottom above the gorge.

I was an hour on the peak and that breeze got cool in spite of my chamois cloth shirt and Kelty. I had the Exakta along but didn't see a picture that I don't already have. One last look at Bonanza Hills country – less snow down that way but a lot in the creek bottom I'm thinking.

On the return trip I stopped to enjoy the scenery. A great difference in the feeling of the air as I reached halfway. I stopped a total of 20 minutes on my way down to timberline. I had a good idea how it would go from there. Going down steep slopes in soft snow can really mess you up. The snow collapses and you settle a foot. The toes of the snowshoes slide down and under, loading the shoes. Then you fall forward into soft snow walking stick deep. Head downhill and feet anchored to the loaded snowshoes. It can be a real struggle to get the center of balance over those snowshoes again. Twice I did it and was trying to avoid it. The snow on the steep south slopes gets the full effect of the sun. It seems to penetrate and all the way to the ground. The snow just at the point of collapsing and does as I have learned many times.

April 10 – Clear, Calm & 10°.

It was eleven when I got to the cabin. A bite to eat and then I would go down to check on the owls. If I knew when the eggs hatched I would have some idea how long she had been on the nest. This time I would take the tripod along but wouldn't get to use it. The sun very bright on the solid snow covered lake – sunglasses a must.

She was on the nest and I got set up a hundred yards away. Would she stay today. I got within about a hundred feet when she raised up and bounced over the edge. I didn't care so much about her as I did the eggs so I hurried up the ladder and into the branches above. Two little white owls about the size of a baby chick from a white rock layer. Also on the nest was the remains of a snowshoe rabbit. The skin and what appeared to be the

skull minus the skin. So – they had hatched during the last day or two. She must have been setting since the first day of spring at least.

I left and went down to check the stream for water birds and saw none. This time I would tuck the 300 mm and camera in the hand warmer pocket of my Kelty and I would climb high and get a shot of those little birds. She left before I got close but both she and the male came hooting and snapping their beaks as I climbed. So close I had trouble focusing and had to climb higher to get farther away. The sun was warm so little danger of them chilling. I did hurry to get away and let the old mother come back and cover them again.

Now to let them get a little growth and able to stand more fresh air. I want to get her with them too if I can. Coming, trudging up the lake I figured it out. Tie my light tripod a straddle of a limb. Build myself a trip mechanism so I can trip the shutter from a hundred yards back. A long string would do that.

April 11 – Clear, Calm & 10°.

I wanted a Bolex shot of the baby owls too. Not early when I got away and it must have been near ten o'clock. I would spent at least three hours going and very near that coming back.

The old biddie shipped off of the nest before I got close. By now I'm an expert at threading up through the limbs above my ladder. That rabbit skin no more than a bare skin now and I'm wondering how many rabbits will come to the nest before the owls make their first flight. Now with them being very small I suspect the old mother up chucks some partly digested meat for them. Today found them still very small but it would take some shoving to get them back into the egg shell again. I got my couple short runs and then hurried back to wait for her to return. Not as soon as I had expected but the sun was warm and the air calm. I suspect she knows how long she can leave them.

I gathered up my camera gear as I passed and cut in towards the cottonwoods to see if Mrs. Owl was on the nest. I didn't use the glasses until about a hundred yards out and when I did I found her gone so I suspect she got the jump on me.

It was five when I arrived to find the temperature 30°. It had been 20° when I left and figuring it would soon be above freezing. I had set my spuds and eggs on the tables out front.

A fire going and a pan of water on to wash away the chill and now the birds came. I fed them and watched to see where they went. They went exactly where they always go – here or yonder to a spruce where they tuck their load and hurry back for more. Two times around and I gave up.

That wind finally came and it was cool. Scattered clouds clutter the sky and the temperature 26° now at 7:55.

April 12 – Clear, Calm & 10°.

She was on the nest alright or at least there was a great horned owl on the nest. Would that old rooster owl stoop so low as to cover those chicks? This owl didn't have that nice neat row of white feathers across its chest where the neck should be. I had paid special attention to that neat row that looked like chin whiskers, short and wide. Anyway there was someone on duty and I was glad to know that there was someone who cared.

I waited awhile and then headed across the flat. No more than a good start when the covers flew off. I hurried over to climb the ladder to see how they were doing. Huddled close and next to them a remnant of a rabbit skin. Back down I took the ladder with me. No more than back on the flat when the …[owl] returned to cover the chicks again.

My ladder made longer I left it lay and headed for home. Let those little ones grow a bit. Get more feathers to cover that pink skin that shows through.

April 14 – Partly Cloudy, Calm & 18°.

She was on the nest and I looked at my modified ladder laying on the flat. It looked like an accident eager to happen. My leg extension poles hadn't been too shookum for size but spruce is tough. I dumped all my excess gear to be as light as possible. Shouldered the thing and headed her way. She knows what is coming and promptly stood up and stepped over the side. The sun warm so the little ones wouldn't suffer. Standing on a high snow bank the ladder was three feet longer than necessary. I set it pretty straight to favor the spindly leg extensions. Two steps up and here came that old sister wide open. She didn't miss me by much as she swooped past. Came back by and broke a dead branch out of a tree after she passed. Much hooting by both and one perched in the top of a tree nearby.

In the nest another rabbit. A fresh one, no doubt about that. One little guy had his head tucked under the rabbit. The other in the clear and not what I would call a pretty baby. Eyes not yet open, it looked pretty flimsy to be a great horned owl some day. Me near the top of that weak ladder with my left arm wrapped around the limb in case it suddenly decided to collapse. 250th at about f7 the exposure and I used my 40 mm wide angle lens. Shot one and then the little guy turned his head to a better position and I shot another and headed for the stability of the snow bank. To the last round of the ladder proper when crack went the legs. There I was standing on the snow and the ladder three feet shorter and still leaning against the tree. Someone must have been holding me by the hand while I was at the top.

I carried the ladder and dragged the extenders to the creek flat again. In order to erase the commotion I headed for the stream. An old track of a fox and a fresh one of a wolverine crossed from left to right on the ice before the open water.

Headed back and again I heard a small plane coming low along the Volcanic Mts. On by it went hugging the slope. Not a track of any kind, what was he looking for. On up past Carrithers' point and to the upper end. Maybe it was 5 minutes later when it came down by Allen & Falls Mts. An old model "T craft" painted dark blue and white. A small engine, maybe 65 hp. Can't prove it but it's my guess that he was looking for a bear just out of hibernation. No state warden protecting this area anymore and the chance of the Park Service showing up is nil. But, I'm thinking they won't shoot one on these mts. with me here and cameras loaded. He continued on down as if to round the point of the Volcanics and head for Lake Clark. My mother owl was back on the nest. I took my pile of sticks apart and headed up the lake wondering how to improve my climbing equipment. The lower half of the ladder skookum enough so I would lash a pole up the center and extend it three feet above. "You can't beat an education!"

April 18 – Clear, Calm & 8°.

She was on the nest and riding high. Something about that climbing to the nest sorta makes me uneasy. I felt the same way before the ladder gave way. Again that old chicken left the nest as soon as she saw me start that way. Much hooting back in the timber and as I poked the ladder up along side the nest. I climbed and was better than halfway when pow! a judo chop to the side of the neck by some unseen attacker. It came suddenly, no sound before or after. I looked to see where she had gone but saw nothing. I rubbed the side of my neck and saw blood on my hand. Very little but she had scratched me. Had she put those talons to good use she could have done real damage. Now the little ones have their eyes open and they appear very light in color. I couldn't see a decent picture there and besides I was too close. The rabbit nearly gone and I suspect a third will come to the nest soon.

I would move the ladder to the other side and see how it looked. I watched for the old biddie as I climbed but she failed to appear. No better, the chicks flattened out and close together. It wasn't worth the film as much as I wanted to get it out of the camera. I packed the ladder away 50 yards and left to go down to the lower lake and my lookout knoll to see what I could see. Calm when I traveled the stream and started down the lower lake. Then a light breeze up and before I went that mile it was blowing cold up the lake. I climbed the knoll and from the lee side of the crest I glassed all the country I could see. I looked at Black Mt. for sign of sheep and bears. I glassed up Emerson valley for I was in line with it. And then Dame Fortune smiled on me. High up and down from Falls Mt. peak in a little saddle of fine stuff that connects a big outcrop to the mt. was a dark blob. A good two miles away but I could see it plain enough. Strange for a rock to lay in that saddle. I settled down to watch it. It changed color, changed shape, it divided. Bears! two bears. One light and the other very dark. A sow and big cub, I thought, for two mature bears wouldn't be together now. Much movement as if playing. One appeared to stand on its hind legs in the scuffle. Playing, that's what they were doing. Where had they come

from and how long had they been out.

Beyond and higher, two hundred yards away was a dark spot and dirty snow around and stringing down the slope. Dirty footprints after leaving the den. From Falls peak a ridge runs directly down towards the lake. The den on the west slope of that ridge in a big snow patch. I watched awhile and headed back for Emerson Creek for a closer look and this time I would set my ladder against the tree ten feet away where I had filmed the nest earlier. Use the 75 mm telephoto lens. This time my Kelty hood was up and snugged up good. As I climbed here she came but I waved her off. The chicks flat in the nest like so much rabbit skin and again I refused to waste the film. So I left. Now I watched for the bears and finally saw three. Make it one more and I would be most sure that it was old limpy and the triplets now two years old. It looked like the cubs for color. One blond one very dark and one a bit lighter. It had been two cubs I had seen playing. The sun moved around and I headed up the lake. Three was all I could see and they appeared to be feeding so they must have been out a few days at least. I kept coming and checking. Finally out onto the big outcrop walked a light bear but not the blond one. The mother that's who it was. Now I had four and I would bet a lot of chips that it's old limpy and her youngun's. I saw her first in '77 raking grass for her winter den. Saw her come out with triplets in '78. Saw her come back in '79 with the now yearlings and now in '80 with two year olds. This has to be her territory.

April 19 – Overcast, Calm & 20°.

I went on to Emerson Creek and now I had a chance to train all that power on the mean old owl. I could still feel soreness in the big cords going up the side of my neck. She was on the nest looking very solemn and not at all friendly. Now while she is on the nest is the perfect time to get a good look at her. That feather pattern is something to see. Why is it that an owl is absolutely silent when it flies? Yesterday proved that. Pow! and that was it, no sound before or after.

April 20 – Overcast, (Snowing), Calm & 21°.

That wise old owl makes me wonder just how wise she is sometimes. There she was pointed down country and her feathers standing on end from the down lake wind. She hadn't seen me come and I had a chance to watch her. Does she ever close her big round eyes. She covered both sides and straight ahead. What was she looking for or expecting to see. I got lined up behind a spruce and would try to move to the edge of the grove. I got halfway and she left the nest. I suspect she heard me crunching snow. So – I went on up and to windward to get protection from the wind by moving close to the brush bordering the flat. By now the snowing had all but quit on the mt. and I searched but not for long. Not 50 yards from where I saw them yesterday they were bedded down in a huddle. Taking

their mid day nap on top of a big outcrop. Below, maybe 150 yards was a ewe and lamb slowly working their way up country. Finally there was movement in that pile of fur. First one cub and then another got up and moved out – started that chore of making a living.

Sometimes in coarse rock and I do believe that bears roll more rocks down the mt. than avalanches and those loosened by frost. If you hear rocks repeatedly rolling down in one area look for bears feeding. The old mother one snoozed on and I got sleepy too so I moved to a snow bent willow, made myself comfortable and finally woke up with a start surprised that I was

> *I do believe that bears roll more rocks down the mt. than avalanches and those loosened by frost. If you hear rocks repeatedly rolling down in one area look for bears feeding. The old mother one snoozed on and I got sleepy too so I moved to a snow bent willow, made myself comfortable and finally woke up with a start surprised that I was still at Emerson Creek.*

still at Emerson Creek. Still she slept while the cubs grubbed. I went back to my bent willow. I was watching when she slowly got up and crouched low in the front like a dog stretching after a nap. One step and she stopped. Another and again she stopped to look around. Then slowly she headed for the cubs and starting scratching in likely places to find whatever she was looking for. They would go no place today I figured and had just as well head back. Now my owl was pointed into the wind. With the scope I could see those big eyes in a dead pan stare.

Snowing again and still blowing. It would be a long three miles. I snugged everything up and headed into it. My packed trail was all but obliterated and at times I strayed away to find I was breaking a new trail. A man could get thoroughly lost on a big lake in a snowstorm. Lost as far as arriving at his destination by dead reckoning.

It had nearly quit by the time I arrived and when after a half hour it came again. I felt better that I hadn't seen all there was on the trail. Five thirty and time for a fire and supper. Temperature was 34°. Very little increase in snow accumulation.

Now at 8 o'clock, snowing, and blowing down, temperature 32°. Ten days till May month – the month that the ice leaves the lake.

April 23 – Partly Cloudy, Breeze dn. & 27°.

I trained the scope on that big owl as I passed and she didn't smile. A good big patch of rabbit fur showing and I knew No. 3 rabbit had paid the full price. From up the creek and looking bear country full in the face I looked at every rock and scree slope and saw no bears or any rock that required a second check. With the scope I checked the snow up along the edge of snow free rock and saw no deep tracks that said they left this side. A good view of Black Mt. and its slope facing the lake. Not even one sheep down that way. Snow was too deep and soft or I would have taken a look up Emerson valley from

the high bench above the high waterfall. I gave them time to move out if kegged up and then decided I had to see how the young owls were doing. Cool and breeze but owls are "tough as an owl."

Going up or down the creek the old lady sits tight but let me head that way and she bails out. So, when she did I hurried for my ladder standing against a tree maybe 75 yards away. Leaned it into a tree twenty five feet from the nest. I watched for that old chicken to come head on but she only hooted and flew around a bit. Say! those owls have grown. Two tone for color – the head still very white but the body a light buff. I could see big wing feather quills showing. Laying flat with heads down and I suspected that is their position after she leaves them. The rabbit skin was that of a rabbit changing color and certainly not the one seen last time I climbed. It appeared to be ready for replacement by rabbit No. 4. I left my ladder there and went back to the flat. I wanted to see what happened when she came back. I was watching through the scope when she came to the edge of the nest. Up came the head of a young owl as if wanting to be fed. She stepped in and spread those big wings slightly to cover the little ones as she settled down. Some day soon I must take camera gear and climb the ladder again.

April 24 – Overcast, Calm & 22°.

Going down and opposite where I saw them last and there was a single sheep exactly where the bears had been an hour before. How could that happen on such short notice. Bears are noted for being very slow unless disturbed. Finally I saw a single dark bear below and quite a ways below. A big rock face there and very brushy at its base. Was it one of the cubs or a new comer to the area. And then the blond showed nearby.

The nest was missing the big horned owl that is always there. Was it warm enough that she would leave them for awhile. I put camera gear together out on the flat and went into the grove. Much hooting and popping of beaks so they were on guard. First I took the Exakta and 300 up the ladder. Didn't look too good. Young ones, headed the other way and crouched down. Here came that old chicken head on and she got me on the right shoulder with a wing. Now I knew how she does it and it is a solid blow that will hurt for a little while. She doesn't stay with the attack but sits in a tree and gets all mad again before she drops off and lines up with me. If I saw her coming I could wave an arm as she came near and she would shear off but if I didn't I would get hit even though I thought the ladder would protect me. It looked no good for the Bolex so I went back out on the flat and parked my gear before going back over my trail to the lake to check on the bears. No bears and I searched good. Then climbing hard up a very steep snow filled wash was the little blond one and it was bawling something awful. Though it was nearly a mile away I could hear it plainly in the dead calm. A very coarse voice and it kept it up until a few minutes after it reached the other three up there in the brush along side the snow. It had been a hundred yards down and below the rock face. What the bawling was about is a mystery.

424

April 25 – Clear, Calm & 15°.

Last night when I took my shirt off I noticed the sore spots on my upper arm. Two short breaks in the skin similar to scratches. My shirt had no sign of a hole in the right sleeve and neither did my Kelty wind breaker. I do believe that a big horned owl could make a man holler for help if she really got with it in using beak, talons, and wings.

This morning even better than yesterday. Totally clear so it would warm early.

I had just finished my spuds when, Airplane! A little one coming and that would be Glen! A little closer and I heard that off beat exhaust of a 150 Super Cub. It came by off shore and not too slow. A dark paint job and on big wheels. Friend or foe? – if it was friendly he might come back and land. If he was a bear hunter he wouldn't – he didn't. Bear season doesn't open until May 10th but that matters not with the monument closed to bear hunting. Period. Lucky for the four bears he flew up the Low Pass Creek side of the lake. He didn't come back down so probably climbed through a pass and to Turquoise.

April 27 – Overcast, Lt. Breeze dn. & 34°.

The owl was on the nest and spread wide as if she had a chick under each wing. She don't mind me looking from across the flat but head her way and she is off and flying. She flew among the cottonwoods but didn't attack as I climbed the ladder. The young ones down flat and not showing much. It appeared that a fourth rabbit had been nearly cleaned up. I went back to my scope on the flat and proceeded to watch the nest. See the action of those little ones when she came back. She was a good while coming but finally did. She didn't cover them but sat to one side of it with the chicks on the sunny side. They raised up when she came and now I could see how big and how active they were. Standing they appeared to be maybe 10 inches tall. Beaks very large and black. They were quite active one picking at the remains of the rabbit and the other picking at its feathers as if having the urge to put them in order. Now if I had my Exakta and 300 mounted in a cottonwood tree and a long string to the flat I could get a masterpiece. Trouble is it's a one shot deal – can't cock the shutter and advance the film.

April 29 – Partly Cloudy, Calm & 30°.

I switched on the flashlight and saw it was 12:30. There had been disturbing of the peace. First a couple licks at the front of the cabin and next it was on the fireplace chimney. I thought – "is that porkypine back so soon." I listened and could tell it was still there.

So – with flashlight in hand I went to check. A porky sure enough and I patted him into a corner until I could get the cage. Head was on the wrong end but no problem.

Put the open cage behind him and touch him on the nose. He will swap ends right now as that front end is not protected with quills. In he went and it was a squeeze. I could hardly get the door closed. I parked him standing on end (rear) down near the lake with a rock on top of the can. I knew he would be scratching tin for the rest of the night.

Another nice morning and more snow would go. The bears had bedded for the night on a little hump of an outcrop in the middle of a snow patch. It happened to be where they had ended the big play session last evening. Still there at five and wouldn't do a tap of work till ten then knock off at one for a long mid day nap.

I had my hotcakes and about 6:30 I was ready to export the latest undesirable. I wouldn't use the sled this trip but lash the cage onto my GI packboard. The lake in pretty good shape to travel and I went to the bare knoll. There I dumped him out and he looked unhappy. Didn't say thank you, go to h---, kiss my foot or anything – just started walking towards the mt. – decided to climb the first tree and I said no and pushed him out. Last I saw of him he had passed a few and still trudging.

May 1 – Partly Cloudy, Calm & 30°.

Morning came too soon – reveille at 4:30. Today I would go shoot the four bears on Falls Mt. and I wanted to be there before they moved from their bed. It was light enough and I didn't even check but started my hotcakes, bacon, and porridge. Last evening I had brought down more film from the cache and got it ready to go.

Dishes done I set up the scope to go to see that they hadn't moved. No bears! that little perfect bed ground was empty. That was a revolting development. I checked the other likely spots and didn't see them. A few sheep scattered about and that didn't look good. It was as if there wasn't a bear on the mt. I headed for Erv Terry's to get high and cover more of the mt. Again I heard the song of a robin and now the white crowned sparrow too. From Erv's I saw no bears and so I went a half mile down the lake to see it from a new angle. Nothing, they must have left the mt. And why would they leave at night. I suspected they smelled a rat (namely me). Years back on a calm day I glassed two bears above timberline on Allen Mt. Then I climbed a half mile down and was well above their elevation when suddenly they came alive and looked down the mt. Promptly they started to climb and passed me a hundred fifty yards away. My scent from below had finally found its way up the mt. carried by the natural flow of air up a slope warmed by the sun.

The snow field where the den is located is very steep and solid. I wished for my crampons for the descent down and across that patch of snow. The den still snow covered and quite deep. A big hole to the living quarters due to the roof caving in and I suspect it did while they were still in hibernation. That would be enough to make them come out early. Bear dens are usually very near the surface and especially near the entrance. I suspect their body heat plus the melt water softens the roof and it falls in for I have found most dens with the entrance caved in. The entrance tunnel went back only a little way and then the living quarters extended right and left. Larger at one end than the other by

eight inches. The big end an even 4 feet and the other 3'4". The room an even 8 feet long and about 3 ½ feet from floor to ceiling. Big claw marks on the walls made by the old mother and I wonder if the cubs helped too. A very big flat sided rock exposed at the big ends back wall so she couldn't have gone farther that way. As big as it was I can't see how four bears could squeeze in and stay for six months without getting cabin fever and eating each other. As playful as they are now it is hard to imagine them inactive for months and months. I climbed back up to the peak where I had left my gear, otherwise I would have been tempted to go on down the snow field and scree slope to the timber and lake. Again I glassed the country and saw a pair of swan on duck pond back of Skywagon point this side of Arlen's cabin.

May 3 – Partly Cloudy, Blowing dn. & 30°.

This afternoon I would go down and check on my owls. Six more days and they will be one month old. This time I would take the Exakta and 300 mm for a couple frames of them growing up. Just enough freezing last night to firm up the soft spots in the lake ice. Going down was the easiest trip I have made this year. I saw where the four caribou had hit my trail and followed it a short distance and then left it to follow the shoreline. Often I have seen where caribou will stop to examine an old track of mine – follow it a few yards and then go on their way.

She was on the nest and I went on up the creek flat to look for moose tracks. I did see one headed this way but deep snow stopped me from getting up to where I saw tracks crossing the creek bottom from Falls peak. I came back and got my camera ready to shoot a close up. The old hen took off and I'm not sure she was covering them or just acting as a wind break.

Those little owls are getting good size. About right for good tender fryers. Big enough and alert enough to look my way when I whistled. The old mother hooted a bit from back in the timber but didn't show herself.

A good steady rest for my big lens was the tripod I had left in the cottonwood. Two frames and I called it good for now. Another week will see them looking pretty good. Then I would like to get them with the old mother again. What I need is a better means of tripping the shutter on my camera. Pulling hard on a cord could be pretty severe on the shutter release. Coming slowly up the lake bucking the cool wind I figured it out. I have a ten second delay shutter release (automatic timer). Don't need the delay so just wind it enough to push the plunger. A gentle tug on the cord would pull the trigger. Sounds like an angry bumble bee and she is sure to look.

May 4 – Partly Cloudy, Lt. Breeze dn. & 33°.

I was seeing more country below the faces but no bears. Better check behind that hump so I circled right across a canyon and along the mt. side. Couldn't see any fur so I went

back, held my breath and eased down. Bears all over! but not behind the hump. Along the slope up country I counted five and that shouldn't be. Then six. A big one just below me and up country. "My god amighty," I had never seen so many bears in such a small area. I suspected the Bell Mt. sow and her twins were mixed up in the mess. It turned out that she was but at the time I found them they hadn't learned that they weren't the only bears on the mt. although two of the two year old triplets were as near to that twin sow as to their own. The Bell Mt. sow and twins were up country maybe 250 yards along a long streak of snow in a wash.

Everybody crapped out for noon break and I had a long wait. The yellow triplet was slowly working up to his mom and the middle colored one. Suddenly the dark one appeared from behind a rock. If I could just get all four together for a picture. It wasn't to be. The yellow one ran out of gas and collapsed fifty yards from the three. Maybe it would come on up when they stirred again. I waited and watched – got a glimpse of the twin sow as she moved up the wash and layed down. Little yeller was the first to stir and what did the rascal do. Headed for the snow filled wash nearby and ran lickity larrup down the mt. and then after a parky squirrel. The remaining three came to life and moved to a nearby facing slope. The yellow one came trudging back. Suddenly the lame sow took off and started walking up country over a low rise. About that time the twin sow decided to play with the twins in the snow. Old limpy knew something wasn't right and when she saw them going helter skelter down the mt. she came running back to round up the triplets who got all excited – heads high and ready to run in my direction. Down the wash the twin sow and cubs went rolling and tumbling. First she would take one and then the other. The snow soft and it was a sight that made me wish for the Bolex.

Now the triplets saw the commotion and sat like big dogs watching. Now the three ran out of snow and came feeding slowly up a scree slope below me. Old limpy watched them a long time and finally decided they would do no harm to her kids who now gathered round for lunch. They still get their milk three times a day I'm thinking. (Morning, and mid day I have seen.)

What a birthday this had been and I have the Bell Mt. sow and twins to thanks for that. It was they who spooked old limpy back and brought the cubs together for pictures. Not quite as close as I would like and there was good cover half the distance but I would be in the wide open on a loose rock slope to get there. I figured I didn't have a chance to make it. I would lose my bears and that I must not do. Let them stay just as long as they like. I don't learn much from bears that run over the mt. Now at 8:15 the sow and twins still hanging tough above the big rock face. The four still bedded on the high point not more than a half mile away.

Nothing special for supper this evening – good well seasoned beans and mashed spuds. Cucumber (by Glen), sourdough bread and grape jelly. A big portion of my famous cold porridge pudding (rolled oats with rice, raisins, whole wheat flour and allspice.) A big cup of hot cocoa with lot of little marshmallows. All that and satisfied – happy to be

in good bear country.

The sun still on the upper lake at 8:30, partly cloudy, calm, and 36°.

That sow with twins – I would like to film on a snow patch.

May 9 – Clear, Blowing dn. & 34°.

Only one cloud in the sky at five and maybe one fourth inch of ice on the open pool along my beach. So – it had been much cooler sometime during the night.

Last evening at sunset I watched the bears call it a day and start climbing, looking for a place to spend the night. It started suddenly. They stopped searching and digging. Two cubs started to climb towards my trail up the ridge, below the big rock face, by waterfall gorge. The old mother and the brown cub followed. I wonder just how old the mother is. On a climb she takes a few steps, stops a few seconds and then up a few more. How many cubs has she raised and how many more before she dies. The cubs climbing next to the base of the face and waited. She climbed but kept going, so, they took the lead again and would their way to the top to scout around and wait. All four went over a rise and I watched to see if they would appear and climb farther. No bears and I figured that I knew where they would bed down.

It was seven this morning when I saw blondy and the dark one playing on a snow patch. Old mom had come up from the shaded side facing the canyon and was laying on the snow in the sun.

They started to move early and today they would go up waterfall canyon. I doubt that I will see them again for awhile. Last year they came back in late May to feed on rank green stuff below the rock faces and to eat willow buds on the scree slopes at timberline.

Swan talk and I saw a lone swan circling over Carrithers' point. Last year there was a lone swan that spent some time on the lakes.

Today I would go visit the owls. One month old today or tomorrow, I can't be sure. Exakta and 300 mm lens to get them growing up. My timer set up along to try for picture of her with them. The lake ice near perfect to travel. A stiff breeze following and I thought about that three mile haul against the wind.

High up in the edge of the rough stuff of Falls Mt. one lone ewe laying close to the rock wall. She could have a lamb between her and the mt. All told about 15 head on the mt. Tracks of two more caribou headed up and again the tracks of a big brown bear and this time on Emerson Creek flat. Going down so I suspect he will end up in caribou calving country.

My owl was on the nest. It was early and light not good so I left her and went on down to the lower lake. The American mergansers still there and also a pair of Barrow's goldeneyes and another pair too far away to identify. Several robins and I heard one singing as if enjoying the very un-May like weather.

So – I came back to my owl and of course she left the nest when she learned I was moving in. Up the ladder and I mounted the lens and camera on the tripod for a portrait. One sitting up and one low in the nest with only one eye showing. A pair of rabbit feet could be seen above nest level. The owls are feathered up completely now. No horns showing yet and faces are very dark. Just as well go all the way and I proceeded to hook up my timer. It would be a real reliable rig, I could see that. All set and I moved across the flat to wait. The lens set at f7 at 250th sec. Cloudy bright and I expected it to last awhile. I waited – no ma owl so I waited. The sky began to clear and soon it was more sunshine than shadows. Still no owl and I suspect it is that the young ones don't need her warmth anymore. Just keep us kids in rabbits and we will be ready to fly in a couple weeks. I waited and waited – moved farther back to the edge of the brush to get out of the wind. I could see a little action by the young ones and I suspect they were feeding on the rabbit. She didn't show and the sun was getting too far around. I would discontinue the operation. Take the tripod down and bring it home. I can see where I can't depend on that old mother any longer. From here on I will shoot close ups of the pair on the nest from a closer tree. So I stripped everything slick and clean. Left my ladder and packed everything else to travel. The wind really strong and I suspect it was blowing 35 or 40 at times. I put my head down and butted into it. I was surprised to find the lake in real good shape to travel. The ewe in the maternity ward was no longer there but farther down a single ewe was feeding very near a popular lambing spot. No sign of the bears in waterfall canyon. Snowing up country and snow in the air against the mts. on both sides of the lake. Five o'clock when I arrived. By the time I got all of my gear stowed it was time for supper.

Of all the birds and animals I wouldn't like to be a young owl and especially in a nest exposed to a Twin Lakes down the lake wind. Set there like a dummy and eat nothing but rabbit until big enough and strong enough to fly. Lambs and bear cubs have a grand time playing. Caribou too enjoy being active. Many young birds are on the move as soon as they are dry. Others go swimming and others get insects poked into them round the clock, nearly. The young owl just sets there with its big eyes blinkin'.

Now at seven thirty, snowing and blowing all down the lakes. Solid grey over head and the temperature 35°.

May 10 – Overcast, Blowing dn. & 32°.

I went on down to find the young owls sitting up in better shape than I have ever seen them. No mother owl at the nest when I came in view of it.

First I searched the gravel where I packed up. No adapter there so I went to the tree. If it had been rattled loose and dropped by the wind it would be melted deep in the

snow. Holes everywhere but at the bottoms. Twigs, leaves, and bits of bark. The mother owl hooted to let me know she wasn't loafing on guard. No adapter but when the snow goes I'll find it if I lost it there. Only need it when using the automatic timers – so – no problem. Of all the birds and animals I wouldn't like to be a young owl and especially in a nest exposed to a Twin Lakes down the lake wind. Set there like a dummy and eat nothing but rabbit until big enough and strong enough to fly. Lambs and bear cubs have a grand time playing. Caribou too enjoy being active. Many young birds are on the move as soon as they are dry. Others go swimming and others get insects poked into them round the clock, nearly. The young owl just sets there with its big eyes blinkin'.

May 13 – Overcast, Blowing dn. & 33°.

The old hen was at the nest but just there to keep those young ones company. She left and I moved in. First thing I noticed the horns. They wasn't there last time. My ladder in and against a tree less than 25 feet away, I unpacked my gear and made ready to climb. Hooting nearby, she wasn't used to me being quite this close. I was climbing the ladder and near the top when here she came head on. I could protect my head and neck with the tree trunk but I had my right arm around the trunk. Wham! and on by she went. Hit pretty hard but I had my quilted jacket, chamois cloth shirt, and sweater under my parky. She didn't make a second pass but sat in a tree nearby.

My owls didn't look like much for pictures. Could only see one and it was pointed the wrong way and had its feathers badly ruffled by the wind. I wouldn't waste 16 mm film on it but did shoot a slide. A couple runs of 16 on the old hen in the tree. Another rabbit on the nest since a few days ago and this one more brown than any I have seen. It seems that if there are rabbits the great horned owl won't go hungry.

Will Troyer was here about June first last year and coming back from the sheep lick we saw young owls flying so I suspect these will leave the nest before June 1st. Enough and I headed up the lake thinking of caribou. I would have a bit to eat and then head for the gravel banks again. Full load of gear this trip. The wind to push me down but I would pay for that coming back.

They might have moved to fox pond so I stayed on the lake until opposite the pond and then climbed the high bank. There they were all four of them and laying sound asleep. Not more than fifty yards away and down at a good angle. Some spruce for me to use as a blind in getting organized. Slowly I inched the tripod out for a clear shot. One was laying facing me and not asleep all the time. Skinny, bleached out caribou bulls. One may have been a yearling or maybe two years old. Two of them had a good growth of new antlers. I was in business if they didn't hear the camera. Exakta first for it seldom spooks game. Laying chewing after they woke up. One got up turned end for end and layed down again. Another got up to move and lay close which made for a good shot. I was doing pretty good. Three got up and brushed those new antlers gently. That third one

was the guy who saw me move but didn't make a big deal of it. The other three fed away and he trotted to join them. Good enough – should have some nice stuff there.

May 15 – Overcast, Breeze dn. & 32°.

Hotcakes and then I would travel the ice. Go down and torment the wise old owl, visit the connecting stream and come back by way of the gravel banks and fox pond. Exakta and 300 mm would be my artillery. The ice was real good but I knew it wouldn't last till noon. Those young owls stand up in the nest nearly as tall as their mother but it doesn't last. The closer you get the lower they sit. Looking more like great horned owls day by day. Now they have the brown faces which improves their looks. No guff from the old one today but she did cooperate by sitting on a big horizontal limb in the wide open and let me as close as 50 feet and less. That is not common of the great horned owl.

    Something I have wondered about – a lot of rabbits have come to the nest. What happens to all the skeletons. Should at least be some big hind feet kicked over the side but I found nothing but owl droppings but plenty of that and the nest edges are well painted.

May 16 – Overcast, Breeze dn. & 40°.

Where could I go on this side if I wore hip boots. I pulled them on and broke trail to the creek flat. Right away I found a job for today. My skinny bridge across Hope Creek had been broken by the settling snow pack. Broke in the middle as you would a match stick. I came back for my big bow saw and pack board. Wrassled the inboard ends out of the snow, sawed it to packing lengths and packed it to the woodshed. I saw no good trees nearby that would make a good bridge log. The closest one was in the little island of spruce this side of the mouth of Hope Creek. It would take some doing to get it moved and in place. On this side of the flat I saw a leaning dead tree that would make good wood so cut it and brought it in while thinking about a bridge log.

    Noon time and I checked for lambs. Now I have four lambs directly across. The two from Falls Mountain have moved to Allen Mt. And the huge ice column at the high waterfall has tumbled down. A huge mass of ice and I would liked to have seen it go tumbling down.

    Now about my new bridge. I had plenty of good nylon rope and my little cable lever hoist. Drop it in the direction of the bridge site, limb it, tie on to the small end and drag it the 100 feet plus to the crossing. Dropped her and proceeded to drag her to the site. I learned a spruce with the bark on doesn't drag easy in soft wet snow. Get my line as tight as a fiddle gut and then lift mightily on the line near the end of the pole. It would jump ahead 6-8 inches and then I would repeat the process. Got it there but not pointed in the right direction so I had to bury a dead man out on the flat to pull the big end around. Then from across the creek hook onto the little end and pull it to get equal footing on each

bank. A much better bridge than the last one and this one will have a support just under the center when it comes time for ice to form in the creek. Past four o'clock when I got everything squared away. This had been a real warm day. The sun bright but after a few hours it cooked up an overcast. I saw the temperature 50° just after one o'clock and doubt that it went higher.

May 20 – Partly Cloudy, Calm & 30°.

Reveille at five and window pane ice on the water out front. The ice would be a little more firm and I would go out to my ice measuring station after spuds. I did and found the ice 19". Coming back I noticed a sparrow size bird working at a small dark object on the ice down towards Hope Creek. It wasn't there yesterday so I went to check. The remains of a tiny porkypine. Some skin, one hind foot the trail and back bone. Black hair and the quills from a quarter to three quarter inch. Sharp as needles but they won't grab and hang on like mature quills. I wondered what had killed it. Now I suspected that the porkies do have some meat eating enemies in this wilderness.

Today I would make another try for the owls nest. Pack a full load of gear and hope for the best. I was away early and it would be warm shirt sleeve hiking with a load. Again I would check for tracks of that big bear. I should have seen them yesterday if he crossed Low Pass Creek.

Past one mile rock at the good beach – another little black object on the ice. Another little porkypine and this time raven tracks. That wise old raven would do that. His heavy sharp beak would kill the slow moving little cabin eater. A half mile farther down I had seen a patch of black hair and a patch of skin yesterday and wondered what it was. Again I checked and found quills. So now I'm thinking the raven may do his share in keeping the porcupine population in check.

On the creek flat and I found the owl nest empty. Not owl one. They had left the nest since I was there two days ago.

So – I claim it takes about six weeks to launch a great horned owl after it hatches. April 9th to May 22nd. I set my ladder up against the nest tree and climbed to inspect their housekeeping. The nest flat on top and littered with bones and bits of bones. It didn't smell very sanitary. Certainly not the housekeeping job that robins would do. No more hooting and popping of the beak. A rapping back in the woods but it was a flicker beating his head against a tree.

May 22 – Clear, Calm & 28°.

On the creek flat and I found the owl nest empty. Not owl one. They had left the nest since I was there two days ago. So – I claim it takes about six weeks to launch a great

horned owl after it hatches. Apr. 9th to May 22nd. I set my ladder up against the nest tree and climbed to inspect their housekeeping. The nest flat on top and littered with bones and bits of bones. It didn't smell very sanitary. Certainly not the housekeeping job that robins would do. No more hooting and popping of the beak. A rapping back in the woods but it was a flicker beating his head against a tree. I took my ladder down and moved it to the edge of the grove. When the lake is open I will canoe it home. Good that I took some pictures two days ago. No more will that old sister perch on a limb at 36 feet for me to take her picture.

The day was young I would visit the falls and see what the water ouzels were up to. I wondered when they start nesting and if they build a new one every year. Water in the creek and running on the surface halfway to the lake. I found shallows to make the two necessary crossings. When I climbed to the observation point close to the pool of the lower falls I saw ouzels active and I sat down to determine where they might be living. A nest in a niche of the shear rock wall beside the falling water that was used two years ago. Last year the nest was on the ledge under the moss covered bench where I now stood. Only a few minutes when one came with a few blades of dry grass and lit on the little ledge at the old nest. Into the opening it went and here came the second one with more grass. Two in the house at the same time. Those kids were putting down a new carpet – moving into the old house. I suspect the ouzel nest would last for years. Made entirely of moss – a big ball of it. The fast water so near keeps it moist. I learned that the grass they use isn't necessarily dry grass. One tugged at a little tuft of fine grass very near the falling water.

By climbing down to a ledge I could get within about 45 feet. The sun fell on the wall and the nest. I set up the Bolex and would shoot 100 feet of the birds and the falls. I switched to the 300 and Exakta. I wanted both of them in front of the nest. As if they had gone to lunch and would take a long nap after – they didn't come back and I stood and listened to the roar of the falls. The sun moved around and no birds. I decided to call it good and climbed back up. Just packed and I saw one come again. Then the other – they were working again. I set up my machinery and got the shots I wanted. Nice birds to work with. They never act as if I am too close – go about their business very unconcerned. Enough and I headed back. Across the stream and I cached the canvas shoes in a little clump of spruce for future use.

May 24 – Partly Cloudy, Blowing dn. & 40°.

I decided to have hotcakes this morning but hadn't started batter last evening. I had part of a bag of Krusteze. I would give it a try. Everything in it – all you add is water but I added a little more dry milk and soda. They looked good and not too bad but compared to sourdoughs they were only slightly better than a poke in the eye with a sharp stick. So – dishes done I wet my roof down and then took the scope up the mt. Maybe between a quarter and a half mile of open water at the upper end of the lower lake. I had thought the wind might have done better than that. A pair of harlequin ducks at the mouth of Hope

Creek when I came down. Last evening I saw a loon in the open pool at Carrithers' point. Here at my cabin I have a rabbit again. Today I opened the door and startled the guy. Around the corner to the back of the cabin it went. So – I went the other way to get a good look. A brown rabbit with white belly, feet and ears bordered with dark brown.

May 27 – Partly Cloudy, Lt. Breeze dn. & 40°.

About 1:30 I was awakened by rasping out front. Not on the cabin or tables so I didn't get too excited. It went on and on and I didn't go back to sleep. Too much and I thought of stopping it but what to do with the porkypine. The lake in no condition to deport him to the far side. Deposit him anywhere on this side and he might be at the cabin door waiting when I arrived. I decided to can him, put him in the lock up and stop that racket at least. Quietly I slipped up on him and was with in touching distance with my walking stick when he whirled facing me. He looked me over in the dim light and started to leave. A touch near the head end, right or left would steer him and finally into the catcher can near by. I backed the open end with the hinged cover against the stump by the clothes line and went back to bed. Soon he was trying to get out and in doing so made more noise than rasping on the antler. I could hear him trying to eat his way out and wondered what kind of mark he could make on gas can tin. All quiet and then he would work at it again. My mistake, I should have carried him out of hearing. Some mosquitoes got into the cabin during the operation. Between them and the porky I didn't get much sleep.

At four I got up. The lake still open out front and towards Erv's hill and down the beach a short distance. I would load him in the canoe and paddle him as far as I could go and dump him out ker-plunk. Maybe he would get the message – remember how it was and not come back for awhile. Just a very light breeze down and a nice early morning short paddle. I dumped him out and he climbed the bank into the timber.

May 30 – Overcast, Calm & 34°.

At 2 am I heard a porkypine complaining about something and it kept it up for sometime. Then, claws against the cabin longs and a few rasping licks on my cache ladder just beyond the wall from my bunk. That did it. I would stuff him in the cooler can. Wouldn't take long so I just pulled on my shoes and eased out the door. Raining lightly but this would be quick and easy. There he was big as a wheelbarrow, under the spruce by the cache. Not an easy place to capture him and besides he got wise and headed for the brush. Me in my skivvies right after him. Through heavy brush that I seldom venture into he headed for the creek flat in a porkypine trot. I was getting wet going through the brush but I was keeping up and steering him a bit. In the open of the flat I tapped him on the front end and turned him around. The can waiting and there was no place to go but in. A real snug fit in face first he wouldn't quite go completely in. Door closed and that end against a willow I

435

stacked a few rocks around and on top. That would humiliate him to no end to stay there till my breakfast dishes were done and maybe he would remember that my cabin is off limits. It took a little time to get back to sleep so I slept in till 5:30 and then it was still raining.

June 3 – Overcast, Lt. Breeze dn & 50°.

A very warm night and the mosquitoes a nuisance. A few in the cabin and I finally sprayed a rag with "Off" and hung it from a roof pole over my head. That did it – I heard no more buzzing.

A dark morning and the lake up considerably from yesterday morning. By this evening it would be 14 ¼ inches above low water. "Taders" for breakfast and I have no more than enough to see me through to plane day. I do have dried, sliced and instant mashed spuds so no problem.

This dark morning I took care of my calouses. An awful lot of hiking makes them thick and no problem unless I am on the mt. Uphill, downhill, side hill makes my feet sore. Some coarse sandpaper and a sanding block is good medicine. Sand them down to the pink and they will behave for a month or two. Another project I have been thinking of. Make an Eskimo "ulu" (womens knife). I have an old rusty worn out cross cut saw blade from Erv's dump. A length of axe handle (broken) to fashion the grip from. I would give it a whirl. To cut a length from the end of the saw blade I used a landing gear leg (broken) that I salvaged from Lofstedt's [Cessna] 180 bust up in the brush at the upper end. ¾ inch thick and sharp edges on the upper end. I laid my length mark on the sharp edge and hit it a few licks with the claw hammer to weaken the metal. Then mashed a line on the sharp edge I weighted the saw blade down with the 8 lb. splitter head and hit the extending end a mighty blow. Broke like glass. I trimmed my rough ulu blade to shape the same way and then filed it to shape. Went pretty good but a file in good shape would have hastened the process. After getting it to shape I thinned and sharpened the cutting edge plus cleaning the rust off down to clean metal. The length of the grip 4⅛ inches. I sawed a saw cut length wise a half inch deep. Now when I get it all dressed and polished I will epoxy the grip on. A thin blade and good steel, it should be a good one.

June 5 – Overcast, Calm & 44°.

This evening I would have a green salad with my beans and porridge. Young and very tender fireweed. Small dandelion, raw potato and dried chopped onion, seasoned with sugar, vinegar, salt, pepper, garlic and celery salt. I do believe that I have discovered a way to improve last years raw potatoes. Peel them and soak them in cold water for a day. Soft spongy spuds become solid and crisp again.

My delinquent birds came again both of them and starved. Grab that hotcake

and tear it apart right there under the shaggy spruce at the corner of the cabin. Still no young ones. I wonder if she was standing in line for welfare when she should have been tending the inkybator.

Overcast, a light breeze down and temp. 60° now at 7:30.

June 6 – Overcast, Lt. Breeze dn. & 50°.

A real good night's sleep except for one small incident. Rasping at the rear of the cabin. Then a few licks at the cache ladder – then porkypine talk out front. If I go to Terry & Vic's I just can't leave those characters in charge here. I quietly opened the door to see ...ten feet out. A big one and a youngish one. How to capture two of them and do a real stroke of managing the big nuisance of Carrithers' point. I reached for my iron shod walking stick and gathered up my catcher can. Got in real close before they got wise. The little one had been educated. It was the log wall climber and knew what to expect. I rapped the big one on the head to slow him down while I captured the runaway. It tried to climb and I poked it out. Then the chase and I finally patted it on the head and it turned around. Into the can and a loose fit. The big one hadn't come around and I didn't have time to wait so I got my war club and finished him. The damage they do balanced against the good they might possibly do makes me think that to thin them down to a minimum number would be fitting and proper. This one I would skin out for the birds and animals that might clean it up but spring summer and fall is not a hungry time. The head, tail and skin I would burn to get rid of the quills. I jammed the cover end of the catcher can up against a boulder at the breakwater and put a rock behind it for this one could turn around in the can. Back to bed and it was five when I woke up again. A nice morning and it was due to be another 70° day. The lake level would climb to 28" and my marker is only 32. Another foot and a half would probably put water in Jerre's cabin.

Sourdoughs and after everything was neatened up I took my paddle and ferried the jail bird across the pond. Dead calm here but out in the long run a light breeze down. Last evening high clouds were moving at a good rate so it would blow today. There happened to be a tall half dead spruce on the bank where I dumped the porkypine. It promptly climbed until it was clinging to the top most dead branches like a masthead lookout on a sailing ship. I wonder if its eyes are good enough to see the homeland!

I came back and skinned out the big one and then went up to water my fresh planted garden. I found the hen robin hopping around looking for food and while on the nest I'll bet she sees every bug that ventures onto the tilled soil.

June 7 – Overcast, Fog, Calm & 40°.

In my sleep I heard rasping and woke up to find it was true. On the cabin in front and I

nearly bumped its head when I opened the door. A young one with quills not yet showing and the rascal was gnawing on the log below the door. What do they like about these logs. Hope's cabin they have never touched and Spike's they pull the chinking out. Just as well break this one of the habit right now. I left him resting peacefully in the Labrador tea next to the path to the lake. It was so nice out that I thought of getting an early breakfast and be ready for Glen until I checked my Baby Ben. It was 11 P.M. Still time for a good night's sleep and I got up at 4:30.

In March or early April and on snowshoes I cut a few dead trees on the Cowgill Creek flat. Now I am reminded how deep the snow was. I had dug down and cut low. With the snow gone one stump two feet high and the other three. I don't like high stumps – a great waste of wood. So – I took saw and axe to the scene and now have a couple loads of dry wood ready to come across the creek but not on the skinny bridge with the water going by miles per hr. I would fix that bridge. It's a neat trick to walk the pole over very fast and plenty deep water. If a person was to end up in that creek now he would end up in the lake and it would be interesting to learn if he would survive. I scouted the jungle for a good straight pole. A green one that I could peel and spike along side and flush with the top of the bridge log. Big end to small end to get a more uniform width of walking surface. Now it is finished and one could walk it blind folded. Might save someone a dunking and possibly an injury during the tourist season.

June 8 – Clear, Calm & 28°.

Last evening after the close encounter with the cow and calf out front, she fed in the brush behind the holding pond on the point and finally moved out on the high bank beyond the breakwater and stood for ten minutes or more just looking out over the lake. Nothing quite like a real gentle cow moose.

A real good night's sleep but I woke up at three and couldn't go back to sleep for thinking this could very well be plane day. I got up at four and was surprised to find the temp. 28°. The beach near water line a little crunchy and window pane ice on the holding pond. Frost on the cabin roof. How about those blueberries at lake level.

Breakfast over and just neatening up the place when I heard the "T craft" coming. Over and around – landing down from the point. Two aboard and darned if little Sig [Alsworth] wasn't in the pilots seat. The "T craft" on Pee Kay floats.[1] "How much free board have you got at Lake Clark," I asked Glen. "Not much and losing what we have," he replied. "About every two days we have to drag the tie down barrels out of the water only to have them soon under again." Did he have his spuds planted? Yes they sure did and under real ideal conditions. How was Babe doing. Improving slowly and when I asked what could possibly have caused the trouble Glen said "I think he had a stroke but of course he won't admit it."

[1] Pee Kay floats are aluminum pontoons for small aircraft made by DeVore Aviation Company of Albuquerque, New Mexico.

June 9 – Partly Cloudy, Calm & 36°.

Again I was awake early and not again till near six. The sun was on the thermometer and 55° but when it moved a bit it dropped to 38°. Ice on the little puddle again so sometime during the night it was frosty cold.

A nice burbot on the trot line and I had another huge porkypine to skin. I don't hate porkypines but I like them scattered some and especially if I plan to be away for a week or two at this time of year. This one was made a gardener.

June 12 – Overcast, Calm & 33°.

I had just finished my morning chores when here came the "T craft" with Glen and Leon [Alsworth]. The weather here hadn't looked too favorable for the trip to the Bonanza Hills but Glen reported it better over the low country. We loaded my gear and I put the night latch on lock. The beach had been raked track free so I could tell if anyone had come to my beach while I was away. Leon in the baggage compartment we took off down the lake. The weather was better over the low country with some fog patches about the Hills of the Bonanza group. Over the fox dens and I looked close for a glimpse of red indicating there would be pups there. On down and nearing the ridge before Victoria Lake,[2] Tom Creek Lakes[3] and Synneva Knob. Out of ground contact for a second or two over the ridge and there was Tom Creek Lakes dead ahead. I asked Glen about them and if he had ever landed there. No, but he would take a look. Two small lakes connected by a very short narrow passage way of water. The upper and larger one looked a little short to me and I said, go on to Victoria Lake, which was only an hrs. hike farther. He circled and said he could make it in ok. It was raining lightly and the windshield messed up. He came in high and a little fast. Dropped her quick and still had half of the lake to go when she touched down. A good beach to come into. I was in real good shape to make Terry's [Gill] camp in an hour and a half.

I had figured on two weeks but Glen thought over his schedule and asked if 13 days would be good. Fine, so, the 25th of June he would pick me up there where we landed. My gear on shore they taxied to the far end, Leon at the controls. Off in half the length of the lake easy. If necessary they could have gone through the narrows on the step but only on the step as there was three big rocks about 10 inches down. They climbed fast and headed for home. I got under my pack saddle and headed for Terry and Vic's camp at the forks of the Big and Little Bonanza [Creeks].[4] One easy climb over the ridge before Synneva Creek and it was downhill all the way. Now, just supposing that for some reason

---

[2] Victoria Lake, a small lake about 6 miles SW of the Gill's camp that drains into Bonanza Creek.

[3] Tom Creek Lakes, a series of very small lakes about 3 miles south of Gill's camp.

[4] Gill's Camp was located at the confluence of Bonanza Creek and Little Bonanza Creeks. The head of Big Bonanza Creek is about 7-miles south of Gill's camp.

Terry and Vic had gone back to Anch. because of any number of reasons. I would be 35 miles from home and 13 days before the plane came.

June 28 – Blue sky showing, Calm.

[RLP was visiting Terry and Vicky Gill at their small placer mining camp in the Bonanza Hills. While there RLP repaired their John Deer bulldozer and helped them placer mine. Glen Alsworth was unable to pick-up RLP so he walked 35 miles back to his Twin Lakes cabin.]

This was the day surely Glen would come and early in the forenoon. Vic was up early to have a good breakfast for I had said I wasn't packing my load back and forth to the lake another time. If he didn't come by noon I was heading for Twin Lakes. I asked Terry for an old gas can that I could cache my Bolex and other excess gear in. Leave it and the tripod in the brush near the pick up spot. Leave a note on a ribboned stick telling him where to find it if he landed.

Terry said he would go with me to the lake and bring back their mail if Glen brought it. He had forgotten to bring it when he took me down. I asked Vic if she would like another mess of trout and I knew she would but she smiled and looked at Terry. He said "no fish" so that was settled. We climbed slow and was there by 8:30. Terry took a much longer route around the head of Synneva than I could see reason for. I cut across the headwaters and was there a half hr. before he arrived. Completely flyable weather but neither of us had any hope that he would come. Terry said he would stay till 9:30. I would stay until 10:30 and see him out of sight headed back. If he saw the plane come he would return if I was still there. I tore my pack down and filled the gas can with heavy unnecessary gear for my hike. My load would be heavy enough by the time I reached my cabin. 9:30 we shook hands the best of friends and he thanked me for all I had done for them. And by me it was, thanks for the good groceries and interesting stay at Bonanza Creek. He circled up country a half mile to measure another lake I had told him about. As long as the one we were on but with better approaches. 10:15 saw him going over the high ridge towards the head of Synneva. 10:25 saw me getting under my pack of maybe 25 lbs. for the long trek to Twin Lakes. I knew about how many hiking hrs. it would take. 15 hrs. should see me there.

I stayed on the slope facing the Ptarmigan Creek and in two hrs. I was on the trail I had traveled years ago on my very first return from the "B" [Bonanza Hills]. Not a bad trail but one alder patch was a bad one. It was raining and like a shower bath in the brush. 4 hrs. saw me around the bend and into some really fine spruce timber. Big trees and many of the nicest tallest straightest cottonwoods I have ever seen. Across the Ptarmigan and in heavy brush and timber I got turned around due to the heavy overcast and calm. Just when I thought I was ready to leave the jungle I came to a completely strange stream flowing in the wrong direction. A high bank on the far side and I was tempted to ford it and climb to see where I was. Looking for a fordable spot I got turned around again and knew where

I was – I climbed out onto the lower slope of the Island Mt. 10 minutes later. Time wise I was on schedule. A real long pull to climb up and around the back side of the mt. to the "erratic Hilton" a huge granite rock where I have slept and listened to the mosquitoes sing – mostly listened, a real cool day and now the rain had stopped. I switched from hip boots to shoe pacs. Four hours in a straight line from the Island Mt. to the drop off into the timber of Lower Twin country. That is always a long stretch. A bunch of five and later a nice bunch of maybe 30 caribou cows and calves along my route and near this end a pair of swans with young. True to nature the parents left the young and headed over land to lead me away.

Now I could see the lower lake was high and how high would the connecting stream be. I was doing good but some how had bruised my left heel a bit and it reminded me of it often. A plane came in Lake Trout bay. A 2nd plane was there and soon they both flew away. I heard a plane down country and wondered if it was Glen coming back from going to pick me up. If it was he didn't come close to Twin Lakes.

Now I could see the head of the Chili River and it was high. I hoped I could ford the connecting stream. Getting a little dark under the heavy overcast as I entered the mile of big rocks towards the upper end of the lower lake. Subtracting the ten or fifteen minutes I had spent in changing from boots to shoes and unbunching my socks I was looking at that awful stream at 10:25. 12 hrs. after the start of the long journey I would have come on up if it hadn't been for the river like stream. I wanted more light and a few hrs. rest before I tried it so I went to the Vanderpool cabin – uncovered the chimney, built a fire – got some water from Emerson Creek – ate the third of the four sandwiches Vic had made for me – layed down and covered with a folded bunkbed mosquito net and went to sleep.

June 29 – Rain, Fog, Calm.

It was five when I woke up feeling a little sore but a few minutes of activity erased that pretty good. I was ready for the crossing. It would be over hip boot deep I was certain but not too fast or chilling cold. No sooner said than done. It sure tasted good to be on my side of the upper lake again. I had worn my L.L. Bean wind pants for the crossing so had a dry start for the home stretch. The lake high and I had to wade the shallows many places which took time. Two hrs. saw me at my bridge across Hope Creek which was running merrily and all in one channel which meant that all was well upstream. My beach still untracked as I had left it. The night latch still in the exact spot I had left it. No one had been here since I left. Everything looked so fresh, neat and clean. Lake level right at the top and 32 inches above winter low water.

A good fire was soon going and a tub of water on the stove. The rest of the day would be spent getting organized to live the no problem life again. Gee! it seemed good to be back home again.

Towards evening I got to the point of looking around a bit. I traveled the beach to Spike's cabin and my garden. Went barging in not thinking of the robins nest. I was surprised to find no one at home and the nest empty. Sugar snap peas looking good. Radishes too and also the rhubarb. Spuds not showing yet. Baby moose calf tracks in the soft earth and did that tame cow calve here on the point. I'm thinking she must have.

At Terry's [Gill] I had seen an ad for a spring wound shaver in a magazine and remarked that I would like to buy one of those. Terry says, "I've got two, I'll give you one." He ordered two and the plastic housing of both were broken in the mailing to him. He sent one back and it finally returned. He thought it took too long to shave with one compared to his battery Norelco. Vic had taped up the broken clear plastic housing on the one he kept. I packed it home and with epoxy and aluminum screen wire I filled the openings of the shell broken and lost. I'm anxious to get it back together. It gives a real close shave but one must shave every day. The holes in the head are small and round. Long whiskers just won't feed through the holes.

During the day I cooked fresh beans and got my sourdough out of the cooler box. I was a little surprised when it came right up during the day. Oleo in there too and it had an odor when it came out but overnight it lost the odor.

My birds came at noon and perched on the spruce buck horns and looked down surprised at me being here. No hotcakes so I put a handfull of rolled oats on the stump. Side by side they worked at it and cleaned it up plus a second handfull.

Overcast, fog patches, and 46° at 8:30. I expected to sleep well and for a long time.

July 6 – Overcast, Calm & 44°.

Here came the fisherman to the breakwater but after repeated casting and no catching he went on up the beach with his two spinning rigs. After maybe a half hr. he came back and after looking at my bone pile parked his gear and came to the door. I invited him in. Stoker was his name and from Illinois below Springfield. A high school boy, big and raw boned. Up on sort of a vacation to Kenai country. Some friends or relatives there.

"Where's the fish," he asked and I told him the water was to high and the fish stuffed and not with metal trinkets with treble hooks attached. He had caught only two since Bud [Lofstedt] landed him there. One a rainbow and on that I really woke up. Turned out it was a pale fish with dark irregular spots – a lake trout I suspect. "Got any porcupines here," he asked. "Yes, I have enough and some to spare." Well, they are climbing up the walls of Bud's cabin. At one time he counted eight. If I were him I wouldn't fish any longer. I would live on mt. seal livers and hearts. He had a million questions about this country. I asked him if he knew he was in national monument country. No, he didn't know and did he know that outboard motors are prohibited on Twin Lakes. Negative again. I told him I would use mine too if I saw fit for safety. He said that Bud intends to fly sport hunters in here again this season.

We had a cup of tea and chewed the fat till noon. He had intended to go to the lower

end of this lake but decided he would go back. "Ever get lonesome," he asked. Be six or seven days before Bud came for him. I told him to stop in again if he got down this way.

July 11 – Overcast, Blowing dn. & 50°.

This afternoon I was writing up a storm when I heard a womans voice out front. I went to the door to find a young man and woman in rain togs. Right away I suspected them to belong to the blue tent up at the upper end. Two Klepper kayaks rested at the water line. I invited them in. She was Betty and he Steve but I noticed they had no last names so I took it to be one of those just real good friends sort of an arrangement. Real friendly Alaskan type and from Cordova.[5] Andy's Flying Service of Kenai had flown them in yesterday. Now they were on their way down to run the Chili River, the Mulchatna River to Dillingham.[6] They figure on about three weeks to make the trip. He was a whitewater kayaker and she had been many places in Alaska since coming up from Minnesota's southeast corner by the Mississippi. Tyonek,[7] Togiak,[8] Sleetmute, Lime Village, Bethel,[9] Flat,[10] and more. Seems she was a swimming instructor teaching the Native kids to swim. We dug out maps and studied their route down the whitewater trail. The Chili would be high and fast but they preferred that to low and gravel bars. Would they have a chance of seeing wolves and grizzly bears. Could be, a couple boys from Maine did a few years ago. How about the weather – rain probably. No problem, Cordova has nothing but rain. No sourdough but they would like to try some if it would work with whole wheat flour. She doesn't use sugar so they would mix the sourdough with their prepared pancake mix. She promised to keep it warm in her sleeping bag and never let it die. I stoked the fire for hot tea and put a sprig of Labrador with each filling of hot water. She liked Labrador [tea], carried some in her pocket for its fragrant aroma. They had planned to camp at the upper end of the lower lake tonight and head on down tomorrow. After examining the cabin, woodshed, and cache they climbed into their squatty little canoes and snapped the spray shield snug about the mid section. They would drop me a card and say how it went from here. When they shoved out she said, "I'll see you again sometime" and as if she meant it. A real outdoorser that gal. The lake was roaring rough but they headed for the outlet and soon when in the trough I could only see half of them.

Later with the scope I could see them nearly there, those goofy kayak double ender paddles waving above their heads like a beginner using a canoe paddle for the first time. It was grey with rain over the lower lake so they would feel right at home while pitching camp. I was surprised to learn that they didn't know they were in the big national monument. I wonder how many visitors would?

[5] Cordova, coastal town along the Gulf of Alaska.

[6] The trip from Twin Lakes runs along the Chilikadrotna, the Mulchatna, and finally the Nushagak River to tidewater at Dillingham, a journey of about 250 river miles.

[7] Tyonek, a small Dena'ina village on Cook Inlet about 40 miles SW of Anchorage; Tubughnen is the Dena'ina word for "beach land."

[8] Togiak, a Yup'ik village on the Bering Sea coast west of Dillingham.

[9] Bethel, the major city in SW Alaska lying between the Yukon and Kuskokwim River deltas.

[10] Flat, a small mining settlement in the Iditarod country NW of Twin Lakes.

July 17 – Partly Cloudy, Calm & 37°.

After lunch I reviewed the program and found that I still hadn't seen the birch trees so I would try again. By now the lake was rippled coming up but no sign of wind to follow.

This time I went up the down country side. I saw where Jerre had cut a batch of nice five and six in. poles and many of them still in the woods. The woods look much different without a lot of snow and I missed the birch trees. Climbed to the game trail – moved a hundred feet farther down to find them. Dead except for a few small branches near the ground. As growing trees they would never be. I picked the worst one and dropped it. Cut it in three lengths for packing and learned that birch is as heavy as lead. The limbs and brushy tips I piled and will take the pack board and bring them too. The only birch I know of in Twin Lakes country and it can't be wasted. Maybe 175 lbs. total came across to be sawed in two and one half foot lengths to season. Three sticks I put in my little holding pond to see what the effect would be. So heavy they nearly sank.

So warm I was afraid I would lose my arctic char so I prepared it for frying and would save half as cold fish. In 30 min. I could run up Cowgill Creek far enough to get a load of hard packed snow which would last for days in my cooler box.

August 14 – Clear, Lt. Breeze dn. & 31°.

[RLP had earlier canoed to upper Twin Lakes and was on his way home when a plane came by.]

So now, I had the whitecaps chasing me and I would beat an hour by ten minutes. Halfway and drifting right along when here came that [Cessna] 185 of yesterday. He rocked his wings as he passed and then turned down to turn again and land below Carrithers' point. It would be the Park Service on patrol and I wouldn't pay them what they are getting for the good they are doing. Little Bill, the pilot of last season was on the beach smoking a cigarette and no doubt he has been doing that every half hour since I saw him last in Oct. of 79 when he flew in my carpet. Another man Mike[11] came from my cabin. He would be Paul Haertel's partner. The two of them in charge of Lake Clark Ntl. Monument. Bill had been flying firefighters and equip. on many fires this summer and happy to be back on this gravy train. Paul was checking Spike and Hope's cabin just to learn where they were and how they looked. He came back saying there should be another that BLM had given them paperwork on. The name Weiser and BLM's last letter to him on Kodiak had been returned undelivered.

No fire and I didn't build one thinking they wouldn't be here long enough. We sat and chewed the fat. I ask them if they would have any more clout than they had last

---

[11] Michael Tollefson, NPS ranger and first chief of park operations for Lake Clark National Monument, presently superintendent of Yosemite National Park.

hunting season. "No, I'm afraid not," Paul said. About all we can do is try to talk them out of the monument. To make it worse the Anch. papers had published words to the effect that the Park Service wouldn't be enforcing game regulations again this year. Bill wondered if Jerre will be back this year. I told them that it is no good, the Park Service bluffing the timid ones out and having the country wide open to those who refuse to be bluffed.

Paul had been on the Chili River floating trip and said it is a good river. He has also been down the Mulchatna from Turquoise [Lake]. A really spectacular gorge opposite the Bonanza Hills on the north. "Walls must be 500 feet high," he said, but the river can be run the full length, gorge included.

August 15 – Overcast, Blowing dn. & 42°.

Raining and I could see new snow coming to Spike's peak and the high ridge on its down country side.

Morning chores squared away I set about bringing my outgoing mail up to date for I expected Glen tomorrow. I was writing up a storm about the black one who left his mark. I thought I heard snuffling but it didn't register. Then from the left of the big window appeared the black bear. Head up and testing the air with that snuffling nose. A good looking black and combed slick and shiny from sliding through the brush. Would he sniff my bear repellent I had placed in a plastic jar on the outside ledge of the window. I had punched holes with a darning needle in the window side of the jar and put mothballs in it thinking the scent, if he tested it, would keep his nose down and those heavy feet off of my Mylar.[12] He came towards the window and was no more than five feet away when he went out of sight headed for the front of the cabin. I would give him a real scare and maybe he would leave the cabin area at least, so I quietly headed for the door – eased it open and not seeing him I rushed out with a whoop and holler. On looking around the corner I saw his rear end go out of sight behind the cabin. I ran the other way and just got a glimpse of his backside as he disappeared into the brush headed for Hope Creek. On checking I found he had again taken the lid off of the cooler can by the holding pond but hadn't disturbed the last ear of sweet corn.

> *He came towards the window and was no more than five feet away when he went out of sight headed for the front of the cabin. I would give him a real scare and maybe he would leave the cabin area at least, so I quietly headed for the door – eased it open and not seeing him I rushed out with a whoop and holler. On looking around the corner I saw his rear end go out of sight behind the cabin. I ran the other way and just got a glimpse of his backside as he disappeared into the brush headed for Hope Creek.*

[12] Mylar, strong flexible, clear polyester RLP used in place of window glass in the Proenneke cabin.

August 20 – Partly Cloudy, Breeze up & 37°.

A strange airplane from Iliamna Air Taxi Service. Who was the first one out, Chuck Hornberger and he said, "I brought you some visitors." Then he fished out a big box of garden truck. Beets, onions, cabbage, carrots, lettuce and more plus a jar of strawberry jam. The pilot I didn't recognize and certainly not the passengers. From Texas a man named Bill and his good looking wife Donna. Just out on a sightseeing trip from Chuck's where they had been attending Boyd Norton's[13] photographers workshop. Both packed new Canon 35 mm cameras – motor drive and lenses to do the job. "We read your book and saw the movie 'One Man's Alaska' at a Sierra Club meeting in Texas," he said and being so close we just had to see the place. So, he had chartered the air taxi to come see Twin Lakes country. Did I mind if he took some pictures. In the cabin and out he kept that Canon busy. Chuck was busy telling me the news of Lake Clark country. The lake coming up and up. Glen Alsworth had one inch to go before it would cover the basement floor. That was a few days ago before the last big rain. Their garden was really producing this summer and he was unhappy that Sara hadn't put some tomatoes in the box. Many black bears close to his place and few blueberries. A brown bear had gone through the area – got spooked, ran into a fence and tore out a stretch of it. This week would wind up his tourist business for now. Norton's workshop had been a great success this time. Even Paul Fritz from Moab, Utah had come up to attend.

August 24 – Clear, Calm & 28°.

Perfect climbing weather with frost on the leaves and now and again a clump of moss with a crunchy feel under foot. High on the mt. I would find ice crystals and the wet ground frozen. I made it a steady climb from the lake to the peak. No stopping except to use the glasses or check my route ahead. Only once before have I seen the "man on the mt."[14] close up and this time I would look down on him as he has done me so often. The breeze from the Kijik was good. I was climbing in a long depression on the point of the mt. Now and then I moved to the edge to check for rams I hadn't seen. High up and rounding to an easy climb I could look down and see a half mile of the Kijik. A perfect end on view of the lower lake and the low country. I was a bit higher than Falls Mt. peak. Flies were bad up there and I went for my GI bug dope.

    Getting in close and I moved a bit to the right to see the long ragged ridge line of Gold Mt. There a half mile away and much lower was a ram and he was walking away. That was a bad sign. My glasses made him not the best of rams but he could still be the leader.

    Then behind him appeared a second and better ram and soon they traveled head

---

[13] Boyd Norton, author and photographer.

[14] RLP's "the man on the mt," a rock spire that appeared from a distance to have a human form in Low Pass.

to tail. Still two some where in between us and soon they came into view following the others. Some how they knew I was on the way or this was just the day that they would head for Hope Creek country. Now and again they stopped to look back and as yet I hadn't appeared on the sky line. Well, the view was worth the climb and I would just shoot a few feet of film. The head of Low Pass basin was quite a spectacular sight and the wide view down country. Airplanes flew by far below me this fine calm morning. One Cub with State Fish and Game colors flew low up the lake and later two Cubs came down from the upper end. One flew around until he passed my canoe on the beach and then back to the upper end as if wanting to know where I was today.

The rams kept a steady pace and climbed snow clad Cowgill peak which was higher than I. From there they would travel the edge of the big hole at the head of Cowgill Creek to another peak and from there they could look down into the head of 1st canyon where I was a few days ago. Against a wall at the upper end of Low Pass basin a lot of snow remains and on it I spotted 16 head of caribou who had climbed the steep snow covered slope of the south wall to rest in the very cool shade of the mt. Cows and calves plus maybe a half dozen bulls. Two bulls even at nearly two miles stood out as being something special. Both the extreme in big racks. One with a very wide spread of the main beams and not many points. The other was even hard to imagine. A real brush pile of antler points. I may have seen one as good at Twin Lakes but none better. I would have to go see him as close up as I could get.

I climbed down the coarse loose rock slope of the peak to the saddle and the scree slope of fine stuff that I had studied yesterday. Here I strapped on the crampons for better traction and not so much over the boot tops plowing in the fine stuff. I had wondered if the rams had gone down there to feed for there was green feed part way up. I found beds nearly to the bottom.

Nearing the bottom I spotted a bull caribou on a snow patch in a hole directly below. I might get real close to him and I did. A frame filler of just his head and antlers. So close he came alive when the Bolex ran. Head turning left and right before he got to his feet and acted foolish trotting around on stiff legs before heading up into the head of the basin. If it wasn't the bull I had lost yesterday it was his twin brother.

A good caribou trail leads to the head of the basin where huge glacier tailing piles surrounded by snow is the terrain. The caribou high on the slope and standing in the shade of the mt. The two good bulls would be the two to be nearest a high pinnacle and the last for the sun to find as it moved to the west. No cover, the best I could do was walk directly towards them but slowly. On the jumble of rock I would be hard to spot but on the snow patches I had to be extra cautious. A wise old cow with a calf did get wise to me and spooked to the extreme head of the basin and took a half dozen with her. In time they came trudging back to join the bunch but she wouldn't forget and kept me pretty well pinned down. A cool breeze came up into this high snow covered land and I wished for my Kelty which I didn't want to pack up the mt.

Those very large racks of antlers are heavy no doubt about it. Those two good

bulls often stood with nose tucked under and let the shovels and brow tines rest on the snow. I wanted them in the sunlight for a few feet of film at least so settled down to wait for them to move or the sun to travel around. Now and again some would start to pull out. Only a step or two and then stand with heads low and as often as not turn back to the shade again. The sun moved slowly but in time I could see that I would be late getting home. The big bulls moved but behind the pinnacle out of sight. I was tempted to pack up and leave but hung tough. Finally it came – a determined effort to move up to the head of the basin and then follow the long snow trail down to grazing country. All headed in that direction and slowly they started to move. The big ones the last of them to come into the sun. The camera ran dry and as soon as they were out of sight I hurried to get out below so as not to disturb them as they moved down.

It is a good trail and down grade all the way from the upper basin to the lake and I rattled right along. The sun casting a shadow on Carrithers' point as I came by the man on the mt. The lake still ruffled from an up the lake breeze which had calmed. 6:20 when I came in the cabin.

First thing a fire going and things warming while I stowed my gear. Later hot water to get cleaned up. It was near nine before I turned in. If the weather was fair tomorrow I would go again and this time take the Exakta and 300 mm. Such bulls as that outstanding one are few and far between. Now Aug. 25 – velvet rubbing time a week away. They will have moved out by then. Today I saw no sign of that rubbing antlers with a hind foot and did see a little bull gently rattle antlers with a larger one. Something that would never happen with soft growing antlers.

At 8:45 clear, a breeze up and 50°. I wouldn't expect frost tonight.

August 29 – Overcast, Breeze up & 43°.

At daylight the weather looked marginal for our tour planned last evening. The overcast low on the mts. but I was up at 5:30 to have my hotcakes and get things in order. Jim and Mardy would be over by eight my time they had said. I finished up the wing screw for my camera and did other small jobs to pass the time. It came eight and eight thirty and no hikers. I finally went over to find Jim washing his socks while Mardy[15] sewed on a big patch that didn't match the seat of her pants. She had ruptured them yesterday. In due time their food supply was hung high in a poplar to save it from bears and we headed up Hope Creek. By now a patch of blue was showing way down.

The way to regulate those two at the start of a hike is to take the lead until you get them worn down a bit. After a while I would be stopping to let them catch up. Near Pop Tent canyon out went a young cow moose. A flighty one and she headed for the hump and timber below. Up 1st canyon and a sheep high on our left. Up farther and a young ram straight ahead. Jim hung on his 200 mm lens and did a little good on him. Then five more high on

---

[15] Jim Alloway from Massachusetts and Mardy Welbourn from Maine were backpackers who visited RLP.

the left and later a young ram and ewe in the head of 1st canyon. I was happy to see that the fog had lifted to clear the saddle and that the snow had melted out since I was there last.

I had let them use my little light Japanese pack frame to carry their camera gear and wind breakers. Jim has saddled Mardy with it at the start and now came loose rock scramble to reach the pass. I felt sorry for the girl but could hardly offer to relieve her of the load. An avalanche had brought down a lot of loose rock and left it in the usual very unstable condition. Very course rock and constantly shifting under our weight Mardy remarked that it was quite a scramble. My first time to climb to the saddle between 1st canyon and Low Pass basin. It looked worse going down than coming up, so after a bite to eat in the shelter of a rock wall I went scouting for a better route down. On a ridge, the "eye of a needle"[16] in giant form it can be seen from a mile away. From it into the basin was a fair route and a good landmark to climb by. A tricky 100 yds. from our climbing route to the eye but no problem if you watch your step. Jim now offered to carry the gear now that she had packed it to the high point of the journey.

Slowly we descended to the snow in the basin. No caribou there today. I learned something about pink snow. Mardy says it is an algae that grows in snow and that it smells like watermelon. Sure enough – scoop up a handful and smell it – as close to watermelon odor as you could ask for. On top the basin was closed in but now as we toured down the caribou trail it was improving fast. We stopped at my lookout rock for more lunch and then headed on down the trail. Five head of sheep on our left across the trench and I had never seen sheep there. Two rams near ¾ curl and a couple half curls. And farther down along the slope on the same side caribou – ten or a dozen of them before we came to the point below the man on the mt. So, since they came they had seen bear, moose, sheep, & caribou and a porkypine heading through the pass to the Kijik. That must seem like a long trail to a porkypine. On down to good blueberry country and its mostly finger licking picking now. Farther along and Jim broke the sad news that he had lost the lens cap from his camera so we went back a quarter to search for it and failed. I will probably find it farther down than he wanted to backtrack.

Slowly we descended to the snow in the basin. No caribou there today. I learned something about pink snow. Mardy says it is an algae that grows in snow and that it smells like watermelon. Sure enough – scoop up a handful and smell it – as close to watermelon odor as you could ask for.

Quarter past four when we arrived at their Hope Creek camp. We figured the tour had taken about seven hrs.

August 30 – Clear, Calm & 30°.

Airplane! and here came a Cessna head on. It looked a little familiar but I couldn't place it. In close I saw the pilot had a Jay Hammond beard. He coasted in to the beach, climbed

---

[16] RLP's "eye of the needle," a rock arch on the divide between the first canyon entering Hope Creek and Low Pass basin.

out, shook hands and said, "Great to see you, how have you been?" He had passengers. His daughter Heidi and a boy and a girl form Calif. "Only brought one letter for you he said." - Park Service had picked up my mail before he got to it. Some garden truck - spuds, carrots, cabbage and such from his garden...And my grocery order of eggs and dry milk.

They came in to sit and visit. Right away he spotted my carpet and asked what I had under it. I asked if anyone would have something hot to drink. He would have tea if I would join him. A sprig of Labrador in it too.

Lake Clark's high water hadn't done any damage to his place but the wild Miller Creek nearly did. A point of rock out into the creek causes the trouble and I asked, "Why not blast it off." "You are an old powder man aren't you?" he said. "Never worked with dynamite." We discussed the subject of hunting and he whole heartedly agreed that subsistence hunting and no sport hunting just don't add up to happy people on both sides. He said, "I am allowed to subsistence hunt – located as I am but if I do those that can't are going to be real unhappy." And he also agreed that if it came to a nationwide vote – hunting or no hunting, it would be no hunting at all.

Had trouble with his Lister light plant – wouldn't put out current at all. No one on the lake could locate the trouble so he flew it to Anch. They charged him $285.00 but used no parts and didn't give any good reason why it didn't put out. Flew it back home and hooked it up. No good, same as before. In the underground line to the lodge one splice and water had gotten to it and shorted it out. It's a happy light plant now.

He was watching the lake roughen up and figured they had better get back. Brought the kids up to see if he could show them some sheep. He went out to check his floats for water while I closed my letters. Heidi stayed and asked if I still had my birds. Only a minute and one came so she fed it. Fishing wasn't so good at Naknek this season. The fishermans strike when the fish were running strong. Jay had said, not many salmon have come to Lake Clark. Millions of them below the rapids in the Newhalen River below Nondalton. The water just to high and fast for them to fight their way up.

Heidi said her mother's health is good now and at present she is at McGrath helping friends mine gold.

A rubber band around my three small parcels and two letters and I handed them to the most distinguished mail carrier I will ever deal with. Not going to Port Alsworth today but would in a couple days. They climbed in, taxied past the mouth of Hope Creek and took off up along the beach and flew down country along the mts. across.

September 3 – Overcast, Blowing up & 28°.

Today seemed the kind of a day to make a man think about making wood for winter. The first big tree I had worked up had dried most of the summer and ready to come in close. A quarter mile back and too much brush to think about sledding it in until late in the winter so I took my pack saddle off of the hook and started the half mile circuit. On the big end a two chunk length made a good heavy pack. Snow in the air as I trudged the trail and I would go over it about 24 times before chunks and limb wood were in. About noon I heard a big Cessna on top headed for the high ones and I guessed it was Kenai Air with the hikers.

[RLP was in Port Alsworth to work on the Cat and to harvest potatoes.]

September 21 – Partly Cloudy, Calm & ?°.

Church service at 10:30 they said. Glen was due to be the minister. I would go as I always intend to do when I am there. Glen is a good minister – an easy talker with a good line. Father-in-law Laddie leads the singing. Mother-in-law Glenda plays the organs. Maybe fifteen or twenty in the congregation.

After supper Glen and I got my list of groceries ready for an early take off to Twin Lakes. He knew I was anxious to get back. Take lots of spuds and anything else that you want or need he said as we looked at his stock. *[RLP spent the night at Port Alsworth].*

October 3 – Clear, Calm & 18°.

At 5:30 a layer of fog over the lower lake. The gravel in front of the cabin lifted and crunchy. This was more like the good October that I remember.

Today I would go way down, I had put it off long enough. Days are getting short fast and soon it would hurry me to paddle the round trip in sunlight.

Spuds for breakfast and that didn't take long. The sun came to the peaks down country and then to the connecting stream as I got away from the beach. Going down at least, I would use the double ender paddle. At 20° there would be lots of ice but it would melt going down the lower lake. No camera gear – instead I took axe & shovel. The main reason for going was to tidy up the lower lake before winter and snow prevented my doing it. I would do more good today than I expected.

Out of the shadow of Cowgill Mt. and into the sun at Emerson Creek. 40 min. for that three mile run. I beached and dumped the water before entering the stream. With my new arrangement I was keeping dry. Into the lower lake and it flat as a pane of

...I stopped there a few minutes to put things in order after someone had spent some time messing it up. 10 minutes on down to the good beach at the extreme lower end and a quarter from Arlen's cabin. From the mt. up here I had seen a camp and plane three weeks ago. The litter there was mostly freeze dried foil envelopes. It says on the envelope "Please pack this foil out with you – don't litter." Some people don't read good unless it's a mistake in their paycheck.

glass. A very beautiful morning to take her right down the middle 50 min to Skywagon point and I stopped there a few minutes to put things in order after someone had spent some time messing it up. 10 minutes on down to the good beach at the extreme lower end and a quarter from Arlen's cabin. From the mt. up here I had seen a camp and plane three weeks ago. The litter there was mostly freeze dried foil envelopes. It says on the envelope "Please pack this foil out with you – don't litter." Some people don't read good unless it's a mistake in their paycheck. At Arlen's cabin it looked as if someone left in a rush. Something moldy in the Teflon skillet. Nearly every pan or camp kettle had a chunk of ice in it. A note telling Terry Hamilton[17] that because he cleaned up the cabin – didn't make it his. Hamilton had left the note of instructions in the spring of 1979.

The door wired shut after storing a bunch of gas cans inside I paddled to the site of the wrecked Stationair Cessna. Glen had said Stu [Ramstad] went down with diving gear and cut the engine loose and dragged it out. Not so, the engine is still there. The wreck out farther as if Stu tried to tow it to deep water with his Beaver but couldn't hack it – so – cut the lines and there she lays a total loss.

Coming back I would use my good old L.L. Bean paddle. 1 hour and 25 min. to the stream and I lined her through which took about 20 min. A light breeze up on the upper lake and gee! it looked like a long three miles. The sun was making a long shadow and would drop behind the mts. as I packed my gear and loot in.

October 10 – Clear, Calm & 7°.

I beached at Emerson Creek which comes no where near reaching the lake with running water. Took the scope and went a quarter mile up for a good view of the den site. A dark spot up there which I took to be the face of a rock. The scope called it a dirt mound and fresh. Looking closely I could see roll marks where small rocks had rolled down the snow covered slope. I searched for tracks and am most sure that I saw some coming across from the left and then down to the den site. I couldn't see evidence of the old den but the new one has to be very close. All it would take to make this find perfect was to see movement there – for that old sister to show even a little bit of her head. I couldn't see the den entrance for it is behind the mound and no doubt goes down at quite an angle. The den was dug after the snow came so can't be more than two days old. Interesting, I would like to see it close up but wouldn't dare risk her learning I was there or she would probably leave the den and not come back. At Port Alsworth, Tony [Balluta],[18] the Native from across Lake Clark told me that before guns the Natives used to use spears to hunt and kill them. Catch them in hibernation – come down to the den entrance from above. Disturb the bear and as it came out, spear it from above. I can imagine the action by the Natives after those spears were planted. Get out of the area fast and wait for the bear to die would be my guess. He also said that a bear lays two ways during hibernation. Lays one way until

[17] Terry Hamilton, an individual from the Kenai Peninsula who stayed in Arlen's cabin on lower Twin Lake for a time.

[18] Tony Balluta (1938-1982) son of Sophie Hobson Balluta Austin, across Lake Clark from Port Alsworth.

about Xmas time and then the other way. Some dens I have seen were so small it would be impossible for me to crawl in and turn around and it appeared that the bear layed stretched out and not curled as I see them, sometimes, on the mt.

October 14 – Overcast, Blowing dn. & 38°.

And the stronger the wind from the gulf the warmer it will be. The wind very strong this morning and would be throughout the day. It didn't look promising for plane day tomorrow.

After breakfast the rains came and I settled down to a good inside chore of sorting, reading, and burning old letters. A lot of fifteen-cent stamps in that tall cardboard box when I packed it by the stove.

My letter writing caught up except for a bundle of a half dozen that had been on hold from '78. I would surprise a few by answering and I ended up at 1 P.M. with 35 letters in my outgoing box. One more I must write and it is to the girl who forwarded that Foley man's letter of inquiry about me. From Minnesota and he had just read the book four times. Was dying to know what happened to me. Did I ever get back to Twin Lakes? Did I ever! I'll bet he will be happy to get my letter. She, Sharon Bacusmo is editorial secretary in Bob Henning's outfit. No doubt she can check and let me know how many copies of the book has sold till now.

October 23 – Overcast, Lt. Breeze up & 35°.

Airplane and here came the "T craft." Glen alone. He had taken Patty and the kids to town. Laddie and Glenda was tending the farm and all its important functions such as weather reports and telephone service plus mail. "Did it blow here?" he asked. "Did it, well I guess." By their instruments there were gusts to 90 m.p.h. and many at 80. Thought he would come in today and maybe we could get rigged up to take the [Cessna] 206 out. If we didn't get done he might just stay here tonight.

The lake was near calm just a light ripple up. We loaded my gear and flew down, landing where I had put the little Crestliner aluminum boat on the beach. "Yup that is our boat sure enough" he said. Into the water with it and we towed it behind the "T craft" for the short taxi to the salvage site. I would rather have had six 55 drums but we would try with 4. I had one here and there was one at Skywagon point. It would have taken more time and I figured we would be lucky if the weather stayed calm for long.

We spiked together a rack for four drums – threaded our block and tackle and rowed out. No problem to hook into a loop of the heavy rope that Stu had tied to the propeller shaft. The lake calmed completely and it was perfect to get rigged for the pull. We anchored the hand cranked winch to a big rock on the beach and started cranking.

The drums started down and when no more than half submerged they didn't go lower. Line was coming in so the [Cessna] 206 had to be moving. Glen went out in the boat and reported "she is moving alright."

Coming to shallow water and we would have to hook closer to the prop. hub. That we did and came in closer. Suddenly Glen said, "She is going to blow, look up the lake." Even with Skywagon point white caps coming and they would soon be with us. We had to go out to make an adjustment and it was a struggle to get there with oars. That detail taken care of we sailed back to the beach and cranked in more line. Getting very rough and Glen would have to get the "T craft" out of there. He climbed in and I cranked her – lifted the tail to get him off the rocky beach. Water was slopping over the nose of the floats and blown back by the prop. He was off in a very short distance. He swung down country to land on the narrow long lake a half mile below the lower lake. Tied her to a tree and came over land but not from the direction of the lake. He was headed to far towards the Chili River.

Now the heavy surf was helping us. The line very tight and the surf action moved the wreckage. The water too shallow for our pontoon over it so we cut it loose and let it come ashore. There we knocked it apart and used the two side members of our bbl. rack to make a bipod A. This we took out as far as the surf would allow. A snatch block at the fork at the top. One end of the line to the wreck and the other to the winch. The snatch block carrying the middle and giving us a lifting action. The winch handle home made and too short so it was a slow hard pull but soon the cowl flaps of the engine were showing in the trough between the waves. The wind very strong but warm, unbelievably warm. In due time we dragged her out on the boulder beach out of reach of the surf. Not much left of the airplane other than the engine. Everything forward of the doors came with the engine. Instrument panel complete. Radios were there and Glen said that John [Alsworth] told him that solid state circuitry in present day radios don't suffer too much. The belly to the rear of the seats came trailing in attached by control cables. The remnant of a right wing came along tied on by a bit of sheet metal work. Glen opened the glove compartment. There, was an Austrian wrist watch with a gold crusted band a jade stone on each side. A lot of gold there, a heavy band. And a plastic case of .22 long rifle cartridges. A water proof flashlight in the pocket behind the seat. That was it for the loot.

Enough for today. He had brought no tools thinking we surely wouldn't need any today and we wouldn't have time anyway. He wanted to take me to Port Alsworth for the night but I said, "No way. This is late October and anything can happen to the weather – take me home." So we packed my gear to the "T craft" and bucked a strong wind coming up. I had the one roll of film and a package containing a half ounce of gold for Terry Gill. Gold that I wouldn't like to keep for the work I had done for them. I would rather they went to Port Alsworth than me. If I had gone they would have stayed.

I asked him when he would be back. "In the morning about nine or ten blowing or not." He wanted to get that engine to John as soon as possible. It weighs 500 lbs. and loading it into his [Cessna] 206 could be a chore, but I have a way figured. Fly a good

heavy gin pole down that I have here. From the top a good guy line back to a big rock. A guy line out to each side to hold her from swinging left or right. Mount the winch at the lower end of the pole. Dead end our hoist line at the top. Come down to a single block at the engine – back up to a single block at the top and then down to the winch with the free end. A two part line and an easy lift. All we will need is calm water to get his [Cessna] 206 on floats in close to the rocky beach.

At the lower end he might need some gas to get home but here he thought he had plenty. Only one way to find out and he took off climbed to clear the Volcanics into the pretty sunset. 7 hrs. from the time we had left my place this morning until we were back. "Unbelievable" was the way he put it. He didn't know I had lost considerable sleep planning for today. Now supper over and dishes done. The wind blowing down and strong. Overcast and 40° at 8:30 P.M.

October 24 – Overcast, Calm & 36°.

Always it snows on top when it is 40° and raining here at lake level but not this Oct. date. Late in the night it rained steadily and was still at it when I got up at 7:15. Yesterday down country a band of new snow about one third of the way up the Volcanics. Less snow above and below. That was a first for me to see such behavior in weather.

Visibility was not good again but Glen would come if he could see even a little bit. That [Cessna] 206 engine represents a lot of money saved for him. How much I wouldn't know but suspect maybe $4,000.00. I wasn't surprised to see the "T craft" coming even though, by now, it was blowing down as well as raining. "Couldn't come direct," he said. Had to take Glen Van Valin's mail up the lake. From there, up and through the notch to Portage Lake. Up the Kijik a few miles to the low pass leading into the Big Valley behind the Volcanics from here. Down the valley and around the end of the mts. and then a straight shot up the lakes.

Did I think it was worth it to work on that junker today. I told him I was game if he was. Rain and wind but warm. We could set up the tripod and wrap some plastic around for a wind break if the rain was too much. We would try it so picked up a pole at the campground across the creek to complete the tripod, lashed it on top of a float and took off. The lower lake too rough to land at the salvage site so we went to the long narrow lake below and packed our gear to the wreck. It was blowing strong but not raining so no shelter was erected. The nose section of the [Cessna] 206 was laying bottom side up so we ripped the cowling off to get at the motor mount bolts. We found one motor mount broken completely off so Stu must have reefed on her for all the Beaver was worth trying to drag her out and deep six her. The engine free it was just a matter of clipping wires and hoses. Disconnect a few flex lines and rolling the shell containing the fire wall controls, instruments, radios, etc. away. We tipped the engine up and stood it on its three bladed prop to finish stripping it of anything that came easy. Then we set the tripod over and used a cable, lever hoist to lift it by its lifting eye on top. Removed the nuts that secured the prop. flange to the crankshaft flange and removed the prop. which was quite heavy. There she was hanging on the hook and not looking so heavy. One of us on either side we could take the weight off of the hoist cable but that's all we could do. Glen allowed three guys could load it into the [Cessna] 206 or if that was too much he would consider lashing it to a float.

The day hadn't been to bad weather wise. Cool to work bare handed because of the wind but no rain while we made the pieces fly. Glen is all for dragging the remains out onto the ice over deep water – cutting a hole and putting her where she will never be seen again ever unless some skin diver is down there prowling around sometime. I said, if it was me, I would tell the Park Service that we took it out of the lake for the engine. If they want to haul it away by hacking it into small pieces and loading it into a Beaver go to it. Glen says it would cost the taxpayers several thousand dollars if they go that route. They don't have money to operate on as it is. So, what happens to the garbage only time will tell. They just might say, "Drag it out cut a hole in the ice and push it in."

We packed our gear and small engine parts and headed for the "T craft" leaving that expensive engine hanging and gently turning a bit in the wind. Tomorrow if it isn't too rough we will complete the job. If it isn't too rough for the aluminum boat we will load the engine in and haul it up near Arlen's cabin where it is calm and then man handle it into the bird that flies.

He flew me up and the lake below rough, plenty rough. It would have taken me three hrs. with the canoe and little kicker. He would be back tomorrow or if it is too bad the next possible day. Off and climbing. It is something how that "T craft" takes off from here and makes a bee line for Port Alsworth. Clears the Volcanics with lots of room to spare.

Still coals from the cottonwood sticks I put in the stove before leaving. My gear put away, supper and dishes done. Now at eight it is overcast, noisy out in the stretch and gusting in the spruce tops. The temp. 37°. Glen said they reported it 50° at Port Alsworth yesterday.

October 25 – Overcast, V. Lt. Breeze up & 30°.

My beach pretty tracked up and rough. I had better rake it before it turned cold tonight. I had just finished and the sun ready to drop behind the mt. when I heard that fast winding [Cessna] 206 coming. Landing light on and close to the water. To my beach and Laddie climbed out one side and Glen the other. He promptly dropped one of the new flashlight batteries I had ordered into the lake and beyond the drop off. Two cans of Jet Fuel "B" for my Aladdin came out. A couple nice chunks of bacon. Some cookies and homemade biscuits. Out of eggs but I have 2 doz. and nine. He would come again in a couple weeks if freeze up didn't crowd him out of Babe's bay.

He remarked about the weather and asked how long it had been this good. Fog

down low and he couldn't get out. Tried twice and couldn't hack it. Had he known it was open he would have climbed on top and come anyway. I climbed in and we took off down the smooth lake. That [Cessna] 206 is a nice flying machine – quiet – and fast. A very quick flight to the lower end and perfect to get against the boulder beach. One thing nice about the beach – the boulders are water worn and no sharp corners.

Just like his pa – he jumps out and says, "Well, what do we do first." I said, "knock that tripod apart and use the 4x6's as a ramp to slide that engine (resting on a piece of plywood) up into those double doors of that good airplane." The engine had to move no more than 25 feet from where it hung overnight on the tripod to its resting place behind the two front seats. Lots of man power with that husky father in law Laddie along so no need to do it the easy way. On the 2x2's we had used on the pontoon we slid the top side down engine on its plywood pallet to the ramp and up. A lot of grunting, heaving and shoving but in less than five minutes the doors could be closed. Laddie would stay and get more parts ready to load when Glen came back from bringing me up to my diggings. At my beach he said, "Say! the mission girls[19] asked me to fly them to Twin Lakes. Not now but after freeze up." I said, "Bring them now it's a nice time of year on days like this." He doubted that they would come now but he would try to get in again before freeze up. With that he blasted off down the lake with that engine safely in his grasp. I asked him what the deal was John [Alsworth] had made. He said, "John had called the insurance adjuster and asked him the status of that [Cessna] 206 in the Lower Twin." They had written it off as Stu had said it was not salvageable. So it's a free engine and I asked how much it would be worth when ready to run again. I said, "Would it be $6,000.00." "Yes, it would be about that," he said.

October 30 – Clear, Calm & 12°.

Hotcakes and dishes done by the time sunlight had came halfway down the mt. I made ready to paddle across. Crampons along in case I saw need for them. Just my glasses, camera gear would go next trip if I saw it worth the film. At the mouth of Falls Creek rabbit tracks and the track of a lynx cat. Five head of sheep at timberline and I got closer than a hundred yds. before they moved away. They showed no fear but didn't want me above, so climbed and went over the point ahead of me. Four ptarmigan on a rock outcrop. In their winter white plumage now. They were the first I have seen in quite sometime.

Up on the point of Falls Mt. and I began to see sheep on the solid snow cover of the big pasture. A couple along the canyon three or four in another place. They were well scattered. Out in the middle the look of rams. Dark heads and that is a sure sign. The glasses made them five good rams, full curl or better. Searching more I found three which made eight. Counting everything I got 36 head. I went as close as I dared without moving them and then decided to climb Falls peak and see what was in view from there. Not a bad climb, a few drifts half knee deep and a solid 2 inches had come since the wind blew last.

---

[19] Florence Hicks and Doris Hagedorn.

Very near calm but what breeze there was cut when the climb was behind me. I dug into my camera bag for wool shirt, down vest, and Kelty. I could look right down on the bear den area a few hundred feet below. Snow fills in there and who would guess there is a big brown bear resting easy under that blanket of white.

Across Emerson I could see sheep trails but no sheep. Down the slope of Falls Mt. towards the mouth of camp creek a little knot of sheep and I settled down to watch them. Rams, every one of them and some good ones in a bunch of five. I buckled on the crampons and went down a few hundred feet for a better view. My best count was 24 head of sheep and six of them good rams. Some horsing around but no serious head bumping. Rams trotting out a few steps, turning and waiting for that other guy to do like wise. Up on their hind legs and the start of a lunge forward but always they stopped before they made contact. Much like they do in May before heading for their high summer pastures. I watched the five and finally as a group, they started, made a move suddenly. One pulled out in front and turned facing the four. I saw heads bump and a second later clack! clack! clack! Three times so that single had taken the blow of two. Above the noise of Emerson Creek I had heard it plain enough. The big contest to see who is the champion on the mt. is about to start.

October 31 – Clear, Calm & 2°.

Still working in the woods and on a second down tree when the unsuspected happened. Chopping a length of top wood on the ground. A hard blow and some how the axe blade got to the toe of my sturdy hiker boot. Boy! that stung, and there was a sharp line top to bottom in front of my big toe. It cut deep I knew and I was thinking I would have to sew up a hole in the toe of my sock. Not that warm wet feeling that goes with blood so I doubted if I was eligible for a purple heart. I came over with a load and in the cabin I pulled the boot off. No damage inside but that heavy sole suffered a cut back to and including the hard toe of my boot. How lucky I was that I had those heavy hikers on. I never wear them making wood. Had it been my L.L. Bean rubber bottomed packs I would start the winter season limping severely. So – I mixed up a little epoxy and filled the gash.

November 1 – Partly Cloudy, V. Lt. Breeze up & 3°.

She ahead and the cubs trudging single file in her tracks. Just far enough away that she couldn't hear the camera and I was running it pretty steady. She came to a smooth grassy slope, now covered with 6 inches of snow, where bears have dug for squirrels but never a den. The soil is deep there and the slope faces southwest. She stopped, scratched a lick or two as if seeing what was under the snow. Then she swung her rear end down the slope and started to dig. I thought, how lucky can you be? She is going to dig a den right here in full view of god and everybody. I had two rolls of film along and would gladly shoot

the full amount to get a den being dug. I have often wondered how long it would take for a working bear to dig a den for one or three. It wasn't to be – she dug a few licks and said "no good" and continued on towards the point of the mt. leading down to the big rock face at the waterfall. Over the point and out of sight and there I was high up across the canyon and wishing I was down on the big rock face so I could follow their route. I felt sure she would den on Allen Mt.

I had a bite to eat while it was clearing and then set up the scope on my beach. Now if she was above snowline I would find her. No sign and I gave it a good try. Finally I picked up their trail near the point of the mt. and followed it angling across and down the mt. They came below snowline just opposite my beach. I watched the brushy slope from there to the moose rutting cottonwoods where bears some times spend some time before hibernation. Many highbush cranberries there. The sun dropped behind the mt. and I hadn't see hide nor hair of the three bears. I'm betting she is headed for the high ones and I might find their tracks at the head of the lake. She was traveling as if she knew exactly where she intended to dig that den. If she hadn't stopped to test that southwest slope along waterfall canyon I would say she was just passing through. Interesting, I must spend a little time learning what her thinking was.

November 2 – Partly Cloudy, Calm & 8°.

Now, a light breeze up so I loaded a 25 lb. stone in the bow of the canoe to make it hold course better. I paddled over in front of the beaver house and there well below the waters surface was a real thicket of grocery brush – not one twig of it showing above the surface. As I paddled out of the bay and near the point marking its entrance I noticed what appeared to be frost free brush on the bank. Curious, I paddled that way. The beaver was there and swimming away. It was their grocery brush supply. A well marked trail from the waters edge and up the bank. A long swim to the lodge towing brush but I have seen them harvesting brush, other years, beyond the point. I had stayed longer than I figured – light was failing. Pretty dark when I came to my beach. As is par for the course the breeze was calming when I beached the canoe and hobbled in on cold feet again. I have the remedy for cold feet. A big granite egg that rests on the stove top. Put it in a shallow box on the floor. Off with shoes and socks and rest those feet on the hot rock.

Overcast, Calm & 15° now at 7:15.

November 14 – Partly Cloudy, Breeze dn. & 23°.

I had a project in mind that fit the day. When Mardy, Jim and I hiked from the connecting stream to the lower waterfall in late Sept. I took them over the old Native trail through the big timber. A blazed trail and it must have been a good one in its day. One of the old Natives at Nondalton told me, it was winter when they came to hunt sheep which they

found at brush line.[20] Cold – bannock would burn on one side and freeze on the other. Now, some of the blazes were well healed over. Trees had fallen across the trail. We followed it part way and I guessed the rest and hit the campsite dead on. Be nice if the trail was kept open enough so it could be followed without searching.

Today I would do that. The sun would be on Emerson Creek full force. And I wanted to check for marten tracks. Have some moved in or just a very few that I may have seen tracks of before and wasn't sure.

My hip boots, axe, and Kelty were lashed on the light pack frame and I was away by ten o'clock. Across Hope Creek, and it has now cut through the ice and running over the rocky stream bed, and I hit the marten track on the beach headed down. Nearly a half mile down it turned up into the timber. Farther on I came onto it again and this time it was coming up. An older track made by the animal when it came to Hope Creek. All the way to Low Pass point I back tracked it and on down I would see its tracks on the snow covered ice of fox pond.

At the stream I switched to boots – left everything but my axe and made the crossing. In the timber I headed for the lower lake end of the trail and followed it towards Emerson Creek and the gorge brightening up the old blazes as I went. A few times I came to a dead end but by covering the area I eventually found an old blaze. A few small dead trees down across the trail and a few big ones. Move them or go around depending on their size. To the campsite in the big trees along the creek flat and I wished I could have snowshoed in and found them camped there.

The day was still young so I went on up to visit the lower falls. A beautiful formation of huge icicles hanging from the wall at the entrance to the gorge. The waterfall running behind a huge shield of ice. No water ouzels there today and I suspect they spend most of their feeding time at the connecting stream.

I headed back over the trail and took the cut off to the Vanderpool cabin and the horned owls nest. Will that old sister use that nest next spring, I wonder? The cabin secure so I took the trail to the lakeshore and down to my crossing. The sun still at the bottom of Spike's Mt. when I started up the beach and it would just leave the peak as I crossed Hope Creek. It was a beautiful sight as I came up the lake. The low sun on the snow white mts. with grey scattered clouds for a background.

The cabin still warm and coals in the stove for a quick start. My birds terribly hungry as they always are when I return after being away a few hrs.

Supper and dishes washed and ironed – now at seven fifteen it is clear. The first qtr. moon is behind Cowgill Mt. The lake still talking from a down lake breeze and the temp. 23°.

Not a great day for wildlife. A couple spruce grouse and an owl. No rabbits and not a lot of tracks.

---

[20] The old Native trail ran from the north shore of lower Twin Lakes near the Herb Wright sheep camp north though the forest to upper Emerson Creek where the Dena'ina had a winter sheep hunting camp.

November 22 – Overcast, Blowing dn. & 32°.

I was getting back early today. I had considered going farther down because it was early. 2:45 when I arrived and none too soon. Some how those smart camp robbers had removed the aluminum lid off of the pressure cooker bean pot. A scattering of beans and gravy on the table and at least two meals of beans missing. Not present so they had worked until they were tired. Soon they came begging for hotcakes and pretending not to know anything about their latest caper. After this there will be a sizable stone on top of the lid when the beans are in the refrig. A sandwich and I popped some corn of which I have a good supply. The mission girls are great popcorn eaters so I must remember to have some when they come.

The heels of my good socks repaired but they wouldn't last without some armor plate. It so happens that I have some wrapping string that is the best I have ever seen for darning heels and making them really last. I had tried some at home and had my sis send 30 feet after I came up. Stitches close together and a good patch of them extending above the wear area. A job well done before I made my journal entry. Blowing down still now at 7:30. Heavy overcast and no sign of that full moon. The temp. 31°.

November 24 – Partly Cloudy, Breeze dn. & 30°.

Suddenly an airplane and close. A little one came over but not the "T craft." This one red and white trim. On floats and who would still be on floats near Thanksgiving. I was on the beach when it came in. Out climbed Jack Ross the expert log construction carpenter from Port Alsworth. He was the passenger, the pilot was Glen. Now I knew the plane. Jack's old "T craft."

Out came a huge mail sack which they said was packages. Another mail sack and that was first class and small parcels and a little box of groceries. "Brought you a Thanksgiving turkey," Glen said. A little bundle in a cardboard box about six inches square. Leave it outside in the cold but watch those two camp robbers.

We came in and I stoked the fire for hot water and tea. Jack is a tea drinker for sure. I ask him if he had ever tasted "Samovar" tea. No he hadn't. Well then he was in for a treat.

They filled me in on the news while I got my outgoing ready. Took me by surprise or I would have written a few more. Reagan won the election. I didn't get to vote but felt good for I would have picked him as my choice. I really like peanuts and think Jimmy Carter should get back to the peanut growing business. Reagan has a tough row to hoe I tell you, and he had better memorize his lines good. Make a boo boo and it will be heard round the world in seconds.

I ask Glen about our Gov. Jay. He is serving his last term as gov. Glen says there is some talk of him being Secretary of Interior.

Jack has been working this summer on a new log house for Doug Butler at Port Alsworth. When I was there they had to have the roof on by Nov. "Didn't make it," Jack said, and now its not safe climbing around on icy logs.

The [Cessna] 206 engine we salvaged is turning out good. A little damage but nothing to reject a lot of expensive parts.

In all the excitement I forgot to get the correct time so must go on guessing. This way I can have daylight and dark at any hour I chose. Glen says, "When is it going to freeze up." "Oh, about Jan.," I figured. So – that's the way we left it. Watch the weather and make a guess.

My outgoing in the sack and they prepared to fly. Glen was pilot again and that little under powered "T craft" must make him wonder if she will ever fly. A big turn out and up the lake into the breeze at full power and finally she broke water. I saw them heading through the notch at the Pyramid Mt. and then got back to my mail and groceries. About 35 letters and eight parcels. "My god amighty" what a batch of stuff. It's a good thing I have Spike and Hope's cabins to catch the overflow.

In groceries – 2 doz. eggs, two onions, one orange, one grapefruit, two apples and that turkey. Oh yes! a $15.00 roll of stamps and a couple small Xmas wrapped packages from Glen and Pat, Laddie & Glenda. Glen says – "Open them any time – who is there to know if you opened them before Xmas."

I read a half dozen letters and then got back to my wood packing. Four loads came in and it was pretty dark on the timber trail.

Now at 8:30 the breeze is down and increased a bit – many stars are looking down and the temp. 30°. All day today it was fluffy pale yellow chinook clouds out of the south east – summer clouds.

Tomorrow will just have to be a Twin Lakes holiday and Thanksgiving till next week.

December 2 – Partly Cloudy, V. Lt. Breeze dn. & 2°.

During the night the temperature hovered real close to 0° and I thought, this will close her up. At six I heard the hollow rackety sound of waves working on the edge of the ice in the vicinity of Carrithers' point. At daylight open water for about a hundred yds. out from my beach and from there ice, beautiful smooth ice as far down as I could see.

Hotcakes and real good ones – thin and light and plenty of them. Today I wanted to check out the country to Beech Creek and while there walk on the ice of the lower lake. It's a real nice experience after weeks and months of trudging over boulders, gravel and uneven ground to walk on something as smooth and level as the salt flats of Utah. Why a

man could walk 50 miles and not feel tired.

Squared away I went up the creek trail to see the extent of the open water. The new ice angled from the bend of the beach at the base of Crag Mt. to a point directly across from Carrithers' point. Just a light breeze down and doing no harm to the ice. To the upper end, open water all the way.

It was eleven thirty before I got away headed down the beach route. At Low Pass point I would follow the creek up to the game trail and then may brush out the trail on down. Many patches of open water along the beach so it is the spring water that prevents ice along shore. A fox track coming and going along the beach. Going up Low Pass Creek I crossed a fairly fresh moose track going both ways. Along the inland trail old tracks of several moose. My bunch of five I suspect. Near Beech Creek tracks of a cow with twin calves. It isn't often that you see a cow with twin calves in the fall. I think that as often as not the brown bear gets one of the twins during the first two weeks after they are born. In the timber of the creek flat many tracks of that cow and calves. One thing for sure I wouldn't see them unless she approved for it is heavy timber and brush.

Down the creek flat to the lower lake and I heard the ice booming. From high ground I had seen the history of the ice. The old ice of the upper end smooth and not a mark. From its lower limit on down a network of fracture lines where the wind had jostled the thin ice crowding it this way.

The ice frosted and a light dusting of snow. The surface not at all slippery. To walk out on it reminded me of driving on the black top after a few days of Alcan gravel. Nice, and I wished that I had time to walk to the lower end.

Coming up I traveled the beach trail to blueberry hill and then up to the game trail crossing of Low Pass Creek. From there my inland timber trail to Cowgill Creek. One place I saw the moose track, but soon after crossing Low Pass Creek. No marten tracks today. A track or two of lynx cat. On Low Pass point the usual plentiful sign of the porkypine and at the den in the creek bank a well worn trail.

Four and one half hrs. of steady going and not easy most of it. Snow with a breaking crust where it had drifted. Snow covering very uneven ground and just plain loose snow seven or eight inches deep.

Clouds had formed during the day but no wind came. The temp. stood at 13° when I arrived. It dropped to 10° before darkness set in and now at 7:30 it is 15°, still the sound of waves chewing on the ice out from the point. Not a star to be seen, so it has closed in since four o'clock.

I would like to see freeze up complete and a few inches of ice before snow comes. A heavy blanket on thin ice forces it down and water comes up to saturate the snow and make a mess of things, but, beggars can't be choosers — we will take it as it comes and make the best of it.

The best freeze up I have ever seen was 1968-69 winter. Freeze up of the entire

lake over night and two inches of ice per day for a few days after. The ice under great pressure and groaning terribly.[21]

December 4 – Partly Cloudy, V. Lt. Breeze dn. & 5°.

A letter writing day along with some reading of the good book *All Creatures Great and Small.* Down country the weather opened up a bit and I could see the peaks in the clear. The temp. had climbed to 8°. Towards sunset I made another inspection tour up the shoreline. A chance to try my brand new GI ice creepers from Army Navy Surplus[22] at $3.95. Halfway to the point and good looking ice I buckled then on. I liked them much better than crampons which are too severe on lake ice.

Up to the open water and still a patch as big as a small farm (60 acres) just beyond the solid expanse that reaches to the lower end. Beyond that patch it was white as far as I could see. New ice was coating that open pool. If it stayed calm tonight would see freeze up complete.

It reminds me of a few lines Jack London wrote about the Yukon country long ago. I thought it fit Twin Lakes too so memorized it. It went – "Then came the autumn – The air grew thin and sharp – the days dim and short. The river ran sluggishly and skin ice formed on the quiet eddies. All migratory wildlife departed south and silence fell upon the land. The first snow flurries came and the running mush ice. Then the hard ice, solid cakes and sheets, till the (Chili River) ran level with its banks. When all this ceased the river and the lakes stood still and the days lost themselves in the darkness."

It was after supper when a light breeze came up the lake. The temperature down to 6° from 7°. A few very weak stars look down now at 7:30.

December 6 – Partly Cloudy, Calm & -19°.

I knew it was getting right down there for the window over the counter was taking on a coat of ice and frost was forming at air leaks around the door. As daylight came I couldn't tell if it was clear or partly cloudy although the stars were very bright overhead. It was pretty crispy sure enough and not a morning to eat ones porridge while standing in shirt sleeves on the beach.

After my breakfast I went for bucket of water and ten feet out I found the ice 2" thick. Good enough, I could cross the lake on that. When Glen and Pat were newlyweds they came in Glen's little Stinson and landed on 2 inches of new ice. Glen had mentioned that several times since Babe used to say, "I can land on 2 but I would rather have four."

---

[21] Alaska National Interest Lands Conservation Act (ANILCA) was signed into law by President Carter on this day creating millions of acres of new wildlife refuges and national parks, including Lake Clark National Park and Preserve.

[22] Army Navy Store on 4th Avenue in Anchorage, long time supplier of rural Alaska clothing needs.

Now a cloud bank over the mountains to the southeast but it appeared to be stationary.

I walked out on the ice and heard no complaint so headed for the bare knoll on the far side. A couple cracks where water had pushed up and spread a few feet but the ice was good. It seemed good to be traveling the ice again. A half inch of frost made a non skid surface and I could step right out. Jets were making bold contrails and that means moisture up there. In -20° dry air they leave no trail at all. Coming back I paced the distance and counted 30" steps and it totaled 1,830, 4,550 feet and about .86 of a mile.

December 7 – Partly Cloudy, Calm & 6°.

Sometime during the night I woke up to hear the wind blowing very strong down and the lake ice was in a continuous uproar of cracking and groaning. Nearly all of it seemed to be towards the lower end of the lake. Daylight saw contrails being distorted so there was wind at high altitude.

Pearl Harbor day and it was Sunday on that fateful day too. What was I doing? I was on the ranch in Oregon and hauling a truck load of saddle horses. I enlisted in the Navy the next day.

Pearl Harbor day and it was Sunday on that fateful day too. What was I doing? I was on the ranch in Oregon and hauling a truck load of saddle horses. I enlisted in the Navy the next day.

A good stack of hotcakes and then to celebrate freeze up I would travel the ice all the way to the lower end. It was still calm and the scattered clouds gave no clue that the wind would blow today.

This upper lake had been scoured clean. It was like one huge skating rink with a few blemishes caused by cracks and water coming to the surface of the ice. It would be a good chance for my GI ice creepers to prove themselves. The lake ice at the water hole measured three inches and the block cut out which formed since yesterday morning was a strong two inches.

I was away and crunching down the lake by 10:30 and suspected the light would be failing by the time I came to my beach again. On the glare ice I learned real soon that it wasn't my good positive traction crampons I was wearing. The GI creepers only cover the soles of my Canadian Sorel shoe pacs. No traction for the heels so those soles must touch the ice almost the instant the heels do or you have a stability problem. And it is worse if you cross a snow patch and get the heels coated with snow. That first step or two on bare ice can be the beginning of fast action. To the stream and the lower lake. A big surprise there. It was still snow white and frost covered. Either the wind didn't blow or the frost was well tied to the ice. No creepers needed and I took them off.

A half mile down I saw where the lake ice had suffered damage by the wind during the last stage of closing up. A strip more than a hundred yds. wide with very rough

ice. Some hefty chunks six inches and more thick tossed on top and frozen there. Pans of ice with turned up edges caused by bumping together in the rough ice choked water. Beyond that strip it was good all the way and the farther I went the deeper the frost. More than an inch of frost and in tufts very close packed. It resembled caribou moss. An old track of a moose crossing to Dry Creek and farther down the large track of a caribou crossing right. The only caribou track I would see.

The high ridge towards Turquoise has very little snow and the Bonanza Hills the same. During the past week or two many small planes on skis headed that way and later coming back. Hardly enough snow for skis so I suppose some caribou meat was very expensive.

At the site of the [Cessna] 206 salvage job I stayed a few minutes. Glen hadn't come back for the propeller hub as he said he might or send Laddie. There lays all the airplane junk on the rocky beach. What will the Park Service do with it if Glen leaves it there. Now before the ice gets thick would be the time to put it out of sight forever but I wouldn't like to see it done.

Coming back I circled over to Arlen's cabin to see how it was entering the winter. A big hole in the up country side and I pushed in a window to see if a brown bear or black was sleeping there. A good big Beaver load of rubbish there and I'm thinking they won't dump that in the lake so why dump the remains of the [Cessna] 206 there. Coming up I faced a cool breeze but it seemed to get warmer as I neared the stream. Creepers for the upper lake and this time I did it. Snow on my heels and my feet went forward. A pretty good fall but no damage done except to the reputation of the Army gear. The ice nearly quiet as I came up but during supper it was noisy and still is now at 7:15. Stars are out but not the full number. It is calm and -1°. Only 3 min. to lose before the evenings get longer.

December 11 – Clear, Calm & -28°.

Tired of sleeping cool, last night I put my sleeping bag inside of a sleeping bag as I have done other winters. I woke up at 5:30 to hear the sound of wind. I listened and heard it again in the spruce tops. Finally I got up and went to the door. It was a breeze down. I checked the temp. which was -28° before I turned in. -20° it said. That was about the last I heard of the wind and this morning it was -28° again.

While it was getting daylight I hauled a couple more loads of wood from beyond Hope Creek and then I noticed the temp. had dropped to -33°. It cut like a knife and I wasn't about to walk to the upper end. I didn't think I should anyway. Those boys [sport hunters] would feel sure that I was watching the country for the Park Service. When they fly away I will go up and see if I can find a kill site. If I do the tongue is most sure to be in the discarded head and that's what I want.

I fooled around at tinkering jobs and improved my fire in the process. I climbed

to the roof and pulled the bonnet off – ran a slim pole down and rattled it around. Added a 7 inch section I had cut from another. A better drawing stove was the result. Enjoying the improvement I wrote letters. An airplane came up the far side and I went out to check. A red & white [Cessna] 185 on wheels and most sure to be the Park Service. A bit later I heard it snarling around at the upper end and then down it came to circle my place before it flew on down country. What do they expect to accomplish without landing.

December 25 – Clear, Calm & -21°.

35 letters and cards, it was 10 o'clock before I was through them once over lightly. I had mailed about thirty and in this batch I kept seeing names and addresses that wasn't on those I sent – sorry bout that.

A good night's sleep and it seems I am doing better since I ran out of Jet fuel "B" for the Aladdin and am now using Glen's oil base diesel fuel. It isn't as hot as Jet "B" - burns without getting wild in my cow barn lantern and doesn't coat the chimney of the Aladdin with the grey deposit.

Ready and willing to roll out at seven. An extra big batch of batter so an extra couple hotcakes on my stack. Lots of real live eggs so one sunny side up on top. It takes that egg on top to make a stack a stack. After dishes I scoured my old aluminum tea kettle and pans – gave the carpet a vigorous sweeping. Washed and ironed the Aladdin chimney and the

This was not just an ordinary morning. So now, I was ready to break into those Christmas wrappers. I hope that if they just had to send something it would be something to eat or to write with and it turned out pretty much that way. Spike and Hope are great at reading my mind. Just yesterday I climbed to the cache for a can of cocoa mix. Most certain there was one there but it was gone. Had it on my list for Jan. 17 (week) delivery. In their box, cocoa mix and popcorn and chocolate and soups and much more including a fruitcake.

cow barn lantern globe. This was not just an ordinary morning. So now, I was ready to break into those Christmas wrappers. I hope that if they just had to send something it would be something to eat or to write with and it turned out pretty much that way. Spike and Hope are great at reading my mind. Just yesterday I climbed to the cache for a can of cocoa mix. Most certain there was one there but it was gone. Had it on my list for Jan. 17 (week) delivery. In their box, cocoa mix and popcorn and chocolate and soups and much more including a fruitcake.

Bibliography

Books and Reports

Brown, Willian E.
2005   *Alaska National Parklands: This Last Treasure,* Alaska Natural History Association, Anchorage (first printing 1982).

Ellanna, Linda J., ed.
1986   *Lake Clark Sociocultural Study: Phase II,* "Dena'ina Place Names In The Lake Clark National Park and Preserve Study Area," by James Kari, Priscilla Russell Kari, and Andrew Balluta.

Hammond, Jay S.
1994   *Tales of Alaska's Bush Rat Governor,* Epicenter Press, Fairbanks/Seattle.

Hirschmann, Fred, ed.
1986   *Lake Clark-Lake Iliamna Country,* Vol. 13, No. 4, Alaska Geographic Society, Anchorage.

Hulten, Eric.
1973   *Flora of Alaska and Neighboring Territories,* Stanford University Press, 1974.

Johnson, Timothy
1998   Richard Proenneke Site, NPS planning document, National Park Service, Anchorage.

Kari, James and James A. Fall
2003   *Shem Pete's Alaska: The Territory of the Upper Cook Inlet Dena'ina ,* Second Edition, University of Alaska Press, Fairbanks.

Kari, Priscilla Russell
1997   *Tanaina Plantlore: An Ethnobotany of the Dena'ina Indians of Southcentral Alaska,* National Park Service, Alaska Region, Anchorage.

Kauffmann, John
1979   "Lake Clark: The Essence of Alaskas: Tundra, Glaciers, Mountains," in *Exploring America's Backcountry,* Robert L. Breeden, ed., National Geographic Society, Washington, D.C.

Karamanski, Theodore J.
1990   National Register of Historic Places Registration Form for the Richard L. Proenneke Complex.

Keith, Sam, ed. and Richard L. Proenneke
1973   *One Man's Wilderness: An Alaskan Odyssey,* Alaska Northwest Publishing Co., Anchorage.

Leopold, Aldo
 1969   *A Sand County Almanac,* Oxford University Press, Inc.: New York.

Montgomery, M. R. and Gerald Foster
 1992   *A Field Guide To Airplanes of North America,* Second Edition, Houghton Mifflin
         Company, Boston-New York City, 1992.

Morgan, Lael
 1978   *Bristol Bay Basin,* Vol.5, No. 3, Alaska Geographic Society, Anchorage.

Nash, Roderick
 1967   *Wilderness and the American Mind,* Yale University Press, New Haven.

National Register of Historic Places Registration Form for the Richard Proenneke Complex,
prepared by Theodore J. Karamanski, August 3, 1990.

"Nessmuk"(George W. Sears)
 1963   *Woodcraft and Camping,* Dover Publications, New York.

Nute, Grace Lee
 1987   *The Voyageur,* Minnesota Historical Society.

Olson, Sigurd F.
 1976   *Reflections From the North Country,* Alfred A. Knopf, New York City, New York.

Orth, Donald J.
 1971   *Dictionary of Alaska Place Names: Geological Survey Professional Paper 567,*
         Government Printing Office, Washington, D.C.

Proenneke, Richard
 1990   Personal interview with Theodore J. Karamanski, 8-2-90.

Ramsay, Cynthia Russ et al
 1983   *Alaska's Magnificent Parklands,* National Geographic Society, Washington, D.C.

Smith, Philip Sidney
 1917   *The Lake Clark-Central Kuskokwim Region Alaska,*Bulletin 655, U. S. Department
         of Interior, Washington D. C., GPO.

Smith, Philip Sidney
 1930   *Mineral Resources of Alaska, Report on Progress of Investigations in 1929,* Bulletin
         824, U.S. Department of Interior, Washington, D.C., GPO.

Thoreau, Henry David
 1960   *Walden,* Signet Classics, New York City.

Unrau, Harlan D.
 1994   *Lake Clark National Park and Preserve, Alaska Historic Resource Study*, draft,
         National Park Service, Anchorage.

Van Horne, Bea
 1975   *The Lake Clark Area Vol.1: Planning For People, Wildlife, and The Land.*
         Environmental Studies Program, University of California Santa Cruz, California.

Williss, Frank G.
 1984   *"Do Things Right the First Time,": The National Park Service and Alaska National
         Interest Lands Conservation Act of 1980*, National Park Service, Anchorage.

Wood, Ginny and Celia Hunter
 1981   *Alaska National Interest Lands*, Vol. 8, Number 4, Alaska Geographic Society,
         Anchorage.

BLM Case Abstracts for Waddell, Cowgill, Carrithers, Wright, and Weisser at BLM Land
Office in Anchorage, Alaska.

File on Tanalian Incorporated at park headquarters in Anchorage, National Park Service v.
Mary A. Alsworth, Native Allotment Claim AA 8209.

Newspapers and Magazines

Hammond, Jay. "Gentle Spirit lived in, loved the wild," *Anchorage Daily News*, 7-27-03.

Medred, Craig. "Spirit of the park: Self-sufficient Proenneke roamed Lake Clark preserve for
decades, making trails," *Anchorage Daily News*, 7-13-03, p 1G, 4G.

Porco, Peter. "Goodbye, Dick: Author, Twin Lakes legend dies at 86," *Anchorage Daily News*,
4-28-03, P1B, 7B.

Obituary, "A Modern Day Thoreau," *Alaska*, 9-03, Vol. 69 Number 7, 78.

Videos

"Alaska: Silence & Solitude," Bob Swerer Productions, 1998.

"Alaska, The Closing Frontier," Nova/PBS, June 28, 1978.

"Alone In the Wilderness," Bob Swerer Productions, 2003.

"Jay Hammond's Alaska," Volume 111, featuring Richard Proenneke, 1993.

"No Place Like Twin Lakes," NPS, 2005.

"One Man's Alaska," National Park Foundation, 1977.

"The Frozen North," Bob Swerer Productions, 1999.

Index